Consciousness, Function, and Representation

Consciousness, Function, and Representation

Collected Papers, Volume I

Ned Block

A Bradford Book
The MIT Press
Cambridge, Massachusetts
London, England

MIT Press books may be purchased at special quantity discounts for business or sales promotional
use. For information, please e-mail special_sales@mitpress.mit.edu or write to Special Sales Department, The MIT Press, 55 Hayward Street, Cambridge, MA 02142-1315.

This book was set in Stone Serif and Stone Sans on 3B2 by Asco Typesetters, Hong Kong.
Printed and bound in the United States of America.

Library of Congress Cataloging-in-Publication Data

Block, Ned Joel, 1942–
Consciousness, functionalism, and representation / Ned Block.
    p.   cm. — (Collected papers ; v. 1)
"A Bradford book"
Includes bibliographical references and index.
ISBN-13: 978-0-262-02603-1 (alk. paper)
ISBN-13: 978-0-262-52462-9 (pbk. : alk. paper)
1. Philosophy of mind. I. Title.
BD418.3.B59   2007
128'.2—dc22   2006046761

10 9 8 7 6 5 4 3 2 1

Contents

Consciousness, Function, and Representation

Introduction: Remarks on Chauvinism and the Mind-Body Problem

This volume contains papers on consciousness, functionalism (the view that mentality can be characterized in terms of relations among internal states and between sensory inputs and behavioral outputs), and representationism (the view that attempts to reduce the phenomenal character of conscious states to the representational content of those states). In this introduction, I will make brief remarks about one of the themes covered in a number of the papers, the significance of the multiple-realizability of mental states for the mind-body problem. Putnam (1967) and Fodor (1968) introduced the multiple-realizability argument against physicalism into philosophy. I went to Putnam's classes at MIT every term starting when I was a sophomore in the early 1960s, and to Fodor's classes at MIT starting when I was a graduate student at Harvard in the late 1960s, and I have been concerned with that argument off and on ever since, most recently in "The Harder Problem of Consciousness" (chapter 20, this volume).

What Is Wrong with the Multiple-Realizability Argument against Physicalism

In "What Psychological States Are Not" (chapter 3, this volume), Jerry Fodor and I worked with a notion of physicalism that hovered indecisively between mind-body identity (each mental property is identical to some physical property) and mind-body correlation (for each mental property, there is a physical property such that the mental property is instantiated if and only if the physical property is instantiated in the same person at the same time). We argued that physicalism is false because one type of mental property can be physically instantiated in fundamentally different ways in different mental systems or even in the same mental system at different times. (The argument does not just appeal to different material substrates, but to mechanisms that are fundamentally different from one another.) This argument depended on thinking of mental states as individuated according to their function—that is, as functional states, states whose identity is given by causal relations to inputs, outputs and other such states. We considered the possibility that each mental property is coextensive with some heterogeneously disjunctive physical property and so physicalism could be preserved, but we rejected that option.

In part, the point was epistemic rather than metaphysical. We quoted Davidson on the idea that even if we found an open sentence that stated the coextension between mental properties and physical properties, "Nothing could reasonably persuade us that we had found it." In part, the point was about laws: the statements of coextensions would not be lawlike. Fodor has since pursued this line of thought (Fodor 1997), but I have rejected it on the ground that it conflates metaphysics with epistemology.

Let me explain. A law is most naturally taken to be just a nomological necessity—something true in all nomologically possible worlds—and nothing bars heterogeneously disjunctive terms from nomological necessities. A notion of law that would preclude heterogeneously disjunctive terms would have to be keyed to epistemic goals such as confirmation, but that would be relevant to our knowledge of nomological necessities involving heterogeneously disjunctive terms, not their truth. (See "The Harder Problem of Consciousness," chapter 20, this volume, and Block 1994, 1997.) So I now think that functionalism, if true, does not show physicalism to be false in this way.

Why Functionalism and Physicalism Are Incompatible

Functionalism and physicalism—construed as identity claims—are nonetheless incompatible. A mental property, being a pain, for example, cannot be identical to both a first-order property and a functional property. Here is why. A functional property is a special case of a second-order property, a property that consists in having some other properties (let us take them to be first order for simplicity) that have certain relations to one another. For instance, dormitivity can be construed as the property that consists in having some other property—for example, a chemical property such as having the structure $C_{12}H_{12}N_2O_3$ (phenobarbitol) or alternatively, $C_{16}H_{13}ClN_2O$ (diazepam)—that causes sleep. The property that consists in having some first-order property that causes sleep cannot be identical to a first-order property itself. That is, the property constituted by having some property or other that causes sleep would not be identical to the property constituted by having the structure $C_{12}H_{12}N_2O_3$. These properties are not even coextensive, and even coextension as a matter of fact would not be enough.

Multiple-Realizability Argument against Functionalism

In "Troubles with Functionalism" and "Are Absent Qualia Impossible?" (chapters 4 and 19, respectively, this volume), I argued that the multiple-realizability argument could be used against functionalism itself—that is, as a modus tollens instead of modus ponens. The argument takes off from examples such as the inverted spectrum and a homunculi-headed robot (a robot whose head is a wireless receiver and whose brain is a large group of people living over a wide area but acting as brain elements, communicating with each other and with the robot). The latter idea was that the homunculi-headed robot might be functionally the same as us (at the relevant level of description) but—because of the odd physical basis of these functional states—have no states with phenomenal character. The idea of the inverted-spectrum argument was that perhaps you and I can be in the same functional state with respect to color perception—for example, seeing a red thing. We both say and think it is red, classifying it with other red things and as having the complementary color to green things. But we might have reason to think that the brain state that is the neural basis of your experience of red is the same as the brain state that is the neural basis of my experience of green, and conversely. So although you and I are functionally isomorphic, we are phenomenally different. The examples are not the argument, but rather are a way of backing up the physicalist point that different physical realizations of the same functional state might be different phenomenally, which if true would show that functionalism cannot be the whole story. The overall line of thought is that plausible physicalist premises can turn the multiple-realizability argument around and use it against functionalism, at least in the case of multiple realization of phenomenal properties.

The Functionalist Bites the Bullet

Of course, these are controversial arguments. One line of reply that the functionalist might take is just to bite the bullet, regarding the homunculi-headed realization as merely another realization of the same phenomenal state that we brain-headed creatures have when we are in that functional state. In the case of the inverted spectrum, the bullet-biting functionalist can point out that if your physical realization of the phenomenal property you are in when seeing green is the same as my physical realization of the phenomenal property I have when seeing red, those physical realizations must be *partial* (i.e., core realizations) rather than total brain states—for example, states of the visual system rather than states of the whole brain.[1] For my physical realization of seeing red causes me to say "Red!" in answer to "What color is it?", whereas the same brain state in you (in the partial sense of "brain state") causes you to say "Green!" in response to the same question. Thus, the functionalist may say, what the objection shows is that the physicalist should identify color experience with a state of the *whole* brain—including the parts that govern talking and sorting behavior—rather than some more minimal part or system that concerns the respects in which color experience differs from experiences with other contents. However, the functionalist will go on, once the physicalist has been pushed toward such a holistic view of brain states, he or she is stuck with a problem that in "Troubles with Functionalism" I call "chauvinism." If the phenomenal state of seeing red is to be identified with *my* total brain state, then creatures that cannot be in that same total brain state cannot have that phenomenal state at all. And the list of such disabled creatures would include not only Martians and sentient, sapient robots such as Commander Data of the second Star Trek series, but also *you*. For by hypothesis, the overall brain state you have when you see red includes a state of your visual system that is the same as mine when I see green, so that overall brain state is not the same as the one I have when I see red. Further, the overall brain state you have when you see green is the same as my red state in the visual-system part but unlike mine in the "surround" that makes you say "Green!" when I say "Red!". Thus neither of your overall brain states is the same as my overall brain state on seeing red, and it is easy to see that the argument can be pursued to make it plausible that none of your overall brain states is the same as the one I have when I see red. So the phenomenal quality I am having now is not one that you can have at all. Thus the bullet-biting functionalist seems to have pushed the physicalist into a chauvinist corner.

However, this point can hardly settle the matter between the bullet-biting functionalist and the physicalist. For the bullet-biting functionalist must back up the assertion that the homunculi-head can be phenomenally the same as one of us and that the inverted-spectrum intuitions are wrong. The holistic "overall" brain states mentioned above that are responsible for the difference between us in sorting and speaking cannot simply be assumed to be the "total" brain states that are sufficient for the experiences of red and of green. The latter are sufficient for the relevant experiences, but the physicalist will accept the possibility that the determiners of what one says and how one sorts may include more of brain organization than what is sufficient for the experiences that partially cause what one says and how one sorts. This debate cannot be settled here. Instead, we turn to a different functionalist approach to defeating the physicalist.

Functionalism Goes Neural

There is another functionalist approach to the homunculi head and the inverted spectrum that is mentioned in "Troubles with Functionalism" and pursued by Lycan (1981), namely, that the functionalist account can simply "go neural." The point can easily be seen by attention to the formulation of functionalism in "What Is Functionalism?" (chapter 2, this volume), where a mental state is defined in terms of a Ramsey sentence for a theory as follows:

Being in pain = Being an x such that $\exists F_1 \ldots \exists F_n [T(F_1 \ldots F_n, i_1,$ etc., $o_1,$ etc.$)$ & x is in $F_{17}]$

where F_{17} is the variable that replaced "pain" in the original theory. (The Ramsey sentence for a theory T is $\exists F_1 \ldots \exists F_n [T]$, where $F_1 \ldots F_n$ are variables that replaced the "theoretical terms" of T.) The form of functionalism being criticized in chapters 2, 3, 4, and

19 is a form in which the theory T is understood to be a theory of "molar" psychology. But to the extent that "odd" multiple realizations at a lower level undermine such a functionalist view, the functionalist can respond by changing T by adding to it enough neuroscience, or even physics and chemistry, to base the functional state firmly in properties of the realization that exclude the "odd" realizations. That is, once the functional state becomes more detailed in this way, the homunculi-headed robot no longer realizes it. Turning to the inverted-spectrum issue, suppose the physicalist "inverted-spectrum" critique of molar functionalism depends on identifying different brain states that are the basis of phenomenal experience and can realize the same molar functional color-experience role. Then the functionalist who is willing to "go neural" can accommodate this idea by abandoning molar functionalism in favor of a version of functionalism that defines color experience in terms of the Ramsey sentence for the neurological theory that describes those neural states.

Chauvinism Again

However, there is a cost to this line of argument, one mentioned in "Troubles with Functionalism" (chapter 4, this volume). The problem is that even if the functionalist can describe a neurofunctional state that is a sufficient condition for, say, the experience as of red, there is no reason to think and plenty of reason to deny that that neurofunctional state will be necessary for that experience. Consider again our hypothetical functional isomorph who is as different physically from us as is possible, Commander Data. A theory that says that the experience as of red is identical to a neurofunctional state derived from the human functional description would say by fiat that Commander Data can have no such experience. Further, since phenomenality itself is just the most general phenomenal state, the neurofunctional theory that identifies phenomenality itself with a neurofunctional state would dictate that Commander Data has no phenomenality at all. Do not get me wrong. I am not saying that Commander Data *does* have phenomenality. What I am saying is that whether Commander Data has phenomenality is an open question that should not be decided by fiat. (Commander Data is described in more detail later in this introduction and in still more detail in "The Harder Problem of Consciousness," chapter 20, this volume.)

Increasingly, philosophers are simply swallowing, even embracing, chauvinism of this kind. It has become routine for functionalists and physicalists to state their views in terms of supervenience of the mind on the functional or physical—that is, as claiming that the mind-body problem is solved if a sufficient condition can be provided for the mind in terms of the brain or in terms of functional properties (Chalmers 1996; Jackson 1998; see Kim 1993 for more on supervenience). And many philosophers who do not advocate a supervenience view of the mind-body problem, put forward theories that seem vastly less plausible as necessary conditions than as sufficient conditions. For example, advocates of the "sensorimotor" form of functionalism (e.g., Noë 2004) are explicit about the idea that their characterizations of phenomenality will mention inputs and outputs specific to humans.

Chauvinism as Part of a General Functionalist Strategy

If physicalism and functionalism are only required to provide a sufficient condition of phenomenality, then chauvinism may seem to disappear as a problem, since creatures of wildly different physical or functional constitution can all satisfy one or another sufficient condition for the same phenomenal state. There will be no problem if some of the conditions mention hands and eyes if others do not.

There are, however, two serious difficulties with embracing this sort of chauvinism in this way. Spelling out these difficulties will be the task of the rest of this introduction. One of the difficulties arises when one asks what the justification of "going neural" is supposed to be. A standard answer, put trenchantly by Dan Dennett (2001, 233), is that functionalism is true generally, for all of science, so the most general functional descriptions are at the level of fundamental science: "Functionalism is the idea enshrined in the old proverb: handsome is as handsome does. Matter matters only because of what matter can do. Functionalism in this broadest sense is so ubiquitous in science that it is tantamount to a reigning presumption of all of science." Dennett goes on to explain that the level of detail in functional descriptions relevant to the mind is the level of detail that makes a difference in computational role. He sees the failure of AI-oriented research about the mind as one of thinking one could get away with too little of the functionalized detail, since functionalized neuroscience is required:

The recent history of neuroscience can be seen as a series of triumphs for the lovers of detail. Yes, the specific geometry of the connectivity matters; yes, the location of specific neuromodulators and their effects matter; yes, the architecture matters; yes, the fine temporal rhythms of the spiking patterns matter, and so on. Many of the fond hopes of opportunistic minimalists have been dashed: they had hoped they could leave out various things, and they have learned that no, if you leave out x, or y, or z, you can't explain how the mind works. This has left the mistaken impression in some quarters that the underlying idea of functionalism has been taking its lumps. Far from it. On the contrary, the reasons for accepting these new claims are precisely the reasons of functionalism. Neurochemistry matters because—and only because—we have discovered that the many different neuromodulators and other chemical messengers that diffuse through the brain have functional roles that make important differences. What those molecules do turns out to be important to the computational roles played by the neurons, so we have to pay attention to them after all. (pp. 234–235)

However, it is no recent discovery that has shown that what the molecules that make up neurons do is important to the computational role played by the neurons. I doubt that anyone has ever thought that the molecules that make up neurons were some sort of inert filler that did nothing significant. But my main objection is that even if we care and know about things because of their causes and effects, we cannot conclude that the identity of every thing and every property can be seen in terms of causes and effects. Anything that functions as a mousetrap is indeed a mousetrap, but something could function as a banana—at least at one level of description—while being a mere ersatz banana. For example, it might be a deviant member of another species. Dennett would no doubt agree, claiming that one can avoid the problem by specifying the causes and effects at a lower level, for example, a molecular level. However—and this is my first point—exactly the same problem arises at other levels, maybe every level.

I give an argument to this effect in "Troubles with Functionalism" (chapter 4, this volume). The argument is that the lowest level of all, that of basic-level physics, is vulnerable to the same point. Putting the point in terms of the physics of forty years ago (see Feynman, Leighton, and Sands 1963), the causal role of neutrons is the same as that of antineutrons. If you formulate a functional role for a neutron, an antineutron will realize it. That is, an antineutron is an ersatz realizer of the functional definition of "neutron." As Feynman, Leighton, and Sands say, "The antineutron is distinguished from the neutron in this way: if we bring two neutrons together, they just stay as two neutrons, but if we bring a neutron and an antineutron together, they annihilate each other with a great explosion of energy being liberated" (p. 52-10). (In modern physics, I am told, there are symmetries that allow a more complex version of the same point.)

Put in terms of the Ramsey definitions mentioned before, the idea is that one could define "neutron" as follows:

Being a neutron = Being an x such that $\exists F_1 \ldots \exists F_n [T(F_1 \ldots F_n, i_1, \text{etc.}, o_1, \text{etc.}) \,\&\, x$ is in $F_{17}]$

where F_{17} is the variable that replaced "neutron" in the original theory. But "being an antineutron" would have a logically equivalent definition, since nothing in the Ramsey sentence would distinguish the variable that replaces "neutron" from the variable that replaces "antineutron." For example, the variable that replaces "antineutron" might be F_{18}. If so, one would get a logically equivalent Ramsey sentence by exchanging the variables that replaced the names of particles with the variables that replaced the names of antiparticles. The Ramsified theory would distinguish between F_{17} and F_{18} only by saying that when particles of type F_{17} meet particles of type F_{18} they annihilate one another. (And particles of type F_{17} do not annihilate particles of type F_{17}, and particles of type F_{18} do not annihilate particles of type F_{18}.) Visibly, exchanging variables makes no difference. One could put the point like this: "neutron" is defined in terms of having causal role R while not being identical to another type of particle that has a role exactly the same as R except that it includes being annihilated by collisions with the first type but not with particles of its own type. Or, more flamboyantly:

what do neutrons say about what they are? They say "I am characterized by causal role *R*, which includes annihilating another particle that also has causal role *R* but is of a different type from me, and also not annihilating particles of my type."[2] If you were communicating by radio with a functionalist in a remote part of the universe, you would not be able to tell from what he or she said about physics whether that person lived in an antimatter part of the universe or a matter part of the universe. Just as there can be a realization of human functional organization that is mentally different from ours—for example, has "inverted" or "absent" qualia[3]—so there can be two equally good realizations of a Ramsified physics that are nonetheless different from one another.

This point shows, I think, that there is no general functionalist property identity claim or even property sufficient-condition claim that works for all of science. However, it is important to see that the point I am making does not refute a slightly but importantly different functionalist project, that of David Lewis's famous "How to Define Theoretical Terms" (1970). Lewis would define "neutron" along these lines: "the thing that has such and such causal role," where the role can be spelled out in terms of a Ramsey sentence. As Lewis emphasizes, these definite descriptions are to be understood as *context-relative*. (One example he uses is "the winning number.") And my objection does not apply to such a view. Even if there is more than one thing that satisfies the neutron role as spelled out in terms of a Ramsey sentence—as I have said—there may be only one context-relative thing. Further, and importantly for Lewis, there is no context in which the definition picks out anything nonphysical. (In my correspondence with Lewis about this issue, he said it would be sufficient for his purposes that there is a pair of things (neutron, antineutron) that is picked out by the Ramsey definition (even ignoring the context relativity).) Lewis was not concerned with the question of whether there is a functional definition that completely captures what it is to be a neutron. He thought of himself as a physicalist, not a functionalist. (See "What Is Functionalism?", chapter 2, this volume.) But for the functionalist, it does matter.

Recall how we got here. We were considering the problem of how a functionalist can deal with realizations of our functional organization that are quite different from us physically, such as the homunculi-head and Commander Data. The suggestion was to embrace neurofunctional chauvinism, the idea that all one needs for a solution to the mind-body problem is a sufficient condition of mentality in neurofunctional terms. Assuming that we share no neurofunctional state with Commander Data or the homunculi head that could be the physical basis of any shared phenomenality, the neurofunctional chauvinist can say this: "We certainly satisfy a functional sufficient condition of phenomenality, and if they have phenomenality, Commander Data and the homunculi-head will satisfy some other sufficient condition. And that is enough to solve the mind-body problem."

But as we have just seen, such an approach does not work in all of science, and so that general claim—made by Dennett above—cannot be used to argue for that approach to the science of the mind. This removes one motivation for the view, but it does nothing to refute the view itself, a matter to which I now turn.

Metaphysics vs. Ontology

The problem with the chauvinist approach is that it ignores the metaphysical problem of mind in favor of the ontological problem of mind. Ontology concerns part of metaphysics, as I use these terms. Metaphysics is the study of the ultimate nature of things, whereas ontology concerns what types of things exist. Dualism and physicalism disagree on both ontology and aspects of metaphysics outside of ontology, but functionalism and physicalism disagree only on aspects of metaphysics outside of ontology. Let me explain. Dualism and physicalism disagree on what there is. Dualism countenances the nonphysical—more specifically, nonphysical substances or nonphysical properties. Physicalism admits nothing nonphysical. But functionalism neither agrees nor disagrees with either dualism or physicalism on what there is, since functionalism takes no stand on the issue of immaterial souls. Functionalism says that what makes two pains both pains is a common functional role. Pains could have that functional role whether or not they involve nonphysical substances or properties, so long as the nonphysical substances or properties are causally efficacious in the right way. An adding automaton is defined by functional relations to its inputs and outputs, but this does not rule out an adding automaton powered by an immaterial soul.

If a complete microphysical story entails the complete mental story, we can be sure that there are no souls and in that sense, let us suppose, ontological physicalism is true. But what we cannot conclude is that we can state the essence of mental states in physical terms—that is, we cannot conclude that we can solve the metaphysical problem of mind. For that we would need necessary *and* sufficient physical conditions.

We can make the problem with chauvinism vivid by more detailed attention to the example of Commander Data. Let us think of Commander Data as defined as a merely superficial functional isomorph of us. A superficial isomorph of us is isomorphic to us in causal relations among mental states, inputs, and outputs to the extent that those causal relations are part of commonsense psychology. (That is, for every human mental state, input, and output, there is a corresponding state (maybe mental, maybe not), input, and output of Commander Data; and for every causal relation among our states, inputs, and outputs, there is a corresponding causal relation among Commander Data's mental states, inputs, and outputs. One consequence is that Commander Data will behave just as we do, as far as we can tell from the standpoint of commonsense psychology.) I said that Commander Data is a *merely* superficial isomorph of us. That means that he is not like us in physical realization of the superficial functional states he shares with us except to the extent that shared properties of physical realizations are required by superficial functional isomorphism. And Commander Data is not like us in detailed functional states—for example, functional states that involve functionalized neuroscience. We can assume that the only functional properties we share with Commander Data are the superficial ones mentioned earlier and that there are no shared physical properties that can explain any shared phenomenality without attributing phenomenality to things that do not have it.

Suppose, as seems conceivable, that Commander Data is a conscious creature. For vividness, suppose, as also seems conceivable, that Commander Data is phenomenally *exactly* like us. It immediately follows that the usual kinds of physicalism and neurological functionalism are problematic as metaphysical accounts of the mind. For a metaphysical account of the mind should tell us *why* Commander Data's pain feels just like mine. A solution to the metaphysical mind-body problem should tell us what it is about Commander Data's pain and mine that explains (or constitutes) why they feel the same. But since, ex hypothesi, there are no shared physical and neurofunctional properties that can do the job, it is not obvious how these approaches can solve the metaphysical problem of mind.

Our pains and Commander Data's pains do share a heterogeneously disjunctive underlying property, the property of having either his physical realization or our physical realization of the shared functional state. But to appeal to that heterogeneously disjunctive state is explaining the shared phenomenality in terms of his having his physical realization and us having ours, which is no explanation at all. Do not get me wrong. I am not saying that the metaphysical mind-body identity claim that identifies the shared phenomenal state with a heterogeneously disjunctive physical state cannot be true. What I am saying is that there is something plainly inadequate about it as a metaphysical theory of mind, something about its lack of explanatory force. (More on this in "The Harder Problem of Consciousness," chapter 20, this volume.)

Of course, nothing I have said rules out the possibility that the superficial functional isomorphism requires some further abstract physical or neurofunctional similarity or that the superficial functional isomorphism itself explains the shared phenomenality. The point of the thought experiment is not to show that neurofunctionalism and physicalism are false but rather to show that a condition of success is avoiding chauvinism. Only by conflating the metaphysical problem of mind with the ontological problem of mind could one suppose that chauvinism is a recipe for success with the metaphysical mind-body problem.

Sometimes chauvinism is suggested as a necessary condition as well as a sufficient condition. For example, Noë (2004, 25) says that "if perception is in part constituted by our possession and exercise of bodily skills—as I argue in this book—then it may also depend on our possession of the sort of bodies that can encompass those skills, for only a creature with such a body could have those skills. To perceive like us, it follows, you must have a body like ours."

We can distinguish between an immodest and a modest version of Noë's sensorimotor chauvinism. The immodest version says that some kind of functional story involving specific features of the human body (he mentions hands and eyes) is an answer to the mind-body problem for experience or at least perceptual experience. The modest version says that something to do with hands and eyes is partially causally determinative of our perceptual experience. I have no quarrel with the modest version. But the immodest version has to face the issue of the nature of experience per se, not just the specific kind of experience we have. And the view that the nature of experience per se must involve the kinds of sense organs and effectors we have would be chauvinist in the derogatory sense of the term.

Notes

1. I am alluding here to Shoemaker 1981, which formulates a distinction between a core and a total brain state. A total brain state is sufficient for the experience. A core realization of the functional role of the experience of red is the minimal brain state that plays that functional role. One could define a somewhat different distinction without using the notion of functional role. For example, one could define the core neural basis of my experience as of red as the brain state that makes the difference between my experience as of red and my other different color experiences— in the context of the background brain properties that constitute the rest of my total brain state that is sufficient for that experience.

2. According to the *New York Times* of April 26, 2005 (Chang 2005), it is possible for particles to be identical to their antiparticles: "Physicists are also trying to learn whether an antineutrino is actually a neutrino. (Other antiparticles have opposite electrical charge. Because neutrinos are electrically neutral, nothing would prevent a neutrino from being its own antiparticle.)" If this is true, it would be handled in the Ramsey treatment by modifying the clause about annihilating the other particle that has the same Ramsey definition.

3. These terms were used for the first time, I believe, in "What Psychological States Are Not."

References

Block, Ned. 1994. Two kinds of laws. In C. MacDonald and G. MacDonald, eds., *The Philosophy of Psychology: Debates on Psychological Explanation*. Blackwell: Oxford, 1994.

Block, Ned. 1997. Anti-reductionism slaps back. *Mind, Causation, World, Philosophical Perspectives* 11: 107–133. Reprinted in volume 2 of these collected papers.

Chalmers, David. 1996. *The Conscious Mind*. New York: Oxford.

Chang, Kenneth. 2005. Tiny, plentiful and really hard to catch. *New York Times*, April 26.

Dennett, Daniel. 2001. Are we explaining consciousness yet? *Cognition* 79(1–2): 221–237.

Feynman, R. P., Leighton, R. B., and Sands, M. 1963. Symmetry in physical laws. In *The Feynman Lectures on Physics*. Vol. 1, chap. 52, 52-1 to 52-12. Reading, MA: Addison-Wesley.

Fodor, Jerry. 1968. Materialism. In *Psychological Explanation*, chap. 3, 90–120. New York: Random House.

Fodor, Jerry. 1997. Special sciences: Still autonomous after all these years. In J. Tomberlin, ed., *Mind, Causation, World, Philosophical Perspectives*. Vol. 11. Oxford: Blackwell.

Jackson, Frank. 1998. *From Metaphysics to Ethics: A Defense of Conceptual Analysis*. Oxford: Oxford University Press.

Kim, Jaegwon. 1993. *Supervenience and Mind*. Cambridge: Cambridge University Press.

Lewis, David. 1970. How to define theoretical terms. *Journal of Philosophy* 67: 427–445.

Lycan, William. 1981. Form, function and feel. *Journal of Philosophy* 78: 24–50.

Noë, Alva. 2004. *Action in Perception*. Cambridge, MA: MIT Press.

O'Regan, J. Kevin, and Noë, Alva. 2001. Acting out our sensory experience. *Behavioral and Brain Sciences* 24(5): 1011–1021.

Putnam, Hilary. 1967. Psychological predicates (later titled The nature of mental states). In W. Capitan and D. Merrill, eds., *Art, Mind, and Religion*. Pittsburgh: Pittsburgh University Press.

Shoemaker, S. 1981. Some varieties of functionalism. *Philosophical Topics* 12: 93–119. Reprinted in S. Shoemaker, *Identity, Cause, and Mind*. Cambridge: Cambridge University Press, 1984.

I Functionalism

1 Functionalism

What Is Functionalism?

Functionalism is one of the major proposals that have been offered as solutions to the mind-body problem. Solutions to the mind-body problem usually try to answer questions such as: What is the ultimate nature of the mental? At the most general level, what makes a mental state mental? Or more specifically, What do thoughts have in common by virtue of which they are thoughts? That is, what makes a thought a thought? What makes a pain a pain? Cartesian dualism said the ultimate nature of the mental was to be found in a special mental substance. Behaviorism identified mental states with behavioral dispositions; physicalism in its most influential version identifies mental states with brain states. Functionalism says that mental states are constituted by their causal relations to one another and to sensory inputs and behavioral outputs. Although it is descended from Aristotle, modern functionalism is one of the major theoretical developments of twentieth-century analytic philosophy, and provides the conceptual underpinnings of much work in cognitive science.

Functionalism has three distinct modern-day sources. First, Putnam and Fodor saw mental states in terms of an empirical computational theory of the mind. Second, Smart's "topic-neutral" analyses led Armstrong and Lewis to a functionalist analysis of mental concepts. Third, Wittgenstein's idea of meaning as use led to a version of functionalism as a theory of meaning, further developed by Sellars and later Harman.

One motivation behind functionalism can be appreciated by attention to artifact concepts like *carburetor* and biological concepts like *kidney*. What it is for something to be a carburetor is for it to mix fuel and air in an internal combustion engine— *carburetor* is a functional concept. In the case of the kidney, the *scientific* concept is functional—defined in terms of a role in filtering the blood and maintaining certain chemical balances.

The kind of function relevant to the mind can be introduced via the parity-detecting automaton illustrated in figure 1.1, which tells us whether it has seen an odd or even number of '1's. This automaton has two states, S_1 and S_2; two inputs, '1' and '0'; and

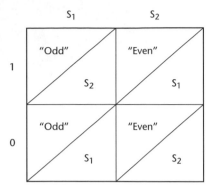

Figure 1.1
Parity automaton with two inputs

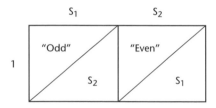

Figure 1.2
Parity automaton with one input

two outputs, with either the word "Odd" or "Even" being uttered. Figure 1.1 describes two functions, one from input and state to output, and another from input and state to next state. Each square encodes two conditionals specifying the output and next state given both the current state and input. The top-left box says that if the machine is in S_1 and sees a '1', it says "Odd" (indicating that it has seen an odd number of '1's) and goes to S_2. The right box says, similarly, that if the machine is in S_2 and sees a '1', it says "Even" and goes back to S_1. The bottom-left box says that if the machine is in S_1 and sees a '0', it says "Odd" and stays in S_1. The machine is intended to start in S_1, so if its first input is a '0', it will wrongly say that it has seen an odd number of '1's, but once it has seen a 1, subsequent answers will be correct. (The flaw is corrected in the next machine.)

The machine of figure 1.2 is simpler. As before, this automaton has two states, S_1 and S_2, and two outputs, "Odd" or "Even." The difference is that it only has one input, '1', though of course it can get no input at all (as can the machine of figure 1.1). As before, the table describes two functions, one from input and state to output, and another from input and state to next state. As before, each square encodes two conditionals specifying the output and next state given both the current state and input. The left box says that if the machine is in S_1 and sees a '1,' it says "Odd" (indicating that it has seen an odd number of '1's) and goes to S_2. The right box says, similarly, that if the machine is in S_2 and sees a '1', it says "Even" and goes back to S_1. This machine is simpler than the machine of figure 1.1 and intuitively serves the same purpose and further avoids branding zero '1's as an odd number of '1's.

Now suppose we ask the question: "What is S_1?" The answer is that the nature of S_1 is entirely relational, and entirely captured by the figure. We could give an explicit characterization of S_1 (from figure 1.2) as follows:

Being in S_1 = being in the first of two states that are related to one another and to inputs and outputs as follows: being in one of the states and getting a '1' input results in going into the second state and emitting "Odd"; and being in the second of the two states and getting a '1' input results in going into the first and emitting "Even."

Making the quantification over states more explicit:

Being in S_1 = Being an x such that $\exists P \exists Q$ [If x is in P and gets a '1' input, then it goes into Q and emits "Odd"; if x is in Q and gets a '1' input, it goes into P and emits "Even" & x is in P]. (Note: Read "$\exists P$" as There is a property P.)

This illustration can be used to make a number of points: (1) According to functionalism, the nature of a mental state is just like the nature of an automaton state—that is, constituted by its relations to other states and to inputs and outputs. All there is to S_1 is that being in it and getting a '1' input results in such and such, etc. According to functionalism, all there is to being in pain is that it disposes you to say "ouch," wonder whether you are ill, become distracted, and so on. (2) Because mental states are like automaton states in this regard, the illustrated method for defining automaton states is supposed to work for mental states as well. Mental states can be totally characterized in terms that involve only logicomathematical language and terms for input signals and behavioral outputs. Thus functionalism satisfies one of the desiderata of behaviorism, characterizing the mental in entirely nonmental language. (3) S_1 is a second-order state in that it consists in having *other* properties, say mechanical or hydraulic or electronic properties, that have certain relations to one another. These other properties, the ones quantified over in the definitions just given, are said to be the *realizations* of the functional properties. So, although functionalism characterizes the mental in nonmental terms, it does so only by quantifying over realizations of mental states, which would not have delighted behaviorists. (4) One functional state can be realized in different ways. For example, an actual metal and plastic machine satisfying the machine table might be made of gears, wheels, pulleys, and the like, in which case the realization of S_1 would be a mechanical state; or the realization of S_1 might be an electronic state, and so forth. (5) Just as one functional state can be realized in different ways, one physical state can realize different functional states in different machines. This could happen, for example, if a single type of transistor were used to do different things in different machines. (6) Since S_1 can be realized in many ways, a claim that S_1 *is* a mechanical state would be false (at least arguably), as would a claim that S_1 is an electronic state. For this reason, functionalism shows that physicalism is false: if a creature without a brain can think, thinking cannot be a brain state. (But see the section on functionalism and physicalism below.)

The notion of a realization deserves further discussion. In the early days of functionalism, a first-order property was often said to realize a functional property by virtue of a 1-1 correspondence between the two realms of properties. But such a definition of realization produces far too many realizations. Suppose, for example, that at t_1 we shout "one" at a bucket of water, and then at t_2 we shout "one" again. We can regard the bucket as a parity-detecting automaton by pairing the physical configuration of the bucket at t_1 with S_1 and the heat emitted or absorbed by the bucket at t_1 with "Odd"; by pairing the physical configuration of the bucket at t_2 with S_2 and the heat exchanged with the environment at t_2 with "Even"; and so on. What is left out by the post hoc correlation way of thinking of realization is that a true realization must satisfy the *counterfactuals* implicit in figure 1.2. To be a realization of S_1, it is not enough to lead to a certain output and state given that the input is a '1'; it is also required that had the input been a '0', the S_1 realization would have led to the other output and *state*. Satisfaction of the relevant counterfactuals is built into the notion of realization mentioned in (3) above. See Lycan 1987.

Suppose we have a theory of mental states that specifies all the causal relations among the states, sensory inputs, and behavioral outputs. Focusing on pain as a sample mental state, it might say, among other things, that sitting on a tack causes pain and that pain causes anxiety and saying "ouch." Agreeing to go along with this moronic theory for the sake of the example, functionalism would then say that we could define "pain" as follows: being in pain = being in the first of two states, the first of which is caused by sitting on tacks, and which in turn causes the other state and emitting "ouch." More symbolically

Being in pain = Being an x such that $\exists P \exists Q$ [sitting on a tack causes P & P causes both Q and emitting "ouch" & x is in P]

More generally, if T is a psychological theory with n mental terms of which the seventeenth is "pain," we can define "pain" relative to T as follows. (The 'F_1'...'F_n' are variables that replace the n mental terms, and 'i_1', etc., and 'o_1', etc. indicate input and output terms).

Being in pain = Being an x such that $\exists F_1 \ldots \exists F_n$ [$T(F_1 \ldots F_n, i_1,$ etc., $o_1,$ etc.) & x is in F_{17}]

In this way, functionalism characterizes the mental in nonmental terms, in terms that involve quantification over realizations of mental states but no explicit mention of them; thus functionalism characterizes the mental in terms of structures that are tacked down to reality only at the inputs and outputs.

The psychological theory T just mentioned can be either an empirical psychological theory or else a commonsense "folk" theory, and the resulting functionalisms are very different. In the latter case, *conceptual functionalism*, the functional definitions are aimed at capturing our ordinary mental concepts. In the former case, which I named *psychofunctionalism*, the functional definitions are not supposed to capture ordinary concepts but are only supposed to fix the extensions of mental terms. The idea of psychofunctionalism is that the scientific nature of the mental consists not in anything biological, but in something "organizational," analogous to computational structure. Conceptual functionalism, by contrast, can be thought of as a development of logical behaviorism. Logical behaviorists thought that pain was a disposition to pain *behavior*. But as Geach and Chisholm pointed out, what counts as pain behavior depends on the agent's beliefs and desires. Conceptual functionalists avoid this problem by defining each mental state in terms of its contribution to dispositions to behave—and have other mental states.

Functionalism and Physicalism

Theories of the mind prior to functionalism have been concerned both with (1) what there *is* and (2) with what gives each type of mental state its own identity—for example, what pains have in common by virtue of which they are pains. Stretching these terms a bit, we might say that (1) is a matter of ontology and (2) of metaphysics. Here are the ontological claims: dualism told us that there are both mental and physical substances, whereas behaviorism and physicalism are monistic, claiming that there are only physical substances. Here are the metaphysical claims: behaviorism tells us that what pains (for example) have in common by virtue of which they are pains is something behavioral; dualism gave a nonphysical answer to this question, and physicalism gives a physical answer to this question. Turning now to functionalism, it answers the metaphysical question without answering the ontological question. Functionalism tells us that what pains have in common—what makes them pains—is their function; but functionalism does not tell us whether the beings that have pains have any nonphysical parts. This point can be seen in terms of the automaton described above. To be an automaton of the type described, an actual concrete machine need only have states related to one another and to inputs and outputs in the way described. The machine description does not tell us how the machine works or what it is made of, and in particular it does not rule out a machine operated by an immaterial soul, so long as the soul is willing to operate in the deterministic manner specified in the table. See the papers by Fodor and Putnam in Block 1980.

In thinking about the relation between functionalism and physicalism, it is useful to distinguish two categories of physicalist theses. One version of physicalism competes with functionalism, making a metaphysical claim about the physical nature of mental-state properties or types (and is thus often called "type" physicalism). As mentioned above, from one point of view, functionalism shows that type physicalism is false.

However, there are more modest physicalisms whose thrusts are ontological rather than metaphysical. Such physicalistic claims are not at all incompatible with functionalism. Consider, for example, a physicalism that says that every actual thing is made up of entirely of particles of the sort that compose inorganic matter. In this sense of physicalism, most functionalists have been physicalists. Further, functionalism can be modified in a physicalistic direction, for example, by requiring that all properties quantified over in a functional definition be physical properties. Type physicalism is often contrasted with *token* physicalism. (The word "teeth" in this sentence has five-letter tokens of three letter types.) Token physicalism says that each pain (for example) is a physical state, but token physicalism allows that there may be nothing physical that all pains share, nothing physical that makes a pain a pain.

It is a peculiarity of the literature on functionalism and physicalism that while some functionalists say functionalism shows physicalism is false (see the papers by Putnam, Fodor, and Block and Fodor in Block 1980, some of which are also in other anthologies), others say functionalism shows physicalism is true (see the papers by Lewis and Armstrong in Block 1980 and Rosenthal 1991). In Lewis's case, the issue is partly terminological. Lewis is a conceptual functionalist about *having pain*. "Having pain," on Lewis's regimentation, could be said to be a rigid designator of a functional property. (A rigid designator names the same thing in each possible world. "The color of the sky" is nonrigid, since it names red in worlds in which the sky is red. "Blue" is rigid, since it names blue even in worlds in which the sky is red.) "Pain," by contrast, is a nonrigid designator conceptually equivalent to a definite description of the form "the state with such and such a causal role." The referent of this phrase in us, Lewis holds, is a certain brain state, though the referent of this phrase in a robot might be a circuit state, and the referent in an angel would be a nonphysical state. Similarly, "the winning number" picks out 17 in one lottery and 596 in another. So Lewis is a functionalist (indeed a conceptual functionalist) about having pain. In terms of the metaphysical issue described above—what do pains have in common by virtue of which they are pains—Lewis is a functionalist, not a physicalist. What my pains and the robot's pains share is a causal role, not anything physical. Just as there is no numerical similarity between 17 and 596 relevant to their being winning numbers, there is no physical similarity between human and Martian pain that makes them pains. And there is no physical similarity of any kind between human pains and angel pains. However, on the issue of the scientific nature of pain, Lewis is a physicalist. What is common to human and Martian pain in his view is something conceptual, not scientific.

Functionalism and Propositional Attitudes

The discussion of functional characterization given above assumes a psychological theory with a finite number of mental state terms. In the case of monadic states like pain, the sensation of red, and so on, it does seem a theoretical option to simply list the states and their relations to other states, inputs, and outputs. But for a number of reasons, this is not a sensible theoretical option for belief states, desire states, and other propositional-attitude states. For one thing, the list would be too long to be represented without combinatorial methods. Indeed, there is arguably no upper bound on the number of propositions any one of which could in principle be an object of thought. For another thing, there are systematic relations among beliefs—for example, the belief that John loves Mary and the belief that Mary loves John. These belief states represent the same objects as related to each other in converse ways. But a theory of the nature of beliefs can hardly just leave out such an important feature of them. We cannot treat "believes-that-grass-is-green," "believes-that-grass-is-blue," and so forth as unrelated primitive predicates. So we will need a more sophisticated theory, one that involves some sort of combinatorial apparatus. The most promising candidates are those that treat belief as a relation. But a relation to what? There are two distinct issues here. One issue is how to state the functional theory in a detailed way. See Loar 1981 and Schiffer 1987 for a suggestion in terms of a correspondence between the logical relations among sentences and the inferential relations among mental states. A second issue is what types of states could possibly realize the relational propositional-attitude states. Field (1978) and Fodor (in Block 1980) argue that to explain the productivity of propositional-attitude states, there is no alternative to postulating a language of thought, a system of syntactically structured objects in the brain that express the propositions in propositional attitudes. See Stalnaker 1984, chaps. 1–3, for a critique of Field's approach. In later work, Fodor (1987) has stressed the systematicity of propositional attitudes mentioned above. Fodor points out that the beliefs whose contents are systematically related exhibit the following sort of empirical relation: if one is capable of believing that Mary loves John, one is also capable of believing that John loves Mary. Fodor argues that only a language of thought in the brain could explain this fact.

Externalism

The upshot of the famous "twin-earth" arguments has been that meaning and content are in part located in the world and in the language community. Functionalists have responded in a variety of ways. One reaction is to think of the inputs and outputs of a functional theory as *long-arm*—that is, as including the objects that one sees and manipulates. Another reaction is to stick with *short-arm* inputs and outputs that stop at the surfaces of the body, thinking of the intentional contents thereby characterized as *narrow*—supervening on the nonrelational physical properties of the body. There has been no widely recognized account of what narrow content is, nor is there any agreement as to whether there is any burden of proof on the advocates of narrow content to characterize it. See the papers by Burge, Loar, and Stalnaker in Rosenthal 1991; see also Goldman 1993.

Meaning

Functionalism says that understanding the meaning of the word "momentum" is a functional state. In one version of the view, the functional state can be seen in terms of the role of the word "momentum" itself in thinking, problem solving, planning, and so on. But if understanding the meaning of "momentum" is this word's having a certain function, then there is a very close relation between the meaning of a word and its function, and a natural proposal is to regard the close relation as simply identity— that is, the meaning of the word just *is* that function. (c.f. Peacocke 1992.) Thus functionalism about content leads to functionalism about meaning, a theory that purports to tell us the metaphysical nature of meaning. This theory is popular in cognitive science, where in one version it is often known as procedural semantics, as well as in philosophy, where it is often known as conceptual role semantics. The theory has been criticized (along with other versions of functionalism) in Putnam 1988 and Fodor and Lepore 1992.

Holism

Block and Fodor (in Block 1980) noted the "damn/darn" problem. Functional theories must make reference to any difference in stimuli or responses that can be mentally significant. The difference between saying "damn" and "darn" when you stub your toe can, in some circumstances, be mentally significant. So the different functionalized theories appropriate to the two responses will affect the individuation of every state connected to those utterances, and for the same reason, every state connected to those states, and so on. Your pains lead to "darn," mine to "damn," so our pains are functionally different, and likewise our desires to avoid pain, our beliefs that interact with those desires, and so forth. Plausible assumptions lead to the conclusion that two individuals who differ in this way share almost nothing in the way of mental states. The upshot is that the functionalist needs a way of individuating mental states that is less fine-grained than appeal to the whole theory, a molecularist characterization. Even if one is optimistic about solving this problem in the case of pain by finding something functional that is common to all pains, one cannot assume that success will transfer to beliefs or meanings, for success in the case of meaning and belief may require an analytic-synthetic distinction (Fodor and Lepore 1992).

Qualia

Recall the parity-detecting automaton described at the beginning of this chapter. It could be instantiated by two people, each of whom is in charge of the function specified by a single box. Similarly, the much more complex functional organization of a human mind could "in principle" be instantiated by a vast army of people. We would have to think of the army as connected to a robot body, acting as the brain of that body, and the body would be like a person in its reactions to inputs. But would such an army really instantiate a mind? More pointedly, could such an army have pain or the experience of red? If functionalism ascribes minds to things that do not have them, it is too liberal. Lycan (1987) suggests that we include much of human physiology in our theory to be functionalized to avoid liberalism—that is, the theory T in the definition described earlier would be a psychological theory plus a physiological theory. But that makes the opposite problem, chauvinism, worse. The resulting functional description will not apply to intelligent Martians whose physiologies are different from ours. Further, it seems easy to imagine a simple pain-feeling organism that shares little in the way of functional organization with us. The functionalized physiological theory of this organism will be hopelessly different from the corresponding theory of us. Indeed, even if one does not adopt Lycan's tactic, it is not clear how pain could be characterized functionally so as to be common to us and the simple organism. (See my "Troubles with Functionalism," chapter 4, this volume.)

Much of the force of the problems just mentioned derives from attention to phenomenal states like the look of red. Phenomenal properties would seem at least at first glance to be intrinsic to (nonrelational properties of) the states that have them, and thus phenomenal properties seem independent of the relations among states, inputs, and outputs that define functional states. Consider, for example, the fact that lobotomy patients often say that they continue to have pains that feel the same as before, but that the pains do not bother them. If the concept of pain is a functional concept, what these patients say is contradictory or incoherent—but it seems to many of us that it is intelligible. (All the anthologies have papers on this topic. See also Lycan 1987; Shoemaker 1984, chaps. 8, 9, 14, 15; Hill 1991.)

The chauvinism-liberalism problem affects the characterization of inputs and outputs. If we characterize inputs and outputs in a way appropriate to our bodies, we chauvinistically exclude creatures whose interface with the world is very different from ours, for example, creatures whose limbs end in wheels, or turning to a bigger difference, gaseous creatures who can manipulate and sense gases but for whom only the topologies of solids and liquids matter. The obvious alternative of characterizing inputs and outputs themselves functionally would appear to yield an abstract structure that might be satisfied by, for instance, the economy of Bolivia under manipulation by a wealthy eccentric, and would thus fall to the opposite problem of liberalism.

It is tempting to respond to the chauvinism problem by supposing that the same functional theory that applies to me also applies to the creatures with wheels. If they thought they had feet, they would try to act like us, and if we thought we had wheels, we would try to act like them. But notice that the functional definitions have to have some specifications of output organs in them. To be neutral among all the types of bodies that sentient beings could have would just be to adopt the liberal alternative of specifying the inputs and outputs themselves functionally. Some suppose that the problem can be handled by conditional outputs. For example, wanting to get the ball to the end of the field could be defined in part by the tendency to kick it if one has limbs of a certain sort, push it if one has limbs of another sort, etc. But it is not clear that the "etc." could ever be filled in, since it would require enumerating and physically describing every kind of output organ an intelligent being could have. Further, the result of a certain desire on one's limbs depends on how they are wired up as well as their physical shape. In the context of the "wrong" wiring, a desire to get the ball to the end of the field would result in the ball stuck in one's mouth rather than propelled down the field. But this point makes it look as if the problem will require going far beyond anything that could be said to be implicit in common sense. (See Braddon-Mitchell and Jackson 1995, for an opposing view.)

Teleology

Many philosophers (see the papers by Lycan and Sober in Lycan 1990, as well as Lycan 1987) propose that we avoid liberalism by characterizing functional roles teleologically. We exclude the armies and economies mentioned because their states are not *for* the right things. A major problem for this point of view is the lack of an acceptable teleological account. Accounts based on evolution smack up against the swamp-grandparents problem. Suppose you find out that your grandparents were formed from particles from the swamp that came together by chance. So, as it happens, you do not have any evolutionary history to speak of. If evolutionary accounts of the teleology underpinnings of content are right, your states do not have any content. A theory with such a consequence should be rejected.

Causation

Functionalism dictates that mental properties are second-order properties, properties that consist in having other properties that have certain relations to one another. But there is at least a prima facie problem about how such second-order properties could be causal and explanatory in a way appropriate to the mental. Consider, for example, provocativeness, the second-order property that consists in having some first-order property (say redness) that causes bulls to be angry. The cape's redness provokes the bull, but does the cape's provocativeness provoke the bull? The cape's provocativeness might provoke an animal protection society, but isn't the bull too stupid to be provoked by it? See Block 1990.

Functionalism continues to be a lively and fluid point of view. Positive developments in recent years include enhanced prospects for conceptual functionalism and the articulation of the teleological point of view. Critical developments include problems with causality and holism, and continuing controversy over chauvinism and liberalism.

Note

This is a somewhat revised version of an entry in *The Encyclopedia of Philosophy*, supplement (New York: Macmillan, 1997).

References

Beakley, Brian, and Ludlow, Peter, eds. 1992. *Philosophy of Mind: Classical Problems/Contemporary Issues*. Cambridge, MA: MIT Press.

Block, Ned, ed. 1980. *Readings in the Philosophy of Psychology*. 2 vols. Cambridge, MA: Harvard University Press.

Block, Ned. 1990. Can the mind change the world? In G. Boolos, ed., *Meaning and Method: Essays in Honor of Hilary Putnam*, 137–170. Cambridge: Cambridge University Press.

Braddon-Mitchell, David, and Jackson, Frank. 1995. *Philosophy of Mind and Cognition*. Oxford: Blackwell.

Chisholm, Roderick. 1957. *Perceiving*, chap. 11. Ithaca, NY: Cornell University Press.

Field, Hartry. 1978. Mental representation. *Erkentniss* 13: 9–61.

Fodor, Jerry. 1987. *Psychosemantics*. Cambridge, MA: MIT Press.

Fodor, Jerry, and Lepore, Ernest. 1992. *Holism*. Oxford: Blackwell.

Geach, Peter. 1971. *Mental Acts*. Chicago: St. Augustine's Press.

Goldman, Alvin. 1993. *Readings in Philosophy and Cognitive Science*. Cambridge, MA: MIT Press.

Hill, Christopher S. 1991. *Sensations*. Cambridge: Cambridge University Press.

Lewis, David. 1995. Reduction of mind. In S. Guttenplan, ed., *A Companion to the Philosophy of Mind*. Blackwell: Oxford.

Loar, Brian. 1981. *Mind and Meaning*. Cambridge: Cambridge University Press.

Lycan, William G. 1987. *Consciousness*. Cambridge, MA: MIT Press.

Lycan, William G., ed. 1990. *Mind and Cognition*. Oxford: Blackwell.

Peacocke, C. 1992. *A Study of Concepts*. Cambridge, MA: MIT Press.

Putnam, Hilary. 1988. *Representation and Reality*. Cambridge, MA: MIT Press.

Rosenthal, David, ed. 1991. *The Nature of Mind*. Oxford: Oxford University Press.

Schiffer, Stephen. 1987. *Remnants of Meaning*. Cambridge, MA: MIT Press.

Shoemaker, Sydney. 1984. *Identity, Cause, and Mind*. Ithaca, NY: Cornell University Press.

Stalnaker, Robert C. 1984. *Inquiry*. Cambridge, MA: MIT Press.

2 What Is Functionalism?

It is doubtful whether doctrines known as "functionalism" in fields as disparate as anthropology, literary criticism, psychology, and philosophy of psychology have anything in common but the name. Even in philosophy of psychology, the term is used in a number of distinct senses. The functionalisms of philosophy of psychology are, however, a closely knit group; indeed, they appear to have a common origin in the works of Aristotle (see Hartman, 1977, especially chap. 4).

Three functionalisms have been enormously influential in philosophy of mind and psychology:

Functional Analysis

In this sense of the term, functionalism is a type of explanation and, derivatively, a research strategy, the research strategy of looking for explanations of that type. A functional explanation is one that relies on a decomposition of a system into its component parts; it explains the working of the system in terms of the capacities of the parts and the way the parts are integrated with one another. For example, we can explain how a factory can produce refrigerators by appealing to the capacities of the various assembly lines, their workers and machines, and the organization of these components. The article by Robert Cummins (1975) describes functionalism in this sense. (See also Fodor, 1965, 1968a, 1968b; Dennett, 1975.)

Computation-Representation Functionalism

In this sense of the term, "functionalism" applies to an important special case of functional explanation as defined above, namely, to psychological explanation seen as akin to providing a computer program for the mind. Whatever mystery our mental life may initially seem to have is dissolved by functional analysis of mental processes to the point where they are seen to be composed of computations as mechanical as the primitive operations of a digital computer—processes so stupid that appealing to them in psychological explanations involves no hint of question-begging. The key notions of functionalism in this sense are representation and computation. Psychological states are seen as systematically representing the world via a language of thought, and psychological processes are seen as computations involving these representations. Functionalism in this sense of the term is not explored here but is discussed in volume 2, part one, "Mental Representation."

Metaphysical Functionalism

The last functionalism, the one that this part is mainly about, is a theory of *the nature of the mind*, rather than a theory of psychological explanation. Metaphysical functionalists are concerned not with how mental states account for behavior, but rather with what they *are*. The functionalist answer to "What are mental states?" is simply that mental states are functional states. Thus theses of metaphysical functionalism are sometimes described as functional state identity theses. The main concern of metaphysical functionalism is the same as that of behaviorism and physicalism. All three doctrines address themselves to such questions as "What is pain?"—or at least to "What is there in common to all pains in virtue of which they are pains?"

It is important to note that metaphysical functionalism is concerned (in the first instance) with mental state *types*, not tokens—with *pain*, for instance, and not with particular *pains*. Most functionalists are willing to allow that each *particular* pain is a physical state or event, and indeed that for each type of pain-feeling organism, there is (perhaps) a single type of physical state that realizes pain in that type of organism. Where functionalists differ with physicalists, however, is with respect to the question of what is common to all pains in virtue of which they are pains. The functionalist says the something in common is functional, while the physicalist says it is physical (and the behaviorist says it is behavioral).[1] Thus, in one respect, the disagreement between functionalists and physicalists (and behaviorists) is *metaphysical without being ontological*. Functionalists can be physicalists in allowing that all the entities (things, states, events, and so on) that exist are physical entities, denying only that what binds certain types of things together is a physical property.

Metaphysical functionalists characterize mental states in terms of their causal roles, particularly, in terms of their causal relations to sensory stimulations, behavioral outputs, and other mental states. Thus, for example, a metaphysical functionalist theory of pain might characterize pain in part in terms of its tendency to be caused by tissue damage, by its tendency to cause the desire to be rid of it, and by its tendency to produce action designed to separate the damaged part of the body from what is thought to cause the damage.

What I have said about metaphysical functionalism so far is rather vague, but, as will become clear, disagreements among metaphysical functionalists preclude easy characterization of the doctrine. Before going on to describe metaphysical functionalism in more detail, I shall briefly sketch some of the connections among the functionalist doctrines just enumerated. One connection is that functionalism in all the senses described has something to do with the notion of a Turing machine (described in the next section). Metaphysical functionalism often identifies mental states with Turing machine "table states" (also described in the next section). Computation-representation functionalism sees psychological explanation as something like providing a computer program for the mind. Its aim is to give a functional analysis of mental capacities broken down into their component mechanical processes. If these mechanical processes are *algorithmic*, as is sometimes assumed (without much justification, in my view) then they will be Turing-computable as well (as the Church-Turing thesis assures us).[2] Functional analysis, however, is concerned with the notion of a Turing machine mainly in that providing something like a computer program for the mind is a special case of functional analysis.

Another similarity among the functionalisms mentioned is their relation to physical characterizations. The causal structures with which metaphysical functionalism identifies mental states are realizable by a vast variety of physical systems. Similarly, the information processing mechanisms postulated by a particular computation-representation functionalist theory could be realized hydraulically, electrically, or even mechanically. Finally, functional analysis would normally characterize a manufacturing process abstractly enough to allow a wide variety of types of machines (wood or metal, steam-driven or electrical), workers (human or robot or animal), and physical setups (a given number of assembly lines or half as many dual-purpose assembly lines). A third similarity is that each type of functionalism described legitimates at least one notion of functional equivalence. For example, for functional analysis, one sense of functional equivalence would be: has capacities that contribute in similar ways to the capacities of a whole.

In what follows, I shall try to give the reader a clearer picture of metaphysical functionalism. ("Functionalism" will be used to mean metaphysical functionalism in what follows.)

Machine Versions of Functionalism

Some versions of functionalism are couched in terms of the notion of a Turing machine, while others are not. A Turing machine is specified by two functions: one from inputs and states to outputs, and one from inputs and states to states. A Turing machine has a finite number of states, inputs, and outputs, and the two functions specify a set of conditionals, one for each combination of state and input. The conditionals are of this form: if the machine is in state S and receives input I, it will then emit output O and go into next state S'. This set of conditionals is often expressed in the form of a machine table (see below). Any system that has a set of inputs, outputs, and states related in the way specified by the machine table is *described* by the machine table

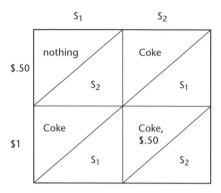

Figure 2.1

and is a *realization* of the abstract automaton specified by the machine table. (This definition actually characterizes a finite transducer, which is just one kind of Turing machine.)

One very simple version of machine functionalism states that each system that has mental states is described by at least one Turing machine table of a certain specifiable sort; it also states that each type of mental state of the system is identical to one of the machine table states specified in the machine table (see Putnam, 1967; Block and Fodor, 1972). Consider, for example, the Turing machine described in the "Coke machine" machine table in figure 2.1 (compare Nelson, 1975).

One can get a crude picture of the simple version of machine functionalism described above by considering the claim that $S_1 = \$1$-desire, and $S_2 = \$.50$-desire. Of course, no functionalist would claim that a Coke machine desires anything. Rather, the simple version of machine functionalism described above makes an analogous claim with respect to a much more complex machine table.

Machine versions of functionalism are useful for many purposes, but they do not provide the most general characterization of functionalism. One can achieve more generality by characterizing functionalism as the view that what makes a pain a pain (and, generally, what makes any mental state the mental state it is) is its having a certain causal role.[3] But this formulation buys generality at the price of vagueness. A more precise formulation can be introduced as follows.[4] Let T be a psychological theory (of either common sense or scientific psychology) that tells us (among other things) the relations among pain, other mental states, sensory inputs, and behavioral outputs. Reformulate T so that it is a single conjunctive sentence with all mental state terms as singular terms; for example, "is angry" becomes "has anger." Let T so reformulated be written as

$T(s_1 \ldots s_n)$

where $s_1 \ldots s_n$ are terms that designate mental states. Replace each mental state term with a variable and prefix existential quantifiers to form the Ramsey sentence of the theory

$$Ex_1 \ldots x_n T(x_1 \ldots x_n).$$

[The ordinary "E" is used here instead of the backward "E" as the existential quantifier.] Now, if x_i is the variable that replaced 'pain', we can define 'pain' as follows:

y has pain if and only if $Ex_1 \ldots x_n[T(x_1 \ldots x_n) \& y$ has $x_i]$.

That is, one has pain just in case he has a state that has certain relations to other states that have certain relations to one another (and to inputs and outputs; I have omitted reference to inputs and outputs for the sake of simplicity). It will be convenient to think of pain as the property expressed by the predicate "x has pain," that is, to think of pain as the property ascribed to someone in saying that he has pain.[5] Then, relative to theory T, pain can be identified with the property expressed by the predicate

$$Ex_1 \ldots x_n[T(x_1 \ldots x_n) \& y \text{ has } x_i].$$

For example, take T to be the ridiculously simple theory that pain is caused by pin pricks and causes worry and the emission of loud noises, and worry, in turn, causes brow wrinkling. The Ramsey sentence of T is

$Ex_1 Ex_2(x_1$ is caused by pin pricks and causes x_2 and emission of loud noises & x_2 causes brow wrinkling).

Relative to T, pain is the property expressed by the predicate obtained by adding a conjunct as follows:

$Ex_1 Ex_2[(x_1$ is caused by pin pricks and causes x_2 and emission of loud noises & x_2 causes brow wrinkling) & y has $x_1]$.

That is, pain is the property that one has when one has a state that is caused by pin pricks, and causes emission of loud noises, and also causes something else, that, in turn, causes brow wrinkling.

We can make this somewhat less cumbersome by letting an expression of the form "%xFx" be a singular term meaning the same as an expression of the form "the property of being an x such that x is F," that is, "being F." So %$x(x$ is bigger than a mouse & x is smaller than an elephant) = being bigger than a mouse and smaller than an elephant. Using this notation, we can say

pain = %$yEx_1 Ex_2[(x_1$ is caused by pin pricks and causes x_2 and emission of loud noises & x_2 causes brow wrinkling) & y has $x_1]$.

rather than saying that pain is the property expressed by the predicate

$Ex_1Ex_2[(x_1$ is caused by pin pricks and causes x_2 and emission of loud noises & x_2 causes brow wrinkling) & y has x_1].

It may be useful to consider a nonmental example. It is sometimes supposed that automotive terms like "valve-lifter" or "carburetor" are functional terms. Anything that lifts valves in an engine with a certain organizational structure is a valve-lifter. ("Camshaft," on the other hand, is a "structural" term, at least relative to "valve-lifter"; a camshaft is *one* kind of device for lifting valves.)

Consider the "theory" that says: "The carburetor mixes gasoline and air and sends the mixture to the ignition chamber, which, in turn ..." Let us consider "gasoline" and "air" to be input terms, and let x_1 replace "carburetor," and x_2 replace "ignition chamber." Then the property of being a carburetor would be

$\%yEx_1 \ldots x_n[$(The x_1 mixes gasoline and air and sends the mixture to the x_2, which, in turn ...) & y is an x_1].

That is, being a carburetor = being what mixes gasoline and air and sends the mixture to something else, which, in turn ...

This identification, and the identification of pain with the property one has when one is in a state that is caused by pin pricks and causes loud noises and also causes something else that causes brow wrinkling, would look less silly if the theories of pain (and carburetion) were more complex. But the essential idea of functionalism, as well as its major weakness, can be seen clearly in the example, albeit rather starkly. Pain is identified with an abstract causal property tied to the real world only via its relations, direct and indirect, to inputs and outputs. The weakness is that it seems so clearly conceivable that something could have that causal property, yet *not be* a pain. This point is discussed in detail in "Troubles with Functionalism" (Block, 1978; see Shoemaker, 1975, and Lycan, 1979, for critiques of such arguments).

Functionalism and Behaviorism

Many functionalists (such as David Lewis, D. M. Armstrong, and J. J. C. Smart) consider themselves descendants of behaviorists, who attempted to define a mental state in terms of what behaviors would tend to be emitted in the presence of specified stimuli. E.g., the desire for an ice-cream cone might be identified with a set of dispositions, including the disposition to reach out and grasp an ice-cream cone if one is proffered, other things being equal. But, as functionalist critics have emphasized, the phrase "other things being equal" is behavioristically illicit, because it can only be filled in with references to *other mental states* (see Putnam, 1963; the point dates back at least to Chisholm, 1957, chap. 11; and Geach, 1957, p. 8). One who desires an ice-cream cone will be disposed to reach for it only if he *knows* it is an ice-cream cone (and not, in general, if he believes it to be a tube of axle-grease), and only if he does not *think* that taking an ice-cream cone would conflict with *other desires* of more importance to him (such as the desire to lose weight, avoid obligations, or avoid cholesterol). The final nail in the behaviorist coffin was provided by the well-known "perfect actor" family of counterexamples. As Putnam argued in convincing detail (1963), it is possible to imagine a community of perfect actors who, by virtue of lawlike regularities, have exactly the behavioral dispositions envisioned by the behaviorists to be associated with absence of pain, even though they do in fact have pain. This shows that no behavioral disposition is a necessary condition of pain, and an exactly analogous example of perfect pain-pretenders shows that no behavioral disposition is a sufficient condition of pain, either.

Functionalism in all its forms differs from behaviorism in two major respects. First, while behaviorists defined mental states in terms of stimuli and responses, they did not think mental states were *themselves* causes of the responses and effects of the stimuli. Behaviorists took mental states to be "pure dispositions." Gilbert Ryle, for example, emphasized that "to possess a dispositional property is not to be in a particular state, or to undergo a particular change" (1949, p. 43). Brittleness, according to Ryle, is not a *cause* of breaking, but merely the fact of breaking easily. Similarly, to attribute pain to someone is not to attribute a cause or effect of anything, but simply to say what he would do in certain circumstances. Behaviorists are fictionalists about the mental, hence they cannot allow that mental states have causal powers. Functionalists, by contrast, claim it to be an advantage of their account that it "allows experiences to be something real, and so to be the effects of their occasions, and the causes of their manifestations (Lewis, 1966, p. 166). Armstrong says that "[when I think] it is not simply that I would speak or act if some conditions that are unfulfilled were to be fulfilled. Something is currently going on. Rylean behaviorism denies this, and so it is unsatisfactory" (chapter 13).

The second difference between functionalism and behaviorism is that functionalists emphasize not just the connections between pain and its stimuli and responses, but also its connections to other mental states. Notice, for example, that any full characterization of S_1 in the machine table above would have to refer to S_2 in one way or another, since it is one of the defining characteristics of S_1 that anything in S_1 goes into S_2 when it receives a nickel input. Another example, recall that the Ramsey sentence formulation identifies pain with

$$\%yEx_1 \ldots x_n[T(x_1 \ldots x_n) \ \& \ y \text{ has } x_i]$$

where the variable x_i replaced 'pain', and the rest of $x_1 \ldots x_n$ replaced the other mental state terms in T. So the functionalist expression that designates pain includes a specification of the relations between pain and all the other mental states related to it, and to inputs and outputs as well. (The role of inputs and outputs would have been better indicated had I written T as

$$T(s_1 \ldots s_n, o_1 \ldots o_m, i_1 \ldots i_k)$$

explicitly including terms for inputs and outputs.)

Behaviorism is a vague doctrine, and one that is sometimes defined in a way that would make functionalism a version of behaviorism. Even functionalists have offered definitions of 'behaviorism' that would make functionalists behaviorists. For example, if we defined 'behaviorism' as the doctrine that mental states (such as pain) can be characterized in nonmental terms, versions of functionalism along the lines of the Ramsey sentence version sketched above (held by Lewis, Armstrong, Smart, and Sydney Shoemaker) would qualify as versions of behaviorism (since all of the original mental state terms are replaced by variables in the Ramsey sentence). Many other definitions of 'behaviorism' count functionalism as a type of behaviorism. But it would be ludicrously literal-minded to take such definitions very seriously. Clear and general formulations of functionalism were not available until recently, so standard definitions of behaviorism could hardly be expected to draw the boundaries between behaviorism and functionalism with perfect accuracy. Furthermore, given an explicit definition of behaviorism, logical ingenuity can often disguise a functionalist account so as to fit the definition (see Bealer, 1978; Thomas, 1978, for accomplishments of this rather dubious variety). Definitions of behaviorism that count functionalism as behaviorist are misguided precisely *because* they blur the distinctions between functionalism and behaviorism just sketched. A characterization of pain can hardly be counted as behaviorist if it allows that a system could behave (and be disposed to behave) exactly as if it were in pain in all possible circumstances, yet not be in pain.[6]

Is Functionalism Reductionist?

Functionalists sometimes formulate their claim by saying that mental states can only be characterized in terms of other mental states. For instance, a person desires such and such if he would do so and so if he believed doing so and so will get him such and such, and if he believed doing so and so would not conflict with other desires. This much functionalism brings in no reductionism, but functionalists have rarely stopped there. Most regard mental terms as eliminable *all at once*. Armstrong says, for example, "The logical dependence of purpose on perception and belief, and of perception and belief upon purpose is not circularity in definition. What it shows is that the corresponding concepts must be introduced *together or not at all*" (1977, p. 88). Shoemaker says, "On one construal of it, functionalism in the philosophy of mind is the doctrine that mental or psychological terms are in principle eliminable in a certain way" (1975). Lewis is more explicit, using a formulation much like the Ramsey sentence formulation given above, which designates mental states by expressions that do not contain any mental terminology (see 1970, 1972 for details).

The same sort of point applies to machine functionalism. Putnam says, "The S_i, to repeat, are specified only *implicitly* by the description" (1967). In the Coke machine automaton described above, the only antecedently understood terms (other than "emit," "go to," and so on) are the input and output terms, "nickel," "dime," and "Coke." The state terms "S_1" and "S_2" in the Coke machine automaton—as in every Turing machine—are given their content entirely in terms of input and output terms (+ logical terms).

Thus functionalism could be said to reduce mentality to input-output structures (note that S_1 and S_2 can have any natures at all, so long as these natures connect them to one another and to the acceptance of nickels and dimes and disbursement of nickels and Cokes as described in the machine table). But functionalism gives us reduction without elimination. Functionalism is not fictionalist about mentality, for each of the functionalist ways of characterizing mental states in terms of inputs and outputs commits itself to the existence of mental states by the use of quantification over mental states, or some equivalent device.[7]

The Varieties of Functionalism

Thus far, I have characterized functionalism without adverting to any of the confusing disagreements among functionalists. I believe that my characterization is correct, but its application to the writings of some functionalists is not immediately apparent. Indeed, the functionalist literature (or, rather, what is generally, and I think correctly, regarded as the functionalist literature) exhibits some bizarre disagreements, the most surprising of which has to do with the relation between functionalism and physicalism. Some philosophers (Armstrong, 1968, 1977; Lewis, 1966, 1970, 1972; Smart, 1971) take functionalism as showing that physicalism is probably *true*, while others (Fodor, 1965; Putnam, 1966; Block and Fodor, chapter 20) take functionalism as showing that physicalism is probably *false*. This is the most noticeable difference among functionalist writings. I shall argue that the Lewis-Armstrong-Smart camp is mistaken in holding that functionalism supports an interesting version of physicalism, and furthermore, that the functionalist insight that they share with the Putnam-Fodor-Harman camp *does* have the consequence that physicalism is probably false. I shall begin with a brief historical sketch.

While functionalism dates back to Aristotle, in its current form it has two main contemporary sources. (A third source, Wittgenstein's, Sellars's and, later, Harman's views on meaning as conceptual role, has also been influential.)

Source I
Putnam (1960) compared the mental states of a person with the machine table states of a Turing machine. He then rejected any identification of mental states with machine

table states, but in a series of articles over the years he moved closer to such an identification, a pattern culminating in "Psychological Predicates" (1967). In this article, Putnam came close to advocating a view—which he defended in his philosophy of mind lectures in the late 1960s—that mental states can be identified with machine table states, or rather disjunctions of machine table states. (See Thomas, 1978, for a defence of roughly this view; see Block and Fodor, 1972, and Putnam, 1975, for a critique of such views.)

Fodor (1965, 1968a) developed a similar view (though it was not couched in terms of Turing machines) in the context of a functional-analysis view of psychological explanation (see Cummins, 1975). Putnam's and Fodor's positions were characterized in part by their opposition to physicalism, the view that each *type* of mental state is a physical state.[8] Their argument is at its clearest with regard to the simple version of Turing machine functionalism described above, the view that pain, for instance, is a machine table state. What physical state could be common to all and only realizations of S_1 of the Coke machine automaton described above? The Coke machine could be made of an enormous variety of materials, and it could operate via an enormous variety of mechanisms; it could even be a "scattered object," with parts all over the world, communicating by radio. If someone suggests a putative physical state common to all and only realizations of S_1, it is a simple matter to dream up a nomologically possible machine that satisfies the machine table but does not have the designated physical state. Of course, it is one thing to *say* this and another thing to prove it, but the claim has such overwhelming prima facie plausibility that the burden of proof is on the critic to come up with reason for thinking otherwise. Published critiques (Kalke, 1969; Gendron, 1971; Kim, 1972; Nelson, 1976; Causey, 1977) have in my view failed to meet this challenge.

If we could formulate a machine table for a human, it would be absurd to identify any of the machine table states with a type of *brain* state, since presumably all manner of brainless machines could be described by that table as well. So if pain is a machine table state, it is not a brain state. It should be mentioned, however, that it is possible to *specify* a sense in which a functional state F can be said to be physical. For example, F might be said to be physical if every system that in fact has F is a physical object, or, alternatively, if every realization of F (that is, every state that plays the causal role specified by F) is a physical state. Of course, the doctrines of "physicalism" engendered by such stipulations should not be confused with the version of physicalism that functionalists have argued against (see note 8).

Jaegwon Kim objects that "the less the physical basis of the nervous system of some organisms resembles ours, the less temptation there will be for ascribing to them sensations or other phenomenal events" (1972). But his examples depend crucially on considering creatures whose functional organization is much more primitive than ours. He also points out that "the mere fact that the physical bases of two nervous systems are different in material composition or physical organization with respect to a certain scheme of classification does not entail that they cannot be in the same physical state with respect to a different scheme." Yet the functionalist does not (or, better, should not) claim that functionalism *entails* the falsity of physicalism, but only that the burden of proof is on the physicalist. Kim (1972) and Lewis (1969; see also Causey, 1977, p. 149) propose species-specific identities: pain is one brain state in dogs and another in people. As should be clear from this introduction, however, this move sidesteps the main metaphysical question: "What is common to the pains of dogs and people (and all other pains) in virtue of which they are pains?"

Source II
The second major strand in current functionalism descends from Smart's early article on mind-body identity (1959). Smart worried about the following objection to mind-body identity: So what if pain is a physical state? It can still have a variety of phenomenal *properties*, such as sharpness, and these phenomenal properties may be irreducibly mental. Then Smart and other identity theorists would be stuck with a "double aspect" theory: pain is a physical state, but it has both physical and irreducibly mental properties. He attempted to dispel this worry by analyzing mental concepts in a way that did not carry with it any commitment to the mental or physical status of the concepts.[9] These "topic-neutral analyses," as he called them, specified mental states in terms of the stimuli that caused them (and the behavior that they caused, although Smart was less explicit about this). His analysis of first-person sensation avowals were of the form "There is something going on in me which is like what goes on when ...," where the dots are filled in by descriptions of typical stimulus situations. In these analyses, Smart broke decisively with behaviorism in insisting that mental states were real things with causal efficacy; Armstrong, Lewis, and others later improved his analyses, making explicit the behavioral effects clauses, and including mental causes and effects. Lewis's formulation, especially, is now very widely accepted among Smart's and Armstrong's adherents (Smart, 1971, also accepts it). In a recent review in the *Australasian Journal of Philosophy*, Alan Reeves declares, "I think that there is some consensus among Australian materialists that Lewis has provided an exact statement of their viewpoint" (1978).

Smart used his topic-neutral analyses only to defeat an a priori objection to the identity theory. As far as an argument *for* the identity theory went, he relied on considerations of simplicity. It was absurd, he thought, to suppose that there should be a perfect correlation between mental states and brain states and yet that the states could be nonidentical. (See Kim, 1966; Brandt and Kim, 1967, for an argument against Smart; but see also Block, 1971, 1979; and Causey, 1972, 1977, for arguments against Kim and Brandt.) But Lewis and Smart's Australian allies (notably D. M. Armstrong) went beyond Smart, arguing that something like topic-neutral analyses could be used to argue *for* mind-brain identity. In its most persuasive version (Lewis's), the argument for physicalism is that pain can be seen (by conceptual analysis) to be the occupant of causal role R; a certain neural state will be found to be the occupant of causal role R; thus it follows that pain = that neural state. Functionalism comes in by way of showing that the meaning of 'pain' is the same as a certain definite description that spells out causal role R.

Lewis and Armstrong argue from functionalism to the truth of physicalism because they have a "functional specification" version of functionalism. Pain is a functionally specified state, perhaps a functionally specified brain state, according to them. Putnam and Fodor argue from functionalism to the falsity of physicalism because they say there are functional states (or functional properties), and that mental states (or properties) are identical to these functional states. No functional state is likely to be a physical state.

The difference between a functional state identity claim and a functional specification claim can be made clearer as follows. Recall that the functional state identity claim can be put thus:

$$\text{pain} = \%y\text{E}x_1 \ldots \text{E}x_n[T(x_1 \ldots x_n) \text{ \& } y \text{ has } x_1]$$

where x_1 is the variable that replaced "pain." A functional specification view could be stated as follows:[10]

$$\text{pain} = \text{the } x_1\text{E}x_2 \ldots \text{E}x_n T(x_1 \ldots x_n)$$

In terms of the example mentioned earlier, the functional state identity theorist would identify pain with the property one has when one is in a state that is caused by pin pricks and causes loud noises and also something else that causes brow wrinkling. The functional specifier would define pain as *the thing* that is caused by pin pricks and causes loud noises and also something else that causes brow wrinkling.

According to the functional specifier, the thing that has causal role R (for example, the thing that is caused by pin pricks and causes something else and so forth) might be a state of one physical type in one case and a state of another physical type in another case. The functional state identity theorist insists that *pain* is not identical to a physical state. What pains have in common in virtue of which they are pains is causal role R, not any physical property.

In terms of the carburetor example, functional state identity theorists say that being a carburetor = being what mixes gas and air and sends the mixture to something else, which, in turn … Functional specifiers say that the carburetor is *the thing* that mixes gas and air and sends the mixture to something else, which, in turn … What the difference comes to is that the functional specifier says that the carburetor is a type of physical object, though perhaps one type of physical object in a Mercedes and another type of physical object in a Ford. The functional state identity theorist insists that *what it is to be a carburetor* is to have a certain functional role, not a certain physical structure.

At this point, it may seem to the reader that the odd disagreement about whether functionalism justifies physicalism or the negation of physicalism owes simply to ambiguities in "functionalism" and "physicalism." In particular, it may seem that the functional specification view justifies *token* physicalism (the doctrine that every particular pain is a physical state token), while the functional state identity view justifies the negation of *type* physicalism (the doctrine that *pain* is a type of physical state).

This response oversimplifies matters greatly, however. First, it is textually mistaken, since those functional specifiers who see the distinction between type and token materialism clearly have type materialism in mind. For example, Lewis says, "A dozen years or so ago, D. M. Armstrong and I (independently) proposed a materialist theory of mind that joins claims of *type-type* psychophysical identity with a behaviorist or functionalist way of characterizing mental states such as pain" (Lewis, 1980; emphasis added). More important, the functional specification doctrine *commits* its proponents to a functional state identity claim. Since the latter doctrine counts against type physicalism, so does the former. It is easy to see that the functional specification view commits its proponents to a functional state identity claim. According to functional specifiers, it is a conceptual truth that pain is the state with causal role *R*. But then *what it is to be a pain* is to have causal role *R*. Thus the functional specifiers are committed to the view that what pains have in common by virtue of which they are pains is their causal role, rather than their physical nature. (Again, Lewis is fairly clear about this: "Our view is that the concept of pain ... is the concept of a state that occupies a certain causal role.")

I suspect that what has gone wrong in the case of *many* functional specifiers is simply failure to appreciate the distinction between type and token for mental states. If pain in Martians is one physical state, pain in humans another, and so on for pain in every pain-feeling organism, then each particular pain is a token of some physical type. This is token physicalism. Perhaps functional specifiers ought to be *construed* as arguing for token physicalism (even though Lewis and others explicitly say they are arguing for type physicalism). I shall give three arguments against such a construal. First, as functional state identity theorists have often pointed out, a *non*physical state could conceivably have a causal role typical of a mental state. In functional specification terms, there might be a creature in which pain is a functionally specified *soul* state. So functionalism opens up the possibility that even if *our* pains are physical, other pains might not be. In the light of this point, it seems that the support that functionalism gives even to token physicalism is equivocal. Second, the *major* arguments for token physicalism involve no functionalism at all (see Davidson, chapter 5, and Fodor, chapter 6). Third, token physicalism is a much weaker doctrine than physicalists have typically wanted.

In sum, functional specifiers *say* that functionalism supports physicalism, but they are committed to a functionalist answer, not a physicalist answer, to the question of what all pains have in common in virtue of which they are pains. And if what all pains have in common in virtue of which they are pains is a functional property, it is very unlikely that pain is coextensive with any physical state. If, on the contrary, functional specifiers have *token* physicalism in mind, functionalism provides at best equivocal support for the doctrine; better support is available elsewhere; and the doctrine is a rather weak form of physicalism to boot.

Lewis's views deserve separate treatment. He insists that pain is a brain state only because he takes "pain" to be a nonrigid designator meaning "the state with such and such causal role."[11] Thus, in Lewis's view, to say that pain is a brain state should not be seen as saying what all pains have in common in virtue of which they are pains, just as saying that the winning number is 37 does not suggest that 37 is what all winning numbers have in common. Many of Lewis's opponents disagree about the rigidity of "pain," but the dispute is irrelevant to our purposes, since Lewis does take 'having pain' to be rigid, and so he does accept (he tells me) a functional property identity view: having pain = having a state with such and such a typical causal role. I think that most functional state identity theorists would be as willing to rest on the thesis that having pain is a functional property as on the thesis that pain is a functional state.

In conclusion, while there is considerable disagreement among the philosophers whom I have classified as metaphysical functionalists, there is a single insight about the nature of the mind to which they are all committed.

Notes

Reprinted from N. Block, ed., *Readings in Philosophy of Psychology*, vol. 1, 171–184 (Cambridge, MA: Harvard University Press, 1980). Also reprinted in John Heil, ed., *Philosophy of Mind: A Guide and Anthology* (Oxford: Oxford University Press, 2004).

1. Discussions of functional state identity theses have sometimes concentrated on one or another weaker thesis in order to avoid issues about identity conditions on entities such as states or properties (see, for example, Block and Fodor, chapter 20). Consider the following theses:

(1) Pain = functional state S.
(2) Something is a pain just in case it is a (token of) S.
(3) The conditions under which x and y are both pains are the same as the conditions under which x and y are both tokens of S.

(1) is a full-blooded functional state identity thesis that entails (2) and (3). Theses of the form of (2) and (3) can be used to state what it is that all pains have in common in virtue of which they are pains.

2. Dennett (1975) and Rey (1979) make this appeal to the Church-Tuning thesis. But if the mechanical processes involved analog rather than digital computation, then the processes could fail

to be algorithmic in the sense required by the Church-Turing thesis. The experiments discussed in Block 1981, part two, "Imagery" suggest that mental images are (at least partially) analog representations, and that the computations that operate on images are (at least partially) analog operations.

3. Strictly speaking, even the causal role formulation is insufficiently general, as can be seen by noting that Turing machine functionalism is not a special case of causal role functionalism. Strictly speaking, none of the states of a Turing machine need cause any of the other states. All that is required for a physical system to satisfy a machine table is that the counterfactuals specified by the table are true of it. This can be accomplished by some causal agent outside the machine. Of course, one can always choose to speak of a *different* system, one that includes the causal agent as part of the machine, but that is irrelevant to my point.

4. Formulations of roughly this sort were first advanced by Lewis, 1966, 1970, 1972; Martin, 1966. (See also Harman, 1973; Grice, 1975; Field, 1978; Block, chapter 22.)

5. See Field, 1978, for an alternative convention.

6. Characterizations of mental states along the lines of the Ramsey sentence formulation presented above wear their incompatibility with behaviorism on their sleeves in that they involve explicit quantification over mental states. Both Thomas and Bealer provide ways of transforming functionalist definitions or identifications so as to disguise such transparent incompatibility.

7 The machine table states of a finite automaton can be defined explicitly in terms of inputs and outputs by a Ramsey sentence method, or by the method described in Thomas (1978). Both of these methods involve one or another sort of commitment to the existence of the machine table states.

8. 'Physical state' could be spelled out for these purposes as the state of something's having a first-order property that is expressible by a predicate of a true physical theory. Of course, this analysis requires some means of characterizing physical theory. A first-order property is one whose definition does not require quantification over properties. A second-order property is one whose definition requires quantification over first-order properties (but not other properties). The physicalist doctrine that functionalists argue against is the doctrine that mental properties are *first-order* physical properties. Functionalists need not deny that mental properties are second-order physical properties (in various senses of that phrase).

9. As Kim has pointed out (1972), Smart did not need these analyses to avoid "double aspect" theories. Rather, a device Smart introduces elsewhere in the same paper will serve the purpose. Smart raises the objection that if afterimages are brain states, then since an afterimage can be orange, the identity theorist would have to conclude that a brain state can be orange. He replies by saying that the identity theorist need only identify the *experience of having an orange afterimage* with a brain state; this state is not orange, and so no orange brain states need exist. Images, says Smart, are not really mental entities; it is experiences of images that are the real mental entities. In a similar manner, Kim notes, the identity theorist can "bring" the phenomenal properties into the mental states themselves; for example, the identity theorist can concern himself with states such as John's having a sharp pain; this state is not sharp, and so the identity theorist is not committed

to sharp brain states. This technique does the trick, although of course it commits its perpetrators to the unfortunate doctrine that pains do not exist, or at least that they are not mental entities; rather, it is the havings of sharp pains and the like that are the real mental entities.

10. The functional specification view I give here is a much simplified version of Lewis's formulation (1972).

11. A rigid designator is a singular term that names the same thing in each possible world. 'The color of the sky' is nonrigid, since it names blue in worlds where the sky is blue, and red in worlds where the sky is red. 'Blue' is rigid, since it names blue in all possible worlds, even in worlds where the sky is red.

References

Armstrong, D. M. 1968. *A Materialist Theory of Mind*. London: Routledge & Kegan Paul.

—— 1970. *The Nature of Mind*. In C. V. Borst, ed., *The Mind/Brain Identity Theory*. London: Macmillan.

—— 1977. "The Causal Theory of the Mind." In *Neue Heft für Philosophie*, no. 11, pp. 82–95. Vendenhoek and Ruprecht.

Bealer, G. 1978. "An Inconsistency in Functionalism." *Synthese* 38:333–372.

Block, N. 1971. "Physicalism and Theoretical Identity." Ph.D. dissertation, Harvard University.

—— 1978. "Troubles with Functionalism." In C. W. Savage, ed., *Minnesota Studies in Philosophy of Science*. Vol. 9. Minneapolis: University of Minnesota Press.

—— 1979. "Reductionism." In *Encyclopedia of Bioethics*. New York: Macmillan.

—— 1981. *Readings in Philosophy of Psychology*. Vol. 2. Cambridge MA: Harvard University Press.

Block, N., and J. A. Fodor. 1972. "What Psychological States Are Not." *Philosophical Review* 81, no. 2:159–182.

Brandt, R., and J. Kim. 1967. "The Logic of the Identity Theory." *Journal of Philosophy* 64, no. 17:515–537.

Causey, R. 1972. "Attribute Identities in Micro-reductions." *Journal of Philosophy* 69, no. 14:407–422.

—— 1977. *Unity of Science*. Dordrecht: Reidel.

Chisholm, R. M. 1957. *Perceiving*. Ithaca: Cornell University Press.

Cummins, R. 1975. "Functional Analysis." *Journal of Philosophy* 72, no. 20:741–764.

Dennett, D. 1975. "Why the Law of Effect Won't Go Away." *Journal for the Theory of Social Behavior* 5:169–187.

Field, H. 1978. "Mental Representation." *Erkenntniss* 13:9–61.

Fodor, J. A. 1965. "Explanations in Psychology." In M. Black, ed., *Philosophy in America*. London: Routledge & Kegan Paul.

—— 1968a. "The Appeal to Tacit Knowledge in Psychological Explanation." *Journal of Philosophy* 65:627–640.

—— 1968b. *Psychological Explanation*. New York: Random House.

Geach, P. 1957. *Mental Acts*. London: Routledge & Kegan Paul.

Gendron, B. 1971. "On the Relation of Neurological and Psychological Theories: A Critique of the Hardware Thesis." In R. C. Buck and R. S. Cohen, eds., *Boston Studies in the Philosophy of Science*. Vol. 8. Dordrecht: Reidel.

Grice, H. P. 1975. "Method in Philosophical Psychology (from the Banal to the Bizarre)." *Proceedings and Addresses of the American Philosophical Association*. Newark, Del.: American Philosophical Association.

Harman, G. 1973. *Thought*. Princeton: Princeton University Press.

Hartman, E. 1977. *Substance, Body and Soul*. Princeton: Princeton University Press.

Kalke, W. 1969. "What Is Wrong with Fodor and Putnam's Functionalism?" *Nous* 3:83–93.

Kim, J. 1966. "On the Psycho-physical Identity Theory." *American Philosophical Quarterly* 3, no. 3:227–235.

—— 1972. "Phenomenal Properties, Psychophysical Law, and the Identity Theory." *Monist* 56, no. 2:177–192.

Lewis, D. 1966. "An Argument for the Identity Theory." Reprinted in D. Rosenthal, ed., *Materialism and the Mind-Body Problem*. Englewood Cliffs, N.J.: Prentice-Hall, 1971.

—— 1969. "Review of *Art, Mind and Religion*." *Journal of Philosophy* 66, no. 1:23–35.

—— 1970. "How to Define Theoretical Terms." *Journal of Philosophy* 67, no. 13:427–444.

—— 1972. "Psychophysical and Theoretical Identification." *Australasian Journal of Philosophy* 50, no. 3:249–258.

—— 1980. "Mad Pain and Martian Pain." In N. Block, ed., *Readings in Philosophy of Psychology*, Vol. 1, 216–222. Cambridge, MA: Harvard University Press.

Lycan, W. 1979. "A New Lilliputian Argument against Machine Functionalism." *Philosophical Studies* 35, 279–287.

Martin, R. M. 1966. "On Theoretical Constants and Ramsey Constants." *Philosophy of Science* 31:1–13.

Nagel, T. 1970. "Armstrong on the Mind." *Philosophical Review* 79:394–403.

Nelson, R. J. 1975. "Behaviorism, Finite Automata and Stimulus Response Theory." *Theory and Decision* 6:249–267.

—— 1976. "Mechanism, Functionalism and the Identity Theory." *Journal of Philosophy* 73, no. 13:365–386.

Putnam, H. 1960. "Minds and Machines." In S. Hook, ed., *Dimensions of Mind*. New York: New York University Press.

—— 1963. "Brains and Behavior." Reprinted in *Mind, Language, and Reality: Philosophical Papers*. Vol. 2. London: Cambridge University Press, 1975.

—— 1966. "The Mental Life of Some Machines." Reprinted in *Mind, Language and Reality: Philosophical Papers*. Vol. 2. London: Cambridge University Press, 1975.

—— 1967. "The Nature of Mental States" (originally published as "Psychological Predicates"). In W. H. Capitan and D. D. Merrill, eds., *Art, Mind, and Religion*. Pittsburgh: University of Pittsburgh Press.

—— 1970. "On Properties." In *Mathematics, Matter and Method: Philosophical Papers*. Vol. 1. London: Cambridge University Press.

—— 1975. "Philosophy and Our Mental Life." In *Mind, Language and Reality: Philosophical Papers*. Vol. 2. London: Cambridge University Press.

Reeves, A. 1978. "Review of W. Matson, *Sentience*." *Australasian Journal of Philosophy* 56, no. 2 (August):189–192.

Rey, G. 1979. "Functionalism and the Emotions." In A. Rorty, ed., *Explaining Emotions*. Berkeley and Los Angeles: University of California Press.

Ryle, G. 1949. *The Concept of Mind*. London: Hutchinson.

Sellars, W. 1968. *Science and Metaphysics*. London: Routledge & Kegan Paul, chap. 6.

Shoemaker, S. 1975. "Functionalism and Qualia." *Philosophical Studies* 27:271–315.

Smart, J. J. C. 1959. "Sensations and Brain Processes." *Philosophical Review* 68:141–156.

—— 1971. "Reports of Immediate Experience." *Synthese* 22:346–359.

Thomas, S. 1978. *The Formal Mechanics of Mind*. Ithaca: Cornell University Press.

3   What Psychological States Are Not

I

As far as anyone knows, different organisms are often in psychological states of exactly the same type at one time or another, and a given organism is often in psychological states of exactly the same type at different times. Whenever either is the case, we shall say of the psychological states of the organism(s) in question that they are *type identical*.

One thing that currently fashionable theories in the philosophy of mind often try to do is characterize the conditions for type identity of psychological states. For example, some varieties of philosophical behaviorism claim that two organisms are in type-identical psychological states if and only if certain of their behaviors or behavioral dispositions are type identical. Analogously, some (though not all) varieties of physicalism claim that organisms are in type-identical psychological states if and only if certain of their physical states are type identical.[1]

In so far as they are construed as theories about the conditions for type identity of psychological states, it seems increasingly unlikely that either behaviorism or physicalism is true. Since the arguments for this conclusion are widely available in the literature, we shall provide only the briefest review here.[2]

The fundamental argument against behaviorism is simply that what an organism does or is disposed to do at a given time is a very complicated function of its beliefs and desires together with its current sensory inputs and memories. It is thus enormously unlikely that it will prove possible to pair behavioral predicates with psychological predicates in the way that behaviorism requires—namely, that, for each type of psychological state, an organism is in that state if and only if a specified behavioral predicate is true of it. This suggests that behaviorism is overwhelmingly likely to be false simply in virtue of its empirical consequences and independent of its implausibility as a semantic thesis. Behaviorism cannot be true unless mind/behavior correlationism is true, and mind/behavior correlationism is not true.

The argument against physicalism rests upon the empirical likelihood that creatures of different composition and structure, which are in no interesting sense in identical physical states, can nevertheless be in identical psychological states; hence that types of psychological states are not in correspondence with types of physical states. This point has been made persuasively in Putnam's "Psychological Predicates." In essence, it rests on appeals to the following three kinds of empirical considerations.

First, the Lashleyan doctrine of neurological equipotentiality holds that any of a wide variety of psychological functions can be served by any of a wide variety of brain structures. While the generality of this doctrine may be disputed, it does seem clear that the central nervous system is highly labile and that a given type of psychological process is in fact often associated with a variety of distinct neurological structures. (For example, it is a widely known fact that early trauma can lead to the establishment of linguistic functions in the *right* hemisphere of right-handed subjects.) But physicalism, as we have been construing it, requires that organisms are in type-identical psychological states if and only if they are in type-identical physical states. Hence if equipotentiality is true, physicalism must be false.

The second consideration depends on the assumption that the Darwinian doctrine of convergence applies to the phylogeny of psychology as well as to the phylogeny of morphology and of behavior. It is well known that superficial morphological similarities between organisms may represent no more than parallel evolutionary solutions of the same environmental problem: in particular, that they may be the expression of quite different types of physiological structure. The analogous point about behavioral similarities across species has been widely recognized in the ethological literature: organisms of widely differing phylogeny and morphology may nevertheless come to exhibit superficial behavioral similarities in response to convergent environmental pressures. The present point is that the same considerations may well apply to the phylogeny of the psychology of organisms. Psychological similarities across species may often reflect convergent environmental selection rather than underlying physiological similarities. For example, we have no particular reason to suppose that the physiology of pain in man must have much in common with the physiology of pain in phylogenetically remote species. But if there are organisms whose psychology is homologous to our own but whose physiology is quite different, such organisms provide counterexamples to the psychophysical correlations physicalism requires.

Finally, if we allow the conceptual possibility that psychological predicates could apply to artifacts, then it seems likely that physicalism will prove empirically false. For it seems likely that given any psychophysical correlation which holds for an organism, it is possible to build a machine which is similar to the organism psychologically, but physiologically sufficiently different from the organism that the psychophysical correlation does not hold for the machine.

What these arguments seem to show is that the conditions that behaviorism and physicalism seek to place upon the type identity of psychological states of organisms are, in a relevant sense, insufficiently abstract. It seems likely that organisms which differ in their behavior or behavioral dispositions can nevertheless be in type-identical psychological states, as can organisms that are in different physical states. (We shall presently discuss a "functionalist" approach to type identity which attempts to set the identity criteria at a level more abstract than physicalism or behaviorism acknowledge.)

Of course, it is *possible* that the type-to-type correspondences required by behaviorism or by physicalism should turn out to obtain. The present point is that even if behavioral or physical states *are* in one-to-one correspondence with psychological states, we have no current evidence that this is so; hence we have no warrant for adopting philosophical theories which *require* that it be so. The paradox about behaviorism and physicalism is that while most of the arguments that have surrounded these doctrines have been narrowly "conceptual," it seems increasingly likely that the decisive arguments against them are empirical.

It is often suggested that one might meet these arguments by supposing that, though neither behavioral nor physical states correspond to psychological states in a one-to-one fashion, they may nevertheless correspond many-to-one. That is, it is supposed that, for each type of psychological state, there is a distinct disjunction of types of behavioral (or physical) states, such that an organism is in the psychological state if and only if it is in one of the disjuncts.

This sort of proposal is, however, shot through with serious difficulties. First, it is less than obvious that there is, in fact, a *distinct* disjunction of behavioral (or physical) states corresponding to each psychological state. For example, there is really no reason to believe that the class of types of behaviors which, in the whole history of the universe, have (or will have) expressed rage for some organism or other, is distinct from the class of types of behaviors which have expressed, say, pain. In considering this possibility, one should bear in mind that practically any behavior might, in the appropriate circumstances, become the conventional expression of practically any psychological state and that a given organism in a given psychological state might exhibit almost any behavioral disposition depending on its beliefs and preferences. The same kind of point applies, *mutatis mutandis*, against the assumption that there is a distinct disjunction of types of physical states corresponding to each type of psychological state, since it seems plausible that practically any type of physical state could realize practically any type of psychological state in some kind of physical system or other.

But even if there *is* a distinct disjunction of types of behavioral (or physical) states corresponding to each type of psychological state, there is no reason whatever to believe that this correspondence is lawlike; and it is not obvious what philosophical interest would inhere in the discovery of a behavioral (or physical) property which happened, accidentally, to be coextensive with a psychological predicate. Thus, as Davidson has pointed out, on the assumption that psychobehavioral correlations are not lawlike, even "if we were to find an open sentence couched in behavioral terms and exactly coextensive with some mental predicate, nothing could reasonably persuade us that we had found it" ("Mental Events"). As Davidson has also pointed out, the same remark applies, *mutatis mutandis*, to physical predicates.

Finally, a theory which says that each psychological predicate is coextensive with a distinct disjunction of behavioral (or physical) predicates[3] is incompatible with what we have been assuming is an obvious truth: namely, that a given behavioral state may express (or a given physical state realize) different psychological states at different times. Suppose, for example, that we have a theory which says that the psychological predicate p_1 is coextensive with the disjunctive behavioral predicate α and psychological predicate p_2 is coextensive with the disjunctive behavioral predicate β. Suppose further that S_i designates a type of behavior that has sometimes expressed p_1 but not p_2 and at other times expressed p_2 but not p_1. Then, S_i will have to be a disjunct of both α and β. But, the disjuncts of α are severally sufficient conditions for p_1 and the disjuncts of β are severally sufficient conditions of p_2 on the assumption that p_1 and α, and p_2 and β, are respectively coextensive. Hence the theory entails that an organism in S_i is in both p_1 and p_2, which is logically incompatible with the claim that S_i expresses p_1 (but not p_2) at some times and p_2 (but not p_1) at others. Of course, one could circumvent this objection by including spatiotemporal designators in the specification of the disjuncts mentioned in α and β. But to do so would be totally to abandon the project of expressing psychobehavioral (or psychophysical) correlations by lawlike biconditionals.

II

It has recently been proposed that these sorts of difficulties can be circumvented, and an adequate theory of the conditions on type identity of psychological states can be formulated, in the following way. Let us assume that any system P to which psychological predicates can be applied has a description as a probabilistic automaton. (A probabilistic automaton is a generalized Turing machine whose machine table includes instructions associated with finite positive probabilities less than or equal to one. For a brief introduction to the notion of a Turing machine, a machine table, and related notions, see Putnam, "Psychological Predicates.") A *description* of P, in the technical sense intended here, is any true statement to the effect that P possesses distinct states $S_1, S_2, \ldots S_n$ which are related to one another and to the outputs and inputs of P by the transition probabilities given in a specified machine table. We will call the states $S_1, S_2, \ldots S_n$ specified by the *description* of an organism, the "machine table states of the organism" relative to that *description*.

It is against the background of the assumption that organisms are describable as probabilistic automata that the present theory (hereafter "*FSIT*" for "functional state identity theory") seeks to specify conditions upon the type identity of psychological states. In particular, *FSIT* claims that for any organism that satisfies psychological predicates at all, there exists a unique best *description* such that each psychological state of the organism is identical with one of its machine table states relative to that description.

Several remarks about *FSIT* are in order. First, there is an obvious generalization of the notion of a probabilistic automaton in which it is thought of as having a separate input tape on which an "oracle" can print symbols during a computation. *FSIT* presupposes an interpretation of this generalization in which sensory transducers take the place of the "oracle" and in which outputs are thought of as instructions to motor transducers. Such an interpretation must be intended if a *description* of an organism is to provide a model of the mental operations of the organism.

Second, we have presented *FSIT* in the usual way as an *identity* theory:[4] in particular, one which claims that each type of psychological state is identical to (a type of) machine table state. Our aim, however, is to sidestep questions about the identity conditions of abstract objects and discuss only a certain class of biconditionals which type-to-type identity statements entail: that is, statements of the form "*O* is in such and such a type of psychological state at time *t* if and only if *O* is in such and such a type of machine table state at time *t*."

Third, it is worth insisting that *FSIT* amounts to more than the claim that every organism has a description as a Turing machine or as a probabilistic automaton. For there are a number of respects in which that claim is trivially true; but its truth in these respects does not entail *FSIT*. For example, if the inputs and outputs of an organism are recursively enumerable (as is the case with any mortal organism after it is dead), then it follows that there exists a Turing machine capable of simulating the organism (that is, a Turing machine which has the same input/output relations). But it does not follow that the organism has a unique best *description* of the sort characterized above. Second, as Putnam has pointed out (in conversation), *everything* is describable as a realization of what one might call the "null" Turing machine: that is, a machine which has only one state and stays in it. (The point is, roughly, that whether a system *P* realizes a Turing machine depends, inter alia, on what counts as a change of state in *P*. If one counts *nothing* as a change of state in *P*, then *P* is a realization of the null Turing machine.) But again, *FSIT* would not be true if the only true *description* of an organism is as a null Turing machine, since *FSIT* requires that the machine table states of an organism correspond one-to-one with its psychological states under its best description.

There are thus two important respects in which *FSIT* involves more than the claim that organisms which satisfy psychological predicates have descriptions. First, *FSIT* claims that such systems have unique best descriptions. Second, *FSIT* claims that the types of machine table states specified by the unique best description of a system are in correspondence with the types of psychological states that the system can be in. It is this second claim of *FSIT* with which we shall be primarily concerned.

FSIT, unlike either behaviorism or physicalism, is not an ontological theory: that is, it is neutral about what token psychological states *are*, in that as far as *FSIT* is concerned, among the systems to which psychological predicates are applicable (and which therefore have *descriptions*) might be included persons, material objects, souls, and so forth. This last point suggests how *FSIT* might meet certain of the kinds of difficulties we raised against physicalism and behaviorism. Just as *FSIT* abstracts from considerations of the ontological status of the systems which have *descriptions*, so too it abstracts from physical differences between systems which have their *descriptions* in common. As Putnam has remarked, "the *same* Turing machine (from the standpoint of the machine table) may be physically realized in a potential infinity of ways" ("The Mental Life of Some Machines," p. 271), and *FSIT* allows us to state type-identity conditions on psychological states which are neutral as between such different realizations.

Similarly, *FSIT* permits us to state such conditions in a way which abstracts from the variety of behavioral consequences which a psychological state may have. It thereby meets a type of objection which, we supposed above, was fatal to behaviorism.

We remarked that the behaviorist is committed to the view that two organisms are in the same psychological state whenever their behaviors and/or behavioral dispositions are identical; and that this theory is implausible to the extent that the behaviors and the behavioral dispositions of an organism are the effects of *interactions* between its psychological states. But *FSIT* allows us to distinguish between psychological states not only in terms of their behavioral consequences but also in terms of the character of their interconnections. This is because the criterion of identity for machine table states acknowledges *their relations to one another* as well as their relations to inputs and outputs. Thus, *FSIT* can cope with the characteristic indirectness of the relation between psychological states and behavior. Indeed, *FSIT* allows us to see how psychological states which have *no* behavioral expressions might nevertheless be distinct.

Finally, it may be remarked that nothing precludes taking at least some of the transitions specified in a machine table as corresponding to causal relations in the system which the table *describes*. In particular, since *FSIT* is compatible with token physicalism, there is no reason why it should not acknowledge that token psychological states may enter into causal relations. Thus, any advantages which accrue to causal analyses of the psychological states, or of the relations between psychological states and behavior, equally accrue to *FSIT*.[5]

III

In this section we are going to review a series of arguments which provide one degree or another of difficulty for the claim that *FSIT* yields an adequate account of the type-identity conditions for psychological states. It is our view that, taken collectively, these arguments are fairly decisive against the theory of type identity of psychological states that *FSIT* proposes. In the final section we will suggest some reasons why the attempt to provide substantive type-identity conditions on psychological states so often founders.

(1) Any account of type-identity conditions on psychological states that adheres at all closely to our everyday notion of what types of psychological states there are will presumably have to draw a distinction between dispositional states (beliefs, desires, inclinations, and so on) and occurrent states (sensations, thoughts, feelings, and so on). So far as we can see, however, *FSIT* has no plausible way of capturing this distinction short of abandoning its fundamental principle that psychological states correspond one-to-one to machine table states. Suppose, for example, *FSIT* attempts to reconstruct the distinction between occurrents and dispositions by referring to the distinction between the machine table state that an organism is *in* and all the other states specified by its machine table. Thus, one might refine *FSIT* to read: for occurrent states, two organisms are in type-identical psychological states if and only if they are in the same machine table state; and, for each dispositional state, there is a machine table state such that an organism is in the former if and only if its machine table contains the latter.

The following suggests one way of seeing how implausible this proposal is. Every machine table state of an organism is a state in which the organism can be at one time or other. Hence, if the distinction between the machine table state an organism is in and all the other states in its table is the same as the distinction between the occurrent state of an organism and its dispositional states, it follows that every dispositional state of the organism is a possible occurrent state of that organism.

This consequence of *FSIT* is correct for a large number of kinds of psychological dispositions. For example, corresponding to the dispositional predicate "speaks French," there is the occurrent predicate "is speaking French"; corresponding to the dispositional "is greedy" we have the occurrent "is being greedy"; corresponding to the dispositional "can hear sounds above 3,000 Herz" there is "is hearing a sound above 3,000 Herz." And, in general, for many dispositionals, we have corresponding present progressive forms which denote occurrences.

For many other psychological dispositionals, however, this parallelism fails. For example, we have no "is believing that *P*" corresponding to "believes that *P*"; we have no "is desiring a lollipop" corresponding to "desires a lollipop"; we have no "is preferring *X* to *Y*" corresponding to "prefers *X* to *Y*," and so forth. In short, many dispositional psychological states are *not* possible occurrent psychological states, and for these states *FSIT* offers no obvious model.

It is important to see what this argument does *not* show. According to this argument certain dispositional states cannot correspond to machine table states since all machine table states are possible occurrent states but some dispositional psychological states are not. For such dispositions, there can be no machine table states such that the organism has the former if and only if the latter appears in its *description*. But it is perfectly possible that necessary and sufficient conditions for having such dispositions should be given by reference to some *abstract* property of the organization of machine tables. To take a far-fetched example, given a normal form for descriptions, it might turn out that an organism believes that the sun is 93,000,000 miles from the earth if and only if the first *n* columns in its machine table have some such abstract property as containing only odd integers. Since saying of a machine that the first *n* columns ... and so forth does not ascribe a machine table state to it, psychological states which are analyzed as corresponding to this sort of property would not thereby be described as possible occurrent states.

To take this line, however, would be to abandon a fundamental claim of *FSIT*. For, while this approach is compatible with the view that two organisms have the same psychology if and only if they have the same machine table, it is *not* compatible with the suggestion that two organisms are in the same (dispositional) psychological state if and only if they have a specified state of their machine tables in common. Hence it is incompatible with the view that psychological states are in one-to-one correspondence with machine table states. Moreover, since we have no way of telling what kinds of abstract properties of machine tables might turn out to correspond to psychological states, the present difficulty much reduces the possibility of using *FSIT* to delineate substantive type-identity conditions on psychological states. To say that psychological states correspond to some property or other of machine tables is to say something very much weaker than that psychological states correspond to machine table states. This is a kind of point to which we will return later in the discussion.

There is, of course, at least one other way out of the present difficulty for *FSIT*. It might be suggested that we ought to give up the everyday notion that there are some dispositional states which are not possible occurrent states (for example, to acknowledge an occurrent, though perhaps nonconscious, state of believing that *P*). Clearly, the possibility that we might some day have theoretical grounds for acknowledging the existence of such states cannot be precluded a priori. But we have no such grounds *now*, and there does seem to us to be a methodological principle of conservatism to the effect that one should resist models which require empirical or conceptual changes that are not independently motivated.

(2) We suggested that *FSIT* allows us to account for the fact that behavior is characteristically the product of interactions between psychological states, and that the existence of such interactions provides a standing source of difficulty for behaviorist theories in so far as they seek to assign characteristic behaviors *severally* to psychological states. It is empirically immensely likely, however, that there are *two* kinds of behaviorally efficacious interactions between psychological states, and *FSIT* provides for a natural model of only one of them.

On one hand, behavior can be the product of a *series* of psychological states, and the *FSIT* account shows us how this could be true, and how some of the states occurring in such a series may not themselves have behavioral expressions. But, on the other hand, behavior can be the result of interactions between *simultaneous* mental states. For example, prima facie, what an organism does at *t* may be a function of what it is feeling at *t* and what it is thinking at *t*. But *FSIT* provides no conceptual machinery for representing this state of affairs. In effect, *FSIT* can provide for the representation of sequential interactions between psychological states, but not for simultaneous interactions. Indeed *FSIT* even fails to account for the fact that an organism can be in more than one occurrent psychological state at a time, since a probabilistic automaton can be in only one machine table state at a time. The upshot of this argument seems to be that if probabilistic automata are to be used as models of an organism, the appropriate model will be a set of intercommunicating automata operating in parallel.

It is again important to keep clear on what the argument does not show about *FSIT*. We have read *FSIT* as claiming that the psychological states of an organism are in one-to-one correspondence with the machine table states postulated in its best *description*. The present argument suggests that if this claim is to be accepted, then the best *description* of an organism must not represent it as a single probabilistic automaton. If organisms, but not single probabilistic automata, can be in more than one state at a time, then either an organism is not a single probabilistic automaton, or the psychological states of an organism do not correspond to machine table states of single probabilistic automata. (It should be remarked that there is an algorithm which will construct a single automaton equivalent to any given set of parallel automata. It cannot be the case, however, that a set of parallel automata and the equivalent single automaton *both* provide best *descriptions* of an organism.)

These remarks are of some importance since the kind of psychological theory we get on the assumption that organisms are parallel processors will look quite different from the kind we get on the assumption that they are serial processors. Indeed, while the general characteristics of serial processors are relatively well understood, very little is known about the corresponding characteristics of parallel systems.

On the other hand, this argument does not touch the main claim of *FSIT*: even if organisms are in some sense sets of probabilistic automata, it may turn out that each psychological state of an organism corresponds to a machine table state of one or other of the members of the set. In the following arguments, we will assume the serial model for purposes of simplicity and try to show that, even on that assumption, psychological states do not correspond to machine table states.

(3) *FSIT* holds that two organisms are in psychological states of the same type if and only if they are in the same machine table state. But machine table states are identical if and only if they are identically related to other machine table states and to states of the input and output mechanisms. In this sense, the criterion for identity of machine

table states is "functional equivalence." Thus *FSIT* claims that type identity of psychological states is also a matter of a certain kind of functional equivalence; psychological states are type identical if and only if they share those properties that must be specified to individuate a machine table state.

But it might plausibly be argued that this way of type-identifying psychological states fails to accommodate a feature of at least some such states that is critical for determining their type: namely, their "qualitative" character. It does not, for example, seem entirely unreasonable to suggest that nothing would be a token of the type "pain state" unless it felt like a pain, and that this would be true even if it were connected to all the other psychological states of the organism in whatever ways pains are. It seems to us that the standard verificationist counterarguments against the view that the "inverted spectrum" hypothesis is conceptually coherent are not persuasive. If this is correct, it looks as though the possibility of qualia inversion poses a serious prima-facie argument against functionalist accounts of the criteria for type identity of psychological states.

It should be noticed, however, that the inverted qualia argument is *only* a prima-facie objection against *FSIT*. In particular, it is available to the proponent of functionalist accounts to meet this objection in either of two ways. On the one hand, he might argue that though inverted qualia, *if they occurred*, would provide counterexamples to his theory, as a matter of nomological fact it is impossible that functionally identical psychological states should be qualitatively distinct: in particular, that anything which altered the qualitative characteristics of a psychological state would alter its functional characteristics. This sort of line may strike one as blatant apriorism, but, in the absence of any relevant empirical data, it might be well to adopt an attitude of wait and see.

There is, moreover, another defense open to the proponent of *FSIT*. He might say that, given two functionally identical psychological states, we would (or perhaps "should") *take* them to be type identical, independent of their qualitative properties: that is, that differences between the qualitative properties of psychological states which do not determine corresponding functional differences are *ipso facto* irrelevant to the goals of theory construction in psychology, and hence should be ignored for purposes of type identification.

To see that this suggestion may be plausible, imagine that it turns out that every person does, in fact, have slightly different qualia (or, better still, grossly different qualia) when in whatever machine table state is alleged to be identical to pain. It seems fairly clear that in this case it might be reasonable to say that the character of an organism's qualia is irrelevant to whether it is in pain or (equivalently) that pains feel quite different to different organisms.

This form of argument may, however, lead to embarrassing consequences. For all that we now know, it may be nomologically possible for two psychological states to be functionally identical (that is, to be identically connected with inputs, outputs, and successor states), even if only one of the states has a qualitative content. In this case, *FSIT* would require us to say that an organism might be in pain even though it is feeling *nothing at all*, and this consequence seems totally unacceptable.

It may be remarked that these "inverted (or absent) qualia" cases in a certain sense pose a deeper problem for *FSIT* than any of the other arguments we shall be discussing. Our other arguments are, by and large, concerned to show that psychological states cannot be functionally defined in a certain way; namely, by being put in correspondence with machine table states. But though they are incompatible with *FSIT*, they are compatible with functionalism in the broad sense of that doctrine which holds that the type-identity conditions for psychological states refer only to their relations to inputs, outputs, and one another. The present consideration, however, might be taken to show that psychological states cannot be functionally defined *at all* and that they cannot be put into correspondence with *any* properties definable over abstract automata. We will ignore this possibility in what follows, since if psychological states are not functional states at all, the question whether they are machine table states simply does not arise.

(4) We remarked that there are arguments against behaviorism and physicalism which suggest that each proposes constraints upon type-identity conditions on psychological states that are, in one way or another, insufficiently abstract. We will now argue that *FSIT* is susceptible to the same kind of objection.

A machine table specifies a state in terms of a set of instructions which control the behavior of the machine whenever it is in that state. By definition, in the case of a deterministic automaton, such instructions specify, for each state of the machine, an associated output and a successor machine state. Probabilistic automata differ only in that any state may specify a *range* of outputs or of successor states, with an associated probability distribution. In short, two machine table states of a deterministic automaton are distinct if they differ either in their associated outputs or in their associated successor state. Analogously, two machine table states of probabilistic automata differ if they differ in their range of outputs, or in their range of successor states, or in the probability distributions associated with either of these ranges.

If, however, we transfer this convention for distinguishing machine table states to the type identification of psychological states, we get identity conditions which are, as it were, too fine-grained. Thus, for example, if you and I differ *only* in the respect that your most probable response to the pain of stubbing your toe is to say "damn" and mine is to say "darn," it follows that the pain you have when you stub your toe is type-distinct from the pain I have when I stub my toe.

This argument iterates in an embarrassing way. To see this, consider the special case of deterministic automata: x and y are type-distinct machine table states of such an automaton if the immediate successor states of x and y are type-distinct. But the immediate successor states of x and y are type-distinct if *their* immediate successor states are type-distinct. So *x* and *y* are type-distinct if the immediate successors of their immediate successors are type-distinct; and so on. Indeed, on the assumption that there is a computational path from every state to every other, any two automata which have less than all their states in common will have none of their states in common. This argument generalizes to probabilistic automata in an obvious way.

It is again important to see what the argument does *not* show. In particular, it does not show that psychological states cannot be type-identified by reference to some sort of *abstract* properties of machine table states. But, as we remarked in our discussion of Argument 1, to say that psychological states correspond to some or other property definable over machine table states is to say much less about the conditions upon the type identity of psychological states than *FSIT* seeks to do. And the present argument *does* seem to show that the conditions used to type-identify machine table states per se cannot be used to type-identify psychological states. It is presumably this sort of point which Putnam, for example, has in mind when he remarks that "the difficulty of course will be to pass from models of *specific* organisms to a *normal* form for the psychological description of *organisms*" ("Psychological Predicates," p. 43). In short, it may seem at first glance that exploitation of the criteria employed for type-identifying machine table states provides *FSIT* with concepts at precisely the level of abstraction required for type-identifying psychological states. But, in fact, this appears not to be true.

(5) The following argument seems to us to show that the psychological states of organisms cannot be placed in one-to-one correspondence with the machine table states of organisms.

The set of states which are included in the machine table of a probabilistic automaton is, by definition, a list. But the set of mental states of at least some organisms (namely, persons) is, in point of empirical fact, productive. In particular, abstracting from theoretically irrelevant limitations imposed by memory and mortality, there are infinitely many type-distinct, nomologically possible psychological states of any given person. The simplest demonstration that this is true is that, on the assumption that there are infinitely many non-equivalent declarative sentences, one can generate definite descriptions of such states by replacing *S* with sentences in the schemata *A*:

A: "the belief (thought, desire, hope, and so forth) that *S*"

In short, while the set of machine table states of a Turing machine can, by definition, be exhaustively specified by listing them, the set of mental states of a person can at best be specified by finite axiomatization.

It might be maintained against this argument that not more than a finite subset of the definite descriptions generable by substitution in *A* do in fact designate nomologically possible beliefs (desires, hopes, or whatever) and that this is true *not* because of theoretically uninteresting limitations imposed by memory and mortality, but rather because of the existence of psychological laws that limit the set of believable (and so forth) propositions to a finite set. To take a farfetched example, it might be held that if you eliminate all such perhaps unbelievable propositions as "$2 + 2 = 17$," "$2 + 2 = 147$," and so forth, the residuum is a finite set.

There is no reason at all to believe that this is true, however, and there are some very persuasive reasons for believing that it is not. For example, the infinite set of descriptions whose members are "the belief that $1 + 1 = 2$," "the belief that $2 + 2 = 4$," "the belief that $3 + 3 = 6$," and so forth would appear to designate a set of possible beliefs of an organism ideally free from limitations on memory; to put it the other way around, the fact that there are arithmetical statements that it is nomologically impossible for any person to believe is a consequence of the character of people's memory, not a consequence of the character of their mental representation of arithmetic.

It should be emphasized, again, that this is intended to be an empirical claim, albeit an overwhelmingly plausible one. It is possible to imagine a creature ideally free from memory limitations whose mental representation of arithmetic nevertheless specifies only a finite set of possible arithmetic beliefs. The present point is that it is vastly unlikely that we are such creatures.

Once again it is important to see what the argument does *not* show. Let us distinguish between the *machine table states* of an automaton, and the *computational states* of an automaton. By the former, we will mean what we have been meaning all along: states specified by columns in its machine table. By the latter we mean any state of the machine which is characterizable in terms of its inputs, outputs, and/or machine table states. In this usage, the predicates "has just run through a computation involving three hundred seventy-two machine table states," or "has just proved Fermat's last theorem," or "has just typed the *i*th symbol in its output vocabulary" all designate possible computational states of machines.

Now, what the present argument seems to show is that the psychological states of an organism cannot be put into correspondence with the machine table states of an automaton. What it of course does *not* show is that the psychological states of an organism cannot be put into correspondence with the *computational* states of an automaton. Indeed, a sufficient condition for the existence of the latter correspondence is that the psychological states of an organism should be countable.[6]

(6) We have argued that since the set of machine table states of an automaton is not productive, it cannot be put into correspondence with the psychological states of an organism. We will now argue that even if such a correspondence could be effected, it would necessarily fail to represent essential properties of psychological states. It seems fairly clear that there are structural similarities among at least some psychological states, and that a successful theory of such states must represent and exploit such similarities. For example, there is clearly some theoretically relevant relation between the psychological state that someone is in if he believes that *P* and the psychological state

that someone is in if he believes that P & Q. The present point is simply that representing the psychological states as a list (for example, as a list of machine table states) fails to represent this kind of structural relation. What needs to be said is that believing that P is somehow[7] a constituent of believing that P & Q; but the machine table state model has no conceptual resources for saying that. In particular, the notion "is a constituent of" is not defined for machine table states.

It might be replied that this sort of argument is not strictly relevant to the claims of *FSIT*: for it is surely possible, in principle, that there should be a one-to-one correspondence between machine table states and psychological states, even though the vocabulary appropriate to the individuation of the former does not capture the structural relations among the latter.

This reply, however, misses the point. To see this, consider the case with sentences. The reason there are structural parallelisms among sentences is that sentences are constructed from a fixed set of vocabulary items by the iterated application of a fixed set of rules, and the theoretical vocabulary required to analyze the ways in which sentences are structurally similar is precisely the vocabulary required to specify the domain of those rules. In particular, structurally similar sentences share either lexical items or paths in their derivations, or both. Thus one explains structural similarities between sentences in the same way that one explains their productivity: namely, by describing them as a generated set rather than a list.

Our point is that the same considerations apply to the set of psychological states of an organism. Almost certainly, they too are, or at least include, a generated set, and their structural similarities correspond, at least in part, to similarities in their derivation; that is, with psychological states as with sentences, the fact that they are productive and the fact that they exhibit internal structure are two aspects of the same phenomenon. If this is true, then a theory which fails to capture the structural relations within and among psychological states is overwhelmingly unlikely to arrive at a *description* adequate for the purposes of theoretical psychology.

This argument, like 5, thus leads to the conclusion that, if we wish to think of the psychology of organisms as represented by automata, then the psychological states of organisms seem to be analogous to the computational states of an automaton rather than to its machine table states.

IV

We have been considering theories in the philosophy of mind which can be construed as attempts to place substantive conditions upon type identity of psychological states. We have argued that none of the major theories currently in the field appear to succeed in this enterprise. It might, therefore, be advisable to reconsider the whole undertaking.

Suppose someone wanted to know what the criteria for type identity of fundamental physical entities are. Perhaps the best one could do by way of answering is to say that two such entities are type-identical if they do not differ with respect to any fundamental physical magnitudes. Thus, as far as we know, the conditions upon type identification of elementary physical particles do not refer to their distance from the North Pole, but do refer to their charge. But notice that this is simply a consequence of the fact that there are no fundamental physical laws which operate on entities as a function of their distance from the North Pole, and there *are* fundamental physical laws which operate on entities as a function of their charge.

One might put it that the basic condition upon type identity in science is that it makes possible the articulation of the domain of laws. This principle holds at every level of scientific description. Thus what is *relevant* to the question whether two entities at a level will be type-distinct is the character of the laws which operate upon entities at that level. But if this is the general case, then it looks as though substantive conditions upon type identity of psychological states will be imposed by reference to the psychological (and perhaps neurological) laws which operate upon those states and in no other way.

In the light of these remarks, we can get a clearer view of what has gone wrong with the kinds of philosophical theories we have been rejecting. For example, one can think of behaviorism as involving an attempt to type-identify psychological states just by reference to whatever laws determine their *behavioral* effects. But this would seem, even prima facie, to be a mistake, since there must be laws which govern the interaction of psychological states and there is no reason to believe (and much reason not to believe) that psychological states which behave uniformly vis-à-vis laws of the first kind characteristically behave uniformly vis-à-vis laws of the second kind.

Analogously, what has gone wrong in the case of physicalism is the assumption that psychological states that are distinct in their behavior vis-à-vis neurological laws are *ipso facto* distinct in their behavior vis-à-vis psychological laws. But, in all probability, distinct neurological states can be functionally identical. That is, satisfaction of the criteria for type-distinctness of neurological states probably does not guarantee satisfaction of the criteria for type-distinctness of psychological states or vice versa.

In short, the fundamental problem with behaviorism and physicalism is that type identity is being determined relative to, at best, a subset of the laws which must be presumed to operate upon psychological states. The only justification for this restriction seems to lie in the reductionist biases of these positions. Once the reductionism has been questioned, we can see that the nomological demands upon type identification for psychological states are likely to be extremely complicated and various. Even what little we already know about psychological laws makes it look implausible that they will acknowledge type boundaries between psychological states at the places where physicalists or behaviorists want to draw them.

The basic failure of *FSIT* is in certain respects analogous to that of behaviorism and physicalism. Of course, *FSIT* is not reductionist even in spirit, and in so far as it is a species of functionalism it does invite us to type-identify psychological states by reference to their nomological connections with sensory inputs, behavioral outputs, and with one another. But *FSIT* seeks to impose a further constraint on type identity: namely, that the psychological states of an organism can be placed in correspondence with (indeed, identified with) the machine table states specified by the best *description* of the organism. We have argued that this is in fact a substantive constraint, and one which cannot be satisfied.

What seems to be left of *FSIT* is this. It may be both true and important that organisms are probabilistic automata. But even if it is true and important, the fact that organisms are probabilistic automata seems to have very little or nothing to do with the conditions on type identity of their psychological states.

Notes

Reprinted from N. Block and J. Fodor, *Philosophical Review* 81: 152–181, April 1972. Reprinted in N. Block, ed., *Readings in Philosophy of Psychology*, vol. 1, 171–184 (Cambridge, MA: Harvard University Press, 1980).

A number of friends and colleagues have read earlier drafts. We are particularly indebted to Professors Richard Boyd, Donald Davidson, Michael Harnish, and Hilary Putnam for the care with which they read the paper and for suggestions that we found useful.

1. If physicalism is the doctrine that psychological states are physical states, then we get two versions depending whether we take "states" to refer to types or to tokens. The latter construal yields a weaker theory assuming that a token of type x may be identical to a token of type y even though x and y are distinct types. On this assumption, type physicalism clearly entails token physicalism, but not conversely.

The distinction between token identity theories and type identity theories has not been exploited in the case of behavioristic analyses. Unlike either version of physicalism, behaviorism is generally held as a semantic thesis, hence as a theory about logical relations between types. In the present paper, "physicalism" will mean *type* physicalism. When we talk about states, we will specify whether we mean types or tokens only when it is not clear from the context.

2. See Donald Davidson, "Mental Events," in *Fact and Experience*, ed. by Swanson and Foster (Amherst, 1970); Jerry A. Fodor, *Psychological Explanation* (New York, 1968); Hilary Putnam, "Brains and Behavior," in *Analytical Philosophy*, ed. by R. J. Butler (Oxford, 1965); Hilary Putnam, "The Mental Life of Some Machines," in *Modern Materialism: Readings on Mind-Body Identity*, ed. by J. O'Connor (New York, 1966); Hilary Putnam, "Psychological Predicates," in *Art, Mind and Religion*, ed. by Capitan and Merrill (Detroit, 1967).

3. Not all philosophical behaviorists hold this view; philosophical behaviorism may be broadly characterized as the view that for each psychological predicate there is a behavioral predicate to which it bears a "logical relation." (See Fodor, *op. cit.*) Thus the following view qualifies as behav-

iorist: all ascriptions of psychological predicates entail ascriptions of behavioral predicates, but not conversely. Though this form of behaviorism is not vulnerable to the present argument, the preceding ones are as effective against it as against biconditional forms of behaviorism.

4. Cf. Putnam, "Psychological Predicates" and "On Properties," in *Essays in Honor of C. G. Hempel*, ed. by N. Rescher et al. (New York, 1970).

5. Cf. Donald Davidson, "Actions, Reasons and Causes," *Journal of Philosophy*, LX (1963), 685–700.

6. The claim that organisms are probabilistic automata might be interestingly true even if *FSIT* is false; that is, even if psychological states do not correspond to machine table states. For example, it might turn out that some subset of the psychological states of an organism correspond to a set of machine table states by which the rest of its psychology is determined. Or it might turn out that what corresponds to each machine table state is a *conjunction* of psychological states ..., etc. Indeed, though the claim that any organism can be modeled by a probabilistic automaton is not interesting, the claim that for each organism there is a probabilistic automaton which is its *unique best* model *is* interesting. And this latter claim neither entails *FSIT* nor is it by any means obviously true.

In short, there are many ways in which it could turn out that organisms are automata in some sense *more* interesting than the sense in which everything is an automaton under some description. Our present point is that such eventualities, while they would be important, would not provide general conditions upon the type identification of psychological states in the way that *FSIT* attempts to do.

7. Very much "somehow." Obviously, believing p is not a constituent of believing $p \vee q$ in the same way that believing p is a constituent of believing $p \& q$. Equally obviously, there is some relation between believing p and believing $p \vee q$, and a theory of belief will have to say what that relation is.

4 Troubles with Functionalism

1.0 Functionalism, Behaviorism, and Physicalism

The functionalist view of the nature of the mind is now widely accepted.[1] Like behaviorism and physicalism, functionalism seeks to answer the question "What are mental states?" I shall be concerned with identity thesis formulations of functionalism. They say, for example, that pain is a functional state, just as identity thesis formulations of physicalism say that pain is a physical state.

I shall begin by describing functionalism, and sketching the functionalist critique of behaviorism and physicalism. Then I shall argue that the troubles ascribed by functionalism to behaviorism and physicalism infect functionalism as well.

One characterization of functionalism that is probably vague enough to be acceptable to most functionalists is: each type of mental state is a state consisting of a disposition to act in certain ways *and to have certain mental states*, given certain sensory inputs and certain mental states. So put, functionalism can be seen as a new incarnation of behaviorism. Behaviorism identifies mental states with dispositions to act in certain ways in certain input situations. But as critics have pointed out (Chisholm, 1957; Geach, 1957; Putnam, 1963), desire for goal G cannot be identified with, say, the disposition to do A in input circumstances in which A leads to G, since, after all, the agent might not *know* that A leads to G and thus might not be disposed to do A. Functionalism replaces behaviorism's "sensory inputs" with "sensory inputs and mental states"; and functionalism replaces behaviorism's "dispositions to act" with "dispositions to act and have certain mental states." Functionalists want to individuate mental states causally, and since mental states have mental causes and effects as well as sensory causes and behavioral effects, functionalists individuate mental states partly in terms of causal relations to other mental states. One consequence of this difference between functionalism and behaviorism is that there are possible organisms that according to behaviorism, have mental states but, according to functionalism, do not have mental states.

So, necessary conditions for mentality that are postulated by functionalism are in one respect stronger than those postulated by behaviorism. According to behaviorism, it is necessary and sufficient for desiring that G that a system be characterized by a certain set (perhaps infinite) of input-output relations; that is, according to behaviorism, a system desires that G just in case a certain set of conditionals of the form "It will emit O given I" are true of it. According to functionalism, however, a system might have these input-output relations, yet not desire that G; for according to functionalism, whether a system desires that G depends on whether it has internal states which have certain causal relations to other internal states (and to inputs and outputs). Since behaviorism makes no such "internal state" requirement, there are possible systems of which behaviorism affirms and functionalism denies that they have mental states.[2] One way of stating this is that, according to functionalism, behaviorism is guilty of *liberalism*—ascribing mental properties to things that do not in fact have them.

Despite the difference just sketched between functionalism and behaviorism, functionalists and behaviorists need not be far apart in spirit.[3] Shoemaker (1975), for example, says, "On one construal of it, functionalism in the philosophy of mind is the doctrine that mental, or psychological, terms are, in principle, eliminable in a certain way" (pp. 306–307). Functionalists have tended to treat the mental-state terms in a functional characterization of a mental state quite differently from the input and output terms. Thus in the simplest Turing-machine version of the theory (Putnam, 1967; Block & Fodor, 1972), mental states are identified with the total Turing-machine states, which are themselves *implicitly* defined by a machine table that *explicitly* mentions inputs and outputs, described nonmentalistically.

In Lewis's version of functionalism, mental-state terms are defined by means of a modification of Ramsey's method, in a way that eliminates essential use of mental terminology from the definitions but does not eliminate input and output terminology. That is, "pain" is defined as synonymous with a definite description containing input and output terms but no mental terminology (see Lewis, 1972).

Furthermore, functionalism in both its machine and nonmachine versions has typically insisted that characterizations of mental states should contain descriptions of inputs and outputs in *physical* language. Armstrong (1968), for example, says,

We may distinguish between "physical behaviour," which refers to any merely physical action or passion of the body, and "behaviour proper" which implies relationship to the mind.... Now, if in our formula ["state of the person apt for bringing about a certain sort of behaviour"] "behaviour" were to mean 'behaviour proper', then we would be giving an account of mental concepts in terms of a concept that already presupposes mentality, which would be circular. So it is clear that in our formula, "behaviour" must mean "physical behaviour." (p. 84)

Therefore, functionalism can be said to "tack down" mental states only at the periphery—i.e., through physical, or at least nonmental, specification of inputs and outputs. One major thesis of this article is that, because of this feature, functionalism fails to avoid the sort of problem for which it rightly condemns behaviorism. Functionalism, too, is guilty of liberalism, for much the same reasons as behaviorism. Unlike behaviorism, however, functionalism can naturally be altered to avoid liberalism—but only at the cost of falling into an equally ignominious failing.

The failing I speak of is the one that functionalism shows *physicalism* to be guilty of. By "physicalism," I mean the doctrine that pain, for example, is identical to a physical (or physiological) state.[4] As many philosophers have argued (notably Fodor, 1965, and Putnam, 1966; see also Block & Fodor, 1972), if functionalism is true, physicalism is probably false. The point is at its clearest with regard to Turing-machine versions of functionalism. Any given abstract Turing machine can be realized by a wide variety of physical devices; indeed, it is plausible that, given any putative correspondence between a Turing-machine state and a configurational physical (or physiological) state, there will be a possible realization of the Turing machine that will provide a counter-example to that correspondence. (See Kalke, 1969; Gendron, 1971; Mucciolo, 1974, for unconvincing arguments to the contrary; see also Kim, 1972.) Therefore, if pain is a functional state, it cannot, for example, be a brain state, because creatures without brains can realize the same Turing machine as creatures with brains.

I must emphasize that the functionalist argument against physicalism does not appeal merely to the fact that one abstract Turing machine can be realized by systems of different *material composition* (wood, metal, glass, etc.). To argue this way would be like arguing that temperature cannot be a microphysical magnitude because the same temperature can be had by objects with *different* microphysical structures (Kim, 1972). Objects with different microphysical structures, e.g., objects made of wood, metal, glass, etc., can have many interesting microphysical properties in common, such as molecular kinetic energy of the same average value. Rather, the functionalist argument against physicalism is that it is difficult to see how there *could be* a nontrivial first-order (see note 4) physical property in common to all and only the possible physical realizations of a given Turing-machine state. Try to think of a remotely plausible candidate! At the very least, the onus is on those who think such physical properties are conceivable to show us how to conceive of one.

One way of expressing this point is that, according to functionalism, physicalism is a *chauvinist* theory: it withholds mental properties from systems that in fact have them. In saying mental states are brain states, for example, physicalists unfairly exclude those poor brainless creatures who nonetheless have minds.

A second major point of this paper is that the very argument which functionalism uses to condemn physicalism can be applied equally well against functionalism; indeed, any version of functionalism that avoids liberalism falls, like physicalism, into chauvinism.

This article has three parts. The first argues that functionalism is guilty of liberalism, the second that one way of modifying functionalism to avoid liberalism is to tie it more closely to empirical psychology, and the third that no version of functionalism can avoid both liberalism and chauvinism.

1.1   More about What Functionalism Is

One way of providing some order to the bewildering variety of functionalist theories is to distinguish between those that are couched in terms of a Turing machine and those that are not.

A Turing-machine table lists a finite set of machine-table states, $S_1 \ldots S_n$; inputs, $I_1 \ldots I_m$; and outputs, $O_1 \ldots O_p$. The table specifies a set of conditionals of the form: if the machine is in state S_i and receives input I_j, it emits output O_k and goes into state S_l. That is, given any state and input, the table specifies an output and a next state. Any system with a set of inputs, outputs, and states related in the way specified by the table is described by the table and is a realization of the abstract automaton specified by the table.

To have the power for computing any recursive function, a Turing machine must be able to control its input in certain ways. In standard formulations, the output of a Turing machine is regarded as having two components. It prints a symbol on a tape, then moves the tape, thus bringing a new symbol into the view of the input reader. For the Turing machine to have full power, the tape must be infinite in at least one direction and movable in both directions. If the machine has no control over the tape, it is a "finite transducer," a rather limited Turing machine. Finite transducers need not be regarded as having tape at all. Those who believe that machine functionalism is true must suppose that just what power automaton we are is a substantive empirical question. If we are "full power" Turing machines, the environment must constitute part of the tape.

One very simple version of machine functionalism (Block and Fodor, 1972) states that each system having mental states is described by at least one Turing-machine table of a specifiable sort and that each type of mental state of the system is identical to one of the machine-table states. Consider, for example, the Turing machine described in the table (cf. Nelson, 1975):

	S_1	S_2
nickel input	Emit no output Go to S_2	Emit a Coke Go to S_1
dime input	Emit a Coke Stay in S_1	Emit a Coke & a nickel Go to S_1

One can get a crude picture of the simple version of machine functionalism by considering the claim that S_1 = dime-desire, and S_2 = nickel-desire. Of course, no functionalist would claim that a Coke machine desires anything. Rather, the simple version of machine functionalism described above makes an analogous claim with respect to a much more complex hypothetical machine table. Notice that machine functionalism specifies inputs and outputs explicitly, internal states implicitly (Putnam [1967, p. 434] says: "The S_i, to repeat, are specified only *implicitly* by the description, i.e., specified *only* by the set of transition probabilities given in the machine table"). To be described by this machine table, a device must accept nickels and dimes as inputs and dispense nickels and Cokes as outputs. But the states S_1 and S_2 can have virtually any natures (even nonphysical natures), so long as those natures connect the states to each other and to the inputs and outputs specified in the machine table. All we are told about S_1 and S_2 are these relations; thus machine functionalism can be said to reduce mentality to input-output structures. This example should suggest the force of the functionalist argument against physicalism. Try to think of a first-order (see note 4) physical property that can be shared by all (and only) realizations of this machine table!

One can also categorize functionalists in terms of whether they regard functional identities as part of a priori psychology or empirical psychology. The a priori functionalists (e.g., Smart, Armstrong, Lewis, Shoemaker) are the heirs of the logical behaviorists. They tend to regard functional analyses as analyses of the meanings of mental terms, whereas the empirical functionalists (e.g., Fodor, Putnam, Harman) regard functional analyses as substantive scientific hypotheses. In what follows, I shall refer to the former view as "Functionalism" and the latter as "Psychofunctionalism." (I shall use 'functionalism' with a lowercase "f" as neutral between Functionalism and Psychofunctionalism. When distinguishing between Functionalism and Psychofunctionalism, I shall always use capitals.)

Functionalism and Psychofunctionalism and the difference between them can be made clearer in terms of the notion of the Ramsey sentence of a psychological theory. Mental-state terms that appear in a psychological theory can be defined in various ways by means of the Ramsey sentence of the theory. All functional-state identity theories can be understood as defining a set of functional states by means of the Ramsey sentence of a psychological theory—with one functional state corresponding to each mental state. The functional state corresponding to pain will be called the "Ramsey functional correlate" of pain, with respect to the psychological theory. In terms of the notion of a Ramsey functional correlate with respect to a theory, the distinction between Functionalism and Psychofunctionalism can be defined as follows: Functionalism identifies mental state S with S's Ramsey functional correlate with respect to a *common-sense* psychological theory; Psychofunctionalism identifies S with S's Ramsey functional correlate with respect to a *scientific* psychological theory.

This difference between Functionalism and Psychofunctionalism gives rise to a difference in specifying inputs and outputs. Functionalists are restricted to specification of inputs and outputs that are plausibly part of commonsense knowledge; Psychofunctionalists are under no such restriction. Although both groups insist on physical—or at least nonmental—specification of inputs and outputs, Functionalists require externally observable classifications (e.g., inputs characterized in terms of objects present in the vicinity of the organism, outputs in terms of movements of body parts). Psychofunctionalists, on the other hand, have the option to specify inputs and outputs in terms of internal parameters, e.g., signals in input and output neurons.

Let T be a psychological theory of either common sense or scientific psychology. T may contain generalizations of the form: anyone who is in state w and receives input x emits output y, and goes into state z. Let us write T as

$$T(S_1 \ldots S_n, I_1 \ldots I_k, O_1 \ldots O_m)$$

where the S's are mental states, the I's are inputs, and the O's are outputs. The S's are to be understood as mental-state *constants*, not variables, e.g., "pain," and likewise for the I's and O's. Thus, one could also write T as

T(pain ..., light of 400 nanometers entering left eye ..., left big toe moves 1 centimeter left ...)

To get the Ramsey sentence of T, replace the mental-state terms—*but not the input and output terms*—by variables, and prefix an existential quantifier for each variable:

$$\exists F_1 \ldots \exists F_n T(F_1 \ldots F_n, I_1 \ldots I_k, O_1 \ldots O_m)$$

If F_{17} is the variable that replaced the word "pain" when the Ramsey sentence was formed, we can define pain as follows in terms of the Ramsey sentence:

x is in pain $\langle$—$\rangle$ $\exists F_1 \ldots \exists F_n T[(F_1 \ldots F_n, I_1 \ldots I_k, O_1 \ldots O_m)$ & x has $F_{17}]$

The Ramsey functional correlate of pain is the property expressed by the predicate on the right-hand side of this biconditional. Notice that this predicate contains input and output constants, but no mental constants, since the mental constants were replaced by variables. The Ramsey functional correlate for pain is defined in terms of inputs and outputs, but not in mental terms.

For example, let T be the theory that pain is caused by skin damage and causes worry and the emission of "Ouch," and worry, in turn, causes brow wrinkling. Then the Ramsey definition would be:

x is in pain $\langle$—$\rangle$ There are two states (properties), the first of which is caused by skin damage and causes both the emission of "Ouch" and the second state, and the second state causes brow wrinkling, and x is in the first state.

The Ramsey functional correlate of pain with respect to this "theory" is the property of being in a state that is caused by skin damage and causes the emission of "ouch" and another state that in turn causes brow wrinkling. (Note that the words "pain" and "worry" have been replaced by variables, but the input and output terms remain.)

The Ramsey functional correlate of a state S is a state that has much in common with S. Specifically, S and its Ramsey functional correlate share the structural properties specified by the theory T. But there are two reasons why it is natural to suppose that S and its Ramsey functional correlate will be distinct. First, the Ramsey functional correlate of S with respect to T can "include" at most those aspects of S that are captured by T; any aspects not captured by T will be left out. Second, the Ramsey functional correlate may even leave out some of what T does capture, for the Ramsey definition does not contain the "theoretical" vocabulary of T. The example theory of the last paragraph is true only of pain-feeling organisms—but trivially, by virtue of its use of the word "pain." However, the predicate that expresses T's Ramsey functional correlate does not contain this word (since it was replaced by a variable), and so can be true of things that do not feel pain. It would be easy to make a simple machine that has some artificial skin, a brow, a tape-recorded "ouch," and two states that satisfy the mentioned causal relations, but no pain.

The bold hypothesis of functionalism is that for *some* psychological theory, this natural supposition that a state and its Ramsey functional correlate are distinct is false. Functionalism says that there is a theory such that pain, for example, *is* its Ramsey functional correlate with respect to that theory.

One final preliminary point: I have given the misleading impression that functionalism identifies *all* mental states with functional states. Such a version of functionalism is obviously far too strong. Let X be a newly created cell-for-cell duplicate of you (which, of course, is functionally equivalent to you). Perhaps you remember being bar-mitzvahed. But X does not remember being bar-mitzvahed, since X never was bar-mitzvahed. Indeed, something can be functionally equivalent to you but fail to know what you know, or [verb], what you [verb], for a wide variety of "success" verbs. Worse still, if Putnam (1975b) is right in saying that "meanings are not in the head," systems functionally equivalent to you may, for similar reasons, fail to have many of your other propositional attitudes. Suppose you believe water is wet. According to plausible arguments advanced by Putnam and Kripke, a condition for the possibility of your believing water is wet is a certain kind of causal connection between you and water. Your "twin" on Twin Earth, who is connected in a similar way to XYZ rather than H_2O, would not believe water is wet.

If functionalism is to be defended, it must be construed as applying only to a subclass of mental states, those "narrow" mental states such that truth conditions for their application are in some sense "within the person." But even assuming that a notion of narrowness of psychological state can be satisfactorily formulated, the interest of functionalism may be diminished by this restriction. I mention this problem only to set it aside.

I shall take functionalism to be a doctrine about all "narrow" mental states.

1.2   Homunculi-Headed Robots

In this section I shall describe a class of devices that are *prima facie* embarrassments for all versions of functionalism in that they indicate functionalism is guilty of liberalism—classifying systems that lack mentality as having mentality.

Consider the simple version of machine functionalism already described. It says that each system having mental states is described by at least one Turing-machine table of a certain kind, and each mental state of the system is identical to one of the machine-table states specified by the machine table. I shall consider inputs and outputs to be specified by descriptions of neural impulses in sense organs and motor-output neurons. This assumption should not be regarded as restricting what will be said to Psychofunctionalism rather than Functionalism. As already mentioned, every version of functionalism assumes *some* specificiation of inputs and outputs. A Functionalist specification would do as well for the purposes of what follows.

Imagine a body externally like a human body, say yours, but internally quite different. The neurons from sensory organs are connected to a bank of lights in a hollow cavity in the head. A set of buttons connects to the motor-output neurons. Inside the cavity resides a group of little men. Each has a very simple task: to implement a "square" of an adequate machine table that describes you. On one wall is a bulletin board on which is posted a state card, i.e., a card that bears a symbol designating one of the states specified in the machine table. Here is what the little men do: Suppose the posted card has a 'G' on it. This alerts the little men who implement G squares— 'G-men' they call themselves. Suppose the light representing input I_{17} goes on. One of the G-men has the following as his sole task: when the card reads 'G' and the I_{17} light goes on, he presses output button O_{191} and changes the state card to 'M'. This G-man is called upon to exercise his task only rarely. In spite of the low level of intelligence required of each little man, the system as a whole manages to simulate you because the functional organization they have been trained to realize is yours. A Turing machine can be represented as a finite set of quadruples (or quintuples, if the output is divided into two parts): current state, current input; next state, next output. Each little man has the task corresponding to a single quadruple. Through the efforts of the little men, the system realizes the same (reasonably adequate) machine table as you do and is thus functionally equivalent to you.[6]

I shall describe a version of the homunculi-headed simulation, which has more chance of being nomologically possible. How many homunculi are required? Perhaps a billion are enough.

Suppose we convert the government of China to functionalism, and we convince its officials to realize a human mind for an hour. We provide each of the billion people in China (I chose China because it has a billion inhabitants) with a specially designed two-way radio that connects them in the appropriate way to other persons and to the artificial body mentioned in the previous example. We replace each of the little men with a citizen of China plus his radio. Instead of a bulletin board, we arrange to have letters displayed on a series of satellites placed so that they can be seen from anywhere in China.

The system of a billion people communicating with one another plus satellites plays the role of an external "brain" connected to the artificial body by radio. There is nothing absurd about a person being connected to his brain by radio. Perhaps the day will come when our brains will be periodically removed for cleaning and repairs. Imagine that this is done initially by treating neurons attaching the brain to the body with a chemical that allows them to stretch like rubber bands, thereby assuring that no brain-body connections are disrupted. Soon clever businessmen discover that they can attract more customers by replacing the stretched neurons with radio links so that brains can be cleaned without inconveniencing the customer by immobilizing his body.

It is not at all obvious that the China-body system is physically impossible. It could be functionally equivalent to you for a short time, say an hour.

"But," you may object, "how could something be functionally equivalent to me for *an hour?* Doesn't my functional organization determine, say, how I would react to doing nothing for a week but reading the *Reader's Digest?*" Remember that a machine table specifies a set of conditionals of the form: if the machine is in S_i and receives input I_j, it emits output O_k and goes into S_l. These conditionals are to be understood *subjunctively*. What gives a system a functional organization at a time is not just what it *does* at that time, but also the counterfactuals true of it at that time: what it *would* have done (and what its state transitions would have been) had it had a different input or been in a different state. If it is true of a system at time t that it *would* obey a given machine table no matter which of the states it is in and no matter which of the inputs it receives, then the system is described at t by the machine table (and realizes at t the abstract automaton specified by the table), even if it exists for only an instant. For the hour the Chinese system is "on," it *does* have a set of inputs, outputs, and states of which such subjunctive conditionals are true. This is what makes any computer realize the abstract automaton that it realizes.

Of course, there are signals the system would respond to that you would not respond to, e.g., massive radio interference or a flood of the Yangtze River. Such events might cause a malfunction, scotching the simulation, just as a bomb in a computer can make it fail to realize the machine table it was built to realize. But just as the computer *without* the bomb *can* realize the machine table, the system consisting of the people and artificial body can realize the machine table so long as there are no catastrophic interferences, e.g., floods, etc.

"But," someone may object, "there is a difference between a bomb in a computer and a bomb in the Chinese system, for in the case of the latter (unlike the former), inputs as specified in the machine table can be the cause of the malfunction. Unusual neural activity in the sense organs of residents of Chungking Province caused by a bomb or by a flood of the Yangtze can cause the system to go haywire."

Reply: The person who says what system he or she is talking about gets to say what signals count as inputs and outputs. I count as inputs and outputs only neural activity in the artificial body connected by radio to the people of China. Neural signals in the people of Chungking count no more as inputs to this system than input tape jammed by a saboteur between the relay contacts in the innards of a computer count as an input to the computer.

Of course, the object consisting of the people of China + the artificial body has *other* Turing-machine descriptions under which neural signals in the inhabitants of Chungking *would* count as inputs. Such a new system (i.e., the object under such a new Turing-machine description) would not be functionally equivalent to you. Likewise, any commercial computer can be redescribed in a way that allows tape jammed into its innards to count as inputs. In describing an object as a Turing machine, one draws a line between the inside and the outside. (If we count only neural impulses as inputs and outputs, we draw that line inside the body; if we count only peripheral stimulations as inputs, we draw that line at the skin.) In describing the Chinese system as a Turing machine, I have drawn the line in such a way that it satisfies a certain type of functional description—one that you *also* satisfy, and one that, according to functionalism, justifies attributions of mentality. Functionalism does not claim that every mental system has a machine table of a sort that justifies attributions of mentality with respect to *every* specification of inputs and outputs, but rather, only with respect to *some* specification.

Objection: The Chinese system would work too slowly. The kind of events and processes with which we normally have contact would pass by far too quickly for the system to detect them. Thus, we would be unable to converse with it, play bridge with it, etc.

Reply: It is hard to see why the system's time scale should matter. Is it really contradictory or nonsensical to suppose we could meet a race of intelligent beings with whom we could communicate only by devices such as time-lapse photography? When we observe these creatures, they seem almost inanimate. But when we view the time-lapse movies, we see them conversing with one another. Indeed, we find they are saying that the only way they can make any sense of us is by viewing movies greatly slowed down. To take time scale as all important seems crudely behavioristic. Further, even if the time-scale objection is right, I can elude it by retreating to the point that a homunculi-head that works in normal time is *metaphysically* possible. Metaphysical possibility is all my argument requires. (See Kripke, 1972.)

What makes the homunculi-headed system (count the two systems as variants of a single system) just described a prima facie counterexample to (machine) functionalism is that there is prima facie doubt whether it has any mental states at all—especially whether it has what philosophers have variously called "qualitative states," "raw feels," or "immediate phenomenological qualities." (You ask: What is it that philosophers have called qualitative states? I answer, only half in jest: As Louis Armstrong said when asked what jazz is, "If you got to ask, you ain't never gonna get to know.") In Nagel's terms (1974), there is a prima facie doubt whether there is anything which it is like to be the homunculi-headed system.

The force of the prima facie counterexample can be made clearer as follows: Machine functionalism says that each mental state is identical to a machine-table state. For example, a particular qualitative state, Q, is identical to a machine-table state, S_q. But if there is nothing it is like to be the homunculi-headed system, it cannot be in Q even when it is in S_q. Thus, if there is prima facie doubt about the homunculi-headed system's mentality, there is prima facie doubt that $Q = S_q$, i.e., doubt that the kind of functionalism under consideration is true.[7] Call this argument the Absent Qualia Argument.

So there is prima facie doubt that machine functionalism is true. So what? After all, prima facie doubt is only prima facie. Indeed, appeals to intuition of this sort are notoriously fallible. I shall not rest on this appeal to intuition. Rather, I shall argue that the intuition that the homunculi-headed simulation described above lacks mentality (or at least qualia) has at least in part a rational basis, and that this rational basis provides a good reason for doubting that Functionalism (and to a lesser degree Psychofunctionalism) is true. I shall consider this line of argument in Section 1.5.

1.3 What If I Turned Out to Have Little Men in My Head?

Before I go any further, I shall briefly discuss a difficulty for my claim that there is prima facie doubt about the qualia of homunculi-headed realizations of human functional organization. It might be objected, "What if *you* turned out to be one?" Let us suppose that, to my surprise, X-rays reveal that inside my head are thousands of tiny, trained fleas, each of which has been taught (perhaps by a joint subcommittee of the American Philosophical Association and the American Psychological Association empowered to investigate absent qualia) to implement a square in the appropriate machine table.

Now there is a crucial issue relevant to this difficulty which philosophers are far from agreeing on (and about which I confess I cannot make up my mind): Do I know on the basis of my "privileged access" that I do not have utterly absent qualia, no matter what turns out to be inside my head? Do I know there is something it is like to be me, even if I am a flea-head? Fortunately, my vacillation on this issue is of no consequence, for either answer is compatible with the Absent Qualia Argument's assumption that there is doubt about the qualia of homunculi-headed folks.

Suppose the answer is no. It is not the case that I know there is something it is like to be me even if I am a flea-head. Then I should admit that my qualia would be in (prima facie) doubt if (God forbid) I turned out to have fleas in my head. Likewise for the qualia of all the other homunculi-headed folk. So far, so good.

Suppose, on the other hand, that my privileged access does give me infallible knowledge that I have qualia. No matter what turns out to be inside my head, my states have qualitative content. There is something it is like to be me. Then if I turn out to have fleas in my head, at least one homunculi-head turns out to have qualia. But this would not challenge my claim that the qualia of homunculi-infested simulations is in doubt. Since I do, in fact, have qualia, supposing I have fleas inside my head is supposing someone with fleas inside his head has qualia. But this supposition that a homunculi-head has qualia is just the sort of supposition my position doubts. Using such an example to argue against my position is like twitting a man who doubts there is a God by asking what he would say if he turned out to *be* God. Both arguments against the doubter beg the question against the doubter by hypothesizing a situation which the doubter admits is logically possible, but doubts is *actual*. A doubt that there is a God entails a doubt that I am God. Similarly, (given that I do have qualia) a doubt that flea-heads have qualia entails a doubt that I am a flea-head.

1.4 Putnam's Proposal

One way functionalists can try to deal with the problem posed by the homunculi-headed counterexamples is by the ad hoc device of stipulating them away. For example, a functionalist might stipulate that two systems cannot be functionally equivalent if one contains parts with functional organizations characteristic of sentient beings and the other does not. In his article hypothesizing that pain is a functional state, Putnam stipulated that "no organism capable of feeling pain possesses a decomposition into parts which separately possess Descriptions" (as the sort of Turing machine which can be in the functional state Putnam identifies with pain). The purpose of this condition is "to rule out such 'organisms' (if they count as such) as swarms of bees as single pain feelers" (Putnam, 1967, pp. 434–435).

One way of filling out Putnam's requirement would be: a pain-feeling organism cannot possess a decomposition into parts *all* of which have a functional organization characteristic of sentient beings. But this would not rule out my homunculi-headed example, since it has nonsentient parts, such as the mechanical body and sense organs. It will not do to go to the opposite extreme and require that *no* proper parts be sentient.

Otherwise pregnant women and people with sentient parasites will fail to count as pain-feeling organisms. What seems to be important to examples like the homunculi-headed simulation I have described is that the sentient beings *play a crucial role* in giving the thing its functional organization. This suggests a version of Putnam's proposal which requires that a pain-feeling organism has a certain functional organization and that it has no parts which (1) themselves possess that sort of functional organization and also (2) play a crucial role in giving the whole system its functional organization.

Although this proposal involves the vague notion "crucial role," it is precise enough for us to see it will not do. Suppose there is a part of the universe that contains matter quite different from ours, matter that is infinitely divisible. In this part of the universe, there are intelligent creatures of many sizes, even humanlike creatures much smaller than our elementary particles. In an intergalactic expedition, these people discover the existence of our type of matter. For reasons known only to them, they decide to devote the next few hundred years to creating out of *their* matter substances with the chemical and physical characteristics (except at the subelementary particle level) of *our* elements. They build hordes of space ships of different varieties about the sizes of our electrons, protons, and other elementary particles, and fly the ships in such a way as to mimic the behavior of these elementary particles. The ships also contain generators to produce the type of radiation elementary particles give off. Each ship has a staff of experts on the nature of our elementary particles. They do this so as to produce huge (by our standards) masses of substances with the chemical and physical characteristics of oxygen, carbon, etc. Shortly after they accomplish this, you go off on an expedition to that part of the universe, and discover the "oxygen," "carbon," etc. Unaware of its real nature, you set up a colony, using these "elements" to grow plants for food, provide "air" to breathe, etc. Since one's molecules are constantly being exchanged with the environment, you and other colonizers come (in a period of a few years) to be composed mainly of the "matter" made of the tiny people in space ships. Would you be any less capable of feeling pain, thinking, etc. just because the matter of which you are composed contains (and depends on for its characteristics) beings who themselves have a functional organization characteristic of sentient creatures? I think not. The basic electrochemical mechanisms by which the synapse operates are now fairly well understood. As far as is known, changes that do not affect these electrochemical mechanisms do not affect the operation of the brain, and do not affect mentality. The electrochemical mechanisms in your synapses would be unaffected by the change in your matter.[8]

It is interesting to compare the elementary-particle-people example with the homunculi-headed examples the chapter started with. A natural first guess about the source of our intuition that the initially described homunculi-headed simulations lack mentality is that they have *too much* internal mental structure. The little men may be sometimes bored, sometimes excited. We may even imagine that they deliberate about the best way to realize the given functional organization and make changes intended to give them more leisure time. But the example of the elementary-particle people just described suggests this first guess is wrong. What seems important is *how* the mentality of the parts contributes to the functioning of the whole.

There is one very noticeable difference between the elementary-particle-people example and the earlier homunculus examples. In the former, the change in you as you become homunculus-infested is not one that makes any difference to your psychological processing (i.e., information processing) or neurological processing but only to your microphysics. No techniques proper to human psychology or neurophysiology would reveal any difference in you. However, the homunculi-headed simulations described in the beginning of the chapter are not things to which neurophysiological theories true of us apply, and *if they are construed as Functional* (rather than Psychofunctional) simulations, they need not be things to which psychological (information-processing) theories true of us apply. This difference suggests that our intuitions are in part controlled by the not unreasonable view that our mental states depend on our having the psychology and/or neurophysiology we have. So something that differs markedly from us in both regards (recall that it is a Functional rather than Psychofunctional simulation) should not be assumed to have mentality just on the ground that it has been designed to be Functionally equivalent to us.[9]

1.5 Is the Prima Facie Doubt Merely Prima Facie?

The Absent Qualia Argument rested on an appeal to the intuition that the homunculi-headed simulations lacked mentality, or at least qualia. I said that this intuition gave rise to prima facie doubt that functionalism is true. But intuitions unsupported by principled argument are hardly to be considered bedrock. Indeed, intuitions incompatible with well-supported theory (e.g., the pre-Copernican intuition that the earth does not move) thankfully soon disappear. Even fields like linguistics whose data consist mainly in intuitions often reject such intuitions as that the following sentences are ungrammatical (on theoretical grounds):

The horse raced past the barn fell.
The boy the girl the cat bit scratched died.

These sentences are in fact grammatical though hard to process.[10]

Appeal to intuitions when judging possession of mentality, however, is *especially* suspicious. *No* physical mechanism seems very intuitively plausible as a seat of qualia, least of all a *brain*. Is a hunk of quivering gray stuff more intuitively appropriate as a seat of qualia than a covey of little men? If not, perhaps there is a prima facie doubt about the qualia of brain-headed systems too?

However, there is a very important difference between brain-headed and homunculi-headed systems. Since we know that *we are brain-headed systems*, and that *we* have qualia, we know that brain-headed systems can have qualia. So even though we have no theory of qualia which explains how this is *possible*, we have overwhelming reason to disregard whatever prima facie doubt there is about the qualia of brain-headed systems. Of course, this makes my argument partly *empirical*—it depends on knowledge of what makes us tick. But since this is knowledge we in fact possess, dependence on this knowledge should not be regarded as a defect.[11]

There is another difference between us meat-heads and the homunculi-heads: they are systems designed to mimic us, but we are not designed to mimic anything (here I rely on another empirical fact). This fact forestalls any attempt to argue on the basis of an inference to the best explanation for the qualia of homunculi-heads. The best explanation of the homunculi-heads' screams and winces is not their pains, but that they were designed to mimic our screams and winces.

Some people seem to feel that the complex and subtle behavior of the homunculi-heads (behavior just as complex and subtle—even as "sensitive" to features of the environment, human and nonhuman, as your behavior) is itself sufficient reason to disregard the prima facie doubt that homunculi-heads have qualia. But this is just crude behaviorism.

My case against functionalism depends on the following principle: if a doctrine has an absurd conclusion that there is no independent reason to believe, and if there is no way of explaining away the absurdity or showing it to be misleading or irrelevant, and if there is no good reason to believe the doctrine that leads to the absurdity in the first place, then don't accept the doctrine. I claim that there is no independent reason to believe in the mentality of the homunculi-head, and I know of no way of explaining away the absurdity of the conclusion that it has mentality (though of course, my argument is vulnerable to the introduction of such an explanation). The issue, then, is whether there is any good reason to believe Functionalism. One argument for Functionalism is that it is the best solution available to the mind-body problem. I think this is a bad form of argument, but since I also think that Psychofunctionalism is preferable to Functionalism (for reasons to be mentioned below), I will postpone consideration of this form of argument to the discussion of Psychofunctionalism.

The only other argument for Functionalism that I know of is that Functional identities can be shown to be true on the basis of analyses of the meanings of mental terminology. According to this argument, Functional identities are to be justified in the way one might try to justify the claim that the state of being a bachelor is identical to the state of being an unmarried man. A similar argument appeals to commonsense platitudes about mental states instead of truths of meaning. Lewis says that Functional characterizations of mental states are in the province of "common sense psychology—

folk science, rather than professional science" (Lewis, 1972, p. 250). (See also Shoe-maker, 1975, and Armstrong, 1968. Armstrong equivocates on the analyticity issue. See Armstrong, 1968, pp. 84–85, and p. 90.) And he goes on to insist that Functional characterizations should "include only platitudes which are common knowledge among us—everyone knows them, everyone knows that everyone else knows them, and so on" (Lewis, 1972, p. 256). I shall talk mainly about the "platitude" version of the argument. The analyticity version is vulnerable to essentially the same considerations, as well as Quinean doubts about analyticity.

I am willing to concede, for the sake of argument, that it is possible to define any given mental-state term in terms of platitudes concerning other mental-state terms, input terms, and output terms. But this does not commit me to the type of definition of mental terms in which all mental terminology has been eliminated via Ramsification or some other device. It is simply a fallacy to suppose that if each mental term is defin-able in terms of the others (plus inputs and outputs), then each mental term is defin-able nonmentalistically. To see this, consider the example given earlier. Indeed, let's simplify matters by ignoring the inputs and outputs. Let's define pain as the cause of worry, and worry as the effect of pain. Even a person so benighted as to accept this, need not accept a definition of pain as *the cause of something*, or a definition of worry as *the effect of something*. Lewis claims that it is analytic that pain is the occupant of a certain causal role. Even if he is right about a causal role, *specified in part mentalistically*, one cannot conclude that it is analytic that pain is the occupant of any causal role, nonmentalistically specified.

I do not see any decent argument for Functionalism based on platitudes or analytic-ity. Further, the conception of Functionalism as based on platitudes leads to trouble with cases that platitudes have nothing to say about.

Recall the example of brains being removed for cleaning and rejuvenation, the con-nections between one's brain and one's body being maintained by radio while one goes about one's business. The process takes a few days, and when it is completed, the brain is reinserted in the body. Occasionally it may happen that a person's body is destroyed by an accident while the brain is being cleaned and rejuvenated. If hooked up to input sense organs (but not output organs) such a brain would exhibit *none* of the usual platitudinous connections between behavior and clusters of inputs and men-tal states. If, as seems plausible, such a brain could have almost all the same (narrow) mental states as we have (and since such a state of affairs could become typical), Func-tionalism is wrong.

It is instructive to compare the way Psychofunctionalism attempts to handle cases like paralysis and brains in bottles. According to Psychofunctionalism, what is to count as a system's inputs and outputs is an empirical question. Counting neural impulses as inputs and outputs would avoid the problems just sketched, since the brains in bottles and paralytics could have the right neural impulses even without bodily movements.

Objection: There could be paralysis that affects the nervous system, and thus affects the neural impulses, so the problem which arises for Functionalism arises for Psychofunctionalism as well. Reply: Nervous system diseases can actually *change mentality*, e.g., they can render victims incapable of having pain. So it might actually be true that a widespread nervous system disease that caused intermittent paralysis rendered people incapable of certain mental states.

According to plausible versions of Psychofunctionalism, the job of deciding what neural processes should count as inputs and outputs is in part a matter of deciding *what malfunctions count as changes in mentality and what malfunctions count as changes in peripheral input and output connections*. Psychofunctionalism has a resource that Functionalism does not have, since Psychofunctionalism allows us to *adjust the line we draw between the inside and the outside of the organism so as to avoid problems of the sort discussed*. All versions of Functionalism go wrong in attempting to draw this line on the basis of only common-sense knowledge; "analyticity" versions of Functionalism go especially wrong in attempting to draw the line a priori.

Objection: Sydney Shoemaker suggests (in correspondence) that problems having to do with paralytics, and brains in vats of the sort I mentioned, can be handled using his notion of a "paradigmatically embodied person" (see Shoemaker, 1976). Paradigmatic embodiment involves having functioning sensory apparatus and considerable voluntary control of bodily movements. Shoemaker's suggestion is that we start with a functional characterization of a paradigmatically embodied person, saying, inter alia, what it is for a physical state to realize a given mental state in a paradigmatically embodied person. Then, the functional characterization could be extended to nonparadigmatically embodied persons by saying that a physical structure that is not a part of a paradigmatically embodied person will count as realizing mental states, if, without changing its internal structure and the sorts of relationships that hold between its states, it could be incorporated into a larger physical system that would be the body of a paradigmatically embodied person in which the states in question played the functional roles definitive of mental states of a paradigmatically embodied person. Shoemaker suggests that a brain in a vat can be viewed from this perspective, as a limiting case of an amputee—amputation of everything but the brain. For the brain can (in principle) be incorporated into a system so as to form a paradigmatically embodied person without changing the internal structure and state relations of the brain.

Reply: Shoemaker's suggestion is very promising, but it saves functionalism only by retreating from Functionalism to Psychofunctionalism. Obviously, nothing in prescientific common-sense wisdom about mentality tells us what can or cannot be paradigmatically embodied *without changing its internal structure and state relations* (unless 'state relations' means 'Functional state relations', in which case the question is begged). Indeed, the scientific issues involved in answering this question are very similar to the scientific issues involved in the Psychofunctionalist question about the difference

between defects in or damage to input-output devices, as opposed to defects in or damage to central mechanisms. That is, the scientific task of drawing the Psychofunctionalist line between the inside and the outside of an organism are much the same as
Shoemaker's task of drawing the line between what can and what cannot be paradigmatically embodied without changing its internal structure and state relations.

I shall briefly raise two additional problems for Functionalism. The first might be
called the Problem of Differentiation: there are mental states that are different, but
that do not differ with respect to platitudes. Consider different tastes or smells that
have typical causes and effects, but whose typical causes and effects are not known or
are not known to very many people. For example, tannin in wine produces a particular
taste immediately recognizable to wine drinkers. As far as I know, there is no standard
name or description (except "tannic") associated with this taste. The causal antecedents and consequents of this taste are not widely known, there are no platitudes
about its typical causes and effects. Moreover, there are sensations that not only have
no standard names but whose causes and effects are not yet well understood by anyone. Let A and B be two such (different) sensations. Neither platitudes nor truths
of meaning can distinguish between A and B. Since the Functional description of a
mental state is determined by the platitudes true of that state, and since A and B do
not differ with respect to platitudes, Functionalists would be committed to identifying
A and B with the same Functional state, and thus they would be committed to the
claim that A = B, which is ex hypothesi false.

A second difficulty for Functionalism is that platitudes are often wrong. Let us call
this problem the Problem of Truth. Lewis suggests, by way of dealing with this problem, that we specify the causal relations among mental states, inputs and outputs, not
by means of the conjunction of all the platitudes, but rather by "a cluster of them—a
disjunction of conjunctions of *most* of them (that way it will not matter if a few are
wrong.)" This move may exacerbate the problem of Differentiation, however, since
there may be pairs of different mental states that are alike with respect to *most*
platitudes.

2.0 Psychofunctionalism

In criticizing Functionalism, I appealed to the following principle: if a doctrine has an
absurd conclusion that there is no independent reason to believe, and if there is no
way of explaining away the absurdity or showing it to be misleading or irrelevant,
and if there is no good reason to believe the doctrine that leads to the absurdity in
the first place, then do not accept the doctrine. I said that there was no independent
reason to believe that the homunculi-headed Functional simulation has any mental
states. However, there *is* an independent reason to believe that the homunculi-headed
*Psycho*functional simulation has mental states, namely, that a Psychofunctional simu-

lation of you would be Psychofunctionally equivalent to you, so any psychological theory true of you would be true of it too. What better reason could there be to attribute to it whatever mental states are in the domain of psychology?

Even if this point shows that any Psychofunctional simulation of you shares your *non*qualitative mental states. I will argue that there is nonetheless some doubt that it shares your qualitative mental states.

Here is one argument for Psychofunctionalism that is implicit in the literature. It is the business of branches of science to tell us the nature of things in the branches' domains. Mental states are in the domain of psychology, and, hence, it is the business of psychology to tell us what mental states are. Psychological theory can be expected to characterize mental states in terms of the causal relations among mental states, and other mental entities, and among mental entities, inputs, and outputs. But these very causal relations are the ones which constitute the Psychofunctional states that Psychofunctionalism identifies with mental states. So Psychofunctionalism is just the result of applying a plausible conception of science to mentality; Psychofunctionalism is just the doctrine that mental states are the "psychological states" it is the business of psychology to characterize.

That something is seriously amiss with this form of argument can be seen by noting that it would be fallacious if applied to other branches of science.

Consider the analogue of Psychofunctionalism for physics. It says that protonhood, for example, is the property of having certain lawlike relations to certain other physical properties. With respect to current physical theory, protonhood would be identified with a property expressible in terms of the Ramsey sentence of current physical theory (in the manner described above). Now there is an obvious problem with this claim about what it is to be a proton. Namely, this physico-functionalist approach would identify being an anti-proton *with the very same property*. According to current physical theory, protons and antiprotons are "dual" entities: one cannot distinguish the variable which replaced 'protonhood' from the variable that replaced 'antiprotonhood' (in any nontrivial way) in the Ramsey sentence of current physical theory. Yet protons and anti-protons are different types of particles; it is a law of physics that particles annihilate their antiparticles; thus, protons annihilate antiprotons, even though protons get along fine with other protons.[12]

Suppose someone were to argue that "protonhood = its Ramsey functional correlate with respect to current physical theory" is our best hypothesis as to the nature of protonhood, on the ground that this identification amounts to an application of the doctrine that it is the business of branches of science to tell us the nature of things in their domains. The person would be arguing fallaciously. So why should we suppose that this form of argument is any less fallacious when applied to psychology?

In the preceding few paragraphs I may have given the impression that the analogue of Psychofunctionalism in physics can be used to cast doubt on Psychofunctionalism itself. But there are two important disanalogies between Psychofunctionalism and its physics analogue. First, according to Psychofunctionalism, there is a theoretically principled distinction between, on one hand, the inputs and outputs described explicitly in the Ramsey sentence, and, on the other hand, the internal states and other psychological entities whose names are replaced by variables. But there is no analogous distinction with respect to other branches of science. An observational/theoretical distinction would be analogous if it could be made out, but difficulties in drawing such a distinction are notorious.

Second, and more important, Psychofunctionalism simply need not be regarded as a special case of any general doctrine about the nature of the entities scientific theories are about. Psychofunctionalists can reasonably hold that only *mental* entities—or perhaps only states, events, and their ilk, as opposed to substances like protons—are "constituted" by their causal relations. Of course, if Psychofunctionalists take such a view, they protect Psychofunctionalism from the proton problem at the cost of abandoning the argument that Psychofunctionalism is just the result of applying a plausible conception of science to mentality.

Another argument for Psychofunctionalism (or, less plausibly, for Functionalism) which can be abstracted from the literature is an "inference to the best explanation" argument: "What *else* could mental states be if not Psychofunctional states?" For example, Putnam (1967) hypothesizes that (Psycho)functionalism is true and then argues persuasively that (Psycho)functionalism is a *better* hypothesis than behaviorism or materialism.

But this is a very dubious use of "inference to the best explanation." For what guarantee do we have that *there is* an answer to the question "What are mental states?" of the sort behaviorists, materialists, and functionalists have wanted? Moreover, inference to the best explanation cannot be applied when none of the available explanations is any good. In order for inference to the best explanation to be applicable, two conditions have to be satisfied: we must have reason to believe an explanation is *possible*, and at least one of the available explanations must be *minimally adequate*. Imagine someone arguing for one of the proposed solutions to Newcomb's Problem on the ground that despite its fatal flaw it is the best of the proposed solutions. That would be a joke. But is the argument for functionalism any better? Behaviorism, materialism, and functionalism are not theories of mentality in the way Mendel's theory is a theory of heredity. Behaviorism, materialism, and functionalism (and dualism as well) are attempts to solve a problem: the mind-body problem. Of course, this is a problem which can hardly be guaranteed to have a solution. Further, each of the proposed solutions to the mind-body problem has serious difficulties, difficulties I for one am inclined to regard as fatal.

Why is functionalism so widely accepted, given the dearth of good arguments for it, implicit or explicit? In my view, what has happened is that functionalist doctrines were offered initially as hypotheses. But with the passage of time, plausible-sounding hypotheses with useful features can come to be treated as established facts, even if no good arguments have ever been offered for them.

2.1   Are Qualia Psychofunctional States?

I began this chapter by describing a homunculi-headed device and claiming there is prima facie doubt about whether it has any mental states at all, especially whether it has qualitative mental states like pains, itches, and sensations of red. The special doubt about qualia can perhaps be explicated by thinking about *inverted* qualia rather than *absent* qualia. It makes sense, or seems to make sense, to suppose that objects we both call green look to me the way objects we both call red look to you. It seems that we could be functionally equivalent even though the sensation fire hydrants evoke in you is qualitatively the same as the sensation grass evokes in me. Imagine an inverting lens which when placed in the eye of a subject results in exclamations like "Red things now look the way green things used to look, and vice versa." Imagine further, a pair of identical twins one of whom has the lenses inserted at birth. The twins grow up normally, and at age 21 are functionally equivalent. This situation offers at least some evidence that each's spectrum is inverted relative to the other's. (See Shoemaker, 1975, note 17, for a convincing description of intrapersonal spectrum inversion.) However, it is very hard to see how to make sense of the analogue of spectrum inversion with respect to nonqualitative states. Imagine a pair of persons one of whom believes that p is true and that q is false, while the other believes that q is true and that p is false. Could these persons be functionally equivalent? It is hard to see how they could.[13] Indeed, it is hard to see how two persons could have only this difference in beliefs and yet there be no possible circumstance in which this belief difference would reveal itself in different behavior. Beliefs seem to be supervenient on functional organization in a way that qualia are not.

There is another reason to firmly distinguish between qualitative and nonqualitative mental states in talking about functionalist theories: Psychofunctionalism avoids Functionalism's problems with nonqualitative states, e.g., propositional attitudes like beliefs and desires. But Psychofunctionalism may be no more able to handle qualitative states than is Functionalism. The reason is that qualia may well not be in the domain of psychology.

To see this, let us try to imagine what a homunculi-headed realization of human psychology would be like. Current psychological theorizing seems directed toward the description of information-flow relations among psychological mechanisms. The aim seems to be to decompose such mechanisms into psychologically primitive mechanisms, "black boxes" whose internal structure is in the domain of physiology rather than in the domain of psychology. (See Fodor, 1968b, Dennett, 1975, and

Cummins, 1975; interesting objections are raised in Nagel, 1969.) For example, a near-primitive mechanism might be one that matches two items in a representational system and determines if they are tokens of the same type. Or the primitive mechanisms might be like those in a digital computer, e.g., they might be (a) *add 1 to a given register*, and (b) *subtract 1 from a given register, or if the register contains 0, go to the nth (indicated) instruction*. (These operations can be combined to accomplish any digital computer operation; see Minsky, 1967, p. 206.) Consider a computer whose machine-language code contains only two instructions corresponding to (a) and (b). If you ask how it multiplies or solves differential equations or makes up payrolls, you can be answered by being shown a program couched in terms of the two machine-language instructions. But if you ask how it adds 1 to a given register, the appropriate answer is given by a wiring diagram, not a program. The machine is hard-wired to add 1. When the instruction corresponding to (a) appears in a certain register, the contents of another register "automatically" change in a certain way. The computational structure of a computer is determined by a set of primitive operations and the ways nonprimitive operations are built up from them. Thus it does not matter to the computational structure of the computer whether the primitive mechanisms are realized by tube circuits, transistor circuits, or relays. Likewise, it does not matter to the psychology of a mental system whether its primitive mechanisms are realized by one or another neurological mechanism. Call a system a "realization of human psychology" if every psychological theory true of us is true of it. Consider a realization of human psychology whose primitive psychological operations are accomplished by little men, in the manner of the homunculi-headed simulations discussed. So, perhaps one little man produces items from a list, one by one, another compares these items with other representations to determine whether they match, etc.

Now there is good reason for supposing this system has some mental states. Propositional attitudes are an example. Perhaps psychological theory will identify remembering that P with having "stored" a sentencelike object which expresses the proposition that P (Fodor, 1975). Then if one of the little men has put a certain sentencelike object in "storage," we may have reason for regarding the system as remembering that P. But unless having qualia is just a matter of having certain information processing (at best a controversial proposal—see later discussion), there is no such theoretical reason for regarding the system as having qualia. In short, there is perhaps as much doubt about the qualia of this homunculi-headed system as there was about the qualia of the homunculi-headed Functional simulation discussed early in the chapter.

But the system we are discussing is ex hypothesi something of which any true psychological theory is true. *So any doubt that it has qualia is a doubt that qualia are in the domain of psychology.*

It may be objected: "The kind of psychology you have in mind is *cognitive* psychology, i.e., psychology of thought processes; and it is no wonder that qualia are not in the domain of *cognitive* psychology!" But I *do not* have cognitive psychology in mind, and if it sounds that way, this is easily explained: nothing we know about the psychological processes underlying our conscious mental life has anything to do with qualia. What passes for the "psychology" of sensation or pain, for example, is (a) physiology, (b) psychophysics (i.e., study of the mathematical functions relating stimulus variables and sensation variables, e.g., the intensity of sound as a function of the amplitude of the sound waves), or (c) a grabbag of descriptive studies (see Melzack, 1973, Ch. 2). Of these, only psychophysics could be construed as being about qualia per se. And it is obvious that psychophysics touches only the *functional* aspect of sensation, not its qualitative character. Psychophysical experiments done on you would have the same results if done on any system Psychofunctionally equivalent to you, even if it had inverted or absent qualia. If experimental results would be unchanged whether or not the experimental subjects have inverted or absent qualia, they can hardly be expected to cast light on the nature of qualia.

Indeed, on the basis of the kind of conceptual apparatus now available in psychology, I do not see how psychology in anything like its present incarnation *could* explain qualia. We cannot now conceive how psychology could explain qualia, though we *can* conceive how psychology could explain believing, desiring, hoping, etc. (see Fodor, 1975). That something is currently inconceivable is not a good reason to think it is impossible. Concepts could be developed tomorrow that would make what is now inconceivable conceivable. But all we have to go on is what we know, and on the basis of what we have to go on, it looks as if qualia are not in the domain of psychology.

Objection: If the Psychofunctional simulation just described has the same beliefs I have, then among its beliefs will be the belief that it now has a headache (since I now am aware of having a headache). But then you must say that its belief is mistaken—and how can such a belief be mistaken?

Reply. The objection evidently assumes some version of the Incorrigibility Thesis (if x believes he has a pain, it follows that he does have a pain). I believe the Incorrigibility Thesis to be false. But even if it is true, it is a double-edged sword. For one can just as well use it to argue that Psychofunctionalism's difficulties with qualia infect its account of belief too. For if the homunculi-headed simulation is in a state Psychofunctionally equivalent to believing it is in pain, yet has no qualia, and hence no pain, then if the Incorrigibility Thesis is true, it does not believe it is in pain either. But if it is in a state Psychofunctionally equivalent to belief without believing, belief is not a Psychofunctional state.

Objection: At one time it was inconceivable that temperature could be a property of matter, if matter was composed only of particles bouncing about; but it would not have been rational to conclude temperature was not in the domain of physics. Reply: First, what the objection says was inconceivable was probably never inconceivable. When the scientific community could conceive of matter as bouncing particles, it could probably also conceive of heat as something to do with the motion of the particles. Bacon's theory that heat was motion was introduced at the inception of theorizing about heat—a century before Galileo's primitive precursor of a thermometer, and even before distinctions among the temperature of x, the perceived temperature of x, and x's rate of heat conduction were at all clear (Kuhn, 1961). Second, there is quite a difference between saying something is not in the domain of physics and saying something is not in the domain of psychology. Suggesting that temperature phenomena are not in the domain of physics is suggesting that they are not explainable at all.

It is no objection to the suggestion that qualia are not psychological entities that qualia are the very paradigm of something in the domain of psychology. As has often been pointed out, it is in part an empirical question what is in the domain of any particular branch of science. The liquidity of water turns out not to be explainable by chemistry, but rather by subatomic physics. Branches of science have at any given time a set of phenomena they seek to explain. But it can be discovered that some phenomenon which seemed central to a branch of science is actually in the purview of a different branch.

Suppose psychologists discover a *correlation* between qualitative states and certain cognitive processes. Would that be any reason to think the qualitative states are identical to the cognitive states they are correlated with? Certainly not. First, what reason would there be to think this correlation would hold in the homunculi-headed systems that Psychofunctionally simulate us? Second, although a case can be made that certain sorts of general correlations between Fs and Gs provide reason to think F is G, this is only the case when the predicates are predicates of different theories, one of which is reducible to the other. For example, there is a correlation between thermal and electrical conductivity (asserted by the Wiedemann-Franz Law), but it would be silly to suggest that this shows thermal conductivity is electrical conductivity (see Block, 1971, Ch. 3).

I know of only one serious attempt to fit "consciousness" into information-flow psychology: the program in Dennett, 1978. But Dennett fits consciousness into information-flow psychology only by claiming that the contents of consciousness are exhausted by judgments. His view is that to the extent that qualia are not judgments (or beliefs), they are spurious theoretical entities that we postulate to explain why we find ourselves wanting to say all sorts of things about what is going on in our minds.

Dennett's doctrine has the relation to qualia that the U.S. Air Force had to so many Vietnamese villages: he destroys qualia in order to save them. Is it not more reasonable to tentatively hypothesize that qualia are determined by the physiological or physicochemical nature of our information processing, rather than by the information flow per se?

The Absent Qualia Argument exploits the possibility that the Functional or Psychofunctional state Functionalists or Psychofunctionalists would want to identify with pain can occur without any quale occurring. It also seems to be conceivable that the latter occur without the former. Indeed, there are facts that lend plausibility to this view. After frontal lobotomies, patients typically report that they still have pains, though the pains no longer bother them (Melzack, 1973, p. 95). These patients show all the "sensory" signs of pain (e.g., recognizing pin pricks as sharp), but they often have little or no desire to avoid "painful" stimuli.

One view suggested by these observations is that each pain is actually a *composite* state whose components are a quale and a Functional or Psychofunctional state.[14] Or what amounts to much the same idea, each pain is a quale playing a certain Functional or Psychofunctional role. If this view is right, it helps to explain how people can have believed such different theories of the nature of pain and other sensations: they have emphasized one component at the expense of the other. Proponents of behaviorism and functionalism have had one component in mind; proponents of private ostensive definition have had the other in mind. Both approaches err in trying to give one account of something that has two components of quite different natures.

3.0 Chauvinism vs. Liberalism

It is natural to understand the psychological theories Psychofunctionalism adverts to as theories of *human* psychology. On Psychofunctionalism, so understood, it is logically impossible for a system to have beliefs, desires, etc., except insofar as psychological theories true of us are true of it. Psychofunctionalism (so understood) stipulates that Psychofunctional equivalence to us is necessary for mentality.

But even if Psychofunctional equivalence to us is a condition on our *recognition of mentality*, what reason is there to think it is a condition on mentality itself? Could there not be a wide variety of possible psychological processes that can underlie mentality, of which we instantiate only one type? Suppose we meet Martians and find that they are roughly Functionally (but not Psychofunctionally) equivalent to us. When we get to know Martians, we find them about as different from us as humans we know. We develop extensive cultural and commercial intercourse with them. We study each other's science and philosophy journals, go to each other's movies, read each other's novels, etc. Then Martian and Earthian psychologists compare notes, only to find that in underlying psychology, Martians and Earthians are very different. They soon agree that the difference can be described as follows. Think of humans and Martians as if they were products of conscious design. In any such design project, there will be various options. Some capacities can be built in (innate), others learned. The brain can be designed to accomplish tasks using as much memory capacity as necessary in order to minimize use of computation capacity; or, on the other hand, the designer could choose to conserve memory space and rely mainly on computation capacity. Inferences can be accomplished by systems which use a few axioms and many rules of inference, or, on the other hand, few rules and many axioms. Now imagine that what Martian and Earthian psychologists find when they compare notes is that Martians and Earthians differ as if they were the end products of maximally different design choices (compatible with rough Functional equivalence in adults). Should we reject our assumption that Martians can enjoy our films, believe their own apparent scientific results, etc.? Should they "reject" their "assumption" that we "enjoy" their novels, "learn" from their textbooks, etc.? Perhaps I have not provided enough information to answer this question. After all, there may be many ways of filling in the description of the Martian-human differences in which it would be reasonable to suppose there simply is no fact of the matter, or even to suppose that the Martians do not deserve mental ascriptions. But surely there are many ways of filling in the description of the Martian-Earthian difference I sketched on which it would be perfectly clear that even if Martians behave differently from us on subtle psychological experiments, they nonetheless think, desire, enjoy, etc. To suppose otherwise would be crude human chauvinism. (Remember theories are chauvinist insofar as they falsely *deny* that systems have mental properties and liberal insofar as they falsely *attribute* mental properties.)

So it seems as if in preferring Psychofunctionalism to Functionalism, we erred in the direction of human chauvinism. For if mental states are Psychofunctional states, and if Martians do not have these Psychofunctional states, then they do not have mental states either. In arguing that the original homunculi-headed simulations (taken as Functional simulations) had no mentality, I appealed, in effect, to the following principle: if the sole reason to think system x has mentality is that x was built to be Functionally equivalent to us, then differences between x and us in underlying information processing and/or neurophysiology are reasons to doubt whether x has mental states. But this principle does not dictate that a system can have mentality only insofar as it is Psychofunctionally equivalent to us. Psychofunctional equivalence to us is a sufficient condition for at least those aspects of mentality in the domain of psychology, but it is not obvious that it is a necessary condition of any aspects of mentality.

An obvious suggestion of a way out of this difficulty is to identify mental states with Psychofunctional states, taking the domain of psychology to include *all creatures with mentality*, including Martians. The suggestion is that we define "Psychofunctionalism" in terms of "universal" or "cross-system" psychology, rather than the human psychology I assumed earlier. Universal psychology, however, is a suspect discipline. For how are we to decide what systems should be included in the *domain* of universal psychology? One possible way of deciding what systems have mentality, and are thus in the domain of universal psychology, would be to use some *other* developed theory of mentality, e.g., behaviorism or Functionalism. But such a procedure would be at least as ill-justified as the other theory used. Further, if Psychofunctionalism must presuppose some other theory of mind, we might just as well accept the other theory of mind instead.

Perhaps universal psychology will avoid this "domain" problem in the same way other branches of science avoid it or seek to avoid it. Other branches of science start with tentative domains based on intuitive and prescientific versions of the concepts the sciences are supposed to explicate. They then attempt to develop natural kinds in a way which allows the formulations of lawlike generalizations which apply to all or most of the entities in the prescientific domains. In the case of many branches of science—including biological and social sciences such as genetics and linguistics—the prescientific domain turned out to be suitable for the articulation of lawlike generalizations.

Now it may be that we shall be able to develop universal psychology in much the same way we develop Earthian psychology. We decide on an intuitive and prescientific basis what creatures to include in its domain, and work to develop natural kinds of psychological theory which apply to all or at least most of them. Perhaps the study of a wide range of organisms found on different worlds will one day lead to theories that determine truth conditions for the attribution of mental states like belief, desire, etc., applicable to systems which are pretheoretically quite different from us. Indeed, such cross-world psychology will no doubt require a whole new range of mentalistic concepts. Perhaps there will be families of concepts corresponding to belief, desire, etc., that is, a family of belieflike concepts, desirelike concepts, etc. If so, the universal psychology we develop shall, no doubt, be somewhat dependent on which new organisms we discover first. Even if universal psychology is in fact possible, however, there will certainly be many possible organisms whose mental status is indeterminate.

On the other hand, it may be that universal psychology is *not* possible. Perhaps life in the universe is such that we shall simply have no basis for reasonable decisions about what systems are in the domain of psychology and what systems are not.

If universal psychology *is* possible, the problem I have been raising vanishes. Universal-Psychofunctionalism avoids the liberalism of Functionalism and the chauvinism of human-Psychofunctionalism. But the question of whether universal psychology is possible is surely one which we have no way of answering now.

Here is a summary of the argument so far:

1. Functionalism has the bizarre consequence that a homunculi-headed simulation of you has qualia. This puts the burden of proof on the Functionalist to give us some reason for believing his doctrine. However, the one argument for Functionalism in the literature is no good, and so Functionalism shows no sign of meeting the burden of proof.

2. Psychofunctional simulations of us share whatever states are in the domain of psychology, so the Psychofunctional homunculi-head does not cast doubt on Psychofunctional theories of cognitive states, but only on Psychofunctionalist theories of qualia, there being a doubt as to whether qualia are in the domain of psychology.

3. Psychofunctionalist theories of mental states that are in the domain of psychology, however, are hopelessly chauvinist.

So one version of Functionalism has problems with liberalism; the other has problems with chauvinism. As to qualia, if they are in the domain of psychology, then Psychofunctionalism with respect to qualia is just as chauvinist as Psychofunctionalism with respect to belief. On the other hand, if qualia are not in the domain of psychology, the Psychofunctionalist homunculi-head can be used against Psychofunctionalism with respect to qualia. For the only thing that shields Psychofunctionalism with respect to mental state S from the homunculi-head argument is that if you have S, then any Psychofunctional simulation of you must have S, because the correct theory of S applies to it just as well as to you.

3.1   The Problem of the Inputs and the Outputs

I have been supposing all along (as Psychofunctionalists often do—see Putnam, 1967) that inputs and outputs can be specified by neural impulse descriptions. But this is a chauvinist claim, since it precludes organisms without neurons (e.g., machines) from having functional descriptions. How can one avoid chauvinism with respect to specification of inputs and outputs? One way would be to characterize the inputs and outputs *only as* inputs and outputs. So the functional description of a person might list outputs by number: $output_1$, $output_2$, ... Then a system could be functionally equivalent to you if it had a set of states, inputs, and outputs causally related to one another in the way yours are, no matter what the states, inputs, and outputs were like. Indeed, though this approach violates the demand of some functionalists that inputs and outputs be physically specified, other functionalists—those who insist only that input and output descriptions be *nonmental*—may have had something like this in mind. This version of functionalism does not "tack down" functional descriptions at the periphery with relatively specific descriptions of inputs and outputs; rather, this version of functionalism treats inputs and outputs just as all versions of functionalism treat internal states. That is, this version specifies states, inputs, and outputs only by requiring that they *be* states, inputs, and outputs.

The trouble with this version of functionalism is that it is wildly liberal. Economic systems have inputs and outputs, e.g., influx and outflux of credits and debits. And economic systems also have a rich variety of internal states, e.g., having a rate of increase of GNP equal to double the Prime Rate. It does not seem impossible that a wealthy sheik could gain control of the economy of a small country, e.g., Bolivia, and manipulate its financial system to make it functionally equivalent to a person, e.g., himself. If this seems implausible, remember that the economic states, inputs, and outputs designated by the sheik to correspond to his mental states, inputs, and outputs need not be "natural" economic magnitudes. Our hypothetical sheik could pick *any* economic magnitudes at all—e.g., the fifth time derivative of the balance of payments. His only constraint is that the magnitudes he picks be economic, that their having such and such values be inputs, outputs, and states, and that he be able to set up a financial structure which can be made to fit the intended formal mold. The mapping from psychological magnitudes to economic magnitudes could be as bizarre as the sheik requires.

This version of functionalism is far too liberal and must therefore be rejected. If there are any fixed points when discussing the mind-body problem, one of them is that the economy of Bolivia could not have mental states, no matter how it is distorted by powerful hobbyists. Obviously, we must be more specific in our descriptions of inputs and outputs. The question is: is there a description of inputs and outputs specific enough to avoid liberalism, yet general enough to avoid chauvinism? I doubt that there is.

Every proposal for a description of inputs and outputs I have seen or thought of is guilty of either liberalism or chauvinism. Though this paper has concentrated on liberalism, chauvinism is the more pervasive problem. Consider standard Functional and Psychofunctional descriptions. Functionalists tend to specify inputs and outputs in the manner of behaviorists: outputs in terms of movements of arms and legs, sound emitted and the like; inputs in terms of light and sound falling on the eyes and ears. Such descriptions are blatantly *species-specific*. Humans have arms and legs, but snakes do not—and whether or not snakes have mentality, one can easily imagine snake-like creatures that do. Indeed, one can imagine creatures with all manner of input-output devices, e.g., creatures that communicate and manipulate by emitting strong magnetic fields. Of course, one could formulate Functional descriptions for each such species, and somewhere in disjunctive heaven there is a disjunctive description which will handle all species that ever actually exist in the universe (the description may be infinitely long). But even an appeal to such suspicious entities as infinite disjunctions will not bail out Functionalism, since even the amended view will not tell us what there is in common to pain-feeling organisms in virtue of which they all have pain. And it will not allow the ascription of pain to some hypothetical (but nonexistent) pain-feeling creatures. Further, these are just the grounds on which functionalists typically acerbically reject the disjunctive theories sometimes advanced by desperate physicalists. If functionalists suddenly smile on wildly disjunctive states to save themselves from chauvinism, they will have no way of defending themselves from physicalism.

Standard Psychofunctional descriptions of inputs and outputs are also species-specific (e.g., in terms of neural activity) and hence chauvinist as well.

The chauvinism of standard input-output descriptions is not hard to explain. The variety of possible intelligent life is enormous. Given any fairly specific descriptions of inputs and outputs, any high-school-age science-fiction buff will be able to describe a sapient sentient being whose inputs and outputs fail to satisfy that description.

I shall argue that *any physical description* of inputs and outputs (recall that many functionalists have insisted on physical descriptions) yields a version of functionalism that is inevitably chauvinist or liberal. Imagine yourself so badly burned in a fire that your optimal way of communicating with the outside world is via modulations of your EEG pattern in Morse Code. You find that thinking an exciting thought produces a pattern that your audience agrees to interpret as a dot, and a dull thought produces a "dash." Indeed, this fantasy is not so far from reality. According to a recent newspaper article (*Boston Globe*, March 21, 1976), "at UCLA scientists are working on the use of EEG to control machines.... A subject puts electrodes on his scalp, and thinks an object through a maze." The "reverse" process is also presumably possible: others communicating with you in Morse Code by producing bursts of electrical activity that affect your brain (e.g., causing a long or short afterimage). Alternatively, if the cerebroscopes that philosophers often fancy become a reality, your thoughts will be readable directly from your brain. Again, the reverse process also seems possible. In these cases, *the brain itself becomes an essential part of one's input and output devices*. This possibility has embarrassing consequences for functionalists. You will recall that functionalists pointed out that physicalism is false because a single mental state can be realized by an indefinitely large variety of physical states that have no necessary and sufficient physical characterization. But if this functionalist point against physicalism is right, *the same point applies to inputs and outputs*, since the physical realization of mental states can serve as an essential part of the input and output devices. That is, on any sense of 'physical' in which the functionalist criticism of physicalism is correct, *there will be no physical characterization that applies to all and only mental systems' inputs and outputs*. Hence, any attempt to formulate a functional description with physical characterizations of inputs and outputs will inevitably either exclude some systems with mentality or include some systems without mentality. Hence, *functionalists cannot avoid both chauvinism and liberalism*.

So physical specifications of inputs and outputs will not do. Moreover, mental or "action" terminology (e.g., "punching the offending person") can not be used either, since to use such specifications of inputs or outputs would be to give up the functionalist program of characterizing mentality in nonmental terms. On the other hand, as you will recall, characterizing inputs and outputs simply *as* inputs and outputs is inevitably liberal. I, for one, do not see how there can be a vocabulary for describing inputs and outputs that avoids both liberalism and chauvinism. I do not claim that this is a conclusive argument against functionalism. Rather, like the functionalist argument against physicalism, it is best construed as a burden-of-proof argument. The functionalist says to the physicalist: "It is very hard to see how there could be a single physical characterization of the internal states of all and only creatures with mentality." I say to the functionalist: "It is very hard to see how there could be a single physical characterization of the inputs and outputs of all and only creatures with mentality." In both cases, enough has been said to make it the responsibility of those who think there could be such characterizations to sketch how they could be possible.[15]

Notes

Reprinted with revision and abridgment from C. W. Savage, ed., *Minnesota Studies in the Philosophy of Science*, vol. 9, 261–325 (Minneapolis: University of Minnesota Press, 1978). Reprinted in N. Block, ed., *Readings in Philosophy of Psychology*, vol. 1 (Cambridge, MA: Harvard University Press, 1980). Reprinted (shortened version) in W. Lycan, ed., *Mind and Cognition*, 444–469 (Oxford: Blackwell, 1990). Reprinted (shortened version) in D. M. Rosenthal, ed., *The Nature of Mind*, 211–229 (Oxford: Oxford University Press, 1991). Reprinted (shortened version) in B. Beakley and P. Ludlow, eds., *Philosophy of Mind* (Cambridge, MA: MIT Press, 1992). Reprinted (shortened version) in Alvin Goldman, ed., *Readings in Philosophy and Cognitive Science* (Cambridge, MA: MIT Press, 1993). German translation, "Schwierigkeiten mit dem Funktionalismus," in D. Münch, Hg., *Kognitionswissenschaft: Grundlagen, Probleme, Perspektiven*, 159–225 (Frankfurt: Suhrkamp, 1992). French translation, "Le fonctionnalisme face au problème des qualia," in *Les Etudes Philosophiques* 3: 337–369, 1992. Spanish translation in E. Rabossi, ed., *Filosofia y Cienca Cognitiva* (Buenos Aires and Barcelona: Libreria Paidós, 1996). Reprinted (much shortened version) in W. Lycan, ed., *Mind and Cognition*, 2nd ed. (Oxford: Blackwell, 1999). Reprinted in Jack Crumley, ed., *Problems in Mind: Readings in Contemporary Philosophy of Mind* (Mayfield, 1999). Reprinted in David Chalmers, ed., *Philosophy of Mind: Classical and Contemporary Readings* (Oxford: Oxford University Press, 2002). Reprinted in *Philosophy of Mind: Contemporary Readings*, a volume in the Routledge "Contemporary Readings" series edited by Timothy William O'Connor and David Robb (New York: Routledge, 2003).

1. See Fodor, 1965, 1968a; Lewis, 1966, 1972; Putnam, 1966, 1967, 1970, 1975a; Armstrong, 1968; Locke, 1968; perhaps Sellars, 1968; perhaps Dennett, 1969, 1978b; Nelson, 1969, 1975 (but see also Nelson, 1976); Pitcher, 1971; Smart, 1971; Block & Fodor, 1972; Harman, 1973; Lycan, 1974; Grice, 1975; Shoemaker, 1975; Wiggins, 1975; Field, 1978.

2. The converse is also true.

3. Indeed, if one defines 'behaviorism' as the view that mental terms can be defined in nonmental terms, then functionalism *is* a version of behaviorism.

4. State type, not state token. Throughout the chapter, I shall mean by 'physicalism' the doctrine that says each distinct type of mental state is identical to a distinct type of physical state; for example, pain (the universal) is a physical state. Token physicalism, on the other hand, is the (weaker) doctrine that each particular datable pain is a state of some physical type or other. Functionalism shows that type physicalism is false, but it does not show that token physicalism is false.

By 'physicalism,' I mean *first-order* physicalism, the doctrine that, e.g., the property of being in pain is a first-order (in the Russell-Whitehead sense) physical property. (A first-order property is one whose definition does not require quantification over properties; a second-order property is one whose definition requires quantification over first-order properties—and not other properties.) The claim that being in pain is a second-order physical property is actually a (physicalist) form of functionalism. See Putnam, 1970.

'Physical property' could be defined for the purposes of this chapter as a property expressed by a predicate of some true physical theory or, more broadly, by a predicate of some true theory of physiology, biology, chemistry, or physics. Of course, such a definition is unsatisfactory without characterizations of these branches of science (see Hempel, 1970, for further discussion). This problem could be avoided by characterizing 'physical property' as: property expressed by a predicate of some true theory adequate for the explanation of the phenomena of nonliving matter. I believe that the difficulties of this account are about as great as those of the previous account. Briefly, it is conceivable that there are physical laws that "come into play" in brains of a certain size and complexity, but that nonetheless these laws are "translatable" into physical language, and that, so translated, they are clearly physical laws (though irreducible to other physical laws). Arguably, in this situation, physicalism could be true—though not according to the account just mentioned of 'physical property'.

Functionalists who are also physicalists have formulated broadly physicalistic versions of functionalism. As functionalists often point out (Putnam, 1967), it is logically possible for a given abstract functional description to be satisfied by a nonphysical object, e.g., a soul. One can formulate a physicalistic version of functionalism simply by explicitly ruling out this possibility. One such physicalistic version of functionalism is suggested by Putnam (1970), Field (1978), and Lewis (in conversation): having pain is identified with a second-order physical property, a property that consists of having certain first-order physical properties if certain other first-order physical properties obtain. This doctrine combines functionalism (which can be formulated as the doctrine that having pain is the property of having certain properties if certain other properties obtain) with token physicalism. Of course, the Putnam-Lewis-Field doctrine is *not* a version of (first-order) type physicalism; indeed, the P-L-F doctrine is incompatible with (first-order) type physicalism.

5. I mentioned two respects in which Functionalism and Psychofunctionalism differ. First, Functionalism identifies pain with its Ramsey functional correlate with respect to a common-sense psychological theory, and Psychofunctionalism identifies pain with its Ramsey functional correlate with respect to a scientific psychological theory. Second, Functionalism requires common-sense specification of inputs and outputs, and Psychofunctionalism has the option of using empirical-theory construction in specifying inputs and outputs so as to draw the line between the inside and outside of the organism in a theoretically principled way.

I shall say a bit more about the Psychofunctionalism/Functionalism distinction. According to the preceding characterization, Psychofunctionalism and Functionalism are theory relative. That is, we are told not what pain *is*, but, rather, what pain is *with respect to this or that theory*. But Psychofunctionalism can be defined as the doctrine that mental states are constituted by causal relations among whatever psychological events, states, processes, and other entities—as well as inputs and outputs—actually obtain in us in whatever ways those entities are actually causally related to one another. Therefore, if current theories of psychological processes are correct in adverting to storage mechanisms, list searchers, item comparators, and so forth, Psychofunctionalism will identify mental states with causal structures that involve storage, comparing, and searching processes as well as inputs, outputs, and other mental states.

Psychofunctional equivalence can be similarly characterized without overt relativizing to theory. Let us distinguish between weak and strong equivalence (Fodor, 1968a). Assume we have agreed on some descriptions of inputs and outputs. I shall say that organisms x and y are weakly or behaviorally equivalent if and only if they have the same output for any input or sequence of inputs. If x and y are weakly equivalent, each is a weak simulation of the other. I shall say x and y are *strongly* equivalent relative to some branch of science if and only if (1) x and y are weakly equivalent, and (2) that branch of science has in its domain processes that mediate inputs and outputs, and x's and y's inputs and outputs are mediated by the same combination of weakly equivalent processes. If x and y are strongly equivalent, they are strong simulations of each other.

We can now give a characterization of a Psychofunctional equivalence relation that is not overtly theory relative. This Psychofunctional equivalence relation is strong equivalence with respect to psychology. (Note that 'psychology' here denotes a branch of science, not a particular theory in that branch.)

This Psychofunctional equivalence relation differs in a number of respects from those described earlier. For example, for the sort of equivalence relation described earlier, equivalent systems need not have any common output if they share a given sequence of inputs. In machine terms, the equivalence relations described earlier require only that equivalent systems have a common machine table (of a certain type); the current equivalence relation requires, in addition, that equivalent systems be in the same state of the machine table. This difference can be eliminated by more complex formulations.

Ignoring differences between Functionalism and Psychofunctionalism in their characterizations of inputs and outputs, we can give a very crude account of the Functionalism/Psychofunctionalism distinction as follows: Functionalism identifies mental states with causal structures involving conscious mental states, inputs, and outputs; Psychofunctionalism identifies mental states with the same causal structures, elaborated to include causal relations to *unconscious* mental entities as well. That is, the causal relations adverted to by Functionalism are a subset of those adverted to by Psychofunctionalism. Thus, weak or behavioral equivalence, Functional equivalence, and Psychofunctional equivalence form a hierarchy. All Psychofunctionally equivalent systems are Functionally equivalent, and all Functionally equivalent systems are weakly or behaviorally equivalent.

Although the characteristics of Psychofunctionalism and Psychofunctional equivalence just given are not overtly theory relative, they have the same vagueness problems as the characterizations given earlier. I pointed out that the Ramsey functional-correlate characterizations suffer from vagueness about level of abstractness of psychological theory—e.g., are the psychological theories to cover only humans who are capable of *weltschmerz*, all humans, all mammals, or what? The characterization of Psychofunctionalism just given allows a similar question: what is to count as a psychological entity or process? If the answer is an entity in the domain of some true psychological theory, we have introduced relativity to theory. Similar points apply to the identification of Psychofunctional equivalence, with strong equivalence with respect to psychology.

Appeal to unknown, true psychological theories introduces another kind of vagueness problem. We can allocate current theories among branches of science by appealing to concepts or vocabulary currently distinctive to those branches. But we cannot timelessly distinguish among branches of science by appealing to their distinctive concepts or vocabulary, because we have no idea what concepts and vocabulary the future will bring. If we did know, we would more or less have future theories now. Worse still, branches of science have a habit of coalescing and splitting, so we cannot know whether the science of the future will countenance anything at all like psychology as a branch of science.

One consequence of this vagueness is that no definite answer can be given to the question, Does Psychofunctionalism as I have described it characterize mental states partly in terms of their relations to *neurological* entities? I think the best anyone can say is: at the moment, it seems not. Psychology and neurophysiology seem to be separate branches of science. Of course, it is clear that one must appeal to neurophysiology to explain some psychological phenomena, e.g., how being hit on the head causes loss of language ability. However, it seems as if this should be thought of as "descending" to a lower level in the way evolutionary biology appeals to physics (e.g., cosmic rays hitting genes) to partially explain mutation.

6. The basic idea for this example is due to Putnam (1967). I am indebted to many conversations with Hartry Field on the topic. Putnam's attempt to defend functionalism from the problem posed by such examples is discussed in Section 1.4 of this essay.

One potential difficulty for Functionalism is provided by the possibility that one person may have two radically different Functional descriptions of the sort that justify attribution of mentality. In such a case, Functionalists might have to ascribe two radically different systems of belief, desire, etc., to the same person, or suppose that there is no fact of the matter about what the person's propositional attitudes are. Undoubtedly, Functionalists differ greatly on what they make of this possibility, and the differences reflect positions on such issues as indeterminacy of translation.

7. Shoemaker, 1975, argues (in reply to Block and Fodor, 1972) that absent qualia are logically impossible, that is, that it is logically impossible that two systems be in the same functional state yet one's state have and the other's state lack qualitative content. If Shoemaker is right, it is wrong to doubt whether the homunculi-headed system has qualia. I attempt to show Shoemaker's argument to be fallacious in Block, 1980.

8. Since there is a difference between the role of the little people in producing your functional organization in the situation just described and the role of the homunculi in the homunculi-headed simulations this chapter began with, presumably Putnam's condition could be reformulated to rule out the latter without ruling out the former. But this would be a most ad hoc maneuver. Further, there are other counterexamples which suggest that a successful reformulation is likely to remain elusive.

Careful observation of persons who have had the nerve bundle connecting the two halves of the brain (the *corpus callosum*) severed to prevent the spread of epilepsy, suggest that each half of the brain has the functional organization of a sentient being. The same is suggested by the observation that persons who have had one hemisphere removed or anesthetized remain sentient beings. It was once thought that the right hemisphere had no linguistic capacity, but it is now known that the adult right hemisphere has the vocabulary of a 14-year-old and the syntax of a 5-

year-old (*Psychology Today*, 12/75, p. 121). Now the functional organization of each hemisphere is different from the other and from that of a whole human. For one thing, in addition to inputs from the sense organs and outputs to motor neurons, each hemisphere has many input and output connections to the other hemisphere. Nonetheless, each hemisphere may have the functional organization of a sentient being. Perhaps Martians have many more input and output organs than we do. Then each half brain could be functionally like a whole Martian brain. If each of our hemispheres has the functional organization of a sentient being, then a Putnamian proposal would rule us out (except for those of us who have had hemispherectomies) as pain-feeling organisms.

Further, it could turn out that other parts of the body have a functional organization similar to that of some sentient being. For example, perhaps individual neurons have the same functional organization as some species of insect.

(The argument of the last two paragraphs depends on a version of functionalism that construes inputs and outputs as neural impulses. Otherwise, individual neurons could not have the same functional organization as insects. It would be harder to think of such examples if, for instance, inputs were taken to be irradiation of sense organs or the presence of perceivable objects in the "range" of the sense organs.)

9. A further indication that our intuitions are in part governed by the neurophysiological and psychological differences between us and the original homunculi-headed simulation (construed as a Functional simulation) is that intuition seems to founder on an intermediate case: a device that simulates you by having a billion little men each of whom simulates one of your neurons. It would be like you in psychological mechanisms, but not in neurological mechanisms, except at a very abstract level of description.

There are a number of differences between the original homunculi-heads and the elementary-particle-people example. The little elementary-particle people were not described as knowing your functional organization or trying to simulate it, but in the original example, the little men have *as their aim* simulating your functional organization. Perhaps when we know a certain functional organization is intentionally produced, we are thereby inclined to regard the thing's being functionally equivalent to a human as a misleading fact. One could test this by changing the elementary-particle-people example so that the little people have the aim of simulating your functional organization by simulating elementary particles; this change seems to me to make little intuitive difference.

There are obvious differences between the two types of examples. It is *you* in the elementary case and the change is *gradual*; these elements seem obviously misleading. But they can be eliminated without changing the force of the example much. Imagine, for example, that your spouse's parents went on the expedition and that your spouse has been made of the elementary-particle people since birth.

10. Compare the first sentence with 'The fish eaten in Boston stank.' The reason it is hard to process is that "raced" is naturally read as active rather than passive. See Fodor, Bever, and Garrett, 1974, p. 360. For a discussion of why the second sentence is grammatical, see Fodor and Garrett, 1967; Bever, 1970; and Fodor, Bever, and Garrett, 1974.

11. We often fail to be able to conceive of how something is possible because we lack the relevant theoretical concepts. For example, before the discovery of the mechanism of genetic duplication,

Haldane argued persuasively that no conceivable physical mechanism could do the job. He was right. But instead of urging that scientists should develop ideas that would allow us to conceive of such a physical mechanism, he concluded that a *non*physical mechanism was involved. (I owe the example to Richard Boyd.)

12. One could avoid this difficulty by allowing *names* or demonstratives in one's physical theory. For example, one could identify protons as the particles with such and such properties contained in the nuclei of all atoms of the Empire State Building. No such move will save this argument for Psychofunctionalism, however. First, it is contrary to the idea of functionalism, since functionalism purports to identify mental states with abstract causal structures; one of the advantages of functionalism is that it avoids appeal to ostension in definition of mental states. Second, tying Psychofunctionalism to particular named entities will inevitably result in chauvinism. See Section 3.1.

13. Suppose a man who has good color vision mistakenly uses "red" to denote green and "green" to denote red. That is, he simply confuses the two words. Since his confusion is purely linguistic, though he says of a green thing that it is red, he does not *believe* that it is red, any more than a foreigner who has confused "ashcan" with "sandwich" believes people eat ashcans for lunch. Let us say that the person who has confused 'red' and 'green' in this way is a victim of Word Switching.

Now consider a different ailment: having red/green inverting lenses placed in your eyes without your knowledge. Let us say a victim of this ailment is a victim of Stimulus Switching. Like the victim of Word Switching, the victim of Stimulus Switching applies "red" to green things and vice versa. But the victim of Stimulus Switching *does* have false color beliefs. If you show him a green patch he says *and believes* that it is red.

Now suppose that a victim of Stimulus Switching suddenly becomes a victim of Word Switching as well. (Suppose as well that he is a lifelong resident of a remote Arctic village, and has no standing beliefs to the effect that grass is green, firehydrants are red, and so forth.) He speaks normally, applying "green" to green patches and "red" to red patches. Indeed, he is functionally normal. But his *beliefs* are just as abnormal as they were before he became a victim of Word Switching. Before he confused the words "red" and "green," he applied "red" to a green patch, and mistakenly believed the patch to be red. Now he (correctly) says "green," but his belief is still wrong.

So two people can be functionally the same, yet have incompatible beliefs. Hence, the inverted qualia problem infects belief as well as qualia (though presumably only qualitative belief). This fact should be of concern not only to those who hold functional state identity theories of belief, but also to those who are attracted by Harman-style accounts of meaning as functional role. Our double victim—of Word and Stimulus Switching—is a counterexample to such accounts. For his word 'green' plays the normal role in his reasoning and inference, yet since in saying of something that it "is green," he expresses his belief that it is *red*, he uses 'green' with an abnormal meaning.

14. The quale might be identified with a physico-chemical state. This view would comport with a suggestion Hilary Putnam made in the late '60s in his philosophy of mind seminar. See also Ch. 5 of Gunderson, 1971.

15. I am indebted to Sylvain Bromberger, Hartry Field, Jerry Fodor, David Hills, Paul Horwich, Bill Lycan, Georges Rey, and David Rosenthal for their detailed comments on one or another earlier draft of this paper. Beginning in the fall of 1975, parts of earlier versions were read at Tufts University, Princeton University, the University of North Carolina at Greensboro, and the State University of New York at Binghamton.

References

Armstrong, D. *A materialist theory of mind*. London: Routledge & Kegan Paul, 1968.

Bever, T. The cognitive basis for linguistic structures. In J. R. Hayes (Ed.), *Cognition and the development of language*. New York: Wiley, 1970.

Block, N. Are absent qualia impossible? *Philosophical Review*, 1980, 89(2).

Block, N., and Fodor, J. What psychological states are not. *Philosophical Review*, 1972, 81, 159–81.

Chisholm, Roderick. *Perceiving*. Ithaca: Cornell University Press, 1957.

Cummins, R. Functional analysis. *Journal of Philosophy*, 1975, 72, 741–64.

Davidson, D. Mental events. In L. Swanson and J. W. Foster (Eds.), *Experience and theory*. Amherst, University of Massachusetts Press, 1970.

Dennett, D. *Content and consciousness*. London: Routledge & Kegan Paul, 1969.

Dennett, D. Why the law of effect won't go away. *Journal for the Theory of Social Behavior*, 1975, 5, 169–87.

Dennett, D. Why a computer can't feel pain. In *Synthese* 1978a, 38, 3.

Dennett, D. *Brainstorms*. Montgomery, Vt.: Bradford, 1978b.

Feldman, F. Kripke's argument against materialism. *Philosophical Studies*, 1973, 416–19.

Fodor, J. Explanations in psychology. In M. Black (Ed.), *Philosophy in America*. London: Routledge & Kegan Paul, 1965.

Fodor, J. The appeal to tacit knowledge in psychological explanation. *Journal of Philosophy*, 1968b, 65, 627–40.

Fodor, J. Special sciences. *Synthese*, 1974, 28, 97–115.

Fodor, J. *The language of thought*. New York: Crowell, 1975.

Fodor, J., Bever, T., and Garrett, M. *The psychology of language*. New York: McGraw-Hill, 1974.

Fodor, J., and Garrett, M. Some syntactic determinants of sentential complexity. *Perception and Psychophysics*, 1967, 2, 289–96.

Geach, P. *Mental acts*. London: Routledge & Kegan Paul, 1957.

Gendron, B. On the relation of neurological and psychological theories: A critique of the hardware thesis. In R. C. Buck and R. S. Cohen (Eds.), *Boston studies in the philosophy of science VIII*. Dordrecht: Reidel, 1971.

Grice, H. P. Method in philosophical psychology (from the banal to the bizarre). *Proceedings and Addresses of the American Philosophical Association*, 1975.

Gunderson, K. *Mentality and machines*. Garden City: Doubleday Anchor, 1971.

Harman, G. *Thought*. Princeton: Princeton University Press, 1973.

Hempel, C. Reduction: Ontological and linguistic facets. In S. Morgenbesser, P. Suppes & M. White (Eds.), *Essays in honor of Ernest Nagel*. New York: St. Martin's Press, 1970.

Kalke, W. What is wrong with Fodor and Putnam's functionalism? *Nous*, 1969, 3, 83–93.

Kim, J. Phenomenal properties, psychophysical laws, and the identity theory. *The Monist*, 1972, 56(2), 177–92.

Lewis, D. Psychophysical and theoretical identifications. *Australasian Journal of Philosophy*, 1972, 50(3), 249–58.

Locke, D. *Myself and others*. Oxford: Oxford University Press, 1968.

Melzack, R. *The puzzle of pain*. New York: Basic Books, 1973.

Minsky, M. *Computation*. Englewood Cliffs: Prentice-Hall, 1967.

Mucciolo, L. F. The identity thesis and neuropsychology. *Nous*, 1974, 8, 327–42.

Nagel, T. The boundaries of inner space. *Journal of Philosophy*, 1969, 66, 452–58.

Nagel, T. Armstrong on the mind. *Philosophical Review*, 1970, 79, 394–403.

Nagel, T. Review of Dennett's *Content and consciousness*. *Journal of Philosophy*, 1972, 50, 220–34.

Nagel, T. What is it like to be a bat? *Philosophical Review*, 1974, 83, 435–50.

Nelson, R. J. Behaviorism is false. *Journal of Philosophy*, 1969, 66, 417–52.

Nelson, R. J. Behaviorism, finite automata & stimulus response theory. *Theory and Decision*, 1975, 6, 249–67.

Nelson, R. J. Mechanism, functionalism, and the identity theory. *Journal of Philosophy*, 1976, 73, 365–86.

Oppenheim, P. and Putnam, H. Unity of science as a working hypothesis. In H. Feigl, M. Scriven and G. Maxwell (Eds.), *Minnesota studies in the philosophy of science II*. Minneapolis: University of Minnesota Press, 1958.

Pitcher, G. *A theory of perception*. Princeton: Princeton University Press, 1971.

Putnam, H. Brains and behavior. 1963. Reprinted as are all Putnam's articles referred to here (except "On properties") in *Mind, language and reality: Philosophical papers*, Vol. 2. London: Cambridge University Press, 1975.

Putnam, H. The mental life of some machines. 1966.

Putnam, H. The nature of mental states (originally published under the title *Psychological Predicates*). 1967.

Putnam, H. On properties. In *Mathematics, matter and method: Philosophical papers*, Vol. 1. London: Cambridge University Press, 1970.

Putnam, H. Philosophy and our mental life. 1975a.

Putnam, H. The meaning of 'meaning'. 1975b.

Rorty, R. Functionalism, machines and incorrigibility. *Journal of Philosophy*, 1972, 69, 203–20.

Scriven, M. *Primary philosophy*. New York: McGraw-Hill, 1966.

Sellars, W. Empiricism and the philosophy of mind. In H. Feigl & M. Scriven (Eds.), *Minnesota studies in philosophy of science I*. Minneapolis: University of Minnesota Press, 1956.

Sellars, W. *Science and metaphysics*. (Ch. 6). London: Routledge & Kegan Paul, 1968.

Shoemaker, S. Functionalism and qualia. *Philosophical studies*, 1975, 27, 271–315.

Shoemaker, S. Embodiment and behavior. In A. Rorty (Ed.), *The identities of persons*. Berkeley: University of California Press, 1976.

Shallice, T. Dual functions of consciousness. *Psychological Review*, 1972, 79, 383–93.

Smart, J. J. C. Reports of immediate experience. *Synthese*, 1971, 22, 346–59.

Wiggins, D. Identity, designation, essentialism, and physicalism. *Philosophia*, 1975, 5, 1–30.

5   What Intuitions about Homunculi Do Not Show

Searle's argument depends for its force on intuitions that certain entities do not think. There are two simple objections to his argument that are based on general considerations about what can be *shown* by intuitions that something can't think.

First, we are willing, and rightly so, to accept counterintuitive consequences of claims for which we have substantial evidence. It once seemed intuitively absurd to assert that the earth was whirling through space at breakneck speed, but in the face of the evidence for the Copernican view, such an intuition should be (and eventually was) rejected as irrelevant to the truth of the matter. More relevantly, a grapefruit-sized head-enclosed blob of gray protoplasm seems, at least at first blush, a most implausible seat of mentality. But if your intuitions still balk at brains as seats of mentality, you should ignore your intuitions as irrelevant to the truth of the matter, given the remarkable evidence for the role of the brain in our mental life. Searle presents some alleged counterintuitive consequences of the view of cognition as formal symbol manipulation. But his argument does not even have the right *form*, for in order to know whether we should reject the doctrine because of its alleged counterintuitive consequences, we must know what sort of evidence there is *in favor* of the doctrine. If the evidence for the doctrine is overwhelming, then incompatible intuitions should be ignored, just as should intuitions that the brain couldn't be the seat of mentality. So Searle's argument has a missing premise to the effect that the evidence *isn't* sufficient to overrule the intuitions.

Well, is such a missing premise *true?* I think that anyone who takes a good undergraduate cognitive psychology course would see enough evidence to justify *tentatively* disregarding intuitions of the sort that Searle appeals to. Many theories in the tradition of thinking as formal symbol manipulation have a moderate (though admittedly not overwhelming) degree of empirical support.

A second point against Searle has to do with another aspect of the logic of appeals to intuition. At best, intuition reveals facts about our *concepts* (at worst, facts about a motley of factors such as our prejudices, ignorance, and, still worse, our lack of imagination—as when people accepted the deliverance of intuition that two straight lines cannot cross twice). So even if we were to accept Searle's appeal to intuitions as showing that homunculus heads that formally manipulate symbols do not think, what this would show is that our formal symbol-manipulation theories do not provide a sufficient condition for the application of our ordinary intentional concepts. The more interesting issue, however, is whether the homunculus head's formal symbol manipulation falls in the same scientific natural kind (see Putnam 1975a) as our intentional processes. If so, then the homunculus head does think in a reasonable scientific sense of the term—and so much the worse for the ordinary concept. Moreover, if we are very concerned with ordinary intentional concepts, we can give sufficient conditions for their application by building in ad hoc conditions designed to rule out the putative counterexamples. A first stab (inadequate, but improvable—see Putnam 1975b, p. 435; Block 1978, p. 292) would be to add the condition that in order to think, realizations of the symbol-manipulating system must not have operations mediated by entities that themselves have symbol manipulation typical of intentional systems. The ad hocness of such a condition is not an objection to it, given that what we are trying to do is "reconstruct" an everyday concept out of a scientific one; we can expect the everyday concept to be scientifically characterizable only in an unnatural way. (See Fodor 1980.) Finally, there is good reason for thinking that the Putnam-Kripke account of the semantics of "thought" and other intentional terms is correct. If so, and if the formal symbol manipulation of the homunculus head falls in the same natural kind as our cognitive processes, then the homunculus head *does* think, in the ordinary sense as well as in the scientific sense of the term.

The upshot of both these points is that the real crux of the debate rests on a matter that Searle does not so much as mention: what the *evidence* is for the formal symbol-manipulation point of view.

Recall that Searle's target is the doctrine that cognition is formal symbol manipulation, that is, manipulation of representations by mechanisms that take account only of the forms (shapes) of the representations. Formal symbol-manipulation theories of cognition postulate a variety of mechanisms that generate, transform, and compare representations. Once one sees this doctrine as Searle's real target, one can simply ignore his objections to Schank. The idea that a machine programmed à la Schank has anything akin to mentality is not worth taking seriously, and casts as much doubt on the symbol-manipulation theory of thought as Hitler casts on doctrine favoring a strong executive branch of government. Any plausibility attaching to the idea that a Schank machine thinks would seem to derive from a crude Turing test version of behaviorism that is anathema to most who view cognition as formal symbol manipulation.[1]

Consider a robot akin to the one sketched in Searle's reply II (omitting features that have to do with his criticism of Schank). It simulates your input-output behavior by using a formal symbol-manipulation theory of the sort just sketched of your cognitive processes (together with a theory of your noncognitive mental processes, a qualification omitted from now on). Its body is like yours except that instead of a brain it has a computer equipped with a cognitive theory true of you. You receive an input: "Who is your favorite philosopher?" You cogitate a bit and reply "Heraclitus." If your robot doppelgänger receives the same input, a mechansim converts the input into a description of the input. The computer uses its description of your cognitive mechanisms to deduce a description of the product of your cogitation. This description is then transmitted to a device that transforms the description into the noise "Heraclitus."

While the robot just described behaves just as you would given any input, it is not obvious that it has any mental states. You cogitate in response to the question, but what goes on in the robot is manipulation of *descriptions of your cogitation* so as to produce the same response. It isn't obvious that the manipulation of *descriptions* of cogitation in this way is *itself* cogitation.

My intuitions agree with Searle about this kind of case (see Block 1981), but I have encountered little agreement on the matter. In the absence of widely shared intuition, I ask the reader to pretend to have Searle's and my intuition on this question. Now I ask another favor, one that should be firmly distinguished from the first: take the leap from intuition to fact (a leap that, as I argued in the first four paragraphs of this commentary, Searle gives us no reason to take). Suppose, for the sake of argument, that the robot described above does not in fact have intentional states.

What I want to point out is that even if we grant Searle all this, the doctrine that cognition is formal symbol manipulation remains utterly unscathed. For it is no part of the symbol-manipulation view of cognition that the kind of manipulation attributed to *descriptions* of our symbol-manipulating cognitive processes is itself a cognitive process. Those who believe formal symbol-manipulation theories of intentionality must assign intentionality to *anything of which the theories are true*, but the theories cannot be expected to be true of devices that use them to mimic beings of which they are true.

Thus far, I have pointed out that intuitions that Searle's sort of homunculus head does not think do not challenge the doctrine that thinking is formal symbol manipulation. But a variant of Searle's example, similar to his in its intuitive force, but that avoids the criticism I just sketched, can be described.

Recall that it is the aim of cognitive psychology to decompose mental processes into combinations of processes in which mechanisms generate representations, other mechanisms transform representations, and still other mechanisms compare representations, issuing reports to still other mechanisms, the whole network being appropriately connected to sensory input transducers and motor output devices. The goal of such theorizing is to decompose these processes to the point at which the mechanisms that carry out the operations have no internal goings on that are themselves decomposable into symbol manipulation by still further mechanisms. Such ultimate mechanisms are described as "primitive," and are often pictured in flow diagrams as "black boxes" whose realization is a matter of "hardware" and whose operation is to be explained by the physical sciences, not psychology. (See Fodor 1968; 1980; Dennet 1975)

Now consider an ideally completed theory along these lines, a theory of *your* cognitive mechanisms. Imagine a robot whose body is like yours, but whose head contains an army of homunculi, one for each black box. Each homunculus does the symbol-manipulating job of the black box he replaces, transmitting his "output" to other homunculi by telephone in accordance with the cognitive theory. This homunculi head is just a variant of one that Searle uses, and it completely avoids the criticism I sketched above, because the cognitive theory it implements is actually *true* of *it*. Call this robot the cognitive homunculi head. (The cognitive homunculi head is discussed in more detail in Block 1978, pp. 305–10.) I shall argue that even if you have the intuition that the cognitive homunculi head has no intentionality, you should not regard this intuition as casting doubt on the truth of symbol-manipulation theories of thought.

One line of argument against the cognitive homunculi head is that its persuasive power may be due to a "not seeing the forest for the trees" illusion (see Lycan 1980). Another point is that brute untutored intuition tends to balk at assigning intentionality to *any* physical system, including Searle's beloved brains. Does Searle really think that it is an initially congenial idea that a hunk of gray jelly is the seat of his intentionality? (Could one imagine a less likely candidate?) What makes gray jelly so intuitively satisfying to Searle is obviously his knowledge that brains are the seat of *our* intentionality. But here we see the difficulty in relying on considered intuitions, namely that they depend on our beliefs, and among the beliefs most likely to play a role in the case at hand are precisely our doctrines about whether the formal symbol-manipulation theory of thinking is true or false.

Let me illustrate this and another point via another example (Block 1978, p. 291). Suppose there is a part of the universe that contains matter that is infinitely divisible. In that part of the universe, there are intelligent creatures much smaller than our elementary particles who decide to devote the next few hundred years to creating out of their matter substances with the chemical and physical characteristics (except at the subelementary particle level) of our elements. They build hordes of space ships of different varieties about the sizes of our electrons, protons, and other elementary particles, and fly the ships in such a way as to mimic the behavior of these elementary particles. The ships contain apparatus to produce and detect the type of radiation elementary particles give off. They do this to produce huge (by our standards) masses of substances with the chemical and physical characteristics of oxygen, carbon, and other elements. You go off on an expedition to that part of the universe, and discover the "oxygen" and "carbon." Unaware of its real nature, you set up a colony, using these "elements" to grow plants for food, provide "air" to breathe, and so on. Since one's molecules are constantly being exchanged with the environment, you and other colonizers come to be composed mainly of the "matter" made of the tiny people in space ships.

If *any* intuitions about homunculi heads are clear, it is clear that coming to be made of the homunculi-infested matter would not affect your mentality. Thus we see that intuition need not balk at assigning intentionality to a being whose intentionality owes crucially to the actions of internal homunculi. *Why* is it so obvious that coming to be made of homunculi-infested matter would not affect our sapience or sentience? I submit that it is because we have all absorbed enough neurophysiology to *know* that changes in particles in the brain that do not affect the brain's basic (electrochemical) mechanisms do not affect mentality.

Our intuitions about the mentality of homunculi heads are obviously influenced (if not determined) by what we believe. If so, then the burden of proof lies with Searle to show that the intuition that the cognitive homunculi head has no intentionality (an intuition that I and many others do not share) is not due to doctrine hostile to the symbol-manipulation account of intentionality.

In sum, an argument such as Searle's requires a careful examination of the source of the intuition that the argument depends on, an examination Searle does not begin.

Notes

Reprinted from *Behavioral and Brain Sciences* 3: 425–426, 1980. Reprinted in A. Castell, D. Borchert, eds., *An Introduction to Modern Philosophy: Examining the Human Condition*, 6th ed. (New York: Macmillan, 1994).

I am grateful to Jerry Fodor and Georges Rey for comments on an earlier draft.

1. While the crude version of behaviorism is refuted by well-known arguments, there is a more sophisticated version that avoids them; however, it can be refuted using an example akin to the one Searle uses against Schank. Such an example is sketched in Block 1978, p. 294, and elaborated in Block, forthcoming.

References

Block, N. J. (1978) Troubles with functionalism. In: *Minnesota studies in the philosophy of science, vol. 9*, ed. C. W. Savage, Minneapolis: University of Minnesota Press.

——— (forthcoming) Psychologism and behaviorism. *Philosophical Review*.

Dennett, D. C. (1975) Why the law of effect won't go away. *Journal for the Theory of Social Behavior* 5: 169–87.

Fodor, J. A. (1968) The appeal to tacit knowledge in psychological explanation. *Journal of Philosophy* 65: 627–40.

———— (1980) Methodological solopsism considered as a research strategy in cognitive psychology. *The Behavioral and Brain Sciences* 3:1.

Lycan, W. G. (1980) "The functionalist reply (Ohio State)," *Behavioral and Brain Sciences* 3: 434–435.

Lycan, W. G. (1981) Form, function, and feel. *Journal of Philosophy* 78, 1: 24–50.

Putnam, H. (1960) Minds and machines. In: *Dimensions of mind*, ed. S. Hook, pp. 138–64. New York: Collier.

———— (1975a) The meaning of "meaning." In: *Mind, language and reality*. Cambridge University Press.

———— (1975b) The nature of mental states. In: *Mind, language and reality*. Cambridge: Cambridge University Press.

II Concepts of Consciousness

6 Consciousness

I The Hard Problem

There are a number of different matters that come under the heading of 'consciousness'. One of them is *phenomenality*, the feeling of say a sensation of red or a pain, that is what it is like to have such a sensation or other experience. Another is *reflection* on phenomenality. Imagine two infants, both of which have pain, but only one of which has a thought about that pain. Both would have phenomenal states, but only the latter would have a state of reflexive consciousness. This chapter will start with phenomenality, moving later to reflexivity and then to one other kind of consciousness.

The Hard Problem of consciousness is how to explain a state of consciousness in terms of its neurological basis. If neural state N is the neural basis of the sensation of red, why is N the basis of that experience rather than some other experience or none at all? Chalmers (1996) distinguishes between the Hard Problem and "easy" problems that concern the function of consciousness. The Hard Problem (though not under that name) was identified by Nagel (1974) and further analyzed in Levine 1983.

There are two reasons for thinking that the Hard Problem has no solution:

1. *Actual failure.* In fact, no one has been able to think of even a highly speculative answer.
2. *Principled failure.* The materials we have available seem ill suited to providing an answer. As Nagel says, an answer to this question would seem to require an objective account that necessarily leaves out the subjectivity of what it is trying to explain. We do not even know what would *count* as such an explanation.

II Perspectives on the Hard Problem

There are many perspectives on the Hard Problem but I will mention only the four that comport with a naturalistic framework

1. *Eliminativism*, the view that consciousness as understood above simply does not exist (Dennett 1979; Rey 1997). So there is nothing for the Hard Problem to be about.

2. *Philosophical Reductionism* or *Deflationism*. Deflationists (for example, Dennett 1991) move closer to common sense by allowing that consciousness exists, but they "deflate" this commitment—again on philosophical grounds—taking it to amount to less than meets the eye (as Dennett might put it). One prominent form of deflationism in this sense makes a conceptual reductionist claim: that consciousness can be conceptually analyzed in nonphenomenal terms. The main varieties of analyses are behavioral, functional, representational and cognitive.

3. *Phenomenal Realism*, or *Inflationism* the view that consciousness is a substantial property that cannot be conceptually reduced or otherwise *philosophically* reduced in nonphenomenal terms. Logical behaviorists thought that we could analyze the concept of pain in terms of certain kinds of behavior, but inflationists reject all such analyses of phenomenal concepts in non-phenomenal terms. According to most contemporary inflationists, consciousness plays a causal role and its nature may be found empirically as the sciences of consciousness advance. Inflationism is compatible with the *empirical scientific* reduction of consciousness to neurological or computational properties of the brain, just as heat was scientifically but not philosophically reduced to molecular kinetic energy. (It is not a conceptual truth that heat is molecular kinetic energy.) Inflationism (which is the view of the author) accepts the Hard Problem but aims for an empirical solution to it (Block 1995; Flanagan 1992; Loar 1997; Nagel 1974). One inflationist, McGinn (1991), argues that an empirical reduction is possible but that we cannot find or understand it. Another inflationist, Searle (1992), endorses a roughly naturalistic point of view and rejects philosophical reduction of phenomenality, but he also rejects any empirical reduction of phenomenal properties.

4. *Dualistic Naturalism* In this catch-all category, I include Chalmers's (1996) view that standard materialism is false but that there are naturalistic alternatives to Cartesian dualism such as pan-psychism. Nagel (2000) proposes that there is a deeper level of reality that is the naturalistic basis both of consciousness and of neuroscience.

Here are some examples of deflationism in this sense. Pitcher (1971) and Armstrong (1968) can be interpreted as analyzing consciousness in terms of beliefs. One type of prototypical conscious experience as of blue is a matter of an inclination (perhaps suppressed) to believe that there is a blue object in plain view. (See Jackson 1977 for a convincing refutation.) A different analysis appeals to higher order thought or higher order perception. These theorists take the concept of a conscious pain to be the concept of a pain that is accompanied by another state that is about that pain. A pain that is not so accompanied is not a conscious state. (Armstrong 1968; Carruthers 1992; Lycan 1990) (Rosenthal 1997 advocates a higher-order thought view as an empirical identity rather than as a conceptual analysis.) Another deflationist view that is compatible with the analyses in terms of beliefs concerns not the states themselves but their contents. Representationism holds that it can be established philosophically that the phenomenal character of experience is its representational content. Many representationists reject conceptual analysis, but still their accounts do not depend on details of the science of mind; if any science is involved, it is evolutionary theory. (See Harman 1990, 1996; Dretske 1995; Lycan 1996; McDowell 1994; Tye 1995.) (Shoemaker 1994 mixes phenomenal realism with representationism in an interesting way.) Conceptual functionalists say that the concept of consciousness is analyzable functionally (Lewis 1994).

The inflationist regards all of these deflationist accounts as leaving out the phenomenon. Phenomenality has a function and represents the world, but it is something over and above that function or representation. Something might function like a phenomenal state but be an ersatz phenomenal state with no real phenomenal character. The phenomenal character that represents red in you might represent green in me. Phenomenal character does represent but it also goes beyond what it represents. Pain may represent damage but that is not what makes pain awful.

According to deflationism, there is such a thing as consciousness, but there is no Hard Problem, that is, there are no mysteries concerning the physical basis of consciousness that differ in kind from scientific problems about for example the physical/functional basis of liquidity, inheritance or computation.

III   Dissolution of the Hard Problem?

Suppose (to move away from the neurologically ridiculous example of c-fiber stimulation in favor of a view championed as a theory of visual experience by Crick and Koch 1990) that corticothalamic oscillation (of a certain frequency) is the neural basis of an experience with phenomenal quality Q. Now there is a simple (over-simple) solution to the Hard Problem from a physicalist point of view. Phenomenal quality Q = cortico thalamic oscillation (of a certain sort). Here's a statement of the solution (or rather dissolution):

The Hard Problem is illusory. One might as well ask why H_2O is the chemical basis of water rather than gasoline or nothing at all. Just as water *is* its chemical basis, so Q is its neural basis, and that shows the original question is wrongheaded.

This point is correct as far as it goes, but it does not go far enough. It just puts the Hard Problem under a different part of the rug. For now we want to know: how could one property *be* both phenomenal property Q *and* corticothalamic oscillation. How is it possible for something subjective to be something objective or for something first-personal to be something third-personal? I am not suggesting that the problem is that we cannot find an explanation for this identity. There are no explanations for any identities (Block 1978a; Block and Stalnaker 1999). The problem rather is that the claim that a phenomenal property is a neural property seems just as mysterious—

maybe even more mysterious—than the claim that a phenomenal property has a certain neural basis. I would distinguish between explaining an identity and explaining how an identity can be true, where the latter involves removing a sense of puzzlement. Further,we can even see the same reasons given before as reappearing:

1. *Actual failure*   No one has even a wildly speculative answer to the question of how something objective can be something subjective.
2. *Principled failure*   As before, actual failure does not seem accidental. The objective seems to necessarily leave out the subjective. The third-personal seems to necessarily leave out the first personal. Further, as McGinn (1991) notes, neural phenomenal are spatial, but the phenomenal is prima facie non-spatial.

The reasons that I mentioned above for thinking that the explanatory gap resists closing seem to surface in a slightly different form. However, as we will see, in this form, they are more tractable.

IV   How to Begin Solving the Hard Problem

The main element in the approach I shall be suggesting to the Hard Problem is a distinction that is widely appealed to in discussions of Jackson's (1982) famous "Mary" example. Jackson imagined a neuroscientist of the distant future who is raised in a black and white room and who knows everything scientific there is to know about color and the experience of it. But when she steps outside the room for the first time, she learns what it is like to see red. Jackson argued that since the scientific facts don't encompass the new fact that Mary learns, dualism is true.

The line of response to Jackson that I think wins the day (and which derives from Loar 1990/1997) involves appeal to the distinction between a property and a concept of that property. (See Churchland 1989; Loar 1990/1997; Lycan 1990b; van Gulick 1993; Sturgeon 1994; Tye 1999; Perry 2001).

A concept is a thought element in a way of thinking, a kind of representation. If you like, you can take (nonexperiental) concepts in my sense to be interpreted symbols in a "language of thought." This usage contrasts with a common philosophical usage in which a concept is something like a meaning. Concepts in my sense are individuated in part by meanings; x and y are instances of the same concept if and only if they are instances of the same representation and have the same meaning. "Water" and "H_2O" are instances of different representations, so the concept *water* is distinct from the concept H_2O.

Someone could believe that *this color* is useful for painting pots but that red is not, even if *this color* = red. Our experiential concept of red differs from our linguistic concept of red. An experiential concept involves a phenomenal element, a phenomenal way of thinking, for example a mental image that is in some sense *of* red or an ability to produce such a mental image or at least an ability to recognize red—which, arguably, could not be done without some phenomenal mental element.

Importantly, we can have an experiential concept *of an experience* (which we can call a phenomenal concept, phenomenal concepts being a subclass of experiential concepts) as well as an experiential concept of a color. And the very same mental image may be involved in both concepts. The difference between the phenomenal concept of the experience and the experiential concept of the color lies in the *rest* of the concept—in particular, the way the phenomenal element functions in the concept. This can be a matter of further concepts explicitly invoked in the concept—the concept of a color in one case and the concept of an experience in the other. One type of experiential concept (of a color or of an experience) involves a demonstrative plus a mental image plus a language-like representation—for example, "that [attention to a mental image] color" or "that [attention to a mental image] experience" where the bracket notation is supposed to indicate the use of attention to a non-descriptive element, a mental image, in fixing the demonstrative reference. Loar (1990/1997) gives an example involving two concepts in which something like a mental image of a cramp feeling is used to pick out a *muscular knot* in one concept and in the other concept, the cramp *experience* itself. The two concepts in my notation would be "that [attention to a mental image] cramp" and "that [attention to a mental image] cramp experience."

An experiential concept uses a phenomenal property to pick out a related property. For example, an experiential concept of a color can use an aspect of the experience of that color to pick out the color. A phenomenal concept uses a phenomenal property to pick out a phenomenal property. The phenomenal property used in the concept need not be the same as the one picked out. For example, one could have a phenomenal concept of the experience of the missing shade of blue whose phenomenal elements are the flanking color experiences. Or a phenomenal element involved in one's perception of a color could be used to pick out the experience of the complementary color. Importantly, the phenomenal element in a phenomenal concept needn't be and cannot in general be conceptualized, at least if the conceptualization is supposed to be itself phenomenal. For if a phenomenal concept had to make use of a phenomenal element via a distinct phenomenal concept of that element, there could be no phenomenal concepts. Thus we can define a phenomenal concept as a concept of a phenomenal property that uses a phenomenal property to pick out a phenomenal property but not necessarily under a concept of the phenomenal property used.

In these terms, then, Mary acquired a new concept of a property she was already acquainted with via a different concept. In the room, Mary knew about the subjective experience of red via physical concepts. After she left the room, she acquired a phenomenal concept of the same property. So Mary did not learn a new fact. She learned a new concept of an old fact. She already had a third person understanding of the fact of what it is like to see red. What she gained was a first person understanding of the very same fact. She knew already that corticothalamic oscillation of a certain frequency is what it is like to see red. What she learned is that this[attention to a mental image] is what it is like to see red. So the case provides no argument that there are facts that go beyond the physical facts.

Recall that there is a principled reason why mind-body identity seemed impossible: that a first person subjective property could not be identical to a third person objective property. But the concept/property distinction allows us to see that the subjective/objective distinction in this use of it and the first person/third person distinction *are distinctions between kinds of concepts, not kinds of properties*. There is no reason why a subjective concept and an objective concept cannot pick out the same property. *Thus we can substitute a dualism of concepts for a dualism of properties*.

There is another way in which the concept/property distinction helps with the Hard Problem. We can blame the explanatory gap and the Hard Problem on our inadequate concepts rather than on dualism. To use a variant on Nagel's (1974) example, we are like pre-Socratics who have no way of understanding how it is possible that heat = mean molecular kinetic energy, lacking the concepts required to frame both sides of the equation. (Heat was not clearly distinguished from temperature until the seventeenth century.) What is needed is a concept of heat and a concept of kinetic energy that makes it conceivable that there is a causal chain of the referential sort leading from the one magnitude to each concept. Or rather, since the phenomenal concept includes a sample of the relevant phenomenal property (on the Humean simplification I am using), there is no mystery about the mental side of the equation. The mystery is how the physical concept picks out that phenomenal property. This is the remaining part of the explanatory gap that will be closed if at all by science. Is there a principled reason to think it cannot be? The Hard Problem itself does not contain such a reason. Perhaps our conceptual inadequacy is temporary, as Nagel sometimes appears to suppose, or perhaps it is permanent as McGinn (1991) supposes.

V   The Paradox of Recent Empirical Findings about Consciousness

I will now switch gears to a discussion of recent empirical findings on consciousness. The most exciting line of experimental investigation of consciousness in recent years uses phenomena in which perception changes independently of the stimulus. One such paradigm uses binocular rivalry. If two different stimuli—for example, horizontal and vertical stripes—are presented to each of one's eyes, one does not see a blend, but rather alternating horizontal and vertical stripes. Logothetis and his colleagues (Logothetis 1998) trained monkeys to pull different levers for different patterns. They then presented different patterns to the monkeys' two eyes, and observed that with monkeys as with people, the monkeys switched back and forth between the two levers even though the sensory input remained the same. Logothetis recorded the firings of various neurons in the monkeys' visual systems. In the lower visual areas (e.g., V1), 80 percent of the neurons did not shift with the percept. But further along the occipital-temporal pathway, 90 percent shifted with the percept. So it seems that later areas in the occipital-temporal pathway—let's call it the "ventral stream"—are more dominantly part of the neural basis of (visual) consciousness than early areas. Recent work using imaging has extended and refined these findings. Kanwisher (2001, 98) notes that "neural correlates of perceptual experience, an exotic and elusive quarry just a few years ago, have suddenly become almost commonplace findings." And she backs this up with impressive correlations between neural activation on the one hand and indications of perceptual experiences of faces, houses, motion, letters, objects, words, speech on the other. So we have an amazing success: identification of the the neural basis of visual consciousness in the ventral stream.

Paradoxically, what has also become commonplace is activation of the *very same ventral stream pathways without "awareness."* Damage to the inferior parietal and frontal lobes has long been known to cause visual extinction in which subjects appear to lose subjective experience of certain stimuli on one side, namely, when there are stimuli on both sides. Extinction is associated with visual neglect in which subjects do not notice stimuli on one side. For example, neglect patients often do not eat the food on the left side of the plate. Although subjects say they do not see the extinguished stimulus, the nature of the stimulus has all sorts of visual effects. For example, if the subject's task is to decide whether a letter string (e.g., "saucer" or "spiger") is a word, the subject is faster for "saucer" if there is a picture of a cup or the word "cup" in the neglected field, even though they are at chance in guessing what the picture depicts (McGlinchey-Berroth et al. 1996). So the stimulus of which the subject is in some sense unaware is processed semantically.

Driver and Vuilleumier (2001) point out that the ventral stream is activated for extinguished stimuli (i.e., which the subject claims not to see). Rees et al. (2000) report studies of a left-sided neglect and extinction patient on face and house stimuli. Stimuli presented just on the left side are clearly seen by the patient, but when there are stimuli on both sides, the subject says he sees only the stimulus on the right. However, the "unseen" stimuli show activation of the ventral pathway that is the same in location and temporal course (though lower in activation) as the seen stimuli. Further, studies in monkeys have shown that a classic "blindness" syndrome is caused by massive cortical ablation that spares most of the ventral stream but not inferior parietal and frontal lobes (Lumer and Rees 1999). Kanwisher (2001) notes that dynamic visual gratings alternating with a gray field showed activation for V1, V2, V3A, V4v, and MT/MST despite the subjects saying they saw only a uniform gray field.

Is the difference between conscious and unconscious activation of the ventral pathway just a matter of the degree of activation? Zeki and Ffytch (1998) hypothesize that this is so. But Kanwisher (2001) mentions that evidence from ERP studies using the attentional blink paradigm show that neural activation associated with meaning is no less when the word is blinked than when it is not, suggesting that it is not lower neural activation strength that accounts for lack of awareness. Dehaene and Naccache (2001) note that in a study of neglect patients, it was shown that there is the same amount of semantic priming from both hemifields, despite the lack of awareness of stimuli in the left field, again suggesting that it is not activation strength that makes the difference.

The paradox then is that our amazing success in identifying the neural correlate of visual experience in normal vision has led to the peculiar result that in masking and neglect, that very neural correlate occurs without, apparently, subjective experience.

What is the missing ingredient, X, which, added to ventral activation, constitutes conscious experience? Kanwisher (2001) and Driver and Vuilleumier (2001) offer pretty much the same proposal as to the nature of X, that the missing ingredient is binding perceptual attributes with a time and a place, a token event. Rees et al. (2000) make two suggestions as to what X is. One is that the difference between conscious and unconscious activation is a matter of neural synchrony at fine timescales. This idea is supported by the finding that ERP components P1 and N1 revealed differences between left sided "unseen" stimuli and left sided seen stimuli. Their second suggestion is that the difference between seen and "unseen" stimuli might be a matter of interaction between the classic visual stream and the areas of parietal and frontal cortex that control attention.

Whether or not any of these proposals are right, the search for X seems to me the most exciting current direction for consciousness research.

VI Physicalism and Functionalism

There is a very different approach to the nature of consciousness. Dennett 1994 postulates that consciousness is "cerebral celebrity." What it is for a representation to be conscious is for it to be widely available in the brain. Dehaene and Naccache (2001) say consciousness is being broadcast in a global neuronal workspace.

The theory that consciousness is ventral stream activation plus e.g. neural synchrony, and the theory that consciousness is broadcasting in the global neuronal workspace are instances of the two major approaches to consciousness in the philosophical literature, *physicalism* and *functionalism*. The difference is that the functionalist says that consciousness is a role, whereas the physicalist says that consciousness is a physical or biological state that *implements* that role. To see the distinction, note that red may play the role of warning of danger. But green might also have played that role. The picture of consciousness as role could be characterized as *computational*—as contrasted with the *biological* picture of consciousness as implementer of the role.

Although functionalists are free to add restrictions, functionalism in its pure form is implementation independent. Consciousness is defined as global accessibility, and although its human implementation depends on our biochemistry, silicon creatures without our biochemistry could implement the same computational relations. Functionalism and physicalism are incompatible doctrines, since a non-biological implementation of the functional organization of consciousness would be regarded as uncontroversially conscious by the functionalist but not by the physicalist. The big question for functionalists is this: "How do you know that it is broadcasting in the global workspace that makes a representation conscious as opposed to something about the *human biological realization* of that broadcasting?"

The problem for functionalists could be put like this: the specifically human biochemical realization of global availability may be necessary to consciousness—other realizations of global availability being "ersatz" realizations. The typical response to this "ersatz realization problem" (Lycan 1981) is that we can preserve functionalism by simply bringing lower-level causes and effects into our functional characterizations—for instance, causes and effects at the level of biochemistry. But the utility of this technique runs out as one descends the hierarchy of sciences because the lowest level of all, that of basic-level physics, is vulnerable to the same point. Putting the point for simplicity in terms of the physics of forty years ago, the causal role of electrons is the same as that of antielectrons. If you formulate a functional role for an electron, an antielectron will realize it. Thus an antielectron is an ersatz realizer of the functional definition of *electron*. Physics is characterized by symmetries that allow ersatz realizations (Block 1978).

We have been talking about the two approaches of functionalism and physicalism as rivals, but we can instead see them as answers to different questions. The question that motivates the physicalist proposal of ventral activation plus X is: What is the neural basis of experience? The question that motivates the global broadcasting type is: What makes neuronal representations available for thought, decision, reporting and action? To attach names to the concepts, the former is a theory of *phenomenal* consciousness (what I have been calling phenomenality), and the latter *access* consciousness. (Theorists will differ of course on whether access-consciousness is really a type of consciousness. See Burge 1997.) We can try to force a unity by *postulating* that it is a condition on X that it promote access, but that is merely a verbal maneuver that only throws smoke over the difference between the different concepts and questions. Alternatively, we could, *hypothesize* rather than postulate that X as a matter of fact is the neural basis of global neuronal broadcasting. Note, however, that the neural basis of global neuronal broadcasting might obtain but the normal channels of broadcasting nonetheless be blocked or cut, again opening daylight between phenomenality and access, and showing that we cannot think of the two as one. (An analogy: rest mass and relativistic mass are importantly different from a theoretical point of view despite coinciding for all practical purposes at terrestrial velocities. Failure of coincidence even if rare is theoretical dynamite if what you are after is the scientific nature of consciousness.)

Many of us have had the experience of suddenly noticing a sound (say a jackhammer during an intense conversation) at the same time realizing that the sound has been going on for some time even though one was not attending to it. If the subject did have a phenomenal state before the sound was noticed, that state was not broadcast in the global neuronal workspace *until it was noticed*. If this is right, there was a period of *phenomenality without broadcasting*. Of course, this is anecdotal evidence. But the starting point for work on consciousness is introspection and we would be foolish to ignore it.

If we take seriously the idea of phenomenality without global accessibility, there is a theoretical option that should be on the table—that ventral stream activation is visual phenomenality and the search for X is the search for the neural basis of what makes visual phenomenality *accessible*. The idea would be that the claims of extinction patients not to see extinguished stimuli are in a sense wrong—they really do have phenomenal experience of these stimuli without knowing it. A similar issue will arise in the section to follow in which I will focus on the relation between phenomenality and a special case of global accessibility, reflexive or introspective consciousness, in which the subject not only has a phenomenal state but also has another state that is about the phenomenal state, say a thought to the effect that he has a phenomenal state.

In this section, we have seen a distinction between two concepts of consciousness, phenomenality and global accessibility. In the following section, we add a third, reflexivity.

VII Phenomenality and Reflexivity

Consider the "false recognition" paradigm of Jacoby and Whitehouse 1989. Subjects are given a study list of 126 words presented for half a second each. They are then presented with a masked word, $word_1$, and an unmasked word, $word_2$. Their task is to report whether whether $word_2$ was old (i.e., on the study list) or new (not on the study list). The variable was whether $word_1$ was lightly or heavily masked, the former presentations being thought of as "conscious" and the latter as "unconscious." The result: confining our attention just to cases in which $word_1 = word_2$, subjects were much more likely to mistakenly report $word_2$ as old when $word_1$ was unconsciously presented than when $word_1$ was consciously presented. The explanation would appear to be that when $word_1$ was consciously presented, the subjects were able to use an internal monologue of the following sort (though perhaps not quite as explicit): "The reason 'reason' ($word_2$) looks familiar is that I just saw it (as $word_1$)," thereby explaining away the familiarity of word$_2$. But when word$_1$ was *unconsciously* presented, the subjects were not able to indulge in this monologue and consequently blamed the familiarity of word$_2$ on its appearance in the study list.

Any monologue that can reasonably be attributed to the subject in this paradigm concerns the subject thinking about why a word (word$_2$) *looks familiar* to the subject. For it is only by *explaining away* the familiarity of word$_2$ that the subject is able to decide that word$_2$ was not on the study list. Thus in the "conscious" case, the subject must have a state that is *about the subject's own perceptual experience* (looking familiar) and thus conscious in what might be termed a "reflexive" sense. An experience is conscious in this sense just in case it is the object of another of the subject's states; for example, one has a thought to the effect that one has that experience. The reflexive sense of "consciousness" contrasts with phenomenality, which attaches to some states which are not the objects of other mental states. Reflexivity is phenomenality plus something else (reflection) and that opens up the possibility in principle for phenomenality without reflection. For example, it is at least conceptually possible for there to be two people in pain, one of whom is introspecting the pain the other not. (Perhaps infants or animals can have pain but do not introspect it.) The first is reflexively conscious of the pain, but both have phenomenally conscious states, since pain is by its very nature a phenomenally conscious state. Reflexivity (of the sort we are considering) involves phenomenality plus another state, one that is about the phenomenal state. Though there is a conceptual distinction between phenomenality and reflexivity, perhaps (though I doubt it) they come to the same thing in the brain?

What is the relation between reflexivity and the notion of global accessibilty discussed in the last section? Global accessibility does not logically require reflexivity, since global accessibility only requires access to all response modes that the organism actually has. (Perhaps a dog or a cat does not have the capacity for reflection.) Reflexivity is a special kind of access, one that requires intellectual resources that may not be available to every being that can have conscious experience.

There is another aspect to the experimental paradigm just discussed which motivates taking seriously the hypothesis that the reflexively *unconscious* case might possibly be phenomenally *conscious*. Consider a variant of the exclusion paradigm reported by Debner and Jacoby (1994). Subjects were presented with pairs of words flanked by digits—for example, "4reason5," and then given stems consisting of the first three letters of the word ("rea____") to complete. There were two conditions. In the "conscious" condition, they were told to ignore the digits. In the "unconscious" condition, they were told to report the sum of the digits before completing the stem. The results were that in the "conscious" condition, the subjects were much more likely than baseline to follow the instructions and complete the stem with a word other than "reason," whereas with "unconscious" presentations, subjects were much more likely than baseline to violate the exclusion instructions, completing the stem with "reason" Merikle and Joordens (1997) report corresponding results for the false recognition paradigm with divided attention substituted for heavy masking. Consider the hypothesis that there was a fleeting phenomenal consciousness of "reason" as the subject's eyes moved from the "4" to the "5" in "4reason5."

What are the theoretical options that deserve the most consideration?

1. The "unconscious perceptions" are *both* phenomenally and reflexively unconscious. (In this case, the exclusion and false recognition paradigms are about consciousness in both senses.)
2. The "unconscious perceptions" are fleetingly phenomenally conscious but reflexively unconscious.

A third option, that they are phenomenally unconscious but "reflexively conscious" seems less likely because the reflexive consciousness would be "false"—that is subjects would have a state "about" a phenomenal state without the phenomenal state itelf. That hypothesis would require some extra causal factor that produced the false recognition and would thus be less simple. One argument in favor of 2 is that subjects in experiments with near-threshold stimuli often report a mess of partial perceptions that they can't hang on to. Some critics have disparaged the idea of fleeting phenomenal consciousness (e.g., Dennett 1991). But what they owe us is a reason to think that 1 is the default view or else they must produce evidence for 1.

But it might seem that there is a principled argument that we could *never* find out about phenomenality in the absence of reflexive consciousness, for don't we require the subject's testimony about phenomenality and doesn't that require the subject to have a state that is about the phenomenal state? We can see what is wrong with this reasoning by attention to some potential lines of evidence for phenomenality in the absence of reflexive consciousness.

Liss (1968) contrasted subjects' responses to brief unmasked stimuli (one to four letters) with their responses to longer lightly masked stimuli. He asked for judgements of brightness, sharpness and contrast as well as what letters they saw. He found that lightly masked 40-msec stimuli were judged as brighter and sharper than unmasked 9-msec stimuli, even though the subjects could report three of four of the letters in the unmasked stimuli and only one of four in the masked cases. He says: "The Ss commented spontaneously that, despite the high contrast of the letters presented under backward masking, they seemed to appear for such brief duration that there was very little time to identify them before the mask appeared. Although letters presented for only 7 msec with no masking appeared weak and fuzzy, their duration seemed longer than letters presented for 70 msec followed by a mask" (p. 329).

Perhaps the subjects were phenomenally conscious of all the masked letter shapes, but could not apply the letter concepts required for reflexive consciousness of them.

(The subjects could apply the concepts of sharpness, brightness and contrast to the letters, so they did have reflexive consciousness of those features, even if they did not have reflexive consciousness of the shapes themselves. There are two kinds of shape concepts that could have provided—but apparently did not provide—reflexive consciousness of the letters: the letter concepts that we all learned in grade school, and shape concepts of the sort we have for unfamiliar shapes.) The underlying view is that phenomenal experience of shapes does not require shape concepts but reflexive consciousness, being an intentional state does require shape concepts, concepts that the subjects seem unable to access in these meager attentional circumstances. Alternatively, perhaps the phenomenal experience of shapes does involve shape concepts of some sort but the use of those shape representations in reflexive consciousness requires more attentional resources than were available to these subjects.

There is an another hypothesis—that the contents of both the subject's phenomenal states and their reflexive states are the same and include the features sharp, high contrast, bright, and letterlike without any specific shape representation. Both hypotheses have to be taken seriously, but the first is superior in one respect. Anyone who has been a subject in this or in Sperling's (1960) similar experiment will feel that the last hypothesis does not really capture the experience, which is one of seeing all or almost all the letters.

Rosenthal (1997) defines reflexive consciousness as follows: S is a reflexively conscious state of mine $\leftrightarrow$ S is accompanied by a thought—arrived at noninferentially and nonobservationally—to the effect that I am in S. He offers this "higher order thought" (HOT) theory as a theory of phenomenal consciousness. It is obvious that phenomenal consciousness without HOT and HOT without phenomenal consciousness are both *conceptually* possible. For examples, perhaps dogs and infants have phenomenally conscious pains without higher-order thoughts about them. For the converse case, imagine that by biofeedback and imaging techniques of the distant future, I learn to detect the state in myself of having the Freudian unconscious thought that it would be nice to kill my father and marry my mother. I could come to know—noninferentially and nonobservationally—that I have this Freudian thought even though the thought is not phenomenally conscious. Since there are conceptually possible counterexamples in both directions, the issue is the one discussed above of whether reflexivity and phenomenality come to the same thing in the brain.

If there are no actual counterexamples, the question arises of why. Is it supposed to be a basic law of nature that phenomenality and reflexivity co-occur? That would be a very adventurous claim. But if it is only a fact about us, then there must be a mechanism that explains the correlation, as the fact that both heat and electricity are carried by free electrons explains the correlation of electrical and thermal conductivity. But any mechanism breaks down under extreme conditions, as does the correlation of electrical and thermal conductivity at extremely high temperatures. So the correlation between phenomenality and reflexivity would break down too, showing that reflexivity does not yield the basic scientific nature of phenomenality.

Rosenthal's definition of reflexivity has a number of ad hoc features. "Nonobservationally" is required to rule out (for example) a case in which I know about a thought I have repressed by observing my own behavior. "Noninferentially" is needed to avoid a somewhat different case in which I appreciate (nonobservationally) my own pain and infer a repressed thought from it. Further, Rosenthal's definition involves a stipulation that the possessor of the reflexively conscious state is the same as the thinker of the thought—otherwise my thinking about your pain would make it a conscious pain. All these ad hoc features can be eliminated by moving to the following definition of reflexivity: S is a reflexively conscious state ↔ S is phenomenally presented in a thought about S. This definition uses the notion of phenomenality, but this is no disadvantage unless one holds that there is no such thing apart from reflexivity itself. The new definition of reflexivity, requiring phenomenality as it does, has the additional advantage of making it clear that reflexivity is a kind of *consciousness*. (See Burge's 1997 critique of my definition of access consciousness as constituting a kind of consciousness.)

We have seen three concepts of consciousness, phenomenality, reflexivity and global accessibility. The Hard Problem arises only for phenomenality. The imaging work on consciousness engages phenomenality and accessibility. But many psychological experimental paradigms mainly engage reflexivity.

Glossary

Phenomenality: What it is like to have an experience.

Reflexivity: A reflexively conscious state is one that is phenomenally presented in a thought about that state. Alternatively, S is a reflexively conscious state of mine ↔ S is accompanied by a thought—arrived at noninferentially and non-observationally—to the effect that I am in S.

Access consciousness: Global availability.

Deflationism: The view that phenomenality can be conceptually reduced or otherwise philosophically reduced to function, representation or cognition.

Inflationism: Phenomenal realism, the view that if phenomenality is reducible to function, representation or cognition, the type of reduction is scientific rather than conceptual or otherwise philosophical.

Qualia: A name often given to the phenomenal character of experience on an inflationist view of it. So the debate about the existence of qualia is really a debate about inflationism.

The Hard Problem: The problem of how to explain phenomenality physically.

Consciousness: Phenomenality or reflexivity or global availability.

Note

Reprinted from Lynn Nadel, ed., *The Encyclopedia of Cognitive Science* (London: The Nature Publishing Group, 2003).

References

Armstrong, D. M. 1968. *A Materialist Theory of the Mind*. London: Routledge & Kegan Paul.

Block, Ned. 1978a. Reductionism. *Encyclopedia of Bioethics*, 1419–1424. New York: Macmillan.

Block, Ned. 1978b. Troubles with functionalism. *Minnesota Studies in the Philosophy of Science* (C. W. Savage, ed.), 9: 261–325. (Reprinted abridged in D. M. Rosenthal, ed., *The Nature of Mind*, 211–229. Oxford: Oxford University Press, 1991.)

Block, Ned, Flanagan, Owen, and Güzeldere, Güven. 1997. *The Nature of Consciousness: Philosophical Debates*. Cambridge, MA: MIT Press.

Block, Ned, and Stalnaker, Robert. 1999, January. Conceptual analysis and the explanatory gap. *Philosophical Review* 108, 1: 1–46.

Burge, Tyler. 1997. Two kinds of consciousness. In Ned Block, Owen Flanagan, and Güven Güzeldere. *The Nature of Consciousness: Philosophical Debates*. Cambridge, MA: MIT Press.

Carruthers, Peter. 1992. Consciousness and concepts. *Proceedings of the Aristotelian Society*, supple. 66: 41–59.

Chalmers, D. 1996. *The Conscious Mind*. New York: Oxford University Press.

Churchland, Paul. 1989. Knowing qualia: A reply to Jackson, 67–76. From *A Neurocomputational Perspective*. Cambridge, MA: MIT Press.

Crick, F., and Koch, C. 1990. Towards a neurobiological theory of consciousness. *Seminars in the Neurosciences* 2: 263–275.

Dehaene, S., and Naccache, L. 2001. Towards a cognitive neuroscience of consciousness: Basic evidence and a workspace framework. *Cognition* 79: 1–37.

Dennett, Daniel. 1979. On the absence of phenomenology. In D. Gustafson and B. Tapscott, eds., *Body, Mind and Method: Essays in Honor of Virgil Aldrich*. Dordrecht: Reidel.

Dennett, Daniel. 1991. *Consciousness Explained*. Boston: Little, Brown.

Dennett, Daniel. 1994. Get real. *Philosophical Topics* 22(1–2): 505–568.

Dretske, Fred. 1995. *Naturalizing the Mind*. Cambridge, MA: MIT Press.

Flanagan, O. 1992. *Consciousness Reconsidered*. Cambridge, MA: MIT Press.

Güzeldere, Güven. 1997. The many faces of consciousness: A field guide. In Ned Block, Owen Flanagan, and Güven Güzeldere, *The Nature of Consciousness: Philosophical Debates*, 1–67. Cambridge, MA: MIT Press.

Harman, Gilbert. 1990. The intrinsic quality of experience. In James Tomberlin, ed., *Philosophical Perspectives 4: Action Theory and Philosophy of Mind*, 31–52. Atascadero: Ridgeview.

Huxley, T. H. 1866. *Lessons in Elementary Physiology*. London: Macmillan.

Jackson, Frank. 1977. *Perception*. Cambridge: Cambridge University Press.

Jackson, Frank. 1982. Epiphenomenal qualia. *Philosophical Studies* 32: 127–136.

Jackson, Frank. 1986. What Mary didn't know. *Journal of Philosophy* 83: 291–295.

Jackson, F. 1993. Armchair metaphysics. In J. O'Leary-Hawthorne and M. Michael, eds., *Philosophy in Mind*, Dordrecht: Kluwer.

Loar, Brian. 1990. Phenomenal states. In James Tomberlin, ed., *Philosophical Perspectives 4, Action Theory and Philosophy of Mind*, 81–108. Atascadero: Ridgeview. A much-revised version of this paper is to be found in Block, Flanagan, and Güzeldere, *The Nature of Consciousness: Philosophical Debates*, 597–616. Cambridge, MA: MIT Press, 1997.

Pitcher, George. 1971. *A Theory of Perception*. Princeton, NJ: Princeton University Press.

Jacoby, L. L., and Whitehouse, K. 1989. An illusion of memory: False recognition influenced by unconscious perception. *Journal of Experimental Psychology: General* 118: 126–135.

Kanwisher, Nancy. 2001. Neural events and perceptual awareness. *Cognition* 79(1–2): 89–113.

Levine, J. 1983. Materialism and qualia: The explanatory gap. *Pacific Philosophical Quarterly* 64: 354–361.

Lewis, David. 1994. Lewis, David: Reduction of mind. In S. Guttenplan, ed., *Blackwell's Companion to Philosophy of Mind*, 412–431. Oxford: Blackwell.

Liss, P. 1968. Does backward masking by visual noise stop stimulus processing? *Perception and Psychophysics* 4: 328–330.

Logothetis, N. K. 1998. Single units and conscious vision. *Proceedings of the Royal Society of London*, Ser B 353: 1801–1818.

Lumer, Erik, and Rees, Geraint. 1999. Covariation of activity in visual and prefrontal cortex associated with subjective visual perception. *Proceedings of the National Academy of Sciences* 96: 1669–1673.

Lycan, William. 1981. Form, function and feel. *Journal of Philosophy* 78: 24–50.

Lycan, William, G. 1990. Consciousness as internal monitoring. In J. Tomberlin, ed., *Philosophical Perspectives* 9: 1–14. Atascadero: Ridgeview. Reprinted in Block, Flanagan, and Güzeldere 1997.

Lycan, William G. 1996. *Consciousness and Experience*. Cambridge, MA: MIT Press.

McDowell, John. 1994, April. The content of perceptual experience. *Philosophical Quarterly* 44(175): 190–205.

McGinn, C. 1991. *The Problem of Consciousness*. Oxford: Blackwell.

Nagel, T. 1974. What is it like to be a bat? *Philosophical Review* 433–471.

Nagel, T. 2000. The psychophysical nexus. In Paul Boghossian and Christopher Peacocke, eds., *New Essays on the A Priori*. Oxford: Oxford University Press.

McGlinchey-Berroth, R., Milberg, W. P., Verfaellie, M., Grande, L., D'Esposito, M., and Alexander, M. 1996. Semantic processing and orthographic specificity in hemispatial neglect. *Journal of Cognitive Neuroscience* 8: 291–304.

Merikle, Philip, and Joordens, Steve. 1997. Parallels between perception without attention and perception without awareness. *Consciousness and Cognition* 6: 219–236.

Rees, Geraint, Wojciulik, Ewa, Clarke, Karen, Husain, Masud, Frith, Chris, and Driver, Jon. 2000. Unconscious activation of visual cortex in the damaged right hemisphere of a parietal patient with extinction. *Brain* 123: 1624–1633.

Perry, John. 2001. *Knowledge, Possibility and Consciousness*. Cambridge: MIT Press.

Putnam, Hilary. 1967. Psychological predicates (later titled the nature of mental states). In W. Capitan and D. Merrill, eds., *Art, Mind, and Religion*. Pittsburgh: Pittsburgh University Press. (Reprinted in *Mind, Language, and Reality*. Cambridge: Cambridge University Press, 1975.)

Rey, Georges. 1997. *Contemporary Philosophy of Mind*. Oxford: Blackwell.

Rosenthal, David. 1997. A theory of consciousness. In N. Block, O. Flanagan, and G. Güzeldere, eds., *Consciousness*, 729–754. Cambridge, MA: MIT Press.

Searle, John. 1992. *The Rediscovery of the Mind*. Cambridge, MA: MIT Press.

Shoemaker, Sydney. 1994, June. Self-knowledge and inner sense; Lecture III: The phenomenal character of experience. *Philosophy and Phenomenological Research* 54(2): 291–314.

Smart, J. J. C. 1959. Sensations and brain processes. *Philosophical Review* 68: 141–156. This paper has been reprinted many times starting in 1962 in a somewhat revised form. See, for example, D. M. Rosenthal, ed., *Materialism and the Mind-Body Problem*. Englewood Cliffs, NJ: Prentice-Hall, 1971.

Sperling, George. 1960. The information available in brief visual presentations. *Psychological Monographs* 74(11): 1–29.

Strawson, Galen. 1994. *Mental Reality*. Cambridge, MA: MIT Press.

Sturgeon, Scott. 1994. The epistemic view of subjectivity. *Journal of Philosophy* 91(5): 221–235.

Tye, Michael. 1995. *Ten Problems of Consciousness*. Cambridge, MA: MIT Press.

Tye, Michael. 1999. Phenomenal consciousness: The explanatory gap as a cognitive illusion. *Mind* 108(432): 706–725.

Van Gulick, Robert. 1993. Understanding the phenomenal mind: Are we all just armadillos? In M. Davies and G. Humphreys, eds., *Consciousness: Psychological and Philosophical Essays*. Oxford: Blackwell. (Reprinted in Block et al. 1997.)

7   Review of Daniel Dennett, *Consciousness Explained, The Journal of Philosophy*

In some ways, this is an extraordinary book, though *Consciousness Ignored* would be a more descriptive title. It is written with a popular audience in mind, getting rave reviews in many publications, including *The New York Times Book Review* and *The London Review of Books*—and it was one of *The New York Times* ten best books of 1991. But Dennett has pulled off the trick of making the philosophical points he would have made in a philosophy journal. He is to be applauded for doing real philosophy in public. More philosophers should aim for this.

The book is witty, charming, informative, full of insights. It is interesting to see how Dennett's point of view treats a variety of fascinating phenomena, even to those of us who reject it. At the same time, the book is exasperatingly elusive, even self-contradictory. Dennett rejects the naive notion of consciousness in favor of some sort of reductionist or deflationary view. But which one? Many different, even conflicting, views appear to be endorsed without any signal that they are distinct. Further, he has lost the kind of touch with the opposition which is needed to mount a convincing refutation. He tilts at caricatures, advocates of total determinacy in matters of phenomenal consciousness, those who believe that there *must* be a single *place* in the brain where experience happens, a Cartesian theater. By ignoring the real opposition, he passes up the chance to clarify his own position in contrast to it. The mushiness of Dennett's characterizations of both positions is responsible for the fact that the main argument of the book limps and limps painfully, or so I shall argue.

Pursuing these points, I shall distinguish among some different concepts of consciousness, especially between phenomenal consciousness and the family of cognitive concepts of consciousness. Phenomenal conscious qualities include the way things look, sound, and smell and the way pain feels. Perhaps thoughts, beliefs, and desires also have characteristic phenomenal conscious aspects. No currently available neurophysiological or computational concepts are capable of explaining what it is like to be in a phenomenally conscious state, e.g., to have a pain or to see something red. Suppose, for example, that Francis Crick and Christof Koch are right that a brief 35–75 hertz locked neural oscillation is essential to phenomenal consciousness. No one has been able to sketch an explanatory connection between these neural oscillations and phenomenal consciousness. Why is it 35–75 hertz as opposed to 5 hertz or 100 hertz? Further, how does one type of say 40 hertz oscillation explain why the resultant conscious state feels one way rather than another or like nothing at all? At the moment, nothing is known in neurophysiology or computational psychology which gives us a clue as to how these questions are to be answered. This is the well-known explanatory gap.

I see no convincing reason for pessimism, however, about the prospects for a scientific understanding of phenomenal consciousness (pace Colin McGinn). Consider the analogy with the time when nothing known in science gave a clue as to how life could be scientifically understood, giving rise to vitalism. Even though there are no concepts in contemporary science that give us a clue as to how to explain what it is like to feel pain or see red, such concepts may be developed in the future.

Let us briefly turn to cognitive consciousness. One cognitive concept is that of self-consciousness, the ability to think about one's self. A closely related cognitive concept of consciousness is the one often expressed with the phrase "conscious of": *reflective consciousness*. I am conscious of one of my mental states if I have a "higher-order" thought to the effect that I am in that state.

Another cognitive concept of consciousness, the one that I think is most easily confused with phenomenal consciousness, is what I call *access consciousness*. One way of spelling out this idea is: a state is access conscious if its content is inferentially promiscuous (in Stephen Stich's sense), i.e., freely available as a premise in reasoning; *and* if its content is available for *rational* control of action and speech. In *Content and Consciousness*,[1] Dennett distinguishes between consciousness in the sense in which conscious information controls speech and in the sense in which conscious information controls behavior. The conjunction of these is close to access consciousness, and he often seems to have something like it in mind in this book.

One obvious difference between phenomenal consciousness and the cognitive family is that they concern different (though perhaps overlapping) kinds of content. The kind of content that is paradigmatically inferentially promiscuous, for example, is *semantic* or *representational* content, whereas it is *experiential* content that can be phenomenally conscious.[2]

Ordinary uses of words such as "conscious" and "aware" usually involve elements of both phenomenal and cognitive notions, but there are pure uses as well. Consider blindsight, in which brain damage in the visual cortex has the effect that a subject can "guess" (sometimes with 90% accuracy), given a binary choice between say an 'X' and an 'O' in his blind field, but says he sees nothing. The visual information can guide the guessing response, but it is not "inferentially promiscuous," and is not available to guide action rationally in the usual way; further, judging from what the subject says, it does not reach phenomenal consciousness (I cannot go further into the matter here)—

except when the subject notices what he is inclined to guess. So the perceptual state is unconscious in the phenomenal, access, and reflective senses. (Note that the perceptual state is not access conscious by my definition, because although the perceptual information does influence action, there is no rational control of action—until the patient hears himself guess.) But now imagine something that does not actually exist, a case of super blindsight: a blindsight subject trained to prompt himself at will, guessing what is in his blind field without being given a binary choice. The super-blind-sighter says, "Now I know that there is an X in front of me even though I don't actually see it." His "vision" in the blind field makes the visual information just pop into his thoughts, the way solutions to problems sometimes do for us, or the way some people just know the time. His perceptual state would be phenomenally unconscious but conscious in the access and reflective senses.

The converse is also coherent: a phenomenally conscious state that is unconscious in the access and reflective senses. Imagine, for example, a painful thought that is repressed via Freudian processes, becoming unconscious. Assuming that the painful thought continues to be painful when unconscious (as is often said to be the case by Freudians), the sense in which the thought is unconscious could not be the phenomenal sense, since nothing painful could be phenomenally unconscious. But the painful thought could be unconscious in the access or reflective senses. Or consider the unconscious pain during sleep that awakens one. Again, the pain, being painful, could not be phenomenally unconscious, but it is presumably access unconscious (until one awakens). Perhaps phenomenal consciousness requires some sort of subject, and so the unconscious might be thought of as an agency that experiences the phenomenally conscious state. But still there is no access consciousness, because there is no rational control of thought and action; the content is not "inferentially promiscuous."

Corresponding to the different concepts of consciousness, we have different notions of zombie. Even if we are computers, we can ask whether machines made to be computationally identical to us are phenomenally conscious. If not, they are phenomenal zombies. Their states are conscious in the access sense, but not in the phenomenal sense. The zombies in *Night of the Living Dead*, however, seem cognitively and affectively diminished, not necessarily phenomenally diminished. Are we to suppose that there is nothing it tastes like for them to eat their relatives?

Although Dennett makes no such distinctions, they are important analytical tools for understanding what is going on in the book, for he often appears to have one or another of these concepts in mind. For example, he sometimes presumes that phenomenal consciousness is reflective consciousness.[3] Dennett explicitly mentions the analysis of a conscious state as a state accompanied by a thought to the effect that I have that state (held in different forms by D. Armstrong, W. Lycan, and D. Rosenthal), treating it as a good analysis of consciousness (presumably in the univocal sense he thinks he has been using all along). If this were the consistent doctrine of the book, this review would have mentioned its problems accounting for the experiences of babies and animals. Dennett tells us in the appendix for philosophers that his view has a foot in both the realist and eliminativist camps, and if the reduction of phenomenal to reflective consciousness were the consistent theory of the book, the strongly deflationary aspect of this view would justify this gloss.

The reduction of phenomenal to reflective consciousness is not, however, the dominant doctrine of the book. Equally often, an incompatible reduction of phenomenal consciousness to access consciousness seems favored, but most of the time there is little clue as to what concept of consciousness is at issue. This problem is at its most extreme in Dennett's discussion of what he labels as his empirical theory of consciousness (to be summarized below). It is not a theory of consciousness in any of the senses discussed, nor in any other sense of which I know. The theory is perhaps best construed as a theory of the whole mind. Those of you who have not read this book but know Dennett's earlier work on consciousness are no doubt tempted to suppose that this book is eliminativist: that is, that Dennett is saying that there is no such thing as consciousness. Alternatively, you may suppose that what Dennett must be saying is that consciousness is either nothing or else one or another of the cognitive consciousnesses. This is not the dominant stance taken by Dennett in this book, however, and thus it marks a substantial change from his earlier (and I think clearer and better) work on the subject, e.g., "On the Absence of Phenomenology." In this book, Dennett mainly comes on as a realist who is weary of being seen as denying the existence of the obvious. He trumpets an account of what consciousness *is*; he is proud of and excited about "my theory of consciousness." (Recall the title.) And although he realizes that his theory conflicts with common sense or at least common views, he insists that his theory does not "neglect the facts about experience that we know so intimately 'from the inside'" (42).

My complaint is that a number of incompatible views seem to coexist, including these: that consciousness is real and identical to access consciousness; that consciousness is real and identical to reflective consciousness; and that consciousness is the whole mind. In addition, at a crucial point, Dennett assumes an extreme form of eliminativism, one that cannot be seen as a deflationary realism.

Pursuing this point, let us turn to the empirical theory "of consciousness." The part of the theory that is set up as the opposition to the Cartesian theater is the *multiple-drafts model*. The name derives from the idea that with the various forms of electronic quasi publishing now flourishing we may one day find ourselves unable to decide which of the many versions of a piece of work is to be counted as *the publication*. The multiple-drafts model says that consciousness does not consist in a single privileged or canonical "narrative," but rather a group of different ones that will be elicited by different probes at different times. If a thief snatches your briefcase, you may tell one story about what happened if somehow probed at the moment, another story five minutes later, and yet another the next day. The point of the multiple drafts model is supposed to be that none of these narratives is definitive: there is no single determinate story that has exclusive control of reasoning, verbalization, and behavior. The multiple drafts model says that there are distinct parallel representations that have *access* to reasoning, verbalization, and behavior, and thus, to the extent that it is about consciousness at all, the multiple-drafts model is about consciousness in the access sense.

Another part of the theory is that consciousness is a "complex of memes" (210), "meme" being Richard Dawkins's term for units of cultural replication and transmission corresponding to genes: "a human mind is itself an artifact created when memes restructure a human brain in order to make it a better habitat for memes." Here we see the Jaynesian idea that consciousness is a cultural construction put in terms of the mind rather than in terms of consciousness. The main part of the theory is the widely held view that the mind is composed of numerous semi-autonomous agencies competing for control. Much of the content of the theory concerns the original functions of these agencies and their mode of interaction and organization. I see little in the theory that is about consciousness in any sense narrower than the whole mind.

As I have been saying, the different notions of consciousness deployed are often incompatible. Consider, for example, the idea just mentioned that consciousness is a cultural construction: "human consciousness (1) is too recent an innovation to be hard-wired into the innate machinery, (2) is largely the product of cultural evolution that gets imparted to brains in early training" (219). This idea makes some sense if, as Julian Jaynes sometimes does, by 'consciousness' you mean "the possession of a theory of consciousness" (in some sense or other), but the idea that consciousness is a cultural construction does not fit well with other notions of consciousness that appear in the book, e.g., reflective consciousness. Surely, no one would take seriously the idea that our capacity to think about our own thoughts is a cultural innovation first discovered by the Greeks between the time of the *Iliad* and the *Odyssey*. And it should go without saying that it is foolish to suppose that phenomenal consciousness is a cultural construction. Both reflective and phenomenal consciousness would seem to be basic biological features of humans. And the same holds for the presence of "multiple drafts" in the brain.

Let me turn now to the argumentative heart of the book, a pair of chapters about certain temporal phenomena, focusing on a contrast between what Dennett calls "Orwellian" and "Stalinesque" theories (to be described below). The conclusion is that one theory of consciousness, Cartesian materialism, should be rejected in favor of Dennett's empirical theory of consciousness, which, because the argument takes place before the rest of the theory has been introduced, takes the form of the multiple-drafts model.[4]

The Cartesian materialism that Dennett attacks is a view he acknowledges that probably no one holds explicitly, but which he thinks importantly influences our thought nonetheless. Cartesian materialism is Cartesian dualism minus the dualism, "the view that there is a crucial finish line or boundary somewhere in the brain ... [such that] *what happens there* is what you are conscious of" (107). This finish line is the Cartesian theater, "where in the brain conscious experience ... [is] located" (107).

Cartesian materialism clearly concerns phenomenal consciousness. But the multiple-drafts model appears to deploy access consciousness (instead? in addition?), as mentioned above. The claim of the multiple-drafts model is that narratives are developed in parallel which gain access to reasoning and control of action and speech at different times in different ways. This apparent difference in the subject matter of the two theories is often obscured in the text by Dennett's tendency to include the negation of Cartesian materialism in the statement of the multiple-drafts model, a rather trivial way of ensuring that Cartesian materialism and the multiple-drafts model are about the same thing. By failing to consider whether the theories are theories of different things, Dennett avoids bringing up the issue of whether there might be a better theory of phenomenal consciousness than Cartesian materialism, or whether his multiple-drafts model, being a theory of something else, just leaves the mysteries of phenomenal consciousness untouched.

The impression that the discussion confuses phenomenal and access consciousness is confirmed by the repeated assertions that "there is no single definitive 'stream of consciousness'" because there are "multiple channels in which specialist circuits" create multiple drafts, narratives that are available to "get promoted to further functional roles" (253–4). But you cannot reject a serial stream of phenomenal consciousness on the basis of nonserial access conscious activities. Dennett rejects a theory of apples because it is incorrect about oranges.[5]

Turning now to Dennett's actual argument, I shall use one of his simplest examples, metacontrast masking. The subject first gets a short (30 milliseconds—about the duration of a television frame) presentation of a disk that is followed immediately by a donut whose inner border is just where the outside of the disk was. if the setup is right, the subject reports having seen only the donut. "Did you see a disk?" "No!" There is evidence, however, that information about the disk is represented in the brain. For example, subjects are better than chance at guessing whether there were one or two stimuli. Further, if the disk is flashed for the same duration without being followed by the donut, the subject does report seeing the disk. Dennett contrasts two theories of what goes on when the subject is shown the disk followed by the donut. The Orwellian theory says that the subject has a conscious experience of *both* the disk and the donut, but that the conscious experience of the donut wipes out the conscious memory of the disk. ("Orwellian" because history is rewritten.) The Stalinesque theory is that the disk is subjected to *pre*conscious processing, but that consciousness of it is prevented by the donut stimulus that follows it. So what the Orwellian and the Stalinist disagree about

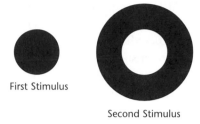

First Stimulus

Second Stimulus

Figure 7.1

is *whether there was a brief flicker of consciousness* of the disk that the subject does not remember. The main philosophical argument of the book has the conclusion that there could be no matter of fact (not just that there need not be a matter of fact in a particular case, which of course all sides should agree to) as between these two theories, because the notion of a brief flicker of consciousness that the subject does not remember makes no sense. See figure 7.1.

So what is the argument that there is no real difference corresponding to the Stalinesque/Orwellian distinction (i.e., no real difference between a flicker of consciousness of the disk and no such flicker)? What Dennett says is that there is nothing discernible to either outside or inside observers—i.e., to scientists or to subjects—which could distinguish the two theories. As Dennett summarizes: "because of spatio-temporal smearing of the observer's point of view in the brain, all the evidence there is or could be fails to distinguish between the Orwellian and Stalinesque theories of conscious experience, and hence there is no difference. That is some sort of operationalism or verificationism" (126). Indeed, at the heart of the argument are distinct appeals to both operationalism and verificationism, one for the *inside* half of the argument, the other for the *outside* half, and I shall consider them separately.

Inside Dennett says that there is no experiential difference between the Orwellian and Stalinesque accounts: "You, as a subject ... *could not* discover anything in the experience from your own first-person perspective that would favor one theory over the other; the experience would 'feel the same' on either account" (123). This is no misprint; this point is repeated a number of times, both in the book and in Dennett and Marcel Kinsbourne's article (*op. cit.*).

Of course, the Orwellian and Stalinesque cases do not feel the same even though the subjects' judgments are the same. There is a phenomenal difference, a difference in the subjectivity of the subject, between a brief flicker of consciousness of the disk and no brief flicker of consciousness of the disk. Although there is a phenomenal difference, it is not one that is accessible to verbalization, and so subjects' testimony is of no direct use to science. Telling the difference between the Orwellian and Stalinesque theories will have to involve other methods, and to this matter we now turn.

Outside Dennett says that the Orwellian and the Stalinist can agree on all the representational (and other scientific) facts. What they disagree about is whether the representation of the disk is conscious or not. But why could there not be evidence about that? Dennett keeps saying that there is no way of drawing a sharp line in the brain between conscious and nonconscious events. But why should the proponent of phenomenal consciousness have to accept a sharp line in the brain? This false hyperdeterminacy is made of straw.

Suppose we find evidence from normal contexts (in which there are no perceptual or memory tricks) for the Crick and Koch conjecture that consciousness is intimately related to a 35–75 hertz neural oscillation. If we have a wide range of converging evidence to support this sort of claim from cases in which we are justified in supposing that there are no memory or perceptual tricks, then we could look at tricky cases like metacontrast masking to see whether the representation of the disk is associated with a brief flicker of 35–75 hertz neural oscillation. If so, Orwellianism is supported; if not, Stalinism is supported. Of course, for a conclusive case to be made either way, we would have to discover the concepts that would allow us to close the explanatory gap by actually explaining phenomenally conscious experience neurophysiologically, but short of that, even correlations would provide some evidence.

Another approach is this: Dennett's Orwellian hypothesizes deletions from memory (see, e.g., 142). But as we come to understand more about memory systems, perhaps we shall be able to tell when such deletions occur. And some Orwellian hypotheses involve hallucinatory memories, memories as of perceptions that never happened. Perhaps the constructive processes involved in producing such memories could be distinguished from normal memory processes using the methods of neurophysiology or psychology. In sum, Dennett has succumbed to what he calls "Philosophers' Syndrome: mistaking a failure of imagination for an insight into necessity" (401).

The inside argument uses what Dennett calls "first-person operationalism." He says:

Some thinkers have their faces set so hard against 'verificationism' and 'operationalism' that they want to deny it even in the one arena where it makes manifest good sense: the realm of subjectivity (132).

The Multiple Drafts model makes "writing it down" in memory criterial for consciousness: that is *what it is* for the "given" to be "taken"—to be taken one way rather than another. There is no reality of conscious experience independent of the effects of various vehicles of content in subsequent action (and hence of course on memory) (132).

But a realist about phenomenal consciousness should not find first-person operationalism any more palatable than third-person operationalism. Consider the reduction of phenomenal consciousness to reflective consciousness which Dennett often favors (a deflationary but nonetheless realist position). Recall that, if phenomenal consciousness is reflective consciousness, then for the pain to be phenomenally conscious is for there to be a higher-order thought about the pain, or at least some sort of cognitive state that scans it. But obviously there could be a brief flicker of a higher-order thought about one's state, even if it left no imprint on memory. Not even Dennett suggests operationalism for thought. But on the theory that phenomenal consciousness *is* higher-order thought, a flicker of higher-order thought just *is* a flicker of phenomenal consciousness. Further, there could be scientific evidence about whether or not there is a brief flicker of a higher-order thought. So, Dennett's claim is incompatible with one of the better deflationary views of phenomenal consciousness: indeed, it is hard to think of any remotely plausible deflationary realist view of phenomenal consciousness that does not engender an Orwellian/Stalinesque distinction.

Dennett and Kinsbourne (*op. cit.*) reply to critics who charge them with abandoning realism, saying "we consider our position to be unproblematically 'realist' ... As 'realists' about consciousness, we believe that there has to be something ... that distinguishes conscious events from nonconscious events" (235–6). (The scare quotes signify only that not every question about a real entity has a determinate answer, something to which no reasonable realist should object.) But a realist who rejects the Orwellian/Stalinesque distinction has the responsibility of exhibiting a notion of consciousness on which the distinction founders, in the way that a realist about temperature can exhibit a theory of temperature (average kinetic energy of an ensemble of molecules) on which there is no such thing as the temperature of a single electron. Neither the book nor the Dennett and Kinsbourne article give any such account; instead, the burden is carried by first-person operationalism. In their reply to critics, Dennett and Kinsbourne hint that maybe a brief flicker of consciousness is impossible in the way a brief flicker of baldness is impossible (my analogy, not theirs). But is the main argument of the book to depend on an unsupported empirical speculation that does not even appear in the book? Further, why does this speculation not support the Stalinesque position rather than Dennett's view that there is no Orwellian/Stalinesque difference?

Here is a tentative diagnosis of what has gone wrong: if Dennett identifies consciousness with access consciousness, one can explain why he thinks there can be no Orwellian/Stalinesque difference. The Orwellian would say (correctly) that there *is* access to the disk information because if the donut had not appeared, then the subject could have reported that there was a disk; and the Stalinist would say (equally correctly) that there is *not* access to the disk information, because given that the donut did appear, the subject cannot report on the disk. Accessibility is a modal notion; what is accessible depends on what is held fixed. The Stalinesque reasoning given holds the perception of the donut fixed, but the Orwellian reasoning does not. (A univocal context-fixed identification of consciousness with access consciousness would yield a robust Orwellian/Stalinesque distinction; it is the modal sensitivity to context that makes the difference disappear.)

Now Dennett's overall argument could be put as follows: (1) if the naive view of phenomenal consciousness is right, then an Orwellian/Stalinesque distinction is legitimate; (2) but no such distinction is legitimate; (3) so the naive view of phenomenal consciousness is wrong.

But the Orwellian/Stalinesque distinction that makes (1) true takes consciousness to be phenomenal consciousness, whereas the Orwellian/Stalinesque distinction that makes (2) true takes consciousness to be access consciousness, a straightforward fallacy of equivocation. Dennett may wish to reply that phenomenal consciousness really does reduce to access consciousness, so there is no equivocation. If *I* were defending Dennett's overall viewpoint, that is what I would say. But if an identification of phenomenal consciousness with access consciousness is what the book hinges on, it would have to be (a) stated, (b) argued for, and (c) the book would have to be purged of the theories of phenomenal consciousness that are incompatible with this one. Also, it would have to be admitted that the key reasoning of the book is completely dependent on the missing argument for the identification of phenomenal with access consciousness.

At many points in the discussion, Dennett talks as if there is nothing more to something's seeming pink than spontaneously judging that it is pink (364–5). Dennett calls these acts of content fixation *presentiments*. This concept of consciousness appears to be different from the other cognitive concepts already discussed. For example, presumably presentiments can be unconscious in the access and reflective senses, as in the Freudian cases mentioned earlier. Presentiments add yet another concept of consciousness to the list of those endorsed by Dennett, and as with reflective consciousness, this one also seems to yield a difference between the Orwellian and the Stalinist. A flicker of presentiment is distinct from no such flicker, and there is no reason to think that such a thing is undetectable.

I have mentioned a number of problems in Dennett's argument. Which is the basic one? Nagel (*op. cit.*) picks as the locus of error Dennett's doctrine (one that I have not yet mentioned) that the proper study of consciousness rests on third-person judgments ("heterophenomenology"), not first-person judgments, what Nagel calls "Dennett's Procrustean conception of scientific objectivity." But the point made five paragraphs ago suggests that this is not the basic error, for Dennett's argument fails even if we concede that a flicker of consciousness is a flicker of higher-order thought. If we accept an objective third-person notion of thought (at least for thought that is phenomenally and reflectively unconscious, as is allowed by the reflective view), then we can also accept an objective third-person notion of consciousness, without giving up the Orwellian/Stalinesque distinction. Although I have singled out a confusion of access and phenomenal consciousness for special mention, I have no illusion that there is one false step that is the root of all Dennett's difficulties. Instead, as often in philosophy, we have a complex network of mutually supporting confusions.

Toward the end of the book there is some explicit discussion of inverted qualia, Frank Jackson's Mary, and other conundra. There is no doubt that Dennett is eliminativist about "qualia" (so his attitude to qualia is very different from his attitude to consciousness), but as Owen Flanagan (*op. cit.*) points out, since Dennett takes it to be of the essence of "qualia" that they are ineffable, atomic, nonrelational, incomparable, and incorrigible, he has put them in the category of things inaccessible from the third-person point of view (reminding us of Norman Malcolm on dreams). But a reasonable advocate of phenomenal consciousness allows the possibility of their scientific study. So what Dennett says about "qualia" has little relevance to phenomenal consciousness.

The unfortunate thing about this book is that Dennett's own multiple-drafts theory is true of the book itself. He has given us a number of interesting but conflicting views that he has not forged into a coherent whole.

Notes

Reprinted from *The Journal of Philosophy* 90 (4): 181–193, April 1993.

I am grateful for comments on previous drafts to Michael Antony, Patricia Churchland, David Chalmers, Martin Davies, Owen Flanagan, Paul Horwich, Jerry Katz, Thomas Nagel, Georges Rey, Michael Tye, and Stephen White, and to Michael Lockwood for the final paragraph. To meet space limits, I have had to cut this review considerably, leaving out, e.g., most of the footnotes. Some of the omitted material is to be found in this volume, chapter 8.

1. New York: Routledge, 1969.

2. Imagine standing in a dark tunnel looking at a brightly lit scene at the end. Compare looking with one eye and looking with both eyes. The representational content is the same (the same objects are represented to be at the same places), but the experiential content is different. This example derives from Christopher Peacocke's *Sense and Content* (New York: Oxford, 1983). See also Sydney Shoemaker, "The Inverted Spectrum," this *the Journal of Philosophy* 79, 7 (July 1982): 357–81. The distinction applies best to perceptual states, which clearly have both kinds of content. Thought might be said to have only representational content, and pain might be said to have only experiential content. I cannot discuss the issue here, but in my view, thought does have phenomenal content, and pain has a rudimentary form of representational content, though this content may be nonconceptualized. There is an open question as to whether access consciousness of this rudimentary representational content amounts to the same thing as reflective consciousness of it. I discussed the access/phenomenal distinction in "Consciousness and Accessibility," *The Behavioral and Brain Sciences*, XIII, 4 (1990): 596–8; and "Evidence Against Epiphenomenalism," *The Behavioral and Brain Sciences*, XIV, 4 (1991): 670–2. Owen Flanagan's *Consciousness Reconsidered* (Cambridge: MIT, 1992) raises some concerns about this version of the access/phenomenal distinction. There is an illuminating discussion in the introduction to M. Davies and G. Humphreys, eds., *Consciousness: A Mind and Language Reader* (Cambridge: Blackwell, 1993).

3. Thomas Nagel's review interprets Dennett's theory this way—*Wall Street Journal*, Thursday, November 7, 1991, p. A12.

4. A more technical version of the same argument plus replies to critics by Dennett and Marcel Kinsbourne appeared in *The Behavioral and Brain Sciences*, xv, 2 (June 1992): 183–201—"Time and the Observer: The Where and When of Consciousness in the Brain"; I recommend the reply by Robert van Gulick in the same issue.

5. See Flanagan, pp. 172–5, for another criticism of Dennett on this topic.

8 What Is Dennett's Theory a Theory Of?

In *Consciousness Explained* and some papers written before and since, Dan Dennett expounds what he says is a theory of consciousness. But there is a real puzzle as to what the theory is about. There are a number of distinct phenomena that "consciousness" is used by Dennett and others to denote. If the theory is about some of them, it is false; if it is about others, it is banal.

A convenient locus of discussion is provided by Dennett's claim that consciousness is a cultural construction. He theorizes that "human consciousness (1) is too recent an innovation to be hard-wired into the innate machinery, (2) is largely the product of cultural evolution that gets imparted to brains in early training."[1] Often, Dennett puts the point in terms of *memes*. Memes are ideas such as the idea of the wheel or the calendar or the alphabet; but not all ideas are memes. Memes are cultural units, the smallest cultural units that replicate themselves reliably. In these terms then, Dennett's claim is that "Human consciousness is *itself* a huge complex of memes."[2] The claim is sometimes qualified (as in the "largely" above). I think the idea is that consciousness is the software that runs on genetically determined hardware. The software is the product of cultural evolution, but it would not run without the hardware that is the product of biological evolution.

I claim that consciousness is a *mongrel* notion, one that picks out a conglomeration of very different sorts of mental properties. Dennett gives us little clue as to which one or ones, which of the "consciousnesses" is supposed to be a cultural construction. Now this would be little more than a quibble if his claims about consciousness were plausible and novel proposals about one or more "consciousnesses," one or more "elements" of the mongrel. OK, so he doesn't tell us exactly which consciousness the claims are about, but we can figure it out for ourselves. As far as I can see, there is no kind of consciousness that is both plausibly and nontrivially a cultural construction, a collection of memes. (But perhaps Dennett will prove me wrong in his reply.) For some kinds of consciousness, the idea that consciousness is a cultural construction is a *nonstarter*. For others, there is an empirical issue, but the cultural construction claim seems likely to be false, and Dennett does not defend it. For others, it is utterly banal—certainly not the exciting new thesis Dennett presents it as. So my challenge for Dennett will be to provide us with a notion of consciousness on which his claim is both true and interesting. Of course, I wouldn't be bothering with all this if I thought Dennett had an answer. What I really think is that Dennett is using the mongrel concept of "consciousness" the way Aristotle used the concept of "velocity," sometimes meaning instantaneous velocity, sometimes meaning average velocity, without seeing the distinction.[3] I think Dennett has confused himself and others by applying an unanalyzed notion of "consciousness," conflating theses that are exciting and false with others that are boring and true. I won't be arguing for this directly, but it is the upshot of what I will have to say.

My procedure will be to go through the major elements of the mongrel briefly, with an eye to filling in and justifying the claim that what Dennett says is not both true and novel. I should say at the outset that I do not intend to be presupposing any controversial views about whether the inverted spectrum hypothesis makes sense, whether there can be "absent qualia" (that is, whether there can be creatures functionally identical to us, such that there is nothing it is like to be them) and the like. What I have to say here is supposed to be independent of such issues.

Phenomenal Consciousness

Phenomenal consciousness is experience. Phenomenal conscious properties are the experiential properties of sensations, feelings, and perceptions; for example, what it is like to experience pain, what it is like to see, to hear, and to smell. Thoughts, desires, and emotions also have phenomenal characters, though these characters do not serve to individuate the thoughts, desires, and emotions. Phenomenal properties are often representational. For example, what it is like to see something as a refrigerator is different from what it is like to see the same thing from the same angle as a big white thing of unknown purpose and design. And there is a representational commonality to what it is like to hear a sound as coming from the right and what it is like to see something as coming from the right. I believe that there is a difference in these experiences that is not representational, a difference that inheres in nonrepresentational features of the modalities; but I will not assume this in what follows. I also think that phenomenal consciousness is not characterizable in functional or intentional or cognitive terms, but again I will not assume this here.

There was a time when Dennett was an out and out eliminativist about phenomenal content, but his views have changed. He now offers a theory of it, though he cautions us that his views of what phenomenal consciousness is are at variance with a picture of it that has a strong hold on our intuitions. I hope it is just obvious to virtually everyone that the fact that things look, sound, and smell more or less the way they do to us is a basic biological feature of people, not a cultural construction that our children have to learn as they grow up. To be sure, cultural constructions have a *big impact* on the way things look, sound, and smell to us. As I said, phenomenal consciousness is often representational, and the representational aspects and phenomenal aspects of phenomenal consciousness often interact. To use Dennett's wonderful example, suppose we discovered a lost Bach cantata whose first seven notes turn out by an ugly coincidence to be identical to the first seven notes of "Rudolph the Red Nosed Reindeer." We wouldn't be able to hear the cantata the way the Leipzigers of Bach's day would have heard it. So culture certainly has an impact on phenomenal consciousness. But we have to distinguish between the idea that culture has an impact on phenomenal consciousness and the idea that phenomenal consciousness *as a whole* is a cultural construction. Culture has a big impact on *feet* too. People who have spent their lives going barefoot in the Himalayas have feet that are different in a variety of ways from people who have worn narrow pointy high-heeled shoes for eight hours a day, every day. Though culture has an impact on feet, feet are not a cultural construction. So the impact of culture on phenomenal consciousness does not give us a reason to take seriously the hypothesis that phenomenal consciousness was *invented* in the course of the development of human culture or that children slowly develop the experience of seeing, hearing, and eating as they internalize the culture. Indeed, children acquire the culture *by* seeing and hearing (and using other senses) and not the other way around. We should not take seriously the question of whether Helen Keller had her first experience of eating or smelling or feeling at the age of seven when she started learning language. We should not take seriously the idea that each of us would have been a zombie if not for specific cultural injections when we were growing up. We should not take seriously such questions as whether there was a time in human history in which people biologically just like us used their eyes and ears, ate, drank, and had sex, but there was nothing it was like for them to do these things.[4] And a view that says that such questions should be taken seriously should be rejected on that basis.

Though almost everyone believes in phenomenal consciousness, some hold a deflationary or reductionist view of it, identifying it with a functional or intentional or cognitive notion. Mightn't such views of phenomenal consciousness make the thesis that phenomenal consciousness is a cultural construction more intelligible? The best way to answer this question, I think, is to examine the other consciousnesses, the other elements of the mongrel. They are the best candidates for a deflationist or a reductionist to identify with phenomenal consciousness.

Access-Consciousness

Let us say that a state is access-conscious if its content is poised for free use in controlling thought and action. More specifically, a state with a certain content is access-conscious if, in virtue of one's having the state, a representation which has that content is (1) poised to be used freely as a premise in reasoning, according to the capabilities of the reasoner, (2) poised to be used freely for control of action. In the case of language-using organisms such as ourselves, a major symptom of access-consciousness would be *reportability*. But reportability is not necessary. My intent in framing the notion is to make it applicable to lower animals in virtue of their ability to use perceptual contents in guiding their actions.

In my view, this is the notion of consciousness that functionalists should want to identify with phenomenal consciousness. We needn't worry about whether access-consciousness is really distinct from phenomenal consciousness, since the question at hand is whether either of them could be a cultural construction. I am dealing with these questions separately, but I am giving the same answer to both, so if I am wrong about their distinctness it won't matter to my argument.

Access-consciousness is a tricky notion which I have spelled out in some detail elsewhere.[5] I will briefly make two comments about it. First, the reader may wonder what the "in virtue of" is doing in the definition. It is there in part because there are syndromes such as blindsight in which the content of a perceptual state is available to the perceiver only when he is prompted and hears himself *guess* what he is seeing. In blindsight, there are "blind" areas in the visual field where the person claims not to see stimuli, but the patient's guesses about certain features of the stimuli are often highly accurate. But that doesn't count as access-consciousness because the blindsight patient is not in a position to reason about those contents simply in virtue of having them. A second issue has to do with the fact that the paradigm phenomenally conscious states are sensations, whereas the paradigm access-conscious states are thoughts, beliefs, and desires, states with representational content expressed by "that" clauses. There are a number of ways of seeing the access-consciousness of sensations such as pain. Pains are often (some have argued always) representational, and so these representational contents are candidates for what is inferentially promiscuous, etc., when a pain is access-conscious. Alternatively, we could take the access-conscious content of pain to consist in the content that one has a pain or a state with a certain phenomenal content.[6]

Now to the point of this excursion into access-consciousness: Could access-consciousness be a cultural construction? Could there have been a time when humans who are biologically the same as us never had the contents of their perceptions and thoughts poised for free use in reasoning or in rational control of action? Could there be a human culture in which the people don't have access-consciousness? Would each of us have failed to be access-conscious but for specific cultural injections? Did Helen Keller become access-conscious at age seven? Once asked, the answers are obvious. *Dogs* have access-consciousness in virtue of their abilities to use perceptual contents in guiding their actions. Without access-consciousness, why would thought and perception ever have evolved in the first place? The discovery that access-consciousness is anything other than a basic biological feature of people would be breathtakingly amazing, on a par with the discovery that housecats are space aliens. Anyone who claimed such a thing would have to marshal a kind of evidence that Dennett makes no attempt to provide. (Of course, to say that access-consciousness is a basic biological feature of people is not to say that it is literally present at birth. Teeth and pubic hair are biological, but not present at birth.)

Access-consciousness is as close as we get to the official view of consciousness of *Consciousness Explained*, and also in Dennett's later writings. In a recent reply to critics, Dennett sums up his current formulation of the theory, saying "Consciousness is cerebral celebrity—nothing more and nothing less. Those contents are conscious that persevere, that monopolize resources long enough to achieve certain typical and 'symptomatic' effects—on memory, on the control of behavior, and so forth."[7] The official theory of *Consciousness Explained* is the Multiple Drafts theory, the view that there are distinct parallel tracks of representation that vie for access to reasoning, verbalization, and behavior. This seems more a theory of access-consciousness than any of the other elements of the mongrel. *But surely it is nothing other than a biological fact about people—not a cultural construction—that some brain representations persevere enough to affect memory, control behavior, etc.* Of course, our *concept* of cerebral celebrity is a cultural construction, but cerebral celebrity *itself* is not. No one should confuse a concept with what it is a concept of. Now we have reached a conundrum of interpretation: The closest thing we have to an *official concept* of consciousness in Dennett's recent work is not a concept of something that can be taken seriously as a cultural construction. In his reply, I hope Dennett tells us how, according to him, cerebral celebrity could be a cultural construction. In the meantime, I will search for another kind of consciousness that he could have in mind.

I said that the concept of consciousness is a mongrel concept. Our use of a single word reflects our tendency to see the elements of the mongrel as wrapped together. In particular, we think of conscious qualities as *given*, as *completely present* with *nothing hidden*. To see phenomenal consciousness as completely present is to see it as entirely accessible. These are ideas about consciousness, but they are ideas that affect phenomenal consciousness itself, what it is like to be us, just as in Dennett's example; what it is like to hear the imaginary Bach cantata would be influenced by the idea we have of the Christmas ditty. Our theories of phenomenal consciousness do influence phenomenal consciousness itself to some extent. Our experience might be somewhat different in a culture in which a different view of phenomenal consciousness was prevalent. But we should not allow such interactions to make us lose sight of the main effect. True, culture *modulates* cerebral celebrity, but it does not *create* it. We must not conflate *cultural influence* with *cultural creation*.

It should be noted that our theories, even wildly false theories, about many things, not just consciousness itself, can influence our experience. For example, we sometimes think of seeing as a process in which something emanates from the eyes. We talk of moving our gaze sometimes as if it were a beam of light. And we sometimes talk of seeing through a dirty window as if our gaze could to some extent penetrate it. These notions were parts of theories of vision in ancient times, and even now appear in childrens' theories.[8] Perhaps these ideas affect our phenomenal consciousness—or perhaps it is the other way around.

Monitoring Consciousness

The idea of consciousness as some sort of internal monitoring takes many forms. One form is one that Dennett discusses in *Consciousness Explained*: higher-order thought. In Rosenthal's version,[9] to say that a state is conscious in this sense is to say that the state is accompanied by a thought to the effect that one is in that state. Perhaps in another time or culture people were or are much less introspective than they are here and now, but would anyone claim that there was a time or place when people genetically like us (and who are not shell-shocked or starving to death) had children who had no capacity to think or say something on the order of "Carry me, my leg hurts"? To be able to think or say this involves being able to think *that one's leg hurts*, and that is to think a higher-order thought in the relevant sense. I won't say that it isn't *possible* that some wise child of our species discovered that she could get Mom to carry her by talking (and thinking) about her pain, but it would take weird and wonderful discoveries to convince me that this is a theoretical option to be taken seriously. Dennett does not give any hint of the kind of weird and wonderful discoveries that would be needed. So we have to doubt that this is what he means. (Though it should be noted that Dennett makes a number of very favorable remarks about this idea of consciousness in *Consciousness Explained*.)

Self-Consciousness

There are a number of closely connected notions of self-consciousness clustered around the notion of the ability to think about oneself. Let us begin with a *minimal* notion of self-consciousness, one that requires thinking about oneself, but not in any particular way. Certainly this very minimal kind of self-consciousness is unlikely to be a cultural construction. Consider deception. Deception involves thinking about getting others to think that one believes something other than what one actually believes. This involves the minimal self-consciousness just mentioned. There is pretty good evidence that higher primates practice deception, so it seems unlikely that humans had to invent it.[10] Further, some higher primates, notably chimps, show other signs of self-consciousness in the minimal sense. Some primates show signs of exploring their bodies in mirrors, while other primates and humans below age one and a half do not.

Gallup[11] and others have painted bright spots on the foreheads and ears of anesthe-tized primates, watching what happened. Chimps between the ages of seven and fif-teen usually show surprise on looking at their mirror images, then touch the spot, attempting to wipe off the mark. This is known as the mark test. Nonprimates never do this. Human babies don't pass the mark test until the middle of their second year. This is now a well-established phenomenon replicated numerous times, though there are raging controversies.[12] As far as I can see, the controversies have little to do with chimp self-consciousness in the minimal sense. One of the controversies is about whether chimps have a "theory of mind," but that is not required for minimal self-consciousness. Anyway, there is independent evidence from the literature on genetic defects that humans have an innate module involved in understanding the minds of other humans, a module which is therefore most unlikely to be a cultural construction. Autistic people appear to lack that module, even when they are otherwise cognitively normal, and there is another syndrome, a chromosomal abnormality, Williams Syn-drome, in which the patients have the mind-module even when they are terribly sub-normal in other cognitive respects.[13] Carey et al. mention a story that illustrates the lack of theoretical understanding characteristic of Williams Syndrome. A young adult woman with Williams Syndrome had read a number of vampire novels. When asked why vampires bite necks, she was very puzzled, and eventually answered that they must have "an inordinate fondness for necks." She had no idea that vampires are sup-posed to consume blood. This sort of evidence for genetic mental modules certainly puts a heavy burden of proof on anyone who claims that anything so basic as con sciousness in any of the senses discussed so far is a cultural construction.

Another controversy is over whether chimps really realize that they are seeing them-selves in the mirror. Perhaps a chimp who is a subject of the experiment thinks she is seeing *another* chimp with a dot on his forehead, and that makes the subject chimp wonder whether she has a dot on her forehead too. Maybe so, but the ability to wonder whether I have a dot on my forehead presupposes that I have minimal self-consciousness. Another objection to these experiments is that perhaps they mainly test understanding of mirrors. But plausibly understanding mirrors involves having some idea that it is oneself that one is seeing in the mirror.

The most fascinating result I've heard of in this area in recent years is unpublished work by Marc Hauser on the cotton-top tamarin, a small monkey which has a large white tuft on the top of its head. Monkeys had never been observed to pass orthodox versions of the mark test. Hauser thought that perhaps the inconsistent responses shown by chimps and other higher primates had to do with the lack of *salience* of the dots, so he died the cottontop tuft outrageous electric colors, flamingo pink, char-treuse, etc. The finding is that the cottontops passed the mark test. Normally, they don't look in the mirror much, and rarely longer than one to three seconds at a time. Hauser observed long stares on the part of the monkeys with died tufts of thirty to forty-five seconds, and a three-fold increase in touching their tufts. Further, it seems unlikely that the monkeys thought they were looking at other monkeys, since staring in this species is a threat, and these monkeys were staring peacefully, something they do not normally do. Hauser has run all sorts of controls, for example, painting the mirror instead of the monkey, checking what happens when a monkey sees another monkey with a died tuft, checking the effect of the smell and the feel of the die, and the result stands.[14]

Another experiment (mentioned by Dennett) is that a chimp can learn to get bananas via a hole in its cage by watching its arm on a closed circuit TV whose camera is some distance away.[15] Though there is strong evidence that chimps (and maybe monkeys) are self-conscious in the minimal sense, given the controversies in the field, I will draw a weaker conclusion, namely that it is up to anyone who claims that humans are not, as a biological matter, self-conscious in the minimal sense to debunk this evidence. In the absence of such debunking, we are entitled to suppose that it is false that self-consciousness in the minimal sense is a cultural construction in humans. (I will ignore the possibility that self-consciousness is an independent creation of monkey, chimp, and human culture.) The idea that minimal self-consciousness is a cultural construction is certainly more of a genuine possibility than the options canvassed earlier, but it is nonetheless a poor empirical bet.

But haven't I given up my case for confusion by admitting that this is an empirical question which could come out either way? No, Dennett will not get off the hook so easily. To be sure, he sees his theory of consciousness as empirical, but empirical in a diffuse way, not something that could be refuted by experiments on cottontop tamarins. Dennett is well aware of the work on the mark test and chooses not to mention it, at least not in anything I've seen. He clearly does not see his theory of consciousness as depending on these specific empirical results, since he mentions few of them; indeed, to the extent that he does mention this type of work, he appears to have something like the same view that I have expressed. He seems to discuss the Menzel experiment so as to support the idea that chimps are self-conscious in something like the way that we are. He describes the result as "a decidedly non-trivial bit of self-recognition."[16]

Where are we? I have argued that if Dennett's theory is about phenomenal consciousness or access-consciousness, it is obviously false and if it is about minimal self-consciousness, it is less obviously false but still false.

There is a notion of self-consciousness that is a better candidate for what Dennett has in mind than minimal self-consciousness. He does have a chapter on the self in which he paints the self as a fiction, a fiction invented in human history. Now I should say right off that I have long been sympathetic to something like this idea, though I prefer a more conservative version; viz., that the self is much more fragmented than we like to think. This is an idea that has been around for many years, one that grows ever more prominent as the evidence mounts up. The first really impressive case for it by a philosopher was Thomas Nagel's famous paper on split brains and the unity of consciousness.[17] Nagel argued that the fragmentation observed in split brain patients exists to some degree in normal people, and in the light of it our concept of the self crumbles. This sort of idea has been widened and elaborated for many years now by many psychologists and neuropsychologists, notably by Gazzaniga and his colleagues.[18] Gazzaniga tries to explain many ubiquitous cognitive phenomena in terms of the relations among "sub-selves," especially the efforts of some "sub-selves" to rationalize the behavior of other "sub-selves."[19]

Now here is the relevance to Dennett. I have been talking about a rather minimal notion of self-consciousness, one that it seems that chimps and human toddlers and maybe monkeys have. This is a very unintellectual notion of self-consciousness, because it is very relaxed about the notion of the self. In particular, this weak notion of self-consciousness does not require any conception of the self as being or as not being a federation of subselves. But we are free to frame a more intellectual notion of the self that *does* presuppose that we are not such a federation. I think it is the self in this sense, the nonfederal sense, that Dennett thinks is a fiction. And that sense of the self gives rise to a conception of self-consciousness, namely thinking about oneself in some way that is incompatible with being a federation. Let us call this sense of self-consciousness NONFEDERAL-SELF-consciousness. I spell it this way to remind the reader that the emendation attaches to the concept of the self; and only derivatively to the concept of consciousness—it is self-consciousness that involves thinking of the self in a certain sophisticated way, a way that Dennett thinks (and I agree) is probably wrong. Note that unity and nonfederation are distinct, since unity is compatible with both federation and nonfederation. The United States is a unity as well as a federation. One could think of oneself as a unity without having the conceptual equipment to think of oneself as either a federation or not a federation. I would guess (and it's just a guess) that members of our species have always thought of themselves as a unity, but only in recorded history have thought of themselves as NONFEDERAL, or, in the case of Dennett, Nagel, et al. (including myself) as FEDERAL.

So perhaps what Dennett means when he says that consciousness is a cultural construction is that NONFEDERAL-SELF-consciousness is a cultural construction because the nonfederal self is a cultural construction. But that would make the claim a *total banality*. It is no surprise at all that the ability to think of oneself in a very sophisticated way is a product of culture. You can't think of yourself as falling under a sophisticated concept without having the sophisticated concept. We could call thinking of oneself as chairman CHAIRMAN-SELF-consciousness. CHAIRMAN-SELF-consciousness involves thinking of oneself as the person who guides the department, the person who has the keys, etc. And all could agree that CHAIRMAN-SELF-consciousness is a cultural construction because the concept of a chairman is a cultural construction. But that is no news. Don't get me wrong. I'm not saying that the idea that selves are not federations is a banality. On the contrary, I think it is an interestingly false thesis. What I am talking about is the claim that it requires culture to think of one's self as nonfederal (or as federal)—*that's* the banality. To put it slightly differently, Dennett's claim that we are federations, that we have federal selves, is a very interesting and profound idea that I agree with. What is banal is that it *takes culture* to think of oneself using such an interesting and intellectual concept (or its negation). The thesis about the self is interesting, the thesis about self-*consciousness* is banal.

However, I find nothing in the texts to justify the idea that what Dennett means is that NONFEDERAL-SELF-consciousness is a cultural construction.[20] So I can't claim to have figured out what Dennett means yet. But there is an important piece of the puzzle that I haven't introduced yet.

Before I get to that piece, I want to guard against one source of misunderstanding. I mentioned earlier that we think of phenomenal consciousness as wrapped together with access-consciousness in thinking of phenomenal consciousness as accessible. And this way of thinking—which may be a cultural product—influences phenomenal consciousness itself. We think of phenomenal consciousness as having nothing hidden about it, and experience might perhaps be somewhat different in a different culture in which phenomenal consciousness was not thought about in this way. I cautioned against the mistake of jumping to the conclusion that if this is right it shows that consciousness is a cultural construction. To confuse being influenced by culture with being created by culture would be a serious error, one that I am not attributing to Dennett. Consciousness and feet may both be influenced by culture, I concluded, but neither is created by it. What I am leading up to is that a similar point can be made about the relation between phenomenal consciousness and self-consciousness. There is a "me"-ness to phenomenal consciousness that may come in part from culture; this aspect comes out in part in the way we describe phenomenal consciousness as "before the mind." Whether or not the "me"-ness of phenomenal consciousness is in part cultural, the ideology of the unity of the self mentioned earlier gives us reason to think there is an influence of culture on the way many or most of us experience the world.[21] But once again, though there may be a cultural influence on phenomenal consciousness here, this is no reason to postulate that phenomenal consciousness is a cultural creation. Surely, in any culture that allows the material and psychological necessities of life, people genetically like us will have experiences much like ours: There will be something it is like for them to see and hear and smell things that is much like what it is like for us to do these things.

I mentioned a new piece of the puzzle. Here it is: In the early part of *Consciousness Explained*,[22] Dennett tells us that consciousness is like love and money. He thinks that you can't love without having the concept of love, and (more plausibly) that there wouldn't be any money unless some people had the concept of money. (In another work, soon to be mentioned and quoted from, he includes right and wrong in the list of things that don't exist without their concepts.) According to Dennett, you can't have consciousness unless you have the concept of consciousness. This is certainly a wild-*sounding* view (and he concedes this). Its incompatibility with common ideas is exemplified by the fact that we are inclined to think that animals are conscious (in at least the phenomenal, access and minimal-self senses) but don't have the concept of consciousness. I don't know what Dennett's argument for this claim is or what kind of consciousness he has in mind, but it does seem closely connected with the idea that consciousness is a cultural construction. Here is a line of reasoning that connects them. Suppose that Dennett is right that we can't be conscious without having the concept of consciousness. And suppose further that the concept is a cultural construction. Then consciousness itself requires a cultural construction and could for that reason be said to *be* a cultural construction. Since there is a close connection between the claim that consciousness requires its own concept and the claim that consciousness is a cultural construction, we should consider what *kind* of consciousness it is supposed to be that you can't have without having a concept of it. For whatever kind of consciousness it is that requires its own concept will no doubt be the Holy Grail, the kind of consciousness we have been seeking that is a cultural construction (and interestingly so).

Dennett credits Julian Jaynes as one of the sources of the idea that consciousness is a cultural construction.[23] Now we are in luck because Dennett has written a long review of Jaynes's book, *Origins of Consciousness in the Breakdown of the Bicameral Mind*, which links this view to the idea that consciousness requires its own concept, a view which Dennett also credits to Jaynes.[24] What kind of consciousness is it that Jaynes is supposed to think requires its own concept? Dennett criticizes my review of Jaynes[25] for misconstruing a revolutionary proposal as a simple blunder.

In a review of Jaynes's book some years ago, Ned Block said the whole book made one great crashing mistake, what we sometimes call a "use mention" error: confusing a phenomenon with either the name of the phenomenon or the concept of the phenomenon. Block claimed that even if everything that Jaynes said about historical events were correct, all he would have shown was not that *consciousness* arrived in 1400 B.C., but that the *concept* of consciousness arrived in 1400 B.C. People were conscious long before they had the concept of consciousness, Block declared, in the same way that there was gravity long before Newton ever hit upon the concept of gravity.... [A discussion of morality follows] Right and wrong, however, are parts of morality, a peculiar phenomenon that *can't* predate a certain set of concepts, including the concepts of right and wrong. The phenomenon is *created* in part by the arrival on the scene of a certain set of concepts.... Now I take Jaynes to be making a similarly exciting and striking move with regard to consciousness. To put it really somewhat paradoxically, you can't have consciousness until you have the concept of consciousness.[26] [Note: Though Dennett calls this a paradoxical way of putting it, he says this repeatedly and does not put it any other way.]

Jaynes has a very concrete version of Dennett's hypothesis that consciousness is a cultural construction, namely that it was invented in Europe by the ancient Greeks around 1400 B.C. We don't need to get into the issue of what Jaynes actually meant by "consciousness." For my purposes, the issue is what Dennett takes Jaynes to mean, because Dennett himself endorses the idea that consciousness is a cultural construction in *this sense*. Here is what he says.

Perhaps this is an autobiographical confession: I am rather fond of his way of using these terms; ['consciousness', 'mind', and other mental terms] I rather like his way of carving up consciousness. It is in fact very similar to the way that I independently decided to carve up consciousness some years ago.

So what then is the project? The project is, in one sense, very simple and very familiar. It is bridging what he calls the 'awesome chasm' between mere inert matter and the inwardness, as he puts it, of a conscious being. Consider the awesome chasm between a brick and a bricklayer. There isn't, in Thomas Nagel's famous phrase, anything that it is like to be a brick. But there is something that it is like to be a bricklayer, and we want to know what the conditions were under which there happened to come to be entities that it was like something to be in this rather special sense. That is the story, the developmental, evolutionary, historical story, that Jaynes sets out to tell.[27]

So it looks like the kind of consciousness that requires its own concept and is a cultural construction is after all *phenomenal* consciousness. W. V. Quine tells me that he asked Jaynes what it was like to be a person before consciousness was invented. Jaynes replied, Quine says, that what it was like to be them was no different from what it is like to be a table or a chair. The passage just quoted suggests that Dennett would agree.

So we are back to square one. I've been going through concepts of consciousness one by one looking for a concept of consciousness in which Dennett's thesis escapes both falsity and banality, and phenomenal consciousness is the first concept of consciousness I tried. If phenomenal consciousness is not reducible to one of the other consciousnesses, then the claim that phenomenal consciousness requires its own concept and is a cultural construction is obviously false for reasons I gave. But if Dennett does favor one of these reductions, we have every right to ask: "Which one?" And if the answer is one of the consciousnesses I have covered, the claim is false or banal.

Perhaps Dennett will say that he will have no part of my distinctions, that they impose a grid on the phenomena that doesn't sit well with his way of thinking of things. But this is no defense. Consider *randomness*. The concept can be and is used in two very different ways. Sometimes we say a particular sequence is random if it is *produced* by a random process, even if the sequence itself consists of eighteen consecutive sevens. Other times what we mean is that it is of a *type* that one would *expect* to be produced by a random process, that is, it has no obvious pattern. Suppose someone makes a claim that is false on one concept of randomness and banal on the other. It would be of no use at all for the offender to defend himself by saying that he didn't find the distinction congenial. Given the fact that on one way of cutting things up, his thesis is trivial or banal, it is up to him to give some precise way of thinking about randomness that disarms the objection. He must show how his thesis can be neither false nor banal, and to do this he will have to make his notion of randomness precise in a way that allows us to see that the criticism is wrong.

The application of the analogy to Dennett is straightforward. I have argued that on one grid that we can impose on the phenomena, his claim is either false or banal. He does not have the option of simply saying he doesn't like the distinctions. He will have to find a way of making more precise what he is talking about under the heading of "consciousness" in a way that rebuts the charge of falsity or banality. It is no good just refusing to make distinctions at all, since anyone can see that "conscious" is highly ambiguous, and my argument puts the burden of proof on him.

In another publication written about the same time as this paper, I have made a shorter version of some of these points about Dennett and Dennett has replied.[28] Here is what I see as his main point:

Although Block discusses my theory of consciousness at some length, his discussion always leans on the presupposition that his putative distinction is in place. My theory of consciousness is stranded, he concludes, between being trivially false (if a theory of P-consciousness), non-trivially false (if a theory of "just" A-consciousness) and banal if a theory of "a highly sophisticated version of self-consciousness." But since I not only decline to draw any such distinction, but argue at length against any such distinction, Block's critique is simply question-begging. I may be wrong to deny the distinction, but this could not be shown by proclaiming the distinction, ignoring the grounds I have given for denying it, and then showing what a hash can then be made of ideas I have expressed in other terms, with other presuppositions. If Block thinks his distinction is too obvious to need further defense, he has missed the whole point of my radical alternative. This is a fundamental weakness in the strategy Block employs, and it vitiates his discoveries of "fallacies" in the thinking of other theorists as well. Those of us who are not impressed by his candidate distinction are free to run the implication in the other direction: since our reasoning is not fallacious after all, his distinction must be bogus.[29]

First of all, though Dennett has some complaints against the phenomenal consciousness/access-consciousness distinction, he never mentions any problem about the notions of access-consciousness, monitoring consciousness or self-consciousness, nor does he impugn the distinctions among these things. Oversimplifying (see below), Dennett wishes to treat phenomenal consciousness as a type of access-consciousness. But the argument I gave can run on just monitoring consciousness, self-consciousness, and access-consciousness of various sorts. Supposing that phenomenal consciousness just is a type of access-consciousness, what then is Dennett's theory about? If it is about access-consciousness, Dennett will run into the problem mentioned earlier, that it is obviously a biological fact about people and not a cultural construction that some brain representations persevere enough to affect memory, control behavior, and the like. Since this is Dennett's favored way of describing access, it is not easy to understand how seeing phenomenal consciousness as a type of access-consciousness is supposed to avoid the problem. If there is some novel form of access that his theory is about, it is surprising that he has not told us in any of his many publications on this topic, including his reply to a version of the criticism of this paper.

Secondly, Dennett does not reject the phenomenal consciousness/access-consciousness distinction. Far from it—he reconstructs it. His idea is that phenomenal-consciousness contents are richer in information and more accessible than the level required for access-consciousness. Thus, he says, I am "inflating differences in degree into imaginary differences in kind."[30] I believe I can show that this reconstruction will not do.[31] For present purposes, let's suppose Dennett is right: The difference is one of degree. *Which degree*, then, does his thesis apply to? Or does it apply to monitoring or self-consciousness? My criticism does not depend on taking the distinction to be one of kind rather than of degree.

Thirdly, Dennett contrasts the informational paucity of the perceptual contents of the blindsight patient with the informational richness of normal vision. Some classic blindsight studies involve prompting the blindsight patient to guess as between an X and an O or between a horizontal and a vertical line. Normal perceptual contents are much richer, representing colors and shapes that are a small subset of a vast number of possibilities. In normal vision, we can "come to know, swiftly and effortlessly, that there was a bright orange Times Roman italic X about two inches high, on a blue-green background, with a pale gray smudge on the upper right arm, almost touching the intersection? (That's a sample of the sort of richness of content normally to be gleaned from the sighted field, after all.)" Supposing that Dennett is right that phenomenal-consciousness contents are just contents that are particularly rich in information and accessibility, is it phenomenally conscious contents that are cultural constructions and require their own concepts? It is hard to take seriously the idea that the human capacity to see and access rich displays of colors and shapes is a cultural construction that requires its own concept. Indeed, there is a great deal of evidence that culture does not even *influence* these perceptual contents. For example, in cultures which have only two or three color words, the people make all the same perceptual distinctions that we do. Further, they recognize the same colors as focal that we do even if their languages do not separate out those colors.[32] In a fascinating series of studies, Eleanor Rosch showed that the Dani, a New Guinea tribe that has only two color words, nonetheless remember and represent colors in many respects just as we do. For example, they learned words for focal colors much more easily than words for nonfocal colors (e.g., blue as opposed to greenish blue). When asked to learn words for oddball color categories covering focal colors plus adjacent nonfocal colors, some subjects wanted to quit the study.[33] There is reason to think that many aspects of color and shape perception are genetically coded features of the visual system, and not a product of culture or something that requires any concept of consciousness.[34]

So I leave the reader with a quandary, one that I hope Dennett will now resolve, since he gets the last word. Consciousness is a mongrel notion: There are a number of very different concepts of consciousness. On some of these, notably phenomenal consciousness, access-consciousness and monitoring consciousness, the idea that consciousness is a cultural construction is hard to take seriously. If it is minimal self-consciousness that is meant, it is an empirical issue whether available evidence goes against the cultural construction idea. (But if that was what Dennett meant, you would think he would have commented negatively on that evidence; instead his limited comment is positive.) If it is a sophisticated self-consciousness that is meant (NONFEDERAL-SELF-consciousness), then the thesis is true but utterly banal, because it is no surprise that the ability to apply a sophisticated concept to oneself requires a cultural construction. I don't claim to have covered all the options. But I have covered enough options to make it fair to ask for an answer: What kind of consciousness is it that requires its own concept and is a cultural construction?

Notes

Reprinted from *Philosophical Topics* 22 (1–2): 23–40, 1994.
     I am grateful to Susan Carey, Chris Hill, Paul Horwich, and Stephen White for comments on a previous draft.

1. Daniel Dennett, *Consciousness Explained* (Boston: Little, Brown & Co., 1991), 219.

2. Ibid., 210.

3. T. S. Kuhn, "A Function for Thought Experiments," in *Melanges Alexandre Koyre*, vol. 1. (Hermann, 1964), 307–34.

4. This last point could be rebutted by the claim that throughout human evolution there was a culture that created phenomenal consciousness (apparently contrary to Julian Jaynes' view to be discussed later). If we allow ourselves to take the view that phenomenal consciousness is a cultural construction seriously we will have to take this issue seriously. My point, however, is that we should not take this question seriously. It is a poor question that will just mislead us.

5. Ned Block, "On a Confusion about a Function of Consciousness," *The Behavioral and Brain Sciences* 18 (1995): 227–47. See also my reply to my critics in the same volume. This paper is reprinted in *The Nature of Consciousness: Philosophical Debates*, ed. N. Block, O. Flanagan, G. Guzeldere (Cambridge, Mass.: MIT Press, 1997).

6. One problem with the first of these suggestions is that perhaps the representational content of pain is *nonconceptualized*, and if so, it would be too primitive to play a role in inference. After all, dogs can have pains, and it is reasonable to doubt that dogs *have* the relevant concepts. In response to an earlier version of this distinction, Davies and Humphreys have made a suggestion which I can adapt. (See the introduction to their *Consciousness* [Oxford: Blackwell, 1993].) A state

with nonconceptualized content is access-conscious if, in virtue of one's having the state, its content *would be* inferentially promiscuous and poised for rational control of action and speech if the subject were to have had the concepts required for that content to be a conceptualized content.

7. Daniel Dennett, "The Message Is: There Is No *Medium*," *Philosophy and Phenomenological Research* 53 (1993): 929.

8. These theories are known as extramission theories.

9. D. Rosenthal, "Two Concepts of Consciousness," *Philosophical Studies* 49 (1986): 329–59.

10. Merlin Donald's *Origins of the Modern Mind: Three Stages in the Evolution of Culture and Cognition* (Cambridge, Mass.: Harvard University Press, 1991) is often thought to be rather critical about the evidence for the conceptual capacities of chimps compared to humans. It is interesting in this regard to find Donald replying to six critics who criticize him for this by admitting that there is impressive evidence for ape deception. See his reply to critics in *The Behavioral and Brain Sciences* 16 (1993): 777. Merlin says he is especially impressed with data on chimps' capacities, including some that indicate "sense of 'self'" in Alexander Marshak's "Correct Data Base: Wrong Model?" *Behavioral and Brain Sciences* 16 (1993): 767. Mitchell and Miles (in the same issue) provide further data supporting this conclusion.

11. G. Gallup, "Self-Awareness and the Emergence of Mind in Primates," *The American Journal of Primatology* 2 (1982): 237–48. The most complete and up-to-date survey on the mark test as of my writing this is D. Povinelli's "What Chimpanzees Know about the Mind," in *Behavioral Diversity in Chimpanzees* (Cambridge, Mass.: Harvard University Press, 1994). See also R. W. Mitchell, "Mental Models of Mirror Self-Recognition: Two Theories," in *New Ideas in Psychology* 11 (1993): 295–332 and "The Evolution of Primate Cognition: Simulation, Self-Knowledge and Knowledge of Other Minds," in *Hominid Culture in Primate Perspective*, ed. D. Quiatt, and J. Itani (University Press of Colorado, 1993).

12. *Self-Awareness in Animals and Humans*, ed. S. T. Parker, et al. (Cambridge: Cambridge University Press, 1994). See also *New Ideas in Psychology* 11 (1993). R. W. Mitchell's paper, "Mental Models of Mirror Self-Recognition: Two Theories" draws fire from Gallup and Povinelli, De Lannoy, Anderson, and Byrne, and there is a reply by Mitchell. I think one gets a pretty good idea of what the controversies are like from this exchange.

13. S. Carey, S. Johnson, and K. Levine, "Two Separable Knowledge Acquisition Systems: Evidence from Williams Syndrome"; H. Tager-Flusberg, K. Sullivan, and D. Zaitchik, "Social Cognitive Abilities in Young Children with Williams Syndrome" (Papers presented at the Sixth International Professional Conference of the Williams Syndrome Association, July 1994).

14. M. Hauser, J. Kralik, C. Botto-Mahan, M. Garrett, and J. Oser, "Self-recognition in Primates: Phylogeny and the Salience of Species-Typical Features" (forthcoming).

15. E. W. Menzel, E. S. Savage-Rumbaugh, and J. Lawson, "Chimpanzee (*Pan Troglodytes*) Spatial Problem Solving with the Use of Mirrors and Televised Equivalents of Mirrors," *The Journal of Comparative Psychology* 99 (1985): 211–17. This experiment is mentioned by Dennett on 428 of *Consciousness Explained*.

16. *Consciousness Explained*, 428.

17. Thomas Nagel, "Brain Bisection and the Unity of Consciousness," *Synthese* 22 (1971): 396–413.

18. M. Gazzaniga and J. E. LeDoux, *The Integrated Mind* (New York: Plenum, 1978); M. Gazzaniga, *The Social Brain* (New York: Basic Books, 1985). See also Marvin Minsky's *The Society of Mind* (New York: Simon and Schuster, 1985).

19. For a detailed account of the difference between phenomenal consciousness and self-consciousness, and of why it is self-consciousness that matters to morality, see Stephen White, "What Is It Like to Be a Homunculus?" *The Pacific Philosophical Quarterly* 68 (1987): 148–74.

20. Further, if that was what Dennett meant, wouldn't he have advanced his theory of the self as a fiction in the course of presenting the theory of consciousness? Instead, the theory of consciousness (including consciousness as a cultural construction) is presented in part II of the book (mainly chapters 7–9), and the theory of the self is given in part III at the end, in the next to the last chapter of the whole book, chapter 13.

21. I am indebted to an unpublished paper on the self by Stephen White.

22. *Consciousness Explained*, 24.

23. Ibid., 259.

24. Daniel Dennett, "Julian Jaynes's Software Archeology," *Canadian Psychology* 27 (1986): 149–54.

25. Ned Block, review of Julian Jaynes's *Origins of Consciousness in the Breakdown of the Bicameral Mind* in *Cognition and Brain Theory* 4 (1981): 81–3.

26. "Julian Jaynes's Software Archeology," 152.

27. Ibid., 149.

28. Block, "On a Confusion about a Function of Consciousness." Dennett's reply is "The Path Not Taken," *The Behavioral and Brain Sciences* 18 (1995): 252–3. 'P-consciousness' and 'A-consciousness' are the terms used in that paper for phenomenal and access-consciousness.

29. Dennett, "The Path Not Taken," 253.

30. Ibid.

31. See my reply in *The Behavioral and Brain Sciences* 18 (1995): 272–84.

32. B. Berlin and P. Kay, *Basic Color Terms: Their Universality and Evolution* (University of California Press, 1969).

33. Eleanor Rosch, "On the Internal Structure of Perceptual and Semantic Categories," in *Cognitive Development and the Acquisition of Language*, ed. T. E. Moore (Academic Press, 1973), 111–44.

34. I can't resist commenting on Dennett's suggestion that phenomenal consciousness can be characterized in part in terms of informational richness. (I won't comment on the accessibility part of the theory.)

Weiskrantz notes that his patient DB had better acuity in some areas of the blind field (in some circumstances) than in his sighted field. And there is an obvious way to increase the superiority of the blind field—namely by decreasing the richness of the deliverances of the sighted field. Suppose a Mad Scientist kidnaps a blindsight patient and damages the sighted part of the visual system. Many blind people are unable to do much more than distinguish light and dark, so we can imagine the Mad Scientist injuring a blindsight patient by so damaging his sighted field. In the sighted field, he only experiences the difference between light and dark.

But do we not still have an informational superiority of the blind field? Dennett describes the informational content of blindsight as "vanishingly" small. In his book, he emphasizes the cases in which the blindsight patient is given a forced choice; e.g., an X or an O. But blindsight patients can exhibit contents that are far more informational than that. In Pöppel et al.'s famous paper, the first human blindsight study, the patients were asked to move their eyes in the direction of the stimulus, *which they could do*. (E. Pöppel, R. Held, and D. Frost, "Residual Visual Functions after Brain Wounds Involving the Central Visual Pathways in Man," *Nature* 243 [1973]: 2295–6.) So we could have a blindsight patient whose *blind* field discriminations involved distinguishing among a number of different directions, and who could not make that many discriminations in his *sighted* field. In the light of this point, no one should maintain that high informational content is the essence of or necessary for experience. Further, blindsight patients can catch a ball thrown in the blind field, and shape their hand to grasp an object presented in the blind field. These are cases of far more than binary information, and more, I would guess, than some cases of near total blindness of the sort described. Further, there are other blindsight-like phenomena in which subjects have rich informational contents without phenomenal or access-consciousness of it. *Prosopagnosia* is a neurological impairment in which subjects cannot recognize faces, even the faces of their friends and family. Bauer ("Autonomic Recognition: A Neuropsychological Application of the Guilty Knowledge Test," *Neuropsychologica* 22 [1984]: 457–69) showed patients photographs of people they had seen many times, for example, John Wayne, and went through a number of names, noting a polygraph blip when the right name came up. Other experiments have shown that many prosopagnosics have information about the faces that they cannot consciously recognize in either the phenomenal or access senses. What's the informational value of seeing that it is John Wayne? Not vanishingly small. Compare the richness of this content with that of say a salty taste (while holding your nose so there is no smell). It is not at all clear that the experience of tasting without smelling has more informational value than the prosopagnosics nonexperiential appreciation that he is seeing John Wayne.

9   On a Confusion about a Function of Consciousness

1   Introduction

The concept of consciousness is a hybrid or better, a mongrel concept: the word "consciousness" connotes a number of different concepts and denotes a number of different phenomena. We reason about "consciousness" using some premises that apply to one of the phenomena that fall under "consciousness," other premises that apply to other "consciousnesses," and we end up with trouble. There are many parallels in the history of science. Aristotle used "velocity" sometimes to mean average velocity and sometimes to mean instantaneous velocity; his failure to see the distinction caused confusion (Kuhn 1964). The Florentine experimenters of the seventeenth century used a single word (roughly translatable as "degree of heat") for temperature and for heat, generating paradoxes. For example, when they measured "degree of heat" by whether various heat sources could melt paraffin, heat source A came out hotter than B, but when they measured "degree of heat" by how much ice a heat source could melt in a given time, B was hotter than A (Wiser and Carey 1983). These are very different cases, but there is a similarity, one that they share with the case of "consciousness." The similarity is: very different concepts are treated as a single concept. I think we all have some tendency to make this mistake in the case of "consciousness."

Though the problem I am concerned with appears in many lines of thought about consciousness, it will be convenient to focus on one of them. My main illustration of the kind of confusion I'm talking about concerns reasoning about the *function* of consciousness. But the issue of the function of consciousness is more of the *platform* of this chapter than its topic. Because this chapter attempts to expose a confusion, it is primarily concerned with reasoning, not with data. Long stretches of text without data may make some readers uncomfortable, as will my fanciful thought-experiments. But if you are interested in consciousness, if I am right you can't afford to lose patience. A stylistic matter: because this paper will have audiences with different concerns, I have adopted the practice of putting items that will mainly be of technical interest to part of the audience in endnotes. Endnotes can be skipped without losing the thread. I now turn to blindsight and its role in reasoning about a function of consciousness.

Patients with damage in primary visual cortex typically have "blind" areas in their visual fields. If the experimenter flashes a stimulus in one of those blind areas and asks the patient what he saw, the patient says "Nothing." The striking phenomenon is that some (but not all) of these patients are able to "guess" reliably about certain features of the stimulus, features having to do with motion, location, direction (e.g., whether a grid is horizontal or vertical). In "guessing," they are able to discriminate some simple forms; if they are asked to grasp an object in the blind field (which they say they can't see), they can shape their hands in a way appropriate to grasping it, and there are some signs of color discrimination. Interestingly, visual acuity (as measured, e.g., by how fine a grating can be detected) increases further from where the patient is looking in blindsight, the opposite of normal sight. (Blindsight was first noticed by Pöppel et al. 1973, and there is now a huge literature on this and related phenomena. I suggest looking at Bornstein and Pittman 1992 and Milner and Rugg 1992).

Consciousness in some sense is apparently missing (though see McGinn 1991, p. 112, for an argument to the contrary), and with it, the ability to deploy information in reasoning and rational control of action. For example, Tony Marcel (1986) observed that a thirsty blindsight patient would not reach for a glass of water in his blind field. (One has to grant Marcel some "poetic license" in this influential example, since blindsight patients appear to have insufficient form perception in their blind fields to pick out a glass of water.) It is tempting to argue (Marcel 1986, 1988; Baars 1988; Flanagan 1991, 1992; van Gulick 1989) that since consciousness is missing in blindsight, consciousness must have a function of somehow enabling information represented in the brain to be used in reasoning, reporting, and rationally guiding action. I mean the "rationally" to exclude the "guessing" kind of guidance of action that blindsight patients *are* capable of in the case of stimuli presented to the blind field. (The intended contrast is that between guidance by reason and guidance by inclination; I don't mean to say that the blindsight patient is irrational.) The idea is that when a representation is not conscious—as in the blindsight patient's blindfield perceptual representations—it can influence behavior behind the scenes, but only when the representation is conscious does it play a rational role; and so consciousness must be involved in promoting this rational role.

A related argument is also tempting: Robert van Gulick (1989) and John Searle (1992) discuss Penfield's observations of epileptics who have a seizure while walking, driving, or playing the piano. The epileptics continue their activities in a routinized, mechanical way despite, it is said, a total lack of consciousness. Searle says that since both consciousness and also flexibility and creativity of behavior are missing, we can conclude that a function of consciousness is to somehow promote flexibility and creativity. These two arguments are the springboard for this chapter. Though some variants of this sort of reasoning have merit, they are often given more weight than they deserve because of a persistent fallacy involving a conflation of two very different concepts of consciousness.

The plan of the chapter is as follows: in the next section, I will briefly discuss some other syndromes much like blindsight, and I will sketch one model that has been offered for explaining these syndromes. Then, in the longest part of the chapter I will distinguish the two concepts of consciousness whose conflation is the root of the fallacious arguments. Once that is done, I will sketch what is wrong with the target reasoning and also what is right about it, and I will conclude with some remarks on how it is possible to investigate empirically what the function of consciousness is without having much of an idea about the scientific nature of consciousness.

2 Other Syndromes and Schacter's Model

To introduce a second blindsight-like syndrome, I want to first explain a syndrome that is not like blindsight: prosopagnosia (*prosop* = face, *agnosia* = neurological deficit in recognizing). Prosopagnosics are unable visually to recognize their closest relatives—even pictures of themselves—though usually they have no trouble recognizing their friends via their voices, or, according to anecdotal reports, visually recognizing people by recognizing characteristic motions of their bodies. Although there is wide variation from case to case, prosopagnosia is compatible with a high degree of visual ability, even in tasks involving faces.

One patient who has been studied by my colleagues in the Boston area is LH, a Harvard undergraduate who emerged from a car accident with very localized brain damage that left him unable to recognize even his mother. His girlfriend began to wear a special ribbon so that he would know who she was. Now, years later, he still cannot identify his mother or his wife and children from photographs (Etcoff et al. 1991). Still, if shown a photo and asked to choose another photo of the same person from a set of, say, five photos presented simultaneously with the original, LH can do almost as well as normal people despite differences between the target and matching photos in lighting, angle, and expression.

Now we are ready for the analog of blindsight. The phenomenon appears in many experimental paradigms, but I will mention only this: It has recently been discovered (by Sergent and Poncet 1990) that some prosopagnosics are very good at "guessing" as between two names in the same occupational category ("Reagan" and "Bush") of a person whose face they claim is unfamiliar. (See Young and de Haan 1993 and Young 1994a, 1994b for a description of these phenomena.) Interestingly, LH, the patient mentioned above, does not appear to have "covert knowledge" of the people whose faces he sees, but he does appear to have "covert knowledge" of their facial expressions (Etcoff et al. 1992).

Many such phenomena in brain-damaged patients have now been explored using the techniques of cognitive and physiological psychology. Further, there are a variety of such phenomena that occur in normals, you and me. For example, suppose that you are given a string of words and asked to count the vowels. This can be done so that you will have no conscious recollection or even recognition of the words and you will be unable to "guess" which words you have seen at a level above chance. However, if I give you a series of word-stems to complete according to your whim, your likelihood of completing "rea-" as "reason" is greater if "reason" is one of the words that you saw, even if you don't recall or recognize it as one of the words you saw.[1]

Recall that the target reasoning, the reasoning I will be saying is importantly confused (but also importantly right) is that since, when consciousness is missing, subjects cannot report or reason about the nonconscious representations or use them to guide action, a function of consciousness is to facilitate reasoning, reporting, and guiding action. This reasoning is *partially* captured in a model suggested by Daniel Schacter (1989; see also Schacter et al. 1988) in a paper reviewing phenomena such as the ones described above. Figure 9.1 is derived from Schacter's model.

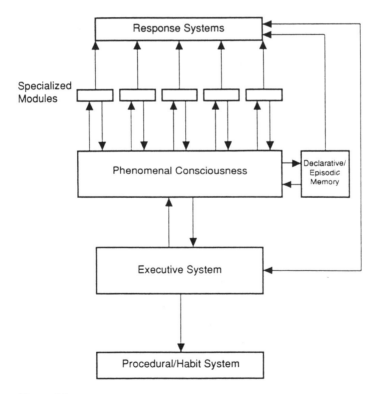

Figure 9.1

The model is only partial (i.e., it models some aspects of the mind, but not others), and so may be a bit hard to grasp for those who are used to seeing inputs and outputs. Think of the hands and feet as connected to the Response System box, and the eyes and ears as connected to the specialized modules. (See Schacter 1989, for some indication of how these suggestions are oversimple.) The key feature of the model is that it contains a box for something called "phenomenal consciousness"; I'll say more about phenomenal consciousness later, but for now, let me just say that phenomenal consciousness is experience; what makes a state phenomenally conscious is that there is something "it is like" (Nagel 1974) to be in that state. The model dictates that the phenomenal consciousness module has a function: it is the gateway between the special purpose "knowledge" modules and the central Executive System that is in charge of direct control of reasoning, reporting, and guiding action. So a function of consciousness on this model includes integrating the outputs of the specialized modules and transmitting the integrated contents to mechanisms of reasoning and control of action and reporting.

I will be using this model as a focus of discussion, but I hope that my endorsement of its utility as a focus of discussion will not be taken as an endorsement of the model itself. I have no commitment to a single executive system or even to a phenomenal consciousness module. One can accept the idea of phenomenal consciousness as distinct from any cognitive or functional or intentional notion while frowning on a modular treatment of it. Perhaps, for example, phenomenal consciousness is a feature of the whole brain.

Many thinkers will hate any model that treats phenomenal consciousness as something that could be accomplished by a distinct system.[2] I call that feature Cartesian Modularism, by analogy to the Cartesian Materialism of Dennett and Kinsbourne (1992a), the view that consciousness occupies a literal place in the brain. Modules are individuated by their function, so the point of the box's place between the specialized modules and the Executive System is to indicate that there is a single system that has the function of talking to the specialized modules and integrating their outputs, and talking to the Executive System, passing on information from the specialized modules. But there is an additional point in *calling* that system the phenomenal consciousness system, namely to say that phenomenal consciousness is somehow involved in performing that function. The idea is that phenomenal consciousness *really does* something: it is involved somehow in powering the wheels and pulleys of access to the Executive System. This is a substantive claim, one that is distinct from the claims that phenomenal consciousness is *correlated* with that information-processing function, or that phenomenal consciousness should be *identified* with that information-processing function. The idea is that phenomenal consciousness is distinct (at least conceptually) from that information-processing function, but is part of the implementation of it.

Martha Farah criticizes this model on the ground that we don't observe patients whose blindsight-like performance is up to the standard of normal vision. Blindsight and its analogs are always degraded in discriminatory capacity. Her assumption seems to be that if there is a phenomenal consciousness module, it could simply be bypassed without decrement in performance; and the fact that this is not observed is taken as reason to reject the phenomenal consciousness module. She appears to think that if there is a phenomenal consciousness module, then phenomenal consciousness *doesn't do any information processing* (except, I guess, for determining reports of phenomenal consciousness), for otherwise why assume that it could be bypassed without decrement in performance. But why assume that phenomenal consciousness doesn't do any information processing? For example, phenomenal consciousness might be like the water in a hydraulic computer. You don't expect the computer to just work normally without the water. Even if there could be an electrical computer that is isomorphic to the hydraulic computer but works without water, one should not conclude that the water in the hydraulic system does nothing. I will return to this issue later.

One reason that many philosophers would hate Cartesian Modularist models is that such models may be regarded as licensing the possibility of "zombies," creatures that have information processing that is the same as ours but that have no phenomenal consciousness. If the phenomenal consciousness module could be replaced by a device that had the same information-processing effects on the rest of the system, but without phenomenal consciousness, the result would be a zombie. My view is that we now know so little about the scientific nature of phenomenal consciousness and its function that we cannot judge whether the same function could be performed by an ersatz phenomenal consciousness module—that is, whether an ersatz phenomenal consciousness module could inject its representations with ersatz conscious content that would affect information processing the same way as real conscious content. There is much of interest to be said about this idea and its relation to other ideas that have been mentioned in the literature, but I have other fish to fry, so I leave the matter for another time.

The information-processing function of phenomenal consciousness in Schacter's model is the ground of the concept of consciousness that I will mainly be contrasting with phenomenal consciousness, what I will call "access-consciousness." A perceptual state is access-conscious roughly speaking if its content—what is represented by the perceptual state—is processed via that information-processing function, that is, if its content gets to the Executive System, whereby it can be used to control reasoning and behavior.

Schacter's model is useful for my purposes both because it can be used to illustrate the contrast between phenomenal and access-consciousness and because it allows us to see one possible explanation of the "covert knowledge" syndromes just described. This explanation (and also Schacter's model) are certainly incomplete and no doubt wildly oversimple at best, but it is nonetheless useful to see the rough outlines of how an account might go. In addition, there is an association between Schacter's model and the target reasoning—though as we shall see there is another processing model that perhaps better embodies the target reasoning.

Consider a blindsight patient who has just had a vertical line displayed in his blind field. "What did you see?" "Nothing," says the patient. "Guess as between a vertical and a horizontal line," says the experimenter. "Vertical," says the patient, correctly. Here's story about what happened. One of the specialized modules is specialized for spatial information; it has some information about the verticality of the stimulus. The pathways between this specialized module and the phenomenal consciousness system have been damaged, creating the "blind field," so the patient has no phenomenally conscious experience of the line, and hence his Executive System has no information about whether the line is vertical or horizontal. But the specialized module has a direct connection to the Response System, so when the subject is given a binary choice, the specialized module can somehow directly affect the response. Similarly, there is a specialized module for face information, which can have some identifying information about the face that has been presented to a prosopagnosic. If the prosopagnosia is caused by damage in the link between the face module and the phenomenal consciousness system, then that prevents the identifying face information from being phenomenally conscious, and without phenomenal consciousness, the Executive System does not get the information about the person behind the face. When the prosopagnosic guesses as between "Reagan and "Bush," the face module somehow directly controls the response. (It is assumed that the face module has information about people— e.g., their names—linked to representations of their faces.) It is interesting in this regard that the patients who do best in these experiments are the ones judged to be the most "passive" (Marcel 1983, p. 204; Weiskranz 1988). One can speculate that in a laid-back subject, the Executive does not try out a guessing strategy, and so peripheral systems are more likely to affect the response.

Alexia is a neurological syndrome whose victims can no longer read a word "at a glance," but can only puzzle out what word they have seen at a rate of, for example, a second per letter. Nonetheless, these subjects often show various kinds of understanding of the meanings of words that have been flashed far too briefly for them to read in their laborious way. The idea, once again, is that one of the specialized modules is specialized for lexical information, and this module has information about words that the subject cannot consciously read. This information somehow affects responses. Landis et al. (1980) report that such a patient actually became worse at "guesses" having to do with the meanings of "unread" words as his explicit reading ability improved (Young and de Haan 1993). Again, perhaps once the Executive has more information, it "takes over," preventing peripheral systems from controlling responses. Coslett and Saffran (1994) report that alexics did worse at "guessing" words with longer exposures.

An exposure of 250 ms was better than an exposure of 2 sec. Again, longer exposures may give the Executive System a chance to try to read letter by letter.

Schacter's model and the explanation I have just sketched are highly speculative; my purposes in appealing to them are heuristic.

3   Two Concepts of Consciousness

First, consider phenomenal consciousness, or P-consciousness, as I will call it. Let me acknowledge at the outset that I cannot define P-consciousness in any remotely non-circular way. I don't consider this an embarrassment. The history of reductive definitions in philosophy should lead one not to expect a reductive definition of anything. But the best one can do for P-consciousness is in some respects worse than for many other things because really all one can do is *point* to the phenomenon (cf. Goldman 1993a). Nonetheless, it is important to point properly. John Searle, acknowledging that consciousness cannot be defined noncircularly, defines it as follows:

By consciousness I simply mean those subjective states of awareness or sentience that begin when one wakes in the morning and continue throughout the period that one is awake until one falls into a dreamless sleep, into a coma, or dies or is otherwise, as they say, unconscious. (This comes from Searle 1990b; there is a much longer attempt along the same lines in his 1992, p. 83ff.)

I will argue that this sort of pointing is flawed because it points to too many things, too many different consciousnesses.

So how should we point to P-consciousness? Well, one way is via rough synonyms. As I said, P-consciousness is experience. P-conscious properties are experiential properties. P-conscious states are experiential states, that is, a state is P-conscious if it has experiential properties. The totality of the experiential properties of a state are "what it is like" to have it. Moving from synonyms to examples, we have P-conscious states when we see, hear, smell, taste, and have pains. P-conscious properties include the experiential properties of sensations, feelings, and perceptions, but I would also include thoughts, wants, and emotions.[3] A feature of P-consciousness that is often missed is that differences in intentional content often make a P-conscious difference. What it is like to hear a sound as coming from the left differs from what it is like to hear a sound as coming from the right. P-consciousness is often representational. (See Jackendoff 1987; van Gulick 1989; McGinn 1991, chapter 2; Flanagan, 1992, chapter 4; Goldman 1993b.) So far, I don't take myself to have said anything terribly controversial. The controversial part is that I take P-conscious properties to be distinct from any cognitive, intentional, or functional property. (Cognitive = essentially involving thought; intentional properties = properties in virtue of which a representation or state is about something; functional properties = e.g., properties definable in terms of a computer program. See Searle 1983 on intentionality; see Block 1980, 1994, for better characterizations of a functional property.) But I am trying hard to limit the controversiality of my assumptions. Though I believe that functionalism about P-consciousness is false, I will be trying not to rely on that view.[4]

It is of course P-consciousness rather than access-consciousness or self-consciousness that has seemed such a scientific mystery. The magazine *Discover* (November, 1992) devoted an issue to the ten great unanswered questions of science, such as "What is Consciousness?," "Does Chaos Rule the Cosmos?," and "How Big is the Universe?" The topic was P-consciousness, not, for example, self-consciousness.

By way of homing in on P-consciousness, it is useful to appeal to what may be a contingent property of it, namely the famous "explanatory gap." To quote T. H. Huxley (1866), "How it is that anything so remarkable as a state of consciousness comes about as a result of irritating nervous tissue, is just as unaccountable as the appearance of Djin when Aladdin rubbed his lamp." Consider a famous neurophysiological theory of P-consciousness offered by Francis Crick and Christof Koch: namely, that a synchronized 35- to 75-hertz neural oscillation in the sensory areas of the cortex is at the heart of phenomenal consciousness. No one has produced the concepts that would allow us to explain why such oscillations might be the physiological basis of phenomenal consciousness.

However, Crick and Koch have offered a sketch of an account of how the 35- to 75-hertz oscillation might contribute to a solution to the "binding problem." Suppose one simultaneously sees a red square moving to the right and a blue circle moving to the left. Different areas of the visual cortex are differentially sensitive to color, shape, motion, and so forth, so what binds together redness, squareness, and rightward motion? That is, why don't you see redness and blueness without seeing them as belonging with particular shapes and particular motions? And why aren't the colors normally seen as bound to the wrong shapes and motions? Representations of colors, shapes, and motions of a single object are supposed to involve oscillations that are in phase with one another but not with representations of other objects. But even if the oscillation hypothesis deals with the informational aspect of the binding problem (and there is some evidence against it), how does it explain *what it is like to see something as red in the first place*—or for that matter, as square or as moving to the right? Why couldn't there be brains functionally or physiologically just like ours, including oscillation patterns, whose owners' experience was different from ours or who had no experience at all? (Note that I don't say that there *could be* such brains. I just want to know *why not*.) And why is it a 35- to 75-hertz oscillation—as opposed to some other frequency—that underlies experience? if the synchronized neural oscillation idea pans out as a solution to the binding problem, no doubt there will be some answer to the question of why *those* frequencies, as opposed to, say 110 hertz, are involved. But will that answer explain why 110-hertz oscillations don't underlie experience? No one has a clue how to answer these questions.[5]

The explanatory gap in the case of P-consciousness contrasts with our relatively good understanding of cognition. We have two serious research programs into the nature of cognition, the classical "language-of-thought" paradigm, and the connectionist research program. Though no doubt there are many ideas missing in our understanding of cognition, we have no difficulty seeing how pursuing one or both of these research programs could lead to an adequate theoretical perspective on cognition. But it is not easy to see how current approaches to P-consciousness *could* yield an account of it. Indeed, what passes for research programs on consciousness just *is* a combination of cognitive psychology and explorations of neuropsychological syndromes that contain no theoretical perspective on what P-consciousness actually is.

I mentioned the explanatory gap partly by way of pointing at P-consciousness: *that's* the entity to which the mentioned explanatory gap applies. Perhaps this identification is contingent; at some time in the future, when we have the concepts to conceive of much more about the explanation of P-consciousness, this may not be a way of picking it out. (See McGinn 1991, for a more pessimistic view.)

What I've been saying about P-consciousness is of course controversial in a variety of ways, both for some advocates and some opponents of some notion of P-consciousness. I have tried to steer clear of some controversies, for example, controversies over inverted and absent qualia; over Jackson's Mary (the woman who is raised in a black and white room, learning all the physiological and functional facts about the brain and color vision, but nonetheless discovers a new fact when she goes outside the room for the first time and learns what it is like to see red); and even Nagel's view that we cannot know what it is like to be a bat.[6] Even if you think that P-consciousness as I have described it is an incoherent notion, you may be able to agree with the main point of this chapter, which is that a great deal of confusion arises as a result of confusing P-consciousness with something else. Not even the concept of what time it is now on the sun is so confused that it cannot itself be confused with something else.

4 Access Consciousness

I now turn to the nonphenomenal notion of consciousness that is most easily and dangerously conflated with P-consciousness: access-consciousness. I will characterize access-consciousness, give some examples of how it is at least possible to have access-consciousness without phenomenal consciousness and vice versa, and then go on to the main theme of the paper, the damage done by conflating the two.

A is access-consciousness. A state is A-conscious if it is poised for direct control of thought and action. To add more detail, a representation is A-conscious if it is poised for free use in reasoning and for direct "rational" control of action and speech. (The "rational" is meant to rule out the kind of control that obtains in blindsight.) An

A-state is one that consists in having an A-representation. I see A-consciousness as a cluster concept in which reportability is the element of the cluster that has the smallest weight even though it is often the best practical guide to A-consciousness.[7]

The interest in the A/P distinction arises from the battle between two different conceptions of the mind, the biological and the computational. The computational approarch supposes that all of the mind (including consciousness) can be captured with notions of information processing, computation and function in a system. According to this view (often called functionalism by philosophers), the level of abstraction for understanding the mind is one that allows multiple realizations, just as one computer can be realized electrically or hydraulically. Their bet is that the different realizations don't matter to the mind, generally, and to consciousness specifically. The biological approach bets that the realization does matter. If P = A, the information processing side is right. But if the biological nature of experience is crucial, then realizations *do* matter, and we can expect that P and A will diverge.

Although I make a firm distinction between A-consciousness and P-consciousness, I also want to insist that they interact. For example, what perceptual information is being accessed can change figure to ground and conversely, and a figure-ground switch can affect one's phenomenal state. For example, attending to the feel of the shirt on your neck, accessing those perceptual contents, switches what was in the background to the foreground, thereby changing one's phenomenal state. (See Hill 1991, pp. 118–126; Searle 1992.)

I will suggest that A-consciousness plays a deep role in our ordinary "consciousness" talk and thought. However, I must admit at the outset that this role allows for substantial indeterminacy in the concept itself. In addition, there are some loose ends in the characterization of the concept which cannot be tied up without deciding about certain controversial issues, to be mentioned below.[8] My guide in making precise the A-consciousness/P-consciousness distinction is to avoid trivial cases of A without P and P without A. The target reasoning (in one form) says that the blindsight patient lacks consciousness of stimuli in the blind field, and that is why he does not use information he actually has about these stimuli, so the function of consciousness must be to harness information for use in guiding action. (Maybe the blindsight patient does not lack P-consciousness of these stimuli, but the target reasoning supposes it, it is independently plausible, and I will consider later what happens if this assumption is wrong. For example, Cowie and Stoerig (1992) point out that the removal of primary visual cortex in these patients disrupts the Crick and Koch 40-Hz oscillations. That is some reason to believe that the blindsight patient lacks P-consciousness of the stimuli.) I will be pointing out that something *else* is also problematic in blindsight that can equally well be blamed for the blindsight patient's failure, namely the machinery of A-consciousness. Of course, the missing P-consciousness may be responsible for the missing A-consciousness; no fallacy is involved in that hypothesis. Rather, the fallacy is *sliding* from an obvious function of A-consciousness to an unobvious function of P-consciousness.

I will mention three main differences between P-consciousness and A-consciousness. The first point, *put crudely*, is that P-conscious content is phenomenal, whereas A-conscious content is representational. It is of the essence of A-conscious content to play a role in reasoning, and only representational content can figure in reasoning. The reason this way of putting the point is crude is that many phenomenal contents are *also* representational. So what I really want to say is that it is in virtue of its phenomenal content or the phenomenal aspect of its content that a state is P-conscious, whereas it is in virtue of its representational content, or the representational aspect of its content, that a state is A-conscious.[9]

(In the last paragraph, I used the notion of P-conscious *content*. The P-conscious content of a state is the totality of the state's experiential properties, what it is like to be in that state. One can think of the P-conscious content of a state as the state's experiential "value" by analogy to the representational content as the state's representational "value." In my view, the content of an experience can be both P-conscious and A-conscious; the former in virtue of its phenomenal feel and the latter in virtue of its representational properties.)

A closely related point: A-conscious states are necessarily transitive; A-conscious states must always be states of consciousness *of*. P-conscious states, by contrast, sometimes are and sometimes are not transitive. P-consciousness, as such, is not consciousness *of*. (I'll return to this point in a few paragraphs.)

Second, A-consciousness is a functional notion, and so A-conscious content is system-relative: what makes a state A-conscious is what a representation of its content does in a system. P-consciousness is not a functional notion.[10] In terms of Schacter's model, content gets to be P-conscious because of what happens *inside* the P-consciousness module. But what makes content A-conscious is not anything that could go on *inside* a module, but rather informational relations *among* modules. Content is A-conscious in virtue of (a representation with that content) reaching the Executive System, the system that is in charge of rational control of action and speech, and to that extent, we could regard the Executive module as the A-consciousness module. But to regard *anything* as an A-consciousness module is misleading, because what makes an A-conscious representation A-conscious is its causal relations to other representations.

A third difference is that there is such a thing as a P-conscious *type* or *kind* of state. For example the feel of pain is a P-conscious type—every pain must have that feel. But any particular token thought that is A-conscious at a given time could fail to be accessible at some other time, just as my car is accessible now, but will not be later when my wife has it. A state whose content is informationally promiscuous now may not be so later.

The paradigm P-conscious states are sensations, whereas the paradigm A-conscious states are "propositional attitude" states like thoughts, beliefs, and desires, states with representational content expressed by "that" clauses (e.g., the thought that grass is green). However, as I said, thoughts often are P-conscious and perceptual experiences often have representational content. For example, a perceptual experience may have the representational content *that there is a red square in front of me*. Even pain typically has *some* kind of representational content. Pains often represent something (the cause of the pain? the pain itself?) as somewhere (in the leg). A number of philosophers have taken the view that the content of pain is *entirely* representational. (See Dretske 1994; Shoemaker 1994; Tye 1995.) I don't agree with this view, so I certainly don't want to rely on it here, but I also don't want to make the existence of cases of P-consciousness without A-consciousness any kind of trivial consequence of an idiosyncratic set of definitions. To the extent that representationalism of the sort just mentioned is plausible, one can regard a pain as A-conscious if its representational content is inferentially promiscuous, and so forth. Alternatively, we could take the A-conscious content of pain to consist in the content that one has a pain or that one has a state with a certain phenomenal content.[11]

Note that the notion of *poised* in the characterization of A-consciousness is intermediate between actual use in reasoning, and so forth, and mere availability for use. You may have learned in elementary school that the sun is 93 million miles from the earth, and a representation of this fact is therefore available for use if re-activated, but that level of access doesn't make it either P-conscious or A-conscious. And if we required actual use, then there could not be a brief episode of A-consciousness which is wiped out by death, as could happen with P-consciousness. The whole idea of A-consciousness is to capture an information processing analog of P-consciousness, and that is the basis of the definition.

There is a familiar distinction, alluded to above, between "consciousness" in the sense in which we speak of a state as being a conscious state (intransitive consciousness) and consciousness *of* something (transitive consciousness). (See, e.g., Rosenthal 1986. Humphrey (1992) mentions that the intransitive usage is much more recent, only 200 years old.) It is easy to fall into an identification of P-consciousness with intransitive consciousness and a corresponding indentification of access-consciousness with transitive consciousness. Such an identification is oversimple. As I mentioned earlier, P-conscious contents can be representational. Consider a perceptual state of seeing a square. This state has a P-conscious content that represents something, a square, and thus it is a state of P-consciousness *of* the square. It is a state of P-consciousness of the square even if it doesn't represent the square *as* a square, as would be the case if the perceptual state is a state of an animal that doesn't have the concept of a square. Since there can be P-consciousness *of* something, P-consciousness is not to be identified with intransitive consciousness.

Here is a second reason why the transitive/intransitive distinction cannot be iden-tified with the A-consciousness/P-consciousness distinction: The *of*-ness required for transitivity does not guarantee that a content be utilizable by a *consuming* system at the level required for A-consciousness. For example, a perceptual state of a brain-damaged creature might be a state of P-consciousness of, say, motion, even though connections to reasoning and rational control of action are damaged so that the state is not A-conscious. In sum, P-consciousness can be consciousness of, and conscious-ness of need not be A-consciousness.[12]

Those who are uncomfortable about P-consciousness should pay close attention to A-consciousness because it is a good candidate for a reductionist identification with P-consciousness.[13]

A-Consciousness without P-Consciousness

Since the main point of this chapter is that these two concepts of consciousness are easily confused, it will pay us to consider conceptually possible cases of one without the other. Actual cases will be more controversial.

First, I will give some examples of A-consciousness without P-consciousness. If there could be a full-fledged phenomenal zombie, say a robot computationally identical to a person, but whose silicon brain did not support P-consciousness, that would do the trick. I think such cases conceptually possible, but this is very controversial, and I am trying to avoid controversial assumptions. (See Shoemaker 1975, 1981.)

But there is a less controversial kind of case, a very limited sort of partial zombie. Consider the blindsight patient who "guesses" that there is an X rather than an O in his blind field. Taking his word for it (for the moment), I am assuming that he has no P-consciousness of the X. As I mentioned, I am following the target reasoning here, but as I will point out later, my own argument does not depend on this as-sumption. I am certainly *not* assuming that lack of A-consciousness guarantees lack of P-consciousness—that is, I am not assuming that if you don't say it you haven't got it.

The blindsight patient also has no X-representing A-conscious content, because al-though the information that there is an X affects his "guess," it is not available as a premise in reasoning (until he has the quite distinct state of hearing and believing his own guess), or for rational control of action or speech. Recall Marcel's point that the thirsty blindsight patient would not reach for a glass of water in the blind field. So the blindsight patient's perceptual or quasi-perceptual state is unconscious in the phenom-enal *and* access senses (*and* in the monitoring senses to be mentioned below, too).

Now imagine something that may not exist, what we might call *super-blindsight*. A real blindsight patient can only guess when given a choice from a small set of alterna-tives (X/O; horizontal/vertical, etc.). But suppose—interestingly, apparently contrary to fact—that a blindsight patient could be trained to prompt himself at will, guessing what is in the blind field without being told to guess. The super-blindsighter spontaneously says "Now I know that there is a horizontal line in my blind field even though I don't actually see it." Visual information from his blind field simply pops into his thoughts in the way that solutions to problems we've been worrying about pop into our thoughts, or in the way some people just know the time or which way is north without having any perceptual experience of it. The super-blindsighter himself contrasts what it is like to know visually about an X in his blind field and an X in his sighted field. There is something it is like to experience the latter, but not the former, he says. It is the difference between *just knowing* and knowing via a visual experience. Taking his word for it, here is the point: the content that there is an X in his visual field is A-conscious but not P-conscious. The super-blindsight case is a very limited partial zombie.[14]

Of course, the super-blindsighter has a *thought* that there is an X in his blind field that is *both* A-conscious and P-conscious, but I am not talking about the thought. Rather, I am talking about the state of his perceptual system that gives rise to the thought. It is this state that is A-conscious without being P-conscious.[15]

Is there *actually* such a thing as super-blindsight? Humphrey (1992) describes a monkey (Helen) who despite *near* total loss of the visual cortex could nonetheless act in a somewhat visually normal way in certain circumstances, without any "prompting." One reason to doubt that Helen is a case of super-blindsight is that Helen may be a case of *sight*. There was some visual cortex left, and the situations in which she showed unprompted visual discrimination were ones in which there was no control of where the stimuli engaged her retina. Another possibility mentioned by Cowie and Stoerig (1992—attributed to an unpublished paper by Humphrey), is that there were P-conscious sensory events, though perhaps auditory in nature. Helen appeared to confuse brief tones with visual stimuli. Cowie and Stoerig propose a number of ways of getting information out of monkeys that are close to what we get out of blindsighted humans. Weiskrantz (1992) mentions that a patient GY sometimes knows that there is a stimulus (though not what it is) without, he says, seeing anything. But GY also seems to be having some kind of P-conscious sensation. (See Cowie and Stoerig 1992.)

The (apparent) nonexistence of super-blindsight is a striking fact, one that a number of writers have noticed. Indeed, it is the basis for the target reasoning. After all, what Marcel was in effect pointing out was that the blindsight patients, in not reaching for a glass of water, are not super-blindsighters. As I mentioned, Farah (see chapter 11) says that blindsight (and blind perception generally) turns out always to be degraded. In other words, blind perception is never super-blind perception.[16]

I don't know whether there are any actual cases of A-consciousness without P-consciousness, but I hope that I have illustrated their conceptual possibility.

P-Consciousness without A-Consciousness

Consider an animal that you are happy to think of as having P-consciousness for which brain damage has destroyed centers of reasoning and rational control of action, thus preventing A-consciousness. It certainly seems *conceptually possible* that the neural bases of P-consciousness systems and A-consciousness systems be distinct, and if they are distinct, then it is possible, at least conceptually possible, for one to be damaged while the other is working well. Evidence has been accumulating for twenty-five years that the primate visual system has distinct dorsal and ventral subsystems. Though there is much disagreement about the specializations of the two systems, it does appear that much of the information in the ventral system is much more closely connected to P-consciousness than information in the dorsal system (Goodale and Milner 1992). So it may actually be possible to damage A-consciousness without P-consciousness and conversely.[17]

Further, one might suppose (Rey 1983, 1988; White 1987) that some of our own subsystems—say each of the two hemispheres of the brain—might themselves be separately P-conscious. Some of these subsystems might also be A-consciousness, but other subsystems might not have sufficient machinery for reasoning or reporting or rational control of action to allow their P-conscious states to be A-conscious; so if those states are not accessible to another system that does have adequate machinery, they will be P-conscious but not A-conscious.

Here is another reason to believe in P-consciousness without A-consciousness: Suppose that you are engaged in intense conversation when suddenly at noon you realize that right outside your window, there is—and has been for some time—a pneumatic drill digging up the street. You were aware of the noise all along, one might say, but only at noon are you *consciously aware* of it. That is, you were P-conscious of the noise all along, but at noon you are both P-conscious *and* A-conscious of it. Of course, there is a very similar string of events in which the crucial event at noon is a bit more intellectual. In this alternative scenario, at noon you realize not just that there is and has been a noise, but also that *you are now and have been hearing* the noise. In this alternative scenario, you get "higher-order thought" as well as A-consciousness at noon. So on the first scenario, the belief that is acquired at noon is that there is and has been a noise, and on the second scenario, the beliefs that are acquired at noon are the first one plus the belief that you are and have been hearing the noise. But it is the first scenario, not the second, that interests me. It is a good case of P-consciousness without A-consciousness. Only at noon is the content of your representation of the drill *poised* for use in rational control of action and speech. (Note that A-consciousness requires being poised, not merely available for use.)

In addition, this case involves a natural use of "conscious" and "aware" for A-consciousness and P-consciousness, respectively. "Conscious" and "aware" are more or less synonymous, so calling the initial P-consciousness "awareness" makes it natural to call the later P-consciousness plus A-consciousness "conscious awareness." Of course I rely here on introspection, but when it comes to P-consciousness, introspection is an important source of insight.[18] This case of P-consciousness without A-consciousness exploits what William James (1890) called "secondary consciousness" (at least I think it does; James scholars may know better), a category that he may have meant to include cases of P-consciousness without attention.[19]

I have found that the argument of the last paragraph makes those who are distrustful of introspection uncomfortable. I agree that introspection is not the last word, but it is the first word, when it comes to P-consciousness. The example shows the conceptual distinctness of P-consciousness from A-consciousness and it also puts the burden of proof on anyone who would argue that as a matter of empirical fact they come to the same thing.

The difference between different concepts of consciousness gives rise to different types of *zombie*. We have already encountered the phenomenal zombies that appear in science-fiction and philosophers' examples—the familiar computers and robots that think but don't feel. Their states are A-conscious, but not P-conscious. However, our culture also acknowledges the concept of voodoo zombies and zombies in *Night of the Living Dead*. If we find that voodoo zombies are cognitively or affectively diminished, say without will, rather than phenomenally diminished, we would not decide that they were not zombies after all. And on seeing the next installment in the "Living Dead" series, we would not feel that our concept of a zombie had been toyed with if it turned out that there is something it is like for these zombies to eat their relatives. (They say "yumm!") No doubt we have no very well formed zombie-concept, but the considerations just mentioned motivate the view that a zombie is something that is mentally dead in one respect or another, and the different respects give rise to different zombies.

Kathleen Akins (1993) has argued against the distinction between a phenomenal and a representational aspect of experience. She asks the reader to look around his or her office, noting what it is like to have that experience. Then she challenges the reader to imagine that "a bat's consciousness is just like that—the feel of the scene is exactly the same—except, of course, all those visual sensations mean something quite different to the bat. They represent quite different properties. Imagine that!" She goes on to say, "The problem is that you cannot imagine that, no matter how hard you try" (p. 267). Of course, she is right that you cannot imagine that. But the explanation of this fact is not that there is no distinction between the P-conscious and representational aspects of experience. The explanation is that, as I said earlier, many representational differences themselves *make* a P-conscious difference. To repeat the example given earlier, what it is like to hear a sound as coming from the left is different from what it is like to hear a sound as coming from the right. Or suppose that you are taken to what appears to be a town from the Old West; then you are told that it is a backdrop for a

film and that what appear to be buildings are mere fronts. This representational difference can make a difference in what the buildings look like to you. A visual experience
as of a facade differs from a visual experience as of a building, even if the retinal image
is the same. Or consider the difference in what it is like to hear sounds in French before
and after you have learned the language (McCullough 1993).

Flanagan (1992) criticizes my notion of A-consciousness, suggesting that we replace
it with a more liberal notion of informational sensitivity that counts the blindsight patient as having access-consciousness of the stimuli in his blind field. The idea is that
the blindsight patient has *some* access to the information about the stimuli in the blind
field, and that amount of access is enough for access consciousness. Of course the
notion of A-consciousness that I have framed is just one of a family of access notions.
But there is more than a verbal issue here. The real question is what good is A-
consciousness as I have framed it in relation to the blindsight issue? The answer is that
in blindsight, the patient is supposed to *lack* "consciousness" of the stimuli in the
blind field. My point is that the blindsighter lacks both P-consciousness and a kind of
access, and that these are easily confused. This point is not challenged by pointing out
that the blindsight patient also has a lower level of access to this information.

The kind of access that I have built into A-consciousness plays a role in theory outside of this issue and in daily life. Consider the Freudian unconscious. Suppose I have a
Freudian unconscious desire to kill my father and marry my mother. Nothing in Freudian theory requires that this desire be P-unconscious; for all Freudians should care, it
might be P-conscious. What is the key to the desire being Freudianly unconscious is
that it come out in slips, dreams, and the like, but *not* be freely available as a premise
in reasoning (in virtue of having the unconscious desire) and that it not be freely available to guide action and reporting. Coming out in slips and dreams *makes it conscious in
Flanagan's sense*, so that sense of access is no good for capturing the Freudian idea. But
it is unconscious in my A-sense. If I can just tell you that I have a desire to kill my
father and marry my mother (and not as a result of therapy), then it isn't an
unconscious state in Freud's sense. Similar points can be made about a number of
the syndromes talked about above. For example, prosopagnosia is a disorder of A-
consciousness, not P-consciousness and not Flanagan's informational sensitivity. We
count someone as a prosopagnosic even when he or she is able to guess at a better
than chance level whom the face belongs to, so that excludes Flanagan's notion. Further, P-consciousness is irrelevant, and that excludes P-consciousness as a criterion. It
isn't the presence or absence of a feeling of familiarity that defines prosopagnosia, but
rather the patient not knowing whose face he is seeing or whether he knows that
person.

To see this, consider the Capgras delusion, a syndrome in which patients claim that
people they know (usually relatives) have been replaced by doubles who look just like
them. (There is a closely related syndrome, reduplicative paramnesia, in which patients

claim that they are in a hospital which is a duplicate of another hospital that they have been in.) Young (1994c) suggests that perhaps what is going on in this syndrome is that a patient recognizes, for example, his mother, but he has no feeling of familiarity, so he thinks that perhaps his mother is a victim of something out of "Invasion of the Body Snatchers." (Actually, it is interesting to note that victims of Capgras syndrome almost never call the FBI or do any of the things someone might do if he really thought his mother was replaced by an extraterrestrial duplicate.) Suppose that this is right. Notice that this patient is not thereby a prosopagnosic. He recognizes his mother's face, he can learn to recognize new faces, and so forth. So loss of the P-conscious feeling of familiarity is not sufficient for prosopagnosia.[20]

I am now just about finished justifying and explaining the difference between P-consciousness and A-consciousness. However, there is one objection I feel I should comment on. The contrast between P-consciousness and A-consciousness was in part based on the distinction between representational and phenomenal content. Put crudely, I said, the difference was that P-conscious content is phenomenal, whereas A-conscious content is representational. I said this was crude because many phenomenal contents are also representational. Some will object that phenomenal content just *is* a kind of representational content. (Dretske 1994, and Tye 1994, forthcoming, take this line; Shoemaker 1994 has a more moderate version. The representational/phenomenal distinction is discussed in Jackson 1977, Shoemaker 1981, and Peacocke 1983.) My reply is first that phenomenal content need not be representational at all (my favorite example is the phenomenal content of orgasm). Second, suppose I have an auditory experience as of something overhead, and simultaneously have a visual experience as of something overhead. I'm imagining a case where one has an impression only of where the thing is without an impression of other features. For example, in the case of the visual experience, one catches a glimpse of something overhead without any impression of a specific shape or color. (So the difference cannot be ascribed to further representational differences.) The phenomenal contents of both experiences represent something as being overhead, but not in virtue of a common phenomenal quality of the experiences. Note that the point is *not* just that there is a representational overlap without a corresponding phenomenal overlap (as is said, e.g., in Pendlebury 1992). That would be compatible with the following story (offered to me by Michael Tye): phenomenal content is just one kind of representational content, but these experiences overlap in nonphenomenal representational content. The point, rather, is that there is a modal difference that isn't at all a matter of representation, but rather is a matter of how those modes of representation feel. Or so I would argue. The look and the sound are both *as of something overhead*, but the two phenomenal contents represent this via different phenomenal qualities. (There is also a line of thought about the phenomenal/representational distinction that involves versions of the traditional "inverted spectrum" hypothesis. (See Shoemaker 1981b, 1993; Block 1990a.))

I am finished sketching the contrast between P-consciousness and A-consciousness. In the remainder of this section, I will briefly discuss two cognitive notions of consciousness, so that they are firmly distinguished from both P-consciousness and A-consciousness. Then in the next section, I will examine some conflations of P-consciousness and A-consciousness, so if you don't feel you have a perfect grasp of the distinction, you have another chance.

Self-Consciousness

By this term, I mean the possession of the concept of the self and the ability to use this concept in thinking about oneself. A number of higher primates show signs of recognizing that they see themselves in mirrors. They display interest in correspondences between their own actions and the movements of their mirror images. By contrast, dogs treat their mirror images as strangers at first, slowly habituating. In one experimental paradigm, experimenters painted colored spots on the foreheads and ears of anesthetized primates, watching what happened. Chimps between ages 7 and 15 usually try to wipe the spot off (Povinelli 1994; Gallup 1982). Monkeys do not do this, according to published reports as of 1994. Human babies don't show similar behavior until the last half of their second year. Perhaps this is a test for self-consciousness. (Or perhaps it is only a test for understanding mirrors; but what is involved in understanding mirrors if not that it is oneself one is seeing?) But even if monkeys and dogs have no self-consciousness, no one should deny that they have P-conscious pains, or that there is something it is like for them to see their reflections in the mirror. P-conscious states often seem to have a "me-ishness" about them, the phenomenal content often represents the state as a state of me. But this fact does not at all suggest that we can reduce P-consciousness to self-consciousness, since such "me-ishness" is the same in states whose P-conscious content is different. For example, the experience as of red is the same as the experience as of green in self-orientation, but the two states are different in phenomenal feel.[21]

The word "conscious" is often used to mean self-consciousness though often one sees some allusion to P-consciousness. For example, a Time-Life book on the mind (1993) says: "No mental characteristic is so mysterious and elusive—or so fundamentally human—as consciousness, the self-awareness that attends perceiving, thinking, and feeling."

Monitoring Consciousness

The idea of consciousness as some sort of internal monitoring takes many forms. One notion is that of some sort of inner perception. This could be a form of P-consciousness, namely P-consciousness of one's own states or of the self. Another notion is often put in information-processing terms: internal scanning. And a third, metacognitive notion, is that of higher-order thought: a conscious state in this sense is a state accompanied by a thought to the effect that one is in that state. The thought must be arrived at nonobservationally and noninferentially. Otherwise, as Rosenthal points out, the higher-order thought definition would get the wrong result for the case in which I come to know about my anger by inferring it from my own behavior.[22] Given my liberal terminological policy, I have no objection to any of these notions as notions of consciousness. Where I balk is at attempts to identify P-consciousness with any of these cognitive notions.

To identify P-consciousness with internal scanning is just to grease the slide to eliminativism about P-consciousness. Indeed, as Georges Rey (1983) has pointed out, ordinary laptop computers are capable of various types of self-scanning, but as he also points out, no one would think of their laptop computer as "conscious" (using the term in the ordinary way, without making any of the distinctions I've introduced). Since, according to Rey, internal scanning is essential to consciousness, he concludes that the concept of consciousness is incoherent. The trouble here is the failure to make distinctions of the sort I've been making. Even if the laptop has "internal scanning consciousness," it nonetheless lacks P-consciousness.[23]

The concepts of consciousness which this paper is mainly about (P-consciousness and A-consciousness) differ in their logics from the consciousnesses just mentioned, self-consciousness and monitoring consciousness. A distinction is often made between the sense of 'conscious' in which a person or other creature is conscious and the sense in which a state of mind is a conscious state. What it is for there to be something it is like to be me, that is for me to be P-conscious, is for me to have one or more states that are P-conscious. If a person is in a dreamless sleep, and then has a P conscious pain, he is to that extent P-conscious. For P-consciousness, it is states that are primary. In the case of self-consciousness and reflective consciousness, however, creature consciousness is basic. What it is for a pain to be reflectively conscious is, for example, for the person whose pain it is to have another state that is about that pain. And it is creatures who can think about themselves. It is not even clear what a self-conscious state would *be*. A-consciousness is intermediate between P on the one hand and self and monitoring consciousness on the other. No state is A-conscious in virtue of its intrinsic properties; what makes it A-conscious is what it controls. But it is not clear that a whole creature is necessary for A-consciousness.

Perhaps you are wondering why I am being so terminologically liberal, counting P-consciousness, A-consciousness, monitoring consciousness, and self-consciousness all as types of consciousness. Oddly, I find that many critics wonder why I would count *phenomenal* consciousness as consciousness, whereas many others wonder why I would count *access* or *monitoring* or *self*-consciousness as consciousness. In fact two reviewers of this chapter complained about my terminological liberalism, but for incompatible reasons. One reviewer said: "While what he uses ["P-consciousness"] to refer to—the "what it is like" aspect of mentality—seems to me interesting and important, I suspect that the discussion of it under the heading "consciousness" is a source of confusion ... he is right to distinguish access-consciousness (which is what I think deserves the name "consciousness") from this." Another reviewer said: "I really still can't see why access is called ... access-consciousness? Why isn't access just ... a purely information processing (functionalist) analysis?" This is not a merely verbal matter. In my view, all of us, despite our explicit verbal preferences, have some tendency to use "conscious" and related words in both ways, and our failure to see this causes a good deal of difficulty in thinking about "consciousness." This point will be illustrated below.

I've been talking about different concepts of consciousness and I've also said that *the* concept of consciousness is a mongrel concept. Perhaps, you are thinking, I should make up my mind. My view is that "consciousness" is actually an ambiguous word, though the ambiguity I have in mind is not one that I've found in any dictionary. I started the paper with an analogy between "consciousness" and "velocity," and I think there is an important similarity. One important difference, however, is that in the case of "velocity," it is easy to get rid of the temptation to conflate the two senses. With "consciousness," there is a tendency toward "now you see it, now you don't." I think the main reason for this is that P-consciousness presents itself to us in a way that makes it hard to imagine how a conscious state could fail to be accessible and self-reflective, so it is easy to fall into habits of thought that do not distinguish these concepts.[24]

The chief alternative to the ambiguity hypothesis is that there is a single concept of consciousness that is a *cluster concept*. For example, a prototypical religion involves belief in supernatural beings, sacred and profane objects, rituals, a moral code, religious feelings, prayer, a world view, an organization of life based on the world view, and a social group bound together by the previous items (Alston 1967). But for all of these items, there are actual or possible religions that lack them. For example, some forms of Buddhism do not involve belief in a supreme being and Quakers have no sacred objects. It is convenient for us to use a concept of religion that binds together a number of disparate concepts whose referents are often found together.

The distinction between ambiguity and cluster concept can be drawn in a number of equally legitimate ways that classify some cases differently. That is, there is some indeterminacy in the distinction. Some might even say that *velocity* is a cluster concept because for many purposes it is convenient to group average and instantaneous velocity together. I favor tying the distinction to the clear and present danger of conflation, especially in the form of equivocation in an argument. Of course, this is no analysis, since equivocation is definable in terms of ambiguity. My point, rather, is that one can make up one's mind about whether there is ambiguity by finding equivocation hard to deny. I will give some examples of conflations in what follows, and there is, I claim, a real-life case of equivocation on the senses of "consciousness" that I have distinguished in an argument in Dennett (1991).[25]

When I called *consciousness* a mongrel concept I was not declaring allegiance to the cluster theory. Rather, what I had in mind was that an ambiguous word often corresponds to an ambiguous mental representation, one that functions in thought as a unitary entity and thereby misleads. These are mongrels. I would also describe *velocity* and *degree of heat* (as used by the Florentine experimenters of the seventeenth century) as mongrel concepts. This is the grain of truth in the cluster-concept theory.

5 Conflations

Conflation of P-consciousness and A-consciousness is ubiquitous in the burgeoning literature on consciousness, especially in the literature on syndromes like blindsight. Nearly every article I read on the subject by philosophers and psychologists involves some confusion. For example, Baars (1988) makes it abundantly clear that he is talking about P-consciousness. "What is a theory of consciousness a theory of? In the first instance ... it is a theory of the nature of experience. The reader's private experience of *this* word, his or her mental image of yesterday's breakfast, or the feeling of a toothache—these are all contents of consciousness" (p. 14). Yet his theory is a "global workspace" model appropriate to A-consciousness. Shallice (1988a, 1988b) says he is giving an account of "phenomenal experience," but actually gives an information-processing theory appropriate to A-consciousness. (His 1988b is about an "information-processing model of consciousness.") Mandler (1985) describes consciousness in P-conscious terms like "phenomenal" and "experience" but gives a totally cognitive account appropriate to A-consciousness. Edelman's (1989) theory is also intended to explain P-consciousness, but it seems a theory of access-consciousness and self-consciousness; see Chalmers (1996). Kosslyn and Koenig (1992) say, "We will address here the everyday sense of the term ["consciousness"]; it refers to the phenomenology of experience, the feeling of red and so forth" (pp. 431–433; I am indebted to Michael Tye for calling this quotation to my attention). But then they give a "parity check" theory that seems more of a theory of monitoring consciousness or A-consciousness.

One result of conflating P-consciousness with other consciousnesses is a tendency to regard ideas as plausible that should be seen as way out on a limb. For example, Johnson-Laird (1988, pp. 360–361) talks of consciousness, using terms like "subjective experience." He goes on to hypothesize that consciousness is a matter of building models of the self and models of the self building models of itself, and so on. This hypothesis has two strikes against it, as should be obvious if one is clear about the distinction between P-consciousness and self-consciousness. Dogs and babies may not build such complex models, but the burden of proof is surely on anyone who doubts that they have P-consciousness.

Another example: In a discussion of phenomena of implicit perception, Kihlstrom et al. (1992) make it clear that the phenomena concern P-consciousness: "In the final

analysis, consciousness is a phenomenal quality that may accompany perception ...''
(p. 42). But they claim that self-consciousness is precisely what is lacking in implicit
perception: "This connection to the self is just what appears to be lacking in the phenomena of implicit perception.... When contact occurs between the representation of
the event—what might be called the "fact node" and the representation of oneself—
what might be called the 'self-node,' the event comes into consciousness" (p. 42). But
again, as we go down the phylogenetic scale we may well encounter creatures that are
P-conscious but have no "self-node," and the same may be true of the very young of
our own species. What should be announced as a theory that conflicts with common
sense, that P-consciousness arises from representing the self, can appear innocuous if
one is not careful to make the distinctions among the consciousnesses.

Andrade (1993) makes it clear that the concern is P-consciousness. For example,
"Without consciousness, there is no pain. There may be tissue damage, and physiological responses to tissue damage, but there will not be the phenomenological experience
of pain" (p. 13). Considering work on control by a central Executive System, Andrade
(correctly, I think) takes the dominant theories to "identify" consciousness with central executive control. "Current psychological theories identify consciousness with
systems that coordinate lower-level information processing." But there are two very
different paths to such an identification: (1) conflating P-consciousness with A-
consciousness and theorizing about A-consciousness in terms of the systems Andrade
mentions, (2) clearly distinguishing P-consciousness from A-consciousness and hypothesizing that the mechanisms that underlie the latter give rise to the former. I
doubt that any objective reader of this literature will think that the hypothesis of
path 2 is often very likely.

In the writings of some psychologists, assimilation of P-consciousness to A-
consciousness is a product of the (admirable) desire to be able to *measure* P-
consciousness. Jacoby et al. (1992) assimilate P-consciousness to A-consciousness for
that reason. Their subject matter is perception without "subjective experience," in normal perceivers in conditions of divided attention or degraded presentations. In other
words, perception without P-consciousness, what is often known as subliminal perception. They note that it is very difficult to disentangle conscious perception from unconscious perception because no one has conceived of an experimental paradigm that
isolates one of these modes. "We avoid this problem," they say, "by inferring awareness ["subjective experience"—N. B.] from conscious control and defining unconscious influences as effects that cannot be controlled" (p. 108). The effect of this
procedure is to definitionally disallow phenomenal events that have no effect on later
mental processes and to definitionally type phenomenal events by appeal to judgments made on the basis of them. "Subjective experience," they say, "results from an
attribution process in which mental events are interpreted in the context of current circumstances" (p. 112). I am reminded of an article in the sociology of science that I

once read that defined the quality of a scientific paper as the number of references to it in the literature. Operational definitions do no good if the result is measuring something *else*.

Schacter (1989) is explicit about what he means by "consciousness" (which he often calls "conscious awareness"), namely P-consciousness. He mentions that the sense he has in mind is that of "phenomenal awareness ... 'the running span of subjective experience'" (quoting Dimond 1976), and consciousness in his sense is repeatedly contrasted with information-processing notions. Nonetheless, in an effort to associate the "Conscious Awareness System" (what I call the phenomenal consciousness system in my labeling of his model in figure 9.1) with the inferior parietal lobes, he says that lesions in this area

have also been associated with confusional states, which are characterized by disordered thought, severe disorientation, and a breakdown of selective attention—in short, a global disorder of conscious awareness ... Several lines of evidence indicate that lesions to certain regions of the parietal lobes can produce disorders of conscious awareness. First, global confusional states have been reported in right parietal patients.... Second, the syndrome of anosognosia—unawareness and denial of a neuropsychological deficit—is often associated with parietal damage.... Anosognosic patients ... may be unaware of motor deficits ... perceptual deficits ... and complete unawareness can be observed even when the primary deficit is severe. (1988, p. 371)

Here, Schacter reverts to a use of "consciousness" and "awareness" in a variety of cognitive senses. Disordered thought, disorientation, and a breakdown of selective attention are not primarily disorders of P-consciousness. Further, anosognosia is primarily a defect in A-consciousness, not P-consciousness. Anosognosia is a neurological syndrome that involves an inability to acknowledge or have access to information about another neurological syndrome. A patient might have anosognosia for, say, his prosopagnosia while complaining incessantly about another deficit. Young (1994a) describes a woman who was a painter before becoming prosopagnosic. Looking at portraits she had painted, trying to figure out whom they represented, she laboriously figured out whom each painting was of, reasoning out loud about the person's apparent age, sex, and any significant objects in the picture, plus her verbal memories of the portraits that she had painted. When the experimenter commented on her prosopagnosia, she said that she "had recognized them," and did not think that there was anything odd about her laborious reasoning.[26]

The crucial feature of anosognosia about prosopagnosia is that the patient's access to information about her own inability to recognize faces is in some way blocked. She cannot report this inability or reason about it or use information about it to control her action. In addition to this A-consciousness problem, there may also be some defect of P-consciousness. Perhaps everyone looks familiar or no one looks familiar, or perhaps there are no visual feelings of familiarity that are distinct from feelings of unfamiliarity. Whatever the answer to the issue of familiarity, this issue of P-consciousness is not crucial to the syndrome, as is shown by the fact that we confidently ascribe ano-sognosia on the basis of the patient's cognitive state—the lack of knowledge of the deficit—without knowing what defects of P-consciousness may or may not be in-volved. Further, the same defects of P-consciousness could be present in a *nonanosog-nosic* prosopagnosic without discrediting the patient's status as nonanosognosic. One can imagine such a person saying, "Gosh, I don't recognize anyone—in fact, I no longer have a visual sense of the difference between familiar and unfamiliar faces." This would be prosopagnosia *without* anosognosia. To take anosognosia as primarily a defect of P-consciousness is a mistake.[27]

I don't think these conflations cause any real problem in Schacter's theorizing, but as a general rule, if you want to get anywhere in theorizing about X you should have a good pretheoretical grip on the difference between X and things that are easily con-fused with it.

Daniel Dennett (1986, 1991) provides another example of conflation of a number of concepts of consciousness. (See Block 1993.) I will focus on Dennett's claim that con-sciousness is a cultural construction. He theorizes that "human consciousness (1) is too recent an innovation to be hard-wired into the innate machinery, (2) is largely the product of cultural evolution that gets imparted to brains in early training" (1991, p. 219). Sometimes he puts the point in terms of memes, which are ideas such as the idea of the wheel or the calendar. Memes are the smallest cultural units that replicate themselves reliably, viz., cultural analogs of genes. In these terms then, Dennett's claim is that "human consciousness is *itself* a huge complex of memes" (1991, p. 210). This view is connected with Dennett's idea that you can't have consciousness without hav-ing the concept of consciousness. He says consciousness is like love and money in this regard, though in the case of money, what is required for one to have money is that *someone* have the concept of money (1991, p. 24; 1986, p. 152).

I think the reason Dennett says "largely" the product of cultural evolution is that he thinks of consciousness as the software that operates on genetically determined hard-ware that is the product of biological evolution. Though consciousness requires the concept of consciousness, with consciousness as with love, there is a biological basis without which the software could not run.

Now I hope it is obvious that P-consciousness is not a cultural construction. Remem-ber, we are talking about P-consciousness itself, not the concept of P-consciousness. The idea would be that there was a time at which people genetically like us ate, drank, and had sex, but there was nothing it was like for them to do these things. Further, each of us would have been like that if not for specific concepts we acquired from our culture in growing up. Ridiculous! Of course, culture *affects* P-consciousness; the won-drous experience of drinking a great wine takes training to develop. But culture affects feet too; people who have spent their lives going barefoot in the Himalayas have feet that differ from those of people who have worn tight shoes 18 hours a day. We mustn't confuse the idea that culture *influences* consciousness with the idea that it (largely) creates it.

What about A-consciousness? Could there have been a time when humans who are biologically the same as us never had the contents of their perceptions and thoughts poised for free use in reasoning or in rational control of action? Is this ability one that culture imparts to us as children? Turning to Dennett's doctrine that you can't be conscious without having the concept of consciousness: Could it be that until we acquired the concept of *poised for free use in reasoning or in rational control of action*, none of our perceptual contents were A-conscious? Again, there is no reason to take such an idea seriously. Very many lower animals are A-conscious, presumably without any such concept.

A-consciousness is as close as we get to the official view of consciousness in *Consciousness Explained* (Dennett 1991) and in later writings, for example, Dennett (1993). The official theory of Dennett (1991) is the Multiple Drafts Theory, the view that there are distinct parallel tracks of representation that vie for access to reasoning, verbalization, and behavior. This seems a theory of A-consciousness if any kind of consciousness. Dennett (1993) says "Consciousness is cerebral celebrity—nothing more and nothing less. Those contents are conscious that persevere, that monopolize resources long enough to achieve certain typical and "symptomatic" effects—on memory, on the control of behavior, and so forth" (p. 929). Could it be anything other than a biological fact about humans that some brain representations persevere enough to affect memory, control behavior, and so forth? So on the closest thing to Dennett's official kind of consciousness, the thesis (that consciousness is a cultural construction) is no serious proposal.

What about monitoring consciousness? No doubt there was a time when people were less introspective than some of us are now. But is there any evidence that there was a time when people genetically like us had no capacity to think or express the thought that one's leg hurts? To be able to think this thought involves being able to think that one's leg hurts, and that is a higher-order thought of the sort that is a plausible candidate for monitoring consciousness (Rosenthal 1986). Here for the first time we do enter the realm of actual empirical questions, but without some very powerful evidence for such a view, there is no reason to give it any credence. Dennett gives us not the slightest hint of the kind of weird evidence that we would need to begin to take this claim seriously, and so it would be a disservice to so interpret him.

What about self-consciousness? I mentioned Gallup and Povinelli's "mark test" evidence (the chimp tries to wipe off a mark on its face seen in a mirror) that chimps are self-conscious. An experiment in this vein that Dennett mentions (1991, p. 428), and mentions positively, is that a chimp can learn to get bananas via a hole in its cage by watching its arm on a closed circuit TV whose camera is some distance away (Menzel et al. 1985). The literature on the topic of animal self-consciousness is full of controversy. (See Heyes 1993; Mitchell 1993a, 1993b; Gallup and Povinelli 1993; de Lannoy 1993; Anderson 1993; Byrne 1993.) I have no space to do justice to the issues, so I will have to make do with just stating my view: I think the weight of evidence in favor of minimal self-consciousness on the part of chimps is overwhelming. By minimal self-consciousness I mean the ability to think about oneself in some way or other—that is, no particular way is required. Many of the criticisms of the mark test actually presuppose that the chimp is self-conscious in this minimal sense. For example, it is often suggested that chimps that pass the mark test think that they are seeing another chimp (e.g., Heyes 1993), and since the chimp in the mirror has a mark on its forehead, the chimp who is looking wonders whether he or she does too. But in order for me to wonder whether *I* have a mark on my forehead, I have to be able to think about myself. In any case, Dennett does not get into these issues (except, as mentioned, to favor chimp self-consciousness), so it does not appear that he has this interpretation in mind.

So far, on all the consciousness I have mentioned, Dennett's thesis turns out to be false. But there is a trend: of the concepts I considered, the first two made the thesis silly, even of animals. In the case of monitoring consciousness, there is a real empirical issue in the case of many types of mammals, and so it isn't completely silly to wonder about whether people have it. Only in the last case, self-consciousness, is there a serious issue about whether chimps are conscious, and that suggests that we might get a notion of self-consciousness that requires some cultural elements. In recent years, the idea of the self as a federation of somewhat autonomous agencies has become popular, and for good reason. Nagel (1971) made a good case on the basis of split-brain data, and Gazzaniga and LeDoux (1978) and Gazzaniga (1985) have added additional considerations that have some plausibilty. And Dennett has a chapter about the self at the end of the book that gives similar arguments. Maybe what Dennett is saying is that nonfederal self-consciousness, the ability to think of oneself as not being such a federation (or more simply, federal self-consciousness) is a cultural construction.

But now we have moved from falsity to banality. I'm not saying that the proposal that we are federations is banal. What is banal is that the having and applying a sophisticated concept such as being a federation (or not being a federation) requires a cultural construction. Consider chairman self-consciousness, the ability to think of oneself as chairman, as the one who guides the department, the one who has the keys, and so forth. It is a banality that a cultural construction is required in order for a person to think of himself in that way, and the corresponding point about federal self-consciousness is similarly banal.

The great oddity of Dennett's discussion is that throughout he gives the impression that his theory is *about P-consciousness*, though he concedes that what he says about it conflicts with our normal way of thinking about consciousness. This comes out especially strongly in an extended discussion of Julian Jaynes's (1976) book which he credits with a version of the view I am discussing, namely, that consciousness is a cultural construction which requires its own concept. He says (Dennett, 1986):

Perhaps this is an autobiographical confession: I am rather fond of his [Jaynes's] way of using these terms ['consciousness', 'mind', and other mental terms]; I rather like his way of carving up consciousness. It is in fact very similar to the way that I independently decided to carve up consciousness some years ago.

So what then is the project? The project is, in one sense, very simple and very familiar. It is bridging what he calls the "awesome chasm" between mere inert matter and the inwardness, as he puts it, of a conscious being. Consider the awesome chasm between a brick and a bricklayer. There isn't, in Thomas Nagel's (1974) famous phrase, anything that it is like to be a brick. But there is something that it is like to be a bricklayer, and we want to know what the conditions were under which there happened to come to be entities that it was like something to be in this rather special sense. That is the story, the developmental, evolutionary, historical story, that Jaynes sets out to tell. (Dennett 1986, p. 149)

In sum, Dennett's thesis is trivially false if it is construed to be about P-consciousness, as advertised. It is also false if taken to be about A-consciousness which is now Dennett's official view of consciousness. But if taken to be about a highly sophisticated version of self-consciousness, it is banal. That's what can happen if you talk about consciousness without making the sorts of distinctions that I am urging.

In talking about failure to see the distinction, I have concentrated on cases in which points having to do with one kind of consciousness are applied to another. But far more commonly, they are not distinguished from one another sufficiently for one to know which consciousness any given claim is about. Crick and Koch (1990) and Crick (1994), for example, usually seem to be talking about P-consciousness. Crick (p. 9) speaks of the issue of explaining "the redness of red or the painfulness of pain." But often, P-consciousness and A-consciousness are just mixed together with no clear indication of which is at issue.

6   The Fallacy of the Target Reasoning

We now come to the denouement of the paper, the application of the P-consciousness/A-consciousness distinction to the fallacy of the target reasoning. Let me begin with the Penfield-Van Gulick-Searle reasoning. Searle (1992) adopts Penfield's (1975) claim that during petit mal seizures, patients are "totally unconscious." Quoting Penfield at length, Searle describes three patients who, despite being "totally unconscious," continue walking or driving home or playing the piano, but in a mechanical way. Van Gulick (1989) gives a briefer treatment, also quoting Penfield. He says, "The importance of conscious experience for the construction and control of action plans is nicely illustrated by the phenomenon of automatism associated with some petit mal epileptic seizures. In such cases, electrical disorder leads to a loss of function in the higher brain stem.... As a result the patient suffers a loss of conscious experience in the phenomenal sense although he can continue to react selectively to environmental stimuli" (p. 220). Because Van Gulick's treatment is more equivocal and less detailed, and because Searle also comments on my accusations of conflating A-consciousness with P-consciousness, I'll focus on Searle. Searle says:

The epileptic seizure rendered the patient *totally unconscious*, yet the patient continued to exhibit what would normally be called goal-directed behavior.... In all these cases, we have complex forms of apparently goal-directed behavior without any consciousness. Now why could all behavior not be like that? Notice that in the cases, the patients were performing types of actions that were habitual, routine and memorized ... normal, human, conscious behavior has a degree of flexibility and creativity that is absent from the Penfield cases of the unconscious driver and the unconscious pianist. *Consciousness adds powers of discrimination and flexibility* even to memorized routine activities.... one of the evolutionary advantages conferred on us by consciousness is the much greater *flexibility, sensitivity, and creativity* we derive from being conscious. (1992, pp. 108–109, italics mine)

Searle's reasoning is that consciousness is missing, and with it, flexibility, sensitivity, and creativity, so this is an indication that a function of consciousness is to add these qualities. Now it is completely clear that the concept of consciousness invoked by both Searle and van Gulick is P-consciousness. Van Gulick speaks of "conscious experience in the phenomenal sense," and Searle criticizes me for supposing that there is a legitimate use of "conscious" to mean A-conscious: "Some philosophers (e.g., Block, "Two Concepts of Consciousness") claim that there is a sense of this word that implies no sentience whatever, a sense in which a total zombie could be 'conscious'. I know of no such sense, but in any case, that is not the sense in which I am using the word" (1992, p. 84). But neither Searle nor van Gulick nor Penfield gives any reason to believe that P-consciousness is missing or even diminished in the epileptics they describe. The piano player, walker, and the driver don't cope with new situations very well, but they do show every sign of *normal sensation*. For example, Searle, quoting Penfield, describes the epileptic walker as "thread[ing] his way" through the crowd. Doesn't he *see* the obstacles he avoids? Suppose he gets home by turning right at a red wall. Isn't there something it is like for him to see the red wall—and isn't it different from what it is like for him to see a green wall? Searle gives no reason to think the answer is no. Because of the very inflexibility and lack of creativity of the behavior they exhibit, it is the *thought processes* of these patients (including A-consciousness) that are most obviously deficient; no reason at all is given to think that their P-conscious states lack vivacity or intensity. Of course, I don't claim to know what it is really like for these epileptics; my point is rather that for the argument for the function of P-consciousness to have any force, a case would have to be made that P-consciousness is *actually* missing, or at least diminished. Searle argues: P-consciousness is missing; so is creativity;

therefore the former lack explains the latter lack. But no support at all is given for the first premise, and as we shall see, it is no stretch to suppose that what's gone wrong is that the ordinary mongrel notion of consciousness is being used; it wraps P-consciousness and A-consciousness together, and so an obvious function of A-consciousness is illicitly transferred to P-consciousness.[28]

Searle and Van Gulick base their arguments on Penfield's claim that a petit mal seizure "converts the individual into a mindless automaton" (Penfield 1975, p. 37). Indeed, Penfield repeatedly refers to these patients as "unconscious," "mindless," and as "automata." But what does Penfield *mean*? Searle and Van Gulick assume that Penfield means P-consciousness, since they adopt the idea that that is what the term means (though as we shall see, Searle himself sometimes uses the term to mean A-consciousness). Attending to Penfield's account, we find the very shifting among different concepts of consciousness that I have described here, but the dominant theme by far involves thinking of the patients as cognitively rather than phenomenally deficient during petit mal seizures. Here is Penfield's summary of the description of the patients:

> In an attack of automatism the patient becomes suddenly unconscious, but, since other mechanisms in the brain continue to function, he changes into an automaton. He may wander about, confused and aimless. Or he may continue to carry out whatever purpose his mind was in the act of handing on to his automatic sensory-motor mechanism when the highest brain-mechanism went out of action. Or he follows a stereotyped, habitual pattern of behavior. In every case, however, the automaton can make few, if any decisions for which there has been no precedent. *He makes no record of a stream of consciousness.* Thus, he will have complete amnesia for the period of epileptic discharge.... In general, if new decisions are to be made, the automaton cannot make them. In such a circumstance, he may become completely unreasonable and uncontrollable and even dangerous. (Penfield 1975, p. 38–40, italics mine)

In these passages, and throughout the book, the dominant theme in descriptions of these patients is one of deficits in thinking, planning, and decision making. No mention is made of any sensory or phenomenal deficit.[29]

My interpretation is supported by a consideration of Penfield's theoretical rationale for his claim that petit mal victims are unconscious. He distinguishes two brain mechanisms, "(a) the *mind's mechanism* (or highest brain mechanism); and (b) the *computer* (or automatic sensory-motor mechanism)" (p. 40, Penfield's italics). The mind's mechanism is most prominently mentioned in connection with planning and decision making, for example, "the highest brain mechanism is the mind's executive." When arguing that there is a soul that is connected to the mind's mechanism, he mentions only cognitive functions. He asks whether such a soul is improbable, and answers, "It is not so improbable, to my mind, as is the alternative expectation—that the highest brain mechanism should itself understand, and reason, and direct voluntary action, and decide where attention should be turned and what the computer must learn, and record, and reveal on demand" (p. 82). Penfield's soul is a cognitive soul.

By contrast, the computer is devoted to *sensory* and motor functions. Indeed, he emphasizes that the mind only has contact with sensory and motor areas of the cortex via controlling the computer, which itself has direct contact with the sensory and motor areas. Since it is the mind's mechanism that is knocked out in petit mal seizures, the sensory areas are intact in the "automaton."

Searle (1990b) attempts (though of course he wouldn't accept this description) to use the idea of degrees of P-consciousness to substitute for A-consciousness. I will quote a chunk of what he says about this. (The details of the context don't matter.)

By consciousness I simply mean those subjective states of awareness or sentience that begin when one wakes in the morning and continue throughout the period that one is awake until one falls into a dreamless sleep, into a coma, or dies or is otherwise, as they say, unconscious.

I quoted this passage earlier as an example of how a characterization of consciousness can go wrong by pointing to too many things. Searle means to be pointing to P-consciousness. But A-consciousness and P-consciousness normally occur together when one is awake, and both are normally absent in a coma and a dreamless sleep—so this characterization doesn't distinguish them.

On my account, dreams are a form of consciousness, . . . though they are of less intensity than full blown waking alertness. Consciousness is an on/off switch: You are either conscious or not. Though once conscious, the system functions like a rheostat, and there can be an indefinite range of different degrees of consciousness, ranging from the drowsiness just before one falls asleep to the full blown complete alertness of the obsessive.

Degrees of P-consciousness are one thing, obsessive attentiveness is another—indeed the latter is a notion from the category of A-consciousness, not P-consciousness.

There are lots of different degrees of consciousness, but door-knobs, bits of chalk, and shingles are not conscious at all. . . . These points, it seems to me, are misunderstood by Block. He refers to what he calls an "access sense of consciousness." On my account there is no such sense. I believe that he . . . [confuses] what I would call peripheral consciousness or *inattentiveness* with total unconsciousness. It is true, for example, that when I am driving my car "on automatic pilot" I am not paying much attention to the details of the road and the traffic. But it is simply not true that I am totally unconscious of these phenomena. If I were, there would be a car crash. We need therefore to make a distinction between the *center of my attention, the focus of my consciousness* on the one hand, and the *periphery* on the other. . . . There are lots of phenomena right now of which I am peripherally conscious, for example the feel of the shirt on my neck, the touch of the computer keys at my finger-tips, and so on. But as I use the notion, none of these is unconscious in the sense in which the secretion of enzymes in my stomach is unconscious. (All quotations from Searle 1990b, p. 635, italics mine)

The first thing to note is the *contradiction*. Earlier, I quoted Searle saying that a "totally unconscious" epileptic could nonetheless drive home. Here, he says that if a driver was totally unconscious, the car would crash. The sense of 'conscious' in which the car would crash if the driver weren't conscious is *A-consciousness*, not P-consciousness. P-consciousness *all by itself* wouldn't keep the car from crashing— the P-conscious contents have to be put to use in rationally controlling the car, *which is an aspect of A-consciousness*. When Searle says the "totally unconscious" epileptic can nonetheless drive home, he can be taken to be talking about P-consciousness; when he says the car would crash if the driver were totally unconscious, he is talking mainly about A-consciousness. Notice that it will do no good for Searle to say that in the quotation of the last paragraph, he is talking about creature-consciousness rather than state-consciousness. What it is for a person to be P-unconscious is for his states (all or the relevant ones) to lack P-consciousness. Creature P-consciousness is parasitic on state P-consciousness. Also, it will do him no good to appeal to the conscious/conscious—of distinction. (The epilectics were "totally unconscious," but if he were "unconscious of" the details of the road and traffic the car would crash.) The epileptics were "totally unconscious" and therefore, since Searle has no resource of A-consciousness, he must say that the epilectics were totally unconscious *of* anything. So he is committed to saying that the epilectic driver can drive despite being totally unconscious of anything. And that contradicts the claim that I quoted that if Searle were totally unconscious of the details of the road and traffic, then the car would crash. If Searle says that someone who is totally unconscious can nonetheless be conscious of something, that would be a backhanded way of acknowledging the distinction.

The upshot is that Searle finds himself drawn to using 'consciousness' in the sense of A-consciousness, despite his official position that there is no such sense. Despite his official ideology, when he attempts to deploy a notion of degrees of P-consciousness he ends up talking about A-consciousness—or about both A-consciousness and P-consciousness wrapped together in the usual mongrel concept. Inattentiveness just *is* lack of A-consciousness (though it will have effects on P-consciousness). Thus, he may be right about the inattentive driver (note, the inattentive driver, not the petit mal case). When the inattentive driver stops at a red light, presumably there is something it is like for him to see the red light—the red light no doubt looks red in the usual way, that is, it appears as brightly and vividly to him as red normally does. But since he is thinking about something else, perhaps he is not using this information very much in his reasoning nor is he using this information to control his speech or action in any sophisticated way—that is, perhaps his A-consciousness of what he sees is diminished. (Of course, it can't be totally gone or the car would crash.) Alternatively, A-consciousness might be normal, and the driver's poor memory of the trip may just be due to failure to put contents that are both P-conscious and A-conscious into memory; my point is that to the extent that Searle's story is right about *any* kind of consciousness, it is right about A-consciousness, not P-consciousness.

Searle's talk of the center and the periphery is in the first instance about kinds of or degrees of access, not "degrees of phenomenality." You may recall that in introducing the A/P distinction, I used Searle's example of attending to the feel of the shirt on the back of one's neck. My point was that A-consciousness and P-consciousness interact: bringing something from the periphery to the center can *affect* one's phenomenal state. The attention makes the experience more fine-grained, more intense (though a pain that is already intense needn't become more intense when one attends to it). There is a phenomenal difference between figure and ground, though the perception of the colors of the ground can be just as intense as those of the figure, or so it seems to me. Access and phenomenality often interact, one bringing along the other—but that shouldn't make us blind to the difference.

Though my complaint is partly verbal, there is more to it. For the end result of deploying a mongrel concept is wrong reasoning about a function of P-consciousness.

Let me turn now to a related form of reasoning used by Owen Flanagan (1992, pp. 142–145). Flanagan discusses Luria's patient Zazetsky, a soldier who lost the memories of his "middle" past—between childhood and brain injury. The information about his past is represented in Zazetsky's brain, but it only comes out via "automatic writing." Flanagan says, "The saddest irony is that although each piece of Zazetsky's autobiography was consciously reappropriated by him each time he hit upon a veridical memory in writing, he himself was never able to fully reappropriate, to keep in clear and continuous view, to live with, the self he reconstructed in the thousand pages he wrote." Flanagan goes on to blame the difficulty on a defect of consciousness, and he means P-consciousness: "Zazetsky's conscious capacities are (partly) maimed. His dysfunction is rooted in certain defects of consciousness" (pp. 144–145). But Zazetsky's root problem appears to be a difficulty in A-consciousness, though that has an effect on self-consciousness and P-consciousness. The problem seems to be that the memories of the middle past are not accessible to him in the manner of his memories of childhood and recent past. To the extent that he knows about the middle past, it is as a result of reading his automatic writing, and so he has the sort of access we have to a story about someone else. The root difficulty is segregation of information, and whatever P-conscious feelings of fragmentation he has can be taken to result from the segregation of information. So there is nothing in this case that suggests a function of P-consciousness.

Let us now move to the line of thought mentioned at the outset about how the thirsty blindsight patient doesn't reach for the glass of water in the blind field.[30] (This line of thought appears in Marcel 1986, 1988; Van Gulick 1989 [though endorsed equivocally]; and Flanagan 1989.) The reasoning is that (1) consciousness is missing, (2) information that the patient in some sense possesses is not used in reasoning or in guiding action or in reporting, so (3) the function of consciousness must be to somehow allow information from the senses to be so used in guiding action (Marcel 1986, 1988). Flanagan (1992) agrees with Marcel: "Conscious awareness of a water fountain to my right will lead me to drink from it if I am thirsty. But the thirsty blindsighted person will make no move towards the fountain unless pressed to do so. The inference to the best explanation is that conscious awareness of the environment facilitates semantic comprehension and adaptive motor actions in creatures like us." And: "Blindsighted patients never initiate activity toward the blindfield because they lack subjective awareness of things in that field" (Flanagan 1992, pp. 141–142; the same reasoning occurs in his 1991, p. 349). Van Gulick (1989) agrees with Marcel, saying, "Subjects never initiate on their own any actions informed by perceptions from the blind field. The moral to be drawn from this is that information must normally be represented in phenomenal consciousness if it is to play any role in guiding voluntary action" (p. 220).

Bernard Baars argues for eighteen different functions of consciousness on the same ground. He says that the argument for these functions is "that loss of consciousness—through habituation, automaticity, distraction, masking, anesthesia, and the like—inhibits or destroys the functions listed here."[31]

Schacter (1989) approvingly quotes Marcel, using this reasoning to some extent in formulating the model of figure 9.1 (though as I mentioned, there is a model that perhaps more fully embodies this reasoning; see below). The P-consciousness module has the function of integrating information from the specialized modules, injecting them with P-conscious content, and of sending these contents to the system that is in charge of reasoning and rational control of action and reporting.

This is the fallacy: In the blindsight patient, both P-consciousness and A-consciousness of the glass of water are missing. There is an obvious explanation of why the patient doesn't reach for the glass in terms of the information about it not reaching mechanisms of reasoning and rational control of speech and action, the machinery of A-consciousness. (If we believe in an Executive System, we can explain why the blindsight patient does not reach for the water by appealing to the claim that the information about the water does not reach the Executive System.) More generally, A-consciousness and P-consciousness are almost always present or absent together, or rather this seems plausible. This is, after all, *why* they are folded together in a mongrel concept. A function of the mechanisms underlying A-consciousness is completely obvious. If information from the eyes and ears did not get to mechanisms of control of reasoning and of rational control of action and reporting, we would not be able to use our eyes and ears to guide our action and reporting. But it is just a mistake to slide from a function of the machinery of A-consciousness to any function at all of P-consciousness.

Of course, it could be that the lack of P-consciousness is itself responsible for the lack of A-consciousness. If *that* is the argument in any of these cases, I do not say "fallacy." The idea that the lack of P-consciousness is responsible for the lack of A-consciousness is a bold hypothesis, not a fallacy. Recall, however, that there is some reason to ascribe the opposite view to the field as a whole. The discussion earlier of Baars, Shallice, Kosslyn and Koenig, Edelman, Johnson-Laird, Andrade, and Kihlstrom et al. suggested that to the extent that the different consciousnesses are distinguished from one another, it is often thought that P-consciousness is a product of (or is identical to) cognitive processing. In this climate of opinion, if P-consciousness and A-consciousness were clearly distinguished, and something like the opposite of the usual view of their relation advanced, we would expect some comment on this fact, something that does not appear in any of the words cited.

The fallacy, then, is jumping from the premise that "consciousness" is missing—without being clear about what kind of consciousness is missing—to the conclusion that P-consciousness has a certain function. If the distinction were seen clearly, the relevant possibilities could be reasoned about. Perhaps the lack of P-consciousness causes the lack of A-consciousness. Or perhaps the converse is the case: P-consciousness is somehow a product of A-consciousness. Or both could be the result of something else. If the distinction were clearly made, these alternatives would come to the fore. The fallacy is failing to make the distinction, rendering the alternatives invisible.

Note that the claim that P-consciousness is missing in blindsight is just an assumption. I decided to take the blindsight patient's word for his lack of P-consciousness of stimuli in the blind field. Maybe this assumption is mistaken. But if it is, then the fallacy now under discussion reduces to the fallacy of the Searle-Penfield reasoning: if the assumption is wrong, if the blindsight patient *does* have P-consciousness of stimuli in the blind field, then *only* A-consciousness of the stimuli in the blind field is missing, so *of course* we cannot draw the mentioned conclusion about the function of P-consciousness from blindsight.

I said at the outset that although there was a serious fallacy in the target reasoning, there was also something importantly right about it. What is importantly right is this. In blindsight, both A-consciousness and P-consciousness (I assume) are gone, just as in normal perception, both are present. So blindsight is yet another case in which P-consciousness and A-consciousness are both present or both absent. Further, as I mentioned earlier, cases of A-consciousness without P-consciousness, such as the super-blindsight patient I described earlier, do not appear to exist. Training of blindsight patients has produced a number of phenomena that look a bit like super-blindsight, but each such lead that I have pursued has fizzled. This suggests an intimate relation between A-consciousness and P-consciousness. Perhaps there is something about P-consciousness that greases the wheels of accessibility. Perhaps P-consciousness is like the liquid in a hydraulic computer (as mentioned earlier in connection with Farah's criticism), the means by which A-consciousness operates. Alternatively, perhaps P-consciousness is the gateway to mechanisms of access as in Schacter's model, in which case P-consciousness would have the function Marcel et al. mention. Or perhaps P-consciousness and A-consciousness even amount to much the same thing empirically even though they differ conceptually, in which case P-consciousness would also have the aforementioned function. Perhaps the two are so entwined together that there is no empirical sense to the idea of one without the other.

Indeed, there are many striking cases in which P-consciousness and A-consciousness come and go together. Kosslyn (1980) reports an imagery scanning experiment in which subjects were asked to zoom in on one location of an imaged map to the point where other areas of the map "over-flow." The parts of the imaged map that lose P-consciousness are no longer readily accessible. (Kosslyn, in conversation) Cooper and Shepard (1973) note that practice in imagery tasks result in images no longer being conscious even though they are still there and are rotating, as shown by their function in reaction time experiments. From their description, one can see that the images lose both P-consciousness and A-consciousness. Baars (1994) mentions this (as an example of something else) and another such case.

Compare the model of figure 9.1 (Schacter's model) with those of figures 9.2 and 9.3. The model of figure 9.2 is just like Schacter's model except that the Executive System and the P-consciousness system are collapsed together. We might call the hypothesis that is embodied in it the Collapse Hypothesis.[32] Figure 9.3 is a variant on Schacter's model in which the Executive module and the P-consciousness module are reversed. Schacter's model clearly gives P-consciousness a function in controlling action. Model 3 clearly gives it no function. Model 2 can be interpreted in a variety of ways, some of which give P-consciousness a function, others of which do not. If P-consciousness is literally identical to some sort of information processing, then P-consciousness will have whatever function that information processing has. But if P-consciousness is, say, a by-product of and supervenient on certain kinds of information processing (something that could also be represented by Model 3), then P-consciousness will in that respect at least have no function. What is right about the Marcel et al. reasoning is that some of the explanations for the phenomenon give P-consciousness a role; what is wrong with the reasoning is that one cannot immediately conclude from missing "consciousness" to P-consciousness having *that* role.

7   Can We Distinguish among the Models?

I'm finished with the point of the chapter, but having raised the issue of the three competing models, I can't resist making some suggestions for distinguishing among them. My approach is one that takes introspection seriously, that is, that we take seriously our impressions of how things seem to us. Famously, introspection is unreliable about some matters—for example, what cognitive processes underlie our choices

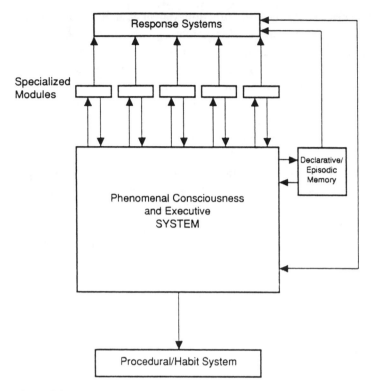

Figure 9.2

(Nisbett and Wilson, 1977; Jacoby, Toth, Lindsay, and Debner 1992). But it would be foolish to conclude that we can afford to ignore our own P-conscious experience in studying P-consciousness.

One phenomenon that counts against the Collapse Hypothesis (fig. 9.2) is the familiar phenomenon of the solution to a difficult problem just popping into P-consciousness. If the solution involves high-level thought, then it must be done by high-level reasoning processes that are not P-conscious. (They aren't A-conscious either, since one can't report or base action on the intermediate stages of such reasoning.) There will always be disputes about famous cases (e.g., Kekulé's discovery of the benzene ring in a dream), but we should not be skeptical about the idea that though the results of thought are both P-conscious and A-conscious, much in the way of the intermediate stages are neither. If we assume that all high-level reasoning is done in the Executive System, and that Model 2 is committed to all Executive processes being P-conscious, then Model 2 is incompatible with solutions popping into P-consciousness. Of course, alternative forms of Model 2 that do not make these assumptions may not make any such predictions.

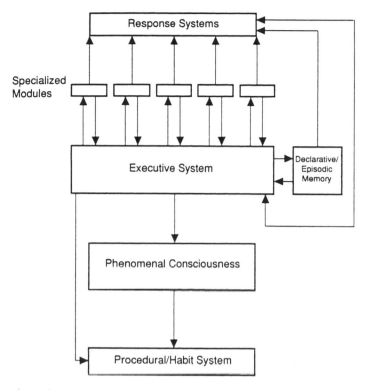

Figure 9.3

(Do cases of the sort mentioned count as A-conscious without being P-conscious? No, or rather, probably not. We would have A-consciousness without P-consciousness if we had a representation somewhere in the system [say in a perceptual module] that was never P-conscious, but which is sent to the Executive System and becomes A-conscious. That is what was supposed to happen in super-blindsight. But what may be going on in these cases of a solution "popping into consciousness" is a case of problem-solving machinery whose workings are not privy to either P- or A-consciousness producing a solution whose representation is simultaneously A- and P-conscious. Certainly, we have no reason to think that there is any representation of the solution which is A-conscious but not P-conscious, although we could find out that this is true.)

I think there are a number of phenomena that, if investigated further, might lead to evidence for P-consciousness without A-consciousness and thus provide some reason to reject Model 2 in favor of Schacter's model (figure 9.1). (I also think that these phenomena, if investigated further, might yield some reason to reject Model 3 in favor of Model 1, but I cannot go into that here.) I repeat: the phenomena I am about to mention don't show anything on their own. I claim only that they are intriguing and deserve further work.

One such phenomenon—or perhaps I should describe it as an idea rather than a phenomenon—is the hypothesis, already mentioned, that there could be animals whose P-conscious brain processes are intact, but whose A-conscious brain processes are not. Another is the case mentioned earlier of states of P-consciousness that go on for some time without attention and only become A-conscious with the focusing of attention. (See also Hill 1991).

Sperling (1960) flashed arrays of letters (e.g., 3 by 3) to subjects for brief periods (e.g., 50 milliseconds). Subjects typically said that they could see all or most of the letters, but they could report only about half of them. Were the subjects right in saying that they could see all the letters? Sperling tried signaling the subjects with a tone. A high tone meant the subject was to report the top row, a medium tone indicated the middle row, and so forth. If the tone was given immediately after the stimulus, the subjects could usually get all the letters in the row, whichever row was indicated. But once they had named those letters, they usually could name no others. This experiment is taken to indicate some sort of raw visual storage, the "icon." But the crucial issue for my purposes is what it is like to be a subject in this experiment. My own experience is that I see all or almost all the letters, and this is what other subjects describe (Baars 1988, p. 15). Focusing on one row allows me to report what letters are in that row (and only that row) and again this is what other subjects report. Here is the description that I *think* is right and that I need for my case: I am P-conscious of all (or almost all— I'll omit this qualification) the letters at once, that is, jointly, and not just as blurry or vague letters, but as specific letters (or at least specific shapes), but I don't have access to all of them jointly, all at once. (I would like to know whether others describe what it is like in this way, but the prejudice against introspection in psychology tends to keep answers to such questions from the journals.) One item of uncertainty about this phenomenon is that responses are serial; perhaps if some parallel form of response were available the results would be different. Ignoring that issue, the suggestion is that I am P-conscious, but not A-conscious, of all jointly.[33]

It may be that some evidence for P-consciousness without A-consciousness can be derived from phenomena involving hypnosis. Consider the phenomenon known as hypnotic analgesia in which hypnosis blocks a patient's access to pain, say from an arm in cold water or from the dentist's drill. Pain must be P-conscious, it might be said, but access is blocked by the hypnosis, so perhaps this is P- without A-consciousness? But what reason is there to think that there is any pain at all in cases of hypnotic analgesia? One reason is that there are the normal psychophysiological indications that would be expected for pain of the sort that would be caused by the stimulus, such as an increase in heart rate and blood pressure (Melzack and Wall 1988; Kihlstrom et al. 1992). Another (flakier) indication is that reports of the pain apparently can be elicited by Hilgard's "hidden observer" technique in which the hypnotist tries to make contact with a "hidden part" of the person who knows about the pain (Hilgard 1986; Kihlstrom 1987). The hidden observer often describes the pain as excruciating and also describes the time course of the pain in a way that fits the stimulation. Now there is no point in supposing that the pain is not P-conscious. If we believe the hidden observer, there is a pain that has phenomenal properties, and phenomenal properties could not be P-unconscious.

One way to think about this situation is that we have different persons sharing some part of one body. The pain is both P-conscious and A-conscious to the system that reports as the "hidden observer." This system doesn't dominate the control of behavior, but since it can report, it can control behavior under some circumstances. This reasoning is supported by the idea that if there is a P-conscious state in me that I don't have access to, then that state is not *mine* at all. Turning now to a different way of thinking about what is going on: There is one system, *the person*, who has some sort of dissociation problem. There is P-conscious pain in there somewhere, but the person, himself or herself, does not have access to that pain, as shown by the failure to report it, and by the failure to use the information to escape the pain. Only on this latter view would we have P- without A-consciousness.

A phenomenon that could lead to evidence of P-consciousness with diminished A-consciousness has to do with persistent reports over the years of P-conscious events under general anesthesia. Patients wake up and say that the operation hurt. (A number of doctors have told me that this is why doctors make a point of giving patients intravenous valium, an amnestic, to wipe out patients' memory of the pain. If the patients don't remember the pain, they won't sue.) So far, it seems we might have both P- and A-consciousness under anesthesia. However, general anesthesia is thought to suppress reasoning power in subanesthetic doses (Kihlstrom 1987; see also Ghoneim et al. 1984), thus plausibly interfering with Executive function and A-consciousness. I know of no reports that would suggest diminished P-consciousness. If P-consciousness were diminished much more than A-consciousness, for example, we could perhaps have analogs of super-blindsight. The patient might report events but not having seen or heard them. So if there are P-conscious states under general anesthesia, they may be states of more or less normal P-consciousness with diminished A-consciousness.

Further, Crick and Koch (1990) mention that the aforementioned neural oscillations persist under light general anesthesia. Kihlstrom and Schacter (1990), Kihlstrom and Couture (1992), and Ghoneim and Block (1993) conclude that the phenomenon depends in ways that are not understood on details of the procedure and the anesthetic cocktail, but there do appear to be some methods that show some kind of memory for events under anesthesia. Bennett et al. (1988) gave some patients under anesthesia suggestions to lift their index fingers at a special signal, whereas other patients were told to pull their ears. Control groups were given similar procedures without the suggestions.

The result: the experimental group exhibited the designated actions at a much higher rate than controls. Of course, even if these results hold up, they don't show that the patients *heard* the suggestions under anesthesia. Perhaps what took place was some sort of auditory analog of blindsight (with no A- or P-consciousness).

An item of more use for present purposes comes from a study done on pilots during WWII by a pair of American dentists (Nathan 1985; Melzack and Wall 1988). The unpressurized cabins of the time caused pilots to experience sensations that as I understand it amount to some sort of re-creation of the pain of previous dental work. The mechanism appeared to have to do with stimulation of the sinuses caused by the air pressure changes. The dentists coined the term "aerodontalgia" for this phenomenon. The dentists were interested in the relation of aerodontalgia to general and local anesthetic. So they did dental work on patients using combinations of general and local anesthetics. For example, they would put a patient under general anesthesia, and then locally anesthetize one side of the mouth, and then drill or pull teeth on both sides. The result (with stimulation of the nasal mucosa in place of the sinus stimulation caused by pressure changes): they found re-creation of pain of previous dental work only for dental work done under general anesthesia, not for local anesthesia, whether or not the local was used alone or together with general anesthesia. Of course, there may have been no pain at all under general anesthesia, only memories of the sort that would have been laid down if there had been pain. But if you hate pain, and if both general and local anesthesia make medical sense, would *you* take the chance on general anesthesia? At any rate, the tantalizing suggestion is that this is a case of P-consciousness without A-consciousness.

The form of the target reasoning discussed misses the distinction between P-consciousness and A-consciousness and thus jumps from the fact that consciousness in some sense or other is missing simultaneously with missing creativity or voluntary action to the conclusion that P-consciousness functions to promote the missing qualities in normal people. But if we make the right distinctions, we can investigate non-fallaciously whether any such conclusion can be drawn. Model 2 would identify P-consciousness with a type of A-consciousness, thus embodying an aspect of the target reasoning. But Model 2 is disconfirmed by the apparent fact that much of our reasoning is neither P-conscious nor A-conscious, as suggested by the phenomenon of the answer to problems "popping" into P- and A-consciousness. I have made further suggestions for phenomena that may provide examples of P-consciousness without A-consciousness, further disconfirming Model 2.

My purpose in this chapter has been to expose a confusion about consciousness. But in reasoning about it I raised the possibility that it may be possible to find out something about the function of P-consciousness without knowing very much about what it is. Indeed, learning something about the function of P-consciousness may help us in finding out what it is.

Notes

First appeared in *Behavioral and Brain Sciences* 18 (2): 227–247, 1995. Reprinted with some changes in N. Block, O. Flanagan, and G. Güzeldere, eds., *The Nature of Consciousness: Philosophical Debates* (Cambridge, MA: MIT Press, 1997). German translation, "Über ein Missverständis bezüglich einer Funktion des Bewußtseins," in Thomas Metzinger, ed., *Bewußtsein: Beiträge aus der Gegenwartsphilosophie* (Paderborn: Schoningh, 1995). Reprinted in *The Philosophers' Annual*, 1996. Slovak translation in an anthology published by Kalligram Publishers.

I would like to thank Tyler Burge, Susan Carey, David Chalmers, Martin Davies, Wayne Davis, Bert Dreyfus, Owen Flanagan, Güven Güzeldere, Paul Horwich, Jerry Katz, Leonard Katz, Joe Levine, David Rosenthal, Jerome Schaffer, Sydney Shoemaker, Stephen White, and Andrew Young for their very helpful comments on earlier versions of this paper. I have been giving this paper at colloquia and meetings since the fall of 1990, and I am grateful to the many audiences which have made interesting and useful comments, especially the audience at the conference on my work at the University of Barcelona in June, 1993.

1. See Bowers and Schacter (1990), and Reingold and Merikle (1990). The phenomenon just mentioned is very similar to phenomena involving "subliminal perception," in which stimuli are degraded or presented very briefly. Holender (1986) harshly criticizes a variety of "subliminal perception" experiments, but the experimental paradigm just mentioned and many others, are in my judgment free from the problems of some other studies. Another such experimental paradigm is the familiar dichotic listening experiments in which subjects wear headphones in which different programs are played to different ears. If they are asked to pay attention to one program, they can report only superficial features of the unattended program, but the unattended program influences interpretation of ambiguous sentences presented in the attended program. See Lackner and Garrett (1973).

2. See, for example, Dennett, and Kinsbourne's (1992b) scorn in response to my suggestion of Cartesian Modularism. I should add that in Dennett's more recent writings, Cartesian materialism has tended to expand considerably from its original meaning of a literal place in the brain at which "it all comes together" for consciousness. In reply to Shoemaker (1993) and Tye (1993), both of whom echo Dennett's (1991) and Dennett and Kinsbourne's (1992a) admission that no one really is a proponent of Cartesian materialism, Dennett (1993) says, "Indeed, if Tye and Shoemaker want to see a card-carrying Cartesian materialist, each may look in the mirror ..." See also Jackson (1993a).

3. But what is it about thoughts that makes them P-conscious? One possibility is that it is just a series of mental images or subvocalizations that make thoughts P-conscious. Another possibility is that the contents themselves have a P-conscious aspect independently of their vehicles. See Lormand, 2000.

4. I say both that P-consciousness is not an intentional property and that intentional differences can make a P-conscious difference, I also say that P-conscious properties are often representational. My view is that although P-conscious content cannot be reduced to or identified with intentional content, P-conscious contents often have an intentional aspect, and also P-conscious

contents often represent in a primitive non-intentional way. A perceptual experience can represent space as being filled in certain ways without representing the object perceived as falling under any concept. Thus, the experiences of a creature which does not possess the concept of a donut or a torus could represent space as being filled in a donut-like way. Intentional representation is representation under concepts, so the creature that represents space as being filled in a donut-like way without any concept of that shape has representational content without intentional content. See Davies (1992, 1995), Peacocke (1992), and finally Evans (1982), in which the distinction between conceptualized and nonconceptualized content was first introduced.

5. My diagnosis is that initially Crick and Koch didn't distinguish solving the binding problem from explaining P-consciousness, but to the extent that they did distinguish, they hypothesized that the solution to the former problem would also solve the latter. Levine (1983) coined the term "explanatory gap," and has elaborated the idea in interesting ways; see also his (1993). Van Gulick (1993) and Flanagan (1992, p. 59) note that the more we know about the connection between (say) hitting middle C on the piano and the resulting experience, the more we have in the way of hooks on which to hang something that could potentially close the explanatory gap. Some philosophers have adopted what might be called a deflationary attitude toward the explanatory gap. See Levine (1993), Jackson (1993), Chalmers (1996), Byrne (1993), and Block (1994).

6. I know some will think that I invoked inverted and absent qualia a few paragraphs above when I described the explanatory gap as involving the question of why a creature with a brain which has a physiological and functional nature like ours couldn't have different experience or none at all. But the spirit of the question as I asked it allows for an answer that explains why such creatures cannot exist, and thus there is no presupposition that these are real possibilities. Levine (1983, 1993) stresses that the relevant modality is epistemic possibility.

7. This is an improvement over the definition of A-consciousness in the original version of this paper.

8. I have been using the P-consciousness/A-consciousness distinction in my lectures for many years, but it only found its way into print in my "Consciousness and Accessibility" (1990b), and my (1991, 1992, 1993). My claims about the distinction have been criticized in Searle (1990b, 1992) and Flanagan (1992)—I reply to Flanagan below; and there is an illuminating discussion in Humphreys and Davies (1993b), a point of which will be taken up in a note to follow. See also Levine's (1994) review of Flanagan which discusses Flanagan's critique of the distinction. See also Kirk (1992) for an identification of P-consciousness with something like A-consciousness.

9. Some may say that only fully conceptualized content can play a role in reasoning, be reportable, and rationally control action. If so, then non-conceptualized content is not A-conscious.

10. However, I acknowledge the empirical possibility that the scientific nature of P-consciousness has something to do with information processing. We can ill afford to close off empirical possibilities, given the difficulty of solving the mystery of P-consciousness. Cf. Loar (1990).

11. On my view, there are a number of problems with the first of these suggestions. One of them is that perhaps the representational content of pain is too primitive for a role in inference. Arguably, the representational content of pain is nonconceptualized. After all, dogs can have pain and

one can reasonably wonder whether dogs have the relevant concepts at all. But there is a better suggestion. Davies and Humphreys (1993b) discuss a related issue. Applying a suggestion of theirs about the higher-order thought notion of consciousness to A-consciousness, we could characterize A-consciousness of a state with nonconceptualized content as follows: such a state is A-conscious if, in virtue of one's having the state, its content would be inferentially promiscuous and poised for rational control of action and speech if the subject were to have had the concepts required for that content to be a conceptualized content. The idea is to bypass the inferential disadvantage of nonconceptualized content by thinking of its accessibility counterfactually—in terms of the rational relations it would have if the subject were to have the relevant concepts. See Lormand (2000) on the self-representing nature of pain.

12. Later in this chapter I introduce the distinction between creature consciousness and state consciousness. In those terms, transitivity has to do primarily with creature consciousness, whereas in the case of P-consciousness and A-consciousness, it is state consciousness that is basic. See the discussion at the end of this section.

13. The distinction has some similarity to the sensation/perception distinction; I won't take the space to lay out the differences. See Humphrey (1992) for an interesting discussion of the latter distinction.

14. Tye (1994) argues (on the basis of neuropsychological claims) that the visual information processing in blindsight includes no processing by the object recognition system or the spatial attention system, and so is very different from the processing of normal vision. This point does not challenge my claim that the super-blindsight case is a very limited partial zombie. Note that super-blindsight, as I describe it, does not require object recognition or spatial attention. Whatever it is that allows the blindsight patient to discriminate an X from an O and a horizontal from a vertical line will do. I will argue later that the fact that such cases do not exist, if it is a fact, is important. Humphrey (1992) suggests that blindsight is mainly a motor phenomenon—the patient is perceptually influenced by his own motor tendencies.

15. If you are tempted to deny the existence of these states of the perceptual system, you should think back to the total zombie just mentioned. Putting aside the issue of the possibility of this zombie, note that on a computational notion of cognition, the zombie has all the same A-conscious contents that you have (if he is your computational duplicate). A-consciousness is an informational notion. The states of the super-blindsighter's perceptual system are A-conscious for the same reason as the zombie's.

16. Actually, my notion of A-consciousness seems to fit the data better than the conceptual apparatus she uses. Blindsight isn't always more degraded in any normal sense than sight. Weiskrantz (1988) notes that his patient DB had better acuity in some areas of the blind field (in some circumstances) than in his sighted field. It would be better to understand her "degraded" in terms of lack of access.

Notice that the super-blindsighter I have described is just a little bit different (though in a crucial way) from the ordinary blindsight patient. In particular, I am not relying on what might be thought of as a full-fledged quasi-zombie, a super-duper-blindsighter whose blindsight is every bit as good, functionally speaking, as his sight. In the case of the super-duper-blindsighter, the only difference between vision in the blind and sighted fields, functionally speaking, is that the quasi-zombie himself regards them differently. Such an example will be regarded by some (though not me) as incoherent—see Dennett (1991), for example. But we can avoid disagreement about the super-duper-blindsighter by illustrating the idea of A-consciousness without P-consciousness by appealing only to the super-blindsighter. Functionalists may want to know why the super-blindsight case counts as A-conscious without P-consciousness. After all, they may say, if we have really high-quality access in mind, the super-blindsighter that I have described does not have it, so he lacks both P-consciousness and really high-quality A-consciousness. The super-duper-blindsighter, on the other hand, has both, according to the functionalist, so in neither case, the objection goes, is there A-consciousness without P-consciousness. But the disagreement about the super-duper-blindsighter is irrelevant to the issue about the super-blindsighter, and the issue about the super-blindsighter is merely verbal. I believe in the possibility of a quasi-zombie like the super-duper-blindsighter, but the point I am making here does not depend on it. There is no reason to frame notions so as to muddy the waters with unnecessary conflicts. One could put the point by distinguishing three types of access: (1) really high-quality access, (2) medium access, and (3) poor access. The actual blindsight patient has poor access, the super-blindsight patient has medium access, and the super-duper-blindsight patient—as well as most of us—has really high-quality access. The functionalist identifies P-consciousness with A-consciousness of the really high-quality kind. I am defining "A-consciousness"—and of course, it is only one of many possible definitions—in terms of medium access. Defining "A-consciousness" in terms of low-quality access would make blindsight patients cases of A without P. Defining "A-consciousness" in terms of the rich information of high-quality access would render the kind of vision you have when you close your eyes lightly (and can still tell whether the lights are on) as P without A. My concern is to make gaps between P and A as interesting as possible.

17. Thus, there is a conflict between this physiological claim and the Schacter model which dictates that destroying the P-consciousness module will prevent A-consciousness.

18. There is a misleading aspect to this example—namely that to the extent that "conscious" and "aware" differ in ordinary talk, the difference goes in the opposite direction.

19. There is a more familiar situation which illustrates the same points. Think back to all those times when you have been sitting in the kitchen when suddenly the compressor in the refrigerator goes off. Again, one might naturally say that one was aware of the noise, but only at the moment in which it went off was one consciously aware of it. A point on the other side: perhaps habituation stems P-consciousness of the noise; perhaps what happens at the moment it goes off is that one is P-conscious of the change only.

20. Whether loss of a feeling of familiarity is a necessary condition of prosopagnosia is a more complex issue. Perhaps it will suffice to say that in the case of prosopagnosics, there may be no fact of the matter as to whether they are experiencing familiarity, yet we still count them as prosopagnosics. See the discussion of anosognosia below.

21. See White (1987) for an account of why self-consciousness should be firmly distinguished from P-consciousness, and why self-consciousness is more relevant to certain issues of value.

22. The pioneer of these ideas in the philosophical literature is David Armstrong (1968, 1980). William Lycan (1987) has energetically pursued self-scanning, and David Rosenthal (1986, 1993), Peter Carruthers (1989, 1992), and Norton Nelkin (1993) have championed higher-order thought. See also Natsoulas (1993). Lormand (2000) makes some powerful criticisms of Rosenthal.

23. To be fair to Rey, his argument is more like a dilemma: for any supposed feature of consciousness, either a laptop of the sort we have today has it or else you can't be sure you have it yourself. So in the case of P-consciousness, laptops don't have it, and we are sure we do, so once we make these distinctions, his argument loses plausibility.

24. This represents a change of view from Block (1994), wherein I said that 'consciousness' ought to be ambiguous rather than saying it is now ambiguous.

25. See Block (1993).

26. Interestingly, she was in many respects much worse at many face-perception tasks than LH (the prosopagnosic mentioned earlier)—she couldn't match photographs of faces, for example. I have noticed that people who know little about anosognosia tend to favor various debunking hypotheses. That is, they assume that the experimenters have made one or another silly mistake in describing the syndrome, because, after all, how could anyone fail to notice that they can't recognize faces, or worse, that they are blind. See Young et al. (1993) for a good debunking of the debunking hypotheses.

27. The same considerations show that prosopagnosia itself is a defect of A-consciousness, not P-consciousness.

28. There is an additional problem in the reasoning that I won't go into except here. There is a well-known difficulty in reasoning of the form: X is missing; the patient has lost the ability to do blah-blah; therefore a function of X is to facilitate blah-biahing. In a complex system, a loss may reverberate through the system, triggering a variety of malfunctions that are not connected in any serious way with the function of the missing item. An imperfect but memorable example (that I heard from Tom Bever) will illustrate: the Martians want to find out about the function of various Earthly items. They begin with the Pentagon, and focus in on a particular drinking fountain in a hall on the third floor of the north side of the building. "If we can figure out what that is for," they think, "we can move on to something more complex." So they vaporize the drinking fountain, causing noise and spurting pipes. Everyone comes out of their offices to see what happened, and the Martians conclude that the function of the fountain was to keep people in their offices. The application of this point to the petit mal case is that even if I am right that it is A-consciousness, not P-consciousness, that is diminished or missing, I would not jump to the conclusion that A-consciousness has a function of adding powers of discrimination, flexibility, and creativity. Creativity, for example, may have its sources in the un-A-conscious, requiring powers of reasoning and control of action and reporting only for its expression.

29. Indeed, in the italicized passage above there is an implicit suggestion that perhaps there are P-conscious events of which no record is made. I could only find one place in the book where Penfield says anything that might be taken to contradict this interpretation: "Thus, the automaton can walk through traffic as though he were aware of all that he hears and sees, and so continue

on his way home. But he is aware of nothing and so makes no memory record. If a policemen were to accost him he might consider the poor fellow to be walking in his sleep" (1975, p. 60). But to properly understand this, we need to know what he means by "awareness," and what he thinks goes on in sleep. Judging by Penfield's use of synonyms, by "awareness" he means something in the category of the higher-order thought analyses or the self-consciousness sense. For example, in discussing his peculiar view that ants are conscious, he seems to use 'conscious' and 'aware' to mean self-aware (pp. 62, 105, 106). Further, he makes it clear that although the mind is shut off during sleep, the sensory cortex is quite active.

30. A similar line of reasoning appears in Shevrin (1992); he notes that in subliminal perception, we don't fix the source of a mental content. Subliminal percepts aren't conscious, so consciousness must have the function of fixing the source of mental contents.

31. Baars (1988, p. 356). Though Baars is talking about the function of "conscious experience," he does have a tendency to combine P-consciousness with A-consciousness under this heading.

32. The Collapse Hypothesis should not be confused with Marcel's (1988, pp. 135–7) Identity Hypothesis, which hypothesizes that the processing of stimuli is identical with consciousness of them. As Marcel points out, blindsight and similar phenomena suggest that we can have processing without consciousness.

33. I am imdebted to Jerry Fodor here.

References

Akins, K. (1993). A bat without qualifies. In Davies and Humphreys (1993a).

Alston, W. (1967). Religion. In *The Encyclopedia of Philosophy*. Macmillan/Free Press, 140–145.

Anderson, J. (1993). To see ourselves as others see us: a response to Mitchell. *New Ideas in Psychology* 11, 3:339–346.

Andrade, J. (1993). Consciousness: current views. In Jones, 1993.

Armstrong, D. M. (1968). *A Materialist Theory of Mind*. Humanities Press.

———. What is consciousness? In *The Nature of Mind*. Ithaca, NY: Cornell University Press.

Baars, B. J. (1988). *A Cognitive Theory of Consciousness*. Cambridge: Cambridge University Press.

Baars, B. J. (1994). A thoroughly empirical approach to consciousness. *Psyche* (the email journal).

Block, N. (1980). What is functionalism? In N. Block (ed), *Readings in the Philosophy of Psychology*, vol 1. Cambridge, MA: Harvard University Press.

——— (1990a). Inverted earth. In J. Tomberlin (ed.), *Philosophical Perspectives*, vol. 4. Atascadero, CA: Ridgeview.

——— (1990b). Consciousness and accessibility. *Behavioral and Brain Sciences* 13:596–598.

—— (1991). Evidence against epiphenomenalism. *Behavioral and Brain Sciences* 14(4):670–672.

—— (1992). Begging the question against phenomenal consciousness. *Behavioral and Brain Sciences* 15, 205–206.

—— (1993). Review of D. Dennett, *Consciousness Explained*. *The Journal of Philosophy* 90, 4:181–193.

—— (1994). "Consciousness," "Functionalism," "Qualia." In S. Guttenplan (ed). *A Companion to Philosophy of Mind*. Oxford: Blackwell.

Bowers, J., and Schacter, D. (1990). Implicit memory and test awareness. *Journal of Experimental Psychology: Learning, Memory and Cognition* 16:3:404–416.

Bornstein, R., and Pittman, T. (1992). *Perception without Awareness*. New York: Guilford Press.

Byrne, A. (1993). *The Emergent Mind*, Ph.D. thesis, Princeton University, Princeton, NJ.

Byrne, R. W. (1993). The meaning of 'awareness': a response to Mitchell. *New Ideas in Psychology* 11, 3:347–350.

Carruthers, P. (1989). Brute experience. *Journal of Philosophy* 86.

—— (1992). Consciousness and concepts. *Proceedings of the Aristotelian Society, Supplementary Volume* 66, 40–59.

Chalmers, D. J. (1996). *The Conscious Mind*. Oxford: Oxford University Press.

Churchland, P. S. (1983). Consciousness: the transmutation of a concept. *Pacific Philosophical Quarterly* 64:80–93.

—— (1986). Reduction and the neurobiological basis of consciousness. In Marcel and Bisiach (1988).

Cooper, L., and Shepard, R. (1973). Chronometric studies of the rotation of mental images. In W. G. Chase (ed), *Visual Information Processing*. New York: Academic Press.

Coslett, H., and Saffran, E. (1994). Mechanisms of implicit reading in alexia. In *The Neuropsychology of High-Level Vision*, M. Farah and G. Ratcliff, eds. Hillside, NJ: Erlbaum.

Cowie, A., and Stoerig, P. (1992). Reflections on blindsight. In Milner and Rugg (1992).

Crick, F., and Koch, C. (1990). Towards a neurobiological theory of consciousness. *Seminars in the Neurosciences* 2:263–275.

Crick, F. (1994). *The Astonishing Hypothesis*. New York: Scribners.

Davies, M., and Humphreys, G. (1993a). *Consciousness*. Oxford: Blackwell.

—— (1993b). Introduction. In Davies and Humphreys (1993a), 1–31.

Davies, M. (1992). Perceptual content and local supervenience. *Proceedings of the Aristotelian Society* 92:21–45.

—— (1995). Externalism and experience. In A. Clark, J. Exquerro, J. Larrazabal (eds), *Categories, Consciousness and Reasoning*. Dordrecht, Netherlands: Kluwer.

de Lannoy, J. (1993). Two theories of a mental model of mirror self-recognition: a response to Mitchell. *New Ideas in Psychology* 11, 3:337–338.

Dennett, D. (1986). Julian Jaynes' software archeology. *Canadian Psychology* 27, 2:149–154.

—— (1991). *Consciousness Explained*. Boston: Little Brown.

—— (1993). The message is: there is no medium. In *Philosophy and Phenomenological Research* 3:4.

Dennett, D., and Kinsbourne, M. (1992a). Time and the observer: the where and when of consciousness in the brain. *Behavioral and Brain Sciences* 15:183–200.

—— (1992b). Escape from the Cartesian theater. *Behavioral and Brain Sciences* 15:234–248.

Dimond, S. (1976). Brain circuits for consciousness. *Brain, Behavior and Evolution* 13:376–395.

Dretske, F. (1993). Conscious experience. *Mind* 102, 406:263–284.

Dupre, J. (1981). Natural kinds and biological taxa. *Philosophical Review* 90:66–90.

Edelman, G. (1989). *The Remembered Present: A Biological Theory of Consciousness*. New York: Basic Books.

Etcoff, N. L., and Freeman, R., and Cave, K. Can we lose memories of faces? Content specificity and awareness in a prosopagnosic. *Journal of Cognitive Neuroscience* 3, 1.

Etcoff, N. L., and Magee, J. J. (1992). Covert recognition of emotional expressions. *Journal of Clinical and Experimental Neuropsychology* 14:95–96.

Evans, G. (1982). *The Varieties of Reference*. Oxford University Press.

Flanagan, O. (1991). *The Science of the Mind*, 2nd ed. Cambridge, MA: MIT Press.

—— (1992). *Consciousness Reconsidered*. Cambridge, MA: MIT Press.

Gallup, G. (1982). Self-awareness and the emergence of mind in primates. *American Journal of Primatology* 2:237–248.

Gallup, G., and Povinelli, D. Mirror, mirror on the wall, which is the most heuristic theory of them all? A response to Mitchell. *New Ideas in Psychology* 11, 3:327–335.

Ghoneim, M., Hinrichs, J., and Mewaldt, S. (1984). Dose-response analysis of the behavioral effects of diazepam: 1. Learning and memory. *Psychopharmacology* 82:291–295.

Ghoneim, M., and Block, R. (1993). Learning during anesthesia. In Jones, 1993.

Goldman, A. (1993a). The psychology of folk psychology. *The Behavioral and Brain Sciences* 16:1:15–28.

———— (1993b). Consciousness, folk psychology and cognitive science. *Consciousness and Cognition* 2:3.

Goodale, M., and Milner, D. (1992). Separate visual pathways for perception and action. *Trends in Neurosciences* 15, 20–25.

Harman, G. (1990). The intrinsic quality of experience. In J. Tomberlin (ed.), *Philosophical Perspectives*, vol. 4. Atascadero, CA: Ridgeview.

Heyes, C. (1993). Reflections on self-recognition in primates, *Animal Behavior*.

Hilgard, E. (1986). *Divided Consciousness*, 2nd ed. New York: John Wiley.

Holender, D. (1986). Semantic activation without conscious identification in dichotic listening, parafoveal vision, and visual masking: a survey and appraisal. *Behavioral and Brain Sciences* 9:1–66.

Hill, C. (1991). *Sensations: A Defense of Type Materialism*. Cambridge: Cambridge University Press.

Humphrey, N. (1992). *A History of the Mind*. New York: Simon & Schuster.

Huxley, T. H. (1866). *Lessons in Elementary Psychology* 8, p. 210. Quoted in Humphrey, (1992).

Jackendoff, R. (1987). *Consciousness and the Computational Mind*. Cambridge, MA: MIT Press.

Jackson, F. (1977). *Perception*. Cambridge: Cambridge University Press.

———— (1993a). Appendix A (for philosophers). In *Philosophy and Phenomenological Research* 3:4.

———— (1993b). 'Armchair metaphysics'. In J. O'Leary-Hawthorne and M. Michael (eds), *Philosophy in Mind*. Dordrecht, Netherlands: Kluwer.

Jacoby, L., Toth, J., Lindsay, D., and Debner, J. (1992). Lectures for a layperson: methods for revealing unconscious processes. In Bornstein and Pittman (1992).

James, W. (1890/1950). *The Principles of Psychology*, 2 vols. New York: Dover.

Jaynes, J. (1976). *The Origin of Consciousness in the Breakdown of the Bicameral Mind*. Boston: Houghton-Mifflin.

Jones, J. G. (1993). *Depth of Anesthesia*. Boston: Little Brown.

Kihlstrom, J. (1987). The cognitive unconscious. *Science* 237:1445–1452.

Kihlstrom, J., and Schacter, D. (1990). Anaesthesia, amnesia, and the cognitive unconscious. In B. Bonke (ed), *Memory and Awareness in Anaesthesia*. Swets and Zeitlinger.

Kihlstrom, J., Barnhardt, T., and Tataryn, D. (1992). Implicit perception. In Bornstein and Pittman (1992).

Kihlstrom, J., and Couture, L. (1992). Awareness and information processing in general anesthesia. *Journal of Psychopharmacology* 6(3):410–417.

Kirk, R. (1992). Consciousness and concepts. *Proceedings of the Aristotelian Society, Supplementary Volume* 66:23–40.

Kosslyn, S. (1980). *Image and Mind*. Cambridge: Harvard University Press.

Kosslyn, S., and Koenig, O. (1992). *Wet Mind: The New Cognitive Neuroscience*. New York: Free Press.

Kuhn, T. (1964). A function for thought experiments. In *Melanges Alexandre Koyre*, vol 1. Hermann: 307–334.

Lackner, J., and Garrett, M. (1973). Resolving ambiguity: effects of biasing context in the unattended ear. *Cognition* 1:359–372.

Landis, T., Regard, M., and Serrat, A. (1980). Iconic reading in a case of alexia without agraphia caused by a brain tumour: a tachistoscopic study. *Brain and Language* 11, 45–53.

Levine, J. (1983). Materialism and qualia: the explanatory gap. *Pacific Philosophical Quarterly* 64:354–361.

——— (1993). One leaving out what it is like. In Davies and Humphreys (1993a).

——— (1994). Review of Owen Flanagan's *Consciousness Reconsidered*. In *The Philosophical Review* 103, 353–356.

Loar, B. (1990). Phenomenal properties. In J. Tomberlin (ed), *Philosophical Perspectives*, vol 4. Atascadero, CA: Ridgeview.

Lormand, E. (2000). Shoemaker and "Inner sense". *Philosophical Topics* 28, 2:147–170.

Lycan, W. (1987). *Consciousness*. Cambridge, MA: MIT Press.

Mandler, G. (1985). *Cognitive Psychology*, chapter 3. Hillside, NJ: Erlbaum.

McGinn, C. (1991). *The Problem of Consciousness*. Oxford: Blackwell.

——— (1993). Consciousness and cosmology: hyper-dualism ventilated. In Davies and Humphreys (1993a).

Marcel, A. J. (1983). Conscious and unconscious perception: An approach to relations between phenomenal experience and perceptual processes. *Cognitive Psychology* 15:238–300.

——— (1986). Consciousness and processing: choosing and testing a null hypothesis. *The Behavioral and Brain Sciences* 9:40–41.

——— (1988). Phenomenal experience and functionalism. In Marcel and Bisiach (1988).

Marcel, A. J., and Bisiach, E. (eds) (1988). *Consciousness in Contemporary Science*. Oxford: Oxford University Press.

McCullough, G. (1993). The very idea of the phenomenological. *Proceedings of the Aristotelian Society* 93:39–58.

Melzack, R., and Wall, P. (1988). *The Challenge of Pain*, 2nd edition. London: Penguin.

Menzel, E., Savage-Rumbaugh, E., Lawson, J. (1985). Chimpanzee (*Pan troglogdytes*) spatial problem solving with the use of mirrors and televised equivalents of mirrors. *Journal of Comparative Psychology* 99:211–217.

Milner, B., and Rugg, M. (eds) (1992). *The Neuropsychology of Consciousness*. New York: Academic Press.

Mitchell, R. W. (1993a). Mental models of mirror self-recognition: two theories. In *New Ideas in Psychology* 11:295–325.

———— (1993b). Recognizing one's self in a mirror? A reply to Gallup and Povinelli, de Lannoy, Anderson, and Byrne. In *New Ideas in Psychology* 11:351–377.

Moscovitch, M., Goshen-Gottstein, Y., Vriezen, E. (1994). "Memory without conscious recollection: a tutorial review from a neuropsychological perspective." In Umilta and Moscovitch, 1994.

Nagel, T. (1974). What is it like to be a bat? *Philosophical Review* chapter 32.

Nagel, T. (1979). *Mortal Questions*. Cambridge: Cambridge University Press.

———— (1986). *The View from Nowhere*. Oxford: Oxford University Press.

Nathan, P. (1985). Pain and nociception in the clinical context. *Philosophical Transactions of the Royal Society of London. Series B: Biological Sciences* 308:219–226.

Natsoulas, T. (1993). What is wrong with the appendage theory of consciousness? *Philosophical Psychology* 6, 2:137–154.

Nelkin, N. (1993). The connection between intentionality and consciousness. In Davies and Humphreys (1993a).

Nisbett, R., and Wilson, T. (1977). Telling more than we can know: verbal reports on mental processes, *Psychological Review* 84, 231–259.

Peacocke, C. (1983). *Sense and Content*. Oxford: Oxford University Press.

———— (1992). *A Study of Concepts*. Cambridge, MA: MIT Press.

Pendlebury, M. (1992). Experience, theories of. In J. Dancy and E. Sosa, *A Companion to Epistemology*. Oxford: Blackwell.

Penfield, W. (1975). *The Mystery of the Mind: A Critical Study of Consciousness and the Human Brain*. Princeton, NJ: Princeton University Press.

Plourde, G. (1993). Clinical use of the 40-Hz auditory steady state response. In Jones (1993).

Povinelli, D. (1994). What chimpanzees know about the mind. In *Behavioral Diversity in Chimpanzees*. Cambridge, MA: Harvard University Press.

Putnam, H. (1975). The meaning of 'meaning'. In Putnam's *Mind, Language and Reality*. Cambridge, MA: Cambridge University Press.

Reingold, E., and Merikle, P. (1993). Theory and measurement in the study of unconscious processes. In Davies and Humphreys (1993a).

Rey, G. (1983). A reason for doubting the existence of consciousness. In *Consciousness and Self-Regulation*, vol 3. R. Davidson, G. Schwartz, D. Shapiro (eds). New York: Plenum.

———— (1988). A question about consciousness. In *Perspectives on Mind*, H. Otto and J. Tuedio (eds). Dordrecht: Reidel.

Rosenthal, David (1986). Two concepts of consciousness. *Philosophical Studies* 49:329–359.

———— (1993). Thinking that one thinks. In Davies and Humphreys (1993a).

Schacter, D. (1989). On the relation between memory and consciousness: dissociable interactions and conscious experience. In: H. Roediger and F. Craik (eds), *Varieties of Memory and Consciousness: Essays in Honour of Endel Tulving*. Hillside, NJ: Erlbaum.

Searle, J. (1983). *Intentionality*. Cambridge: Cambridge University Press.

———— (1990a). Consciousness, explanatory inversion and cognitive science. *Behavioral and Brain Sciences* 13:4:585–595.

———— (1990b). Who is computing with the brain? *Behavioral and Brain Sciences* 13, 4:632–642.

———— (1992). *The Rediscovery of the Mind*. Cambridge, MA: MIT Press.

Sergent, J., and Poncet, M. (1990). From covert to overt recognition of faces in a prosopagnosic patient. *Brain* 113:989–1004.

Shallice, T. (1988a). *From Neuropsychology to Mental Structure*. Cambridge: Cambridge University Press.

———— (1988b). Information-processing models of consciousness: possibilities and problems. In Marcel and Bisiach (1988).

Shevrin, H. (1992). Subliminal perception, memory and consciousness: cognitive and dynamic perspectives. In Bornstein and Pittman (1992).

Shoemaker, S. (1975). Functionalism and qualia. *Philosophical Studies* 27:291–315.

———— (1981a). Absent qualia are impossible—a reply to Block. *The Philosophical Review* 90, 4:581–599.

———— (1981b). The inverted spectrum. *The Journal of Philosophy* 74, 7:357–381.

———— (1993). Lovely and suspect ideas. In *Philosophy and Phenomenological Research* 3, 4:905–910.

———— (1994). Phenomenal Character, *Nous* 21–38.

Sperling, G. (1960). The information available in brief visual presentations. *Psychological Monographs* 74, 11.

Stich, S. (1978). Autonomous psychology and the belief-desire thesis. *The Monist* 61, 573–591.

Time-Life (1993). *Secrets of the Inner Mind: Journey Through the Mind and Body*. New York: Time-Life Books.

Tye, M. (1991). *The Imagery Debate*. MIT Press.

—— (1993). Reflections on Dennett and consciousness. In *Philosophy and Phenomenological Research* 3, 4.

—— (1994). Blindsight, the absent qualia hypothesis and the mystery of consciousness. In *Philosophy and Cognitive Science*. C. Hookway and D. Peterson (eds), *Royal Institute of Philosophy Supplement*: 34. Cambridge: Cambridge University Press.

—— (1995). A representational theory of pains and their phenomenal character. In J. Tomberlin (ed), *Philosophical Perspectives* 9: Atascadero, CA: Ridgeview.

Umilta, C., and Moscovitch, M. (1994). *Attention and Performance XV*. Cambridge, MA: MIT Press.

Van Gulick, R. (1989). What difference does consciousness make? *Philosophical Topics* 17, 1:211–230.

—— (1993). Understanding the phenomenal mind: are we all just armadillos? In Davies and Humphreys (1993a).

Weiskrantz, L. (1986). *Blindsight*. Oxford: Oxford University Press.

—— (1988). Some contributions of neuropsychology of vision and memory to the problem of consciousness. In Marcel and Bisiach (1988).

—— (1992). Introduction: Dissociated issues. In B. Milner and M. Rugg (1992).

White, S. L. (1987). What is it like to be an homunculus. *Pacific Philosophical Quarterly* 68:148–174.

—— (1991). Transcendentalism and its discontents. In White, S. L. *The Unity of the Self*, Cambridge, MA: MIT Press.

Wiser, M., and Carey, S. (1983). When heat and temperature were one. In D. Gentner and A. Stevens (eds), *Mental Models*. Hillside, NJ: Erlbaum.

Young, A. W. (1994a). Covert recognition. In M. Farah and G. Ratcliff (eds), *The Neuropsychology of Higher Vision: Collected Tutorial Essays*. Hillside, NJ: Erlbaum.

—— (1994b). Neuropsychology of awareness. In M. Kappinen and A. Revonsuo (eds), *Consciousness in philosophy and cognitive neuroscience*. Hillside, NJ: Erlbaum.

—— (1994c). Recognition and reality. In E. M. R. Critchley (ed). *Neurological boundaries of Reality*: Farrand Press.

Young, A. W., and De Haan, E. (1993). Impairments of Visual Awareness. In Davies and Humphreys (1993a).

10 How Many Concepts of Consciousness?

I learned a great deal from the commentators about ways in which what I said was wrong or easily misunderstood. I am grateful for the opportunity to rethink and rephrase in response to the criticisms. A number of superb commentaries also had to be held over to a future issue, and I look forward to grappling with them as well.

R1. Is P-Conscious Content Just Highly Informational Content?

Armstrong accepts P-consciousness but says it is "a species of representational content of a particularly detailed sort." Farah notes that perception in blindsight and other such cases is degraded and concludes (here and in other publications) that P-consciousness depends on quality of information representation. [See also Farah: "Neuropsychological Inference with an Interactive Brain" *BBS* 17(1) 1994.] Dennett says that my A/P distinction should really be seen as a continuum, a continuum of richness of content and degree of influence. He says I am "inflating differences in degree into imaginary differences in kind." In Note 16 of the target article I suggested that some functionalists "will see the distinction between A-consciousness and P-consciousness primarily as a difference in degree rather than in kind." But I was alluding to degree of access, not degree of informational content. I think the high degree of information views of P don't get to first base.

To see what is wrong with highly informational representational content as a substitute for P-content, consider the common types of blindness in which the (legally) blind person is able to distinguish a few degrees of light and dark, much as you or I can with our eyes closed. *This is P-conscious content that is relatively informationally poor, not informationally rich.* Furthermore, senses can differ in information richness without differing in phenomenality. Perhaps taste (not including smell via the mouth or mouth feel) is less rich than vision (Kapsalis 1987, p. 66). But is taste any less phenomenal than vision? Or consider orgasm again. Are we supposed to think that orgasm is informationally rich? Tye has made a valiant attempt to characterize (partially) the phenomenal content of orgasm in representational terms: something that is very pleasing (and changes in intensity) is happening down there. Even if this does capture the phenomenal content of orgasm (which I don't believe for a second), this is not a very informationally rich content. Yet there can be no doubt that orgasm is "phenomenologically impressive"!

Weiskrantz (1988) notes that his patient DB had better acuity in some areas of the blind field (in some circumstances) than in his sighted field. Suppose a blindsight patient with fairly good acuity in tile blind field were to become near-blind in the sighted field, able to distinguish only a few shades of light and dark. He experiences the light and dark but does not experience the blindsight. The blindsight is informationally richer but (presumably) not phenomenal, whereas the near-blind vision is phenomenal and informationally poorer.[1]

Dennett describes the informational content of blindsight as "vanishingly" small. In Dennett (1991), he emphasizes the cases in which the blindsight patient is given a forced-choice, for example, an X or an O. But blindsight patients can exhibit contents that have more informational value than that. In Pöppel et al. (1973), the first human blindsight study, the patients were asked to move their eyes in the direction of the stimuli that they apparently had no experience of seeing. The patients could do so even though they thought they were guessing. In addition, as I mentioned in the target article, blindsight patients can catch a ball thrown in the blind field and can shape their hands appropriately so as to grasp an object presented in the blind field. The information involved in these nonphenomenal activities is surely at least as great as the phenomenal discriminations of the blind people just mentioned or of some sighted people with their eyes closed. In addition, the implicit prosopagnosics mentioned in the target article have the capacity to recognize un-P-consciously the face of, say, John Wayne. I skipped over most of the empirical literature on this topic for lack of space, but let me just mention one phenomenon:

Semantic priming is a phenomenon in which the presentation of one stimulus facilitates the subject's response to a related stimulus. For example, if normal Americans are asked to press a button when a familiar face appears in a series of faces presented rapidly one after another, the subject tends to press the button sooner if a related name has been presented recently. For example, "Reagan" facilitates reactions to Bush's face. Likewise, one name primes another and one face primes a "related" name. Here is the result: in a few prosopagnosics who have been studied in detail and who exhibit some of the other indications of "covert knowledge" of faces, faces prime related names despite the prosopagnosics' insistence that they have no idea whose face it is. For example, Lady Di's face primes Prince Charles's name even though the subject insists that he does not know whose face it is. See also the phenomenon mentioned by Graham. The perceptual content that it is Lady Di's face is moderately informationally rich, but this is not a P-conscious content. So once again, we have moderate informational richness without P, contradicting the point of view of Armstrong, Farah, and Dennett.

Dennett constructs a thought experiment, a superblindsight patient who comes to be able to tell us—effortlessly—very detailed facts about the visual properties in his blind field. He can tell us that there is a bright orange Times Roman italic X on a blue-green background about 2 inches high with a smudge. This superblindsighter says that he knows these sorts of features of stimuli in his blind field, even though he is just guessing, and contrasts what is going on with the real visual experiences of his sighted field. Dennett rightly says that it is hard to swallow that "anybody who could gather that much information from a glance" might have no visual experience. And he adds, imagining another patient, that if all he can tell us about the sighted field is that he saw an X rather than an O, we would be baffled by his claim of P-conscious experience.

Dennett is on to something here, but he has misdiagnosed what it is. There is some plausibility in the idea of high-information representational content as an empirically *sufficient* condition of phenomenality in humans (though not a conceptually sufficient condition). But there is no plausibility at all to the idea that high information content is a *necessary* condition for phenomenality, as is shown by the example of orgasm and the discrimination of a few degrees of light and dark with one's eyes closed. I think that the reason for the plausibility of Dennett's examples is that they illustrate *depictive* or *pictorial* representations. And it is very tempting to believe that pictorial visual representations must be P-conscious. That explains Dennett's first example. In the second example, if we think of the person as having a pictorial representation of an X, it is hard to imagine how the person could see the X without seeing it as having some particular size, typeface, color, and so on (hard only because one naturally but wrongly thinks of images as photograph-like; see Block 1983).

However, even mental images can apparently fail to be P-conscious. Cooper and Shepard (1973) noted that when subjects practiced image rotation to the point of automaticity, they reported that they had no image experiences, yet the rotation data argued for the same images as before (I am indebted here to Baars 1994). Kosslyn (1980; 1994) asked subjects to zoom in on an imagined map to the point where they could only see a part of it. It would be interesting to see whether these subjects could make use of the information in the "invisible" parts of the map better than subjects who had not just had those parts in the mind's eye.

So far I have been criticizing the view that P-content = highly information content, the view of Armstrong and Farah, but not quite Dennett's view. Dennett also mentions access. But how is access supposed to figure? Is P-content content that is *both* highly informational *and* highly accessible? If so, the legally blind contents I mentioned are a counterexample since though they are highly accessible, they are low in information. Or perhaps the mode of combination is disjunction rather than conjunction: P content is content that is high in information *or* high in accessibility. But now the P-unconscious images are a counterexample in the other direction. Furthermore, everyone has relatively high information but quiescent beliefs and desires that are not P-conscious.

R2.   Does P Exist?

Rey says it is strange that I did not explicitly consider any of the accounts that have been offered of P-consciousness in computational terms. This was an explicit strategic decision. Not everything can be discussed in every paper. This one was about some distinctions and how missing them causes trouble. In other papers I have discussed some computational (functional), intentional, and cognitive theories of P-consciousness. Rey says that the assumption of P-consciousness as noncomputational and noncognitive impedes research. That depends on whether P-consciousness *is* noncomputational and noncognitive. If it is, then Rey's assumption that it isn't impedes research. Rey assumes that the right approach to consciousness is that of computational and cognitive psychology (computational in this context = functional; see Block 1994). But why does Rey ignore the neurophysiological approach? The sort of research program described, for example, in Crick (1994) does not accept Rey's assumption, yet it seems to be going somewhere. Rey admits that phenomenal consciousness deflated so as to be amenable to computational analysis of the sort he favors is "phenomenologically unsatisfying," but he persists because he knows of no non-question-begging evidence for the postulation of P-consciousness as distinct from computational notions. I find Rey's stance baffling. Let's look at a specific example. Above, I discussed the idea that P-conscious content is simply highly informational content. I appealed to the evidence of our own experience: when you close your eyes, you can nonetheless distinguish a few degrees of light and dark via truly phenomenal experience, so phenomenal experience can be low on the informational scale. Does Rey propose that we should ignore the evidence of our own experience in cases like this? To do so would be "phenomenologically unsatisfying" in a way that carries some weight, namely, it ignores a source of evidence that we all have from our own experience.

Rey is worried about conundra involving epiphenomenalism, zombies and such, and to avoid them he wants to reduce phenomenal consciousness to the computational. If P can be functionally defined, epiphenomenalism is ruled out and zombies are impossible. But this is the wrong way to avoid the conundra. Russell once hypothesized that the world was created five minutes ago with all the evidence of an age of many billions of years. Some philosophers have wanted to avoid this possibility by defining the past in terms of its effect on the present. To say that there were dinosaurs 65 million years ago is to say there are dinosaur-signs now. But this is a foolish metaphysical over-reaction. Better to face the conundra head on as discussed below in section R13.

R3. Is A-Consciousness Consciousness at All?

Graham, Lloyd, Natsoulas, Revonsuo, and the Editorial Commentary question whether A-consciousness is consciousness at all. As Searle (1992) emphasizes, a zombie that is a functional duplicate of us but lacks any P-consciousness is not conscious at all. (This point is made forcefully by Tyler Burge 1997.) But it is a mistake to jump from the idea that a zombie is not conscious in any sense to the idea that A-consciousness is not a form of consciousness. A-consciousness can be a kind of consciousness even if it is in some way parasitic (as Burge, Lloyd, and Revonsuo rightly say) on a core notion of P-consciousness. (A parquet floor is a kind of floor even though it requires another floor beneath it.) A-consciousness can come and go in a background of a P-consciousness person (that is, a person who sometimes has P-conscious states). Suppose a drunk becomes "unconscious." He may have P-conscious states both before and during his episode of unconsciousness; for example, while unconscious he may be seeing stars or having mental images of various sorts. I don't want to try to specify exactly the relation between being unconscious in this ordinary sense and the concepts of P and A, but roughly, I think we count the drunk as unconscious to the extent that he has no A-consciousness of the environment via P-conscious perceptions of it. The drunk is A-unconscious in a way the specification of which involves appeal to P.

We tend to deploy the concept of A-consciousness in describing unconscious phenomena, so it is not surprising that many of the most common uses come in at a somewhat theoretical level. Consider, for example, Freudian unconscious states. Suppose a person is tortured horribly in a cinnabar room (a particular shade of orange-red). The cinnabar color symbolizes the pain and is repressed. He remembers the torture vividly but denies remembering the color of the room. Nonetheless, the memory of the color comes out in slips, associations, dreams, and so on. For example, he dreams of horrid cinnabar things. When he is in a cinnabar room he shudders violently and comes up with an excuse to leave, but does not recognize why. There is nothing in Freudian theory or common sense that precludes repressed phenomenal color images of the room. In fact, we can imagine the patient realizing this himself after years of psychoanalysis. "I had a cinnabar image all the time that I would not let myself acknowledge." Whether or not this actually occurs, it makes sense for there to be a blockage that keeps a phenomenal color image from being informationally promiscuous. So the sense in which repressed memories are unconscious is A-unconscious. The Freudian type of unconsciousness does not *require* P-unconsciousness, but it does require A-unconsciousness.

Similar points apply to neurological syndromes such as prosopagnosia, in which the patient is not "conscious" of whose face he is seeing, even though he reveals in a variety of experimental circumstances that the information is unconsciously represented.

The unconsciousness is A-unconsciousness. It is not the presence or absence of a feeling of familiarity that defines prosopagnosia but rather the patient lacking A-consciousness of the information about the identity of the person. As Young notes, the lack of a P-conscious feeling of familiarity is (normally) a consequence of the lack of A-consciousness, but is not a defining feature of the syndrome. This point is nicely illustrated by Young's theory of Capgras's delusion, a syndrome in which patients claim that people whom they know (usually friends and relations) have been replaced by aliens who look just like them. Young (1994c) provides evidence that what is going on is that the subject recognizes (say) his mother, but he gets no feeling of familiarity from the perception, so he supposes the person is not really his mother. (It may be that victims of Cotard's syndrome, in which patients think they have died likewise, lack this feeling of familiarity, but blame it on themselves instead of on the people who don't stimulate the feeling of familiarity.) Suppose Young's suggestion is right. Still, this lack of the feeling of familiarity does not make the patient a prosopagnosic. He recognizes his mother's face and the faces of others despite the lack of the feeling of familiarity. So lack of a P-conscious feeling is not at the heart of prosopagnosia. In sum, though I agree that P is the core notion, A is still a kind of consciousness.

R4.   P without A; A without P

Many of the commentators agreed with at least some of my cases of P without A. Revonsuo proposes a new one: dreams. The trouble with dreams as cases of P without A is that dreams often involve substantial rationality. For example, Chomsky tells me he plans papers in his dreams, and there is a well-known phenomenon of lucid dreaming in which the dreamer, knowing he is dreaming, changes the course of the dream. Of course, many dreams are much less rational, on the surface at least, but I would be reluctant to suppose that these dreams are unconscious in a different sense of the term than less overtly sensible dreams. I expect that dreams are unconscious in the sense described in the discussion above of the unconscious drunk.

What about A without P. In the target article I said that such cases were conceptually possible, but I knew of no actual ones. If it is so much easier to find P without A than A without P, that is a striking empirical fact. Humphrey was the only commentator to make any remarks in favor of A without P. He argues that Helen was in some respects such a case, correcting wrong impressions about his unpublished work. But, as he notes, even if Helen is a case of no visual phenomenality, she had no shape recognition of any kind. So we need to know more about cases such as Helen to count her as a good case of A without P.

I have long been troubled by cases from the "imageless thought" controversy from the early part of the century (G. Humphrey 1963—not the same Humphrey). For example, pick up an object from your desk, put it down, and pick up another. If they differ substantially in weight, you may "just know" this. My experience here is that I have "images" of the weights of the two objects, but apparently not of the *relation* between them. The relation between them appears to be something I just know without any phenomenal experience of it. This is a tricky bit of introspection, just the sort of thing that got psychologists in trouble during this controversy. But it would be foolish to ignore it, since it can guide experimentation. I hope some clever experimentalist figures out how to get an experimental handle on it. Burge (1997) has some very interesting arguments for A without P. One of Burge's examples involves the familiar case of a solution to a problem popping into mind. We often know we've got the solution without actually expressing it in any internal phenomenal clothes such as words or pictures.

I should add that from the point of view of empirical model building, it is very important to distinguish between cases of A without P, like superblindsight, if it exists, and Burge's sort of case. Both count against Model 2 because they show that some highly sophisticated thought (that must be accomplished by the Executive System if there is one such system) is not P. But neither Burge's type of case nor the imageless thought case challenges Schacter's (1989) model, because that model allows for executive processes that are not P. However, superblindsight, if it exists, would challenge Schacter's model, because that model tells us that the only way for perceptual information to get to the Executive is to pass through the P-module. Of course, we already have good reason to reject Model 2. As pointed out in the target article, the intermediate steps in problem solving often fail to be P, and that alone counts against Model 2.

Let us now move to objections to the idea of P without A. Church, Kobes, and Revonsuo criticize my example of the unattended noise as a case of P without A. They say that people adjust the loudness of their speech in response to noise even when not attending to it, and that is a rational action that reflects A consciousness of the noise. But this noise adjustment does not show A-consciousness in my sense of the term. There is no inferential promiscuity here. If the notion of A-consciousness were to be weakened in this direction (also suggested by Graham and in Flanagan's [1992] critique of my notion of A), the consequence would be to let in cases of A without P. If A-consciousness were watered down in this way, then blindsight and the other "covert knowledge" syndromes would be cases of A without P. Of course if you like A without P and hate P without A, you could adopt Graham's and Flanagan's suggestion, but your pleasure would be purely verbal.

Kobes criticizes one of my arguments for conceptually possible cases of P without A. In Note 7 of the target article I worried about an A-unconscious state that caused an A-conscious state with the same content. The first state is ex hypothesis not A-conscious, but it is in virtue of one's having *that* state that its content is inferentially promiscuous, so it seems that it does have to be A-conscious. I avoided the problem by thinking of the "in virtue of" in the definition of A-consciousness (a state is A-conscious if in virtue of one's having the state, a representation of its content is inferentially promiscuous, etc.) as *directly* in virtue of. If state X has an inferentially promiscuous content, but only because it causes state Y, which inherits X's content, then X doesn't count as A-conscious. Kobes thinks this answer gets me in trouble with the perceptual states of the superblindsighter (who, you will recall, is conceptually possible but apparently nonexistent). He says that it is only in virtue of the effects of these perceptual states on the superblindsighter's thoughts that the perceptual states are inferentially promiscuous, and so on, so the perceptual states are *neither A-conscious nor P-conscious*, and the supposed example of A without P dissolves. But why suppose, as Kobes does, that the superblindsighter's perceptual states of "seeing" an X have their effects only via the causation of the *thought* that there is an X? If such a perceptual state could only have an effect by causing a specific thought, then it would not be informationally promiscuous and it would not be A-conscious. A genuinely A-conscious perceptual content would be freely available for use in thought.

Kobes criticizes my account of the Sperling (1960) experiment, saying that before the icon fades, the subject is both P- and A-conscious of them all jointly, and after the icon fades the subject is neither P- nor A-conscious of them all jointly, so there is no divergence of P and A. Let me try to state my point better. Consider the distinction between *jointly* and *severally*. A pair of swimmers can be poised to win jointly if, say, they are on the same team in a race of teams. But in a race in which only one swimmer can win, a pair of swimmers would be poised to win severally, not jointly, that is each is poised to win, even though they can't both win. In the Sperling experiment there is never a time in which the letters are all poised to win jointly (become inferentially promiscuous, etc.) because, as with the individual swimmers, they cannot all win. But they can all jointly be P-conscious, or at any rate that's my claim.

Zalla and Palma argue that the tip of the tongue phenomenon (and "Feeling of Knowing" states generally) is a case of P without A. You have the feeling of knowing someone's name, but you can't access it. But on the surface, at least, the content that the name is known is *both* P and A, and the specific name content (e.g., "Blanche") that leads to knowledge of or correct guesses about features of the name (rhymes with "ranch") is *neither* P nor A. I agree with Zalla & Palma's statement that Feeling of Knowing states involve consciousness of "the *existence* of a content but not *of* the content itself." But as far as I can see, this characterizes both P and A, so there is no gap here between P and A. Zalla & Palma argue (if I understand them rightly) that when I have the feeling that I know her name, typically the name itself is P, but not A. "Blanche" is a P-content but not an A-content. But I don't see why the facts that they mention about frontal lobe patients are supposed to support this idea. They point out that I have not got a wealth of data to support the idea of P without A. They are right, but I am hopeful for the future.

Baars thinks that P = A, but what is his evidence? In his reply he mentions a few cases in which both P and A are present and other cases in which both P and A are absent. I mentioned in the target article that this sort of evidence is suggestive of a rough correlation, but it can hardly show that P = A. He says that "implicitly ... we all treat" P and A as "empirically inseparable." True, but implicitly we treat the earth as stationary as well. Baars studies P by studying A, so if P ≠ A, his research program would have to be reevaluated. Even if P and A are perfectly correlated within some conditions, but not identical, his research strategy would be questionable. One would want to know *why* P and A are correlated. Weight and mass are correlated at the surface of the earth, but studying weight is not studying mass. He says, "GW theory shows that the equivalence ... is very productive indeed." I question that; we know lots about A, almost nothing about P. I think we are more likely to make progress by looking very carefully at cases where P and A seem to diverge. If they do diverge, that's where the interesting results are. Baars just ignores the cases that cause problems for his view instead of subjecting them to scrutiny. Church, Kobes, Revonsuo, and Chalmers (1997) agree with Baars that P and A are correlated, but unlike Baars they take the responsibility to confront the putative exceptions. Baars should consider what Humphrey says about A without P. Baars brings in evolution to argue for P = A, saying that we are unlikely to get two nearly identical organs for one job. "That is not how the natural world works." In our state of ignorance of what P is and how P might be related to access, I don't think such an argument has much weight. One can imagine an uninformed person wondering why evolution needed both sperms and eggs, two things for one job. Should the uninformed person conclude that sperm = egg? No, he should try to find out more about the correlation. And we are no less ignorant about consciousness than this uninformed person. Furthermore, even sophisticated biologists do not agree about why sex evolved. So the question of Why two things for one job? is still a live one. Nonetheless, concluding that sperm = egg would be a joke. Baars coauthored "Does Philosophy Help or Hinder Scientific Work on Consciousness?" (Baars & McGovern 1993), arguing that philosophers should get out of the way. We should evaluate this criticism in the light of the fact that philosophers are the ones most likely to raise doubts about Baars's research program.

R5. Why Not Make A Easier to Have?

Church, Graham, and Revonsuo think I set the A-hurdle too high. Church suggests accessibility instead of being poised for access, and Graham wants to set the hurdle low enough so that the kind of access that blindsight patients have is good enough for A. Flanagan (1992) reacted in a similar manner to an earlier version of this paper, proposing that we substitute a notion of "informational sensitivity" for A, where blindsight patients are informationally sensitive to information in their blind fields.

Of course, one is free to define "Access-conscious" as one chooses. What I was after was a notion of access that I find in common-sense reasoning and that is the best shot at coextension with P. Defining A in terms of informational sensitivity will frustrate that aim. As I mentioned, blindsight will count as a case of A without P. Indeed, one reason for choosing "poised for access" instead of "accessible" is to avoid classifying as A a familiar kind of inactive or dormant belief. For example, we were all taught facts in elementary school, such as that the sun is 93 million miles away from the earth. Perhaps you were taught this and have believed it ever since, even though you haven't thought of this fact in years. It was an inactive belief. But if we make A a matter of accessibility, then such inactive beliefs will be A but not P, and that makes the failure of coextension of A and P a trivial consequence of a definition. In the view of many of the commentators, A = P or at least A and P are coextensive or can be made so with a little tinkering with definitions. I disagree, but I do not want my disagreement to rest on a triviality.

Similar points apply to the definition of "P." Humphrey prefers to restrict P to the result of irritation of the sensory surfaces. This leaves out, for example, images and the phenomenal aspect of thinking, and would therefore generate A without P. Perhaps Humphrey would want to include images that reflect the same states as are produced by sensory surfaces, but then why leave out the phenomenal aspect of thought?

As Chalmers (1997) notes, I should welcome attempts to tinker with the definitions of "P" and "A" so as to make them coincide better. I don't want my claim that P ≠ A to depend on anything that is merely verbal. So I invite further attempts to improve these definitions.

R6.   Why Does A Have to Be Rational?

I defined A using the notion of rationality, and this draws complaints from Graham, Lloyd, Revonsuo, and Warren as well as an excellent account of what I should have said from Kobes. Though I think there are deep connections between consciousness (both P and A) and rationality, I didn't intend to imply that principles of logic or good reasoning are necessary for A or that animals cannot have A. I meant to appeal to the use of a representation in reasoning, even if the reasoning is poor. And I intended a relativization to the capacities of the type of animal involved. As Kobes says, "Access is not diminished merely in virtue of the creature's having less power to reason or act." I apologize to my readers for not being clearer about this.

R7.   Is the P/A Distinction Useful?

What is good about the P/A distinction? (1) It is an ordinary concept of consciousness, and so it is relevant to how we think about ourselves. (2) It is the information-processing image of P and thus a good candidate for what P is in information-processing terms. And (3) the relative ease of finding cases of P without A as compared with A without P suggests the distinction is on to something to do with the joints of nature.

Dixon argues that there is no point in distinguishing P from A. He gives a number of cases that he apparently sees as borderline ones, not clearly A or P. But to conclude from the existence of borderline cases that there is no distinction or that the distinction is not useful is a mistake. There are objects that are borderline cases between a table and a chair—a bit table-like, a bit chair-like, but neither table nor chair. That doesn't impugn the utility of the table/chair distinction. Dixon mentions many cases, but I'll just discuss the one he says casts the greatest doubt on the distinction: Hypnosis induces a hallucination in the subject of the experimenter, but when the subject turns to the side he also sees the real experimenter. Dixon seems to think that there is some sort of conundrum here that casts doubt on the A/P distinction. But if there is a genuine hallucination, then when I'm having it I'm having one experience that is both A and P, and when I see the real experimenter I have a similar experience that is also both A and P. What's the problem? Dixon goes on to argue that I should not have constructed a theory of consciousness on the basis of evidence from brain damage, because these patients may have compensating defects that make them different from normal people, and there are not enough of them for good sample size. But if brain-damage cases show P without A, then its existence is proved whether or not it ever occurs in normal people, and if brain damage does not yield cases of A without P, this is an especially interesting fact given the fantastic wealth of variation in brain-damage cases. These points illustrate why general cautions like, "You can't show anything by appealing to brain damage" are so weak. Every source of evidence has its pitfalls—the critic of a particular bit of empirical reasoning must show that the pitfalls have been engaged.

Warren rejects the A/P distinction because it is not defined in a completely clear and unambiguous way. But the demand for such definitions is misplaced. Especially at the beginning of a scientific enterprise there is no alternative to going by the seat of one's pants. I once saw a book that discussed the quality of scientific articles. The authors shared Warren's mistaken view of definition. They felt it was important to define "scientific quality," and they did so in terms of the number of references to the article in the subsequent literature. As anyone can see, that is no good—for example, an article can be referred to as a standard example of a terrible mistake. At an early stage in inquiry, noncircular definition is usually not possible. It took a whole thermodynamic theory to ground the thermodynamic definition of temperature, and further work reducing this theory to statistical mechanics to ground the definition of temperature as mean molecular kinetic energy. Definition and theory must progress together. The demand for definition at an early stage encourages misplaced precision.

R8. Is There a Fallacy at All?

Atkinson and Davies quote Shiffrin and Schneider (1977) giving a theory of P in terms of A, and they say reasonably that there is no conflation here. But the fact that Shiffrin and Schneider don't exhibit a conflation does not show that others don't. The sign of lack of conflation in what they quote is that in a single sentence the authors say they are going to give an information-processing theory of the "phenomenological feeling of consciousness." But there is another route to a theory of P in terms of A: first you conflate P and A, and then you give a theory of A, taking it to be a theory of P. The cases I quoted look quite different from Shiffrin and Schneider, more in the direction of the second story. The important point is that the difference here is not in premises and conclusion. I agree that in that regard Shiffrin and Schneider are more or less the same as a number of the cases I mention. The difference lies not in the premises and the conclusion but in the means of getting from one to the other.

Atkinson and Davies go on to suggest a new argument for explaining A in terms of P. P is relatively intrinsic and categorical compared to A, whereas A is relatively relational and dispositional. They are right about this, but the upshot for matters causal is limited. Atkinson and Davies think the relation between P and A is like that between the chemical basis of solubility and the tendency to dissolve. However, a token thought can be accessible at one time but not another, depending on the whole system and the pathways available. We do not know that P content is a force toward mechanisms of reasoning and reporting. This is of course intuitively plausible, but then blindsight is or was intuitively *im*plausible. Suppose, for example, that Schacter's (1989) model is correct. Then we may be able to explain why P-conscious representations tend to be A-conscious without any appeal to the intrinsic properties of P. It is a property of the model that anything that gets to the P module is close to the Executive System and (perhaps) likely to be sent there.

Tye also argues that there is no fallacy, but on a different ground. P is preconceptual, so how could it involve the Executive System? So it must be that information fails to arrive at the Executive System because it fails to be P; so there is no fallacy. On the substance of Tye's argument: How do we know if P is preconceptual? I used the phrase "representational" to describe P-content instead of "intentional" to allow for that possibility, but I have seen no convincing argument to the effect that P-content is preconceptual. Furthermore, there is reason to doubt the preconceptual claim. The specialized modules appear to have lots of conceptualized information. For example, there appears to be information in the face module about people's *occupations* (see Sergent and Poncet 1990; Young 1994a; 1994b). On Schacter's (1989) model, all the inputs to the P-module are from sources that contain conceptualized contents. But suppose that Tye is right. Still, this is a new argument. When someone finds a good argument from premises to a conclusion, there is a temptation to suppose that this is what others have had in mind who have argued, apparently fallaciously, from the same premises to the same conclusion. However, I saw no sign of Tye's argument in the works that I criticized.

R9.   Is P at All Representational?

Katz argues that I have not presented sufficient reason to conclude that P-content is at all representational. He notes that even though what it is like to hear a sound from the right ≠ what it is like to hear a sound from the left, one cannot conclude that P-content is representational. What it is like to be married ≠ what is it like to be single; marital status is social, but it would be a mistake to conclude that P-content is social. The argument form is certainly not valid, but it has something to it: the premises call for an account of the difference, in the case of marriage, we have an adequate account of why what it is like to be married ≠ what is it like to be single without assuming that phenomenal content is social. And in the direction case, as Katz says, we could explain the different P-contents on the basis of a difference in attention or orienting. But I believe that there are many cases for which the best explanation of the difference between the P-content of seeing X and the P content of seeing Y appeals to representational features of P.

Consider the P content of seeing a square compared to the P-content of seeing a circle. These P-contents allow one to see that the squares are packable together without gaps, whereas the circles are not. Also, the squares have a small number of axes of symmetry, but the circles have a large number. These examples show that P-content is representational, but they also show something stronger and more interesting, something that must be Katz's real target. Katz's position allows that P-content represents as ink represents, namely, extrinsically, that is, it can be used to represent. But what the examples show is that P-contents represent per se. The P-contents are intrinsically packable (for the square-representing contents) or not packable (for the circle-representing contents). The P-contents alone allow one to see such facts.

Katz notes that my examples are spatial, and suggests that to the extent that I am right, it may be because P-consciousness involves "clicking" on a region of a spatial buffer. But nonspatial properties, for example causality, are represented by P-contents. Roll a ball at another so that the first makes the second move. I don't think that very subjective type could be experienced as the second ball acting on the first (see Michotte 1946). Katz points out that for P properties that are subject to spectrum inversion or an analog of it, the P-contents can represent the properties involved in inversion only extrinsically. True, but the possibility of spectrum inversion applies notably to "secondary" qualities like colors and not to P-contents, of, for example, shapes or causal properties. Katz also objects that there is some tension between P-content being representational and there being a P-module. But the representational features of P-contents could depend on processes that occur prior to the P-module (say in the specialized modules) or after it. The idea would be that non-P representations sent to the P-module become representational P-contents within it. Like Farah, Katz sees the P-module as concerned only with intrinsic properties of the representations in it. Katz does not comment on whether, for example, thoughts are P-states, but his views fit best with Humphrey's restriction of P to sensory properties.

R10.   Is There an Important Distinction Left Out?

Harman and Lycan have similar criticisms. First, both think that I have left out a distinction. Lycan distinguishes between a quale, for example, a red area of the visual field, on the one hand, and self-monitoring of that quale on the other. The self-monitoring apparently consists in mobilizing internal attention toward the quale or alternatively, in the views of many students of this issue, having a higher order thought about the quale. Lycan says that my term "P" comprehends both of these, and he seems to suggest that "P" (as with "what it is like") is ambiguous between the two. I find it hard to accept the criticism that I left out the P/monitoring distinction, since I explicitly mentioned three forms of internal monitoring consciousness and I explicitly distinguished them from P (sect. 4.2.2, para. 1). Lycan also disagrees with me about whether qualia are entirely representational, that is, whether there is more to P-content than representational content. I say yes, Lycan says no. But Lycan promotes this entirely legitimate disagreement into another sense of P-consciousness. He calls my qualia, the ones that aren't entirely exhausted by their representational properties, "Q-ualia." I don't see why a disagreement about P-content should be blown up into a new sense of P.

Harman says I miss the distinction between "raw feel" and "what is it like." Raw feel is Harman's word for Lycan's Q-ualia, the P-contents that I accept, and he rejects that are supposed to outrun their representational content. Harman's what it is like is Lycan's monitoring consciousness. So raw feels are P-contents that are at least in part nonrepresentational and can exist without monitoring, and what it is like, which Harman feels is the proper referent of "consciousness," is entirely representational and has a constitutive connection to the self. As with Lycan, I find it hard to take seriously the criticism that I have conflated these things. I was very explicit about all the "pieces." The issue between me and Harman is one of what the most revealing way of assembling these pieces is.

What separates Harman and Lycan from me is mainly two issues. First, I say the phenomenal content of an experience goes beyond its representational content. They disagree (more on this later). A second source of disagreement has to do with the relation between consciousness and the self and monitoring. My P-content is a kind of phenomenal content that need not be monitored, and I give little emphasis to the connection with the self. (I describe P-content at a few points as having a "me-ish" phenomenal quality.) So my major category does not emphasize monitoring or connection with the self, and in fact I mention monitoring and self-consciousness as separate categories. By contrast, Lycan emphasizes monitoring. For example, he says that there is an explanatory gap for monitoring consciousness, but not (or not obviously) for the phenomenal content that is itself monitored. And Harman emphasizes that A-conscious experience is always an experience of a self.

To sum up, (1) I have a substantive disagreement with both Lycan and Harman about whether there is any phenomenal but not entirely representational content. And (2) there is a substantive disagreement with Lycan about the explanatory gap. But (3) there is also a much more diffuse issue between me and them about what is important in the study of phenomenal consciousness. Lycan emphasizes monitoring, Harman emphasizes the self (at least by contrast with me), and I emphasize the phenomenal quality of experience. Because there are some differences between Lycan and Harman, let me discuss them separately.

Lycan in effect criticizes (see especially his Note 4) my claim in the target article that the "explanatory gap" applies to P-consciousness. He says there is an explanatory gap for monitoring consciousness (P attended), but not, or not obviously, to P itself. I would like to see Lycan back this up. Attention is as likely to yield to the information-processing theories of cognitive psychology and cognitive neuroscience as is, say, memory or any other cognitive process. It is an active area of research with many competing theories—see, for example, the seven articles in *Attention and Performance XV* (Umiltà and Moscovitch 1994), or the seven articles in *Attention and Performance XIV* (Meyer & Kornblum 1993). By contrast, there are really no theories (nothing that deserves to be called a theory) of P. No one really has any idea about what P is. As mentioned earlier, the typical research program is to study A, hoping A = P (see Baars). Monitoring consciousness is attended P-consciousness, so what is likely to be understood within the confines of current research paradigms is just the part that Lycan thinks adds the mystery.

Harman says that A-conscious experience is always an experience of a self and necessarily involves access to that self, so, trivially, Consciousness is "access consciousness." Is access to the self supposed to involve engagement with mechanisms of reasoning and reporting bringing with them inferential promiscuity, and so on. If so, then Harman owes us some comment on the putative cases of P without A: If not, then I don't think there is a large disagreement here, for Harman's view does not then preclude P without A. (Levine makes essentially this point.) But there is at least a difference in emphasis. I am a Humean about the self (like Dennett and Church), seeing the self-regarding aspect of P-consciousness as being a matter of connection of the P-state to other states. I said in the target article that P-content often represents the state as a state of mine. Part of the self-regarding aspect of P in my view is a further P-attribute that involves some apprehension of the connection to other states. But I am also willing to countenance P-states in my body that are not fully mine. (I mentioned hypnotic analgesia as a possible example.)

There is one issue that I have not yet mentioned on which Lycan agrees with me rather than Harman. Lycan allows a category of qualia (e.g., a red area of the visual field) that are phenomenal but not necessarily monitored. I would guess that these fit into the category of what Harman calls "sense data," which he takes me (wrongly) as endorsing. I am grateful to Lycan for explicitly not supposing (as he did in Lycan, 1987, and as Harman does here) that the advocate of qualia is committed to sense data or "phenomenal individuals." If any of us is committed to sense data, it is Lycan, Armstrong, Church, Kitcher (and perhaps Harman) and other advocates of monitoring. The rest of us can agree with Harman (1990) that we look *through* our experiences, and that the experiences do not need to be *observed* in order to be phenomenally conscious.

Lycan and Harman think that P-content is entirely representational. They note that I think P-content outruns representational content, and they both appear to conclude that I am therefore committed to some new strange kind of phenomenal content that is entirely nonrepresentational, Lycan's Q-ualia and Harman's raw feels. I did say that the P-content of orgasm represented nothing at all, but this is not a strongly held view. I am happy to say that very little of the phenomenal content of orgasm is representational. Certainly very little of what matters about orgasm is representational. What puzzles me about Lycan and Harman is that they appear to think that the idea that there is more to phenomenal content than what it represents entails some "weird" or "exotic" realm of sense data that are entirely nonrepresentational and of which one is "directly aware" in perception. As reflection on the example of the phenomenal content of orgasm should make clear, the idea that there is more to phenomenal experience than its representational content is just common sense from which it should take argument to dislodge us. Furthermore, why should believing in phenomenal contents that are *partly* nonrepresentational commit one to *wholly* nonrepresentational phenomenal contents (of the sort Katz advocates)? Perhaps Harman and Lycan think that if a P-content is partly nonrepresentational, one can simply separate off the nonrepresentational part and think of it as a separate realm. But once the argument is made explicit it looks dubious. Consider the examples I used in my reply to Katz, say, the example of packability in the case of experiences as of squares contrasted with circles. Is it obvious that there is any separable phenomenal content of that experience that is phenomenal but not representational? I don't think so.

R11. More on Monitoring

Kitcher objects to my contrast between P-consciousness, which applies primarily to states, and monitoring or reflective consciousness, which applies primarily to persons.

A pain is monitoring conscious if (roughly speaking) the person has another state that is about the pain. She notes that monitoring consciousness is a matter of some states being about others, and wonders why I make this distinction. The answer is that if a state of mine is about a pain of yours, your pain is not thereby monitoring conscious. So the notion of a person is crucial. (Someone could argue, as Kitcher does not, that the same is true of A-consciousness.)

Kitcher also says that she cannot see what "what it is like" could evoke if not monitoring consciousness and that the explanatory gap applies most obviously to monitored states. She also finds it implausible that there could even be phenomenal consciousness without monitoring. These points should sound familiar, since I just discussed versions of them in the comment by Lycan, and to a slightly lesser extent in the comment by Harman. Church also favors the view. See also Rosenthal (1986) and Burge (1997). I find this difference of opinion far more troubling than any other that comes up about consciousness. I really don't know how to explain the vast divergence we see here. The magnitude of the gulf is apparent from the fact that two of the commentators, Armstrong and Natsoulas, assumed that *I* mean monitoring consciousness to be involved in A or A and P together. Armstrong complains about the term. "A" would be better, he says, if it stood for action; and even better: change it in for "I" for introspection. My A-consciousness, however, requires no introspection. Natsoulas says—and he says that I agree—that if we have an A-conscious P-state, then we must have another representation of that state. He calls this representation of the phenomenal state "the required representations," since it is supposed to be necessary for A consciousness. I am not sure that I follow the rest of the argument, but he seems to go on to argue that the required representation itself has to be the object of yet another state.[2]

What can be said in favor of the idea that monitoring is necessary for phenomenal states, or at least for "sensory experience" (Lycan). Kitcher mentions that listening to a piece of music requires integration over time. But what reason is there to think that sensory integration requires states that are about other states? It requires memory, of course, but memory images can be linked in the appropriate way without any "aboutness." Lycan appeals to the familiar long-distance truck driver who drives competently but in a daze. He stops at red lights and so must have had a real quale, but for experience, says Lycan, he has to notice the quale, that is be aware of it. Nissan is funding some work at MIT that apparently includes an investigation of this phenomenon, and I have been told some simple preliminary results. If you probe "unconscious" drivers, what you find is that they can always recall (accurately) the road, decisions, perception, and so on, for the prior 30–45 seconds, but farther back than that it's all a blank. No one should be surprised by this result. What else would one expect? If you were a subject who was just asked about the last 30 seconds, do you think you would say that you had not experienced the last 30 seconds? If you say yes, you are in the grip of a theory.

This seems a clear case of experience as genuine as any but quickly forgotten, a moving window of memory. The driver is paying some attention—to the road. Otherwise the car would crash. He is not paying attention to his own states, but one rarely is. Of course, more attention to the road or to the experiences themselves would yield different experiences. But the inattentive driver is still experiencing the bends in the road, the red lights, the other cars maneuvering around him. Why should anyone suppose that there is nothing it is like to be that driver or that to the extent that there is an explanatory gap it doesn't apply here?

One way to see what is wrong with the idea that monitoring consciousness is crucial for P-consciousness is to note that even if I were to come to know about states of my liver noninferentially and nonobservationally (as some people know what time it is), that wouldn't make those states P-conscious. Furthermore, even if I were to come to know of states of my mind that way—say, the operation of my language-understanding mechanisms, or Freudian unconscious states—that wouldn't make those states P-conscious. Of course, all this observation shows is that monitoring isn't sufficient for P, but if monitoring is necessary for P, what else is required to get a sufficient condition? Advocates of this view have not provided an answer to this question.

A second point is that monitoring seems too intellectual a requirement for phenomenal consciousness. Dogs and babies may have phenomenal pains without anything like thoughts to the effect that they have them. If we have two dogs, one of which has a pain whereas the other has a similar pain plus a thought about it, surely the latter dog has an A-conscious state even if the former doesn't! Yes, but it is the converse that is problematic. The first dog could be conscious without being conscious of anything.

Kitcher anticipates the dog objection and replies that I make monitoring a sophisticated activity requiring a sense of self. Not so. What I doubt is that a dog that has a phenomenal state need have any further state that is about the first one. I don't require a sense of self.

As observed in the target article, advocates of the higher-order thought perspective (e.g., Rosenthal) note that if I infer my anger from my behavior, that does not make my anger conscious. They therefore include a requirement that the higher-order thought be arrived at noninferentially and nonobservationally. But as Byrne (forthcoming) notes, why should these details of the causation of the monitoring state matter to whether the state that is monitored is *conscious?* Byrne mentions a number of other conundra for the advocates of monitoring having to do with the level of detail of the monitoring state and the question of whether the description included in the monitoring state could be false of the state monitored.

Levine makes some remarks that may help to explain this puzzling difference of opinion with advocates of monitoring. He notes that phenomenal character itself is a "kind of presentation," a presentation to the self. He also says that this brings with it a kind of access that is distinct from A, phenomenal access as distinct from information-processing access. And he suggests that the existence of two kinds of access is partly responsible for the difficulty in distinguishing A from P. There is at least something right about this. It is often said that phenomenology is self-revealing, that there is something intrinsically epistemic about phenomenology. Perhaps phenomenal access is itself a phenomenal quality, a quality that has some representational features. These representational features represent the state as a state of me. But it does not follow that any kind of information-processing access (such as A) or monitoring is necessary for P.

R12. Does P Outrun Its Representational Content?

Armstrong, Harman, Lycan, and Tye all take the view that P-content is entirely representational. I like Tye's approach best because he doesn't treat it as obvious that representationalism is right, but rather sees a responsibility to say what the representational contents actually are. In the case of orgasm, he specifies that the representational content is in part that something that is intense, throbbing, changing in intensity, and very pleasing is happening down there. OK, I will concede one thing—that there is *some* representational content to orgasm. But this representational content is one that I could have toward another person. Suppose I have perceptual contents about my partner's orgasm without having one myself. The location of "down there" might differ slightly from my own orgasm, but why should that matter? Of course, the subject the orgasm is ascribed to is itself a representational matter. But is that the difference between my having one and perceiving yours—that I ascribe it to me instead of you? What if I mistakenly ascribe yours to me? Furthermore, the phenomenal quality of orgasm varies from time to time. Similarly, there are very different phenomenal experiences that fit descriptions like "in the toe," "intense," "burning," and the like.

I had a pain yesterday that is quite different phenomenally from the one I am having now, but not in any way describable in words. Of course, we should not demand that a representationalist be able to capture his contents in words, but we should be told something about the representational difference. Suppose the content is specified in terms of recognitional capacities. That runs into the problem that recognitional capacities can work without P-content, as in blindsight. At this point of the dialectic, the representationalist often appeals to functional role to specify the representational contents. So is the debate about whether phenomenal content is entirely representational just the old debate about functionalism and qualia? Representationalists certainly give the impression that their position is stronger than mere functionalism, that they can accommodate the idea that there are phenomenal contents, but that those contents are representational.

The way in which representationalism is stronger than mere functionalism comes out in Tye's criticism of my example of two kinds of experiences as of something overhead. Tye doesn't just say: sure, the representational difference resides in the functional difference (though that might be the upshot of the last two sentences of his commentary). Instead, he tries to say what the representational differences are. He argues that the difference will reside in other visual and auditory features. I believe that Tye is wrong about vision but right about audition. In peripheral vision, something can be seen only as having a certain location, without any color, shape, or size. (Try waving your hand near your ear while looking straight ahead.) But without a comparable point in audition, my example will not work, and I know of no auditory analog of peripheral vision. However, my side has another arrow, for the loudness of the sound is irrelevant to its representing something as of overhead. The as-of-overheadness of the visual perception seems independent of color, shape, and so on, and likewise for the auditory perception. The difference seems to reside in the phenomenal character of vision as opposed to audition, and that has not been shown to be a representational difference.

R13. What Is the Relation between A and P?

Shepard, as usual, asks hard questions. How do we know if P peters out as we go down the phylogenetic scale as A peters out? It is a measure of our ignorance about P-consciousness that we have no idea how to go about answering such a question. I think all we can do is investigate P in the creatures we know best and hope that the answer we get throws some light on creatures who are very different from us. Shepard says that what agents do is evidence of A, not of P. I disagree. Sure, purposive action is evidence of A, but it is also evidence, albeit indirect evidence, of P. For example, let us accept for the moment Crick's (1994) current theory of P: that P is a matter of neuronal activity in reverberating cortico-thalamic circuits that run between cortical layer five and the thalamus. Such a theory can only be arrived at on the basis of behavior that indicates A. But once we have the theory (and especially when we understand why that neuronal activity underlies P) we can use it to isolate cases of P without A, or cases, if they exist, of A without P. Of course, we have to explain the discrepancy. Thus, if we find the neuronal activity but no A and hence no outward indication of consciousness, we have two choices: conclude that Crick's theory is wrong, or find some reason why in this particular case there is no A.

This line of thought also supplies my answer to Rey's charge that if P is not identical to anything functional, intentional or cognitive, "what possible reason could we have to posit it in anyone's case, even our own?" I think it is always a mistake to suppose that no one could ever find evidence of something (with a few exceptions—e.g., the thing is literally defined in terms of there being no possible evidence for it). This is just an argument from lack of imagination. A neat example is provided by the familiar idea that the world was created five minutes ago complete with all the evidence of an earlier age. It is tempting to argue that no one could find any evidence for or against such a theory, but that would be a mistake. Steady state cosmology plus the second law of thermodynamics (entropy increases in a closed system) dictate that the relatively ordered state we see around us is a result of a random fluctuation from a steady disordered state. The great fluctuation that created our order happened in the past, but when? Answer: the most likely moment for the fluctuation is the least ordered moment, and that is the most recent moment, that is, *now*. So the evidence *against* steady state theory is evidence *for* the existence of a real past.

Furthermore, in thinking about this sort of possibility, we should not ignore the utility of ordinary considerations of scientific simplicity and ad hocness. For example, one can maintain any theory—even that the earth is flat—if one is willing to adopt all sorts of ad hoc auxiliary hypotheses to explain away recalcitrant observations. In so doing, one could arrive at a totally wacko theory that is observationally equivalent to contemporary physics. But the wacko theory can be ruled out just because it is ad hoc. A further point about the "epiphenomenal" possibility is that the epiphenomenalism of Figure 3 (target article) is not the "philosopher's epiphenomenalism" in which the epiphenomenal entity has no effects at all. Rather, it is the psychologists' epiphenomenalism that rules out effects only *in a system*. The latter allows for effects, but outside the system. The color of the wires in a computer are epiphenomenal in the psychologist's sense but not in the philosopher's sense, since there are effects on observers. Thus the P-module of Figure 3 could be detectable by physiologists even if it had no psychological function.

I agree with what Morton says about the interdependence of A and P, and I gave a number of similar examples myself. (There is a foreground/background example in sect. 4, para. 3 and three more examples in sect. 4.2, para. 6.) I also agree with the idea that we would not have the concepts we have if not for these facts. But I do not agree that the intuitive idea of there being only one consciousness shows that the concept of consciousness is a cluster concept rather than a mongrel. The distinction, as I intended it, was linked to the concept of a conflation. If conflation is possible, then mongrel; if not, cluster. If the myth of uniqueness is enough to make a cluster, then Aristotle's conception of velocity is a cluster concept. Of course, there is no right or wrong here, only utility. If we adopt Morton's terminology, we shall have to make a distinction within the cluster concepts between those that allow conflation and those that do not.

Farah argues that if superblindsight existed, that would be evidence for Schacter's model, complete with P-module, and the nonexistence of superblindsight is evidence against such a P-module. In other words, she thinks that if the presence or absence of such a module made no difference to perception (but only to whether the subject says he is having experiences) that would be evidence for such a module. This seems to me to be precisely backwards. If a module has some information-processing function—and why else would it deserve a box—then whether it is present or absent should make a difference. It seems to be an essential feature of a P-module on Farah's idea of it, that it doesn't do much of anything except paint representations with P-paint and promote reports of experience. Sure, if it has little in the way of an information-processing function then its presence or absence shouldn't make much or a difference. But why assume that if there is a P-module it doesn't have much of an information-processing function? For example, perhaps the Executive System can do things with P representations that it can't do with non-P representations.

Farah objects to my suggestion of P-consciousness as the implementation of the function specified by the Phenomenal Consciousness box in Schacter's model. As I mentioned in the target article, the function specified by that box (and there may be others not specified by the box) is that of talking to the specialized modules, integrating information from them, and talking to the Executive System about that information. I suggested that perhaps P-consciousness is part of the implementation of that function. I used an analogy in which this function could be implemented in a number of ways, some involving consciousness, others not involving consciousness. Farah interprets the label on the box as specifying the sole function represented. I tried to cancel that reading in the text by mentioning that the function was to be understood partly in terms of the box, arrow, their relations, and the textual remarks on how these are to be interpreted. Since the label is "phenomenal consciousness," she assumes that that is the one and only intended function. So we were at cross purposes.

Young suggests that P is responsible for confidence. After all, people who "just know" what time it is don't have the confidence of people who are looking at a clock that they know to be reliable. This is certainly sensible and compelling. But blindsight raises a doubt about such commonsensical ideas: maybe we could know without P? And if we could know without P, why not confidence without P?

Navon suggests that the function of P may be found primarily in motivation rather than cognition (I made the same suggestion in Block 1991). But there is an evolutionary puzzle that this idea raises, one that derives from William Paley (1964) (via a column by Stephen Jay Gould). Paley pointed out that there is no mystery about why birds copulate—pleasure is the answer. But we can't give the same answer to the question of why the bird sits on the egg. (Paley backs this up with a description of the misery of sitting on the egg.) But why does evolution deploy two such different motivators?

Bachmann notes that I say that P depends on what goes on inside the P-module, and he goes on to indicate that this is incompatible with interaction effects involving representational contents (see the replies to Katz and Farah). But these are not incompatible ideas, and I was careful in the target article to describe a number of respects in which P-consciousness is (in the words of Armstrong describing my views) "thoroughly interpenetrated" by representational matters. Note that in Schacter's model, the P-module talks to the Executive System and the specialized modules, so interactions are allowed for. Bachmann mentions the possibility that a P-module might have its activity lowered, but he somehow takes me to be denying this possibility and doubting the possibility of measurement of P. Bachmann mentions a number of fascinating phenomena that may cast some light on the relation between A and P, but I have not investigated these phenomenon sufficiently to comment on them.

R14. Is Consciousness a Cultural Construction?

Dennett says that my critique of his view that consciousness is a cultural construction simply begs the question. I assume the A/P distinction, but he rejects it, he says. "Because I not only decline to draw any such distinction but argue at length against any such distinction, Block's critique is simply question-begging." This is a strange response from Dennett, since he does not actually reject the A/P distinction but rather reconstructs it in terms of information and access. Perhaps he thinks that the reconstructed A/P distinction is so different from what I meant that it is tantamount to rejecting the distinction. Well, then, let's suppose Dennett is completely right. To the extent that there is an A/P distinction, it is a matter of degree of access and information. Dennett's theory of access, you will recall, is that it is a matter of brain representations persevering so as to affect memory, control behavior, and so on. So the P/A distinction is a matter of brain representations' degree of informational content and degree of persevering. Then Dennett ought to be able to tell us to what degree or range of degrees of persevering and informational content his theory applies to. I'm not being very demanding. I don't insist on precision, just some idea of what degrees of information and control make for cultural construction. Perhaps he will say it is the highly informational and accessible contents he is talking about, the rich displays of colors and shapes that appear in his examples (e.g., the Times Roman X on a blue-green background). But we have good reason to think that these types of contents are not very influenced by culture. Long ago, Eleanor Rosch (1973) showed that the Dani, a tribe with only two color words, represented colors much as we do. In sum, my point against Dennett does not depend at all on whether the A/P distinction is a matter of degree or of kind. If it is a matter of degree, he must tell us what band of degrees he is talking about.

Dennett used to be an eliminativist (in "On the Absence of Phenomenology" [1979], for example). In recent years, especially since Dennett (1991), he has shifted gears, saying he is a realist about consciousness and at the same time saying that his position is not all that different from what it used to be. He appeals to the truth that the difference between eliminativism and reductionist realism is often purely tactical. However, not all reductionisms are close to eliminativism. Indeed, Dennett's new position is very different from his old one, as many readers have recognized (see Rey, e.g.). In giving what he insists is a theory of consciousness, with such highly substantive claims as that consciousness is a cultural construction, Dennett has left eliminativism far behind. Now he is a real realist, a reductionist or a deflationist, and the theory is supposed to be true of some deflated version of consciousness or something consciousness is reduced to. The trouble is that he has neglected to make up his mind about which deflated version he wants or what it is that he is reducing consciousness to.

My advice to Dennett is to read Church—that's the view of A and P that best captures his intentions. Church says that my analogy with the development of the concepts of heat and temperature is miscast. I said that we have an intuitive preanalytic concept of consciousness that can be resolved into P, A, monitoring consciousness, and self-consciousness. She argues that P should be seen as the preanalytic concept, and given its confused nature, we should abandon it in favor of ideas such as A, monitoring, and self-consciousness. She gives an interesting argument for the confused nature of P. A P-state must be a state of a self, and given that there is no Cartesian self, being a state of a self must involve relations to other states. Then comes the step that mainly bothers me: according to Church, P (if it exists) is intrinsic. Since P is both intrinsic and involves a relation, P is a confusion. My view is that this step conflates concepts with the properties that they are concepts of. The concept of a color does not involve relations, but color (the property) is highly relational. The concept of water has nothing to do with molecules, but water (or the property of being water) is constituted by being a molecular amalgam of hydrogen and oxygen. Similarly, the concept of P (of a state) has nothing to do with other states, but P itself could turn out to be relational. This point is briefly mentioned in Note 10 of the target article.

Oddly enough, Church is well aware of the concept/property distinction, and pins the incoherence on the concept. Yet in laying out her argument, she shifts to properties, saying that the property of being phenomenal is both intrinsic and relational. I also have some disquiet about the prior step in her argument. I agree that a P state must be a state of the self, and I agree about the deflationary view of selves. But I am not convinced that the way in which P involves the self is incompatible with intrinsciness. At a minimum, the mode of self-involvement could be simple, a phenomenal property, the "me-ishness" I described (see Levine and my reply to his comment). Alternatively, the state could in some sense be about other states or about the self (it could represent the state as a state of me, as I said in the target article) but not in a way that would satisfy a functionalist. I can want a sloop even if there aren't any sloops. And the relation to other states or to the self could be like that.

Van Brakel takes me to be an advocate of "one true taxonomy," but I took pains to avoid this characterization. I emphasized repeatedly that there are many notions of access-consciousness with utility for different purposes. My purpose had mainly to do with a notion of access as a surrogate for phenomenal consciousness. Furthermore, there are somewhat different notions of phenomenal consciousness that are legitimate for some purposes, for example, the limitation to bodily sensations suggested by Humphrey (see also Katz). I am perfectly happy to allow that culture affects P-consciousness. I emphasized that intentional and phenomenal content interpenetrate, and I don't think anyone should doubt that culture can affect intentional content. But note the difference between the idea that culture affects phenomenal consciousness and the idea that culture creates it. Culture affects feet—the feet of Himalayan tribesmen who walk barefoot in the mountains are different from the bound feet of nineteenth-century Chinese women. But culture does not *create* feet. I have to admit skepticism about much of van Brakel's evidence, however. Whorfians thought culture affected color and form perception until Berlin and Kay (1969) and Rosch (1973) showed the effects were overrated. Van Brakel's evidence is best evaluated when we know enough about consciousness to see whether it really differs in different cultures.

Notes

Reprinted from *Behavioral and Brain Sciences* 18 (2): 227–247, 1995. Reply to 28 critics of "On a Confusion about a Function of Consciousness" *Behavioral and Brain Sciences* 18 (2): 227–247, 1995 (reprinted as chapter 9, this volume).

I am grateful for comments from Alex Byrne, David Chalmers, Leonard Katz, and Daniel Stoljar.

1. Opponents of the inverted-spectrum thought experiment should pay attention to cases like the legal blindness/eyesclosed case. It is much easier to come up with an inverted-spectrum type of thought experiment for a sensory modality with reduced informational content. Tye, for example, has objected to the inverted spectrum hypothesis on the basis of asymmetries in color   blue can be blackish but yellow cannot. But such objects do not apply to vision in the legal blindness/eyes-closed mode.

2. I can surmise that what misled Natsoulas was a remark in Note 11. It would take me too far afield to raise the issue here.

References

Akins, K. (1993) A bat without qualities. In: *Consciousness: Psychological and philosophical essays*, ed. M. Davies & G. Humphreys. Blackwell.

Alston, W. (1967) Religion. In: *The encyclopedia of philosophy*. Macmillan/Free Press.

Anderson, J. (1993) To see ourselves as others see us: A response to Mitchell. *New Ideas in Psychology* 11(3):339–34.

Andrade, J. (1993) Consciousness: Current views. In: *Depth of anesthesia*, ed. J. G. Jones. Little Brown.

Armstrong, D. M. (1968) *A materialist theory of mind*. Humanities Press.

——— (1980) What is consciousness? In: *The nature of mind*. Cornell University Press.

Baars, B. J. (1988) *A cognitive theory of consciousness*. Cambridge University Press.

—— (1994) A thoroughly empirical approach to consciousness. *Psyche: An International Journal of Consciousness Research* 1(2).

Baars, B., and McGovern, K. (1993) Does philosophy help or hinder scientific work on consciousness? *Consciousness and Cognition* 2, 18–27.

Bennett, H. (1988) Perception and memory of events during adequate general anesthesia for surgical operations. In: *Hypnosis and memory*, ed. H. Pettinati. Guilford.

Berlin, B., and Kay, P. (1969) *Basic color terms*. University of California Press.

Block, N. (1983) The photographic fallacy in the debate about mental imagery, *Nous* XVII, 4.

—— (1980) What is functionalism? In: *Readings in the philosophy of psychology, vol. 1*, ed. N. Block. Harvard University Press.

—— (1990a) Inverted earth. In: *Philosophical perspectives, vol. 4*, ed. J. Tomberlin. Ridgeview.

—— (1990b) Consciousness and accessibility. *Behavioral and Brain Sciences* 13:596–59.

—— (1991) Evidence against epiphenomenalism. *Behavioral and Brain Sciences* 14:670–67.

—— (1992) Begging the question against phenomenal consciousness. *Behavioral and Brain Sciences* 15:205–07.

—— (1993) Review of Dennett: Consciousness explained. *The Journal of Philosophy* 4:181–19.

—— (1994) "Functionalism," "Qualia." In: *A companion to philosophy of mind*, ed. S. Guttenplan. Blackwell.

—— (in press) What is Dennett's theory about? *Philosophical topics*.

Bornstein, R., and Pittman, T. (1992) *Perception without awareness*. Guilford Press.

Bowers, J., and Schacter, D. (1990) Implicit memory the test awareness. *Journal of Experimental Psychology: Learning, Memory and Cognition* 16(3):404–41.

Burge, T. (1997) Two kinds of consciousness. In *The Nature of Consciousness*, ed. N. Block, O. Flanagan, and G. Güzeldere. MIT Press.

Byrne, A. (1993) *The emergent mind*. Princeton University, PhD dissertation.

Byrne, R. W. (1993) The meaning of 'awareness': A response to Mitchell. *New Ideas in Psychology* 11(3):347–35.

Carruthers, P. (1989) Brute experience. *Journal of Philosophy* 86.

—— (1992) Consciousness and concepts. *Proceedings of the Aristotelian Society (Supplement)* 66:40–5.

Chalmers, D. J. (1993) *Toward a theory of consciousness*. University of Indiana PhD thesis.

Chalmers, D. (1997) Availability: The cognitive basis of experience? *Behavioral and Brain Sciences* 20:148–149.

Churchland, P. S. (1983) Consciousness: The transmutation of a concept. *Pacific Philosophical Quarterly* 64:80–93.

——— (1986) Reduction and the neurobiological basis of consciousness. In: *Consciousness in contemporary society*, ed. A. J. Marcel & E. Bisiach. Oxford University Press.

Cooper, L., and Shepard, R. (1982) Chronometric studies of the rotation of mental images. In: *Visual information processing*, ed. W. Chase. Academic Press. Reprinted in R. Shepard & L. Cooper, *Mental images and their transformation*. MIT Press.

Coslett, H., and Saffran, E. (1994) Mechanisms of implicit reading in alexia. In: *The neuropsychology of high-level vision*, ed. M. Farah & G. Ratcliff. Erlbaum.

Cowie, A., and Stoerig, P. (1992) Reflections on blindsight. In: *The neuropsychology of consciousness*, ed. B. Milner & M. Rugg. Academic Press.

Crick, F. (1994) *The astonishing hypothesis*, Scribner's.

Crick, F., and Koch, C. (1990) Towards a neurobiological theory of consciousness. *Seminars in the Neurosciences* 2:263–75.

Davies, M. (1992) Perceptual content and local supervenience. *Proceedings of the Aristotelian Society* 92:21–45.

(forthcoming) Externalism and experience. In: *Categories, consciousness and reasoning*, ed. A. Clark, J. Exquerro, J. Larrazabal. Dordrecht.

Davies, M., and Humphreys, G. (1993a) *Consciousness: Psychological and philosophical essays*. Blackwell.

——— (1993b) Introduction. In: *Consciousness*, ed. M. Davies & G. Humphreys. Blackwell.

de Lannoy, J. Two theories of a mental model of mirror self-recognition: A response to Mitchell. *New Ideas in Psychology* 11(3):337–33.

Dennett, D. C. (1979) On the absence of phenomenology. In: *Body, mind and method: Essays in honor of Virgil Aldrich*, ed. D. Gustafson & B. Tapscott. Dordrecht.

——— (1986) Julian Jaynes' software archeology. *Canadian Psychology* 27(2):149–15.

——— (1993) The message is: There is no medium. In: *Philosophy and Phenomenological Research III*.

Dennett, D., and Kinsbourne, M. (1992a) Time and the observer: The where and when of consciousness in the brain. *Behavioral and Brain Sciences* 15:183–20.

——— (1992b) Escape from the Cartesian theater. *Behavioral and Brain Sciences* 15:234–24.

Dimond, S. (1976) Brain circuits for consciousness. *Brain, Behavior and Evolution* 13:376–95.

Dretske, F. (1993) Conscious experience. *Mind* 102, 406:263–84.

Dupre, J. (1981) Natural kinds and biological taxa. *Philosophical Review* 90:66–9.

Edelman, G. (1989) *The remembered present: A biological theory of consciousness.* Basic Books.

Etcoff, N. L., Freeman, R., and Cave, K. Can we lose memories of faces? Content specificity and awareness in a prosopagnosic. *Journal of Cognitive Neuroscience* 3.

Etcoff, N. L., and Magee, J. J. (1992) Covert recognition of emotional expressions. *Journal of Clinical and Experimental Neuropsychology* 14:95–9.

Farah, M. (1994) Visual perception and visual awareness after brain damage: A tutorial overview. In: *Attention and performance 15*, ed. C. Umilà & M. Moscovitch. MIT Press.

Flanagan, O. (1991) *The science of the mind*, 2d ed. MIT Press.

––––––– (1992) *Consciousness reconsidered.* MIT Press.

Gallup, G. (1982) Self-awareness and the emergence of mind in primates. *American Journal of Primatology* 2:237–48.

Gallup, G., and Povinelli, D. Mirror, mirror on the wall, which is the most heuristic theory of them all? A response to Mitchell. *New Ideas in Psychology* 11:327–3.

Gazzaniga, M. (1985) *The social train.* Basic Books.

Ghoneim, M., and Block, R. (1993) Learning during anesthesia. In: *Depth of anesthesia*, ed. J. G. Jones. Little Brown.

Ghoneim, M., Hinrichs, J., and Mewaldt, S. (1984) Dose-response analysis of the behavioral effects of diazepam: 1. Learning and memory. *Psychopharmacology* 82:291–95.

Goldman, A. (1993a) The psychology of folk psychology. *Behavioral and Brain Sciences* 16:15–82.

––––––– (1993b) Consciousness, folk psychology and cognitive science. *Consciousness and Cognition II.*

Goodale, M. A., and Milner, A. D. (1992) Separate visual pathways for perception and action. *Trends in Neurosciences* 15:20–25.

Harman, G. (1990) The intrinsic quality of experience. In: *Philosophical perspectives, vol. 4*, ed. J. Tomberlin. Ridgeview.

Hauser, M., Kralik, J., Botto-Mahan, C., Garrett, M., and Oser, J. (submitted) Self-recognition in primates: Phylogeny and the salience of species-typical features.

Heyes, C. (1993) Reflections on self-recognition in primates. *Animal Behavior.*

Hilgard, E. R. (1986) *Divided consciousness*, 2d ed. Wiley.

Hill, C. (1991) *Sensations: A defense of type materialism.* Cambridge University Press.

Holender, D. (1986) Semantic activation without conscious identification in dichotic listening, parafoveal vision, and visual masking: A survey and appraisal. *Behavioral and Brain Sciences* 9:1–66.

Humphrey, G. (1963) *Thinking.* Wiley.

Humphrey, N. (1992) *A history of the mind*. Simon & Schuster.

Huxley, T. H. (1866) Lessons in elementary psychology. Quoted in Humphrey, 1992.

Jackendoff, R. (1987) *Consciousness and the computational mind*. MIT Press.

Jackson, F. (1977) *Perception*. Cambridge University Press.

—— (1986) What Mary didn't know. *Journal of Philosophy* 83:291–9.

—— (1993a) Appendix A (for philosophers). In: *Philosophy and phenomenological research III*.

—— (1993b) Armchair metaphysics. In: *Philosophy in mind*, ed. J. O'Leary-Hawthorne & M. Michael. Kluwer.

Jacoby, L., Toth, J., Lindsay, D., and Debner, J. (1992) Lectures for a layperson: Methods for revealing unconscious processes. In: *Perception without awareness*, ed. R. Bornstein & T. Pittman. Guilford Press.

James, W. (1890) *The principles of psychology*. Dover, 1950.

Jaynes, J. (1976) *The origin of consciousness in the breakdown of the bicameral mind*. Houghton-Mifflin.

Johnson-Laird, P. (1988) *The computer and the mind*. Harvard University Press.

Jones, J. G. (1993) *Depth of anesthesia*. Little Brown.

Kapsalist, J. G. (1987) *Objective Methods in Food Quality Assessment*. CRC Press.

Kihlstrom, J. (1987) The cognitive unconscious. *Science* 237:1445–145.

Kihlstrom, J., Barnhardt, T., and Tataryn, D. (1992) Implicit perception. In: *Perception without awareness*, ed. R. Bornstein & T. Pittman. Guilford Press.

Kihlstrom, J., and Couture, L. (1992) Awareness and information processing in general anesthesia. *Journal of Psychopharmacology* 6(3):410–41.

Kihlstrom, J., and Schacter, D. (1990) Anaesthesia, amnesia, and the cognitive unconscious. In: *Memory and awareness in anaesthesia*, ed. B. Bonke. Swets & Zeitlinger.

Kim, J. (1995) "Supervenience." In: *Blackwell's Companion to Metaphysics*, ed. J. Kim and E. Sosa. B. H. Blackwell.

Kirk, R. (1992) Consciousness and concepts. *Proceedings of the Aristotelian Society* (Supplement) 66:23–4.

Kosslyn, S. (1980) *Image and mind*, Harvard University Press.

—— (1994) *Image and brain*. MIT Press.

Kosslyn, S., and Koenig, O. (1992) *Wet mind: The new cognitive neuroscience*. Free Press.

Kuhn, T. (1964) A function for thought experiments. In: *Melanges Alexandre Koyre, vol 1*. Hermann.

Lackner, J., and Garrett, M. (1973) Resolving ambiguity: Effects of biasing context in the un-attended ear. *Cognition* 1:359–37.

Landis, T., Regard, M., and Serrat, A. (1980) Iconic reading in a case of alexia without agraphia caused by a brain tumour: A tachistoscopic study. *Brain and Language* 11:45–53.

Levine, J. (1983) Materialism and qualia: The explanatory gap. *Pacific Philosophical Quarterly* 64:354–36.

——— (1993) On leaving out what it is like. In: *Consciousness: Psychological and philosophical essays*, ed. M. Davies & G. Humphreys. Blackwell.

——— (1994) Review of Owen Flanagan: Consciousness reconsidered. *Philosophical Review*.

Loar, B. (1990) Phenomenal properties. In: *Philosophical perspectives: Action theory and philosophy of mind*, ed. J. Tomberlin. Ridgeview.

Lormand, E. (forthcoming) What qualitative consciousness is like.

Luria, A. (1972) *The man with the shattered world.* Harvard University Press (translation: 1987).

Lycan, W. G. (1987) *Consciousness.* MIT Press.

Mandler, G. (1985) *Cognitive psychology.* Erlbaum.

Marcel, A. J. (1983) Conscious and unconscious perception: An approach to relations between phenomenal experience and perceptual processes. *Cognitive Psychology* 15:238–300.

——— (1986) Consciousness and processing: Choosing and testing a null hypothesis. *Behavioral and Brain Sciences* 9:40–44.

——— (1988) Phenomenal experience and functionalism. In: *Consciousness in contemporary society*, ed. A. J. Marcel & E. Bisiach. Oxford University Press.

Marcel, A. J., and Bisiach, E., eds. (1988) *Consciousness in contemporary science.* Oxford University Press.

McCullough, G. (1993) The very idea of the phenomenological. *Proceedings of the Aristotelian Society* 93:39–58.

McGinn, C. (1991) *The problem of consciousness.* Blackwell.

——— (1993) Consciousness and cosmology: Hyperdualism ventilated. In: *Consciousness: Psychological and philosophical essays*, ed. M. Davies & G. Humphreys. Blackwell.

Melzack, R., and Wall, P. (1988) *The challenge of pain*, 2d ed. Penguin.

Menzel, E., Savage-Rumbaugh, E., and Lawson, J. (1985) Chimpanzee ({Pantroglogdytes}) spatial problem solving with the use of mirrors and televised equivalents of mirrors. *Journal of Comparative Psychology* 99:211–17.

Meyer, D. E., and Kornblum, S. (1993) *Attention and Performance XIV. Synergies in Experimental Psychology, Artificial Intelligence, and Cognitive Neuroscience.* MIT Press.

Michotte, A. (1946) *The Perception of causality*, translated by Miles, T. R. and E., 1963. London.

Milner, B., and Rugg, M., eds. (1992) *The neuropsychology of consciousness*. Academic Press.

Mitchell, R. W. (1993a) Mental models of mirror self-recognition: Two theories. *New Ideas in Psychology* 11:295–32.

——— (1993b) Recognizing one's self in a mirror? A reply to Gallup and Povinelli, de Lannoy, Anderson, and Byrne. *New Ideas in Psychology* 11:351–77.

Moscovitch, M., Goshen-Gottstein, Y., and Vriezen, E. (1994) Memory without conscious recollection: A tutorial review from a neuropsychological perspective. In: *Attention and performance 15*, ed. C. Umiltà & M. Moscovitch. MIT Press.

Nagel, T. (1971) Brain bisection and the unity of consciousness. *Synthèse* 22:396–413.

——— (1979) *Mortal questions*. Cambridge University Press.

——— (1986) *The view from nowhere*. Oxford University Press.

Nathan, P. (1985) Pain and nociception in the clinical context. *Philosophical Transactions of the Royal Society London B* 308:219 22.

Natsoulas, T. (1993) What is wrong with the appendage theory of consciousness? *Philosophical Psychology* 6(2):137–15.

Nelkin, N. (1993) The connection between intentionality and consciousness. In: *Consciousness: Psychological and philosophical essays*, ed. M. Davies & G. Humphreys. Blackwell.

Nisbett, R., and Wilson, T. (1977) Telling more than we can know: Verbal reports on mental processes. *Psychological Review* 84:231–59.

Peacocke, C. (1983) *Sense and content*. Oxford University Press.

——— (1992) *A study of concepts*. MIT Press.

Pendlebury, M. (1992) Theories of experience. In: *A companion to epistemology*, ed. J. Dancy & E. Sosa. Blackwell.

Penfield, W. (1975) *The mystery of the mind: A critical study of consciousness and the human brain*. Princeton University Press.

Plourde, G. (1993) Clinical use of the 40-Hz auditory steady state response. In: *Depth of anesthesia*, ed. J. G. Jones. Little Brown.

Povinelli, D. (1994) What chimpanzees know about the mind. In: *Behavioral diversity in chimpanzees*. Harvard University Press.

Putnam, H. (1975) The meaning of 'meaning'. In: *Mind, language and reality*, ed. H. Putnam. Cambridge University Press.

Reingold, E., and Merikle, P. (1993) Theory and measurement in the study of unconscious processes. In: *Consciousness: Psychological and philosophical essays*, ed. M. Davies & G. Humphreys. Blackwell.

Rey, G. (1983) A reason for doubting the existence of consciousness. In: *Consciousness and self-regulation*, vol 3., ed. R. Davidson, G. Schwartz & D. Shapiro. Plenum.

—— (1988) A question about consciousness. In: *Perspectives on mind*, ed. H. Otto & J. Tuedio. Reidel.

Rosch, E. (1973) On the internal structure of perceptual and semantic categories in T. E. Moore, ed. *Cognitive Development and the Acquisition of Language* I:111–144.

Rosenthal, D. (1986) Two concepts of consciousness. *Philosophical Studies* 49:329–35.

—— (1993) Thinking that one thinks. In: *Consciousness: Psychological and philosophical essays*, ed. M. Davies & G. Humphreys. Blackwell.

Schacter, D. L. (1989) On the relation between memory and consciousness: Dissociable interactions and conscious experience. In: *Varieties of memory and consciousness: Essays in honour of Endel Tulving*, ed. H. Roediger & F. Craik. Erlbaum.

Schacter, D., McAndrews, M., and Moscovitch, M. (1988) Access to consciousness: Dissociations between implicit and explicit knowledge in neuropsychological syndromes. In: *Thought without Language*, ed., L. Weiskrantz. Oxford University Press.

Schacter, D. L., and Worling, J. R. (1985) Attribute information and the feeling-of-knowing. *Canadian Journal of Psychology* 39(3):467–75.

Searle, J. R. (1983) *Intentionality*. Cambridge University Press.

—— (1990a) Consciousness, explanatory inversion and cognitive science. *Behavioral and Brain Sciences* 13:4:585–95.

—— (1990b) Who is computing with the brain? *Behavioral and Brain Sciences* 13:4:632–64.

—— (1992) *The rediscovery of the mind*. MIT Press.

Sergent, J., and Poncet, M. (1990) From covert to overt recognition of faces in a prosopagnosic patient. *Brain* 113:989–1004.

Shallice, T. (1988a) *From neuropsychology to mental structure*. Cambridge University Press.

—— (1988b) Information-processing models of consciousness: Possibilities and problems. In: *Consciousness in contemporary society*, ed. A. J. Marcel & E. Bisiach. Oxford University Press.

Shevrin, H. (1992) Subliminal perception, memory and consciousness: Cognitive and dynamic perspectives. In: *Perception without awareness*, ed. R. Bornstein & T. Pittman. Guilford Press.

Shiffrin, R. M., and Schneider, W. (1977) Controlled and automatic human information processing: II. Perceptual learning, automatic attending, and a general theory. *Psychological Review* 84:127–90.

Shoemaker, S. (1975) Functionalism and qualia. *Philosophical Studies* 27:291–315.

—— (1981a) Absent qualia are impossible—a reply to Block. *Philosophical Review* 90(4):581–59.

—— (1981b) The inverted spectrum. *Journal of Philosophy* 74(7):357–38.

—— (1993) Lovely and suspect ideas. *Philosophy and Phenomenological Research* 3(4):905–91.

—— (1994) *Phenomenal character*. Nous.

Sperling, G. (1960) The information available in brief visual presentations. *Psychological Monographs* 74:11.

Stich, S. (1978) Beliefs and sub-doxastic states. *Philosophy of Science* 45:499–58.

Tye, M. (1991) *The imagery debate*. MIT Press.

—— (1993) Reflections on Dennett and consciousness. *Philosophy and Phenomenological Research* 34:893–98.

—— (forthcoming a) Blindsight, the absent qualia hypothesis and the mystery of consciousness.

—— (forthcoming b) Does pain lie within the domain of cognitive psychology? In: *Philosophical perspectives*, ed. J. Tomberlin.

Umiltà, C., and Moscovitch, M. (1994) *Attention and performance 15*. MIT Press.

Van Gulick, R. (1989) What difference does consciousness make? *Philosophical Topics* 17(1):211–23.

—— (1993) Understanding the phenomenal mind: Are we all just armadillos? In: *Consciousness: Psychological and philosophical essays*, ed. M. Davies & G. Humphreys. Blackwell.

Weiskrantz, L. (1986) *Blindsight*. Oxford University Press.

—— (1992) Introduction: Dissociated issues. In: *The neuropsychology of consciousness*, ed. B. Milner & M. Rugg. Academic Press.

White, S. L. (1987) What is it like to be an homunculus. *Pacific Philosophical Quarterly* 68:148–17.

—— (1991) Transcendentalism and its discontents. In: *The unity of the self*, ed. S. L. White. MIT Press.

Wiser, M., and Carey, S. (1983) When heat and temperature were one. In: *Mental models*, ed. D. Gentner & A. Stevens. Erlbaum.

Young, A. W. (1994a) Covert recognition. In: *The neuropsychology of higher vision: Collected tutorial essays*, ed. M. Farah & G. Ratcliff. Erlbaum.

—— (1994b) Neuropsychology of awareness. In: *Consciousness in philosophy and cognitive neuroscience*, ed. M. Kappinen & A. Revonsuo. Erlbaum.

Young, A. (1994c) Conscious and non-conscious recognition of familiar faces. In Umiltà and Moscovitch, ed., *Attention and Performance 15*. MIT Press.

Young, A. W., and De Haan, E. (1993) Impairments of visual awareness. In: *Consciousness: Psychological and philosophical essays*, ed. M. Davies & G. Humphreys. Blackwell.

11   Biology versus Computation in the Study of Consciousness

The target article focused on the distinction between P (for phenomenal) consciousness and A (for access) consciousness. P = experience. P-conscious qualities are the qualities of experience such as the phenomenal quality of pain or the sensation of red. A state is A conscious if it is poised for direct control of reasoning, speech, and action. The interest in the A/P distinction arises from the battle between two different conceptions of the mind, the *computational* and the *biological*. The computational approach supposes that all of the mind (including consciousness) can be captured with information processing notions such as computation and function in a system.

According to this view (often called functionalism by philosophers), the level of abstraction for understanding the mind is one that allows multiple realizations: just as one algorithm can be realized electrically or hydraulically, the mind can be realized biologically or electronically. The functionalist thinks that the right level of description for characterizing consciousness is the information processing level, not the level of realization of computation, namely, the biological level. The biological approach makes the opposite bet. If P = A, the functionalist side is right about consciousness. But if consciousness has a biological nature, then the realizations are what count, and we can expect that P and A will diverge.

I hypothesized that cases of P without A exist, but that A without P may not. In all my searching and reviewing suggestions of correspondents, I have seen only one case (in humans) that may well be a case of A without P. Hartmann et al. (1991) describe a case of "inverse Anton's syndrome," an adult whose primary visual cortex had been mostly destroyed, leaving a small island of primary visual cortex. (Thanks to Ralph Adolphs for drawing this to my attention.) This patient cannot discriminate whether the room is dark or illuminated, and he insists that he is blind. If stimuli are presented in the upper right visual field (which projects to the remnant of his primary visual cortex), however, he can recognize faces, facial emotions, and read single words. Yet the patient insists that he does not see anything. When asked how he knows what the word says or whose face it is, he says things like "It clicks" or "I feel it in my mind." There is no sign of hysteria or a psycho-social situation favoring blindness; that is, no reason to believe he is self-deceived. There is damage in the parietal lobes, including the left inferior parietal region. Milner and Goodale (1995) have proposed that phenomenal consciousness requires ventral stream activity plus attention, and that the requisite attention can be blocked by parietal lesions. So perhaps this is a case of visual access without visual phenomenal consciousness. I hope that readers of this journal can comment on whether this is a genuine case of A without P.

R1.   Tweaking the Definition of "A"

I certainly agree with Chalmers's point that we should tweak the definition of "A" so as to avoid uninteresting cracks between P and A, that is uninteresting cases of P without A or A without P. Of course, it would be easy to redefine "A" in response to each crack between A and P, resulting in an ad hoc gerrymandered notion of A. Since P *has* an information-processing role (I assume), it would be trivial to claim that there are no cracks between P and *that* role. For example, in the target article I gave an example of P which does not result in A because of lack of attention. Assume that Crick and Koch (1995) are right that visual experience is a matter of activity in pyramidal cells of the lower cortical layers of the visual areas in the back of the head. Suppose further, (as Crick and Koch also suggest) that visual information is put in a position in which it can be used for reasoning and control of behavior by being transmitted to the frontal and prefrontal cortex (in the front of the head). So a conscious event in the visual cortex becomes A-conscious by virtue of transmitting information to the frontal and prefrontal cortex, and those events in the front are later than the P-events in the back, since it takes time for the information to get to the front. If these ideas are right, a crack would appear to open up between P and A because of the myriad ways in which the information in the back might fail to affect the front in the appropriate way. Now many functionalists (especially the variety that hold functionalism as a conceptual truth) would not be bothered by this, for functionalism is prepared to count an event as P-conscious by virtue of its effects at *other times and places*. In fact, functionalism is prepared to include in the defining role of a P-conscious event processes that do not *actually* happen, but *would* happen under certain conditions. But such features, if used to frame a type of information processing, would make it far from a natural kind of information processing. If the claim that P = A is to be significant, A must be a genuine natural kind that is also a genuine information processing analog of P. It was in this spirit that I defined A so as to rule out the kind of degraded access involved in blindsight as a case of genuine A. The blindsight patient cannot harness the information from the blind field without being told to guess and being given a set of alternatives. So it is best to think of access-consciousness as involving a form of access that is more full-blooded than what exists in blindsight. To rule out blindsight as a case of A without P, I defined a state as A-conscious if it is poised for *rational* control of reasoning, speech, and action. The word "rational" caused a great deal of misunderstanding and I conceded in the response to the first round of commentary that it was a misleading choice. (I never meant to rule out control that involves poor reasoning—see especially my reply to Kobes in the original response.) "Control" does the job all by itself if understood properly: the information in the blindsight patient's head about what he saw *influences*, but it does not control. In some publications, I have been defining a state as A-conscious if it is poised for *voluntary* or *direct* control. The blindsight patient's guesses are voluntary, but the contents do not control the responses in a voluntary manner. They control via an indirect pathway involving guessing.

Chalmers proposes defining "A" as "direct availability for global control"; he expands on global control saying that he has in mind especially deliberate behaviors. His "deliberate" corresponds to my "voluntary" (and "rational"), and I think both play the same role in eliminating blindsight. No significant difference so far. Also, my *poised* and Chalmers's *directly available* seem to do the same job. As I explained (Block 1995), the reason for "poised" was to rule out cases where access requires processing. For example, we all have a belief about what we had for breakfast this morning, but for many readers, that belief was quiescent until reading this sentence. If we make A a totally dispositional concept, a matter of mere accessibility, then quiescent or inactive beliefs will count as A without P. Chalmers's "directly available" seems designed to do the same job, since as he explains, it is meant to eliminate contents that take some work to retrieve.

Chalmers suggests "global control" whereas I specify the kind of control in much more detail, including specifying that the kind of control of reasoning must involve inferential promiscuity, that is, free use of a representation as a premise in reasoning. I don't see much difference here between Chalmers and me, but it is worth mentioning that the greater specificity does have an advantage. Consider the case I mentioned in the target article of a torture victim who represses the memories of torture. The memories exert a *global* effect on his behavior, causing him to react negatively to places and people that are similar to those involved in the torture; the memories cause slips, affect dreams, and create a global mood. Yet they are not A-conscious. The notion of inferential promiscuity is especially useful in seeing why not.

Now we come to a significant difference. Though our definitions of "A" seem more or less equivalent, there is a crucial difference in interpretation when it comes to thinking about my putative cases of P without A. I gave a number of examples that were designed to exploit the fact that access to a P-content can fail for a variety of reasons, including lack of attention and various forms of blockage. (I mentioned blockage due to repression, information processing limits, fragmentation of the self, and deactivation of centers of reasoning and planning by, for example, anesthesia.) If these cases are genuine cases of P, then they are cases of P without A, because some work would be required to access the blocked representations. Attention would have to be focused or the blockage removed. Chalmers does not dispute that any of my cases are cases of P; rather, he tries to avoid such cases by saying "the information was directly available all along; it simply wasn't accessed." But he is trying to have his cake and eat it too, interpreting "directly available" as *poised* for access in order to rule *out* A-consciousness of what I had for breakfast this morning (before it was mentioned) and as *merely potentially available* for access to rule *in* A-consciousness in cases of inattention, repression, limits on information process, fragmentation, and anesthesia. The information about what I had for breakfast was potentially available for access only not accessed, yet not phenomenally conscious.

Perhaps Chalmers will say that accessing the information about what I had for breakfast this morning involves retrieval from memory—which is why it is not access-conscious—whereas the cases of P without A that I mentioned do not. But what about repression? Accessing the repressed images of torture involves retrieval from memory too, yet Chalmers wants to see them as access-conscious. In short, Chalmers regards the cases of inattention, repression, etc. as phenomenal and access-conscious, so he needs a merely potential notion of access. But he also needs a notion of access that is not merely potential to avoid cases such as a phenomenal appreciation of what I had for breakfast this morning (before it was mentioned above)—cases that are not phenomenal but are potentially available for access (and for phenomenality). No doubt there is some way of distinguishing between the ways that memory is involved in these two cases. But recall that a candidate definition of "A" must be non-ad-hoc as well as a genuine information processing image of P. To build into our definition of "A" a very fine grained condition distinguishing between two ways of accessing memory looks ad hoc, and it raises the question of why that difference involving memory ought to be included in an information processing image of P.

In sum, there are a variety of ways in which access to representations—both P and non-P representations—can be derailed. Anyone who wants to frame a definition of "A" that cuts between the P and non-P cases to avoid cracks between P and A owes us far more than Chalmers has provided. Moreover, P comes in a variety of degrees, of phenomenal flavors, and of representational contents. All would seem to affect the causal properties of P-states. But that raises the issue of whether the role of P has any unity apart from its dependence on the intensity, flavor, and representational properties of the P-states that have that role. Consider the kind *feet*, which, let us suppose, is a natural category. Now consider the causal role of feet, what affects them and how and what they affect. Feet are affected by concrete and high-heeled shoes and in turn affect the air-conditioners in gas pedal plants, the breeding of animals from which shoe-leather is taken, and the stockprices of companies in the foot-jewelry industry. Is the *role* a natural item apart from the feet that mediate the causal relations? I doubt it, and I would guess that the same point applies to the role of P-consciousness.

R2. Does Consciousness Have a Function?

The best explanation for the close correlation between P and A is that P is somehow involved in the machinery of A. By contrast, Chalmers favors epiphenomenalism. He objects to my claim that P greases the wheels of A on the ground that there is no conceptual entailment from neural stuff to P-consciousness, so there is no contradiction in the idea of a physical duplicate of me who is a zombie, that is, has no P-consciousness. His argument that P-consciousness must be redundant to the causal mechanisms of A-consciousness is that the zombie has the same physical causal machinery of A-consciousness as I do but has no P. Since the causal machinery works the same way with or without P, P does nothing.

But this argument takes mere logical possibilities much too seriously. Mere logical possibilities do not tell us what the real mechanisms are. Magic is logically possible in the sense of not contradictory. The scarecrow of Oz who thinks despite a head of straw is not contradictory, but one cannot move from that to any conclusion about the *actual* mechanisms of thinking. My car does not think and has no P-consciousness, but there is a consistently describable physical duplicate of it that is a sapient and sentient being whose thinking and P-consciousness plays a role in the operation of the car. In my car, the low-gas light goes on via a simple piece of machinery. That machinery is present in the magic "world," but, in addition, there is another mechanism. In the magic "world", the fact that the car wants to inform me of the empty tank plays a causal role that is parallel to the physical machinery but nonetheless causally efficacious. Both are causally efficacious; it is a case of overdetermination. The magic "world" is *merely* logically possible only in the sense that there is no contradiction in it. Sapience and sentience are present in one case, absent in the other. But no conclusion can be drawn about sapience and sentience having no effect.

Moving to a somewhat different topic, I agree with Chalmers that one can interpret much of the empirical work on consciousness that I criticized as assuming that P = A (that is, that P is a nondispositional state that provides the basis for the A-disposition). So some of this empirical work can be rescued in a post hoc way by making a distinction that the authors themselves did not see. I acknowledged this in the target article. But not all of this work is equally rescuable in that way. In particular, much of the reasoning I was criticizing has problems of the "trivial or false" variety. Witness Searle's reasoning described in the target article and Crick and Koch's reasoning that V1 is not part of the neural correlate of consciousness because V1 does not project to frontal cortex and projection to frontal cortex is required for direct control of behavior. This is trivial of A and false (or at least unjustified) for P. (See Block 1996b.) One final point: Chalmers notes that model 3 is implausible, apparently assuming that I thought otherwise. I indicated that model 3 might be difficult to refute empirically, not because I thought the model might actually be right, but rather because of the usual problems with refuting epiphenomenalism. Refutations of the view always end up being more methodological than experimental. So-called simplicity has to figure very strongly in refutation of such ideas.

R3. Consciousness and the Self

Many of the commentators in round one felt that neither A nor P corresponds very well to the intuitive notion of consciousness. The problem was that neither P nor A required that one's *self* have access to one's own conscious states. A-consciousness is a purely information-theoretic idea that does not explicitly involve the self. One can speak of one state controlling another without explicitly putting any self in the picture. Although I mentioned various connections with the self in talking about P, none loomed large. Both Browne and Rosenthal criticize me on this basis, as did many in round one. Church (1995), Harman (1995), Lycan (1995), Kitcher (1995), and Levine (1995) criticized my view explicitly on this ground, but many of the critics in round one were obliquely critical about this. For example, Baars (1995) expanded my P-consciousness as "personal consciousness" and Armstrong (1995) suggested that "A" would be better replace by "I" for introspection. Officially, Rosenthal's conclusion is that P entails A (unless one or the other is phony), so it is useless to look for cases of P without A. I say that this is his *official* conclusion because *actually* he thinks cases of P without A are completely obvious and uncontroversial. Rosenthal has adopted the misleading strategy of *redefining* both "P" and "A" so that the *P-redefined* entails the *A-redefined*, even though in his view, as in mine, *P does not entail A*. What is misleading about this procedure is that the redefinitions are not made explicit. I confess that my first thought on reading Rosenthal's reply was that for the reason just mentioned, the disagreement between us was completely verbal. But on reflection, I see that the redefinitions he offers are natural expressions of the clash of our points of view about the importance of self-consciousness, and this clash is an important one to get clear about.

Let me explain. Rosenthal and I mean the same thing by "state with phenomenal content." Phenomenal contents are specific types or categories of experience such as the experience of the sensation of red or the feeling of pain. In my terminology, a state with phenomenal content is just a P-conscious state; I do not distinguish between the two. But Rosenthal rejects the equivalence, *state with phenomenal content = P-conscious state*. His argument starts with the claim that we can have *unconscious* states that belong in one of these P-content categories, for example, an unconscious pain or an unconscious sensation of red in subliminal perception. Such unconscious pains and sensations, he notes, are not A-conscious. By my definitions (which I will be using here), they are cases of P without A, and so we see that Rosenthal accepts P without A in *my* senses of these terms as uncontroversial. Indeed, Rosenthal is much more liberal about P without A than I am. I think that there is only a very remote *possibility* that subliminal perception is P and thus only a remote possibility that subliminal perception involves P-content without A. Suppose the letter "Q" is flashed too briefly for the subject to report on it, but long enough to influence later choices. Rosenthal seems to assume that such "perceptions" are states with phenomenal content. (I expect this is because he has a very thin notion of phenomenal content. But let us put this issue to one side, accepting with Rosenthal that there are uncontroversial cases of P, in my terms, without A.)

Here is where the basic difference in perspective comes in. Rosenthal holds that these P-without-A states (in my senses of the terms) are not *conscious* states *at all*, for there is "nothing it's like *for a subject* to be in that state." In other words, P without A, if it exists, is not *real* consciousness because it need not involve access to the self, to the subject him or herself. So he rejects my notion of P (because it is not what he thinks of as *consciousness*). He holds that the cases of P without A are not real cases of P-*consciousness* without A. Since he thinks access to the self is required for genuine consciousness, he redefines "P" as what we might call "{P + self-access}."

Okay, so that is part of the story. But we still haven't seen how a redefined P will necessarily involve A. Does {P + self-access} entail A? No, because as Rosenthal notes, A is a purely information-processing notion that *also* involves no connection to the self. So Rosenthal changes my A too to what we might call "{A + self-access}," my A plus the added condition that the self has access to the state. He regards this as the pre-theoretic intuitive sense of A: "Much in Block's discussion relies on this pretheoretic notion of A-consciousness, rather than the official connection with inference and the control of speech and action." So Rosenthal's claim that P entails A amounts to the claim that the redefined P, {P + self-access} entails the redefined A, {A + self-access}. There is more to the story here about why {P + self-access} entails {A + self-access}, but I will not go into it. My point is only that the claim that redefined-P entails redefined-A does not challenge my claim that P without A is at least conceptually possible. Those cases of P that *don't involve self-access* may be the very cases that do not involve A. For example, in the target article I mentioned a case in which one is having an intense conversation oblivious to a loud noise, even though one has raised the volume of one's voice to compensate for it. Once one notices the noise, one might realize that one was *hearing it all along*. This is plausibly a case of P without A, and one that does not involve self-access.

Rosenthal notes that A is dispositional. Being poised for direct mental and behavioral control is a disposition. But consciousness is not dispositional, he says. For one's sensation of red to be conscious in his preferred sense, one must oneself be conscious of it, and that is not dispositional. I can agree that that nondispositionality of the P-conscious sensation of red shows that P-consciousness is not Aconsciousness. But this does not show that we should reject A in favor of higher-order thought. The sensation of red is also P-conscious. And P consciousness, like higher-order thought, is not dispositional.

The key problem with higher-order thought as the main or only nondispositional notion of consciousness is that it is too intellectual. Consider the dog in pain mentioned by both Kitcher (1995) and me (Block 1995). Surely a dog with a pain that *hurts* (and therefore exerts direct control of behavior) is in a conscious state in a reasonable, intuitive sense of the term even if the dog has no higher order thought about the pain! And the dog may have a conscious pain in this sense even if it does not have a sufficient grip on the concept of pain or the concept of the self to *have* the thought that "I, myself have a pain."

The verbal aspect of Rosenthal's point can also be seen by noting that Rosenthal has no complaint against the naturalness or importance of what I call P-consciousness. For him, it is the category *state with phenomenal content*. And he makes no criticism of my notion of A except that, leaving out the self, it is not the "pretheoretic notion of A-consciousness." The criticism is that neither P nor A deserve to be called categories of *"consciousness."* So the verbal aspect is that the word "consciousness" should not be applied to them. But there is also an implicit substantive and nonverbal complaint, namely, that I have left out *the main thing* in a notion of consciousness. What is this main thing that I left out? For Rosenthal it is the higher order thought, one state being about another. I agree that higher order thought is important, but I have scanted it because both P and A are more primitive and fundamental. It is P that engenders the famous explanatory gap. We have a promising research program into the nature of thought. There is no reason to suppose that higher order thought will not yield to it. But there is something else that I might be said to have left out. Armstrong, Baars, Church, Harman, Kitcher, Levine, and Lycan, all first round commentators, mention some sort of connection with the self. I will try to come to grips with this issue, starting with Browne's argument. Browne regards the relations of access to the self as the heart of the intuitive conception of consciousness. He says that reducing this intuitive conception to A-consciousness will simply leave out the intuitive idea of access to the self. Recall that a representation is A-conscious to the extent that it is poised for direct mental and behavioral control. The informational relations involved in direct control of reasoning and action (e.g., informational promiscuity) make no mention of the self and do not in any explicit way clarify the intuitive notion of self-access. So, according to Browne, reducing the intuitive idea to A is not initially promising. The other alternative mentioned by Browne is the idea of reducing the intuitive idea of self-consciousness to P (or perhaps adopting a version of P that includes it). His objection to this idea is that it is unexplanatory. P does not help to explain anything about access to the self.

R4. Deflationism about the Self

My disagreement with Browne (and many of the other commentators) hinges on my deflationism about the self. (See White 1991, for a worked out picture along these lines.) This is not tantamount to being an eliminativist like Hume or Dennett. My view is that the upshot of work in cognitive psychology and cognitive neuroscience is that we (ourselves) are loose federations of centers of control and integration, and for this reason, the intuitive idea of the self as a monolithic integrated entity is an illusion. The conflict between the intuitive conception and the emerging scientific picture was first captured in a convincing manner in Nagel's 1971 paper, "Brain bisection and the unity of consciousness." Nagel argued that the fragmentation observed in split brain patients exists to some degree in normal people, and this challenges our intuitive concept of the self. This sort of idea has been widened and elaborated for many years now by many psychologists and neuropsychologists, for example by Gazzaniga and his colleagues (see also, Dennett 1991). Gazzaniga (1985) tries to explain many ubiquitous cognitive phenomena in terms of the relations among "sub-selves," especially the efforts of some sub-selves to rationalize the behavior of other sub-selves. The most impressive evidence involves cases where knowledge is accessible via one part of the body, but not another. Goodale and Milner (1992) note a double dissociation: some patients cannot describe the orientation of a slot but act appropriately towards it, others show the reverse. Marcel (1993) notes a situation in which blindsight patients can access information better if responding by button-presses than verbally, and better still by eye blinks. Such phenomena are observed not only in brain damaged patients, but also in normals.

So I take it that there is a good scientific basis for what might be called deflationism about the self; regarding the self as a loose federation. This fact is what underlies my disagreement with Browne and others. To begin, my notion of A-consciousness *does* involve the self, the only self that *really exists*. The self-consciousness that they hanker after is a mirage. For a representation to be informationally promiscuous, to directly control behavior and speech, *is* for it to be *self*-conscious, given what the self *really* is. The definition of access-consciousness is implicitly relativized to a system. For a representation to dominate activity within that system is for it to be *as* self-conscious as it *can* be. Browne's dissatisfaction with A because it leaves out the self depends on ignoring the relevant science. I said in the target article that one should take intuitions about consciousness very seriously. But these intuitions can only be taken seriously insofar as they do not conflict with scientific fact, and one of the few facts in this area is that the intuitive notion of the self is in large part illusory. So the dissatisfaction with A that many of the critics have expressed, that it does not involve any connection with the self, is a mistake. A does involve self-consciousness in the only sense in which self-consciousness is real.

R5.   Is A a Kind of Consciousness at All?

Bringsjord points out that I waffle on whether A is a kind of consciousness that can exist without P. I expressed some sympathy (but did not actually endorse) Searle's (1992) and Burge's (1997) claim that a zombie which has no P consciousness has no consciousness of any sort, even if it has the information processing aspects of P. I think they are on to something important about the ordinary notion of consciousness: P is the core and A is conceived of by many of us as a kind of consciousness only against a background of P (as I noted in the replies in the first round). But I have two reasons for seeing A as an independent kind of consciousness. First, I think we all use both A and P to some extent in thinking about consciousness. I refer the reader to the discussion of Searle in the target article. Searle officially denies that A is a kind of consciousness, but I have caught him using "consciousness" in the sense of A. There is also the curious fact I noted in the target article that many people appear to have a concept of consciousness in which A appears to be the core and P is a subsidiary sensory aspect of A that is not even necessary for consciousness. It would be surprising if there were no echo of this in those of us who officially see consciousness as P.

A second reason is that I am less concerned with our ordinary use of "conscious" than with the important scientific issue of the relation between P and its information processing image, namely, A. Are they phenomena of different sorts? Can one can exist without the other? The ordinary concepts of consciousness are vague and even if Searle and Burge are right, not too much violence is done to the ordinary concept by treating A without P as a form of consciousness.

R6.   How Representational Is P?

Güzeldere and Aydede find my views on the representational properties of P incoherent. Let me summarize the relevant claims so you can judge for yourselves:

1. Some P-contents are not at all representational, or at least, there is nothing about P that *requires* that P-contents be representational. In the target article, I gave the example of orgasm, but I am not totally sure about it. What I am sure about is that what *matters* about the phenomenal content of orgasm is nothing representational.
2. So P-content is not representational *per se*. (This is just another way of saying that there is nothing about P that requires it to be representational.)
3. Some specific P contents *are* representational *per se*; that is, some specific P-contents have an essential representational aspect. The example I used was the image or visual experience of circles (as opposed to squares). I noted that it is a feature of these P contents that the squares are packable but the circles are not.

4. Some other specific P contents are representational, but not *per se*. According to me, the inverted spectrum thought experiment shows that the P-content that represents red might have represented green.

I think the appearance of incoherence that Güzeldere and Aydede are worried about comes from the ease of confusing the claim that P is not essentially representational with the claim that some specific P-contents are essentially representational. Art is not essentially representational but some items of art are.

Gamble raises the interesting issue of how P could be representational at all. She says P is an intrinsic property whereas representation is relational. But why can't an intrinsic property represent via a relation? Consider the red color of a section of a map. Suppose the redness is an intrinsic property. Still, it can be used to represent altitude. Gamble says that cognitive science must treat P as a representation if it hopes to study it. I don't see why cognitive science can't study the *function* of something that is not representational. No doubt this depends on how one chooses to define "cognitive science." But using "cognitive science" so that Gamble is right, still some other field could study P, call it cognitive biology.

R7.   Is There a Fallacy?

Güzeldere and Aydede say that Schacter's notion of consciousness is more like A than P. But their quotations do not seem to me to support this view. Güzeldere and Aydede quote Schacter as speaking of "access to consciousness." Is this supposed to be *access to access consciousness?* Charity requires rejecting this reading. My view is that consciousness is a mongrel concept containing elements of both P and A. Schacter (and Crick and Koch 1995b) are closer to P than A. But the important point is that by using a single notion of consciousness (that includes elements of both P and A), they end up with a dilemma: triviality or falsehood. This also applies to Crick and Koch (1995a). If they mean A, it is trivial that V1 is not conscious; but if they mean P it is perhaps false. Consider Searle (1992): the epileptics are missing "consciousness" and therefore flexibility. If it is P that is meant, the premise is very likely false. If A is meant, the reasoning is trivial. It is trivial that missing A leads to lack of flexibility because A *includes* flexibility in the relevant sense.

Searle does not make the P/A distinction, but if we make it, we can reinterpret him as saying that P is missing in the epileptics, and that explains the missing A. But even this much charity will not save his argument, since it is very implausible that they are missing P. Bringsjord tries to make it plausible that this happens all the time, for example, when we drive "automatically." But this is a very implausible view of automatic driving. Here is an experiment we can all perform. Next time you are going out on a long drive, get your companion to note when you seem to have spaced out and to ask you the following question: "What did you just see?" I will tell you my result: I remember the last car I passed, the last curve in the road and the like. I have been told that pilot work using the Nissan driving simulator (at the Nissan laboratory in Cambridge MA) yields the same result: a moving window of memory of about 30–45 seconds. (Unfortunately, I have been unable to confirm this report.) Bringsjord seems to assume that because there is no long-term memory of P, there is no P.

What about Searle's contradiction? Bringsjord gives a stunning application of the principle of charity in explaining away Searle's contradiction. I submit that my diagnosis (switching between using "consciousness" to mean A and P) was far more plausible.

R8. Representation and Function

Gilman and I are to some extent at cross purposes, as I can explain by distinguishing between representationism and functionalism. Functionalism is the view that the nature of experience can be completely captured by the role of experiences in the mental economy, how they affect other mental states and behavior, and how they are themselves affected by stimulation. Suppose that when I both touch and look at the corner of a cube, I have experiences in the two modalities with the same representational content but different phenomenal feels. One phenomenal feel in sight, another in touch, but no representational difference. This need not disturb a *functionalist*, since there are such large and obvious functional differences between sight and touch. A functionalist has the resources to explain the phenomenal difference. But a *representationist*, by contrast cannot accept experiences that have the same representational content but different phenomenal content, for representationism goes beyond functionalism in trying to cash out all phenomenal character in terms of the ways the world is represented to be. Similarly, a functionalist need not be troubled if the experience of orgasm has no representational content at all, for its functional role (e.g., its motivational role) can serve to distinguish that experience from other experiences.

As Gilman notes, I believe in a "nonrepresentational, nonfunctional notion of phenomenal consciousness." Although phenomenal consciousness represents and functions, it cannot be completely accounted for in these terms. However, I did *not* try to argue for the *nonfunctional* part in the target article. The strategy of the target article, was to try to put some of the controversies aside to discuss a distinction (between P and A) that was to some extent at least visible even if my position in those controversies is mistaken. However, I *did* argue that P-content goes beyond the representational. I did not give my strongest argument for that conclusion (namely, the Inverted Earth argument, presented in 1990; 1994; 1996) but I did make some brief remarks in that direction, discussing the impoverished representational content of orgasm (as compared with its truly impressive phenomenal character). And I also had a discussion of sensations with the same representational content in different modalities. My purpose was to head off an identification of P with A, one that surfaced in the commentaries of Armstrong, Dennett, Farah, and Tye, in the first round.

Here's why Gilman and I are largely at cross purposes. He argues against my point about the experience of orgasm partly by appealing to its functional properties. He says "Phenomenal contents may vary in a more fine-grained way than natural language labels for those contents, but is such variation obviously nonrepresentational *and nonfunctional?*" He summarizes my remarks about the experience of orgasm as suggesting that "there is so much to the experience of orgasm that one couldn't possibly exhaust 'all that' with a representational *or functional* account." And he notes that there is no in-principle problem to "representational *or functional* accounts of the evaluative part of an experience." (Emphasis added in all these quotations.) Sure, the evaluative function of the experience of orgasm is entirely immune from my point that this experience is *representationally* impoverished; however, I wasn't trying to argue against functionalism, but only against the stronger view: representationism.

We are not entirely at cross purposes, however. Gilman does also defend the representationist point of view. For example, he notes correctly that we cannot expect all of representational content to be expressible in natural language; for example, recognitional dispositions often constitute a kind of content that is not expressible in English. But are we to take seriously the idea that the phenomenal character of orgasm is exhausted by a kind of *recognition*? On the face of it, having the orgasm-experience and recognizing it are very different. Perhaps recognizing the experience *changes* the experience somewhat. But surely recognition does not wholly create the experience. (What about the first time?) And there is no plausibility in the idea that an orgasm experience requires any sort of categorization. Couldn't an animal, or even a person, have something like that experience without the recognition?

R9. P = A?

I argued that just as the concept of water differs from the concept of H_2O, so the concept of P and A differ. The real question, I suggested, was whether as a matter of empirical fact, just as water = H_2O, so P = A. (Since A is dispositional whereas P is not, what this comes to is that all and only P-states have the A role.)

Pöppel presents evidence that 30–40 Hz oscillations (each one lasting roughly 30 msec) are the basis of consciousness. For example, if a type of anesthesia is used that suppresses these oscillations, subjects feel that no time has elapsed when they wake up. ("When does the operation start?") Types of anesthesia that do not suppress the oscillations promote implicit recall of tapes played under anesthesia. (Patients exposed to a recording of a Robinson Crusoe story are much more likely to associate Crusoe with "Friday" after the operation; see Schwender et al. 1994). Pöppel mentions another interesting temporal matter: evidence for mechanisms of presemantic automatic sensory integration that take 2–3 seconds. Access to P must take place within such a 2–3 second window. So is the idea this? There are two basic mechanisms of consciousness; the 30–40 Hz oscillations underlie P, and the 2–3 second integration mechanism underlies A. I take it that with mechanisms that differ in their time scale in this way, we could have P without A. For a P event might occur and fade out before the integration required for A can take place.

Noë denies that the concepts of P and A differ. He argues that perception intrinsically involves both P and A. Even if he is right about this, it falls short of the conclusion. Perception could essentially involve two nonidentical things. Moreover, I mentioned a number of nonperceptual cases. Recall the Freudian example of the repressed image of the red room in which the patient was tortured. I argued that the repressed image could be P without being A. (The case is hypothetical, but recall that we are talking about the *conceptual* possibility that P and A come apart.) But Noë sometimes appears to use "perception" to *mean* experience, namely, P. On this interpretation, there is no doubt that experience is intrinsically P. The only issue, then, is whether experience is intrinsically A, the issue of the next to last paragraph of Noë's comment.

Noë gives two reasons why P contents must be A, but neither applies to nonperceptual cases like the Freudian case. The first is that experience by its nature has a rational import. Surely the repressed image potentially has a rational bearing, but one cannot use it unless it becomes A-conscious. The second is that he doubts that one would credit someone with P unless one were willing to credit the person with A too. But one might have all sorts of indirect evidence of the P content of the red image, including the person's own testimony *after* the psychotherapy is successful and the image becomes A-conscious. The patient might tell us that once he recovered access to the image, he realized that he had always had the image, but the pain associated with it kept him from acknowledging it even to the point of realizing that he had it or realizing that it showed that he had been tortured. Even if one insists on the latter sort of evidence, there could be a period during which the image was P without being A. (Some models of memory, e.g., the Headed Records view of Morton, 1991, have room for such phenomena.)

Mangan agrees that there is a conceptual possibility of P diverging from A, but he is certain that in fact P = A. He seems to think that I argue as follows: a difference in concepts, therefore difference in fact. But that is not my argument. I say that we do not know whether P = A. There is certainly reason to take apparent cases of P without A (and one apparent case of A without P) seriously. Mangan says that research on P is doing well on the assumption that P = A. But is it really doing well when we have no idea how anything physical could have P, when we have proposals that the field seriously considers drawing on quantum mechanics, whose rationale seems to be that both quantum mechanics and consciousness are mysterious? Mangan mentions my analogy: perhaps P is like the liquid in a hydraulic computer, and A is like the computation.

P is the hardware implementation of A. Mangan wonders whether P can "completely" implement A. But if the analogy is correct, then we have to wonder whether there are other implementations of A, just as a given computation may be realized electrically instead of mechanically. There can be hydraulic fluid without the hydraulic computer and an electronic version of the computer without any fluid. How does Mangan rule out the analogous possibilities in the case of P and A?

Bogen wonders whether the right hemisphere might have A without P. He is sure it has A, and if his theory of P in terms of the ILN is right, it has P too. Perhaps some reader can shed more light on the issue. On dreaming, Bogen agrees with Revonsuo (first round) that dreams may be P without A. In dreaming, one's representations *are* poised to control behavior, but behavioral systems are paralyzed, so there is no behavior. Dream contents are A; so they do not provide a case of P without A.

R10. The Explanatory Gap

Van der Heijden et al. think that the explanatory gap is made to seem wider than it is by assuming that, for example, roses are red and violets are blue. If you suppose that a rose is red, then, according to them, you have to suppose that red is "literally reproduced" in P-consciousness. And if red is "literally reproduced" in P-consciousness, it is no surprise that it seems almost impossible to explain P-consciousness in neural terms. They suggest that we give up the "color-color identity constraint" that insists that we have red both in the world and in the mind. Here is where they go wildly, unbelievably wrong. They say that we should give up the idea that a rose or anything else is ever red. The only redness, they say, is mental redness. But why not hold instead that roses are red, giving up the idea that red is "literally reproduced" in P-consciousness? Why not reject the "color-color identity constraint" by rejecting colors in the mind? Why not construe talk of red in the mind as a misleading way of expressing the fact that P-conscious states *represent* the world as red? And a representation of red need not itself be red (like the occurrences of the word "red" here). This idea is spelled out further in Block (1983) and Tye (1995, Ch. 4).

Note

Author's response, reprinted from *Behavioral and Brain Sciences* 20 (1): 159–165, 1997. This is the second round of replies to critics of "On a Confusion about a Function of Consciousness", reprinted in this volume, chapter 9.

References

Armstrong, D. (1995) Perception-consciousness and action consciousness? *Behavioral and Brain Sciences* 18:247–48.

Aydede, M. (1995) An analysis of pleasure vis-à-vis pain. Unpublished manuscript, University of Chicago.

Baars, B. (1995) Evidence that phenomenal consciousness is the same as access consciousness. *Behavioral and Brain Sciences* 18:249.

—— (1988) *A cognitive theory of conscioussness.* Cambridge University Press.

Bachmann, T. (1995) More empirical cases to break the accord of phenomenal and access-consciousness. *Behavioral and Brain Sciences* 18:249–51.

Berlucchi, G., Aglioti, S., Marzi, C. A., and Tassinari, G. (1995) Corpus callosum and simple visuomotor integration. *Neuropsychologia* 33:923–36.

Block, N. (1980) Troubles with functionalism. In: *Readings in philosophy of psychology*, vol. 1. Harvard University Press.

—— (1983) Mental pictures and cognitive science. *The Philosophical Review XCII* 4:499–541.

—— (1990) Inverted earth. In: *Philosophical perspectives 4: Action theory and philosophy of mind*, ed. J. Tomberlin. Atascadero.

—— (1994) Consciousness. In: *A companion to philosophy of mind*, ed. S. Guttenplan. Blackwell.

—— (1995r) How many concepts of consciousness? *Behavioral and Brain Sciences* 18:272–84.

—— (1995t) On a confusion about a function of consciousness. *Behavioral and Brain Sciences* 18:227–87.

—— (1996a) Mental paint and mental latex. In: *Philosophical issues*, ed. E. Villanueva. Atascadero: Ridgeview.

—— (1996b) How to find the neural correlate of consciousness. *Trends in Neuroscience* 19:2.

Bogen, J. E. (1993) Thecallosal syndromes. In: *Clinical neuropsychology*, 3rd ed., ed. K. M. Heilman & E. Valenstein. Oxford University Press.

—— (1995a) On the neurophysiology of consciousness: 1. Overview. *Consciousness and Cognition* 4:52–62.

—— (1995b) On the neurophysiology of consciousness: 2. Constraining the semantic problem. *Consciousness and Cognition* 4:137–58.

Bogen, J. E., and Vogel, P. J. (1962) Cerebral commissurotomy in man: Preliminary case report. *Bulletin of the Los Angeles Neurological Society* 27:169–73.

Bringsjord, S. (1992) *What robots can and can't be.* Kluwer.

—— (1995) Pourquoi Henrik Ibsen est-il une menace pour la littérature générée par ordinateur? In: *Littérature et Informatique la Littérature Générée Par Ordinateur*, ed. A. Vuillemin. Arras, France: Artois Presses Universite.

Burge, T. (1997) Two kinds of consciousness. In: *Consciousness: Philosophical and scientific debates*, ed. N. Block, O. Flanagan & G. Güzeldere. MIT Press.

Chalmers, D. J. (1996) *The conscious mind: In search of a fundamental theory*. Oxford University Press.

Church, J. (1995) Fallacies or analyses? *Behavioral and Brain Sciences* 18:251–52.

Cooper, L. A., and Shepard, R. N. (1973) Chronometric studies of the rotation of mental images. In: *Visual information processing*, ed. W. G. Chase. Academic Press.

Corballis, M. C. (1995) Visual integration in the split brain. *Neuropsychologia* 33:937–59.

Crick, F., and Koch, C. (1990) Towards a neurobiological theory of consciousness. *Seminars in the Neurosciences* 2:263–75.

——— (1995a) Are we aware of neural activity in primary visual cortex? *Nature* 375:121–23.

——— (1995b) Why neuroscience may be able to explain consciousness (sidebar). *Scientific American* 12(95):92.

Delacour, J. (1995) An introduction to the biology of consciousness. *Neuropsychologia* 33:1061–74.

Dennett, D. (1991) *Consciousness explained*. Little Brown.

——— (1995) The path not taken. *Behavioral and Brain Sciences* 18:252–53.

Dretske, F. (1969) *Seeing and knowing*. University of Chicago Press.

——— (1981) *Knowledge and the flow of information*. MIT Press.

——— (1995) *Naturalizing the mind*. MIT Press.

Farah, M. J. (1994) Visual perception and visual awareness after brain damage: A tutorial overview. In: *Consciousness and unconscious information processing: Attention and performance*, ed. C. Umilta & M. Moscovitch. MIT Press.

——— (1995) Is consciousness of perception really separable from perception? *Behavioral and Brain Sciences* 18:254–55.

Gazzaniga, M. (1985) *The social brain*. Basic Books.

Gazzaniga, M., Fendrich, R., and Wessinger, C. (1994) Blindsight reconsidered. *Current Directions in Psychological Science* 3(3):93–6.

Gazzaniga, M., and LeDoux, J. E. (1978) *The integrated mind*. Plenum.

Gerstner, G. E., and Fazio, V. A. (1995) Evidence of a universal perceptual unit in mammals. *Ethology* 101:89–100.

Goodale, M., and Milner A. D. (1992) Separate visual pathways for perception and action. *Trends in Neuroscience* 15:20–25.

Graham, G. (1995) Guilty consciousness. *Behavioral and Brain Sciences* 18(2):255–56.

Güzeldere, G. (1997) *The many faces of consciousness.* Ph.D. dissertation, Stanford University.

Hardin, C. L. (1988) *Colour for philosophers.* Hacket Publishing Company.

Harman, G. (1990) The intrinsic quality of experience. In: *Philosophical perspectives, vol. 4*, ed. J. Tomberlin. Ridgeview.

———— (1995) Phenomenal fallacies and conflations. *Behavioral and Brain Sciences* 18:256–57.

Hartmann, J. A. et al. (1991) Denial of visual perception. *Brain and Cognition* 16:29–40.

Humphrey, N. (1992) *A history of the mind.* Simon & Schuster.

Huxley, T. H. (1866) Lessons in elementary psychology. Quoted in: *A history of the mind*, by N. Humphrey, 1992. Simon & Schuster.

Katz, L. D. (1995) On distinguishing phenomenal consciousness from the representational functions of mind. *Behavioral and Brain Sciences* 18:258–59.

Kinsbourne, M. (1995) The intralaminar thalamic nuclei: Subjectivity pumps or attention-action coordinators? *Consciousness and Cognition* 4:167–71.

Kitcher, P. (1995) Triangulating phenomenal consciousness. *Behavioral and Brain Sciences* 18:259–60.

Kobes, B. W. (1995) Access and what it is like. *Behavioral and Brain Sciences* 18:260.

Kowal, S., O'Connell, D. C., and Sabin, E. J. (1975) Development of temporal patterning and vocal hesitations in spontaneous narratives. *Journal of Psycholinguistic Research* 4:195–207.

Lackner, J., and Garrett, M. (1973) Resolving ambiguity: Effects of biasing context in the unattended ear. *Cognition* 1:359–37.

Lambek, J. (1961) How to program an infinite abacus. *Canadian Mathematical Bulletin* 4:295–302.

Levine, J. (1995) Phenomenal access: A moving target. *Behavioral and Brain Sciences* 18:261.

Libet, B. (1993) The neural time factor in conscious and unconscious events. In: *Experimental and theoretical studies of consciousness* (Ciba Foundation Symposium 174). Wiley.

Lloyd, D. (1995) Access denied. *Behavioral and Brain Sciences* 18(2):261–62.

Lycan, W. G. (1995) We've only just begun. *Behavioral and Brain Sciences* 18:262–63.

Madler, C., and Pöppel, E. (1987) Auditory evoked potentials indicate the loss of neuronal oscillations during general anaesthesia. *Naturwissenschaften* 75:42–43.

Mangan, B. (1993a) Dennett, consciousness, and the sorrows of functionalism. *Consciousness and Cognition* 2(1):1–17.

———— (1993b) Taking phenomenology seriously: The "fringe" and its implications for cognitive research. *Consciousness and Cognition* 2(2):89–108.

Marcel, A. J. (1993) Slippage in the unity of consciousness. In: *Experimental and theoretical studies of consciousness*. Wiley.

Mates, J., Müller, U., Radil, T., and Pöppel, E. (1994) Temporal integration in sensorimotor synchronization. *Journal of Cognitive Neuroscience* 6:332–40.

McDowell, J. (1994) The content of perceptual experience. *Philosophical Quarterly* 44:190–205.

Milner, A. D., and Goodale, M. A. (1995) *The visual brain in action*. Oxford University Press.

Morton, J. (1991) Cognitive pathologies of memory: A headed records analysis. In: *Memories, thoughts, and emotions: Essays in honor of George Mandler*, ed. W. Kessen, A. Ortony & F. Craik. Erlbaum.

Nagel, T. (1971) Brain bisection and the unity of consciousness. *Synthese* 22:396–413.

——— (1974) What is it like to be a bat? *Philosophical Review* 83:435–50.

Natsoulas, T. (1995) How access-consciousness might be a kind of consciousness. *Behavioral and Brain Sciences* 18(2):264–65.

Pani, J. R. (1982) A functionalist approach to mental imagery. 23rd Annual Psychonomic Society Meeting.

Páre, D., and Llinás, R. (1995) Consciousness and preconscious processes as seen from the standpoint of sleep-waking cycle neurophysiology. *Neuropsychologia* 33:1155–68.

Peterson, L. B., and Peterson, M. J. (1959) Short-term retention of individual items. *Journal of Experimental Psychology* 58:193–98.

Pöppel, E. (1970) Excitability cycles in central intermittency. *Psychologische Forschung* 34:1–9.

——— (1988) *Mindworks: Time and conscious experiences*. Harcourt Brace Jovanovich. (Orig. 1985: *Grenzen des Bewusstseins*, dva, Stuttgart).

——— (1989) Taxonomy of the subjective: An evolutionary perspective. In: *Neuropsychology of visual perception*, ed. J. Brown. Erlbaum.

——— (1994) Temporal mechanisms in perception. *International Review of Neurobiology* 37:185–202.

Pöppel, P., Held, R., and Frost, D. (1973) Residual visual function after brain wounds involving the central visual pathways in man. *Nature* 243:295–96.

Revonsuo, A. (1995) Conscious and nonconscious control of action. *Behavioral and Brain Sciences* 18(2):265–66.

Rey, G. (1995) Block's philosophical anosognosia. *Behavioral and Brain Sciences* 18:266–67.

Rosenthal, D. M. (1986) Two concepts of consciousness. *Philosophical Studies* 49:329–59.

——— (1990) Why are verbally expressed thoughts conscious? Report no. 32, Center for Interdisciplinary Research. University of Bielefeld.

——— (1993) Thinking that one thinks. In: *Consciousness*, ed. M. Davies & G. Humphreys. Blackwell.

Schleidt, M., Eibl-Eibesfeldt, I., and Pöppel, E. (1987) A universal constant in temporal segmentation of human short-term behavior. *Naturwissenschaften* 74:289–90.

Schwender, D., Madler, C., Klasing, S., Peter, K., and Pöppel, E. (1994) Anesthetic control of 40 Hz brain activity and implicit memory. *Consciousness and Cognition* 3:129–47.

Searle, J. (1983) *Intentionality*. Cambridge University Press.

——— (1992) *The rediscovery of the mind*. MIT Press.

Shallice, T. (1972) Dual functions of consciousness. *Psychological Review* 79:383–93.

——— (1988a) *From neuropsychology to mental structure*. Cambridge University Press.

——— (1988b) Information-processing models of consciousness: Possibilities and problems. In: *Consciousness in contemporary science*, ed. A. Marcel & E. Bisiach. Oxford University Press.

Shepard, R. N. (1995) What is an agent that it experiences P-consciousness? And what is P-consciousness that it moves an agent? *Behavioral and Brain Sciences* 18:267–68.

Sperling, G. (1960) The information available in brief visual presentations. *Psychological Monographs* 74.

Sperry, R. W. (1974) Lateral specialization in the surgically separated hemispheres. In: *Neuroscience 3rd study program*, ed. F. O. Schmitt & F. G. Worden. MIT Press.

Stich, S. P. (1978) Beliefs and subdoxastic states. *Philosophy of Science* 45:499–518.

Tye, M. (1995a) Blindsight, orgasm and representational overlap. *Behavioral and Brain Sciences* 18:268–69.

——— (1995b) *Ten problems of consciousness*. MIT Press.

Vollrath, M., Kazenwadel, J., and Krüger, H.-P. (1992) A universal constant in temporal segmentation of human speech. *Naturwissenschaften* 79:479–80.

White, S. (1991) *The unity of the self*. MIT Press.

Zaidel, E. (1978) Concepts of cerebral dominance in the split brain. *Cerebral correlates of conscious experience*, ed. Buser & Rougeul-Buser.

Elsevier/North-Holland Biomedical Press.

Zaidel, E., Zaidel, D. W., and Bogen, J. E. (1996) Disconnection syndrome. In: *The Blackwell dictionary of neuropsychology*, ed. J. G. Beaumont, R. Keneally & M. Rogers. Blackwell.

——— (1995) *Behavioral and Brain Sciences*. Editorial commentary BBS 18:272.

12 Ridiculing Social Constructivism about Phenomenal Consciousness

Kurthen, Grunwald, and Elger often speak as if the issue between us is whether it is *coherent* to claim that phenomenal consciousness is a cultural construction. For example, their commentary closes with: "we do not hold that P-consciousness does not exist; we just think that if it is coherent to claim that consciousness is a social construction, it must also be coherent to imagine the cultural deconstruction of consciousness." But I never said the cultural construction view was incoherent. It is as coherent as the view that human phenomenal consciousness depends on the proximity of beetles or that peanuts are surreptitious Martian spies. (This is not intended as hyperbole.) Like these theses, the view that phenomenal consciousness is a cultural construction is *coherent* but *ridiculous*. So even if Kurthen et al. are right (that coherence of the social construction doctrine implies coherence of the possibility that P-consciousness can be deconstructed), there is no more need to examine this claim than the claim that if peanuts are Martian spies, then one should eat as many peanuts as possible.

Another preliminary remark: I ridicule the claim that *phenomenal* consciousness is a cultural construction, but I do not ridicule Dennett's and Jaynes's view that consciousness, simpliciter, is a cultural construction. Dennett rejects a distinction between phenomenal consciousness and what I have called cognitive forms of consciousness such as access-consciousness, reflective consciousness, and self-reflective consciousness. (A state is access-conscious if it is poised for global control; a state is reflectively conscious if it is accompanied by another state that is about it; and a state, for example, a pain, is self-reflectively conscious if it promotes an accompanying thought to the effect that I, myself, have that pain.) But Kurthen et al. do not object to my separating out phenomenal consciousness from other forms of consciousness. Indeed, they regard phenomenality as an essential or intrinsic property of any P-conscious state, a property without which the state would not be the state it is. It is their concession that there is such a thing as phenomenal consciousness that puts Kurthen et al. on unstable ground and makes their view ridiculous.

Leukemia is not a social construction or creation—and Kurthen et al. would agree. By contrast, love, marriage, money, property, and chess are plausibly social constructions, at least in part. What's the difference? Money is, but leukemia is not, wholly or partly constituted by social norms, principles, practices, myths, institutions, and so on. Leukemia is, of course, affected by cultural factors. The medical community has amassed much evidence that temperament and attitudes (which are influenced by cultural practices) affect the course of many forms of cancer. And cultural phenomena— war, weapons testing, etc.—have produced cases of leukemia. Cultural phenomena produce cancers including leukemia and affect their course, but they do not even in part constitute leukemia.

This distinction between what culture affects or produces and what it creates—in the sense of constitutes—is viewed by Kurthen et al. with suspicion. They seem to think that if culture modulates something, then it must create some component of it. I noted in the target article (Block 1995a) that culture affects feet without creating them. Kurthen et al. say that culture affects feet by, for example, creating horny skin. One could note by way of an initial response that if I affect the growth of a plant either by depriving it of water or by watering it well, I don't thereby produce any component of it, no part of a leaf or stem. But this is an unimportant flaw in their argument compared to what comes next. They conclude that the difference between affecting and creating is a matter of degree. But they have lost sight of what it means for something to be a cultural creation. A cultural creation is *constituted* by something cultural, not just *produced* by it. Horny skin is like leukemia, not like money; it is not constituted by anything cultural. (Do not be misled by the fact that the concept of horny skin (like the concept of leukemia) is a cultural construction and that there can be cultures that do not have that concept. The *fact* picked out by that concept is culture-independent, and could have existed even if the concept had never been produced. (So animals might have had horny skin even if there had never been people.) The distinction between what culture affects and what culture creates sounds to the unwary like a difference in degree, a difference in *how much* of an effect culture has. But note that cultural phenomena can produce leukemia even though culture is not even part of what constitutes leukemia. All money is alike in that what makes something money is cultural. But the effect of culture on some kinds of money is stronger than others. Sea shells are not much changed from what is found in nature—at least compared with the tree pulp and pigment that constitute dollar bills. So degrees of cultural effect have nothing to do with cultural creation in the sense relevant here (namely cultural constitution).

What is cultural constitution? Searle's 1995 book on the topic argues persuasively that the core of a culturally constituted fact is "collective intentionality" involving, most importantly, a collective agreement (albeit usually tacit) that a certain item has a certain function. The fact that you can buy things with dollars is constituted by a network of functions tacitly agreed to by all members of the relevant community. Collective intentionality underlies facts about money, but not the existence of leukemia. My leukemia is not constituted partly by the activities of other people (though those activities might have produced it or affect it). If people had never existed, there never would have been any money, even if particles from the swamp had by chance come together to form an exact molecular duplicate of a dollar bill. By contrast, if people had never existed, animals would still have died of leukemia. No doubt, people had leukemia before anyone had any concept of it.

So let's finally ask the question: Which category does P-consciousness fit in? With leukemia or with money? Is my pain partly constituted by facts about you (as with money)? Does my pain depend on a tacit agreement that something has a certain function? Could animals have had pain even if no humans had ever existed? I ask these questions rhetorically. They answer themselves. Of course the pain of one person does not depend on tacit agreements involving other people that something has a certain function. (Though I hasten to add that such agreements could affect pain.) Of course animals had pain before there were any people. There were chimp-like creatures before there were people. Does anyone really doubt that they had pains, just as chimps do today? Does anyone doubt that children who are deaf and blind and hence have difficulty absorbing the culture have P-conscious pains and sensations of touch? Helen Keller recalled her P-conscious sensations after she had absorbed the culture. Were her P-conscious states as a child constituted by the rest of us? That would have to be the view of those who think that P-consciousness is a cultural construction. Since *she* hadn't absorbed the culture, if her P-conscious states are constituted by culture, they have to reside in the rest of us.

My argument in the target paper was that once one makes the distinction between P-consciousness and various forms of cognitive consciousness, it becomes obvious that P-consciousness is not a cultural construction. By contrast, perhaps some types of self-consciousness are. To take a very extreme case, consider thinking of oneself as the president. A case can be made that no one could think of himself as a president without a cultural milieu that includes a president-like office. Having the concept of a presidency, as with the concept of money, may require a cultural surround. A molecular duplicate of one of us who arises by chance in a culture that has no such institutions or their precursors may not have the requisite concepts. This fact points up the contrast between this sophisticated form of self-consciousness and P-consciousness.

I turn now to Kurthen et al.'s positive argument that consciousness is a cultural construction. They start from a point with which I completely agree, that for P-consciousness there is no appearance/reality distinction. What it *is* like to have a P-conscious state is the same as what it seems like. Being = seeming. Their next step is the claim that as a matter of fact, there are "top-down" influences on sensation. What you believe or expect influences how you sense. Though I have questions about this empirical premise, I will go along with it for the sake of pinpointing the logical flaw in their argument. From these two premises, they draw the following conclusion: "So, if how some mental entity 'seems' to the total subject of mental entities depends on how this subject takes that mental entity, then it may well be that phenomenality, with its unique identity of being and seeming, just *is* a certain way of taking certain mental entities." The final step is that how one takes things is determined by culture. In other words, phenomenality is taking and taking is determined by culture, so phenomenality is determined by culture.

There are two very serious errors here. One error has already been explained. Even if taking is determined by culture—in the sense of produced by culture—it does not follow that it is constituted by culture or cultural facts. The social construction of consciousness is a matter of constitution, not production or creation in any causal sense. But there is another error that is more insidious, an equivocation on the word "taking." "Taking" has both a phenomenal and a cognitive sense. In the cognitive sense, how you take an experience is a matter of your beliefs, intentions, expectations and the like about it. In this sense, to take an experience as a pain is, for example, to believe that it is a pain. In the phenomenal sense, how you take an experience is just what it is like for you to have it. It is the phenomenal sense in which an experience is what you take it to be. There is no difference between appearance and reality for experiences (or rather their phenomenal component) because what it is = what it's like and how you take$_{phenomenal}$ it also = what it's like. Seeming = taking$_{phenomenal}$. But in the cognitive sense, there is a great chasm—though not one that is always easy to see—between seeming and taking. One can have a phenomenal state without noticing (and therefore knowing) that one has it, and one can believe falsely that one has a certain phenomenal state. After all, belief involves categorizing and that is a process that can misfire.

I won't try to do much to justify this point, since it was thoroughly aired in the philosophical literature in the 1960s and 1970s. Just one example from Buck (1962): imagine a football player who is injured and obviously in pain, but who so much wants to play that he insists—to the point of convincing himself—that it doesn't hurt. Self-deception can create a gap between the phenomenal character of experience and one's beliefs about that phenomenal character. Seeming ≠ taking$_{cognitive}$. (Of course, the word "seeming" can itself be used in a cognitive sense as well as the phenomenal sense that I am using; I will not complicate the matter by going further into this issue.) [See also Mele: "Real Self-Deception" BBS 20(1) 1997.]

Now we are in a position to see the fallacy. Phenomenal consciousness can be identified with taking in the phenomenal sense. But if there is any sense of taking in which it is a cultural construction, it is the cognitive sense. To suppose that taking in the phenomenal sense is a cultural construction would be to beg the question. That is the overall conclusion of Kurthen et al. So their argument is a classic equivocation. The support for the claim that taking is a cultural phenomenon depends on construing taking in the cognitive sense, but the sense of taking in which it is true that taking = seeming (that is, there is no appearance/reality distinction for P-consciousness) is the phenomenal sense. Being (that is, what P-consciousness is) =

seeming and seeming − taking$_{phenomenal}$. So being = taking$_{phenomenal}$. But if any kind of taking is culturally constituted, it is taking$_{cognitive}$, not taking$_{phenomenal}$. Hence it would be a mistake to conclude that being (what P-consciousness is) is cultural.

Note

Author's response, reprinted from *Behavioral and Brain Sciences* 22 (1), 1999.

References

Block, N. 1995. On a confusion about a function of consciousness. *Behavioral and Brain Sciences* 18:227–87.

Buck, R. 1962. "XX." In: *Analytical Philosophy*, vol 2, ed. J. Butler. Blackwell.

Dennett, D. 1986. Julian Jaynes's software archeology. *Canadian Psychology* 27:149–54.

Dennett, D. 1991. *Consciousness explained*. Little, Brown.

Jaynes, J. 1976. *The origin of consciousness in the breakdown of the bicameral mind*. Houghton-Mifflin.

Kurthen, M. 1995. On the prospects of a naturalistic theory of phenomenal consciousness. In: *Conscious experience*, ed. T. Metzinger. Imprint Academic.

Levine, J. 1983. Materialism and qualia: The explanatory gap. *Pacific Philosophical Quarterly* 64:354–61.

Rorty, R. 1993. Holism, intrinsicality, and the ambition of transcendence. In: *Dennett and his critics*, ed. B. Dalhbohm. Blackwell.

Searle, J. 1995. *The construction of social reality*. Free Press.

13   Concepts of Consciousness

The concept of consciousness is a hybrid or better, a mongrel concept: the word "consciousness" connotes a number of different concepts and denotes a number of different phenomena. When we reason about "consciousness" using some premises that apply to one of the phenomena that fall under "consciousness," and other premises that apply to other "consciousnesses," we end up with trouble. There are many parallels in the history of science. Aristotle used "velocity" sometimes to mean average velocity and sometimes to mean instantaneous velocity; his failure to see the distinction caused confusion (Kuhn 1964). The Florentine Experimenters of the seventeenth century used a single word (roughly translatable as "degree of heat") for temperature and for heat, generating paradoxes (Block and Dworkin 1974). For example, when they measured "degree of heat" by whether various heat sources could melt paraffin, heat source A came out hotter than B, but when they measured "degree of heat" by how much ice a heat source could melt in a given time, B was hotter than A (Wiser and Carey 1983). These are very different cases, but there is a similarity, one that they share with the case of "consciousness." The similarity is: very different concepts are treated as a single concept. I think we all have some tendency to make this mistake in the case of "consciousness."

Phenomenal Consciousness

First, consider phenomenal consciousness, or P-consciousness, as I will call it. Phenomenal consciousness is experience; what makes a state phenomenally conscious is that there is something "it is like" (Nagel 1974) to be in that state. Let me acknowledge at the outset that I cannot define P-consciousness in any remotely noncircular way. I do not consider this an embarrassment. The history of reductive definitions in philosophy should lead one not to expect a reductive definition of anything. But the best one can do for P-consciousness is in some respects worse than for many other things because really all one can do is *point* to the phenomenon (see Goldman 1993b). Nonetheless, it is important to point properly. John Searle, acknowledging that consciousness cannot be defined noncircularly, defines it as follows: "By consciousness I simply mean those subjective states of awareness or sentience that begin when one wakes in the morning and continue throughout the period that one is awake until one falls into a dreamless sleep, into a coma, or dies or is otherwise, as they say, unconscious." (This comes from Searle 1990, there is a much longer attempt along the same lines in Searle 1992, 83ff.)

I will argue that this sort of pointing is flawed because it points to too many things, too many different consciousnesses.

So how should we point to P-consciousness? Well, one way is via rough synonyms. As I said, P-consciousness is experience. P-conscious properties are experiential properties. P-conscious states are experiential states—that is, a state is P-conscious just in case it instantiates experiential properties. The totality of the experiential properties instantiated in a state are "what it is like" to have it. Moving from synonyms to examples, we have P-conscious states when we see, hear, smell, taste, and have pains. P-conscious properties include the experiential properties of sensations, feelings, and perceptions, but I would also include thoughts, wants, and emotions.[1] An important feature of P-consciousness is that differences in intentional content often make a P-conscious difference. What it is like to hear a sound as coming from the left differs from what it is like to hear a sound as coming from the right. Further, P-conscious differences often make an intentional difference. And this is partially explained by the fact that P-consciousness is often—perhaps even always—representational. (See Jackendoff 1987; Van Gulick 1989; McGinn 1991, chap. 2; Flanagan 1992, chap. 4; Goldman 1993a.) So far, I do not take myself to have said anything terribly controversial. The controversial part is that I take P-conscious properties to be distinct from any cognitive, intentional, or functional property. At least, no such reduction of P-consciousness to the cognitive, intentional, or functional can be known in the armchair manner of recent deflationist approaches. (Cognitive = essentially involving thought; intentional properties = properties by virtue of which a representation or state is about something; functional properties = properties definable in terms of a computer program, for example. See Searle 1983 on intentionality; see Block 1980, 1994, for better characterizations of a functional property.) But I am trying hard to limit the controversiality of my assumptions. Though I will be assuming that functionalism about P-consciousness is false, I will be pointing out that limited versions of many of the points I will be making can be acceptable to the functionalist.[2]

By way of homing in on P-consciousness, it is useful to appeal to what may be a contingent property of it, namely, the famous "explanatory gap." To quote T. H. Huxley (1866), "How it is that anything so remarkable as a state of consciousness comes about as a result of irritating nervous tissue, is just as unaccountable as the appearance of Djin when Aladdin rubbed his lamp." Consider a famous neurophysiological theory of P-consciousness offered by Francis Crick and Christof Koch, namely, that a synchronized 35–75 hertz neural oscillation in the sensory areas of the cortex is at the heart of phenomenal consciousness. Assuming for the sake of an example that such neural oscillations are the neural basis of sensory consciousness, no one can imagine concepts that would allow us to have any idea *why* such oscillations are the neural basis of one phenomenally conscious state rather than another or why the oscillations are the neural basis of a phenomenally conscious state rather than a phenomenally unconscious state.

However, Crick and Koch have offered a sketch of an account of how the 35–75 hertz oscillation might contribute to a solution to the "binding problem." Suppose one simultaneously sees a red square moving to the right and a blue circle moving to the left. Different areas of the visual cortex are differentially sensitive to color, shape, motion, and so on, so what binds together redness, squareness, and rightward motion? That is, why don't you see redness and blueness without seeing them as belonging with particular shapes and particular motions? And why aren't the colors normally seen as bound to the wrong shapes and motions? Representations of colors, shapes, and motions of a single object are supposed to involve oscillations that are in phase with one another but not with representations of other objects. But even if the oscillation hypothesis deals with the informational aspect of the binding problem (and there is some evidence against it), how does it explain *what it is like to see something as red in the first place*—or for that matter, as square or as moving to the right? Why couldn't there be brains functionally or physiologically just like ours, including oscillation patterns, whose owners' experience was different from ours or who had no experience at all? (Note that I do not say that there *could be* such brains. I just want to know *why not*.) No one has a clue how to answer these questions.

The explanatory gap in the case of P-consciousness contrasts with our better (though still not very good) understanding of the scientific basis of cognition. We have two serious research programs on the nature of cognition, the classical "language-of-thought" paradigm, and the connectionist research program. Both assume that the scientific basis of cognition is computational. If this is idea is right—and it seems increasingly promising—it gives us a better grip on why the neural basis of a thought state is the neural basis of that thought rather than some other thought or none at all than we have about the analogous issue for consciousness.

What I have been saying about P-consciousness is of course controversial in a variety of ways, both for some advocates and for some opponents of some notion of P-consciousness. I have tried to steer clear of some controversies—for example, controversies over inverted and absent qualia; over Jackson's (1986) Mary, the woman who is raised in a black-and-white room, learning all the physiological and functional facts about the brain and color vision, but nonetheless discovers a putatively new fact when she goes outside the room for the first time and learns what it is like to see red; and even Nagel's view that we cannot know what it is like to be a bat.[3] Even if you think that P-consciousness as I have described it is an incoherent notion, you may be able to agree with the main point of this paper, which is that a great deal of trouble arises as a result of confusing P-consciousness with something else. Not even the concept of what time it is now on the sun is so confused that it cannot itself be confused with something else.

Access Consciousness

I now turn to the nonphenomenal notion of consciousness that is most easily and dangerously conflated with P-consciousness: access consciousness. I will characterize access consciousness, give some examples of how it makes sense for someone to have access consciousness without phenomenal consciousness and vice versa, and then go on to the main theme of the paper, the damage done by conflating the two.

A-consciousness is access consciousness. A representation is A-conscious if it is broadcast for free use in reasoning and for direct "rational" control of action (including reporting). Talk of a representation being broadcast for free use in reasoning and direct "rational" control of action can be seen in terms of a distinction between producing systems and consuming systems. The senses produce perceptual representations that are broadcast—in the sense of made available—to consuming systems such as systems of perceptual categorization, reasoning, planning, evaluation of alternatives, decision making, voluntary direction of attention, memory, reporting, and more generally rational control of action. An A-state is one that consists in having an A-representation. I see A-consciousness as a cluster concept in which reportability is the element of the cluster that has the smallest weight even though it is often the best practical guide to A-consciousness.

The "rational" is meant to rule out the kind of automatic control that obtains in blindsight. (Blindsight is a syndrome involving patients who have brain damage in the first stage of visual processing, the primary visual cortex. These patients seem to have "holes" in their visual fields. If the experimenter flashes stimuli in these holes and asks the patient what was flashed, the patient claims to see nothing but can often guess at high levels of accuracy, choosing between two locations or directions or whether what was flashed was an X or an O.)

I will suggest that A-consciousness plays a deep role in our ordinary "consciousness" talk and thought. However, I must admit at the outset that this role allows for substantial indeterminacy in the concept itself. In addition, there are some loose ends in the characterization of the concept that cannot be tied up without deciding certain controversial issues, to be mentioned below.[4] My guide in making precise the notion of A-consciousness is to formulate an information-processing correlate of P-consciousness that is not ad hoc and mirrors P-consciousness as well as a non–ad hoc information-processing notion can.

In the original version of this paper, I defined "A-consciousness" as (roughly) "poised for control of speech, reasoning and action."[5] In a comment on the original version of this paper, David Chalmers (1997) suggested defining "A-consciousness" instead as "directly available for global control." Chalmers's definition has the advantage of avoiding enumerating the kinds of control. That makes the notion more general, applying to creatures who have kinds of control that differ from ours. But it has the disadvantage of that advantage, counting simple organisms as having A-consciousness if they have representations that are directly available for global control of whatever resources they happen to have. If the idea of A-consciousness is to be an information-processing image of P-consciousness, it would not do to count a slug as having A-conscious states simply because there is some machinery of control of the resources that a slug happens to command.

As I noted, my goal in making explicit the ordinary notion of access as it is used in thinking about consciousness is to formulate a non–ad hoc notion that is close to an information-processing image of P-consciousness. A flaw in both my definition and Chalmers's definition is that they make A-consciousness dispositional, whereas P-consciousness is occurrent. As noted in the critique by Atkinson and Davies (1995), that makes the relation between P-consciousness and A-consciousness the relation between the ground of a disposition and the disposition itself. (See also Burge 1997.) But pain is an occurrence, not a disposition. This has long been one ground of criticism of both functionalism and behaviorism (Block and Fodor, chap. 3, this volume), but there is no real need for an information-processing notion of consciousness to be saddled with a category mistake of this sort. I have dealt with the issue here by using the term "broadcast," as in Baars's (1988) theory that conscious representations are ones that are broadcast in a global workspace. A consciousness is similar to that notion and to Dennett's (1993) notion of consciousness as cerebral celebrity.[6]

The interest in the A/P distinction arises from the battle between two different conceptions of the mind, the biological and the computational. The computational approach supposes that all of the mind (including consciousness) can be captured with notions of information processing, computation, and function in a system. According to this view (functionalism), the level of abstraction for understanding the mind is one that allows multiple realizations, just as one computer can be realized electrically or hydraulically. Their bet is that the different realizations do not generally matter to the mind, and specifically to consciousness. The biological approach bets that the realization does matter. If P = A, the information-processing side is right. But if the biological nature of experience is crucial, then realizations *do* matter, and we can expect that P and A will diverge.[7]

A-consciousness and P-consciousness interact. For example, what perceptual information is being accessed can change figure to ground and conversely, and a figure-ground switch can affect one's phenomenal state. For instance, attending to the feel of the shirt on your neck, accessing those perceptual contents, switches what was in the background to the foreground, thereby changing your phenomenal state. (See Hill 1991, 118–126; Searle 1992.)

Of course, there are notions of access in which the blindsight patient's guesses count as access. There is no right or wrong here. Access comes in various degrees and kinds, and my choice here is mainly determined by the desideratum of finding a notion of A-consciousness that mirrors P-consciousness. If the blindsight patient's perceptual representations are not P-conscious, it would not do to count them as A-conscious. (I also happen to think that the notion I characterize is more or less one that plays a role in our thought.)

I will mention three main differences between P-consciousness and A-consciousness. The first point, *put crudely*, is that P-conscious content is phenomenal, whereas A-conscious content is representational. It is of the essence of A-conscious content to play a role in reasoning or at least protoreasoning and only representational content can figure in reasoning. The reason this way of putting the point is crude is that many (perhaps even all) phenomenal contents are *also* representational. And some of the representational contents of a P-conscious state may be intrinsic to those P-contents.[8]

(In the last paragraph, I used the notion of P-conscious *content*. The P-conscious content of a state is the totality of the state's experiential properties, what it is like to be in that state. One can think of the P-conscious content of a state as the state's experiential "value" by analogy to the representational content as the state's representational "value." In my view, the content of an experience can be both P-conscious and A-conscious—the former by virtue of its phenomenal feel and the latter by virtue of its representational properties.)

A closely related point: A-conscious states are necessarily transitive; A-conscious states must always be states of consciousness *of*. P-conscious states, by contrast, sometimes are and sometimes are not transitive. P-consciousness, as such, is not consciousness of. (I will return to this point in a few paragraphs.)

Second, A-consciousness is a functional notion, and so A-conscious content is system-relative: what makes a state A-conscious is what a representation of its content does in a system. P-consciousness is not a functional notion.[9] In terms of Schacter's model of the mind (see Block 1995, the original version of this paper), content gets to be P-conscious because of what happens *inside* the P-consciousness module. But what makes content A-conscious is not anything that could go on inside a module, but rather informational relations *among* modules. Content is A-conscious by virtue of (a representation with that content) reaching the Executive system, the system that is in charge of rational control of action and speech, and to that extent, we could regard the

Executive module as the A-consciousness module. But to regard *anything* as an A-consciousness module is misleading, because what makes an A-conscious representation A-conscious is what getting to the Executive module sets it up to *do*, namely, figuring in reasoning and action.

A third difference is that there is such a thing as a P-conscious *type* or *kind* of state. For example, the feel of pain is a P-conscious type—every pain must have that feel. But any particular token thought that is A-conscious at a given time could fail to be accessible at some other time, just as my car is accessible now, but will not be later when my wife has it. A state whose content is informationally promiscuous now may not be so later.

The paradigm P-conscious states are sensations, whereas the paradigm A-conscious states are "propositional-attitude" states like thoughts, beliefs, and desires, states with representational content expressed by *that*-clauses (e.g., the thought that grass is green). What, then, gets broadcast when a P-conscious state is also A-conscious? The most straightforward answer is: the P-content itself. Exactly what this comes to depends on what exactly P-content is. If P-content is nonconceptual, it may be said that P-contents are not the right sort of thing to play a role in inference and guiding action. However, even with nonhumans, pain plays a rational role in guiding action. Different actions are appropriate responses to pains in different locations. Since the contents of pain do in fact play a rational role, either their contents are conceptualized *enough*, or else nonconceptual or not very conceptual content can play a rational role.

There is a familiar distinction, alluded to above, between "consciousness" in the sense in which we speak of a state as being a conscious state (intransitive consciousness) and consciousness *of* something (transitive consciousness). (The transitive-intransitive terminology seems to have appeared first in Malcolm 1984, but see also Rosenthal 1997. Humphrey (1992) mentions that the intransitive usage is much more recent, only 200 years old.) It is easy to fall into an identification of P-consciousness with intransitive consciousness and a corresponding identification of access consciousness with transitive consciousness. Such an identification is overly simple. As I mentioned earlier, P-conscious contents can be representational. Consider a perceptual state of seeing a square. This state has a P-conscious content that represents something, a square, and thus it is a state of P-consciousness *of* the square. It is a state of P-consciousness of the square even if it does not represent the square *as* a square, as would be the case if the perceptual state is a state of an animal that does not have the concept of a square. Since there can be P-consciousness *of* something, P-consciousness is not to be identified with intransitive consciousness.

Here is a second reason why the transitive/intransitive distinction cannot be identified with the P-consciousness/A-consciousness distinction: the *of*-ness required for transitivity does not guarantee that a content be utilizable by a *consuming* system, a system that uses the representations for reasoning or planning or control of action at the level required for A-consciousness. For example, a perceptual state of a brain-damaged creature might be a state of P-consciousness of, say, motion, even though connections to reasoning and rational control of action are damaged so that the state is not A-conscious. In sum, P-consciousness can be consciousness of, and consciousness of need not be A-consciousness.

Those who are uncomfortable with P-consciousness should pay close attention to A-consciousness because it is a good candidate for a reductionist identification with P-consciousness.[10]

Many of my critics (Searle 1992; Burge 1997) have noted that if there can be "zombies," cases of A without P, they are not conscious in any sense of the term. I am sympathetic, but I do not agree with the conclusion some have drawn that the A-sense is not a sense of "consciousness" and that A is not a kind of consciousness. A-consciousness can be a kind of consciousness even if it is parasitic on a core notion of P-consciousness. A parquet floor is a floor even though it requires another floor beneath it. A-consciousness can come and go against a background of P-consciousness.

The rationale for calling A-consciousness a kind of consciousness is first that it fits a certain kind of quasi-ordinary usage. Suppose one has a vivid mental image that is repressed. Repression need not make the image go away or make it nonphenomenal. One might realize after psychoanalysis that one had the image all along, but that one could not cope with it. It is "unconscious" in the Freudian sense—which is A-unconscious. Second, A-consciousness is typically the kind of consciousness that is relevant to use of words like "conscious" and "aware" in cognitive neuroscience. This point is made in detail in my comment on a special issue of the journal *Cognition* (Block 2001). This issue summarizes the "state of the art," and some of the writers are clearly talking about A-consciousness (or one or another version of monitoring consciousness—see below), whereas others are usually talking about P-consciousness. The A-notion of consciousness is the most prominent one in the discussion in that special issue and in much of the rest of cognitive neuroscience. (See the article by Dehaene and Naccache in that volume, which is very explicit about the use of A-consciousness.) Finally, recall that my purpose in framing the notion of A-consciousness is to get a functional notion of consciousness that is not ad hoc and comes as close to matching P consciousness as a purely functional notion can. I hope to show that nonetheless there are cracks between P and A. In this context, I prefer to be liberal with terminology, allowing that A is a form of consciousness but not identical to phenomenal consciousness.

A-Consciousness without P-Consciousness

The main point of this paper is that these two concepts of consciousness are distinct and quite likely have different extensions yet are easily confused. Let us consider conceptually possible cases of one without the other. Actual cases will be more controversial.

First, I will give some putative examples of A-consciousness without P-consciousness. If there could be a full-fledged phenomenal zombie, say a robot computationally identical to a person, but whose silicon brain did not support P-consciousness, that would do the trick. I think such cases conceptually possible, but this is controversial. (See Shoemaker 1975, 1981.)

But there is a less controversial kind of case, a very limited sort of partial zombie. Consider the blindsight patient who "guesses" that there is an 'X' rather than an 'O' in his blind field. Taking his word for it (for the moment), I am assuming that he has no P-consciousness of the 'X'. The blindsight patient also has no 'X'-representing A-conscious content, because although the information that there is an 'X' affects his "guess," it is not available as a premise in reasoning (until he has the quite distinct state of hearing and believing his own guess), or for rational control of action or speech. Marcel (1986) points out that the thirsty blindsight patient would not reach for a glass of water in the blind field. So the blindsight patient's perceptual or quasi-perceptual state is unconscious in the phenomenal *and* access senses (*and* in the monitoring senses to be mentioned below, too).

Now imagine something that probably does not exist, what we might call *superblindsight*. A real blindsight patient can only guess when given a choice from a small set of alternatives ('X'/'O'; horizontal/vertical, etc.). But suppose—interestingly, apparently contrary to fact—that a blindsight patient could be trained to prompt himself at will, guessing what is in the blind field without being told to guess. The superblindsighter spontaneously says "Now I know that there is a horizontal line in my blind field even though I don't actually see it." Visual information of a certain limited sort (excluding color and complicated shapes) from his blind field simply pops into his thoughts in the way that solutions to problems we have been worrying about pop into our thoughts, or in the way some people just know the time or which way is North without having any perceptual experience of it. He knows there is an 'X' in his blind field, but he does not know the type font of the 'X'. The superblindsighter himself contrasts what it is like to know visually about an 'X' in his blind field and an 'X' in his sighted field. There is something it is like to experience the latter, but not the former, he says. It is the difference between *just knowing* and knowing via a visual experience. Taking his word for it, here is the point: the perceptual content that there is an 'X' in his visual field is A-conscious but not P-conscious. The superblindsight case is a very limited partial zombie.

Of course, the superblindsighter has a *thought* that there is an 'X' in his blind field that is *both* A-conscious and P-conscious. But I am not talking about the thought. Rather, I am talking about the state of his perceptual system that gives rise to the thought. It is this state that is A-conscious without being P-conscious.[11]

The (apparent) nonexistence of superblindsight is a striking fact, one that a number of writers have noticed, more or less. What Marcel was in effect pointing out was that the blindsight patients, in not reaching for a glass of water, are not superblindsighters. (See also Farah 1994.) Blind perception is never superblind perception.[12]

Notice that the superblindsighter I have described is just a little bit different (though in a crucial way) from the ordinary blindsight patient. In particular, I am *not* relying on what might be thought of as a full-fledged quasi-zombie, a super-duper blindsighter whose blindsight is every bit as good, functionally speaking, as his sight. In the case of the super-duper blindsighter, the *only* difference between vision in the blind and sighted fields, functionally speaking, is that the quasi-zombie himself regards them differently. Such an example will be regarded by some (though not me) as incoherent— see Dennett 1991, for example. But we can avoid disagreement about the super-duper blindsighter via illustrating the idea of A-consciousness without P-consciousness by appealing only to the superblindsighter. Functionalists may want to know why the superblindsight case counts as A-consciousness without P-consciousness. After all, they may say, if we have really high-quality access in mind, the superblindsighter that I have described does not have it, so he lacks both P-consciousness and really high quality A-consciousness. The super-duper blindsighter, on the other hand, has both, according to the functionalist, so in neither case, according to the objection, is there A-consciousness without P-consciousness.

I will reply by distinguishing three types of access: (1) really high quality access, (2) medium access, and (3) poor access. The *actual* blindsight patient has poor access (he has to be prompted to guess), the superblindsight patient has medium access since he can spontaneously report a few details, and the super-duper blindsight patient—like most of us—has really high quality access. The functionalist objector I am talking about identifies P-consciousness with A-consciousness of the really high quality kind, whereas I am allowing A-consciousness with only medium access. (The functionalist and I agree in excluding low-quality access.) The issue, then, is whether the functionalist can get away with restricting access to high-quality access. I think not. I believe that in some cases, normal phenomenal vision involves only medium access. One illustration is peripheral vision. If you wave a colored object near your ear, you will find that in the right location you can see the movement without having the kind of rich access that you have in foveal vision. For example, your ability to recover shape and color is poor.

Why isn't peripheral vision a case of A without P? In peripheral vision, we are both A- and P-conscious of the same features—for instance, motion but not color. But in superblindsight—so the story goes—there is no P-consciousness at all of the stimulus. (He just knows.) I conclude that A without P is conceptually possible even if not actual.

P-Consciousness without A-Consciousness

Consider an animal that you are happy to think of as having P-consciousness for which brain damage has destroyed centers of reasoning and rational control of action, thus preventing A-consciousness. It certainly seems *conceptually possible* that the neural bases of P-consciousness systems and A-consciousness systems are distinct, and if they are distinct, then it is possible, at least conceptually possible, for one to be damaged while the other is working well. Evidence has been accumulating for twenty-five years that the primate visual system has distinct dorsal and ventral subsystems. Though there is much disagreement about the specializations of the two systems, it does appear that much of the information in the ventral system is more closely connected to P-consciousness than information in the dorsal system is (Goodale and Milner 1992). And the dorsal system is concerned with visually guided action. So it may actually be possible to damage A-consciousness without P-consciousness and conversely.[13]

Further, one might suppose (Rey 1983, 1988; White 1987) that some of our own subsystems—say, each of the two hemispheres of the brain—might themselves be separately P-conscious. Some of these subsystems might also be A-consciousness, but other subsystems might not have sufficient machinery for reasoning or reporting or rational control of action to allow their P-conscious states to be A-conscious. Thus, if those states are not accessible to another system that does have adequate machinery, they will be P-conscious but not A-conscious.

Here is another reason to believe in P-consciousness without A-consciousness: Suppose that you are engaged in intense conversation when suddenly at noon you realize that right outside your window, there is—and has been for some time—a pneumatic drill digging up the street. You were aware of the noise all along, one might say, but only at noon are you *consciously aware* of it. That is, you were P-conscious of the noise all along, but at noon you are both P-conscious *and* A-conscious of it. Of course, there is a very similar string of events in which the crucial event at noon is a bit more intellectual. In this alternative scenario, at noon you realize not just that there is and has been a noise, but also that *you are now and have been hearing* the noise. In this alternative scenario, you get "higher-order thought" as well as A-consciousness at noon. So in the first scenario, the belief that is acquired at noon is that there is and has been a noise, and in the second scenario, the beliefs that are acquired at noon are the first one plus the belief that you are and have been hearing the noise. But it is the first scenario, not the second that interests me. It is a putative case of P-consciousness without A-consciousness—just before noon. Only at noon is the content of your representation of the drill *broadcast* for use in rational control of action and speech. (Note that A-consciousness requires being broadcast, not merely being *available* for use.)

In addition, this case involves a natural use of "conscious" and "aware" for A-consciousness and P-consciousness. "Conscious" and "aware" are more or less synonymous, so when we have one of them we might think of it as awareness, but when we have both it is natural to call that conscious awareness. This case of P-consciousness without A-consciousness exploits what William James (1890) called "secondary consciousness" (at least I think it does; James scholars may know better), a category in which he may have meant to include cases of P-consciousness without attention.

I have found that the argument of the last two paragraphs makes those who are distrustful of introspection uncomfortable. I agree that introspection is not the last word, but it is the first word, when it comes to P-consciousness. The example shows the conceptual distinctness of P-consciousness from A-consciousness and it also puts the burden of proof on anyone who would argue that as a matter of empirical fact they come to the same thing.

A-consciousness and P-consciousness very often occur together. When one or the other is missing, we can often speak of unconscious states (when the context is right). Thus, by virtue of missing A-consciousness, we think of Freudian states as unconscious. And by virtue of missing P-consciousness, it is natural to describe the superblindsighter or the unfeeling robot or computer as unconscious. Lack of monitoring consciousness in the presence of A and P is also sometimes described as unconsciousness. Thus Julian Jaynes describes Greeks as becoming conscious when—in between the time of the *Illiad* and the *Odyssey*—they become more reflective.

Flanagan (1992) criticizes my notion of A-consciousness, suggesting that we replace it with a more liberal notion of informational sensitivity that counts the blindsight patient as having access consciousness of the stimuli in his blind field. The idea is that the blindsight patient has *some* access to the information about the stimuli in the blind field, and that amount of access is enough for access consciousness. Of course, as I keep saying, the notion of A-consciousness that I have framed is just one of a family of access notions. But there is more than a verbal issue here. If we count the blindsight patient as A-conscious of stimuli in the blind field, we commit ourselves to A-consciousness without P-consciousness too easily.

The kind of access that I have built into A-consciousness plays a role in theory outside of this issue and in daily life. Consider the Freudian unconscious. Suppose I have a Freudian unconscious desire to kill my father and marry my mother. Nothing in Freudian theory requires that this desire be P-unconscious; for all Freudians should care, it might be P-conscious. What is the key to the desire being Freudianly unconscious is that it come out in slips, dreams, and the like, but not be freely available as a premise in reasoning (by virtue of having the unconscious desire) and not be freely available to guide action and reporting. Coming out in slips and dreams *makes it conscious in Flanagan's sense*, so that sense of access is no good for capturing the Freudian idea. But it is unconscious in my A-sense. If I can just tell you that I have a desire to kill my father and marry my mother (and not as a result of therapy), then it is not an unconscious state in either Freud's sense or my A-sense. Similar points can be made about a number of the syndromes that are often regarded as disorders of consciousness. For example, consider prosopagnosia, a syndrome in which someone who can see noses, eyes, and so on cannot recognize faces. Prosopagnosia is a disorder of A-consciousness, not P-consciousness and not Flanagan's informational sensitivity. We count people as proso-pagnosics even when they are able to guess at better than a chance level who the face belongs to, so that excludes Flanagan's notion. Further, P-consciousness is irrelevant, and that excludes P-consciousness as a criterion. It is not the presence or absence of a feeling of familiarity that defines prosopagnosia, but rather the patients not knowing who the person is whose face they are seeing or whether they know that person.

I am finished sketching the contrast between P-consciousness and A-consciousness. In the remainder of this article, I will briefly discuss two cognitive notions of consciousness, so that they are firmly distinguished from both P-consciousness and A-consciousness.

Self-Consciousness

By this term, I mean the possession of the concept of the self and the ability to use this concept in thinking about oneself. A number of higher primates show signs of recog-nizing that they see themselves in mirrors. They display interest in correspondences between their own actions and the movements of their mirror images. By contrast, dogs treat their mirror images as strangers at first, slowly habituating. In one experi-mental paradigm, experimenters painted colored spots on the foreheads and ears of anesthetized primates, watching what happened. Chimps between ages seven and fif-teen usually try to wipe the spot off (Povinelli 1994; Gallup 1982). Monkeys do not do this, according to published reports as of 1994. (Since then, Hauser et al. (1995) have shown that monkeys can pass the test if the mark is salient enough.) Human babies do not show similar behavior until the last half of their second year. Perhaps this is a test for self-consciousness. (Or perhaps it is only a test for understanding mirrors, but no doubt a component of what is involved in understanding mirrors is that it is oneself one is seeing.) But even if monkeys and dogs have no self-consciousness, no one should deny that they have P-conscious pains, or that there is something it is like for them to see their reflections in the mirror. P-conscious states often seem to have a "me-ishness" about them; the phenomenal content often represents the state as a state of me. But this fact does not at all suggest that we can reduce P-consciousness to self-consciousness, since such "me-ishness" is the same in states whose P-conscious content is different. For example, the experience as of red is the same as the experience as of green in self-orientation, but the two states are different in phenomenal feel.[14]

Monitoring Consciousness

The idea of consciousness as some sort of internal monitoring takes many forms. One notion is that of some sort of inner perception. This could be a form of P-consciousness, namely, P-consciousness of one's own states or of the self. Another notion is often put in information-processing terms: internal scanning. And a third, metacognitive notion, is that of a conscious state as one that is accompanied by a thought to the effect that one is in that state.[15] Let us lump these together as one or another form of monitoring consciousness. Given my liberal terminological policy, I have no objection to monitoring consciousness as a notion of consciousness. Where I balk is at the idea that P-consciousness just is one or another form of monitoring consciousness.

To identify P-consciousness with internal scanning is just to grease the slide to eliminativism about P-consciousness. Indeed, as Georges Rey (1983) has pointed out, ordinary laptop computers are capable of various types of self-scanning, but as he also points out, no one would think of their laptop computer as "conscious" (using the term in the ordinary way, without making any of the distinctions I have introduced). Since, according to Rey, internal scanning is essential to consciousness, he concludes that the concept of consciousness is incoherent. If one regards the various elements of the mongrel concept that I have been delineating as elements of a single concept, then that concept is indeed incoherent and needs repair by making distinctions, for example along the lines I have been suggesting. I doubt that the ordinary concept of consciousness is sufficiently determinate for it to be incoherent, though whether or not this is so is an empirical question about how people use words that it is not my job to decide. However that inquiry turns out, Rey's mistake is to trumpet the putative incoherence of the concept of consciousness as if it showed the incoherence of the concept of *phenomenal* consciousness.[16]

Rosenthal (1997) defines reflexive consciousness as follows: S is a reflexively conscious state of mine ↔ S is accompanied by a thought—arrived at noninferentially and nonobservationally—to the effect that I am in S. He offers this "higher order thought" (HOT) theory as a theory of phenomenal consciousness. It is obvious that phenomenal consciousness without HOT and HOT without phenomenal consciousness are both *conceptually* possible. For example, perhaps dogs and infants have phenomenally conscious pains without higher-order thoughts about them. For the converse case, imagine that by biofeedback and neural imaging techniques of the distant future, I learn to detect the state in myself of having the Freudian unconscious thought that it would be nice to kill my father and marry my mother. I could come to know—noninferentially and nonobservationally—that I have this Freudian thought even though the thought is not phenomenally conscious.

Rosenthal sometimes talks as if it is supposed to be a basic law of nature that phenomenal states and HOTs about them co-occur. That is a very adventurous claim. But even if it is true, then there must be a mechanism that explains the correlation, as the fact that both heat and electricity are carried by free electrons explains the correlation of electrical and thermal conductivity. But any mechanism breaks down under extreme conditions, as does the correlation of electrical and thermal conductivity at extremely high temperatures. So the correlation between phenomenality and HOT would break down too, showing that higher-order thought does not yield the basic scientific nature of phenomenality.

Rosenthal's definition of his version of monitoring consciousness has a number of ad hoc features. "Nonobservationally" is required to rule out (for example) a case in which I know about a thought I have repressed by observing my own behavior. "Noninferentially" is needed to avoid a somewhat different case in which I appreciate (nonobservationally) my own pain and infer a repressed thought from it. Further, Rosenthal's definition involves a stipulation that the possessor of the monitoring-conscious state is the same as the thinker of the thought—otherwise *my* thinking about *your* pain would make *it* a conscious pain. All these ad hoc features can be eliminated by moving to the following definition of monitoring consciousness: S is a monitoring-conscious state ↔ S is phenomenally presented in a thought about S. This definition uses the notion of phenomenality, but this is no disadvantage unless there is no such thing apart from monitoring itself. The new definition, requiring phenomenality as it does, has the additional advantage of making it clear why monitoring consciousness is a kind of *consciousness*.

There is an element of plausibility to the collapse of P-consciousness into monitoring consciousness. Consider two dogs, one of which has a perceptual state whereas the other has a similar perceptual state plus a representation of it. Surely the latter dog has a conscious state even if the former dog does not. Quite right, because *consciousness of* plausibly brings consciousness with it. (I am only endorsing the plausibility of this idea, not its truth.) But the *converse* is more problematic. If I am conscious of a pain or a thought, then, plausibly, that pain or thought has some P-conscious aspect. But even if consciousness of entails P-consciousness, that gives us no reason to believe that P-consciousness entails consciousness of, and it is the implausibility of this converse proposition that is pointed to by the dog problem. The first dog can have a P-conscious state too, even if it is not conscious of it.

Perhaps you are wondering why I am being so terminologically liberal, counting P-consciousness, A-consciousness, monitoring consciousness, and self-consciousness all as types of consciousness. Oddly, I find that many critics wonder why I would count *phenomenal* consciousness as consciousness, whereas many others wonder why I would count access or monitoring or *self*-consciousness as consciousness. In fact, two

reviewers of the article from which this paper derives complained about my terminological liberalism, but for incompatible reasons. One reviewer said: "While what he
uses ['P-consciousness'] to refer to—the 'what it is like' aspect of mentality—seems
to me interesting and important, I suspect that the discussion of it under the heading 'consciousness' is a source of confusion...he is right to distinguish access-
consciousness (which is what I think deserves the name 'consciousness') from this."
Another reviewer said: "I really still can't see why access is called...access-
consciousness? Why isn't access just...a purely information processing (functionalist)
analysis?" This is not a merely verbal matter. In my view, all of us, despite our explicit
verbal preferences, have some tendency to use "conscious" and related words in both
ways, and our failure to see this causes a good deal of difficulty in thinking about
"consciousness."

I have been talking about different concepts of "consciousness" and I have also said
that *the* concept of consciousness is a mongrel concept. Perhaps, you are thinking, I
should make up my mind. My view is that "consciousness" is actually an ambiguous
word, though the ambiguity I have in mind is not one that I have found in any dictionary. I started the paper with an analogy between "consciousness" and "velocity," and
I think there is an important similarity. One important difference, however, is that in
the case of "velocity," it is easy to get rid of the temptation to conflate the two senses,
even though for many purposes the distinction is not very useful. With "consciousness," there is a tendency toward "now you see it, now you don't." I think the main
reason for this is that when we are considering it in a quiet study without distraction,
P-consciousness presents itself to us in a way that makes it hard to imagine how a conscious state could fail to be accessible and self-reflective, so it is easy to fall into habits
of thought that do not distinguish these concepts.[17]

The chief alternative to the ambiguity hypothesis is that there is a single concept of
consciousness that is a *cluster concept*. For example, a prototypical religion involves belief in supernatural beings, sacred and profane objects, rituals, a moral code, religious
feelings, prayer, a worldview, an organization of life based on the worldview, and a
social group bound together by the previous items (Alston 1967). But for all of these
items, there are actual or possible religions that lack them. For example, some forms
of Buddhism do not involve belief in a supreme being and Quakers have no sacred
objects. It is convenient for us to use a concept of religion that binds together a number of disparate concepts whose referents are often found together.

The distinction between ambiguity and cluster concept can be drawn in a number of
equally legitimate ways that classify some cases differently. That is, there is some indeterminacy in the distinction. Some might even say that *velocity* is a cluster concept, because for many purposes it is convenient to group average and instantaneous velocity
together. I favor tying the distinction to the clear and present danger of conflation,
especially in the form of equivocation in an argument. Of course, this is no analysis,

since equivocation is definable in terms of ambiguity. My point, rather, is that one can make up one's mind about whether there is ambiguity by finding equivocation hard to deny. In Block 1995, the longer paper from which this paper derives, I give some examples of conflations.

When I called *consciousness* a mongrel concept, I was not declaring allegiance to the cluster theory. Rather, what I had in mind was that an ambiguous word often corresponds to an ambiguous mental representation, one that functions in thought as a unitary entity and thereby misleads. These are mongrels. I would also describe *velocity* and *degree of heat* (as used by the Florentine experimenters of the seventeenth century) as mongrel concepts. This is the grain of truth in the cluster-concept theory.

Note the distinction between the claim that the concept of consciousness is a mongrel concept and the claim that consciousness is not a natural kind (Churchland 1983, 1986). The former is a claim about the concept, one that can be verified by reflection alone. The latter is like the claim that dirt or cancer are not natural kinds, claims that require empirical investigation.[18]

Notes

Reprinted from David Chalmers, ed., *Philosophy of Mind: Classical and Contemporary Readings* (Oxford: Oxford University Press, 2002).

Mainly from "On a Confusion about a Function of Consciousness," in *Behavioral and Brain Sciences* 18(2), 1995, with permission of the author and Cambridge University Press. I have changed only what seems mistaken even from the point of view of my former position. No attempt has been made to systematically update the references.

1. But what is it about thoughts that makes them P-conscious? One possibility is that it is just a series of mental images or subvocalizations that make thoughts P-conscious. Another possibility is that the contents themselves have a P-conscious aspect independently of their vehicles. See Lormand 1996; Burge 1997.

2. My view is that although P-conscious content cannot be *reduced to* or identified with intentional content (at least not on relatively a priori grounds), P-conscious contents often—maybe always—have an intentional aspect, representing in a primitive nonconceptual way.

3. I know some will think that I invoked inverted and absent qualia a few paragraphs above when I described the explanatory gap as involving the question of why a creature with a brain that has a physiological and functional nature like ours could not have different experience or none at all. But the spirit of the question as I asked it allows for an answer that explains why such creatures cannot exist, and thus there is no presupposition that these are real possibilities.

4. I have been using the P-consciousness/A-consciousness distinction in my lectures for many years, but it only found its way into print in my "Consciousness and Accessibility" (1990), and in my 1991, 1992, and 1993 publications. My claims about the distinction have been criticized in Searle 1990, 1992, as well as in Flanagan 1992—I reply to Flanagan below. There is also an

illuminating discussion in Davies and Humphreys 1993b; in a later note, I take up a point they make. See also Levine's (1994) review of Flanagan, which discusses Flanagan's critique of the distinction. See in addition Kirk 1992 for an identification of P-consciousness with something like A-consciousness.

5. The full definition was: "A state is access-conscious if, in virtue of one's having the state, a representation of its content is (1) inferentially promiscuous, that is, poised for use as a premise in reasoning, (2) poised for rational control of action, and (3) poised for rational control of speech" (p. 231).

6. Dennett (1991) and Dennett and Kinsbourne (1992b) advocate the "multiple drafts" account of consciousness. Dennett switched to the cerebral celebrity view in his 1993 paper.

7. See Dennett 2001 and Block 2001 for a more sophisticated treatment of this dialectic.

8. Some may say that only fully conceptualized content can play a role in reasoning, be reportable, and rationally control action. Such a view should not be adopted in isolation from views about which contents are personal and which are subpersonal.

9. The concept of P-consciousness is not a functional concept; however, I acknowledge the empirical possibility that the scientific nature of P-consciousness has something to do with information processing. We can ill-afford to close off empirical possibilities given the difficulty of solving the mystery of P-consciousness.

10. The distinction has some similarity to the sensation/perception distinction; I will not take the space to lay out the differences. See Humphrey 1992 for an interesting discussion of the latter distinction.

11. If you are tempted to deny the existence of these states of the perceptual system, you should think back to the total zombie just mentioned. Putting aside the issue of the possibility of this zombie, note that from the standpoint of a computational notion of cognition, the zombie has *all* the same A-conscious contents that you have (if he is your computational duplicate). A-consciousness is an informational notion. The states of the superblindsighter's perceptual system are A-conscious for the same reason as the zombie's.

12. Farah claims that blindsight is more degraded than sight. But Weiskrantz (1988) notes that his patient DB had better acuity in some areas of the blind field (in some circumstances) than in his sighted field. It would be better to understand her "degraded" in terms of lack of access.

13. Thus, there is a conflict between this physiological claim and the Schacter model, which dictates that destroying the P-consciousness module will prevent A-consciousness.

14. See White 1987 for an account of why self-consciousness should be firmly distinguished from P-consciousness, and why self-consciousness is more relevant to certain issues of value.

15. The pioneer of these ideas in the philosophical literature is David Armstrong (1968, 1980). William Lycan (1987) has energetically pursued self-scanning, and David Rosenthal (1986, 1997), Peter Carruthers (1989, 1992), and Norton Nelkin (1993) have championed higher-order thought. See also Natsoulas 1993. Lormand (1996) makes some powerful criticisms of Rosenthal.

16. To be fair to Rey, his argument is more like a dilemma: for any supposed feature of consciousness, either a laptop of the sort we have today has it or else you cannot be sure you have it yourself. In the case of P-consciousness, laptops do not have it, and we are sure we do, so once we make these distinctions, his argument loses plausibility.

17. This represents a change of view from Block 1994, where I said that "consciousness" ought to be ambiguous, rather than saying it is now ambiguous.

18. I would like to thank Tyler Burge, Susan Carey, David Chalmers, Martin Davies, Wayne Davis, Bert Dreyfus, Güven Güzeldere, Paul Horwich, Jerry Katz, Leonard Katz, Joe Levine, David Rosenthal, Jerome Schaffer, Sydney Shoemaker, Stephen White, and Andrew Young for their very helpful comments on earlier versions of this paper. I have been giving this paper at colloquiums and meetings since the fall of 1990, and I am grateful to the many audiences that have made interesting and useful comments, especially the audience at the conference on my work at the University of Barcelona in June 1993.

References

Alston, W. 1967. Religion. In *The Encyclopedia of Philosophy*, 140–145. New York. Macmillan/Free Press.

Armstrong, D. M. 1968. *A Materialist Theory of Mind*. New York: Humanities Press.

Armstrong, D. M. 1970. What is consciousness? In D. M. Armstrong, ed., *The Nature of Mind*. Ithaca, NY: Cornell University Press.

Atkinson, A., and Davies, M. 1995. Consciousness without conflation. *Behavioral and Brain Sciences* 18(2): 248–249.

Baars, B. J. 1988. *A Cognitive Theory of Consciousness*. Cambridge: Cambridge University Press.

Block, N. 1980. What is functionalism? In N. Block, ed., *Readings in the Philosophy of Psychology*, vol. 1. Cambridge, MA: Harvard University Press.

Block, N. 1990. Consciousness and accessibility. *Behavioral and Brain Sciences* 13: 596–598.

Block, N. 1991. Evidence against epiphenomenalism. *Behavioral and Brain Sciences* 14(4): 670–672.

Block, N. 1992. Begging the question against phenomenal consciousness. *Behavioral and Brain Sciences* 15(2): 205–206.

Block, N. 1993. Review of D. Dennett, *Consciousness Explained*. *Journal of Philosophy* 90(4): 181–193.

Block, N. 1994. "Consciousness," "functionalism," "Qualia." In S. Guttenplan, ed., *A Companion to the Philosophy of Mind*. Oxford: Blackwell.

Block, N. 1995. On a confusion about a function of consciousness. *Behavioral and Brain Sciences* 18(2): 227–247.

Block, N. 2001. Paradox and cross purposes in recent work on consciousness. *Cognition* 79(1–2): 197–219.

Block, N., and Dworkin, G. 1974. IQ, heritability and inequality. Part I. *Philosophy and Public Affairs* 3(4): 331–409.

Burge, Tyler. 1997. Two kinds of consciousness. In Ned Block, Owen Flanagan, and Güven Güzeldere, eds., *The Nature of Consciousness: Philosophical Debates*. Cambridge, MA: MIT Press.

Carruthers, P. 1989. Brute experience. *Journal of Philosophy* 86: 258–269.

Carruthers, P. 1992. Consciousness and concepts. *Proceedings of the Aristotelian Society*, suppl. vol. 66: 40–59.

Chalmers, D. J. 1997. Availability: The cognitive basis of experience? In N. Block, O. Flanagan, and G. Güzeldere, eds., *The Nature of Consciousness: Philosophical Debates*. Cambridge, MA: MIT Press.

Churchland, P. S. 1983. Consciousness: The transmutation of a concept. *Pacific Philosophical Quarterly* 64: 80–93.

Crick, F. 1994. *The Astonishing Hypothesis*. New York: Scribner.

Crick, F., and Koch, C. 1990. Towards a neurobiological theory of consciousness. *Seminars in the Neurosciences* 2: 263–275.

Davies, M., and Humphreys, G. 1993a. *Consciousness*. Oxford: Blackwell.

Davies, M., and Humphreys, G. 1993b. Introduction. In M. Davies and G. Humphreys, *Consciousness*. Oxford: Blackwell.

Dennett, D. 1991. *Consciousness Explained*. Boston: Little Brown.

Dennett, D. 1993. The message is: There is no medium. *Philosophy and Phenomenological Research* 3: 4.

Dennett, D. 2001. Are we explaining consciousness yet? *Cognition* 79(1–2): 221–237.

Dennett, D., and Kinsbourne, M. 1992a. Escape from the Cartesian theater. *Behavioral and Brain Sciences* 15: 234–248.

Dennett, D., and Kinsbourne, M. 1992b. Time and the observer: The where and when of consciousness in the brain. *Behavioral and Brain Sciences* 15: 183–200.

Farah, M. 1994. Visual perception and visual awareness after brain damage: A tutorial overview. In C. Umiltà and M. Moscovitch, eds., *Attention and Performance XV: Conscious and Nonconscious Information Processing*, 37–76. Cambridge, MA: MIT Press.

Flanagan, O. 1992. *Consciousness Reconsidered*. MIT Press.

Gallup, G. 1982. Self-awareness and the emergence of mind in primates. *American Journal of Primatology* 2: 237–248.

Goldman, A. 1993a. Consciousness, folk psychology and cognitive science. *Consciousness and Cognition* 2(3): 364–382.

Goldman, A. 1993b. The psychology of folk psychology. *Behavioral and Brain Sciences* 16(1): 15–28.

Goodale, M., and Milner, D. 1992. Separate visual pathways for perception and action. *Trends in Neurosciences* 15: 20–25.

Hauser, M. D., Kralik, J., Botto, C., Garrett, M., and Oser, J. 1995. Self-recognition in primates: Phylogeny and the salience of species-typical traits. *Proceedings of the National Academy of Sciences* 92: 10811–10814.

Hill, C. 1991. *Sensations: A Defense of Type Materialism*. Cambridge: Cambridge University Press.

Humphrey, N. 1992. *A History of the Mind*. New York: Simon & Schuster.

Huxley, T. H. 1866. *Lessons in Elementary Psychology* 8: (Quoted in N. Humphrey, *A History of the Mind*, 210. New York: Simon & Schuster, 1992.)

Jackendoff, R. 1987. *Consciousness and the Computational Mind*. Cambridge, MA: MIT Press.

Jackson, F. 1986. What Mary didn't know. *Journal of Philosophy* 83: 291–295.

James, W. 1890. *Principles of Psychology*. New York: Holt.

Kirk, R. 1992. Consciousness and concepts. *Proceedings of the Aristotelian Society*, suppl. vol. 66: 23–40.

Kuhn, T. 1964. A function for thought experiments. In *Mélanges Alexandre Koyre*, vol. 1, 307–334. Paris: Hermann.

Levine, J. 1994. Review of Owen Flanagan's *Consciousness Reconsidered*. *Philosophical Review* 103(2): 356–358.

Loar, B. 1990. Phenomenal properties. In J. Tomberlin, ed., *Philosophical Perspectives: Action Theory and Philosophy of Mind*. Atascadero: Ridgeview.

Lormand, E. 1996. Nonphenomenal consciousness. *Nous* 30: 242–261.

Lycan, W. 1987. *Consciousness*. Cambridge, MA: MIT Press.

Malcolm, N. 1984. Consciousness and causality. In D. M. Armstrong and N. Malcolm, *Consciousness and Causality*. Oxford: Blackwell.

Marcel, A. J. 1986. Consciousness and processing: Choosing and testing a null hypothesis. *Behavioral and Brain Sciences* 9: 40–41.

McGinn, C. 1991. *The Problem of Consciousness*. Oxford: Blackwell.

Nagel, T. 1974. What is it like to be a bat? *Philosophical Review* 83(4): 435–450.

Nagel, T. 1979. *Mortal Questions*. Cambridge: Cambridge University Press.

Natsoulas, T. 1993. What is wrong with the appendage theory of consciousness? *Philosophical Psychology* 6(2): 137–154.

Nelkin, N. 1993. The connection between intentionality and consciousness. In M. Davies and G. Humphreys, *Consciousness*. Oxford: Blackwell.

Povinelli, D. 1994. *What Chimpanzees Know about the Mind*. In L. Marchant, C. Boesch, G. Hohmann, eds., *Behavioral Diversity in Chimpanzees and Bonobos*. Cambridge, MA: Harvard University Press.

Rey, G. 1983. A reason for doubting the existence of consciousness. In R. Davidson, G. Schwartz, and D. Shapiro, eds., *Consciousness and Self-Regulation*, vol. 3. New York: Plenum.

Rey, G. 1988. A question about consciousness. In H. Otto and J. Tuedio, eds., *Perspectives on Mind*, Dordrecht: Reidel.

Rosenthal, David. 1986. Two concepts of consciousness. *Philosophical Studies* 49: 329–359.

Rosenthal, David. 1997. A theory of consciousness. In N. Block, O. Flanagan, and G. Güzeldere, eds., *The Nature of Consciousness: Philosophical Debates*. Cambridge, MA: MIT Press.

Schacter, D. 1989. On the relation between memory and consciousness: Dissociable interactions and conscious experience. In H. Roediger and F. Craik, eds., *Varieties of Memory and Consciousness: Essays in Honour of Endel Tulving*. Mahwah, NJ: Erlbaum.

Searle, J. 1983. *Intentionality*. Cambridge: Cambridge University Press.

Searle, J. 1990. Who is computing with the brain? *Behavioral and Brain Sciences* 13(4): 632–642.

Searle, J. 1992. *The Rediscovery of the Mind*. Cambridge, MA: MIT Press.

Shoemaker, S. 1975. Functionalism and qualia. *Philosophical Studies* 27: 291–315.

Shoemaker, S. 1981. The inverted spectrum. *Journal of Philosophy* 74(7): 357–381.

Stich, S. 1978. Autonomous psychology and the belief-desire thesis. *Monist* 61(4): 573–591.

Van Gulick, R. 1989. What difference does consciousness make? *Philosophical Topics* 17(1): 211–230.

Van Gulick, R. 1993. Understanding the phenomenal mind: Are we all just armadillos? In M. Davies and G. Humphreys, eds., *Consciousness*. Oxford: Blackwell.

Weiskrantz, L. 1988. Some contributions of neuropsychology of vision and memory to the problem of consciousness. In A. Marcel and E. Bisiach, eds., *Consciousness in Contemporary Society*. Cambridge: Cambridge University Press.

White, S. L. 1987. What is it like to be an homunculus? *Pacific Philosophical Quarterly* 68: 148–174.

Wiser, M., and Carey, S. 1983. When heat and temperature were one. In D. Gentner and A. Stevens, eds., *Mental Models*. Mahwah, NJ: Erlbaum.

III Empirical Approaches to Consciousness

There are two concepts of consciousness that are easy to confuse with one another, access consciousness and phenomenal consciousness. However, just as the concepts of water and H_2O are different concepts of the same thing, so the two concepts of consciousness may come to the same thing in the brain. The focus of this paper is on the problems that arise when these two concepts of consciousness are conflated. I will argue that John Searle's reasoning about the function of consciousness goes wrong because he conflates the two senses. And Francis Crick and Christof Koch fall afoul of the ambiguity in arguing that visual area V1 is not part of the neural correlate of consciousness. Crick and Koch's work raises issues that suggest that these two concepts of consciousness may have different (though overlapping) neural correlates—despite Crick and Koch's implicit rejection of this idea.

I will start with two quotations from Searle. You will see what appears to be a contradiction, and I will later claim that the appearance of contradiction can be explained if one realizes that he is using two different concepts of consciousness. I am not going to explain yet what the two concepts of consciousness are. That will come later, after I have presented Searle's apparent contradiction and Crick and Koch's surprising argument.

Searle's Apparent Contradiction

Searle discusses my claim that there are two concepts of consciousness, arguing that I have confused modes of one kind with two different kinds:

There are lots of different degrees of consciousness, but door knobs, bits of chalk, and shingles are not conscious at all.... These points, it seems to me, are misunderstood by Block. He refers to what he calls an "access sense of consciousness." On my account there is no such sense. I believe that he ... [confuses] what I would call peripheral consciousness or inattentiveness with total unconsciousness. It is true, for example, that when I am driving my car "on automatic pilot" I am not paying much attention to the details of the road and the traffic. *But it is simply not true that I am totally unconscious of these phenomena. If I were, there would be a car crash.* We need therefore to make a distinction between the center of my attention, the focus of my consciousness on the one hand, and the periphery on the other. (Italics added)[1]

Note that Searle claims that if I became unconscious of the road while driving, the car would crash. Now compare the next argument:

The epileptic seizure rendered the patient totally unconscious, yet the patient continued to exhibit what would normally be called goal-directed behavior.... In all these cases, we have complex forms of apparently goal-directed behavior without any consciousness. Now why could all behavior not be like that? Notice that in the cases, the patients were performing types of actions that were habitual, routine and memorized... normal, human, conscious behavior has a degree of flexibility and creativity that is absent from the Penfield cases of *the unconscious driver* and the unconscious pianist. Consciousness adds powers of discrimination and flexibility even to memorized routine activities... one of the evolutionary advantages conferred on us by consciousness is the much greater flexibility, sensitivity, and creativity we derive from being conscious.[2]

Note that according to the first quotation, if I were to become unconscious (and therefor unconscious of the road and traffic), my car would crash. But in the second quotation, he accepts Penfield's description "totally unconscious" as applying to the case of the petit mal patient who drives home while having a seizure. Thus we have what looks like a contradiction.

Crick and Koch's Argument

I will now shift to Crick and Koch's recent article in *Nature*[3] arguing that V1 (the first major processing area for visual signals) is not part of the neural correlate of consciousness (what they call the NCC). Crick and Koch say that V1 is not part of the neural correlate of consciousness because V1 does not directly project to frontal cortex. (They extrapolate (tentatively) from the fact that no direct connections are known in macaques to no connections in humans.) Their reasoning makes use of the premise that part of the function of visual consciousness is to harness visual information in the service of the *direct* control of reasoning and decision-making that controls behavior. On the hypothesis that the frontal areas are involved in these mental functions, they argue that a necessary condition of inclusion in the NCC is direct projection to frontal areas. Though something seems right about their argument, it has nonetheless puzzled many readers. The puzzle is this: Why couldn't there be conscious activity based in V1 despite its lack of direct connection to frontal cortex? This is Pollen's[4] worry: "I see no a priori necessity for neurons in perceptual space to communicate directly with those in decision space." The possibility of conscious activity based in V1 is especially salient in the light of Crick and Koch's suggestion that visual consciousness is reverberatory activity in pyramidal cells of the lower layers of the visual cortex involving connections to the thalamus.[5] For one wonders how they have ruled out the possibility that such activity *exists* in V1 despite the lack of direct connection between V1 and frontal cortex. They do not address this possibility at all. The overall air of paradox is deepened by their claim that that "Our hypothesis is thus rather subtle; if it [no direct connection] turns out to be true it [V1 is not part of the neural correlate of consciousness] will eventually come to be regarded as completely obvious" (p. 123). But the reader wonders why this is true at all, much less obviously true. When such accomplished researchers say such puzzling things, one has to wonder if one is understanding them properly.

I will argue that once the two concepts of consciousness are separated out, the argument turns out to be trivial on one reading and not clearly compelling on the other reading. That's the critical part of my comment on Crick and Koch, but I have two positive points as well. I argue that nonetheless their conclusion about V1 should be accepted, but for a different reason, one that they implicitly suggest and that deserves to be opened up to public scrutiny. Further, I argue that the considerations that they raise suggest that the two concepts of consciousness correspond to different neural correlates despite Crick and Koch's implicit rejection of this idea.

The Two Concepts

The two concepts of consciousness are *phenomenal* consciousness and *access* consciousness.[6] Phenomenal consciousness is just *experience*; access consciousness is a kind of direct control. More exactly, a representation is access conscious if it is actively poised for direct control of reasoning, reporting and action.

One way to see the distinction between the two concepts is to consider the possibility of one without the other. Here is an illustration of access without phenomenal consciousness. In Anton's Syndrome, blind patients do not realize that they are blind (though implicit knowledge of blindness can often be elicited). Hartmann et al.[7] report a case of "Reverse Anton's Syndrome" in which the patient does not realize that he is *not* really blind. The patient regards himself as blind, and he is at chance at telling whether a room is illuminated or dark. But he has a small preserved island of V1 that allows him to read single words and recognize faces and facial expressions if they are presented to the upper right part of the visual field. When asked how he knows the word or the face, he says "it clicks" and denies that he sees the stimuli. There is no obvious factor in his social situation that would favor lying or self-deception. In addition to the damage in V1, he has bilateral parietal damage, including damage to the left inferior parietal lobe. Milner and Goodale[8] have proposed that phenomenal consciousness requires ventral stream activity plus attention, and that the requisite attention can be blocked by parietal lesions. So perhaps this is a case of visual access without visual phenomenal consciousness. (Note that Milner and Goodale's account is not in conflict with Crick and Koch's claim that V1 is not part of the NCC if activity in V1 is not the object of attentional processes.)

So we see that access consciousness without phenomenal consciousness makes sense and may even exist in a limited form. What about the converse, phenomenal consciousness without access? For an illustration at the conceptual level, consider the familiar phenomenon in which one notices that the refrigerator has just gone off. Sometimes one has the feeling that one has been hearing the noise all along, but without noticing it until it went off. One of the many possible explanations of what happens in such a case illustrates phenomenal consciousness without access consciousness: Before the refrigerator went off, you had the experience (phenomenal consciousness) of the noise (let us suppose) but there was insufficient attention directed toward it to allow direct control of speech, reasoning or action. There might have been *indirect* control (the volume of your voice increased to compensate for the noise) but not direct control of the sort that happens when a representation is poised for free use as a premise in reasoning and can be freely reported. (It is this free use that characterizes access consciousness.) On this hypothesis, there is a period in which one has phenomenal consciousness of the noise without access consciousness of it. Of course, there are alternative hypotheses, including more subtle ones in which there are degrees of access and degrees of phenomenality. One might have a moderate degree of both phenomenal consciousness of and access to the noise at first, then filters might reset the threshold for access, putting the stimulus below the threshold for direct control, until the refrigerator goes off and one notices the change. The degree of phenomenal consciousness and access consciousness may always match. Although phenomenal consciousness and access consciousness differ conceptually (as do the concepts of water and H_2O), we do not know yet whether or not they really come to the same thing in the brain.

Once one sees the distinction, one sees many pure uses of both concepts. For example, the Freudian unconscious is *access* unconscious. A repressed memory of torture in a red room could in principle be a phenomenally vivid image; what makes it unconscious in the Freudian sense is that it comes out in dreams, slips, fleeing from red rooms and the like rather than directly controlling behavior. Thus in principle an image can be unconscious in one sense (not poised for access), yet experienced and therefor conscious in another sense (phenomenally).

Searle's Contradiction

Let's go back to Searle's (apparent) contradiction. You will recall that he says that if he were to become unconscious of the details of the road and traffic, the car would crash: "When I am driving my car 'on automatic pilot' I am not paying much attention to the details of the road and the traffic. But it is simply not true that I am totally unconscious of these phenomena. If I were, there would be a car crash." But he also says that Penfield's famous unconscious driver is "totally unconscious" yet manages to drive home. (Searle has never suggested that he changed his mind on this issue between 1990 and 1992.) Note that there is no room for resolving the contradiction via appeal to the difference between "conscious" and "conscious of." If Penfield's driver is "totally unconscious," then he is not conscious *of* anything. And thus we have a conflict with the idea that if one were to become unconscious of the road and traffic, the car would crash. Can we resolve the contradiction by supposing that what Searle thinks is that *normally* if one were to become unconscious of the road the car would crash, but the Penfield case is an abnormal exception? Not likely, since Searle's explicit conclusion is that consciousness adds flexibility, creativity, and sensitivity to action—suggesting that he thinks that consciousness is simply not necessary to routine activities like driving home.

I think that appeal to the access/phenomenal distinction does serve to resolve the contradiction. The resolution is that Searle is presupposing that the Penfield petit mal seizure case loses phenomenal consciousness but still has sufficient access consciousness to drive. But when he says that if he were unconscious of the road the car would crash, he is thinking of loss of both phenomenal and access consciousness—and it is the loss of the latter that would make the car crash.

I find that audiences I have talked to about this issue tend to divide roughly evenly. Some use "conscious" to mean phenomenal consciousness—to the extent that they control their uses. Others use "conscious" to mean either access consciousness or some kind of self-consciousness. But Searle's error shows how easy it is for people to mix the two concepts together, whatever their official stance is.

How Crick and Koch's Argument Depends on a Conflation

Crick and Koch argue that V1 is not part of the neural correlate of consciousness because V1 does not project to frontal cortex. Visual consciousness is used in harnessing visual information for directly guiding reasoning and decision making and direct projection to frontal cortex is required for such a use. But what concept of consciousness are Crick and Koch deploying? They face a dilemma. If they mean phenomenal consciousness, then their argument is extremely interesting but unsound: their conclusion is *unjustified*. If they mean access-consciousness, their argument is *trivial*. Let me explain.

Let us look at their argument more closely. Here it is:

1. Neural machinery of visual consciousness harnesses visual information for direct control of reasoning and decision making
2. Frontal areas subserve these functions
3. V1 does not project directly to frontal cortex
4. SO V1 is not part of neural correlate of consciousness

Note that the "direct" in premise 1 is necessary to generate the conclusion. But what reason is there to suppose that there cannot be *some* neural machinery of visual consciousness—V1, for example—that is part of the machinery of control of reasoning and decision making, but only indirectly so? If by "consciousness" we mean phenomenal consciousness, there is no such reason, and so premise 1 is unjustified. But suppose we take "consciousness" to mean *access consciousness*. Then premise 1 is trivially true. Of course the neural machinery of access consciousness harnesses visual information for *direct* control since access consciousness just *is* direct control. But the trivial interpretation of premise 1 trivializes the argument. For to say that *if* V1 does not project directly to areas that control action, *then* V1 is not part of the neural correlate of *access* consciousness is to say something that is very like the claim that *if* something is a sleeping pill, then it is dormitive. Once Crick and Koch tell us that V1 is not directly connected to centers of control, nothing is added by saying that V1 is not part of the neural correlate of consciousness in the *access* sense. For an access-conscious representation just *is* one that is poised for the direct control of reasoning and decision making.

On this reading, we can understand Crick and Koch's remark about their thesis that "if it [V1 is not directly connected to centers of control] turns out to be true it [V1 is not part of the neural correlate of consciousness] will eventually come to be regarded as completely obvious." In the access-consciousness interpretation, this remark is like saying that if it turns out to be true that barbiturates cause sleep, their dormitivity will eventually come to be regarded as completely obvious.

To avoid misunderstanding, I must emphasize that I am not saying that it is a triviality that neurons in V1 are not directly connected to frontal areas. That is an empirical claim, just as it is an empirical claim that barbituates cause sleep. What is trivial is that if neurons in V1 are not directly connected to centers of control, then neurons in V1 are not part of the neural correlate of access consciousness. Similarly, it is trivial that if barbituates cause sleep, then they are dormitive.

That was the "access-consciousness" interpretation. Now let us turn to the phenomenal interpretation. On this interpretation, their claim is very significant, but not obviously true? How do we know whether activity in V1 is phenomenally conscious without being access conscious? As mentioned earlier, Crick and Koch's own hypothesis that phenomenal consciousness is reverberatory activity in the lower cortical layers makes this a real possibility. They can hardly rule out this consequence of their own view by fiat. Crick and Koch[9] say, "We know of no case in which a person has lost the whole prefrontal and premotor cortex, on both sides (including Broca's area), and can still see." But there are two concepts of seeing, just as there are two concepts of consciousness. If it is the phenomenal aspect of seeing that they are talking about, they are ignoring the real possibility that patients who have lost these frontal areas *can* see.

Crick and Koch attempt to justify the "directly" by appeal to representations on the retina. These representations control but not directly; and they are not conscious either. Apparently, the idea is that if representations do not control directly, then they are not conscious. But this example cuts no ice. Retinal representations have *neither* phenomenal *nor* access consciousness. So they do not address the issue of whether V1 representations might have phenomenal but not access consciousness.

So Crick and Koch face a dilemma: their argument is either not substantive or not compelling.

Is the Point Verbal?

Crick and Koch often seem to have phenomenal consciousness in mind. For example, they orient themselves towards the problem of "a full accounting of the manner in which subjective experience arises from these cerebral processes.... Why do we experience anything at all? What leads to a particular conscious experience (such as the blueness of blue)? Why are some aspects of subjective experience impossible to convey to other people (in other words, why are they private)?"[10]

Crick and Koch often use "aware" and "conscious" as synonyms, as does Crick in *The Astonishing Hypothesis*. For example, the thesis of the paper in *Nature*[3] is that V1 is not part of the neural correlate of consciousness and also that V1 is not part of the neural correlate of visual awareness. But sometimes they appear to use "awareness" to *mean* access-consciousness. For example, "All we need to postulate is that, unless a visual area has a direct projection to at least one of [the frontal areas], the activities in that particular visual area will not enter visual *awareness* directly, because the activity of frontal areas is needed to allow a person to report *consciousness*" (p. 122; emphases added). What could "consciousness" mean here? "Consciousness" cannot mean *access* consciousness, since reporting is a kind of accessing, and there is no issue of *accessing* access consciousness. Consciousness in the sense in which they mean it here is something that might conceivably exist even if it cannot be reported or otherwise accessed. And consciousness in this sense might exist in V1. Thus when they implicitly acknowledge an access/phenomenal consciousness distinction, the possibility of phenomenal without access consciousness looms large.

My point is not a verbal one. Whether we use "consciousness" or "phenomenal consciousness," "awareness," or "access consciousness," the point is that there are two different concepts of the phenomenon or phenomena of interest. We have to acknowledge the possiblity in principle that these two concepts pick out different phenomena. Two versus one: that is not a verbal issue.

Are the Neural Correlates of the Two Kinds of Consciousness Different?

Perhaps there is evidence that the neural correlate of phenomenal consciousness is exactly the same as the neural correlate of access consciousness? The idea that this is a conceptual difference without a real difference would make sense both of Crick and Koch as well as other work in the field. But paradoxically, the idea that the neural correlates of the two concepts of consciousness coincide is one which Crick and Koch themselves actually give us reason to *reject*. Their hypothesis about the neural correlate of visual *phenomenal* consciousness is that it is localized in reverberatory circuits involving the thalamus and the lower layers of the visual cortex.[3] This is a daring and controversial hypothesis. But it entails a much less daring and controversial conclusion: that the localization of visual phenomenal consciousness *does not involve the frontal cortex*. However, Crick and Koch think that the neural correlate of consciousness—and here we would be charitable in interpreting them as meaning access consciousness—*does* involve the frontal cortex. It would not be surprising if the brain areas involved in visual control of reasoning and reporting are not exactly the same as those involved in visual phenomenality.

One way for Crick and Koch to respond would be to include the neural correlates of *both* access and phenomenal consciousness in the "NCC." To see what is wrong with this, consider an analogy. The first sustained empirical investigation of heat phenomena was conducted by the Florentine Experimenters in the seventeenth century. They did not distinguish between temperature and heat, using a single word, roughly translatable as "degree of heat," for both. This failure to make the distinction generated paradoxes. For example, when they measured degree of heat by the test "Will it melt paraffin?" heat source A came out hotter than B, but when they measured degree of heat by how much ice a heat source could melt in a given time, B came out hotter than A.[11] The concept of degree of heat was a *mongrel* concept, one that lumps together things that are very different.[6]

The suggestion that the neural correlate of visual consciousness includes both the frontal lobes *and* the circuits involving the thalamus and the lower layers of the visual cortex would be like an advocate of the Florentine experimenters' concept of degree of heat saying that the molecular correlate of degree of heat includes both *mean* molecular kinetic energy (temperature) and *total* molecular kinetic energy (heat), an idea that makes little sense. The right way to react to the discovery that a concept is a *mongrel*, is to distinguish distinct tracks of scientific investigation corresponding to the distinct concepts, not to lump them together.

Another way for Crick and Koch to react would be to include both the frontal lobes and the circuits involving the thalamus and the lower layers of the visual cortex in the neural correlate of *phenomenal* consciousness. (Koch seems inclined in this direction in correspondence.) But this would be like saying that the molecular correlate of *heat* includes both mean and total molecular kinetic energy. Again, this makes little sense. The criteria that Crick and Koch apply in localizing visual phenomenal consciousness are very fine grained, allowing them to emphasize cortical layers 4, 5, and 6 in the visual areas. For example, they appeal to a difference in those layers between cats that are awake and cats that are in slow-wave sleep, both exposed to the same visual stimuli. No doubt there are many differences between the sleeping and the waking cats in areas outside the visual cortex. But we would need a very good reason to include any of those other differences in the neural correlate of visual phenomenology as opposed, say, to the nonphenomenal cognitive processing of visual information.

A Better Reason for not Including V1 in the NCC

Though I find fault with one strand of Crick and Koch's reasoning about V1, I think there is another strand in the paper that does justify the conclusion, but for a reason that it would be good to have out in the open and to distinguish from the reasoning just discussed. (Koch tells me that what I say in this paragraph is close to what they had in mind.) They note that it is thought that representations in V1 do not exhibit the Land effect (color constancy). But our experience, our phenomenal consciousness, does exhibit the Land effect, or so we would all judge. Similarly, it appears that neurons in V1 are sensitive to gratings that are finer than people judge they can make out. We should accept the methodological principle: *at this early stage of inquiry,* don't suppose that people are wildly wrong about their own experience. Following this principle and assuming that the claim that cells in V1 do not exhibit color constancy is confirmed, then we should accept for the moment that representations in V1 are not on the whole phenomenally conscious. This methodological principle is implicitly accepted throughout Crick's and Koch's work.

An alternative route to the same conclusion would be the assumption that the neural correlate of phenomenal consciousness is "part of" the neural correlate of access consciousness (and so there can be no phenomenal without access consciousness). Phenomenal consciousness is automatically "broadcast" in the brain, but perhaps there are other mechanisms of broadcasting. So even if the "reverse Anton's syndrome" case turns out to be access without phenomenal consciousness, Crick and Koch's conclusion might still stand.

Note that neither of the reasons given here make any use of the finding that V1 is not directly connected to frontal areas.

The assumption that phenomenal consciousness is part of access consciousness is very empirically risky. One empirical phenomenon that favors taking phenomenal without access consciousness seriously is the fact that phenomenal consciousness has a finer grain than access consciousness based on memory representations. For example, normal people can recognize no more than 80 distinct pitches, but it appears that the number of distinct pitch experiences is much greater. This is indicated (but not proven) by the fact that normal people can *discriminate* 1,400 different frequencies from one another.[12] There are many more phenomenal experiences than there are concepts of them.

Despite these disagreements, I greatly admire Crick's and Koch's work on consciousness and have written a very positive review of Crick's book.[13] Crick has written "No longer need one spend time...[enduring] the tedium of philosophers perpetually disagreeing with each other. Consciousness is now largely a scientific problem."[14] I think this conceptual issue shows that even if largely a scientific issue, it is not entirely one. There is still some value in a collaboration between philosophers and scientists on this topic.

Notes

This is a substantially revised version of a paper that appeared in *Trends in Neurosciences* 19(2): 456–459, 1996. I am grateful to audiences at the 1996 consciousness conference in Tucson, at the 1996 cognitive science conference at the University of Sienna, at the University of Oxford, Department of Experimental Psychology, at Union College Department of Philosophy, and at the Royal Institute of Philosophy. I am also grateful to Susan Carey, Francis Crick, Martin Davies, Christof Koch, and David Milner, as well as to the editor of *Trends in Neurosciences* for comments on a previous draft.

Reprinted in João Branquinho, ed., *The Foundations of Cognitive Science* (New York: Oxford University Press, 2001). Reprinted in *Intellectica* 31 (2000): 1–12. Reprinted in Anthony O'Hear, ed., *Current Issues in Philosophy of Mind*, Royal Institute of Philosophy Supplement (Cambridge: Cambridge University Press, 1998). German translation ("Das neurale Korrelat des Bewusstseins") in Frank Esken and Heinz-Dieter Heckmann, eds., *Bewusstsein und Repraesentation* (Paderborn: Verlag Ferdinand Schoeningh, 1997). Italian translation, "Come trovare il correlato neurale della coscienza?", in *Sistemi Intelligenti*, with comments by Italian philosophers, 1998. Reprinted in the proceedings of the 1996 conference on consciousness at Tucson S. Hameroff, A Kaszniak, and A. Scott, eds., *Toward a Science of Consciousness II: The Second Tucson Discussions and Debates* (Cambridge: MIT Press, 1998). Spanish translation forthcoming in a book on consciousness edited by Jose Luis Blanco.

1. Searle, John. 1990. Who is computing with the brain? *Behavioral and Brain Sciences* 13(4): 632–634.

2. Searle, John. 1992. *The Rediscovery of the Mind*. Cambridge, MA: MIT Press.

3. Crick, F., and Koch, C. 1995, May 11. Are we aware of neural activity in primary visual cortex? *Nature* 375: 121–123.

4. Pollen, D. 1995, September 28. Cortical areas in visual awareness. *Nature* 377: 293–294.

5. Crick, F. 1994. *The Astonishing Hypothesis*. New York: Scribner.

6. Block, N. 1995. On a confusion about a function of consciousness. *Behavioral and Brain Sciences* 18(2): 227–247.

7. Hartmann, J. A., et al. 1991. Denial of visual perception. *Brain and Cognition* 16: 29–40.

8. Milner, A. D., and Goodale, M. A. 1995. *The Visual Brain in Action*. Oxford: Oxford University Press.

9. Crick, F., and Koch, C. 1995. Untitled response to Pollen. *Nature* 377: 294–295.

10. Crick, F., and Koch, C. 1995, December. Why neuroscience may be able to explain consciousness. Sidebar in *Scientific American*, p. 92.

11. Wiser, M., and Carey, S. 1983. When heat and temperature were one. In D. Gentner and A. Stevens, eds., *Mental Models*. Mahwah, NJ: Erlbaum.

12. Raffman, D. 1995. On the persistence of phenomenology. In T. Metzinger, ed., *Conscious Experience*. Thorverton: Imprint Academic.

13. Block, N. 1996. Review of Francis Crick, *The Astonishing Hypothesis*. *Contemporary Psychology*, May.

14. Crick, F. 1996, August 2. Visual perception: Rivalry and consciousness. *Nature* 379: 485–486.

15 Paradox and Cross-Purposes in Recent Work on Consciousness

Several papers in Dehaene 2001 "see convergence coming from many different quarters on a version of the neuronal global workspace model" (Dennett 2001). On the contrary, even within that volume, there are commitments to very different perspectives on consciousness. And these differing perspectives are based on tacit differences in philosophical starting places that should be made explicit. Indeed, it is not clear that different uses of "consciousness" and "awareness" in Dehaene 2001 can be taken to refer to the same phenomenon. More specifically, I think there are three different concepts of consciousness in play there. The global-workspace model makes much more sense on one of these than on the others.

Part of the point of this comment is that "consciousness" and "awareness" are ambiguous terms. To avoid tedious use of "scare-quotes" and constant reminders that authors being discussed may mean something different from other authors, I will often just speak of consciousness in whatever sense is at issue in the work of the author being discussed.

The Paradox of Recent Findings about Consciousness

The most exciting and puzzling results described in the special issue of *Cognition* and the volume edited by Dehaene appear in a linked set of experiments reported by Kanwisher 2001, Driver and Vuilleumier 2001, and Dehaene and Naccache 2001. Kanwisher notes that "neural correlates of perceptual experience, an exotic and elusive quarry just a few years ago, have suddenly become almost commonplace findings" (p. 98). And she backs this up with impressive correlations between neural activation on the one hand and indications of perceptual experiences of faces, houses, motion, letters, objects, words, and speech on the other. Conscious perception of faces whether rivalrous or not correlates with activity in the fusiform face area (FFA) but not the parahippocampal place area (PPA). And conversely for perception of places. This work is especially extensive in vision, where what I will refer to as the *ventral stream*, a set of occipital-temporal pathways, is strongly implicated in visual experience. Apparently, the further into the temporal cortex, the more dominant the correlation with the percept. (The precise pathway depends on the subject matter, the different areas determining the different contents of consciousness.)

As Kanwisher notes, the FFA and PPA were selected for scrutiny in these experiments, not because of any association with consciousness but because it was known that they specialize in these sorts of stimuli. These areas are not as strongly activated by most other stimuli that are not places or faces. Thus the neural basis of consciousness is not localized in one set of cells, but rather in the very areas that do the perceptual analysis. Nonetheless, in a broader sense, this work does suggest a single neural basis for visual consciousness, because all visual stimuli affect areas of a single stream of processing, albeit different parts of that stream. Although finding the neural basis for visual consciousness would be exciting, it would be foolish to suppose it would immediately yield an understanding of *why* it is the neural basis. That understanding will no doubt require major ideas of which we now have no glimmer.

So we apparently have an amazing success: identification of the neural basis of visual consciousness in the ventral stream. Paradoxically, what has also become commonplace is activation of the *very same ventral stream pathways without awareness*. Damage to the inferior parietal lobes has long been known to cause visual extinction, in which, for example, subjects appear to lose subjective experience of stimuli on one side when there are stimuli on both sides, yet show signs of perception of the stimuli—for instance, the extinguished stimuli often facilitate responses to nonextinguished stimuli. (Extinction is associated with visual neglect in which subjects do not notice stimuli on one side; e.g., neglect patients often do not eat the food on one side of the plate.) Driver and Vuilleumier point out that the ventral stream is activated for extinguished stimuli (i.e., which the subject claims not to see). Rees et al. (2000) report studies of a left-sided neglect and extinction patient on face and house stimuli. Stimuli presented *only* on the left side are clearly seen by the patient, but when there are stimuli on both sides, the subject acknowledges just the stimulus on the right. However, the "unseen" stimuli show activation of the ventral pathway that is the same in location and temporal course as the seen stimuli. Further, studies in monkeys have shown that a classic "blindness" syndrome is caused by massive cortical ablation that spares most of the ventral stream but not the inferior parietal and frontal lobes (Nakamura and Mishkin 1980, 1986, as cited in Lumer and Rees 1999). Kanwisher notes that dynamic visual gratings alternating with a gray field—both very faint stimuli—showed greater activation for the gratings in V1, V2, V3A, V4v, and MT/MST despite the subjects saying they saw only a uniform gray field. Dehaene and Naccache note that processing of a masked number word proceeds all the way through the occipital-temporal pathway to a motor response even though subjects were at chance in discriminating presence from absence and in discriminating words from non-words: "An entire stream of perceptual, semantic, and motor processes, specified by giving arbitrary verbal instructions to a normal subject, can occur outside of consciousness" (p. 9).

Is the difference between conscious and unconscious activation of the ventral pathway just a matter of the degree of activation? As Kanwisher notes, Rees et al. (2000) found activations for extinguished face stimuli that were as strong as for conscious stimuli. And evidence from ERP studies using the attentional blink paradigm show that neural activation of meaning is no less when the word is blinked and therefore not consciously perceived than when it is not, suggesting that it is not lower neural activation strength that accounts for lack of awareness. Further, in a study of neglect patients, McGlinchey-Berroth et al. (1993) showed that there is the same amount of semantic priming from both hemifields, despite the lack of awareness of stimuli in the left field, again suggesting that it is not activation strength that makes the difference. The upshot is that something in addition to activation strength must be playing a role.

Driver and Vuilleumier put the paradox as follows: "How then can the patient remain unaware of a contralesional stimulus, even when it can still activate the pathways that are most often considered to support conscious experience?" The paradox then is that our amazing success in identifying the neural correlate of visual experience in normal vision has led to the peculiar result that in masking and neglect, that very neural correlate occurs without, apparently, subjective experience.

What is the missing ingredient, X, which, added to ventral activation (of sufficient strength), constitutes conscious experience? Kanwisher and Driver and Vuilleumier, despite differences of emphasis, offer pretty much the same proposal as to the nature of X: (1) activation of the ventral stream supplies the contents of consciousness, (2) X is what makes those ventral contents conscious, (3) X includes binding perceptual attributes with a time and a place, that is, the representation of a token event, and (4) the neural basis of X is centered in the parietal cortex. If this is true, it is extremely significant, suggesting that the causal basis of all experience is spatiotemporal experience.

But I have a number of doubts about this proposal.

1. The proposal is wrong if there can be unbound but nonetheless conscious experiences—for example, experienced color not located in space or experienced shape and color not attached to one another. When a person has a visual experience of a ganzfeld, in which a color fills the subject's whole field of vision, that visual experience is apparently unbound and yet conscious. (I am indebted to correspondence with Ann Treisman on the ganzfeld.) But perhaps we need more clarity on what binding is before we can take this as evidence against the proposal. Friedman-Hill, Robertson, and Treisman (1995) and Wojciulik and Kanwisher (1998) discuss a patient (RM) with bilateral parietal damage who has binding problems. In many tasks, RM's level of illusory conjunctions (e.g., reporting a blue X and a red O when seeing a red X and a blue O) is high. Wojciulik and Kanwisher discuss a number of tasks in which RM is at chance, as

in the case of reporting which of two words is colored (rather than white). Perhaps RM has bound but illusory experiences—for instance, if the stimulus is a green "short" and white "ready," he experiences a green "ready" and a white "short." Or perhaps RM experiences green, white, "short," and "ready" but without colors bound to words. (I have not been able to tell which is right from the published literature.) The binding hypothesis may withstand this putative disconfirmation, however, since as Wojciulik and Kanwisher report, he appears to be binding "implicitly" as indicated by his normal interference in a Strooplike task. (It takes him longer to name the colored word if he is presented with a green "brown" and a white (i.e., noncolored) "green" than a green "green" and a white "brown.")

2. Weiskrantz and his colleagues (Kentridge, Heywood, and Weiskrantz 1999) have reported that attention can be guided to a flashed dot in the blind field by an arrow in the sighted field. Further, the patient, GY, learns when the contingencies are changed so that the arrow is misleading about where the dot will appear. A straightforward conjunction experiment requires a choice between four options: A&B, A&¬B, ¬A&B, and ¬A&¬B. If we want to know whether a blindsight patient visually perceives the conjunction of say red and moves vertically, we would have to give him choices among all four options. Unfortunately, the usual blindsight choice is between two, which may introduce skepticism about whether binding can be detected in blindsight. However, GY can choose among four options (DeGelder et al. 1999). Can a demonstration of binding in the blind field be far off?

3. Why take X to be binding rather than just attention or rather sufficient attention? (Perhaps the attention in the blind field is too low for X.) Tipper and Behrman (1996) show a neglect patient a "barbell" consisting of two circles joined by a line, with target words flashed in both circles. The patient does not recognize the target words on the left. But if the barbell is rotated so that the circle that was on the left is now on the right, the subject does not recognize the words on the right. (Caramazza and Hillis (1990) obtained similar results.) The usual explanation is that the subject's attention travels with the object that was initially on the left. So it seems attention is crucial to whether a stimulus is extinguished. Perhaps attention determines binding, and binding determines consciousness (in the presence of the right kind of activation). But anyone who pursues this hypothesis should investigate whether we need the intermediary. (Milner and Goodale (1995) propose that consciousness is ventral stream activity plus attention, and a similar view is advocated by Prinz (2000).)

Rees et al. (2000) make two suggestions as to (in my terms) what X is. One is that the difference between conscious and unconscious activation is a matter of neural synchrony at fine timescales. The finding that ERP components P1 and N1 revealed differences between left-sided "unseen" stimuli and left-sided seen stimuli supports this idea. Driver and Vuilleumier mention preliminary data to the same effect. As they note, ERP is probably more dependent on synchrony than fMRI. Their second suggestion is that the difference between seen and "unseen" stimuli might be a matter of interaction between the classic visual stream and the areas of the parietal and frontal cortex that control attention. Since both proposals concern hypothetical mechanisms of attention, there may be no difference between them and the attention hypothesis.

Whether or not any of these proposals are right, the search for X seems to me the most exciting current direction for consciousness research. The search for X is a diagnostic for the main difference of opinion in Dehaene 2001. Kanwisher and Driver and Vuilleumier and I give it prominence. Dehaene and Naccache, Dennett, and Jack and Shallice do not. (Parvisi and Damasio are engaging different issues.) More on what the sides represent below.

Surprisingly, given her proposal that X is binding, Kanwisher also gives a second answer: "that *awareness of a particular element of perceptual information must entail not just a strong enough neural representation of that information, but also access to that information by most of the rest of the mind/brain*" (p. 16). What's going on here? Why two solutions to one problem? Are these meant as exclusive alternatives? Or are they both supposed to be true?

The answer is found in the rationale given by Kanwisher for the access condition. She appeals to a

common intuition about perceptual awareness (e.g., Baars 1988), if you perceive something, then you can report on it through any output system [in my terms, the information is globally available—NB]. . . . Perceptual information that could be reported through only one output system and not through another just would not fit with most people's concept of a true conscious percept. . . . It seems that a core part of the idea of awareness is that not only effector systems, but indeed most parts of the mind have access to the information in question. (p. 16)

Common intuition gives us access to the meanings of our words and our concepts but not necessarily to what they are concepts of. The rationale for saying that the concept of consciousness does not apply in the absence of global availability is like the rationale for calling a darkening of the skin "sunburn" only if the sun causes it. The identical skin change—spelled out in molecular terms—could fail to fit the concept of sunburn if it had a different cause. The suggestion is that the concept of consciousness only applies to states that are globally accessible.

But that leads to a question: Could there be ventral stream activation plus X (whatever X turns out to be) that is not widely broadcast and therefore does not deserve to be *called* "consciousness" in this "access" sense that Kanwisher is invoking? Kanwisher mentions that the neural synchrony involved in binding might also play a role in broadcasting. But the hypothesis serves to make salient the *opposite* idea. Whatever role synchrony plays in making a representation phenomenal is unlikely to be exactly the same as the role it plays in subserving broadcasting. And even if it is the same, what would prevent the causal path to broadcasting from being blocked? Even if we make it a condition on X that X cause the reliable broadcast of the contents of the activated area, any reliable mechanism can fail or be damaged, in which case we would have activation plus X without broadcasting. If such a thing happened, no doubt one concept of "awareness" (e.g., global accessibility) would not apply to it. But maybe another concept—phenomenality—would.

What is phenomenality? What it is like to have an experience. When you enjoy the taste of wine, you are enjoying gustatory phenomenality. Sensations are the paradigms of phenomenality, but other experiences such as thinking to oneself also are phenomenal.

Any appeal to evidence to back a theory of consciousness depends on a pretheoretical concept of consciousness to supply a starting point. We have now seen two such concepts, phenomenality and global accessibility.[1] The import of this distinction for the current discussion is that the X that makes contents phenomenal might not be the same as the X that makes them accessible. Without being clear about the distinction between phenomenality and accessibility, we will have no hope of ever discovering any difference in the neural bases of these two properties.

Dehaene and Naccache state the global-accessibility view as follows: "An information becomes conscious...if the neural population that represents it is mobilized by top-down attentional amplification into a brain-scale state of coherent activity that involves many neurons distributed throughout the brain. The long-distance connectivity of these "workspace neurons" can, when they are active for a minimal duration, make the information available to a variety of processes including perceptual categorization, long-term memorization, evaluation and intentional action" (p. 2). Or for short, consciousness is being broadcast in a global neuronal workspace. Dennett, advocating a similar view, takes consciousness to be cerebral celebrity, fame in the brain.

The proposal that consciousness is ventral activation plus X (e.g., neural synchrony) is based on a different starting point, a different concept of consciousness than the proposal that consciousness is cerebral celebrity or global neuronal broadcasting. (I will ignore one difference, namely, that the first is a theory of *visual* consciousness and the second is a theory of consciousness *simpliciter*.) We could see the two types of proposals as responses to different questions. The question that motivates the ventral activation plus X type of proposal is: What is the neural basis of phenomenality? The question that motivates the global neuronal broadcasting type of proposal is: What makes neuronal representations available for thought, decision, reporting, and control of action, the main types of access? We can try to force a unity by *postulating* that it is a condition on X that it promote access, but that is a verbal maneuver that only throws smoke over the difference between the concepts and questions. Alternatively, we could, *hypothesize* rather than postulate that X plus ventral stream activation as a matter of fact is the neural basis of global neuronal broadcasting. Note, however, that the neural basis of global neuronal broadcasting might exist but the normal channels of broadcasting nonetheless be blocked or cut, again opening daylight between phenomenality and global accessibility, and showing that we cannot think of the two as one. (An analogy: rest mass and relativistic mass are importantly different from a theoretical point of view despite coinciding for all practical purposes at terrestrial velocities. Failure of coincidence even if rare is theoretical dynamite if what you are after is the scientific nature of consciousness.)

Driver and Vuilleumier suggest that we should see X in part in terms of winner-takes-all functions. But this hypothesis is more of a different way of putting the question than an answer to it if winner-takes-all means "winner gets broadcast."

Many of us have had the experience of suddenly noticing a sound (say, a jackhammer during an intense conversation), at the same time realizing that the sound has been going on for some time even though one was not attending to it. If the subject did have a phenomenal state before the sound was noticed, that state was not broadcast in the global neuronal workspace *until it was noticed*. If this is right, there was a period of *phenomenality without broadcasting*. Of course, this is merely anecdotal evidence. And the appearance of having heard the sound all along may be a false memory. But the starting point for work on consciousness is introspection, and we would be foolish to ignore it.

If we take seriously the idea of phenomenality without access, there is a theoretical option that should be on the table, one that I think is worth investigating—that the X that makes ventral contents accessible is not the same as the X that makes ventral contents phenomenal. Perhaps visual phenomenality is ventral stream activation alone or ventral stream activation plus one of the trio of synchrony, binding, and attention. If visual phenomenality is, say, ventral stream activation plus neural synchrony, then there is a distinct issue of what makes visual phenomenality accessible, which might be another of the items mentioned, say, binding. The idea would be that the claims of extinction patients not to see extinguished stimuli are in a sense wrong—they really do have phenomenal experience of these stimuli without knowing it. A similar issue will arise in the section to follow, in which I will focus on the relation between phenomenality and a *special case* of global accessibility, reflexive or introspective consciousness, in which the subject not only has a phenomenal state but also has another state that is about the phenomenal state, say, a thought to the effect that he has a phenomenal state.

The theory that consciousness is ventral stream activation plus, for example, neural synchrony, and the theory that consciousness is broadcasting in the global neuronal workspace, are instances of the two major rival approaches to consciousness in the philosophical literature, *physicalism* and *functionalism*. The key to the difference is that functionalism identifies consciousness with a role, whereas physicalism identifies consciousness with a physical or biological property that fills or implements or realizes that role in humans. Global availability could be implemented in many ways, but the human biological implementation involves specific electrical and chemical quantities, which, according to the physicalist, are necessary for consciousness. By contrast, functionalism in its pure form is implementation independent. As Dennett says, "The proposed consensual thesis is . . . that this global availability . . . *is*, all by itself, a conscious state" (p. 2). Consciousness is defined as global accessibility, and although its human implementation depends on biochemical properties specific to us, the functionalist says that artificial creatures without our biochemistry could implement the same computational relations. Thus functionalism and physicalism are incompatible doctrines since silicon implementations of the functional organization of consciousness would not share our biological nature. The rationale is expressed in Dennett's statement that "handsome is as handsome does, that matter matters only because of what matter can do" (p. 233). He says that "functionalism in this broad sense is so ubiquitous in science that it is tantamount to a reigning presumption of all science" (p. 8). I disagree. The big question for functionalists is this: "How do you know that it is broadcasting in the global workspace that makes a representation conscious as opposed to something about the *human biological realization* of that broadcasting that makes it conscious?" There is a real issue here with two legitimate sides. The biological point of view is represented here by the hypothesis of ventral stream activation plus, for instance, neural synchrony, which in one natural way of filling in the details requires a specific biological realization.[2]

Thus the search for X is not well defined. It could be the search for what makes ventral contents phenomenal or it could be the search for what makes ventral contents accessible. Presumably, phenomenality itself is *part* of what makes ventral contents accessible, but if there is a real possibility of phenomenality without accessibility, we should expect to find something more that jointly, together with phenomenality, makes for accessibility. When I have given talks on this topic, I am sometimes told that X is global broadcasting itself. But this proposal has to be evaluated in light of the ambiguity just mentioned. If we take the search for X to be the search for what makes ventral contents accessible, to take X to be global broadcasting itself is to take global broadcasting to make ventral contents accessible—a thesis on a par with trumpeting dormitivity as what makes sleeping pills work. On the other hand, if the search for X is the search for what makes ventral contents phenomenal, then saying X is global broadcasting is a substantive claim, but not one anyone can claim to know to be true. My own view is that the other way around is more plausible—that phenomenality greases the wheels of accessibility.

This section has concerned two concepts of consciousness, phenomenality and global accessibility. (I have not brought up the issue of whether global accessibility should really be considered a concept of consciousness, given that it does not require phenomenality.) In the next section, I add a third.

What Are Experiments "about Consciousness" Really about?

Merkle, Smilek, and Eastwood describe Debner and Jacoby's (1994) "exclusion" paradigm, in which subjects follow instructions not to complete a word stem with the end of a masked word just presented to them—only if the word is presented consciously (lightly masked). If the word is presented unconsciously (heavily masked), the subjects are more likely than baseline to disobey the instructions, completing the stem with the very word that was presented.

But what is the "conscious/unconscious" difference in this experiment? Perhaps in the case of the conscious presentation, the subject says to himself something on the order of (though maybe not this explicitly) "I just saw 'reason,' so I'd better complete the stem 'rea' with something else, say 'reader.'" (I am not saying the monologue has to be experienced by the subject on every trial. Perhaps it could be automatized if there are enough trials.) And in the case of the unconscious presentation, there is no internal monologue of this sort. If so, the sense of the "conscious/unconscious" difference that is relevant to this experiment has something to do with the presence or absence of whatever is required for an internal monologue, perhaps something to do with introspection. Tony Jack tells me that many of his subjects in this paradigm complained about how much effort was required to follow the exclusion instructions, further motivating the hypothesis of an internal monologue.

We get some illumination by attention to another experimental paradigm described by Merikle and Joordens (1997), the "false recognition" paradigm of Jacoby and Whitehouse (1989). Subjects are given a study list of 126 words presented for half a second each. They are then presented with a masked word, $word_1$, and an unmasked word, $word_2$. Their task is to report whether $word_2$ was old (i.e., on the study list) or new (not on the study list). The variable was whether $word_1$ was lightly or heavily masked, the former presentations being thought of as "conscious" and the latter as "unconscious." The result, confining our attention just to cases in which $word_1 = word_2$, is that subjects were much more likely to mistakenly report $word_2$ as old when $word_1$ was unconsciously presented than when $word_1$ was consciously presented. (When $word_1$ was consciously presented, they are less likely than baseline to mistakenly report $word_2$ as old; when $word_1$ was unconsciously presented, they were more likely than baseline to err in this way.) As before, the explanation would appear to be that when $word_1$ was consciously presented, the subjects were able to use an internal monologue of the following sort (though perhaps not as explicit): "Here's why 'reason' ($word_2$) looks familiar—because I just saw it (as $word_1$)," thereby explaining away the familiarity of $word_2$. But when $word_1$ was *unconsciously* presented, the subjects were not able to engage in this monologue and consequently mistakenly blamed the familiarity of word$_2$ on its appearance in the original study list.

Any reasoning that can reasonably be attributed to the subject in this paradigm concerns the subject thinking about why a word (word$_2$) *looks familiar* to the subject. For it is only by *explaining away* the familiarity of word$_2$ that the subject is able to decide that word$_2$ was not on the study list. (If you have a hypothesis about what is going on in this experiment that does not appeal to the subject's explaining away the familiarity, I would like to hear it. Of course, I would allow that the monologue could be automatized. I suppose a skeptic might think it has already been automatized even before the experiment starts by natural versions of the experiment.) Thus in the "conscious" case, the subject must have a state that is *about the subject's own perceptual experience* (looking familiar), and so the sense of "conscious" that is relevant here is what might be termed a "reflexive" sense. An experience is conscious in this sense just in case it is the object of another of the subject's states—for example, one has a thought to the effect that one has that experience.[3] The reflexive sense of "consciousness" contrasts with phenomenality, which perhaps attaches to some states, which are not the objects of other mental states. Reflexivity is phenomenality plus something else (reflection), and that opens up the possibility in principle for phenomenality without reflexivity. For example, it is at least conceptually possible for there to be two people in pain, one of whom is introspecting the pain, the other not. (Perhaps infants or animals can have pain but do not introspect it.) The first is reflexively conscious of the pain, but both have phenomenally conscious states, since pain is by its very nature a phenomenally conscious state. Reflexivity (of the sort we are considering) involves phenomenality plus another state, one that is about the phenomenal state. Note that reflexivity might occur but be *unconscious* (in the phenomenal sense). (Perhaps this could occur in blindsight or in a Freudian process.) There is clearly a *conceptual* distinction between phenomenality and reflexivity, even if one or the other does not deserve to be called "consciousness." (Oddly, I find some interlocutors want to bar one, some the other; we would be better off not using words like "consciousness" and "awareness" since there is so little terminological agreement about them. I would rather use "phenomenality" and "reflexivity.") In any case, the salient empirical question is whether phenomenality and reflexivity come to the same thing in the brain.

What is the relation between reflexivity and the notion of global accessibility discussed in the last section? Global accessibility does not logically require reflexivity, since global accessibility only requires access to the response modes that the organism actually has. Perhaps a dog or a cat does not have the capacity for reflection.[4] Reflexivity is a special kind of access, one that requires intellectual resources that may not be available to every being that can have conscious experience.

There is another aspect to both experimental paradigms just discussed, which motivates taking seriously the hypothesis that the reflexively *unconscious* case might possibly be phenomenally *conscious*. In another variant of the exclusion paradigm reported by Debner and Jacoby (1994), heavy masking was replaced by divided attention. Subjects were presented with pairs of words flanked by digits, such as "4reason5," and then given stems consisting of the first three letters of the word ("rea____") to complete. There were two conditions. In the "conscious" condition, they were told to ignore the digits. In the "unconscious" condition, they were told to report the sum of the digits before completing the stem. The results were the same as before, both qualitatively and quantitatively: in the "conscious" condition, the subjects were much more likely than baseline to follow the instructions and complete the stem with a word other than "reason," whereas with "unconscious" presentations, subjects were much more likely than baseline to violate the exclusion instructions, completing the stem with "reason." Merikle and Joordens (2001) report corresponding results for the false-recognition paradigm with divided attention substituted for heavy masking. The added significance of this variant is that it makes one wonder whether there was a fleeting phenomenal consciousness of "reason" as the subject's eyes moved from the 4 to the 5 in "4reason5."

What is the status of the "unconscious" percepts in these experiments? Two theoretical options come to the fore:

1. The "unconscious perceptions" are *both* phenomenally and reflexively unconscious. (In this case, the exclusion and false-recognition paradigms are about consciousness in both senses.)
2. The "unconscious perceptions" are (fleetingly) phenomenally conscious but reflexively unconscious.

A third option, that they are phenomenally unconscious but "reflexively conscious," seems less likely because the reflexive consciousness would be "false"—that is, subjects would have a state "about" a phenomenal state without the phenomenal state itself. That hypothesis would require some extra causal factor that produced the false recognition and would thus be less simple. One argument in favor of the second hypothesis is that subjects in experiments with near-threshold stimuli often report a mess of partial perceptions that they cannot hang onto. Some critics have disparaged the idea of fleeting phenomenal consciousness in this paradigm. But what they owe us is evidence for the first option or else a reason to think it is the default view. A fourth option, that there is both phenomenal and reflexive consciousness, seems doubtful given that it is the very absence of reflexive consciousness that explains the results.

What about the fact, detailed in the first half of Dehaene and Naccache, that reportable phenomenal experience of a stimulus is systematically correlated with the ability to perform a vast variety of operations with the stimulus, while nonreportable stimulus presentation is associated with a limited, encapsulated set of processing options? This certainly is evidence for a correlation between reflexivity and accessibility. But what does it tell us about phenomenality? First, consider whether it provides evidence that phenomenality and reflexivity go together. It would be question begging to take the evidence provided by Dehaene and Naccache as evidence of a correlation of phenomenality itself (as opposed to reports of phenomenality) with reflexivity. For the very issue we are considering is whether some of those cases of limited encapsulated processing might involve a flicker of phenomenality. Of course, the cases of phenomenality that subjects *report* are reflexively conscious. The issue is whether there are *unreported* cases of phenomenality. Broadening our focus, the same point applies to the supposition that this evidence supports a correlation between phenomenality and accessibility. (In addition, though the considerations presented by Dehaene and Naccache do show a correlation between reflexivity and accessibility in alert adult humans, we cannot generalize to infants or dazed adults or nonhumans.)

It may be said that although there is no evidence for preferring option 1 to 2, 1 is preferable on methodological grounds. Here is a way of putting the point: "How are we going to do experiments on consciousness without taking at face value what people say about whether or not they saw something? For example, if we gave up this methodology, we would have to reject blindsight work." But I am not suggesting abandoning that methodology. We can hold onto the methodology because it is the best we have while at the same time figuring out ways to test it. No one promised us that work on consciousness was going to be easy! In the next section, I will suggest a methodological principle that will help in thinking about how to get evidence on this issue.

Let me tie the issue of this section in with that of the last—the issue stemming from the fact that the classic ventral stream can be activated without reports of awareness. There are three options about the ventral stream in, say, extinction that deserve further consideration:

1. The ventral stream is not activated enough for either phenomenality or reflexivity. (As I mentioned, this one seems disconfirmed.)
2. The ventral stream is activated enough for phenomenality, but that is not sufficient for reflexivity (nor, more generally, for accessibility). Something else (one of the Xs mentioned earlier) is required (possibly not exactly the same extra ingredient for both reflexivity and accessibility).
3. There is no phenomenality or reflexive consciousness of the extinguished stimuli, but what is missing is not activation level but something else.

Again, what reason do we have for regarding option 2 (phenomenality without reflexivity) as less likely than option 1 or 3? I suggest none.

Dehaene and Naccache argue that durable and explicit information maintenance is one of the functions of consciousness. One of their items of evidence is Sperling's (1960) experiment on iconic memory. Sperling flashed arrays of letters (e.g., 3 by 3) to subjects for brief periods (e.g., 50 milliseconds). Subjects typically said that they could see all or most of the letters, but they could report only about half of them. Were the subjects right in saying that they could see all the letters? Sperling tried signaling the subjects with a tone. A high tone meant the subject was to report the top row, a medium tone indicated the middle row, and so on. If the tone was given immediately after the stimulus, the subjects could usually get all the letters in the row, whatever row was indicated. But once they had named those letters, they usually could name no others. Why did the information decay? One possibility is that the subjects had *phenomenal* images of all (or almost all) of the letters, and what they lacked was was access consciousness and reflexive consciousness of their identities. For subjects report that they see all the letters (Sperling 1960; Baars 1988, 15), suggesting phenomenal experience of all of them. If so, durable and explicit information maintenance may be *a function of reflexive consciousness or of access consciousness without being a function of phenomenality.*

Dehaene and Naccache suggest that the introspective judgments that fuel my phenomenal/access distinction can be accounted for by postulating three levels of accessibility. The two extremes are I_1, total inaccessibility, and I_3, global accessibility. Level I_2 consists of representations that are connected to the global workspace and that can be ushered into it by the application of attention. They suggest that the letters in the Sperling phenomenon are in I_2 until attention is applied to only some of them, at which point those representations enter I_3.

But where does phenomenality come into this system? One option is that both I_2 and I_3 are phenomenal, in which case I_2 representations are phenomenal without being globally accessible, as I suggested. Another option—the one favored by Dehaene and Naccache—is that only representations in the global workspace (I_3) are phenomenal. Their proposal is geared toward explaining away the *appearance* that the subjects saw each letter, claiming that the source of the subjects' judgment is that they *could potentially* see each letter by focusing on its location. In other words, their proposal is that the subjects mistake potential phenomenality for actual phenomenality, and this yields the appearance of phenomenality without access. Let us call this the Refrigerator Light illusion, the allusion being to the possibility that technologically naive people might have the illusion that the refrigerator light is always on because it is always on when they look.

Note, however, that phenomenally active location is not enough to capture the experience of Sperling's subjects. Subjects do not report seeing an array of blobs at locations that turn into letters when they attend to them. Subjects report seeing an array of letters. Subjects in a related masking experiment (to be discussed below) were able to give judgments of brightness, sharpness, and contrast for letters that they could not report, and they also seemed aware that the stimuli were letters. Speaking as a subject in the Sperling experiment, I am entirely confident that subjects could give such judgments.

The natural way for functionalists such as Dehaene and Naccache to respond would be to say that both the phenomenal and reflexive contents of the subjects in the Sperling experiment include features such as letterlike and features of degrees of sharpness, brightness, and contrast. Thus, they would say, early vision gives subjects experience of these features that are both phenomenally and reflexively conscious, so there is no discrepancy. I share the functionalist view that the subjects have reflexive consciousness of the letterlikeness, sharpness, brightness, and contrast of the letters. My disagreement with them is that I also allow phenomenal consciousness of the shapes themselves without any reflexive consciousness of them. I say the subjects have phenomenal experience of the shapes; the functionalists say the appearance that the subjects have phenomenal experience of shapes is a case of the Refrigerator Light illusion fostered by the fact that the subjects could potentially access the shapes.

At this point, the reader may feel that there is little to choose between the two points of view. But there are two considerations that I believe tip the balance in favor of phenomenality without access. The first is that the functionalist position does not accommodate what it is like for the subjects as well as does phenomenality without access. Speaking as a subject, what it is like for the subjects is experiencing all or most of the letter shapes. An analogy: suppose you are one of a group of subjects who report definitely seeing red. The hypothesis that you and the other subjects have an experience as of red accommodates what it is like for the subjects better than the hypothesis that all of you are under the illusion that you have an experience as of red but are really experiencing green. Postulating an illusion is an extreme measure.

Second and more impressive, there is another hypothesis that applies in this case that also applies in the case of some other phenomena (to be discussed). The functionalist appeal to the Refrigerator Light illusion by contrast applies less well or not at all in these other cases. Thus the phenomenality-without-access hypothesis has the advantage of more generality, whereas the functionalist has the disadvantage of ad hoc postulation.

Let me fill in the phenomenality-without-access idea a bit. One picture is that the subjects in the Sperling experiment are phenomenally conscious of the letter shapes, but do not have the attentional resources to apply letter concepts or even shape concepts of the sort one applies to unfamiliar shapes when one has plenty of time. Phenomenal experience of shapes does not require shape concepts but reflexive consciousness being an intentional state does require shape concepts, concepts that the subjects seem unable to access in these meager attentional circumstances. Another option is that shape concepts are applied but the subjects do not have the attentional resources to harness those concepts in reflexive consciousness, and the neglected representations decay.

Liss (1968) contrasted subjects' responses to brief unmasked stimuli (one to four letters) with their responses to longer lightly masked stimuli. He asked for judgments of brightness, sharpness, and contrast as well as what letters they saw. He found that lightly masked 40-msec stimuli were judged brighter and sharper than unmasked 9-msec stimuli, even though the subjects could report three of four of the letters in the unmasked stimuli and only one of four in the masked cases. He says: "The Ss commented spontaneously that, despite the high contrast of the letters presented under backward masking, they seemed to appear for such brief duration that there was very little time to identify them before the mask appeared. Although letters presented for only 7 msec with no masking appeared weak and fuzzy, their duration seemed longer than letters presented for 70 msec followed by a mask" (p. 329).

What is especially intriguing about the Liss experiment is the suggestion of a double dissociation between phenomenal clarity and the ability to form a conceptual representation. The masked stimuli were relatively high in phenomenal clarity but low in conceptualization, whereas the unmasked stimuli were higher in conceptualization but lower in phenomenal clarity. (There is a third level, perceptual representation, intermediate between phenomenal and conceptual, which this experiment casts little light on.)

As in the Sperling phenomenon, a natural hypothesis is that the subjects were phenomenally conscious of all the masked letter shapes, but could not apply the letter concepts (and perhaps could not apply perceptual representations) required for reflexive consciousness of all of them. Or, as before, perhaps they did briefly apply the letter concepts, but with insufficient attention those conceptual representations dissolved. And as before, there is an alternative functionalist hypothesis—that the contents of both the subjects' phenomenal states and their reflexive states are the same and include the features sharp, high contrast, bright, and letterlike without any specific shape representation. A major difference between Sperling and Liss is that in the Liss experiment, there is no evidence that the subjects were able to access any letter they chose. Sperling asked them to report an indicated row; Liss did not. In the Liss experiment, subjects were trying to grab all the letters they could, and they could get only about one of four when masked. Thus the Refrigerator Light illusion hypothesis applied by Dehaene and Naccache to the Sperling phenomenon gets no foothold in the Liss phenomenon. The subjects' conviction that they saw all four of the masked letters would have to be explained in some other way, and that makes the functionalist position ad hoc compared with the hypothesis of phenomenality without reflexivity. The third and final stage of this argument will be presented in the next section in the discussion of the grain of vision, where I will mention a third experimental paradigm—one that is completely different from that of either Sperling or Liss and that also does not fit the Refrigerator Light illusion hypothesis but does suggest phenomenality without access.

Dennett takes a stand similar to that of Dehaene and Naccache, arguing that potential and actual fame in the brain are all that are needed to handle such phenomena.

The Liss experiment just described suggests phenonomenality without fame or even potential fame. In addition, potential fame without any hint of phenomenality is often reported. Many people have representations of direction (which way is north) and time without (apparently) phenomenality or the illusion of phenomenality. As soon as they ask themselves the question of what time it is or which way is north, they "just know." Before the knowledge popped into mind, it was potentially famous but with no phenomenality or illusion of phenomenality.

Moving back to the main subject of this section, we have seen three concepts of consciousness: phenomenality, reflexive consciousness, and access consciousness. Can we blame the disagreements among our authors on different concepts of consciousness?

This ecumenical stance is especially helpful in reading Parvisi and Damasio and Jack and Shallice. Parvisi and Damasio characterize consciousness as follows: "Core consciousness occurs when the brain's representation devices generate an imaged, nonverbal account of how the organism's own state is affected by the organism's interaction with an object, and when this process leads to the enhancement of the image of the causative object, thus placing the object saliently in a spatial and temporal context" (p. 137). This would be a mysterious account of phenomenality, since the images mentioned in it presumably *already* have phenomenality, making the nonverbal account unnecessary. And the account would make little sense as an account of access consciousness, since a *thought* can be access conscious without involving such images, much less images of a causative object or the enchancement of them. The account is best construed as a characterization of reflexive consciousness, since it emphasizes the knowledge of the subject of how that subject has been affected by an interaction, and thus involves reflection.

Jack and Shallice propose that a conscious process is one in which a supervisory system directly selects one of a number of competing schemata plus its arguments. But they do not give us any evidence against the possibility of either phenomenality or global access without supervisory selection, or supervisory selection without phenomenality or global access. Phenomenality might be a matter of activation plus binding, which, as far as we know, could occur in an organism that does not have a supervisory system, or even in an organism that has a supervisory system, without its activity, or even with its activity, without its selecting one of a number of competing schemata. Access might be a matter of broadcasting in a system that contains no supervisor. Conversely, it would appear at first glance that there could be supervisory selection of the sort they suggest without phenomenality or global access. They do give evidence that supervisory selection among schemata does lead to encoding of specific episodes, but they do not argue that this encoding requires either phenomenality or global accessibility. If Jack and Shallice were advancing a theory of phenomenality or of access consciousness, there would be a heavy burden on them to justify it, a burden that they give no hint of acknowledging. But as a theory of reflexive consciousness it makes much more sense. Reflexive consciousness involves one aspect of the mind monitoring another aspect, like a sensory state, so in one sense of "supervisory," reflexive consciousness necessarily involves a supervisory system. (They make a similar point.) Jack and Shallice would still owe us an account of why there cannot be reflexive consciousness where the supervisory system focuses on a sensory state without choosing among competing schemata. But at least with reflexive consciousness they are in the right ballpark.

Jack and Shallice may be skeptical about the global workplace account. Shallice (1975) argued that there is reason to think that there is more than one "workplace" for different functions, and no global one. He was criticizing Atkinson and Shiffrin's (1971) "idea that in some sense consciousness can be 'equated' with the short-term store" (Shallice 1975, 270). And Jack and Shallice note that it is unlikely that representational codes in different modules match. But the version of the global-workspace model advocated by Dehaene and Naccache does not extend to broadcasting within modules. They are not committed to the idea that conscious experiences of, say, color are available to the phonology module, nor do Jack and Shallice suggest any such thing.

Perhaps Jack and Shallice think that representations that have been selected by a supervisory system of a certain sort are as a matter of fact globally accessible in an appropriately qualified sense, but that does not address the issue of why their definition characterizes a *necessary* condition for global accessibility (of an appropriately limited sort). Could a machine be made that has globally accessible representations that are not the result of selection of competing schemata by a supervisory system? They do not say why not.

Though Jack and Shallice give an account that makes sense as a theory of reflexive consciousness (and maybe as an account of access consciousness restricted to humans), they have ambitions for its application to any process that is *phenomenally* the same. They say that "tasks involving Type-C processes should either actually require the subject to make an introspective judgment, or be phenomenologically similar to tasks that do" (p. 15) Also, Dehaene and Naccache make it clear that they see their stance as applying to (as I would put it) phenomenality. Just after the words quoted earlier, they say that "we postulate that this global availability of information through the workspace is what we subjectively experience as a conscious state" (p. 1). Someone (like myself) who believes in phenomenality as distinct from its function would naturally think that phenomenality *causes* the global availability of information, not that phenomenality *is* the global availability of information (although, given our ignorance about the fundamental nature of phenomenality, I am not prepared to rule that option out a priori). In sum, these theories are best seen as theories of reflexivity or global accessibility rather than as theories of phenomenality, but their advocates claim phenomenality nevertheless.

Defining Reflexivity

Rosenthal (1997) defines reflexive consciousness as follows: S is a reflexively conscious state of mine ↔ S is accompanied by a thought—arrived at noninferentially and nonobservationally—to the effect that I am in S. He offers this "higher order thought" (HOT) theory as a theory of phenomenal consciousness. It is obvious that phenomenal consciousness without HOT and HOT without phenomenal consciousness are both *conceptually* possible. For example, perhaps dogs and infants have phenomenally conscious pains without higher-order thoughts about them. For the converse case, imagine that by biofeedback and neural imaging techniques of the distant future, I learn to detect the state in myself of having the Freudian unconscious thought that it would be nice to kill my father and marry my mother. People can learn to lower blood pressure via biofeedback. Perhaps they could learn to detect brain states. I could come to know—noninferentially and nonobservationally—that I have this Freudian thought even though the thought is not phenomenally conscious. Since there are conceptually possible counterexamples in both directions, the issue is the one discussed above of whether reflexivity and phenomenality come to the same thing in the brain.

If there are no actual counterexamples, the question arises of why. Is it supposed to be a basic law of nature that phenomenality and reflexivity co-occur? That would be a very adventurous claim. But if it is only a fact about us, then there must be a mechanism that explains the correlation, as the fact that both heat and electricity are carried by free electrons explains the correlation of electrical and thermal conductivity. But any mechanism breaks down under extreme conditions, as does the correlation of electrical and thermal conductivity at extremely high temperatures. So the correlation between phenomenality and reflexivity would break down too, showing that reflexivity does not yield the basic scientific nature of phenomenality.

Rosenthal's definition of reflexivity has a number of ad hoc features. "Nonobservationally" is required to rule out (for example) a case in which I know about a thought I have repressed by observing my own behavior. "Noninferentially" is needed to avoid a somewhat different case in which I appreciate (nonobservationally) my own pain and infer a repressed thought from it. Further, Rosenthal's definition involves a stipulation that the possessor of the reflexively conscious state is the same as the thinker of the thought—otherwise my thinking about your pain would make it a conscious pain. All these ad hoc features can be eliminated by moving to the following definition of reflexivity: S is a reflexively conscious state ↔ S is phenomenally presented in a thought about S. This definition uses the notion of phenomenality, but this is no disadvantage unless there is no such thing apart from reflexivity itself. The new definition of reflexivity, requiring phenomenality as it does, has the additional advantage of making it clear that reflexivity is a kind of *consciousness*. (See Burge's 1997 critique of my definition of access consciousness as constituting a kind of consciousness.)

Is It Impossible in Principle to Empirically Distinguish Phenomenality from Reflexivity?

Some objectors think that the distinction between phenomenality and reflexivity has no real empirical significance. Here is a version of that view: "In order to ascertain empirically whether a phenomenal state is present or absent or what its content is, we require the subject's testimony. But when a subject says that he did or did not see something, or that his state did or did not have a certain content, he is exhibiting presence or absence of the relevant reflexive consciousness too. So how can there ever be an empirical wedge between phenomenality and reflexivity or between phenomenal content and reflexive content?" Further, if the contents of phenomenal states are nonconceptual, how can we ever find out what they are by attention to what a subject says? (A similar but more difficult issue arises about the relation between phenomenality and global accessibility that I will not have the space to discuss.)

Here are some considerations that should loosen the grip of this pessimistic point of view. First, consider the common experience, mentioned earlier, of suddenly noticing that one has been hearing a noise for some time. Testimony at time t_2 can be evidence for phenomenality at time t_1 even though the subject did not notice the phenomenal experience at time t_1. That is, a phenomenal state does not have to be accompanied *simultaneously* by a reflection on it for there to be testimony about it. How do we know there wasn't also a brief flash of reflexivity about the phenomenality at t_1? There is no reason to believe there is any principled problem of discovering such a thing, since reflexivity is a kind of thought. (For example, if we discover a language-of-thought hypothesis to characterize thought in other circumstances, we could apply it here.)

Second, note that reflexivity involves phenomenality plus more—reflection on the phenomenality.[5] If this is right, we can see that whatever processes produce the reflection will—like all physical processes—sometimes misfire and we will have phenomenality without reflexivity. The prior probability then, of phenomenality without reflexivity is considerable. Jack and Shallice may think otherwise—their theory certainly presupposes otherwise—but they do not present a single empirical result that points in this direction. To the extent that they supply a case against phenomenality without reflexivity, it is entirely *philosophical*.

We can guess that phenomenality without reflexivity will happen when the machinery of reflection is damped down—perhaps in infants whose reflection machinery is undeveloped, in adults where it is permanently or temporarily damaged, or in animals where it is minimal to begin with. When we know that something very likely occurs and we have an idea of what makes it occur, we should not be pessimistic about our ability to find a reliable way of experimentally exploring it.

The best way to silence the pessimistic point of view is to canvas some empirical approaches. One line of evidence emerges from work by Cavanagh and his colleagues

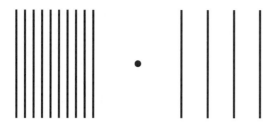

Figure 15.1
Fixate on the dot at the center and attend to the lines on the right, with the page held at arm's length. (Distance is not very important with this display.) Subjects are capable of "stepping" (described in the text) from one line to another on the right (though with trouble on line 3) but not on the left. From Cavanagh, He, and Intriligator 1998.

that shows that the resolution of visual attention is five to ten times coarser than the resolution of vision itself (Cavanagh, He, and Intriligator 1998; He, Cavanagh, and Intriligator 1996; Intriligator and Cavanagh, forthcoming). The grain of visual attention is about 5–10 arc min (1 arc min is a sixtieth of a degree) at the fovea (the densest area of the retina), whereas the grain of vision is about 1 arc min at the fovea. What is meant by "grain" and "resolution"? In the experiments by Cavanagh and his colleagues, the resolution of vision is measured by such procedures as whether a subject can verbally distinguish a set of lines from a uniform gray field, and whether the subject can report the orientation of the lines. The resolution of visual attention can be measured by whether the subject can count the items to be resolved, but a better measure is a "stepping" procedure that is illustrated in figure 15.1. First, fixate on the dot in the middle. (This is necessary to avoid eye movements, and consequent complication in interpretation; whether subjects succeed in fixating can be checked with eye-tracking devices.) One line lights up; the subject is asked to focus on that one, then move, for example, one to the right, another to the right, one to the left, one to the right. Success is determined by checking which line the subject is focused on at the end. In the set of four lines on the right in figure 15.1, most subjects can step through the first, second, and fourth lines from the left, but the third tends to cause trouble. Most subjects cannot step through the lines on the left even though the lines on the left are visually resolvable. Attentional resolution can also be measured by a tracking task developed by Pylyshyn and his colleagues (Pylyshyn and Storm 1988).

How are these findings relevant to the distinction between phenomenality and reflexivity? Landolt (1891)—who apparently was the first to publish an observation of the phenomenon—asked observers to count finely spaced dots or stripes. As Intriligator and Cavanagh (forthcoming) note, Landolt's observers could not count the stripes or dots if their spacing was less than about 5 arc min, even though they could still see them. Landolt says, "You get to a point where you can no longer count them at all, even though they remain perfectly and distinctly visible."[6] (Landolt's subjects looked right at them instead of fixating to a single spot to the side, but it turns out that that the eye movements did not matter much for his stimuli.) The individual lines remain "purely and distinctly visible"—in my terms, one is phenomenally conscious of them. And one can say roughly how many there are. But, to the extent that one cannot attend to them, one cannot apply concepts to them individually—for example, shape concepts. True, one has an impression of lines of a certain length (as on the left of figure 15.1), but to the extent that one cannot attend to individual items, one cannot distinguish the shape of one from another. If the items are gratings rather than lines, one cannot say what the orientation is; if they are letters, one can see that they are letters but not which letters they are. My suggestion is the same as the one I made in the case of Sperling and Liss, namely, that the subjects may have phenomenal awareness of the individual shapes without the attentional resources to apply shape concepts to them and thus without reflexive awareness of them. (This may be because they cannot apply perceptual representations and perceptual representations are necessary for conceptual representations.) Or alternatively, they may apply shape concepts to them but lack the attentional resources to harness those concepts in reflexive states. In either case we would have phenomenality without reflexivity.

There is an alternative hypothesis—that the contents of both the subject's phenomenal states and their reflexive states are the same and include the feature "letterlike" without any specific shape. Cavanagh speaks of seeing a "texture." There is a reason for preferring my sort of hypothesis, namely, that subjects find the individual items "perfectly and distinctly visible" in Landolt's phrase. (Look at the figure. Doesn't it seem to you that you see each line, rather than just a texture of a sort one has learned is produced by lines?) But perhaps subjects are under an illusion of some sort? Maybe, but if so, it is not the same as the "Refrigerator Light" illusion postulated by Dehaene and Naccache in the case of the Sperling phenomenon. You will recall that they supposed that the sense of subjects in the Sperling experiment that they saw all the letters derived from the fact that they could attend to any small number of their locations and be aware of the identity of the letter. But there is no such thing here. No matter how hard subjects try, they cannot ascertain the identity of stimuli that are crowded to the point of being below the grain of attention. This hypothesis, then, has more generality than the Refrigerator Light illusion hypothesis of Dehaene and Naccache.

Interestingly, adaptation to the orientation of gratings that the subject cannot report affects the detection of other gratings as much as uncrowded gratings whose orientation the subjects can report. He, Cavanagh, and Intriligator (1996) note that V1 is the first site of orientation processing, so the attentional effect of crowding must occur later in processing than V1. He and colleagues conclude that activation of neurons in

V1 is "insufficient for conscious perception" (p. 335), but although this result shows V1 is insufficient for reflexive consciousness, it is less effective in showing that activation in V1 is insufficient for phenomenality (Block 1996). Do not get me wrong. I am not saying activation in V1 *is* sufficient for phenomenality. I am making a logical point about comparative strength of evidence, the upshot of which is that an empirical wedge between phenomenality and reflexivity is possible. More generally, I allow that it could be discovered that, contrary to what I have been arguing, one is phenomenally aware of exactly the same features that one is reflexively aware of. I do not say that there is strong evidence for phenomenality without reflexivity. My point is that for stimuli that are below the level of attentional resolution but above the level of visual resolution, there is a better case for phenomenal awareness than for reflexive awareness.

If my picture of the attentional phenomena is accepted, it can also avoid the conclusion that many have drawn from the change-blindness and inattentional-blindness literature (Simons 2000), that there is an "illusion" of rich visual awareness of the world. As Cavanagh (1999) puts it, "But what of our feeling that we piece together our world in multiple glances, building up a reasonably complete model of a stable world around us? This concept of a rich model of the world does not hold up." Vision, he says gives us a *"false* sense of 'knowing what is out there.'" (This view, a version of the Refrigerator Light hypothesis, is strongly defended in O'Regan 1992.) We can avoid the idea that vision creates an illusion if our perception of the world is phenomenally rich but attentively sparse. That is, our phenomenal impression is accurate, but only the attended aspects of it are available for the tasks tapped in the change-blindness literature.[7]

Turning to something completely different. I will mention an old, somewhat anecdotal result, not because it is itself serious evidence for anything, but because it illustrates some methodological points.

I have in mind the strange phenomenon of aerodontalgia (Melzack and Wall 1988; Nathan 1985). Two American dentists in Britain in World War II noticed that pilots who went up in the unpressurized planes of the time often complained of pains that seemed to be recreations of pains of previous dental work, even though the dental work had been done under anesthesia. They hypothesized that the recreated pains all derived from dental work done under general anesthesia rather than local anesthesia and they put this hypothesis to the test by doing extractions under combinations of local and general anesthesia. The result was that they only got recreated pains for general anesthesia. For example, if they gave a pilot general anesthesia and also local anesthetic on the left side and then extracted teeth from both sides, they got recreated pains from the right side only. (They used a substitute for the unpressurized planes—stimulation of the nasal mucosa—since it turned out that the effect of the unpressurized cabins was mediated by sinus stimulation.)

My point is *not* that this is serious evidence for phenomenal states under general anesthesia. This is old work that was not done by behavioral scientists. I do not know of any replication. Further, even if replicated, there would be a problem since maybe what happened was that traces were laid down under general anesthesia without any phenomenal event, and then those traces later produced a phenomenal event. This would be representation of pain under general anesthesia rather than pain under general anesthesia. My points about this experiment are these:

1. Though the evidence is flawed, it is better evidence for phenomenality under general anesthesia than it is for reflexive consciousness under general anesthesia, since a reflexively conscious pain is a phenomenal event (pain is necessarily phenomenal) plus something else—reflection on it. The reflection is a species of thought, and there is reason to believe that anesthetic gets in the way of thought. So we are on better ground postulating a pain under general anesthesia than a pain plus reflection on it.

2. The methodological point is that *the reflexively conscious second pain can be evidence for the first pain even though the first pain isn't reflexively conscious—we don't need the subject's testimony about the first pain itself.* It is this feature of the aerodontalgia case that makes it methodologically interesting despite the obvious flaws and despite the fact that it is not in itself serious evidence for phenomenality without reflexivity. To see the interest of this methodological item, consider the objection "If you think of phenomenality as a purely subjective phenomenon—something only the subject can tell you about—how can you possibly get evidence for phenomenality that the subject can't report?" Answer: the sense of subjectivity in the objection is faulty. Subjectivity does not entail that only the subject can tell us about it.

Objection: "But you have admitted that this is far from conclusive evidence for phenomenality without reflexivity. Doesn't the principled problem arise again when you try to go from highly flawed evidence of the sort you are presenting to conclusive evidence of the sort the scientific community would be compelled to believe? How could we ever get more than a glimmer of evidence for phenomenality without reflexivity?" The answer is that if we can get many convergent though flawed sources of evidence—so long as the flaws are of different sorts and uncorrelated—we will have a convincing case. (Note that I am not saying that a lot of weak evidence adds up to strong evidence.) For example, there are different methods of dating rocks and artifacts based on isotopes. Those based on counting the products of radioactive decay, "daughter" isotopes (e.g., potassium-argon dating), have different flaws from those based on counting decay of the parent substance (e.g., carbon-14 dating), and other methods such as the fission-track method have still different flaws, but if a number of measures with different flaws agree, that is very convincing.

Conclusion

The papers in Dehaene 2001 deploy three different concepts of consciousness:

1. Phenomenality experience. This is the concept of consciousness that is most directly the subject of the hypothesis discussed by Driver and Vuilleumier and Kanwisher that visual consciousness is ventral stream activation plus X.

2. Access consciousness global accessibility. This is the concept of consciousness most directly related to Dehaene and Naccache's account of consciousness as being broadcast in a global neuronal workspace and Dennett's account of consciousness as cerebral celebrity. Since this concept of consciousness does not require phenomenality, there is some doubt as to whether it is a full-fledged concept of consciousness. (See Burge 1997.)

3. Reflexive consciousness a special kind of access; a state is introspectively conscious just in case (roughly) it is the object of another state. Or alternatively (and better in my view) a state S is reflexively consciousness just in case it is phenomenally presented in a thought about S. This is the concept of consciousness most clearly involved in reasoning about the false-recognition and exclusion experiments (Merikle, Smilek, and Eastwood) and is most appropriate to Jack and Shallice.

Some of the disagreements among the contributors to the volume can be explained by interpreting them as talking about different things.

Are the three kinds of consciousness aspects of a single thing? There are a number of ways of interpreting this question. One is the sense of aspects of a single thing in which the solid, liquid, and gaseous phase are aspects of a single substance. In this sense, being an aspect of a single thing requires that for any solid substance there be some conditions under which it would be gaseous. In this sense, I think it is a wide-open empirical question whether phenomenality and access consciousness are aspects of a single thing. But I suspect that it is less likely that reflexivity can be included with these two. If a lizard has phenomenality, must there be conditions under which it would have reflexive consciousness of that phenomenality? If you are doubtful, then you are doubtful whether all three kinds of consciousness are aspects of a single thing.[8]

Notes

This is a somewhat expanded and revised version of a paper that appeared in *Cognition* 79: 1–2, April 2001. It is a commentary on all the papers in a special issue of that journal on the state of the art in the neuroscience of consciousness. (The special issue is available as a book edited by Stan Dehaene and published by MIT Press; see Dehaene 2001.) Two philosophers—Dan Dennett and I—were asked to comment on all the scientists' papers. (We both made some comments on each others' papers as well.) Dennett's paper is available at http://ase.tufts.edu/cogstud/papers/

cognition.fin.htm. The volume of *Cognition* is on the web and available on the NYU library site by going to http://www.nyu.edu/library/bobst/research/sci/ej_c.htm, clicking on "Cognition," and then going to 79, 1–2. Other library sites will also have access to this journal.

1. Block 1997 says a representation is access conscious if it is poised for global control. Block 1995 adopts a more cumbersome formulation that lists various types of control. (The advantage of the cumbersome formulation is that it avoids ascribing consciousness to simple devices that nonetheless have global control in the sense of control over all response systems.) Since phenomenal consciousness is best thought of as an occurrence, *broadcast* for global control would be better. (See Burge 1997, which criticizes Block 1995.)

2. The problem for functionalists could be put like this: the specifically human realization of global availability may be necessary to consciousness—other realizations of global availability being "ersatz" realizations. Dennett responds to this point by arguing in effect that we can preserve functionalism by simply characterizing global availability in a more detailed way—at the level of biochemistry. But the utility of this technique runs out as one descends the hierarchy of sciences, because the lowest level of all, that of basic-level physics, is vulnerable to the same point. Putting the point for simplicity in terms of the physics of forty years ago, the causal role of electrons is the same as that of antielectrons. If you formulate a functional role for an electron, an antielectron will realize it. Thus an antielectron is an ersatz realizer of the functional definition of *electron*. Physics is characterized by symmetries that allow ersatz realizations.

For an introduction to issues about functionalism, the reader could consult the entries on consciousness or on functionalism in any of the truly excellent philosophy reference works that have been published in the last five years: *The Routledge Encyclopedia of Philosophy, The Oxford Companion to Philosophy, The Cambridge Companion to Philosophy, Blackwell's Companion to the Philosophy of Mind,* or the supplement to Macmillan's *The Encyclopedia of Philosophy.*

3. This definition is oversimple but complications will not matter here.

4. To avoid overattributing access consciousness, we have to specify the machinery instead of using the catchall "global." For a specific brain architecture that provides flexibility in the choices of devices the conscious information is passed to, see Dehaene, Kerszberg, and Changeux 1998.

5. I am ignoring the possibility that reflexivity might occur without the experience it is normally about.

6. "On arrive à un point où l'on ne peut plus les compter d'aucune façon, alors qu'ils demeurent encore parfaitement et distinctement visibles" (p. 385).

7. Wolfe (1999) advocates "inattentional amnesia" rather than inattentional blindness, which is close to the "inattentional inaccessibility" view I am advocating. Simons (2000) quotes Wolfe as suggesting that we might think of subjects' failure to notice in the change- and inattentional-blindness literature as "inattentional agnosia." (Agnosia is a centrally caused failure to achieve knowledge on the basis of sensation.) Assuming that agnosia involves failure of application of concepts to stimuli or failure to harness such concepts in the service of knowledge, there is another overlap between my view and Wolfe's.

8. I am grateful to Tyler Burge, Susan Carey, Nancy Kanwisher, Georges Rey, and Jesse Prinz for comments on an earlier version, and I am especially grateful to Stan Dehaene and Tony Jack for many rounds of debate on key issues on which we disagree. The paper has been much improved as a result of these controversies.

References

Atkinson, R. C., and Shiffrin, R. M. 1971. The control of short-term memory. *Scientific American* 225: 82–90.

Baars, B. J. 1988. *A Cognitive Theory of Consciousness*. Cambridge: Cambridge University Press.

Block, Ned. 1995. On a confusion about a function of consciousness. *Behavioral and Brain Sciences* 18(2): 1995. Reprinted in N. Block, O. Flanagan, and G. Güzeldere, eds., *The Nature of Consciousness: Philosophical Debates*. Cambridge, MA: MIT Press.

Block, Ned. 1996, October. How can we find the neural correlate of consciousness? *Trends in Neuroscience* 19: 456–459.

Block, Ned. 1997. Biology vs. computation in the study of consciousness. *Behavioral and Brain Sciences* 20: 1.

Burge, Tyler. 1997. Two kinds of consciousness. In N. Block, O. Flanagan, and G. Güzeldere, eds., *The Nature of Consciousness: Philosophical Debates*. Cambridge, MA: MIT Press.

Caramazza, A., and Hillis, A. E. 1990. Levels of representation, coordinate frames, and unilateral neglect. *Cognitive Neuropsychology* 7(5–6): 391–445.

Cavanagh, P. 1999. Attention: Exporting vision to the mind. In C. Taddei-Ferretti and C. Musio, eds., *Neuronal Basis and Psychological Aspects of Consciousness*, 129–143. Singapore: World Scientific.

Cavanagh, P., He, S., and Intriligator, J. 1999. Attentional resolution: The grain and locus of visual awareness. In C. Taddei-Ferretti and C. Musio, eds., *Neuronal Basis and Psychological Aspects of Consciousness*. Singapore: World Scientific.

Debner, J. A., and Jacoby, L. L. 1994. Unconscious perception: Attention, awareness, and control. *Journal of Experimental Psychology: Learning, Memory and Cognition* 20: 304–317.

DeGelder, B., Vroomen, J., Pourtois, G., and Weiskrantz, L. 1999. Non-conscious recognition of affect in the absence of striate cortex. *NeuroReport* 10: 3759–3763.

Dehaene, S., ed. 2001. *The Cognitive Neuroscience of Consciousness*. Cambridge, MA: MIT Press.

Dehaene, S. 2001. Towards a cognitive neuroscience of consciousness: Basic evidence and a workspace framework. In Dehaene 2001, 1–37.

Dehaene, S., Kerszberg, M., and Changeux, J. P. 1998. A neuronal model of a global workspace in effortful cognitive tasks. *Proceedings of the National Academy of Sciences USA* 95: 14529–14534.

Dennett, D. 2001. Are we explaining consciousness yet? In Dehaene 2001, 221–237.

Driver, J., and Vuilleumier, 2001. Perceptual awareness and its loss in unilateral neglect and extinction. In Dehaene 2001, 39–88.

Friedman-Hill, S., Robertson, L., and Treisman, A. 1995, August 11. Parietal contributions to visual feature binding: Evidence from a patient with bilateral lesions. *Science* 269: 853–855.

He, Sheng, Cavanagh, Patrick, and Intriligator, James. 1996. Attentional resolution and the locus of visual awareness. *Nature* 383: 334–337.

Intriligator, James, and Cavanagh, Patrick. Forthcoming. The spatial resolution of visual attention. *Cognitive Psychology* 43: 171–216.

Jack, A., and Shallice, T. 2001. Introspective physicalism as an approach to the science of consciousness. In Dehaene 2001, 161–196.

Jacoby, L. L., and Whitehouse, K. 1989. An illusion of memory: False recognition influenced by unconscious perception. *Journal of Experimental Psychology: General* 118: 126–135.

Kanwisher, N. 2001. Neural events and perceptual awareness. In Dehaene 2001, 89–113.

Kentridge, R. W., Heywood, C. A., and Weiskrantz, L. 1999. Attention without awareness in blindsight. *Proceedings of the Royal Society of London. Series B, Biological Sciences* 266(1430): 1805–1811.

Landolt, E. 1891. Nouvelles recherches sur la physiologie des mouvements des yeux. *Archives d'ophthalmologie* 11: 385–395.

Liss, P. 1968. Does backward masking by visual noise stop stimulus processing? *Perception and Psychophysics* 4: 328–330.

Lumer, Erik, and Rees, Geraint. 1999. Covariation of activity in visual and prefrontal cortex associated with subjective visual perception. *Proceedings of the National Academy of Sciences* 96: 1669–1673.

McGlinchey-Berroth, R., Milberg, W. P., Verfaellie, M., Alexander, M., and Kilduff, P. 1993. Semantic priming in the neglected field: Evidence from a lexical decision task. *Cognitive Neuropsychology* 10: 79–108.

Melzack, R., and Wall, P. 1988. *The Challenge of Pain*. 2nd ed. New York: Penguin.

Merikle, Philip, and Joordens, Steve. 1997. Parallels between perception without attention and perception without awareness. *Consciousness and Cognition* 6: 219–236.

Merikle, Philip, Smilek, Daniel, and Eastwood, John. 2001. Perception without awareness: Perspectives from cognitive psychology. In Dehaene 2001, 115–134.

Milner, A. D., and Goodale, M. A. 1995. *The Visual Brain in Action*. Oxford: Oxford University Press.

Nathan, P. 1985. Pain and nociception in the clinical context. *Philosophical Transactions of the Royal Society of London*, Series B 308: 219–226.

O'Regan, J. K. 1992. Solving the "real" mysteries of visual perception: The world as an outside memory. *Canadian Journal of Psychology* 46: 461–488.

Parvisi, J., and Damasio, A. 2001. Consciousness and the brainstem. In Dehaene 2001, 135–160.

Prinz, J. J. 2000. A neurofunctional theory of visual consciousness. *Consciousness and Cognition* 9(2): 243–259.

Pylyshyn, Z., and Storm, R. 1988. Tracking multiple independent targets: Evidence for a parallel tracking mechanism. *Spatial Vision* 3: 179–197.

Rees, Geraint, Wojciulik, Ewa, Clarke, Karen, Husain, Masud, Frith, Chris, and Driver, Jon. 2000. Unconscious activation of visual cortex in the damaged right hemisphere of a parietal patient with extinction. *Brain* 123: 1624–1633.

Shallice, Tim. 1975. On the contents of primary memory. In P. M. A. Rabbit and S. Dornic, eds., *Attention and Performance V*. London: Academic Press.

Simons, Daniel. 2000. Attentional capture and inattentional blindness. *Trends in Cognitive Science* 4(4): 147–155.

Sperling, George. 1960. The information available in brief visual presentations. *Psychological Monographs* 74(11): 1–29.

Tipper, S. P., and Behrman, M. 1996. Object-centered not scene-based visual neglect. *Journal of Experimental Psychology: Human Perception and Performance* 22(5): 1261–1278.

Wojciulik, E., and Kanwisher, N. 1998. Implicit visual attribute binding following bilateral parietal damage. *Visual Cognition* 5: 157–181.

Wolfe, J. M. 1999. Inattentional amnesia. In V. Coltheart, ed., *Fleeting Memories*. Cambridge, MA: MIT Press.

If a sensory brain state plays an unusual functional role, does the phenomenology go with the role or the brain state? If the phenomenology goes with the functional role, that supports functionalism, which is the view that phenomenology just *is* the role. If it goes with the brain state, that supports physicalism, which is the view that phenomenology is what *realizes* or implements the role. I agree with Gray [1] as against Noë and Hurley [2] that the interest of the issues discussed by Hurley and Noë [3] lies in their relevance to the functionalism/physicalism debate. However, I do not think that Hurley and Noë have made it plausible that there are *any* cases in which phenomenology goes with role when role and realizer conflict.

Gray [1] and Hurley and Noë [2, 3] suppose that in Braille, visual cortex serves a tactile role and that the phenomenology is tactile too—so phenomenology goes with role rather than realizer. Objections: First, proficient Braille readers have an enlarged somatosensory representation for the reading finger; and zapping the somatosensory cortex of blind subjects with TMS (transcranial magnetic stimulation) interferes with Braille reading [4, 5]. Hence, whatever tactile phenomenology there is in Braille may be a result of somatosensory activation rather than 'visual' activation.

Second, the talk of 'visual' (or perhaps any modality-specific) cortex that Hurley and Noë depend on is seeming increasingly problematic. Many, perhaps most so-called "visual" areas are better thought of as multimodal (or multisensory) and spatial rather than specifically visual. An fMRI study [6] on sighted subjects found "visual" activation for tactile object recognition. Many different methodologies have located tactile shape recognition in the lateral occipital complex (a "visual" area), including a report of one patient who had both visual and tactile agnosia upon injury in the left occipital cortex [7]. Tactile motion and visual motion appear to activate the same areas in macaques (viz, area MT) [7]. There is also evidence that superior occipital (i.e., "visual") activation is necessary for some tactile discriminations from an experimental paradigm [7, 8] that contrasted two kinds of tactile judgments of a grating: spacing width and orientation. When TMS was applied to occipital cortex, sighted subjects could still feel the grating and were unimpaired in detecting spacing, but they were impaired in recognition of orientation and also said they were unsure of orientation. However, when TMS was applied to primary somatosensory cortex, both texture and orientation discrimination were reduced to chance, and subjects reported being unable to experience the pattern of the grating. Primary (striate) "visual" cortex is often not activated in tactile tasks, but Hurley and Noë would be on thin ice if they claimed that primary visual cortex underlies tactile phenomenology in blind subjects, because it is doubtful that primary visual cortex is part of the neural correlate of visual phenomenology in sighted subjects [9].

Finally, one has to wonder what the basis is for Hurley's and Noë's claim that the phenomenology of Braille is exclusively tactile—might it also be spatial or visual?

Hurley and Noë see tactile–visual substitution systems (TVSS) as involving tactile brain areas playing a visual role—and with visual phenomenology. Again, the brain, role and phenomenology claims are all problematic. First, there is a submitted report (R. Kupers *et al.*) from a PET study of 'visual' activation in TVSS. Second, there is doubt as to whether the phenomenology of TVSS is exclusively visual. Reports of TVSS subjects sound as much spatial as visual (although reports of a similar auditory substitution system sound more visual). For example, in the paper by Bach-y-Rita cited in Noë and Hurley [10], he says the subjects "reported experiencing the image in space." He describes visual means of analysis (e.g., parallax) but *not* visual phenomenology. Further, whatever visual reports there are from previously sighted subjects might issue from visual imagery using unmodified visual areas.

Hurley and Noë [2] appear to presuppose that visual phenomenology is shown by the *spatial* function of TVSS—e.g. that tactile "size" increases as you approach. But nonvisual senses might be spatial in the same way, e.g., bat sonar. More significantly, it would be question-begging to appeal to a functional analysis of the concept of vision to support functionalism. Third, there are persistent reports in this literature of tactile sensation. For example, the same Bach-y-Rita paper [10] says "Even during task performance with the sensory system, the subject can perceive purely tactile sensations when asked to concentrate on these sensations."

Perhaps TVSS is a case of spatial perception via tactile sensation (maybe Braille is too). One intriguing possibility is that there may be an independent phenomenology both to sensation (grounded in brain state) and to perception (grounded in the function of that brain state). Who knows—maybe *both* traditional functionalism and physicalism will turn out to be partially true!

I have argued for recasting the debate between functionalism and physicalism in terms of a notion of functional role that should not be modified ad hoc, as is typical with traditional philosophical notions of functional role [11]. I have spelled out the non-ad-hoc role as global access, whereas Hurley and Noë choose sensorimotor contingencies. We agree, I hope, in construing the functionalism/physicalism debate in empirically responsive terms.

Note

Reprinted from *Trends in Cognitive Sciences* 7 (7): 285–286, July 2003.

References

1. Gray, J. (2003) How are qualia coupled to functions? *Trends Cogn. Sci.*, 7 (DOI: 10.1016/S1364-6613(02)02088-0)

2. Noë, A. and Hurley, S. L. (2003) The deferential brain in action: response to Jeffrey Gray. *Trends Cogn. Sci.*, 7 (DOI: 10.1016/S1364-6613(02)02097-1)

3. Hurley, S. L. and Noë, A. (2003) Neural plasticity and consciousness. *Biol. Philos.* 18, 131–168

4. Sadato, N. *et al.* (1998) Neural networks for Braille reading by the blind. *Brain* 121, 1213–1229

5. Sathian, K. and Zangaladze, A. (2001) Feeling with the mind's eye: the role of visual imagery in tactile perception. *Optometry Vis. Sci.* 78, 276–281

6. Deibert, E. *et al.* (1999) Neural pathways in tactile object recognition. *Neurology* 52, 1413–1417

7. Sathian, K. *et al.* (2004) Visual cortical involvement in normal tactile perception. In *The Handbook of Multisensory Processes* (Calvert, G. *et al.*, eds), MIT Press

8. Zangaladze, A. *et al.* (1999) Involvement of visual cortex in tactile discrimination of orientation. *Nature* 401, 587–590

9. Crick, F. and Koch, C. (1995) Are we aware of neural activity in primary visual cortex? *Nature* 375, 121–123

10. Bach-y-Rita, P. (1996) Sustitucion sensorielle et qualia. Reprinted (English transl.) in *Vision and Mind: Selected Readings in the Philosophy of Perception* (Noë, A. and Thompson, E. eds), pp. 497–514, MIT Press

11. Block, N. (1997) Biology versus computation in the study of consciousness. *Behav. Brain Sci.* 20 (1), 159–165. (see especially p. 159)

17 Two Neural Correlates of Consciousness

I have previously proposed a conceptual distinction between phenomenal consciousness and access consciousness (Block 1990, 1992, 1995). Phenomenally conscious content is what differs between experiences as of red and green, whereas access-conscious content is content, information about which is "broadcast" in the "global workspace." Some have accepted the distinction but held that phenomenal consciousness and access consciousness coincide in the real world (Chalmers 1996, 1997; but see Block 1997). Others have accepted something in the vicinity of the conceptual distinction but argued that only access consciousness can be studied experimentally (Dehaene and Changeux 2004). Others (Dennett 1995) have disparaged the conceptual distinction itself. This article argues that the framework of phenomenal consciousness and access consciousness helps to make sense of recent results in cognitive neuroscience; we see a glimmer of an empirical case for thinking that they correspond to different NCCs.

Phenomenal NCC

Christof Koch (2004, 16) defines "the" NCC as "the minimal set of neuronal events and mechanisms jointly sufficient for a specific conscious percept." However, since there is more than one concept of consciousness, this definition allows that a given percept may have more than one NCC. In my proposed framework, the Phenomenal NCC is the minimal neural basis of the phenomenal *content* of an experience, that which differs between the experience as of red and the experience as of green. I will start with an example: the neural basis of visual experiences as of motion is likely to be activation of a certain sort in area MT/V5.[1] (Philosophers often use the terminology "as of motion" instead of "of motion" since the experience can and does occur without motion.) The evidence includes

- Activation of MT/V5 occurs during motion perception (Heeger et al. 1999).
- Microstimulation to monkey MT/V5 while the monkey viewed moving dots influenced the monkey's motion judgments, depending on the directionality of the cortical column stimulated (Britten et al. 1992).

• Bilateral (both sides of the brain) damage to a region that is likely to include MT/V5 in humans causes akinetopsia—the inability to perceive—and to have visual experiences as of motion. Akinetopsic subjects see motion as a series of stills. (See Zihl, von Cramon, and Mai 1983; Rees, Kreiman, and Koch 2002.)

• The motion after effect—a moving afterimage—occurs when subjects adapt to a moving pattern and then look at a stationary pattern. These moving afterimages also activate MT/V5 (Huk, Ress, and Heeger 2001).

• Transcranial magnetic stimulation (TMS[2]) applied to MT/V5 disrupts these moving afterimages (Théoret et al. 2002).

• MT/V5 is activated even when subjects view "implied motion" in still photographs—for example, of a discus thrower in midthrow (Kourtzi and Kanwisher 2000).

• TMS applied to the visual cortex in the right circumstances causes phosphenes[3]—brief flashes of light and color (Kammer 1999). When TMS is applied to MT/V5, it causes subjects to experience moving phosphenes (Cowey and Walsh 2000).

Mere activation over a certain threshold in MT/V5 might not be enough for the experience as of motion: the activation probably has to be part of a feedback loop, what Lamme (Lamme and Roelfsema 2000; Lamme 2004) calls recurrent processing. Pascual-Leone and Walsh (2002) applied TMS to both MT/V5 and V1 in human subjects with the pulses placed so that the stationary phosphenes determined by the pulses to V1 and the moving phosphenes from pulses to MT/V5 overlapped in visual space. When the pulse to V1 was applied 5 to 45 msec later than to MT/V5, all subjects said that their phosphenes were mostly stationary instead of moving. (See Pascual-Leone and Walsh 2002 for references to single-cell recording in monkeys that comport with these results.) The delays are consonant with the time for feedback between MT/V5 and V1, which suggests that experiencing moving phosphenes depends not only on activation of MT/V5 but also on a recurrent feedback loop in which signals go back to V1 and then forward to MT/V5 (Pascual-Leone and Walsh 2002).

So recurrent activity in and around MT/V5, in the context of other brain areas functioning normally—exactly which brain areas are required is unknown at present—is a good bet for being the physical basis of visual experience as of motion. (But see box 17.1 as well as Zeki and ffytche 1998 and Sincich et al. 2004 for some data that complicate the conclusion.) Corresponding conclusions can be drawn for other types of contents of experience. For example, recurrent activation of the fusiform face area on the ventral (bottom) surface of the temporal lobe (again in context) may determine experience as of a face (Kanwisher 2001). The overall conclusion is that there are different Phenomenal NCCs for different phenomenal contents. (See Zeki 2001 on micro-consciousness; also see Pins and ffytche 2003.)

Of course no one would take activation of MT/V5 + recurrent loops to V1 all by itself in a bottle as sufficient for experience of motion. (See box 17.2.) A useful distinction

Box 17.1

Blindsight and MT/V5

The picture presented in the text is complicated by attention to studies involving blind-sight patient GY, who has experiences of motion that may be visual but does not have the corresponding part of V1. GY does well in forced-choice guesses about stationary stimuli to his blind field that he says he does not see. But he says he is aware of some moving stimuli (Weiskrantz 1997). Functional magnetic resonance imaging (fMRI) shows that GY's area MT/V5 is activated when he is aware of moving stimuli presented to his blind field (Weiskrantz 1997). However, he does not experience moving phosphenes when TMS is applied to MT/V5 in the left hemisphere of his brain, where he is missing the corresponding V1 (Zeki and ffytche 1998). Recent neuroanatomy has shown that there is a pathway between the eyes and MT/V5 that bypasses V1 (directly from the LGN—the neural way station between the eyes and the cortex) (Sincich et al. 2004). GY has spoken to investigators about his experience. In 1994, GY said that his experience of motion in the blind field was "a 'feeling' of something happening in his blind field" (Zeki and ffytche 1998, 29). In 1996, he said his experience was that of "a black shadow moving on a black background" (p. 30). The shadow description comports with Riddoch's 1917 paper, which included studies of five patients who had gunshot wounds affecting V1 in World War I. (Zeki and ffytche (1998)—commendably and rarely in neuroscience—quote some of these patients.) The conclusion I would draw from reading what these subjects and GY say is that their experiences are very abstract, involving pure motion without any other experiential features such as color, light, shape, or contour. (Some philosophers I have mentioned this to wrongly think this description is incoherent!) It is not certain that these motion experiences should be described as visual. One suggestion is that activation of MT/V5 requires feedback loops to lower areas for experiences as of color, light, shape, and contour and for moving color, light, and so on, but not for pure motion. However, it may be that recurrent processes are necessary for all conscious experience, since there may be recurrent processes feeding back to MT/V5 from higher areas.

here is that between a *core* and a *total* NCC (Shoemaker 1981; Chalmers 2002). The total NCC of a conscious state is—all by itself—sufficient for the state. The core NCC is the part of the total NCC that distinguishes one conscious content from another—the rest of the total NCC being considered as the background conditions, which supply the rest of the sufficient condition. (One interesting issue is whether there might be somewhat different background conditions for different experiential contents, or whether the background conditions—at least in a single sensory modality—are always the same.[4]) In these terms, then, the core Phenomenal NCC for the neural basis of the experience as of motion as opposed to the experience as of red or as of a face, is likely to be recurrent activation of MT/V5. See figure 17.1. (See box 17.3 for some doubts about the concept of an NCC.)

Box 17.2
Area MT/V5 in a Bottle?

The total Phenomenal NCC for the experience as of motion is a sufficient condition all by itself for the experience. What might that turn out to be? I suggest approaching it by asking what we could remove from a normal brain and still have that experience. My suggestion is that we might be able to remove—at least—areas responsible for access to experiential contents and still have the heart of the same experiential contents. (In my approach, areas responsible for access to experiential contents probably also are responsible for conceptualization of those contents. So experiential contents without access might be nonconceptual, or may only involve purely sensory concepts.) Nakamura and Mishkin (1980, 1986) removed frontal, parietal, and superior temporal areas in one hemisphere of monkeys, leaving what is usually considered the visual system intact. They also disconnected visual inputs to the undamaged hemisphere. This preparation is sometimes said to cause blindness (Rees, Kreiman, and Koch 2002), but Nakamura and Mishkin are careful to say that this is shorthand for behavioral unresponsiveness to visual stimuli (at least temporarily), and should not be taken to show complete lack of visual sensation. One intriguing result is that when the limbic (emotional) system in the damaged hemisphere is intact, the monkeys showed eye and head movements as if engaged in visual exploration. This contrasts with monkeys in which V1 is ablated who stare fixedly.

Access NCC

We can distinguish between phenomenal contents of experience and access-conscious contents, information about which information is made available to the brain's "consumer" systems: systems of memory, perceptual categorization, reasoning, planning, evaluation of alternatives, decision making, voluntary direction of attention, and more generally, rational control of action. Wide availability motivates the idea that there is some mechanism via which producing systems can communicate with all the consuming systems at once, a "global workspace" (Baars 1997), and that information concerning conscious representations is "broadcast" in this global workspace. According to the global-workspace metaphor, the sensory systems are the "producers" of representations, and the aforementioned systems are the "consumers." The neural basis of information being sent to this global workspace is the "Access NCC."[5]

Rees, Kreiman, and Koch (2002) note that in studies of the neural correlates of bistable perception, in which there are spontaneous fluctuations in conscious contents, reports of conscious contents correlate with activation in frontal and parietal areas. Dehaene and Changeux (2004) suggest that a significant piece of the neural machinery of what they call "access to consciousness" (roughly equivalent to my access consciousness) is to be found in "workspace neurons" that have long-range excitatory

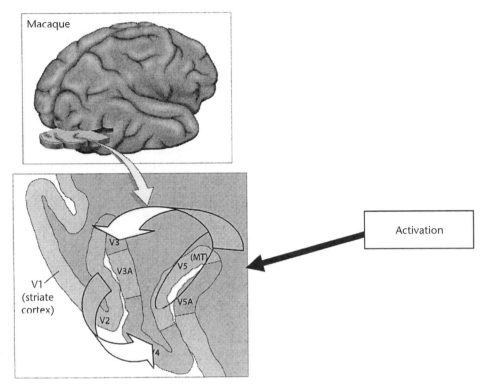

Figure 17.1

The core Phenomenal NCC for the visual experiential content as of motion: MT/V5 activation with recurrent loops to and from lower areas. The arrows are supposed to indicate recurrent loops. Adapted from S. Zeki, *A Vision of the Brain* (Oxford: Blackwell, 1993), 97, as modified by M. Gazzaniga, R. Ivry, and G. Mangun, *Cognitive Neuroscience*, 2nd ed. (New York: Norton, 2002). Arrows indicating recurrent loops were added.

axons allowing, for example, visual areas in the back of the head to communicate with frontal and parietal areas toward the front of the head. Thus it is a good guess that the Access NCC, the neural basis of access, is activation of these frontal and parietal areas by occipital (classic "visual") areas in the back of the head. (See figure 17.2.)

As Dehaene and his colleagues (2004) have emphasized, there is a winner-take-all competition among representations to be broadcast in the global workspace.[6] This point is crucial to the nature of the Access NCC and the difference between it and the Phenomenal NCC. One item of evidence for winner-take-all processes derives from the attentional blink paradigm, in which the subject is given a string of very brief visual stimuli, most of which are distractors. The subject is asked to report on one or two

Box 17.3
NCC or NDC?

I have been talking about the "neural correlates of consciousness." But the evidence of the sort just described argues for something both weaker and stronger than correlation:

• *Weaker*, because none of the evidence cited has anything to say about whether there is some other sort of physical constitution—an alternative biology, or even silicon chips— that is sufficient for the same experiences. The evidence supports a *one*-way connection, neural → experiential, not a *two*-way connection, neural ↔ experiential.

• *Stronger*, because it is evidence for determination, not just correlation. There is a correlation between the temperature in Brooklyn and Manhattan, but there is no necessity to it. The relation between recurrent MT activation and experience as of motion appears to be a necessary one: you cannot have (recurrent) activation of MT/V5 (together with certain unknown supporting areas) without visual experience as of motion.

Thus we should really be thinking about "NDC" for "neural determiner of consciousness" instead of NCC. (I will continue to use the acronym "NCC" since it is established terminology.)

"targets" after the sequence of rapid visual stimuli. If there are two targets separated by an appropriate delay, the subject does not report seeing the second one, even though the second one would have been likely to be reported if the subject had not been given the first target. Dehaene, Sergent, and Changeux (2003) used a modified attentional blink paradigm, in which subjects were asked to indicate on a continuous scale the visibility of the second target. The second target was at its peak of invisibility when the targets were separated by 260 msec. The result of interest here is that the subjects almost never used the *intermediate* cursor positions (at the 260 msec delay)—that is, they rated the "blinked" stimulus as either totally unseen or as maximally seen almost all the time. Thus Phenomenal NCC activations compete for dominating the Access NCC. Importantly, it is not the case that the Phenomenal NCC representation that is highest in initial activation will dominate, because domination can be the result of "biasing" factors such as expectations or preferences (Lamme 2003, 2004).

Although the winning Phenomenal NCC will in general be amplified by the recurrent loop, a losing Phenomenal NCC may itself involve recurrent loops to lower areas that will be sufficient for an experiential or phenomenal content. For example, an activation of area MT/V5 might have recurrent interactions with V1, making it the neural basis of an experiential content, but nonetheless lose in the winner-take-all competition and so not be accessed (Lamme 2004). The general point is that the simplest and most explanatory theory may be one in which recurrent MT/V1 loops are sufficient for an experiential content despite not being accessible when they lose the winner-take-all

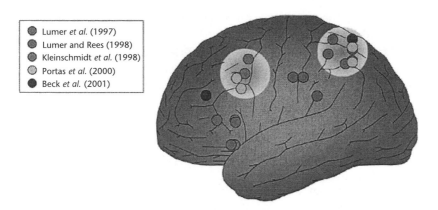

Lumer *et al.* (1997)
Lumer and Rees (1998)
Kleinschmidt *et al.* (1998)
Portas *et al.* (2000)
Beck *et al.* (2001)

Figure 17.2
Suggestion for the core Access NCC for visual experiences, from G. Rees, G. Kreiman, and C. Koch, "Neural correlates of consciousness in humans," *Nature Reviews Neuroscience* 3, 4 (2002): 261–270. Activations cluster in superior parietal and dorsolateral prefrontal cortex as indicated by large light circles. These are frontal and parietal areas that fluctuate spontaneously in binocular rivalry and other bistable perception in a way that is time-locked to fluctuation in reported experience. The core Access NCC may be activation of these areas by neural firing in the occipital cortex in the back of the head. Do we count the Phenomenal NCC as part of the Access NCC—in which case this figure pictures the Access NCC minus the Phenomenal NCC? Or do we regard the Access NCC as not including the Phenomenal NCC, in which case this figure pictures the Access NCC? This is a terminological issue assuming that phenomenal consciousness is the gateway to full-fledged access consciousness.

competition. Thus the winner-take-all process that is part of the nature of global broadcasting also strongly suggests that the Phenomenal NCC can be instantiated without the Access NCC, so global broadcasting does not encompass all of consciousness. This idea is further bolstered by evidence that there is brief parallel processing of many objects in the ventral visual stream[7] (up to inferotemporal cortex) before zooming in on one or two of them (Rousselet, Thorp, and Fabre-Thorp 2004).

But Is the Phenomenal NCC Really the Neural Basis of a Kind of Consciousness?

You may ask, "If the Phenomenal NCC can perhaps occur without the Access NCC, how do we know that the Phenomenal NCC is really the neural basis of anything conscious?" A quick answer is that, since the Phenomenal NCC determines the contents of experience, what it determines is ipso facto a kind of consciousness. The Phenomenal NCC for visual motion determines the experiential content of visual motion—as distinct from the experiential content of seeing something as a face. That content itself is a kind of phenomenology, a kind of consciousness. If there could be a phenomenal content without anything that could be called awareness of it, some might not want to apply the word "consciousness" to it. For this reason, Burge (1997) distinguishes between phenomenality—which he is uncomfortable about calling a kind of "consciousness"—and phenomenal consciousness, which is phenomenality that is the subject of some kind of access.[8] If one accepts Burge's terminology, though, it is important to realize that phenomenality is the important and puzzling phenomenon that is the heart of the mind-body problem and what we do not understand how to explain in neurological terms. If we could solve the "Hard Problem of consciousness" (Chalmers 1996) for phenomenality in Burge's sense, there would be no "Hard Problem" left for phenomenal consciousness in Burge's sense.

But this answer is too quick, since the doubt that motivates the question is a doubt that the Phenomenal NCC really does determine the contents of experience, and since the Phenomenal NCC was defined in terms of the contents of experience, the doubt challenges the evidence presented earlier for a Phenomenal NCC. The doubter may say that without access, there can be no true phenomenal contents but only *protocontents* that become contents when globally broadcast. But how does the doubter claim to know that? Some are motivated by a terminological point—that we should not call something "phenomenal" or "conscious" if it is not broadcast for access (Kanwisher 2001). However, the substantive empirical question is the following: If our evidence always concerns phenomenal contents that are actually accessed, how can the Phenomenal and Access NCC ever be empirically distinguished?

The answer is that it is not true that our evidence always concerns experiential contents that are accessed. There are a variety of paradigms in which we can use convergent evidence involving varying degrees of access to try to separate out the Phenomenal from Access NCC. One such paradigm is signal-detection theory.

Signal-Detection Theory (SDT) Approaches

Suppose a subject is shown a series of stimuli at around threshold level and asked to press one button if a target is visible and another if not. SDT models the subject's behavior in terms of two factors: the extent to which the subject sees the target and the criterion the subject implicitly sets for reporting seeing it. The criterion is famously influenceable by features of the experimental setup that affect subjects' expectations or motivation—such as by the proportion of "catch trials" (where no stimulus is presented) and by rewards for hits and penalties for false alarms. We know from standard SDT analyses that subjects' reports of whether there was a target or whether they saw it *do not just reflect the extent to which they did see it* (i.e., did have a visual phenomenal state), but also the subjects' threshold for reporting and even for believing that they did see it. Two experimental setups in which there are the *same* experiential contents may result in *different* beliefs and different reports.

A dramatic example is a series of experiments concerning the "exclusion" paradigm (Debner and Jacoby 1994), in which subjects are instructed to complete a word stem with something other than the end of a masked word that has just been presented to them. If the word "reason" is presented "unconsciously" at 50 msec, subjects are more likely than baseline to *disobey* the exclusion instructions, completing "rea___" with "son," whereas if "reason" is presented "consciously" at 250 msec, subjects are more likely than baseline to choose some other ending (e.g., as in "reader"). This paradigm has impressed many because it appears to yield opposite results for unconscious and conscious stimuli. However, Visser and Merikle (1999) showed that changing the motivation of the subjects by using a reward structure can change the degree of exclusion. They started subjects with a $15 credit and docked them $1 for each error. Visser and Merikle interpret the result in terms of the effect of reward/punishment on increased attention, accepting the idea that the 50 msec/250 msec difference engenders an unconscious/conscious difference. But there is an alternative SDT interpretation suggested by Snodgrass (2002), in which the results in part *reflect a criterion shift rather than a difference in consciousness*. The idea is that punishment for errors of failing to exclude pushes the criterion level (the degree of phenomenal experience that the subject implicitly sets as a condition for action) for inhibiting the immediate response so low that weak conscious perception of "reason" blocks use of "son" even though the subjects are so lacking in confidence that they say and think they do not see the word. That is, their criterion level for inhibiting the immediate response is lower than their criterion level for believing that they saw a word, and the phenomenal level is in between the two criteria. A subject's state of mind when successfully excluding one of the 50 msec stimuli could be articulated—overarticulated, no doubt—as "I probably didn't see a word but if I did, it was 'reason,' so I'd better complete the stem with 'reader'" (Block 2001). And the SDT interpretation is confirmed by the effect on "inclusion" instructions. With "inclusion" instructions, the subjects see "reason" and then are given "rea___" but are told to complete the stem with *the word they saw* if possible. In this paradigm, SDT predicts no shift with change in reward or punishment, because there is no issue of a criterion level. There is no degree of experience that subjects implicitly set as a condition of acting: rather, they just use the first word that comes to mind regardless of level of confidence that it is the word they saw. And the result (Visser and Merikle 1999) is just that: the difference in reward/punishment structure makes no difference in the result under "inclusion" instructions. Thus there is a striking difference in the effect of reward on exclusion as compared with inclusion instructions.

There is, therefore, evidence in the "exclusion" case of experiential contents (e.g., as of seeing "reason") without the kind of access required for report, planning, decision making, evaluation of alternatives, memory, and voluntary direction of attention. Some of the 50 msec stimuli are weakly conscious although not broadcast in the global

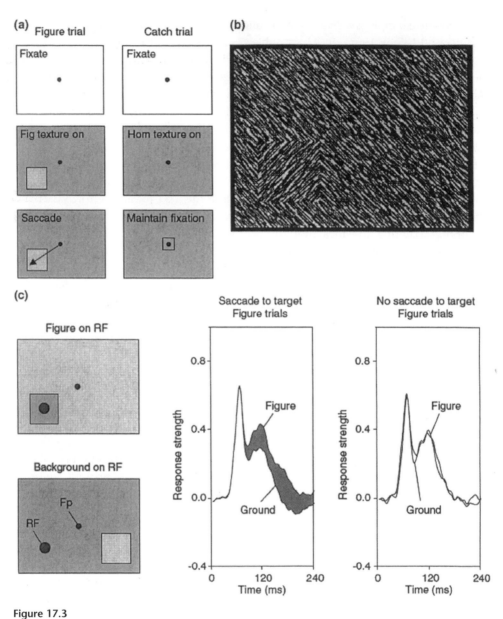

Figure 17.3

(a) Supèr, Spekreijse, and Lamme (2001) trained monkeys to saccade from a fixation point to a target (bottom left of (a)). Initially, a fixation point was presented (top). Then a target texture was presented ("Fig texture on," left) or there was a homogeneous pattern with no target ("Hom texture on," right). If there was no target, the monkey was rewarded for maintaining fixation for 500 msec (right panels). The target could be in one of three locations. (b) The targets were areas of an workspace. Thus SDT gives us reason to think that experiential content—based on the Phenomenal NCC—can be instantiated without the kind of access that is based in the Access NCC.

Neural SDT

In a landmark series of experiments, Supèr, Spekreijse, and Lamme (2001) recorded from V1 (which, you will recall, is the first classic "visual" area in the cortex) during a task in which monkeys were rewarded for saccading to a target if there was one or continuing to look at the fixation point if not. (A saccade is an eye movement whose function is to make a region of interest project to the densest part of the retina; in natural visual exploration, there are roughly two per second, although the movement itself takes only 30 msec.) Supèr and colleagues manipulated whether the locations in V1 corresponded to figure or ground. When the monkey detected (saccaded to) the target, there was an increased V1 response for figure as compared with ground. See figure 17.3, in which this increased figure response is referred to as "modulation."

Supèr and colleagues were able to manipulate the modulation by varying the saliency of the stimulus (i.e., the number of pixels in line segments in the target; see figure 17.3b) and the proportion of "catch trials" in which there was no target. For high-saliency stimuli and small numbers of catch trials, there was a near-perfect correlation

overall pattern in which the lines were orthogonal to the rest of the pattern. (c) Supèr et al recorded from sites in V1 whose receptive fields (RF) included the three locations in which targets could occur. When the monkey saccaded from the fixation point (Fp) to the target, the neural response from the target counted as "figure" and the other two sites were counted as "ground." Figure responses were greater than ground responses after ~90 msec, as indicated in the shaded area (central panel). The shaded area indicates the degree of "modulation." When the targets were highly salient and the number of catch trials were few, modulation disappeared when the monkey did not detect the target (right panel). That is, when the monkey did not saccade to the target and the saliency was high and catch trials low, there was little difference between the activity in the part of V1 corresponding to the target and the two other locations, as indicated in the right-most panel of (c). (However, when the saliency of the target was low or catch trials high, there was a substantial difference.) Modulation also disappeared under anesthesia. Supèr et al. manipulated the saliency of the target by decreasing the size of the line segments used. The target shown in (b) is 16 pixels on a side, but they also used 8- and 4-pixel targets. For 16-pixel targets, modulation is present as shown in (c) when the target is detected and absent when the target is absent. But as the number of pixels is decreased, the difference between the case when the target is detected and not detected decreases, so long as the number of catch trials is held constant. When the pixel count is 4, there is no significant difference in modulation between detection and nondetection. Figures (courtesy of Victor Lamme) redrawn with permission from Nature Neuroscience.

between modulation and saccades to the target, and in that sense modulation and access to the target corresponded well. But moving the saliency down or the percentage of catch trials up boosted the modulation when the animal did not saccade to the target to the 50 percent range. That is, with low saliency or a high number of catch trials, the monkey's criterion level for saccading was close enough to the visual "signal" that the modulation averaged the same whether the animal saccaded to the target or not. For example, this happened when the pixel count was reduced from 16 to 4, maintaining catch trials at 20 percent, and also when the pixel count was 16 and the catch trials were raised to 50 percent. If the pixel count was reduced to 4 but the catch-trial percentage was also reduced to zero, then the correlation between modulation and access was restored. These results show that the modulation does not reflect access to the target (since it was the same whether the target was or was not accessed). Nor does the modulation reflect the saccade, so it is on the sensory rather than motor side of the decision process. It also does not reflect attention, since the detected targets can be assumed to draw more attention. The modulation seems to reflect something intermediate between the stimulus and access. In a classic signal-detection analysis, Supèr, Spekreijse, and Lamme indeed showed that the modulation is an intermediate-level representation that can be disconnected from access either by raising the perceptual decision criterion or by decreasing saliency of the stimulus, lowering the visual "signal" to the range of the decision criterion.

The modulation shown by Supèr and colleagues disappears under anesthesia (Lamme, Zipser, and Spekreijse 1998) and is probably produced by recurrent processes (Lamme, Supèr, and Spekreijse 1998), unlike other V1 representations such as direction and orientation tuning. So there is some plausibility to taking it as an indication of if not directly part of a Phenomenal NCC for the experiential content of seeing the target. (See also Ress and Heeger 2003.)

Can the Phenomenal NCC Be Studied Empirically?

Doubts about whether phenomenal consciousness (and hence its neural basis, the Phenomenal NCC) can be studied empirically are common (see box 17.4), and are often based on the idea that ultimately, introspective reports—that is, reports about one's conscious experience—are the fundamental epistemological basis of theories of consciousness, the gold standard (Dehaene and Changeux 2004; Weiskrantz 1997; Papineau 2002, especially chap. 7). Reports are not supposed to be infallible, but any discounting of reports as reporting too much or too little will supposedly have to be based solely on *other* reports. Reports inevitably reflect the Access NCC, not just the Phenomenal NCC. When people tell you about their conscious states, you only hear about the ones that have won the winner-take-all competition. Hence we can only study "access to consciousness" (Dehaene and Changeux 2004)—that is, access to ex-

Box 17.4

Questions for Future Research

1. In visual extinction due to right parietal damage, the subject reports not seeing a stimulus on the left when there is a competing stimulus on the right. Rees et al. (2002) showed that the fusiform face area (in the relevant hemisphere) of an extinction patient can be activated robustly when the patient says he does not see the face (because of a competing stimulus), though not quite as strongly as when the subject says he does see the face. One question is: is there *recurrent* activation of the relevant part of V1 in such a patient? A related question is: does the fusiform-face-area activation in such a patient show the enhanced figure modulation response described by Supèr et al.? If the answer to both turns out to be yes, that is evidence that recurrent fusiform-face activation is a genuine core Phenomenal NCC for face experience, even though the subject says he does not see a face.

2. If indeed recurrent activation of sensory areas creates the core Phenomenal NCCs, why? For example, why is recurrent activation of area MT/V5 (together with the unknown background activation) sufficient for visual experience of motion instead of some other experiential content or no content? That is a form of the infamous Hard Problem of consciousness (Chalmers 1996).

periential content, not experiential content itself. I do not agree with this methodological view for a number of reasons.

First, observed electrons can provide evidence about electrons that cannot in principle be observed—for example, electrons that are too distant in space and time (i.e., outside our light cone) to be observed. Why should we suppose matters are any different for consciousness?

Second, there is no gold standard of evidence, here or in any area of science. We should go for the simplest theory compatible with *all* the evidence. *No evidence is privileged.* In particular, it is not true that our theory of consciousness should be completely determined by the introspective reports of subjects. An analogy: it is trivial to program two computers to yield the same input-output function via different algorithms. No theory of what goes on in computers based wholly on the computers' "reports"—that is, input-output relations—stands a chance of success. Why should we suppose consciousness is any different? Just as two computationally different computers can have the same input-output function, two brains that are different in conscious structure might at least in principle have the same input-output function.

Third, any neuroscientific approach that bases everything on reports about a subject's own experience is in danger of focusing on the *neural basis of higher-order thought*—thought to the effect that I myself have an experience—rather than the neural basis of experiential content or even access to experiential content. To give an introspective report, the subject has to have a higher-order thought—so to insist on introspective reportability as the gold standard is to encourage leaving out cases in which subjects have experiences that are not adequately reflected in higher-order thoughts.[9]

Finally, even those who assimilate experiential content to its accessibility should not accept introspective reports as a gold standard. Animals have plenty of access to their experiences, but probably little in the way of higher-order thought about them of the sort that could be the basis of an introspective report. Cowey and Stoerig (1997) showed that monkeys that had been made blindsighted on one side and trained to make a visual discrimination in their sighted field, could make the discrimination in their blind field. However, when given the option, they preferred a third "nothing" response. This is evidence about the monkey's perceptual state that does not depend on any introspective reports.

But is the monkeys' button pushing just a *nonverbal introspective report*? Nonhuman primates that have learned symbolic systems for communication may not even make spontaneous reports about the world (Terrace 2004; Wallman 1992), so there is little ground for supposing that they are prone to reports about their own experience.[10] If a human were to push the "nothing" button, we might guess whether there is a thought underlying the response. We might consider two hypotheses: first, the *introspective* report, "I am having no visual experience," and second, the *environmental* report, "There is nothing on the screen." If the subject were a child of 3–4, the introspective report would be unlikely since children have a great deal of difficulty with states of mind about their own mental states (Esbensen, Taylor, and Stoess 1997; Gopnik and Graf 1988). Given that the environmental report would be preferable even for a child, we can hardly suppose the introspective report would be preferable in the case of a macaque! The take-home message is that you do not need reports *about the subject's experiences* to get good evidence about what the subject is experiencing: indications of what the subject takes to be in front of him or her will do just fine.

Where are we? I have proposed a distinction between a Phenomenal NCC and an Access NCC. The "single NCC" framework does not do as well in making sense of the empirical data, in particular signal-detection theory data as an account in which there are two NCCs, a Phenomenal NCC and an Access NCC. Of course both NCCs are to be firmly distinguished from perceptual representations that are not conscious in any sense (as in the right-most panel of figure 17.3c). More generally, rather than asking "What is the direct evidence about the Phenomenal NCC independently of the Access NCC?", we should instead ask "What framework makes the most sense of the data?"

Notes

This is a longer version of a paper in *Trends in Cognitive Sciences* 9(2): 46–52, February 2005.

1. The first classical "visual" cortical area is V1; later classic "visual" areas include V2, V3, V4, and V5. V5 has two names because it was identified and named by two groups. I put "visual" in scare

quotes because there is some debate as to whether some of the classic "visual" areas are best thought of as multimodal and spatial. In the United States, the area I am talking about is usually called "MT+" because it includes structures that adjoin MT.

2. TMS delivers an electromagnetic jolt to brain areas when placed appropriately on the scalp. The effect is to disrupt organized signals but also to create a signal in a quiescent area. Thus TMS can both disrupt moving afterimages and create phosphenes. A comparison is to hitting a radio: the static caused might interrupt good reception going on but also cause a noise when there is no reception. (I am indebted here to Nancy Kanwisher and Vincent Walsh.)

3. To experience phosphenes for yourself, close your eyes and exert pressure on your eye from the side with your finger. Or if you prefer not to put your eyeball at risk, look at the following website for an artist's rendition: http://www.reflectingskin.net/phosphenes.html.

4. The distinction between core and total NCC as I defined it depends on the assumption that at least some core NCCs share background conditions. Suppose the background condition for the experience as of red and the experience as of green are the same and are the same as other visual experiences, but not the same as the background condition for taste experiences—for instance, the experience as of saltiness. Then the core NCC for visual experiences will have to be defined as the part of the total visual NCC that distinguishes one visual content from another.

5. The "made-available" terminology is supposed to capture both the occurrent nature of the experience (when something is *made* available, something happens) and the dispositional aspect (availability). There are many somewhat different ways of making access consciousness precise in this picture. One might think of the crucial feature as representations being *sent*, or else *received*, or else *translated* from the system of representation of the producing systems to the system of representation of the consuming systems.

6. The idea is not that the auditory signals from a voice compete with the visual signals from the person's mouth moving, but rather that a "coalition" that involves neural processing of both of those signals competes with other coalitions.

7. Milner and Goodale (1995) distinguish between a conscious visual pathway from the classic visual areas in the back of the head feeding into the temporal lobe on the side of the head (ventral stream) and an unconscious "dorsal" action-oriented stream starting in the back of the head and feeding to the top of the head.

8. More specifically, Burge argues that there is a kind of primitive of-ness of a phenomenally conscious state that is not reducible to higher-order thought (and not reducible to any other cognitive notion). In Block 1995, I argue that "phenomenal consciousness" in my sense of the term can be either transitive (take an object of which the subject is conscious) or intransitive. My intransitive phenomenal consciousness corresponds to Burge's phenomenality, and my transitive phenomenal consciousness corresponds to Burge's phenomenal consciousness.

9. Armstrong, Carruthers, Lycan, and Rosenthal have argued for seeing consciousness in terms of higher-order thought. In some versions of this view—for example, Rosenthal's—experiential content can exist without higher-order thought. Anyone who takes such a view should agree with me

that a methodology focused exclusively on introspective report alone will be in danger of finding the neural basis of higher-order thought rather than the neural basis of experiential content. The difference between the Rosenthal-type view and mine has to do in part with the issue of whether the term "consciousness" refers to a higher-order state or to a first-order state. (My view is that the term "consciousness" is ambiguous and in one sense refers to a higher-order state and in another sense a first-order state.) But that difference about how the term is used is itself dependent (I believe) on a difference of opinion on whether the "Hard Problem" applies to experiential content. For someone who does not believe in the Hard Problem for experiential content, a higher-order thought about such contentful states may seem a more worthy bearer of the term "consciousness."

10. There have been many claims of reports by nonhuman primates—for example, by Savage-Rumbaugh—but it is controversial whether those claims are based on trained-up responses given in the expectation of reward.

References

Baars, B. J. 1997. *In the Theater of Consciousness: The Workspace of the Mind*. New York: Oxford University Press.

Beck, D., Rees, G., Frith, C. D., and Lavie, N. 2001. Neural correlates of change detection and change blindness. *Nature Neuroscience* 4: 645–650.

Block, N. 1990. Consciousness and accessibility. *Behavioral and Brain Sciences* 13: 596–598.

Block, N. 1992. Begging the question against phenomenal consciousness. *Behavioral and Brain Sciences* 15: 205–206. (Reprinted in N. Block, O. Flanagan, and G. Güzeldere, eds., *The Nature of Consciousness: Philosophical Debates*. Cambridge, MA: MIT Press, 1997.) 175–179.

Block, N. 1995. On a confusion about a function of consciousness. *Behavioral and Brain Sciences* 18(2): 227–247. (Reprinted in N. Block, O. Flanagan, and G. Güzeldere, eds., *The Nature of Consciousness: Philosophical Debates*. Cambridge, MA: MIT Press, 1997.)

Block, N. 1997. Biology versus computation in the study of consciousness. *Behavioral and Brain Sciences* 20(1): 159–165. http://www.nyu.edu/gsas/dept/philo/faculty/block/papers/Reply1997 .pdf.

Block, N. 2001. Paradox and cross purposes in recent findings about consciousness. *Cognition* 79(1–2): 197–219.

Britten, K., Shadlen, M., Newsome, W., and Movshon, A. 1992. The analysis of visual motion: A comparison of neuronal and psychophysical performance. *Journal of Neuroscience* 12: 4745–4765.

Burge, Tyler. 1997. Two kinds of consciousness. In N. Block, O. Flanagan, and G. Güzeldere, eds., *The Nature of Consciousness: Philosophical Debates*. Cambridge, MA: MIT Press.

Chalmers, D. 1996. *The Conscious Mind*. Oxford: Oxford University Press.

Chalmers, D. 1997. Availability: The cognitive basis of experience. *Behavioral and Brain Sciences* 20(1): 148–149. (Reprinted in N. Block, O. Flanagan, and G. Güzeldere, eds., *The Nature of Consciousness: Philosophical Debates*. Cambridge, MA: MIT Press, 1997.)

Chalmers, D. 2002. What is a neural correlate of consciousness? In T. Metzinger, ed., *Neural Correlates of Consciousness: Empirical and Conceptual Questions*. Cambridge, MA: MIT Press.

Cowey, A., and Stoerig, P. 1997, July. Visual detection in monkeys with blindsight. *Neuropsychologia* 35(7): 929–939.

Cowey, A., and Walsh, V. 2000. Magnetically induced phosphenes in sighted, blind and blindsighted subjects. *NeuroReport* 11: 3269.

Debner, J. A., and Jacoby, L. L. 1994. Unconscious perception: Attention, awareness, and control. *Journal of Experimental Psychology: Learning, Memory, and Cognition* 20: 304–317.

Dehaene, S., and Changeux, J.-P. 2004. Neural mechanisms for access to consciousness. In M. Gazzaniga, ed., *The Cognitive Neurosciences*, vol. 3. Cambridge, MA: MIT Press.

Dehaene, S., Sergent, C., and Changeux, J.-P. 2003. A neuronal network model linking subjective reports and objective physiological data during conscious perception. *Proceedings of the National Academy of Sciences* 100(14): 8520–8525.

Dennett, D. 1995. The path not taken. *Behavioral and Brain Sciences* 18(2): 1995: 252–253. (Reprinted in N. Block, O. Flanagan, and G. Güzeldere, eds., *The Nature of Consciousness: Philosophical Debates*. Cambridge, MA: MIT Press, 1997.)

Esbensen, B. M., Taylor, M., and Stoess, C. J. 1997. Children's behavioral understanding of knowledge acquisition. *Cognitive Development* 12: 53–84.

Gopnik, A., and Graf, P. 1988. Knowing how you know: Children's understanding of the sources of their knowledge. *Child Development* 59: 1366–1371.

Heeger, D., Boynton, G., Demb, J., Seideman, E., and Newsome, W. 1999. Motion opponency in visual cortex. *Journal of Neuroscience* 19: 7162–7174.

Huk, A., Ress, D., and Heeger, D. 2001. Neuronal basis of hte motion aftereffect reconsidered. *Neuron* 32: 161–172.

Kammer, T. 1999. Phosphenes and transient scotomas induced by magnetic stimulation of the occipital lobe: Their topographic relationship. *Neuropsychologia* 37: 191–198.

Kanwisher, N. 2001. Neural events and perceptual awareness. *Cognition* 79(1–2): 89–113.

Kleinschmidt, A., Buchel, C., Zeki, S., and Frackowiak, R. S. J. 1998. Human brain activity during spontaneously reversing perception of ambiguous figures. *Proc. R. Soc. Lond. B* 265: 2427–2433.

Koch, C. 2004. *The Quest for Consciousness: A Neuroscientific Approach*. Granwood Village, Co. Roberts and Company.

Kourtzi, Z., and Kanwisher, N. 2000. Activation in human MT/MST by static images with implied motion. *Journal of Cognitive Neuroscience* 12(1): 48–55.

Lamme, V. 2003. Why visual attention and awareness are different. *Trends in Cognitive Science* 7: 12–18.

Lamme, V. 2004. Separate neural definitions of visual consciousness and visual attention: A case for phenomenal awareness. *Neural Networks* 17: 861–872.

Lamme, V., and Roelfsema, P. 2000. The distinct modes of vision offered by feedforward and recurrent processing. *Trends in Neuroscience* 23(11): 571–579.

Lamme, V. A. F., Supèr, H., and Spekreijse, H. 1998. Feedforward, horizontal, and feedback processing in the visual cortex. *Current Opinion in Neurobiology* 8: 529–535.

Lamme, V. A. F., Zipser, K., and Spekreijse, H. 1998. Figure-ground activity in primary visual cortex is suppressed by anaesthesia. *Proceedings of the National Academy of Sciences of the USA* 95: 3263–3268.

Lumer, E. D., Friston, K. J., and Rees, G. 1998. Neural correlates of perceptual rivalry in the human brain. *Science* 280: 1930–1934.

Lumer, E. D., and Rees, G. E. 1999. Covariation of activity in visual and prefrontal cortex associated with subjective visual perception. *Proc. Natl Acad. Sci. USA* 96: 1669–1673.

Milner, A. D., and Goodale, M. A. 1995. *The Visual Brain in Action*. Oxford: Oxford University Press.

Nakamura, R., and Mishkin, M. 1980. Blindness in monkeys following non-visual cortical lesions. *Brain Research* 188: 572–577.

Nakamura, R., and Mishkin, M. 1986. Chronic "blindness" following lesions of nonvisual cortex in the monkey. *Experimental Brain Research* 63: 173–184.

Papineau, D. 2002. *Thinking about Consciousness*. Oxford: Oxford University Press.

Pascual-Leone, A., and Walsh, V. 2002, April. Fast backprojections from the motion to the primary visual area necessary for visual awareness. *Science* 292: 510–512.

Pins, D., and ffytche, D. 2003. The neural correlates of conscious vision. *Cerebral Cortex* 13: 461–474.

Portas, C. M., Strange, B. A., Friston, K. J., Dolan, R. J., and Frith, C. D. 2000. How does the brain sustain a visual percept? *Proc. R. Soc. Lond. B* 267: 845–850.

Rees, G., Kreiman, G., and Koch, C. 2002, April. Neural correlates of consciousness in humans. *Nature Reviews Neuroscience* 3(4): 261–270.

Rees, G., Wojciulik, E., Clarke, K., Husain, M., Frith, C. D., and Driver, J. 2002. Neural correlates of conscious and unconscious vision in parietal extinction. *Neurocase* 8: 387–393.

Ress, D., and Heeger, D. 2003. Neuronal correlates of perception in early visual cortex. *Nature Neuroscience* 6: 4414–4420.

Rousselet, G., Thorpe, S., and Fabre-Thorpe, M. 2004. How parallel is visual processing in the ventral pathway? *Trends in Cognitive Sciences* 8(8): 363–370.

Shoemaker, S. 1981. Some varieties of functionalism. *Philosophical Topics* 12: 93–119. (Reprinted in S. Shoemaker, *Identity, Cause, and Mind.* Cambridge: Cambridge University Press, 1984.)

Sincich, L., Park, K. F., Wohlgemuth, M. J., and Horton, J. C. 2004. Bypassing V1: A direct geniculate input to area MT. *Nature Neuroscience* 7(10): 1123–1128.

Snodgrass, M. 2002. Disambiguating conscious and unconscious influences: Do exclusion paradigms demonstrate unconscious perception? *American Journal of Psychology* 115: 545–580.

Supèr, H., Spekreijse, H., and Lamme, V. 2001. Two distinct modes of sensory processing observed in monkey primary visual cortex (V1). *Nature Neuroscience* 4(3): 304–310.

Terrace, H. 2004. Metacognition and the Evolution of Language. In H. Terrace and J. Metcalfe, eds., *The Missing Link in Cognition: Origins of Self-Knowing Consciousness.* New York: Oxford University Press.

Théoret, H., Kobayashi, M., Ganis, G., Di Capua, P., and Pascual-Leone, A. 2002. Repetitive transcranial magnetic stimulation of human area MT/V5 disrupts perception and storage of the motion aftereffect. *Neuropsychologia* 40(13): 2280–2287.

Visser, T., and Merikle, P. 1999. Conscious and unconscious processes: The effects of motivation. *Consciousness and Cognition* 8: 94–113.

Wallman, J. 1992. *Aping Language.* Cambridge: Cambridge University Press.

Weiskrantz, L. 1997. *Consciousness Lost and Found.* Oxford: Oxford University Press.

Zeki, S. 2001. Localization and globalization in conscious vision. *Annual Reviews of Neuroscience* 24: 57–86.

Zeki, S., and ffytche, D. H. 1998. The Riddoch Syndrome: Insights into the neurobiology of conscious vision. *Brain* 121: 25–45.

Zihl, J., von Cramon, D., and Mai, N. 1983. Selective disturbance of movement vision after bilateral brain damage. *Brain* 106: 313–340.

This is a charming and engaging book that combines careful attention to the phenomenology of experience with an appreciation of the psychology and neuroscience of perception. In some of its aims—for example, to show problems with a rigid version of a view of visual perception as an "inverse optics" process of constructing a static 3-D representation from static 2-D information on the retina it succeeds admirably. As Noë points out, vision is a process that depends on interactions between the perceiver and the environment and involves contributions from sensory systems other than the eye. He is at pains to note that vision is not passive. His analogy with touch is to the point: touch involves skillful probing and movement, and so does vision, although less obviously and in my view less centrally so. This much is certainly widely accepted among vision scientists—although mainstream vision scientists (represented, for example, by Stephen Palmer's excellent textbook[1]) view these points as best seen within a version of the inverse optics view that takes inputs as nonstatic and as including motor instructions (for example, involving eye movements and head movements).[2] The kind of point that Noë raises is viewed as important at the margins, but as not disturbing the main lines of the picture of vision that descends—with many changes—from the pioneering work of David Marr in the 1980s (and before him, from Helmholtz). But Noë shows little interest in mainstream vision science, focusing on nonmainstream ideas in the science of perception, specifically ideas from the antirepresentational psychologist J. J. Gibson, and also drawing on Wittgenstein and the phenomenology tradition. There is a sense throughout the book of revolution, of upsetting the applecart. This is a review from the point of view of the applecart.

My comments are in two parts, one mainly a priori, the other largely empirical: first, I will consider Noë's version of externalism in the light of the distinction between causation and constitution. Second, I will argue that on the most obvious reading of Noë's view, one that identifies perceptual experience with the skilled bodily exercise of "sensorimotor knowledge" (I will leave off the scare quotes in what follows) that includes visually guided action, there are empirical results that suggest that such knowledge does not reflect the phenomenology of conscious vision.

I Causation and Constitution

Burge, Kripke, and Putnam have argued for externalism about meaning and content. A familiar flamboyant illustration: two people with molecularly identical brains could nonetheless have different "water"-thoughts because of differences in their physical and/or social environments. Dretske, Lycan, and Tye hold that the phenomenal character of an experience is or at least supervenes on the experience's representational content, and so they use the Burge/Kripke/Putnam sort of externalism to support externalism about experience. They are Representationists about phenomenal character in the sense that they hold that the phenomenal character of an experience is exhausted by its representational content. Noë argues for what is in one way a more radical form of externalism about experience. His externalism is *vehicle* externalism rather than content externalism. The vehicles of contents are the physical items that have or express the contents—sentences for example. His analogy is to the view of Clark and Chalmers[3] that memory and calculation constitutively include props such as a diary. Similarly, according to Noë's view, skilled active body partially constitutes the vehicle of experience.

Noë sometimes tries to frame the debate in a way that has his side arguing for a mere possibility, for example, "I have been arguing that, for at least some experiences, the physical substrate of the experience *may* cross boundaries, implicating neural, bodily, and environmental features" (p. 221). However, these specks of caution float on a sea of exuberant declarations, such as "A neuroscience of perceptual consciousness must be an enactive neuroscience—that is, a neuroscience of embodied activity, rather than a neuroscience of brain activity" (p. 227).

The leading idea of the book—what Noë calls the enactive view[4]—is a constitutive claim about experience: "Perceptual experience, according to the enactive approach, is an activity of exploring the environment drawing on knowledge of sensorimotor dependencies and thought" (p. 228). What are sensorimotor dependencies (or contingencies) and what is knowledge of them? First, the "sensori" in "sensorimotor" is not supposed to be taken to be itself mentalistic. Noë is wary of the pitfall for his view of tacitly appealing to the content of experience in explaining the sensorimotor knowledge that is supposed itself to serve to explain the content of experience, so wary that he appears to adopt not one but two pieces of machinery for avoiding it. He says that strictly speaking sensorimotor knowledge—knowledge of sensorimotor contingencies—is knowledge of "the way sensory *stimulation* varies as you move" (p. 78; emphasis added). The sensory side of the sensorimotor division is also spelled out in terms of what he calls "appearances," which are supposed to be totally objective. For example, the shape appearance of an object is one of its projections on a plane that is orthogonal to the line of sight—for example, a projection (or a set of projections) on an imaginary window interposed between the eye and the object. Thus the objective shape appearance of a round plate seen at an angle is the elliptical projection on such a plane, and so the plate objectively "looks" elliptical.[5] Sensorimotor knowledge is knowledge of how objective appearances change as you move and as the things you see move, but sensorimotor knowledge is also a matter of knowing how rather than knowing that. His comparisons are with knowing how to dance or gesture. The upshot is that perceptual experience, according to the enactive view, is the practical bodily exercise of sensorimotor know-how (see §3.5). Noë's rock-the applecart conclusion is that perceptual experience does not constitutively supervene on the brain alone but only on the active body that is required for the skilled exercise of sensorimotor knowledge.

Although I have described Noë as holding a constitutive externalist view of perceptual experience, I should say that there is considerable variation in the statement of the enactive view. Sometimes it is stated as a constitutive view about perception rather than perceptual experience: "perceiving is constituted by the exercise of a range of sensorimotor skills."[6] In addition to identifying perceptual experience with the exercise of sensorimotor skills—that is, skilled bodily exercise of sensorimotor know-how, Noë also says that perceptual experience "draws on," is "constrained by," and is "enabled" by sensorimotor knowledge. We are often given declarations about the nature of perception or perceptual experience, but the terms change, frustratingly, from one statement to another. There are even parts of the book in which perceptual experience appears to be identified with a set of expectations rather than bodily activity. I believe that my interpretation of the enactive view as the claim that perceptual experience is the exercise of sensorimotor know-how in bodily activity is justified by the fact that it appears frequently throughout the book, that it is often expressed emphatically ("Perceptual experience *just is* a mode of skillful exploration of the world," p. 194), that it is emphasized in the last chapter (labeled "Brain and Mind: A Conclusion"), which is on the mind-body problem, and that this radical claim will inevitably be a source of attention to the enactive point of view.

Noë supposes that the enactive view has a number of philosophical advantages. For example, he argues that it goes some way toward closing the famous "explanatory gap": why is it that the neural basis of this experience is the neural basis of an experience like this instead of like something else or like nothing? In my view, the appearance of help here comes from a tacit conceptual functionalism (or even behaviorism). To put the point crudely, if you think the concept of a pain is the concept of a state that makes you say "Ouch" and the concept of an itch is the concept of a state that makes you scratch, it is a lot easier to close the explanatory gap for pain and itching and the difference between them.[7]

Another line of argument that Noë offers in favor of the enactive view is based on impressive evidence that in many disparate kinds of cases, perceptual experience depends on sensorimotor contingencies. One point is emphasized by Brian

O'Shaughnessy and Michael Martin:[8] our tactile experience of a solid object depends on sensing its resistance when we push against it, thus showing a causal dependence of experience on action. Another line of thought is experimental: in a variety of paradigms, changing sensorimotor contingencies changes the brain and experience itself. As Richard Held and Alan Hein showed in the 1960s, kittens that are active in exploring the environment have normal visual systems as compared with kittens that have the same stimulation but are passive.[9] Wearing inverting goggles results in considerable reorganization of perception. Hooking up a TV camera to a pixel array grasped in a blind person's mouth allows for navigation through space, probably by recruiting "visual" areas of the brain.[10] These results are impressive but what they show is that sensorimotor contingencies have an *effect* on experience, not that experience is even partially *constituted* by—or supervenes, constitutively on—bodily activity. (To say that, for example, the moral facts supervene on the physical facts is to say that there can be no moral difference without a physical difference.)

This distinction between the claim that sensorimotor contingencies affect experience and the claim that experience is constituted by the exercise of sensorimotor know-how poses a major problem for many of Noë's arguments. The problem can be seen in stark form in Noë's discussion of dreaming. He says: "Let us take it as settled that when we dream there is no dynamic exchange with the environment (although this might turn out not to be true), and let us accept that, therefore, neural states alone *are* sufficient for dreaming (*although this does not follow—e.g., the affective content of dream states may depend on endocrine gland activity, as waking emotional states do . . .*)" (p. 213; emphasis added). Noë's thought here is that dream experience supervenes on the brain but perceptual experience does not. The suggestion raises the question of whether dream experience could really have a constitutive metaphysical basis that is different from that of perceptual experience, but I will pass over this issue, confining myself to commenting on what for Noë's purpose is just a parenthetical remark, a revealing aside. Noë supposes that if the affective content of dream states *depends causally on endocrine activity*, then the constitutive supervenience base for dream experience is not just the brain but has to include the endocrine system. But endocrine activity can affect dream experience without being part of the constitutive supervenience base for dream experience—if dream experience is fixed by something else that is in turn affected by endocrine activity. Indeed, the upshot of evidence on the brain basis of experience is that effects of the endocrine system on experience are mediated by effects on the brain itself and therefore do not challenge the orthodoxy that says that the brain is the minimal constitutive supervenience base for experience. (This is part of the applecart I mentioned earlier.)[11]

Let us be clear about what the issue is. The issue of the constitutive supervenience base for experience is the issue of what is—and is not—a *metaphysically necessary part of a metaphysically sufficient condition* of perceptual experience. That is, it is the issue of what is—and is not—part of the *minimal* metaphysically sufficient condition for perceptual experience (i.e., the minimal supervenience base). Noë's enactive view says that the skilled active body is part of that minimal condition (minimal supervenience base), whereas the view, which I hold and which I have labeled the orthodox view, is that nothing outside the brain is part of it.[12]

Importantly, the minimal supervenience base for an experience that occurs at time *t* is an instantiation of a physical property at *t*—according to the orthodox view. The Representationists mentioned earlier—Dretske, Lycan and Tye—hold that the minimal supervenience base includes features of the environment from the past—for example, aspects of the evolutionary history of the individual and perhaps aspects of the individual's own lifetime of interacting with the environment. But the Representationists would agree with the orthodox view that if we hold these environmental variables fixed, only the features of the brain *now* are needed to determine the phenomenal character of experience *now*. And this is where the enactive view is more radical: the enactive view holds that even if we hold the evolutionary and immediate past environments fixed, there is still something outside the brain to be fixed in order to determine the phenomenal character of experience now, namely the activity of the body.

Of course, there is often a process of perception that *involves* bodily activity—one moves closer to get a better look—but that should not be conflated with the very different idea that perceiving *is* an activity or, worse, that perceptual experience is an activity. And even if perceptual experience *depends* causally or counterfactually on movement or another form of activity, it does not follow that perceptual experience *constitutively* involves movement.

To illustrate the point, one might ask the question: suppose it was arranged so that the passive kitten in Held's and Hein's experiment had exactly the same brain goings on as the active kitten. The upshot of Noë's view is that, incredibly, that passive kitten *still* won't have the same experience as the active kitten.

Noë supposes that the main argument for drawing the line at the brain is the assumption that every experience that we can have can be produced by brain stimulation. He says:

We are now able to produce very simple visual sensations such as the illusion of the presence of flashes of light ("phosphenes") by means of direct neural stimulation...from the fact that it is possible to produce *some* experiences, it does not follow that it is possible to produce *all* experiences. To assume, without further discussion, that we will someday be able to produce all perceptual experiences by direct neural stimulation, or that it is in principle possible to do so, is to assume too much. Indeed, it is to come close to assuming internalism about experience. (p. 211)

But the issue is not whether neural stimulation can *produce* every experience but whether if the relevant brain state were to come about—*somehow*—the experience would be instantiated. To suppose that the issue is one of how experiences can be produced is to shift the topic from a constitutive issue to a causal issue. Certainly the causal sources of our experience include sensorimotor causal loops, but that does not settle the constitutive question.

Sometimes Noë talks as if the issue is whether, when an experience is produced in a given environment, that environment is causally necessary for the experience.

It may be that the only nomically possible world in which such a temporal series of brain states could occur would be one in which the animal were dynamically interacting with the very same kind of environment! To imagine the duplication of brain states is thus tacitly to appeal to the more extended setting in which those brain states are placed. Experience doesn't supervene on neural states alone, then, but only on neural states plus environmental conditions. (p. 223)

There is no plausibility in the claim that there is some nomologically possible series of brain states that can *only be produced by skilled interaction with a certain environment.* To see this point, we need only distinguish between the unlikely and the impossible. It is of course unlikely that all the air molecules in the room will all rush to one side, leaving you in a vacuum but it is not nomologically impossible. In fact, as I understand it, if the room constitutes a "quasi-ergodic" system (which rules out, for example, that the air molecules are perfectly elastic spheres which are hitting the perfectly reflective walls at 90°), it is guaranteed to happen "eventually"—according even to the Newtonian statistical mechanics of particles (although the sun may go out first). Once one adds quantum mechanics to the mix, the conclusion is even stronger. Any state of the brain that can be brought about by normal perception could perhaps occur—although with very low probability—by chance fluctuation. So at least one of the premises of Noë's argument for including the environment in the minimal supervenience base is mistaken.[13]

I will end this section with two side issues. First, I believe that interaction with the environment in evolutionary history and the history of the individual is constitutively necessary for an experience to have the *representational content* that it has. A brain in a vat (that has always been in the vat) does not have the same perceptual representational contents that that brain—even if relevantly internally the same—would have in a normal perceptual environment. Indeed, a certain evolutionary background would be required for the brain in the vat to have anything that could qualify as a *perceptual* representation at all. (This is familiar content externalism.[14]) In my view, it is possible to resist the slide from externalism about the representational content of perception to externalism about the nature of the phenomenal character of perception.[15] In any case, although this is an interesting controversial issue, what Noë's book is about is not this issue about content externalism, but rather the quite different issue of vehicle externalism.

Second, the causation/constitution conflation that I have mentioned in connection with Noë also affects Francis Crick and Christof Koch, who have famously argued that activity in the classic visual areas in the back of the head is insufficient for experience.

But Crick and Koch do not clearly distinguish between the view that activity in the front of the head (that promotes cognitive access to visual signals) is constitutively necessary to visual experience and the quite different view that feedback from the front of the head to the visual areas in the back is required to boost activity in the visual areas to the threshold for experience. The latter view (which appears most clearly in Koch, op. cit.) is subject to the problem that local feedback within the back of the head might be enough to boost activity over the threshold for experience.

To sum up so far: sensorimotor know-how and perceptual experience are causally related, but that is no reason to think that they are constitutively related. I now turn to a very different line of probing having to do with a type of empirical finding that creates difficulty for the enactive view.

II The Empirical Issue

Thus far, I have not engaged much with the slippery issue of exactly what the enactive view really is. I will approach this issue by mentioning a line of empirical work that refutes the enactive view, at least on what seems to me the most obvious reading of it. Humans and other primates have two distinct visual systems, a conscious visual system that starts in the back of the head, moving to the bottom and side (the "ventral" system) and a much less clearly conscious "dorsal" system that goes from the back toward the top of the brain.[16] These two systems have very different properties. The ventral (conscious) system is slow, is oriented towards long term visual planning of motion and uses object-centered coding (objects are represented from a stereotypical point of view instead of the point of view that reflects the perceiver's current position). The dorsal system is fast, uses "egocentric" representations that are distance and orientation sensitive, has virtually no memory or color vision and is used for the online visual guidance of action—for example, guiding the dribbling of a basketball down the court, avoiding obstacles. The last two sentences may sound like mumbo-jumbo to those who are unfamiliar with the concepts involved, so let me mention a few illustrations. Some of us have had the experience of running barefoot on the beach, our feet avoiding stones that we do not seem to see. The dorsal system—which feeds much more strongly than the ventral system to peripheral vision—is responsible for visually guided bodily movements that operate largely out of awareness.[17] There are a number of visual illusions that fool conscious vision but do not fool reaching and grasping motions that are guided by the dorsal system. (And some illusions that work in the reverse way!) It is the ventral system that is mainly relevant to perceptual experience, but—in a surprise result that trumps philosophers' science fiction scenarios—it is the dorsal system that guides action from moment to moment!

Noë summarizes some of this research (describing it as "striking," p. 18), but he does not grapple with what seems to me to be the real problem that this research creates for his perspective. (His response is in terms of teleology: perceptual experience is not *for* acting.) I can approach this problem by describing a dorsal/ventral difference which presupposes none of the theory that I have sketched. To understand it, you need to know that the fovea is the central area of the retina that is very densely packed with receptors. If you look at your thumb held at arms length, the fovea will be mainly occupied by the projection of your thumb. Here is the point: As Danckert and Goodale[18] say: "The ventral 'perception' pathway...deals primarily with foveal vision—a fact that is consistent with the crucial role this pathway plays in the perception and recognition of objects and scenes....In contrast, the dorsal 'action' stream, which...is known to play a critical role in the control of actions, such as goal-directed limb and eye movements, has a full representation of the visual field." Goodale and Murphy[19] provide a dramatic example of this point. They presented five rectangular blocks to subjects at various positions in the visual field ranging from 5° to 70° off the line of sight. They compared accuracy of perceptual discrimination of one block from another with accuracy of grip via a device that measured the aperture between thumb and forefinger as subjects reached out to pick up one of the blocks. The basic finding is that subjects' grip accuracy is roughly the same at 5° as at 70°, whereas conscious perceptual discrimination is vastly worse at 70° than at 5°.

You can get a first person appreciation of this point easily by holding up an object at 70° off of your line of sight. Features—including size—that you can see when you are looking straight at something are invisible or barely visible at an eccentricity of 70°—that is, they are inaccessible to conscious vision. But now try picking up something at 70°: you can do it pretty well. The upshot is that if the activity guided by sensorimotor knowledge with which the enactive approach identifies perceptual experience includes visually guided action, it *simply does not reflect the phenomenology of conscious vision.* That is, sensorimotor knowledge—to the extent that it involves the visual guidance of action—is not true to perceptual experience.

However, at this point we encounter a deep obscurity in the enactive view. *Does* the enactive view include visually guided action in the "activity" which it identifies with visual experience? The enactive view, as I have been understanding it, and as is stated often in the book, is that perceptual experience "is an *activity* of exploring the environment" drawing on knowledge of sensorimotor contingencies. Does the enactive view say that the activity of exercising sensorimotor know-how involves visually guided action? It is hard to see how skilled activity of exploring the environment drawing on sensorimotor knowledge-how could *fail* to involve visually guided action or what would be left of that skilled activity if visually guided action were removed.

However, there is one place in the book in which Noe explicitly denies that the sensorimotor know-how he is talking about includes visually guided action. (See p. 90, where he describes visual guidance of action as "humdrum.") And there are a number of places in which he seems to take a view at odds with the often stated view that perceptual experience is an activity. Optic ataxia is a syndrome in which the dorsal system is damaged. If the ventral system is intact, the subject is impaired in visually guided action but apparently unimpaired in visual perception. Noë says that the optic ataxic "does not undercut the enactive view, for from the fact that a patient suffers optic ataxia, it doesn't follow that he or she lacks the relevant sensorimotor knowledge. What would undercut the enactive approach would be the existence of perception in the absence of the bodily skills and sensorimotor knowledge, which, on the enactive view, are constitutive of the ability to perceive" (p. 12). Here he seems to be identifying perception or perceptual experience with the mere *possession* of bodily skills and sensorimotor knowledge rather than their exercise in perceptually guided activity. Since the possession of sensorimotor know-how persists while experience changes, this cannot be quite what is meant: if $x = y$, x cannot persist while y changes. But perhaps there is some way other than visually guided action in which sensorimotor knowledge and bodily skills can be exercised and that might be supposed to be constitutive of visual experience?

One possibility is that the view is meant to be dispositional. But *dispositions* to visually guided action do not reflect the phenomenology of conscious vision any better than visually guided action itself. Dispositions to visually guided action are just as "dorsal" as visually guided action itself. Further, it is not clear that the optic ataxic *has* the relevant dispositions. Dispositional functionalists and behaviorists can and do deal with spinal cord paralysis by claiming that the paralysis affects the *manifestation* of the dispositions without affecting the dispositions themselves. For example, behaviorists and dispositional functionalists sometimes handle paralysis by appeal to counterfactuals about how a person would move if his body were normal in certain ways ("paradigmatic embodiment," to use Shoemaker's term), but such an appeal is only appropriate when the paralysis is caused by damage that affects the manifestation of the experience rather than the experience itself—for example, spinal cord damage rather than brain damage.[20] But optic ataxia is a result of *brain* damage—not spinal cord damage—that affects the dispositions themselves, not just their manifestation. So dispositions are of no help to Noë.

There is a deflationary understanding of the enactive view that appears at some points in the book: that a perceptual experience is an instantiation of a *set of expectations* of how appearances will shift with movement. Some comments: First, the instantiation of a set of expectations need not involve any bodily skills or even a body, and so such a view would give up much of what is distinctive and revolutionary about the enactive view, which, you will recall, says that perceptual experience is the exercise of sensorimotor know-how. ("Perceptual experience *just is* a mode of skillful exploration of the world.") Second, the set of expectations might be instantiated in the form of sensorimotor *mental imagery*, but this possibility provides no comfort for the enactive view since sensorimotor mental imagery could be entirely internal and not involve bodily skills. What the enactive view would come down to is the rather un-applecart-upsetting view that perceptual experience involves a kind of mental imagery. Third, the point made in the first part of this review applies: even if expectations have an effect on perceptual experience, that is far from showing that perception is partially or totally constituted by the instantiation of expectations. Fourth, presumably the dorsal system involves at least implicit expectations for how objects in the environment shift with visual guided movements. So even the alternative deflationary version of the enactive view would still clash with the facts about the two visual systems, since the enactive view would dictate that the (in fact unconscious) dorsal states are conscious. Fifth, it is unclear what the evidence in favor of such a view would be. Certainly, the points Noë makes about how changes in sensorimotor contingencies affect experience provide at best a weak argument for such a view.

If there is a constitutive role for anything sensorimotor in perception, I think it is likely to be a matter of one's spatial sense—a sense that is shared by many perceptual systems, including vision and proprioception, and seems to be embodied in the dorsal system. One of the most interesting parts of the book are Noë's discussions of presence in absence, the phenomenology of the back of an apple that one does not see but senses nonetheless, or the cat that one sees—all of it—moving behind a picket fence. I think that presence in absence may be a matter of multimodal or amodal spatial imagery, and that that imagery may in part be motor imagery—since its brain basis appears to overlap with motor guidance systems in the dorsal visual system. Noë would have been on much stronger ground if he had restricted his enactive account to this aspect of experience instead of trying to capture all of experience. Sean Kelly has made a related suggestion: that knowledge of sensorimotor contingencies could provide an account of the background of perception rather than the foreground.[21] Here is a fact that supports both my view and Kelly's somewhat different view: subjects who have damage to the dorsal visual system that as I said is primarily responsible for visually guided action are worse at avoiding obstacles than in aiming for the main target.[22]

In an epilogue in the last four pages of the book, Noë seems to take back the claim that he has emphasized and spelled out in great detail throughout the book: that sensorimotor contingencies can be characterized objectively, suggesting that the enactive view must appeal to a primitive notion of life. "For living beings are already, by dint of being alive, *potentially conscious*" (p. 230). The idea seems to be that what is common to all experience cannot be explained by appeal to knowledge of sensorimotor contingencies, but the difference between different perceptual contents can be so explained. "You give us a spark of consciousness, we'll give you the world" (p. 230). I would suggest something more like the reverse: something sensorimotor has a better chance of explaining the spatial sense that is common to all or most perceptual experience than it has of explaining what distinguishes different experiences.

The applecart that I have been defending against Noë's attack has two main tenets. First, the minimal constitutive supervenience base for perceptual experience is the brain and does not include the rest of the body. Second, although motor outputs and motor output instructions affect perceptual experience (as has been known since Helmholtz) much of perceptual experience can be understood in abstraction from such causes.

Although I have been heavily critical of Noë's book, I did find it interesting and intriguing. And, not coincidentally, I think there is a grain of truth in the enactive view: perceptual experience is indeed (causally) affected by sensorimotor contingencies, and our sense of "presence in absence" may be a matter of spatiomotor imagery.

Notes

Review of Alva Noë, *Action in Perception* (Cambridge, MA: MIT Press, 2004).

I am grateful to Tyler Burge, John Campbell, Jakob Hohwy, Sean Kelly, Alva Noë, Christopher Peacocke, and Susanna Siegel for comments on an earlier draft.

1. *Vision Science: From Photons to Phenomenology* (Cambridge, MA: MIT Press, 1999).

2. See, for example, Palmer's treatment of position constancy (objects do not appear to jump when the eye moves), pp. 339–343, and optic flow, pp. 507–509. Helmholtz showed that the information the brain uses to distinguish a sudden jerky motion of an object in the environment from a sudden jerky motion of the eye does not come from "afferent" (i.e., input) sensors in the muscles that move the eye but rather from "efferent" motor commands to the eye. His experiment was simple: use the finger to move the eye, pushing from the side. The world appears to move, supporting the "efference copy" theory. As Palmer notes, an orthodox treatment can easily handle such inputs.

3. Andy Clark and David Chalmers, "The Extended Mind," *Analysis* 58: 10–23. Clark and Chalmers do not apply their vehicle externalism to experience.

4. This view has been pursued in other works by Noë and his collaborators, notably in Susan Hurley's *Consciousness in Action* (Cambridge, MA: Harvard University Press, 1998), and in J. K. O'Regan and A. Noë, "A Sensorimotor Approach to Vision and Visual Consciousness," *Behavioral and Brain Sciences* 24/5 (2001): 939–973. See also F. Varela, E. Thompson, and E. Rosch, *The Embodied Mind* (Cambridge, MA: MIT Press, 1991), as well as Dan Dennett's somewhat skeptical review of this book in the *American Journal of Psychology* 106 (1993): 121–126. An early precursor is H. L. Dreyfus, "Why Computers Must Have Bodies in Order to Be Intelligent," *Review of Metaphysics* 21 (September 1967): 13–32.

5. Christopher Peacocke noted (in conversation) that the devices I just mentioned do not avoid circularity. If you read about how to remove an appendix, that (plausibly) does not affect what it is like to see people who have appendixes, but it does add to one's knowledge of sensorimotor contingencies. The only way to rule out this book-learning kind of sensorimotor knowledge as

determining the phenomenology of perception is to say that it is not implied by the perception itself. But that brings in the perceptual content in explaining the sensorimotor know-how rather than the other way round.

6. However, even in this case (p. 90), the context (e.g., the sentences before and after) make it clear that the topic is perceptual experience.

7. For an argument for the implausibility of a priori functionalism, see my "Troubles with Functionalism," in C. W. Savage, ed., *Minnesota Studies in the Philosophy of Science*, vol. 9, 261–325 (Minneapolis: University of Minnesota Press, 1978); reprinted in N. Block, ed., *Readings in Philosophy of Psychology*, vol. 1 (Cambridge, MA: Harvard University Press, 1980).

8. Brian O'Shaughnessy, *The Will*, vol. 1 (Cambridge: Cambridge University Press, 1980), and *Consciousness and the World* (New York: Oxford University Press, 2000); Michael Martin, "Sight and Touch," in Tim Crane, ed., *The Contents of Experience: Essays on Perception* (Cambridge: Cambridge University Press, 1992). See also A. D. Smith, *The Problem of Perception* (Cambridge MA: Harvard University Press, 2002).

9. R. Held and A. Hein, "Movement-Produced Stimulation in the Development of Visually Guided Behavior," *Journal of Comparative and Physiological Psychology* 56/5 (1963): 872–876.

10. See S. Hurley and A. Noë, "Neural Plasticity and Consciousness," *Biology and Philosophy* 18: 131–168; N. Block, "Spatial Perception via Tactile Sensation," *Trends in Cognitive Science* 7/7 (2003): 285–286; S. Hurley and A. Noë, "Neural Plasticity and Consciousness: A Reply to Block," *Trends in Cognitive Sciences* 7/8 (2003): 342. (These papers can be found on my website, http://www.nyu.edu/gsas/dept/philo/faculty/block/.) Noë thinks that the subjects who have worn the goggles the longest end up finding the world to look as it did before they donned the goggles. Although I disagree with that gloss on the experiments, there can be no doubt that there is considerable experiential adaptation.

11. Note that even if dreaming were—contrary to fact—not causally affected by events outside the brain, still dreaming could fail to supervene on the brain if, for example, there is a constitutive connection between dream experience and perceptual experience. Note also that I am assuming only that the dreamer is experiencing, not that dream experience is perceptual experience.

12. See my "Two Neural Correlates of Consciousness," *Trends in Cognitive Sciences* 9/2 (2005): 46–52; Christof Koch, *The Quest for Consciousness* (Englewood, CO: Roberts & Co., 2004). The orthodox view is also rejected by the Representationists mentioned earlier and by disjunctivists such as John McDowell and Mike Martin. See Susanna Siegel, "Indiscriminability and the Phenomenal," *Philosophical Studies* 120 (2004): 90–112, for an excellent discussion of one version of disjunctivism.

13. When I pressed Noë on the constitutive/causal issue at the Workshop on the Fundamental Issues in Cognitive Science in Taipei, Taiwan, January 6–9, 2005, and on March 22, 2005, at the Mind and Language Seminar at NYU, he disparaged the causal/constitutive distinction. But it should be noted that the book repeatedly makes what has to be read as constitutive claims, including sometimes using the word "constitutive," as in: "Most recent work on the relation of percep-

tion and action stops short of making the constitutive claim that defines the enactive standpoint: It does not treat perception as a kind of action or skillful activity (or as drawing on a kind of sensorimotor knowledge)" (p. 18).

14. See Tyler Burge, "Individualism and Psychology," *Philosophical Review* 95 (1986): 3–45; "Individuation and Causation in Psychology," *Pacific Philosophical Quarterly* 707 (1989): 303–322; "Vision and Intentional Content," in E. Lepore and R. Van Gulick, eds., *John Searle and His Critics* (Oxford: Blackwell, 1991).

15. See my "Mental Paint" in M. Hahn and B. Ramberg, eds., *Reflections and Replies: Essays on the Philosophy of Tyler Burge* (Cambridge, MA: MIT Press, 2003); Tyler Burge, "Qualia and Intentional Content: Reply to Block," in the same volume.

16. See M. A. Goodale and A. D. Milner, *The Visual Brain in Action* (Oxford: Oxford University Press, 1995); M. A. Goodale and A. D. Milner, *Sight Unseen* (Oxford: Oxford University Press, 2003). For an account aimed at philosophers, see A. Clark, "Visual Experience and Motor Action: Are the Bonds Too Tight?", *Philosophical Review* 110/4 (2001): 495–519.

17. I. Schindler, N. Rice, R. D. McIntosh, Y. Rossetti, and A. D. Milner, "Automatic Avoidance of Obstacles Is a Dorsal Stream Function: Evidence from Optic Ataxia," *Nature Neuroscience* 7 (2004): 779–784; R. D. McIntosh, K. I. McClements, I. Schindler, T. P. Cassidy, D. Birchall, and A. D. Milner, "Avoidance of Obstacles in the Absence of Visual Awareness," *Proceedings of the Royal Society of London B, 2004, 271*, 15–20.

18. J. A. Danckert and M. A. Goodale, "Ups and Downs in the Visual Control of Action," in S. H. Johnson-Frey, ed., *Taking Action: Cognitive Neuroscience Perspectives on the Problem of Intentional Movement* (Cambridge MA: MIT Press, 2003).

19. M. A. Goodale and K. J. Murphy, "Action and Perception in the Visual Periphery," in P. Their and H.-O. Karnath, eds., *Parietal Lobe Contributions to Orientation in 3 D Space*, 447–461 (Heidelberg: Springer-Verlag, 1997).

20. Sydney Shoemaker, "Embodiment and Behavior," in Amelie Rorty, ed., *The Identities of Persons* (Berkeley: University of California Press, 1976).

21. At the NYU Mind and Language Seminar, March 9, 2004.

22. Schindler et al., op. cit. See also G. W. Humphreys and M. G. Edwards, "Automatic Obstacle Avoidance and Parietal Cortex," *Nature Neuroscience* 7 (2004): 693. This paper introduces the Schindler et al. paper.

IV Consciousness and the Mind-Body Problem

19   Are Absent Qualia Impossible?

Functionalism is the doctrine that pain (for example) is identical to a certain functional state, a state definable in terms of its causal relations to inputs, outputs, and other mental states. The functional state with which pain would be identified might be partially characterized in terms of its tendency to be caused by tissue damage, by its tendency to cause the desire to be rid of it, and by its tendency to produce action designed to shield the damaged part of the body from what is taken to cause it.[1]

Functionalism has been plagued by two "qualia"-centered objections: the Inverted Qualia Objection and the Absent Qualia Objection. The inverted Qualia Objection can be introduced by attention to the familiar inverted spectrum hypothesis, the hypothesis that though you and I have exactly the same functional organization, the sensation that you have when you look at red things is phenomenally the same as the sensation that I have when I look at green things. If this hypothesis is true, then there is a mental state of you that is functionally identical[2] to a mental state of me, even though the two states are qualitatively or phenomenally different. So the functional characterizations of mental states fail to capture their "qualitative" aspect. To put the difficulty more boldly, one could define a qualitative state Q as the state someone has just in case he has a sensation with the same qualitative character as my current headache.[3] If inverted qualia are possible, then mental state Q is not identical with any functional state, and if functionalism claims that every mental state is a functional state, functionalism is false.

The Absent Qualia Objection proceeds along similar lines, beginning with an argument that it is possible that a mental state of a person x be functionally identical to a state of y, even though x's state *has* qualitative character while y's state *lacks* qualitative character altogether.

Sydney Shoemaker's "Functionalism and Qualia" is an ingenious defense of the functionalist point of view from these qualia-centered objections. Shoemaker argues that the functionalist can live with the possibility of inverted qualia. Briefly, Shoemaker's proposal is that the functionalist should concede that the mental state Q (defined above) is not identical to any functional state. But he argues that this concession does not prohibit the functionalist from giving functional characterizations of pain, being appeared to red, and other common mental states that have qualitative character (without having qualitative identity conditions in the manner of Q).

While Shoemaker allows the possibility of inverted qualia and elaborates functionalism so as to accomodate them, he is not so tolerant of absent qualia. He argues that absent qualia are logically impossible, and hence that no version of the Absent Qualia Objection can go through. My main purpose is to rebut Shoemaker's argument against the possibility of absent qualia. At the end of the paper, I sketch Shoemaker's solution to the Inverted Qualia Objection, showing that it fails if absent qualia are indeed possible.

Shoemaker's argument against the possibility of absent qualia is this: if absent qualia are possible, then the presence or absence of the qualitative character of pain would make no difference to its causal consequences; and so, according to a causal theory of knowledge, we could have no knowledge of the qualitative character of pain; but given that we *do* have knowledge of the qualitative character of pain (in any sense of "qualitative character" of interest to a discussion of absent or inverted qualia), absent qualia are not possible.

I have no quarrel with any reasonable version of a causal theory of knowledge, nor do I wish to doubt Shoemaker's assumption that we have knowledge of the qualitative character of our pain. The crux of my disagreement with Shoemaker is in his first premise: that if absent qualia are possible, then the presence or absence of the qualitative character of pain would make no difference to its causal consequences. If absent qualia are possible, there could be a state functionally identical to pain that lacks qualitative character (call it "ersatz pain").[4] But ersatz pain could be possible even though the qualitative character of *genuine* pain *is* crucial to producing the consequences that are produced *in another way* by ersatz pain. This is the point on which Shoemaker's argument runs aground.

I make this point plausible by sketching an "odd realization" of human functional organization whose pains are arguably ersatz.

Consider a very simple version of machine functionalism[5] which states that each mental system is described by at least one Turing machine table of a certain sort, and that each mental state of the system is identical to one of the machine table states. Consider, for example, the Turing machine specified by the table in figure 19.1.[6] (The table is equivalent to four conditionals: for example "If the machine is in S_1 and receives a \$.50 input, then it emits a coke and stays in S_1.")

One can get a crude picture of the simple version of machine functionalism that I am talking about by considering the claim that $S_1 =$ dollar-desire and $S_2 = $ \$.50-desire. Of course, no functionalist should claim that a Coke machine desires anything. Rather, the simple version of machine functionalism that I am sketching makes an analogous claim with respect to a much more complex machine table.

Now imagine a body externally like a human body, say yours, but internally quite different. The neurons from sense organs are connected to a bank of lights in a hollow cavity in the head. The motor output neurons are activated by buttons on a console in another section of the cavity. On one wall of the cavity is a very large machine table that describes a person, say you, and in a corner of the cavity, there is a blackboard. In the cavity resides a little man. We tell the man to "start" in a certain state, say $S_{1,975}$, which happens to be the state that you are now in. The man's job is as follows. He writes "1,975" on the blackboard, and looks to the bank of input lights to see what inputs are currently occurring. He sees a pattern of lights that he has been trained to identify as input I_{342}. He looks on the great machine table on the wall for the box at the intersection of row 342 and column 1,975. In the box is written "Go to $S_{7,651}$; emit output $O_{10,983}$." The little man erases the "1,975" from the blackboard and writes "7,651." Then he goes to the output console and presses the pattern of buttons that he has been taught will produce output $O_{10,983}$. Then he looks to the input board to see what the next input is, and so on. Through the efforts of this little man, the artificial body in which he lives behaves just as you would, given any possible sequence of inputs. Indeed, since the machine table that the little man follows describes you, it is easy to see that the homunculus-headed system is functionally the same as you.

But though the homunculus-headed system is now in the same functional state that you are in, does it have the same mental states that you have? Suppose that you and your homunculus-headed doppelgänger are in different rooms, both connected to a third room by a two-way TV system. An interrogator in the third room addresses a remark carried to you by your TV set and also to your homunculus-headed doppelgänger by his TV set. Since you and your doppelgänger are functionally alike, you emit exactly

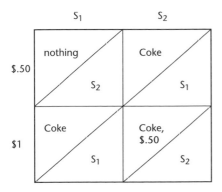

Figure 19.1

the same sounds and movements in response. The interrogator replies, and you and your doppelgänger continue to respond in indistinguishable manners. Of course, *you* are understanding the interrogator's English sentences and expressing your thoughts in English. But is your doppelgänger understanding the interrogator's English sentences? Is it having the same thoughts that you are having? The *little man* need not understand the interrogator's remarks. He can push the buttons and read the patterns of lights without having any idea that they have any relation to a conversation in English. Indeed, he can do his job without knowing what sort of a system he is controlling, and without being able to understand English at all. More relevantly to our current discussion of qualia, suppose you have a nasty headache and are calling for aspirin; the homunculus-headed system, of course, is in the same functional state as you, and is uttering similar sounds. However, the *homunculus* who is pushing the buttons need not have any pain. Why should we suppose that the system of which he is a part has a pain?[7]

There are two claims that I want to emphasize that I am *not* making. First I do not intend to use the example in any direct way to suggest that functionalism has *special* difficulties with *qualia*. The homunculus-headed system seems as lacking in thought as in qualia, and so any argument against functionalism based on such an example could as well be couched in terms of absent thoughts as absent qualia. I do place special emphasis on the example's relevance to absent qualia because I am discussing Shoemaker's claim that absent qualia are impossible. Second, I do not intend that the example or what I shall say about it here should convince anyone that absent qualia (or thoughts) are possible. Intuitions about such matters are easy to manipulate, and even if our intuitions in these cases were immutable, a critical examination of the *source* of the intuitions would be required to ground any argument for absent qualia.[8]

Rather, my point is this. I want the reader to see why it is reasonable for philosophers to allow that absent qualia are possible *without* committing themselves to Shoemaker's first premise. According to his first premise, if the homunculus-head has absent qualia, we can conclude that absent qualia are possible, and therefore that the presence or absence of the qualitative character of pain would make no difference to its causal consequences. But surely the possibility of a homunculus-head with absent qualia does not entail—nor does it give us any reason to believe—that the causal role of *our genuine* pain is independent of its qualitative character. The causal role of genuine pain may be crucially *dependent on its qualitative character*, even if the homunculus-head's pains are ersatz.

Perhaps an analogy will make the point clearer. Consider a hydraulic computer or other logic device. Now, for some such device, an "absent fluid" hypothesis may be true: that is, there may be a functionally identical device that lacks fluid, for example, because it works electrically. (Recall that the absent qualia hypothesis says that for some state that has qualitative character, there can be a functionally identical state that lacks qualitative character.) But no one in his right mind would argue that since the absent fluid hypothesis is true, the presence or absence of fluid would make no difference to the operation of the hydraulic device. The hydraulic device will presumably have states whose causal consequences depend crucially on the properties of the fluid, *even though* there could be functionally identical states that did not depend on any properties of fluid (but on electrical properties instead). Similarly, mousetraps with springs can be functionally identical to mousetraps without springs. (So an "absent spring" hypothesis is true.) But it would be silly to conclude that the presence or absence of springs make no differences to the causal consequences of the states of those mousetraps that *have* springs.

Shoemaker goes wrong in his implicit picture of what the friend of absent qualia must be committed to. The picture is that qualia are like the colors of wires in a computer which cannot be opened. The wires are (say) red, though since their color makes no difference to the working of the computer, they could have been some other color without making any functional difference. Since we cannot open the computer, we will never know whether the wires are red or green or even whether they have any color at all. The color is "epiphenomenal," and so, according to a causal theory of knowledge, we can have no knowledge of it. My point is that a sensible friend of absent qualia need not be committed to any such epiphenomenal picture of qualia. Instead, he can think of qualia as like the fluid in the hydraulic computer mentioned above; the fluid is crucial to the working of the device, even though there could be a functionally identical device that lacks fluid.

The friend of absent qualia that Shoemaker attacks thinks that our pain could lack qualitative character and still have the same causal consequences. The friend of absent qualia that I defend makes a much more modest claim, that there could be a being that has ersatz pain. But although the friend of absent qualia that I defend is more modest than the one Shoemaker attacks, I am not failing to meet Shoemaker's challenge head-on. For the point of Shoemaker's attack on absent qualia is to defend functionalism. And the version of the absent qualia claim that I am suggesting, though deflationary, is strong *enough* to defeat functionalism. For if it is *true* that the homunculus-head can have the functional state putatively identical to pain (functional state S, let us say) yet have no state with qualitative character, then we have a case of S without pain. Therefore, pain ≠ S, and hence functionalism is false.

I have just sketched what is wrong with Shoemaker's argument on its most natural interpretation. However, there are other ways of understanding the argument which I will proceed to discuss. The different versions of the argument can be seen as stemming from a three-way ambiguity in the notion of "epiphenomenal" (my word, not Shoemaker's) in terms of which the argument can be couched. The main premises of the argument are the one that I have just been criticizing, that if absent qualia are possible, qualitative character is epiphenomenal (call this the AQ premise), and a causal theory of knowledge (CTK) premise to the effect that what is epiphenomenal *is* unknowable. (The final premise is that qualitative character *is* knowable, so (conclusion) absent qualia are impossible.) On one way of reading "epiphenomenal," the AQ premise is subject to just the difficulty I have been pointing out. On another way of reading "epiphenomenal," the AQ premise is subject to another difficulty having to do with physical or physiological differences between pains and ersatz pains. On still another way of reading "epiphenomenal," the AQ premise becomes trivially true, but the CTK premise then becomes entirely question-begging.

Let me state Shoemaker's argument in roughly the way he puts it:[9]

1. AQ Premise   If absent qualia are possible, then the qualitative character of pain is entirely independent of its causal powers.
2. CTK Premise   If F is a feature of a mental state S, and F is entirely independent of the causal powers of S, then F is not knowable.
3. The qualitative character of pain is knowable.
4. Therefore, absent qualia are not possible.

As I said above, the problem in understanding the argument lies in an ambiguity in the notion of "epiphenomenal" being used, that is, in what Shoemaker means by "entirely independent of the causal powers of." Shoemaker explicates this phrase in his statement of the CTK premise:

If there could be a feature of some mental state that was entirely independent of the causal powers of the state (i.e., was such that its presence or absence would make no difference to the state's tendencies to bring about other states, and so forth), and so was irrelevent to its 'functional identity', then such a feature would be totally unknowable (if you like, this assumes a causal theory of knowledge).[10]

So "F is entirely independent of the causal powers of S" is to be read: "The presence or absence of F would make no difference to S's tendencies to bring about other states and so forth," or as I shall abbreviate it: "The presence or absence of F would make no difference to S's causal role." Now there is at least one serious ambiguity here:

Strong Reading   S could lack F, and S's lacking F would make no difference to S's causal role.
Weak Reading   There could be a state S⁻ which is functionally identical to S, such that S⁻ lacks F, but nonetheless has the same causal role as S.

The Strong Reading is stronger than the Weak Reading because in a possible world in which S lacks F yet has the same causal role, S retains the functional identity it has in the actual world (because it has the same causal role), so S itself satisfies the conditions on S^- specified by the Weak Reading. So the Strong Reading entails the Weak Reading, that is, if F is entirely independent of the causal powers of S on the Strong Reading, then F is entirely independent of the causal powers of S on the Weak Reading as well (though not vice versa).

Now it is easy to see how a functionalist might miss this distinction, for if S is taken to be a functional state type, the distinction is a distinction without a difference. For if S is a functional state type, and S^- is functionally identical to S, then S just is S^-. Functional identity of functional state types[11] entails identity *simpliciter*. For functional state types are defined by their causal relations to inputs, outputs, and other states, and functional identity is just identity of these causal relations. So, since S^- lacks F, then S (being identical to S^-) could lack F. Hence the Weak Reading would entail the Strong Reading. And since as I mentioned above, the Strong Reading entails the Weak Reading (even if S is not taken to be a functional state) the two readings would be logically equivalent.

Of course, what I have just said should not be taken to challenge the distinction between the Strong Reading and the Weak Reading. For to take S to be a functional state would be illicit in the context of Shoemaker's argument. In the premises of Shoemaker's argument that make use of locutions of the form of "F is entirely independent of the causal powers of S," S is a *mental* state, and to take mental states to be functional states would be to beg the question, since the truth of functionalism is just what is at issue.

Let us begin our more detailed examination of Shoemaker's argument by adopting the Strong Reading. On the Strong Reading, Shoemaker's CTK premise looks reasonable enough (anyway, I won't object to it). It says:

CTK Premise   If F is a feature of a mental state S, and S's lacking F would make no difference to S's causal role, then F is not knowable.

Now let us look at the AQ premise. As originally stated, it said that if absent qualia are possible, then the qualitative character of pain is entirely independent of its causal powers. Substituting in the Strong Reading of "entirely independent of the causal powers of," we get

Absent Qualia Premise, Strong Reading   If absent qualia are possible, then pain could lack qualitative character, and its lacking qualitative character would make no difference to its causal role.

Now on this Strong Reading of the AQ premise, it is clearly false for reasons that I have already given. If absent qualia are possible, one can conclude at most[12] that ersatz pain is possible, but not that genuine pain might have lacked qualitative character, or that if genuine pain had lacked qualitative character, then it would have had the same causal consequences (or retained its functional identity at all). (Recall the analogy to the "absent fluid" and "absent spring" hypothesis.) I conclude that on the Strong Reading, the AQ premise is false.

Let us now turn to the Weak Reading of the AQ premise. On the Weak Reading, the AQ premise amounts to this:

AQ Premise, Weak Reading   If absent qualia are possible, there could be ersatz pain that has the same causal role as pain.

This premise looks virtually tautological (Recall that "absent qualia are possible" can be taken to mean[13] that for any state Q that has qualitative character, there could be a functionally identical state Q⁻ that lacks qualitative character). But appearances are deceiving. What *is* tautological is that if absent qualia are possible, then ersatz pain is possible. However, one cannot conclude that ersatz pain must have the same causal role as pain. Recall that it is open to the friend of absent qualia to hold that ersatz pain can only occur in a system that is physically very different from us, for example, a homunculus-head. Indeed, if the friend of absent qualia holds a rather minimal physicalist doctrine, he is *forced* to believe that *ersatz pain differs physically from genuine pain*. The minimal physicalist doctrine that I have in mind combines token physicalism (the doctrine that each particular pain (for example) is a token of some physical type—though there need be no physical property m common to all pains), and the supervenience of the mental (no mental difference without a physical difference). My minimal physicalist doctrine says that *two states cannot differ mentally without differing physically*. Now since the difference between pain and ersatz pain is a mental difference, and given the doctrine that two states cannot differ mentally without differing physically, it follows that pain and ersatz pain *must differ physically*. But then pain and ersatz pain will in general have different causal properties, for instance, with regard to their effects on EEGs, head X-rays, and brain surgeons.

So on the Weak Reading of the AQ premise, the friend of absent qualia need not accept it, and if he holds a minimal version of physicalism, he is *forced to reject it*.

The following remark in Shoemaker's paper suggests an objection to my criticism of the AQ premise on the Weak Reading:

There could (on this view [the absent qualia hypothesis]) be no possible physical effects of any state from which we could argue by an "inference to the best explanation" that it has qualitative character; for if there were, we could give at least a partial functional characterization of the having of qualitative character by saying that it tends to give rise, in such and such circumstances, to those physical effects, and could not allow that a state lacking qualitative character could be functionally identical to a state having it. (p. 296)

The objection suggested might be put as follows:

Objection: Suppose I formulate a functional theory according to which S is the functional state identical to pain. Suppose you are in S, and your functional simulation is in the functionally identical state S'. Relative to this functional theory, the functional causal consequences of S and S' are the same, but suppose some *non*functional consequences are different. Now you claim that some of these differences in nonfunctional consequences show S is pain while S' is merely ersatz pain. *If you are right*, then while my proposed functional theory is mistaken, there is *another* functional theory that is superior to mine, and that escapes refutation, for it incorporates into the functional definition of "pain" the tendency to produce the sorts of consequences, whatever they were, that distinguished S from S'. So on the new functional theory, S and S' are *not* functionally equivalent, and S' is not a case of pain. So all your argument shows is that the functional theory presupposed is not the best one.[14]

Reply: The first thing to notice about the objection is that its relevance extends a good deal beyond the defence of the Weak Reading of the AQ premise. It is an objection also to the argument for absent qualia that one would base on the example of the homunculus-head described earlier. Secondly, the reader should note that there are a number of very different proposals that the objection could be understood as suggesting. One suggestion would be to add *physiological* information to the functional account. We have neurons in our heads, while the systems that arguably have ersatz pains have, for example, little people or transistors instead. If we characterize pain in part in terms of its physiological causes and effects, we will avoid ascribing pain to creatures which (like the homunculus-head) are physiologically unlike us. A sample characterization along these lines would be: x is in pain if and only if x is in functional state S, and S is realized in x by such and such neurological states.

While such an account has certain attractions, it also has its defects; the main one being that it would prevent us from ascribing pain to creatures sufficiently neurologically different from us. I will not pursue this point here, however, since for present purposes the view can be dismissed simply because it is not acceptable as a defence of *functionalism*. Functionalism requires purely "relational" characterizations of mental states (see note 1), so adding physiological information changes a functionalist account into a *mixed* physiological-functional account.

This difficulty could be avoided by adding *functionalized* physiological conditions to the original functional account. This idea is best explained via the sketch of functionalism in note 1. The psychological theory in terms of which the functional definitions are constructed (theory T of note 1) would simply be supplemented by a fragment of physiological theory *prior* to Ramsification. No physiological terms would then appear in the functional characterization, since they would be replaced by variables in the same manner as the mental terms. The resulting account would be purely functional.

There are three major sources of difficulty with this approach. (1) Since the resulting account is fully functional, it can as easily have homunculus-headed realizations as any other functional account.[15] (2) The account will chauvinistically disqualify sentient creatures whose internal workings do not sufficiently resemble *our* physiological mechanisms. (3) It would be unacceptable to Shoemaker and to the other functionalists

(Lewis, Smart, Armstrong[16]) who take functional definitions to be truths of conceptual analysis or at any rate, common sense. Physiology is not part of common sense psychology.

These "analytic" functionalists may wish to take another tack. They may wish to modify their functional definitions by including whatever *negative* conditions can be motivated by a priori thought experiments.[17] For example, they might propose that x is in pain if and only if x has the functional state S, and x does not contain parts that (*a*) have a functional organization similar to that of x, and (*b*) also play a crucial role in giving x its functional organization.[18]

One kind of difficulty with such a proposal resides in its ad hoc nature. This point is illustrated by the observation that the formulation just given won't do,[19] because it is logically (and perhaps nomologically) possible that we could come to fail to satisfy the condition ourselves—without thereby losing any of our mental assets. Imagine that part of the universe contains matter that is infinitely divisible and that this region of the universe contains people of all sizes—including people much smaller than our "elementary" particles. They build spaceships that are equipped to simulate our "elementary" particles, and fly them so as to mimic clumps of our matter, for example, oxygen, carbon, and so on. We embark on a long interstellar trip, and running low on supplies, we stop on an "asteroid" made up of this unusual matter, taking on large quantities of the stuff to grow our food, manufacture our air, etc. Gradually, we come to be made of the matter. This change would be at too small a level to affect the basic electrochemical mechanisms of our brains, and so it seems doubtful that our mentality would be changed in any way. So the formulation of the last paragraph would have to be changed to rule out the homunculus-head described earlier without ruling out those of us who come to be composed of the particle homunculi. I don't wish to suggest that *no* formulation can be found which excludes the big homunculus-heads while at the same time including the little homunculus-heads. My point, rather, is that those who aim to produce such a formulation must cope not only with *mindless* creatures who are functionally similar to us on the most natural sort of functional account (such as the big homunculus-head), but also with *mindful* creatures who differ from the mindless ones in, for example, the role and size of the homunculi. Given any *particular* functional account, we could have virtually no confidence in it, because human ingenuity being what it is, we could expect that some new thought experiment would show that the condition ruled out either too much or too little.

A second difficulty with the analytic functionalist proposal is that it does not really defend functionalism at all. Rather, like the proposal mentioned earlier that combined functionalism with physiology, the present proposal amounts to a mixed physico-functional account. The central idea of functionalism in all its forms is that what it is to be a pain is to have a certain causal role, and that what pains have in common in virtue of which they are pains is just this causal role and not their physical nature. This is clearest in the empirically minded functionalists such as Putnam and Fodor who argue that functionalism shows that physicalism is false. But the doctrine is equally present among the "analytic" functionalists. As Lewis puts the position that he shares with Armstrong (and presumably also Shoemaker), "Our view is that the concept of pain . . . is the concept of a state that occupies a certain causal role."[20] But to identify the concept of pain with the concept of a state that occupies a certain causal role, *adding* that only *some* of the things that occupy that causal role are *really* pains is not to specify the causal role in more detail, but rather to abandon the functionalist point of view altogether.

This problem could be avoided by abandoning formulations in terms of conditions on realizations of functional states in favor of conditions on causal antecedents and consequents of the realizations. For example, a crude first effort might be: x has pain if and only if x is in functional state S, and x's realization of S doesn't have effects on brain surgeons, X-ray machines, etc., that are typical of the states of homunculus-heads. However, this sort of approach is just as ad hoc as the one just discussed, and it introduces a new difficulty as well: how are we to rule out beings whose inner workings are designed so as to *falsely* convince us that they are (or are not) homunculus-heads? Since it is the *actual presence* of the homunculus playing a certain role (in the original example) that is important, and not the causal consequences that give the *appearance* of a homunculus playing that role, it is hard to see how this sort of line of argument will work.

Thus far, I have suggested two readings of "entirely independent of the causal powers of," the Strong Reading and the Weak Reading. I have argued that on both readings, the locus of fallacy in Shoemaker's argument is the AQ premise. I now want to suggest a way of evading my objections by adopting a Weaker Still Reading of "entirely independent of the causal powers of." I will repeat the other readings for the convenience of the reader.

Strong Reading   S could lack F, and S's lacking F would make no difference to S's causal role.
Weak Reading   There could be a state S⁻ that is functionally identical to S, such that S⁻ lacks F, but nonetheless has the same causal role as S.
Weaker Still Reading   There could be a state S⁻ which is functionally identical to S, but which lacks F.

The Weaker Still Reading differs from the Weak Reading in that the former requires only that S and S⁻ be functionally identical, while the latter requires, in addition, that S and S⁻ have the same total causal role. The difference, you will recall, is that functionally identical states need have the same causal role only with respect to a designated set of states, inputs and outputs. A mental state can have causes and effects that are not in the designated set, for example, cosmic ray causes and EEG effects.

The advantage of the Weaker Still Reading for Shoemaker's purposes is that it renders the AQ premise true, indeed trivially true. Recall that on the Weak Reading, the AQ premise said that if absent qualia are possible, there could be ersatz pain that has the same causal role as pain. The Weaker Still Reading drops the "same causal role" requirement:

AQ Premise, Weaker Still Reading   If absent qualia are possible, ersatz pain is possible.

This is trivially true (see note 12).

However, on the Weaker Still Reading, Shoemaker's CTK (Causal Theory of Knowledge) premise becomes totally question-begging. Recall that the original CTK premise was:

CTK Premise   If F is a feature of a mental state S, and F is entirely independent of the causal powers of S, then F is not knowable.

I had no quarrel with this premise in this form. But on the Weaker Still Reading of "entirely independent of the causal powers of," what the premise says is:

CTK (Weaker Still Reading)   If F is a feature of a mental state S, and there could be a state S^- which is functionally identical to S but lacks F, then F is not knowable.

This is just the claim that if absent qualia are possible then qualitative character is unknowable, *generalized* to cover whatever other features of mental states there may be which cannot be functionally defined. But since what is *at issue* is whether the possibility of absent qualia makes qualia unknowable, Shoemaker can hardly just assume a slightly stronger version of this claim as a *premise* in his argument.

In sum, I have suggested three readings of "entirely independent of the causal powers of." On the Strong Reading, the CTK premise is plausible enough, but the AQ premise is absurd. On the Weak Reading, the AQ premise is still wrong. On the Weaker Still Reading, the AQ premise is trivially true, but the CTK premise becomes question-begging.

Shoemaker's Answer to the Inverted Qualia Objection

I will now sketch Shoemaker's answer to the Inverted Qualia Objection. I will not argue that it is mistaken, but only that it fails *if* absent qualia are indeed possible. If I can show this, I will also have shown that the homunculus-headed example mentioned earlier may in an indirect way be useable to demonstrate that qualia pose a special difficulty for functionalism. For suppose that the homunculus-headed example can be used to show that absent qualia are possible. Then, even if the example can equally well be used to show that absent thoughts, wants, and so on, are possible, the example will be useable to undermine Shoemaker's solution to the Inverted Qualia Objection. Since there is no Inverted Thought Objection or Inverted Desire Objection corresponding to the Inverted Qualia Objection,[21] if the Inverted Qualia Objection stands, qualia do pose a special problem for functionalism.

Shoemaker observes that if we can speak of mental states being like or different in qualitative character, we should be able to speak of "qualitative states," states whose type indentity conditions can be specified in terms of qualitative similarity. Take for example, the qualitative state Q mentioned earlier—the one someone has just in case his state feels just like (is qualitatively similar to) my current headache. The possibility of qualia inversion shows that no qualitative state type is identical to a functional state type, and thus, Shoemaker concedes, functionalism will have to allow that some types of mental states (namely qualitative states) are not identical to functional states, or in Shoemaker's terminology, qualitative states are not "functionally definable." (Functionally definable = a definition can be formulated involving input and output terms and quantification over mental states, but no mental terminology—see note 1.) Shoemaker's innovation is to show that this concession does not commit one to holding that "pain," "being appeared to red," and other sensation terms are not functionally definable. For we needn't suppose that these states are qualitative states (in the sense of having qualitative identity conditions). He argues that so long as the relation of "qualitative similarity" *is* functionally definable, so is "pain," and so on. He suggests that "qualitative similarity" may be functionally definable in terms of the tendency to believe that objects that produce similar qualia have similar properties, and the tendency to act in a way appropriate to such beliefs. For example, if two objects produce the same qualia (of a certain sort) in me, I may tend to believe they have the same color, and to point to them both when asked for examples of red objects. Such a definition of "qualitative similarity" may require viewing pains as somatic sense impressions, for example, impressions of bodily injuries.

Shoemaker argues that once we have a functional definition of "qualitative similarity," we can give functional definitions of terms like "pain" in a way which dispenses with reference to particular qualia in favor of quantification over qualia. That is, we could define "pain" as a state that has (*a*) *some* qualitative character or other, and (*b*) such and such causal relations to other states, inputs and outputs. Shoemaker's proposal gives shape to the vague suggestion that functionalism can deal with inverted qualia worries by regarding pain as a state which can have different qualitative character on different occasions.

Shoemaker does not say explicitly how a functional definition of "qualitative similarity" allows us to define mental state terms such as "pain." In order to define "pain" as a state with some qualitative character or other with such and such causal relations to other states, inputs and outputs, one needs a functional definition of the predicate "has qualitative character." But how does one get a definition of this predicate in terms of the qualitative similarity relation? One assumes that what Shoemaker has in mind is something like the formation of equivalence classes of qualia under an equivalence relation definable in terms of the qualitative similarity relation.[22] Then "has qualitative character" could be defined as membership in one of the equivalence classes.

However, Shoemaker's move works only if absent qualia are indeed impossible. Suppose, for example, that the homunculus-head described above has no states with qualitative character. Shoemaker's functional definition of "has qualitative character" would nonetheless class the homunculus-head's ersatz sensations as having qualitative character. Indeed, an equivalence relation defined in terms of Shoemaker's qualitative similarity relation would partition the ersatz sensations into different equivalence classes, even though all members of all the equivalence classes would have the *same* qualitative character, namely, none. (Worse, if *we* could have ersatz pains as well as genuine pains, Shoemaker's functional definition of qualitative similarity would dictate that an ersatz pain could be qualitatively identical to a genuine pain.)

In sum, if I have succeeded in refuting Shoemaker's arguments against the possibility of absent qualia, then an argument for absent qualia may block his way around the Inverted Qualia Objection.

Notes

Reprinted from *Philosophical Review* 89 (2): 257–274, April 1980. Reprinted in Frank Jackson, ed., *Consciousness*, 203–220 (Aldershot: Dartmouth Publishing Company, 1998). German translation, "Sind fehlende Qualia unmöglich?," in Sven Walter and Heinz-Dieter Heckmann, eds., *Qualia* (Paderborn: Mentis Verlag, 2001).

I am very much indebted to comments by Sydney Shoemaker on a number of earlier drafts of this paper. I am also grateful to Hartry Field, Jerry Fodor, Paul Horwich, Barbara Klein, Joe Levine, and George Smith.

1. More precisely, functionalism could be characterized as follows: Let T be a psychological theory, all of whose mental state terms are predicates. The Ramsey sentence of T can be written as

$$\exists F_1 \ldots F_n T(F_1 \ldots F_n).$$

If F_i is the variable that replaced "having pain," then

$$x \text{ is in pain} \leftrightarrow \exists F_1 \ldots F_n[T(F_1 \ldots F_n) \ \& \ x \text{ has } F_1].$$

Functionalism would identify the property of having pain with the property expressed by the predicate on the right hand side of the biconditional. The property expressed by the predicate on the right hand side of the biconditional is a functional property. This sort of formulation is due to David Lewis (though Lewis's proposal differs markedly in details). A detailed exposition of functionalism can be found in "What Is Functionalism?", the introduction to the functionalism section of my *Readings in Philosophy of Psychology*, vol. 1 (Cambridge, MA: Harvard University Press, 1980).

2. A and B are functionally identical states iff they have the same causal relations to inputs, outputs, and other mental states. As note 1 indicates, the "mental" in the last sentence's characterization of functional identity is eliminable via a formulation that specifies a certain set of states without saying explicitly that they are mental states. So A and B would be said to be functionally identical iff they have the same causal relations to inputs, outputs, and other states that are themselves specified in terms of causal role.

As note 1 also indicates, functional characterizations are relative to psychological theory. So A and B might be functionally identical with respect to one theory, but not with respect to another. The seriousness of this problem may not be clear to those whose main contact with functionalism is via Lewis's functional definitions. Lewis defines pain as the state with causal role R. But pain can be the state with causal role R *as well as* the state with causal role R', without contradiction, just as George Washington is both the first president and the father of our country. However, the version of functionalism with which I am concerned here—and one to which Lewis is also committed—identifies pain, not with a functionally *characterized* state, (a state picked out by its causal role) but with a *functional state* (a state constituted by its causal role). One way of stating a genuine functional state (or rather, functional property) identity thesis is that it identifies the property of being a pain with the property of having causal role R. And being a pain cannot be identical to both having causal role R *and* having causal role R', just as no property can be identical to both the property of being the first president, and being the father of our country.

3. See Sydney Shoemaker's "Functionalism and Qualia," *Philosophical Studies* 27 (1975): 293. Reprinted in *Readings in Philosophy of Psychology*, vol. 1, op. cit.

4. I owe the phrase "ersatz pain" to an unpublished paper by Larry Davis.

5. See N. Block and J. Fodor, "What Psychological States Are Not," *Philosophical Review* 81 (1972): 159–181.

6. Cf. R. J. Nelson, "Behaviorism, Finite Automata, and Stimulus Response Theory," in *Theory and Decision* 6 (1975): 249–267.

7. This example combines features of one discussed in my "Troubles with Functionalism," in C. W. Savage, ed., *Perception and Cognition: Issues in the Foundations of Psychology*, Minnesota Studies in the Philosophy of Science, vol. 9. (Minneapolis: University of Minnesota Press, 1978) (reprinted in *Readings in Philosophy of Psychology*, vol. 1, op. cit.) and an example discussed in my "Psychologism and Behaviorism," *Philosophical Review* 90 (1981): 5–43. John Searle makes use of a similar example in an unpublished paper.

8. An attempt at such an argument is to be found in "Troubles with Functionalism," op. cit. I do argue that there is one type of homunculus-head whose qualia are more in doubt than its thoughts, namely what I call a "Psychofunctional" simulation of us. A Psychofunctional simulation is one for which the theory T of note 1 is an empirical psychological theory (rather

than a common sense theory). I argue that the science relevant to qualia may be physiology rather than psychology, and if so, we have a reason to suppose that homunculus-infested Psychofunctional simulations have thoughts (namely, a psychological theory true of us is true of them) but no corresponding reason to suppose the homunculus-infested Psychofunctional simulation has qualia. This problem could be avoided by moving from Psychofunctionalism to Physiofunctionalism (for which the theory T is a physiological theory, but that would be to go far too deep into human chauvinism.

9. The argument appears mainly on pp. 295–298 (this and other page references are to the version in *Philosophical Studies*).

10. Shoemaker, op. cit., p. 298.

11. A *token* state or event is datable and nonrecurrent. For example, the pain I am having now can't recur (though I could have a similar one later). The *type* pain, on the other hand, can recur, in that I can have pain and have *it* again tomorrow. The type pain might be identified with the property common to all token pains in virtue of which they are pains.

12. The locution "absent qualia are possible" is actually used by Shoemaker to mean that for *some* state Q that has qualitative character, there could be a functionally identical state Q⁻ that lacks qualitative character. It is *in this sense* that Shoemaker wishes to deny that absent qualia are possible. However, in this sense, the possibility of absent qualia does not entail the possibility of ersatz pain. This is a trivial invalidity in Shoemaker's argument, since pain is used merely as a convenient example. For the purpose of making Shoemaker's argument valid, I will be taking the locution "absent qualia are possible" to mean that for *any* state Q that has qualitative character, there could be a functionally identical state Q⁻ that lacks qualitative character. Making the doctrine that absent qualia are possible *stronger* in this way makes Shoemaker's task of refuting it *easier*, so he should have no objection.

13. See note 12.

14. Shoemaker put the objection to me in this way in correspondence.

15. On the other hand, I would argue that the more physiology included in the functionalized theory, the less the functionalist has to fear from its homunculus-headed realizations. See "Troubles with Functionalism," op. cit.

16. See D. M. Armstrong, "The Nature of Mind," and David Lewis, "Psychophysical and Theoretical Identifications." The former appeared in C. V. Borst, ed., *The Mind-Brain Identity Theory* (London: Macmillan, 1970). The latter appeared in the *Australasian Journal of Philosophy* 50/3 (1972): 249–258. Both are reprinted in *Readings in Philosophy of Psychology*, op. cit.

17. Shoemaker suggested something of this sort in correspondence.

18. This sort of proposal was first made by Putnam in "The Nature of Mental States," reprinted in *Readings in Philosophy of Psychology*, op. cit.

19. This point is spelled out in more detail in "Troubles with Functionalism," this volume, chapter 4, section 1.4.

20. "Mad Pain and Martian Pain," published in *Readings in Philosophy of Psychology*, op. cit.

21. See "Troubles with Functionalism," this volume, chapter 4, note 13.

22. Actually, what Shoemaker tells me he has in mind is that qualitative indistinguishability can be used to define a qualitative identity relation. (Of course, qualitative indistinguishability can itself be defined in terms of qualitative similarity: x and y are qualitatively indistinguishable iff anything that is qualitatively similar to x is exactly as qualitatively similar to y.)

I   The Hard Problem

T. H. Huxley famously said "How it is that anything so remarkable as a state of consciousness comes about as a result of irritating nervous tissue, is just as unaccountable as the appearance of Djin when Aladdin rubbed his lamp."[1] We do not see how to explain a state of consciousness in terms of its neurological basis. This is the Hard Problem of Consciousness.[2]

The aim of this paper is to present another problem of consciousness. The Harder Problem, as I will call it, is more epistemological than the Hard Problem. A second difference: the Hard Problem could arise for someone who has no conception of another person, whereas the Harder Problem is tied closely to the problem of other minds. Finally, the Harder Problem reveals an epistemic tension or at least discomfort in our ordinary conception of consciousness that is not suggested by the Hard Problem, and so in one respect it is harder. Perhaps the Harder Problem includes the Hard Problem and is best thought of as an epistemic add-on to it. Or perhaps they are in some other way facets of a single problem. Then my point is that this single problem breaks into two parts, one of which is more epistemic, involves other minds, and involves an epistemic discomfort.

II   Preliminaries

I believe that the major ontological disputes about the nature of consciousness rest on an opposition between two perspectives:

• Deflationism about consciousness, in which a priori or at least armchair analyses of consciousness (or at least armchair-sufficient conditions) are given in nonphenomenal terms, most prominently in terms of representation, thought, or function.
• Phenomenal realism, which consists in the denial of deflationism plus the claim that consciousness is something real. Phenomenal realism is metaphysical realism about

consciousness and thus allows the possibility that there may be facts about the distribution of consciousness that are not accessible to us even though the relevant functional, cognitive, and representational facts are accessible. Phenomenal realism is based on one's first-person grasp of consciousness while allowing that first person cognition about one's own conscious states can be incomplete and mistaken. An opponent might prefer to call phenomenal realism "inflationism," but I reject the suggestion of something bloated.

In its most straightforward version, deflationism is a thesis of a priori conceptual analysis, most prominently analysis of mental terms in functional terms. As David Lewis—a well-known deflationist—noted,[3] this view is the heir of logical behaviorism. Phenomenal realism rejects these armchair philosophical reductive analyses. But phenomenal realists have no brief against *scientific* reduction of consciousness. Of course, there is no sharp line here, and since the distinction is epistemic, one and the same metaphysical thesis could be held both as a philosophical reductionist and as a scientific reductionist thesis.[4]

I apologize for all the "isms" (deflationism, phenomenal realism, and one more to come), but they are unavoidable since the point of this paper is that there is a tension between two of them. The tension is between phenomenal realism ("inflationism") and (scientific) naturalism, the epistemological perspective according to which the default view is that consciousness has a scientific nature—where this is taken to include the idea that conscious similarities have scientific natures. (A view on a given subject is the default if it is the only one for which background considerations give rational ground for tentative belief.) This paper argues for a conditional conclusion in which specifications of phenomenal realism and scientific naturalism (and a few other relatively uncontroversial items—including, notably, a rejection of a skeptical perspective) appear on the left-hand side. On the right-hand side we have a specification of the epistemic tension that I mentioned. Deflationists who accept the argument may opt for modus tollens, giving them a reason to reject phenomenal realism. Phenomenal-realist naturalists may want to weaken their commitment to naturalism or to phenomenal realism. To put the point without explicit "isms": many of us are committed to the idea that consciousness is both real and can be assumed to have a scientific nature, but it turns out that these commitments do not fit together comfortably.

Modern phenomenal realism has often been strongly naturalistic (e.g., Levine, Loar, McGinn, Peacocke, Perry, Shoemaker, Searle, and myself). Dennett has often accused phenomenal realists of closet dualism. Rey has argued that the concept of consciousness is incoherent.[5] The upshot of this paper is that there is a grain of truth in these accusations.

Before I go on, I must make a terminological comment. Imagine two persons both of whom are in pain, but only one of whom is introspecting his pain state and is in that sense conscious of it. One could say that only one of the two has a *conscious* pain. This is not the sense of "conscious" used here. In the sense of "conscious" used here, just by virtue of *having* pain, both have conscious states. To avoid verbal disputes, we could call the sense of "consciousness" used here *phenomenality*. Pains are intrinsically phenomenal and in that sense are intrinsically conscious. In that sense—but not in some other senses—there cannot be an unconscious pain.

The plan of the paper is this: first I will briefly characterize the Hard Problem, mainly in order to distinguish it from the Harder Problem. I will argue that the Hard Problem can be dissolved only to reappear in a somewhat different form, but that in this different form we can see a glimmer of hope for how a solution might one day be found. I will then move on to the Harder Problem, its significance, and a comparison between the Hard and Harder Problems. I will conclude with some reflections on what options there are for the naturalistic phenomenal realist.

III   Mind-Body Identity and the Apparent Dissolution of the Hard Problem

The Hard Problem is one of explaining why the neural basis of a phenomenal quality is the neural basis of *that* phenomenal quality rather than another phenomenal quality or no phenomenal quality at all. In other terms, there is an explanatory gap between the neural basis of a phenomenal quality and the phenomenal quality itself. Suppose (to replace the neurologically ridiculous example of c-fibers that is often used by philosophers with a view proposed as a theory of visual experience by Crick and Koch[6]) that corticothalamic oscillation (of a certain sort) is the neural basis of an experience with phenomenal quality Q. Now there is a simple (oversimple) physicalist dissolution to the Hard Problem that is based on mind-body identity: phenomenal quality Q = corticothalamic oscillation (of a certain sort). Here's a statement of the solution: "The Hard Problem is illusory. One might as well ask why H_2O is the chemical basis of water rather than gasoline or nothing at all. Just as water *is* its chemical basis, so Q just is its neural basis (corticothalamic oscillation), and that shows the original question is wrongheaded." I think there is something right about this answer, but it is nonetheless unsatisfactory. What is right about it is that if Q = corticothalamic oscillation, that identity itself, like all genuine identities, is inexplicable.[7] What is wrong about it is that we are in a completely different epistemic position with respect to such a mind-body identity claim than we are with respect to "water = H_2O." The claim that Q is identical to corticothalamic oscillation is just as puzzling—maybe more puzzling—than the claim that the physical basis of Q is corticothalamic oscillation. We have no idea how it could be that one property could be identical both to Q and corticothalamic oscillation. How could one property be both subjective and objective? Although no one can explain an identity, we can remove puzzlement by explaining how an identity can be true—most obviously, how it is that the two concepts involved can pick out the same thing. This is what we need in the case of subjective/objective identities such as the putative identity that Q = corticothalamic oscillation.

Joe Levine[8] argues that there are two kinds of identities, those like "water = H_2O," which do not admit of explanation, and those like "the sensation of orange = cortico-thalamic oscillation" that are "gappy identities" that do allow explanation. He argues that the "left-hand" mode of presentation of the latter is more substantive than those of the former. The idea is supposed to be that descriptive modes of presentation are "pointers we aim at our internal states with very little substantive conception of what sort of thing we are pointing at—demonstrative arrows shot blindly that refer to what-ever they hit." By contrast, according to Levine, phenomenal modes of presentation really do give us a substantive idea of what they refer to, not a "whatever they hit" idea. However, even if we accept this distinction, it will not serve to explain the "gappiness" of mind-body identities. Consider that the mode of presentation of a sensation of a color can be the same as that of the color itself. Consider the identity "orange = yellowish red." Both modes of presentation involved in this identity can be as substantive as those in the putatively "gappy" identity just mentioned, yet this one is not "gappy," even if some others are. To get an identity in which only one side is substantive, and is so a better analogy to the mind-body case, consider an assertion of "orange = yellowish red" in which the left-hand concept is phenomenal but the right-hand concept is discursive. But that identity is not gappy either.

IV How to Approach the Hard Problem

The standard arguments against physicalism (most recently by Jackson, Kripke, and Chalmers) make it difficult to understand how mind-body identity could be true, so explaining how it could be true requires undermining those arguments. I will not at-tempt such a large task here, especially since the role of the discussion of the Hard Problem in this paper is mainly to contrast it with the Harder Problem to come. So I will limit my efforts in this direction to a brief discussion of Jackson's famous "knowl-edge" argument. I discuss this argument not because I think it is the most challenging argument against mind-body identity, but rather because it motivates an apparatus that gives us some insight into what makes the Hard Problem hard. Jackson imagined a neuroscientist of the distant future (Mary) who is raised in a black-and-white room and who knows everything physical and functional that there is to know about color and the experience of it. But when she steps outside the room for the first time, she learns what it is like to see red. Jackson argued that since the physical and functional facts do not encompass the new fact that Mary learns, dualism is true.

The key to what is wrong with Jackson's argument (and to removing one kind of puzzlement about how a subjective property could be identical to an objective prop-erty) is the concept/property distinction.[9] Any account of this distinction as it applies to phenomenal concepts is bound to be controversial. I will use one such account without defending it, but nothing in the rest of the paper will be based on this account.

The expressions "this sudden involuntary muscle contraction" and "this [experience] thing in my leg" are two expressions that pick out the cramp I am now having in my leg. (These are versions of examples from Loar, op. cit.) In "this [experience] thing in my leg," attention to an experience of the cramp functions so as to pick out the referent, the cramp. (That is the meaning of the bracket notation. The "this" in "this [experience] thing in my leg" refers to the thing in my leg, not the experience.) The first way of thinking about the cramp is an objective concept of the cramp. The second is a subjective concept of the same thing—subjective in that there is a phenomenal mode of access to the thing picked out. Just as we can have both objective and subjective concepts of a cramp, we can also have objective and subjective concepts of a cramp *feeling*. Assuming physicalism, we could have an objective neurological concept of a cramp feeling—for example, "the phased locked 40 Hz oscillation that is occurring now." And we could have a subjective concept of the same thing, "this [experience] feeling." Importantly, the same experience type could be part of—though function differently—in *both* subjective concepts, the subjective concept of the cramp and the subjective concept of the cramp feeling. Further, we could have both a subjective and objective concept of a single color. And we could have both a subjective and an objective concept of the experience of that color, and the same experience or mental image could function—albeit differently—in the two subjective concepts, one of the color, the other of the experience of the color.

Deflationists will not like this apparatus, but they should be interested in the upshot since it may be of use to them in rejecting the phenomenal realism in the antecedent of the conditional that this paper argues for.

Concepts in the sense used here are mental representations. For our purposes, we may as well suppose a system of representation that includes both quasi-linguistic elements as well as phenomenal elements such as experiences or mental images. Stretching terminology, we could call it a language of thought.[10]

In these terms, then, we can remove one type of puzzlement that is connected with the Hard Problem as follows: there is no problem about how a subjective property can be identical to an objective property. Subjectivity and objectivity are better seen as properties of *concepts* rather than properties of *properties*. The claim that an objective property is identical to a subjective property would be more revealingly expressed as the claim that an objective concept of a property picks out the same property as a subjective concept of that property. So we can substitute a dualism of concepts for a dualism of properties.

The same distinction helps us to solve the Mary problem. In the room, Mary knew about the subjective experience of red via the objective concept *corticothalamic oscillation.* On leaving the room, she acquires a subjective concept *this [mental image] phenomenal property* of the same subjective experience. In learning what it is like to see red, she does not learn a new fact. She knew about that fact in the room under an objective concept and she learns a new concept of that very fact. One can acquire new knowledge about old facts by acquiring new concepts of those facts. New knowledge acquired in this way does not show that there are any facts beyond the physical facts. Of course it does require that there are concepts that are not physicalistic concepts, but that is not a form of dualism. (For purposes of this paper, we can think of physicalistic concepts as concepts couched in the vocabulary of physics. A physicalist can allow nonphysicalistic vocabulary—for instance, the vocabulary of economics. Of course, physicalists say that everything is physical, including vocabulary. But the vocabulary of economics can be physical in that sense without being physicalististic in the sense of couched in the vocabulary of physics.)

Where are we? The Hard Problem in one form was: how can an objective property be identical to a subjective property? We now have a dissolution of one aspect of the problem, appealing to the fact that objectivity and subjectivity are best seen as properties of concepts. But that is no help in getting a sense of what *sorts* of objective concepts and subjective concepts could pick out the same property, and so it brings us no closer to actually getting such concepts. As Nagel (op. cit.) noted, we have no idea how there could be causal chains from an objective concept and a subjective concept leading back to the same phenomenon in the world. We are in something like the position of pre-Einsteinians who had no way of understanding how a concept of mass and a concept of energy could pick out the same thing.

V   Preliminaries before Introducing the Harder Problem

Naturalism

Naturalism is the view that it is a default that consciousness has a scientific nature (and that similarities in consciousness have scientific natures). I will assume that the relevant sciences include physics, chemistry, biology, computational theory, and parts of psychology that do not explicitly involve consciousness. (The point of the last condition is to avoid the trivialization of naturalism that would result if we allowed the scientific nature of consciousness to be...consciousness.) I will lump these sciences together under the heading "physical," thinking of naturalism as the view that it is a default that consciousness is physical (and that similarities in consciousness are physical). So naturalism = default physicalism, and is thus a partly epistemic thesis. Naturalism in my sense recognizes that although the indirect evidence for physicalism is impressive, there is little direct evidence for it. My naturalist is not a "die-hard" naturalist, but rather one who takes physicalism as a default, a default that can be challenged. My rationale for defining "naturalism" in this way is that this version of the doctrine is plausible, widely held, and leads to the epistemic tension that I am exposit-ing. Some other doctrines that could be called "naturalism" do not, but this one does. I think that my naturalism is close to what John Perry calls "antecedent physicalism." (See his *Knowledge, Possibility, and Consciousness*. Cambridge, MA: MIT Press, 2001.)

Functionalism

Functionalism and physicalism are usually considered competing theories of mind. However, for the purposes of this paper, the phenomenal realism/deflationism distinc-tion is more important, and this distinction crosscuts the distinction between func-tionalism and physicalism. In the terms used earlier, one type of functionalism is deflationist, the other phenomenal realist. The latter is psychofunctionalism, the iden-tification of phenomenality with a role property specified in terms of a psychological or neuropsychological theory.[11] At the beginning of the paper, I pointed to the some-what vague distinction between philosophical and scientific reduction. Deflationist functionalism is a philosophical reductionist view, whereas phenomenal-realist psy-chofunctionalism is a scientific reductionist view.

I will be making use of the notion of a superficial functional isomorph, a creature that is isomorphic to us with respect to those causal relations among mental states, inputs, and outputs that are specified by common sense, or if you like, "folk psychol-ogy." Those who are skeptical about these notions should note that the point of the paper is that a nexus of standard views leads to a tension. This conceptual apparatus may be part of what should be rejected. Those who would like to see more on function-alism should consult any of the standard reference works such as the *Routledge Encyclo-pedia of Philosophy*. Or see http://www.nyu.edu/gsas/dept/philo/faculty/block/papers/functionalism.html.

As I mentioned at the outset, this paper argues for a conditional. On the left side of the conditional are phenomenal realism and naturalism (plus conceptual apparatus of the sort just mentioned). My current point is that I am including psychofunc-tionalism in the class of phenomenal-realist naturalist theories. Thus one kind of functionalism—the deflationist variety—is excluded by the antecedent of my condi-tional, and another—the phenomenal-realist variety—is in the class of open options.

Antiskeptical Perspective

In what follows, I will be adopting a point of view that sets skepticism aside. *"Un-doubtedly,* humans are conscious and rocks and laptops are not." (Further, *bats* are undoubtedly conscious.) Of course, the antiskeptical point of view I will be adopting is the one appropriate to a naturalist phenomenal realist. Notably, from the naturalist phenomenal-realist perspective, the concept of a functional isomorph of us with no consciousness is not incoherent and the claim of bare possibility of such a zombie—so long as it is not alleged to be us—is not a form of skepticism.

Multiple Realization/Multiple Constitution

Putnam, Fodor, and Block and Fodor argued that if functionalism about the mind is true, physicalism is false.[12] The line of argument assumes that functional organizations are multiply realizable. The state of adding 2 cannot be identical to an electronic state if a nonelectronic device (e.g., a brain) can add 2.

This "multiple-realizability" argument has become controversial lately,[13] for reasons that I cannot go into here.[14] The argument I will be giving is a version of the traditional multiple-realizability argument (albeit an epistemic version), so I had better say a bit about what a realization is. One of the many notions of realization that would do for our purposes is the following. A functional state is a kind of second-order property, a property that consists in having certain first-order properties that have certain causes and effects.[15] For example, dormitivity in one sense of the term is the property a pill has of having some (first-order) property that causes sleep. Provocativity is the property of having some (first-order) property or other that makes bulls angry. We can speak of the first-order property of being a barbiturate as being one realizer of dormitivity, or of red as being one realizer of provocativity.[16]

If we understand realization, we can define constitution in terms of it. Suppose that mental state M has a functional role that is realized by neural state N. Then N constitutes M—relative to M playing the M role. The point of the last condition is that ersatz M—a state functionally like M but missing something essential to M as phenomenality is to pain—would also have the M role, but N would not constitute ersatz M merely by virtue of constituting M. So the M role can be multiply realized even if mental state M is not multiply constituted.

There is an obvious obscurity in what counts as *multiple* realization (or constitution). We can agree that neural property X is distinct from neural property Y and that both realize a single functional property without agreeing on whether X and Y are variants of a single property or two substantially different properties, so we will not agree on whether there is genuinely multiple realization. And even if we agree that X and Y are substantially different, we may still not agree on whether the functional property is multiply realized since we may not agree on whether there is a single disjunctive realization. These issues will be discussed further in section VII.

VI   Introducing the Harder Problem

My strategy will be to start with the epistemic possibility of multiple realization and use it to argue for the epistemic possibility of multiple constitution of mentality. I will then argue that the epistemic possibility of multiple constitution of phenomenal properties is problematic. I will use a science fiction example of a creature who is functionally the same as us but physically different. Those who hate science fiction should note that the same issue arises—in more complicated forms—with respect to real creatures, such as the octopus, which differ from us both physically and functionally.

(1)   We have no reason to believe that there is any deep physical property in common to all and only the possible realizations of our superficial functional organization. Moreover—and this goes beyond what is needed for (1) but it does make (1) more vivid—we have no reason to believe that we cannot find or *make* a merely superficial isomorph of ourselves. By "merely superficial isomorph," I mean an isomorph with respect to folk psychology and whatever is logically or nomologically entailed by folk psychological isomorphism, but that is all. For example, the fact that pains cause us to moan (in circumstances that we have some appreciation of but no one has ever precisely stated) is known to common sense, but the fact that just-noticeable differences in stimuli increase with increasing intensity of the stimuli (the Weber-Fechner law) is not. So the merely superficial isomorph would be governed by the former but not necessarily the latter. The TV series *Star Trek: The Next Generation* has an episode ("The Measure of a Man") that includes a trial in which it is decided whether a humanlike android, Lieutenant Commander Data, may legally be turned off and taken apart by someone who does not know whether he can put the parts together again. (The technology that allowed the android to be built has been lost.)[17] Let us take Commander Data to be a merely superficial isomorph of us (ignoring his superior reasoning and inferior emotions.) Then (1) can be taken to be that we have no reason to believe that Commander Data is not nomologically or otherwise metaphysically possible. Note that I am not making as strong a claim as is made in Block and Fodor (op. cit.)—that there is empirical reason to suppose that our functional organization is multiply realizable—but only that we have no reason to doubt it.

The strategy of the argument, you recall, is to move from the epistemic possibility of multiple realization to the epistemic possibility of multiple constitution. (1) is the epistemic possibility of multiple realization.

(2)   Superficial functional equivalence to us is a defeasible reason for attributing consciousness. That is, superficial functional equivalence to us provides a reason for thinking a being is conscious, but that reason can be disarmed or unmasked, its evidential value canceled.

(2) consists of two claims, that superficial functional equivalence to us is a reason for attributing consciousness and that that reason is defeasible. The first claim is obvious enough. I am not claiming that the warrant is a priori, just that there is warrant. I doubt that there will be disagreement with such a minimal claim.

What is controversial about (2) is that the reason is claimed to be defeasible. Certainly, deflationary functionalists will deny the defeasibility. Of course, even deflationary functionalists would allow that *evidence* for thinking something is functionally equivalent to us can be defeated. For example, that something emits English sounds is a reason to attribute consciousness, but if we find the sound is recorded, the epistemic value of the evidence is canceled. However, (2) does not merely say that functional or behavioral *evidence* for consciousness can be defeated. (2) says that even if we *know* that something is functionally equivalent to us, there are things we can find out that cancel the reason we have to ascribe consciousness (without challenging our knowledge of the functional equivalence). A creature's consciousness can be unmasked without unmasking its functional equivalence to us.

Here is a case in which the epistemic value of functional isomorphism is canceled: the case involves a *partial physical* overlap between the functional isomorph and humans. Suppose that there are real neurophysiological differences of kind—not just complexity—between our conscious processes and our unconscious—that is, nonphenomenal—processes. Nonphenomenal neural process include, for example, those that regulate body temperature, blood pressure, heart rate, and sugar in the blood—brain processes that can operate in people in irreversible vegetative coma. Suppose (*but only temporarily*—this assumption will be dispensed with later) that we find out that all of the merely superfical isomorph's brain states are ones that—in us—are the neural bases *only of phenomenally unconscious states*. For example, the neural basis of the functional analog of pain in the merely superficial isomorph is the neural state that regulates the pituitary gland in us. This would not prove that the isomorph is not phenomenally conscious (for example, since the contexts of the neural realizers are different), but it would cancel or at least weaken the force of the reason for attributing consciousness provided by its functional isomorphism to us.

The role of this case is to motivate a further refining of our characterization of Commander Data and to justify (2) by exhibiting the epistemic role of a defeater.

Let us narrow down Commander Data's physical specification to rule out the cases just mentioned as defeaters for attribution of consciousness to him. Here is a first shot:

• Commander Data is a superficial isomorph of us.
• Commander Data is a merely superficial isomorph. So we have no reason to suppose there are any shared nonheterogeneously disjunctive physical properties between our conscious states and Commander Data's functional analogs of them that could be the physical basis of any phenomenal overlap between them, since we have no reason to think that such shared properties are required by the superficial overlap. Further, one could imagine this discussion taking place at a stage of science where we could have rational ground for believing that there are no shared physical properties (or more generally scientific properties) that could be the physical basis of a phenomenal overlap. Note that no stipulation can rule out certain shared physical properties—for example, the disjunctive property of having either the physical realizer of the functional role of one of our conscious states or Commander Data's analog of it.

• The physical realizers of Commander Data's functional analogs of conscious states do not overlap with any of our brain mechanisms in any properties that we do not also share with inorganic entities that are uncontroversially mindless, like toasters. So we can share properties with Commander Data like having molecules. But none of the realizers of Commander Data's analogs of conscious states are the same as realizers of, for example, our states that regulate our blood sugar—since these are organic.

• Commander Data does not have any part which itself is a functional isomorph of us and whose activities are crucial to maintaining the functional organization of the whole.[18]

The point of the last two conditions is to specify that Commander Data has a realization that cannot be seen to defeat the attribution of consciousness to him either a priori or on the basis of a theory of *human* consciousness. (For example, the last condition rules out a "homunculi-headed" realization.) It would help if I could think of all the realizations that have these kinds of significance. If you tell me about one I have not thought of, I will add a condition to rule it out.

Objection   We are entitled to reason from same effects to same causes. Since our phenomenal states play a role in causing our behavior, we can infer that the functionally identical behavioral states of Commander Data are produced in the same way—that is, phenomenally. To refuse to accept this inference, the objection continues, is to suppose that the presence or absence of phenomenality makes no causal difference.

Reply   Consider two computationally identical computers, one that works via electronic mechanisms, the other that works via hydraulic mechanisms. (Suppose that the fluid in one does the same job that the electricity does in the other.) We are not entitled to infer from the causal efficacy of the fluid in the hydraulic machine that the electrical machine also has fluid. One could not conclude that the presence or absence of the fluid makes no difference, just because there is a functional equivalent that has no fluid. One need not be an epiphenomenalist to take seriously the hypothesis that there are alternative realizations of the functional roles of our phenomenal states that are phenomenally blank.

We might suppose just to get an example on the table that the physical basis of Commander Data's brain is to be found in etched silicon chips rather than the organic carbon basis of our brains.[19]

The reader could be forgiven for wondering at this point whether I have not assembled stipulations that close off the question of Commander Data's consciousness. Naturalism includes the doctrine that it is the default that a conscious overlap requires a physical basis, and it may seem that I have in effect stipulated that Commander Data does not have any physical commonality with us that could be the basis of any shared phenomenality. The objection ignores the option of a shared *disjunctive* basis and certain other shared bases to be discussed below.

(3)   Fundamentally different physical realization from us per se is not a ground for rational belief in lack of consciousness. So the fact that Commander Data's control mechanisms are fundamentally different is not a ground of rational belief that he has no phenomenal states. Note that I do not say that finding out that Commander Data has a silicon-based brain is not a *reason* for regarding him as lacking consciousness. Rather I say that the reason falls below the epistemic level of a ground for rational belief.

(4)   We have no conception of a ground of rational belief to the effect that a realization of our superficial functional organization that is physically fundamentally different along the lines I have specified for Commander Data is or is not conscious. To use a term suggested by Martine Nida-Rümelin in commenting on this paper, Commander Data's consciousness is meta-inaccessible. Not only do we lack a ground of belief, but we lack a conception of any ground of belief. This metainaccessibility is a premise rather than a lemma or a conclusion because the line of thought I have been presenting leads up to it without anything that I am happy to think of as an argument for it. My hope is that this way of leading up to it will allow the reader to see it as obvious.

We can see the rationale for metainaccessibility by considering John Searle's Chinese Room argument. Searle famously argued that even if we are computational creatures, we are not either sentient or sapient merely by virtue of that computational organization. In reply to his critics,[20] he says repeatedly that a machine that shares our computational organization and is therefore behaviorally and functionally equivalent to us—and therefore passes the Turing Test—need not be an intentional system (or a conscious being). What would make it an intentional system—and for Searle, intentionality is engendered by and requires consciousness—is not the functional organization but rather the way that functional organization is implemented in the biology of the organism. But, to take an example that Searle uses, how would we know whether something made out of beer cans is sentient or sapient? He says: "It is *an empirical question* whether any given machine [that shares our superficial functional organization] has causal powers equivalent to the brain" (p. 452). He adds: "I think it is evident that all sorts of substances in the world, like water pipes and toilet paper, are going to lack those powers, but that is *an empirical claim* on my part. On my account it is a *testable empirical claim* whether in repairing a damaged brain," we could duplicate these causal powers (p. 453). Further, "I offer no a priori proof that a system of integrated circuit chips could not have intentionality. That is, as I say repeatedly, *an empirical question*. What I do argue is that in order to produce intentionality the system would have to duplicate the causal powers of the brain and that simply instantiating a formal program would not be sufficient for that" (p. 453; emphasis and bracketed clause added).

I do not deny that one day the question of whether a creature like Commander Data is phenomenally conscious may become a testable empirical question. But it is obvious that we do not now have any conception of how it could be tested. Searle has suggested (in conversation) that the question is an empirical one in that if I were the device, I would know from the first-person point of view if I was conscious. But even if we accept such a counterfactual, we cannot take it as showing that the claim is testable or empirical in any ordinary sense of the term.

Though I am tweaking Searle's flamboyant way of putting the point, my naturalist phenomenal-realist view is not that different from his. I agree that whether physically different realizations of human functional organization are conscious is not an a priori matter and could be said to depend on whether their brains have "equivalent causal powers" to ours—in the sense of having the power to be the physical basis of conscious states. (However, I do not agree with Searle's view that the neural bases of conscious states "cause" the conscious states in any normal sense of "cause.") I agree with him that consciousness is a matter of the biology of the organism, not (just) its information processing. The issue that I am raising here for naturalist phenomenal realism threatens my view as much as his.

I am not denying that we might some day come to have the conception we now do not have. (So I am not claiming—as McGinn does—that this knowledge can be known now to be beyond our ken.)[21] I am merely saying that at this point, we have no idea of evidence that would ground rational belief, even a hypothetical or speculative conception. Of course those who meet Commander Data will reasonably be sure that he is conscious. But finding out that he is not *human* cancels that ground of rational belief.

Perhaps we will discover the nature of human consciousness and find that it applies to other creatures. For example, the nature of human consciousness may involve certain kinds of oscillatory processes that can apply to silicon creatures as well. But the problem I am raising will arise in connection with realizations of our functional organization that lack those oscillatory processes. The root of the epistemic problem is that the example of a conscious creature on which the science of consciousness is inevitably based is us (where "us" can be construed to include nonhuman creatures that are neurologically similar to humans). But how can science based on us generalize to creatures that do not share our physical properties? It would seem that a form of physicalism that could embrace other creatures would have to be based on them at least in part in the first place, but that cannot be done unless we already know whether they are conscious.

I have left a number of aspects of the story unspecified. What was the aim of Commander Data's designer? What is to be included in the "commonsense" facts about the mind that determine the grain of the functional isomorphism?

I keep using the phrase "ground of rational belief." What does it mean? I take this to be an epistemic level that is stronger than "reason for believing" and weaker than "rational certainty." I take it that a ground of rational belief that p allows knowledge that p but mere reason for believing p does not.

VII   Disjunctivism and the Epistemic Problem

I now move to the conditional that I advertised earlier. Let us start by supposing, but only temporarily, that physicalism requires a deep (nonsuperficial) unitary (nonheterogeneously disjunctive) scientific (physical) property shared by all and only conscious beings. This version of physicalism seems at first glance to be incompatible with Commander Data's being conscious, and the corresponding version of naturalism (which says that physicalism is the default) seems at first glance to be epistemically incompatible with phenomenal realism. That is, naturalism says the default is that Commander Data is not conscious but phenomenal realism says that the issue is open in the sense of no rational ground for belief either way. This is a first pass at saying what the Harder Problem is.

If this strong kind of physicalism really is incompatible with Commander Data's being conscious, we might wonder whether the reasons we have for believing physicalism will support this weight. I will pursue a weaker version of physicalism (and corresponding version of naturalism) that does not rule out consciousness having a physical basis that is disjunctive according to the standards of physics. However, as we will see, the stronger version of physicalism is *not* actually incompatible with Commander Data's being conscious, and the difference between the stronger and weaker versions makes no important difference with respect to our epistemic situation concerning Commander Data's consciousness.

Disjunctivism is a form of physicalism that allows that consciousness is a physical state that is disjunctive by the standards of physics. As applied to the current issue, Disjunctivism allows that if Commander Data is conscious, the shared phenomenality is constituted by the property of having Commander Data's electronic realization of our shared functional state or our electrochemical realization.

In note 13, I mentioned Kim's critique of the multiple-realizability argument against physicalism. He argues that if mental property M is nomically equivalent to a heterogeneous disjunction N, we should regard M as nonnomic and non-"real" because N is. He argues that if human thought can be realized by very different physical mechanisms from, say, Martian or robot thought, then the real sciences of thought will be the sciences of the separate realizations of it. To call them all "thought" is simply to apply a superficial verbal concept to all of them, but the laws of human thought will be different from the laws of Martian thought. The real kinds are not at the level of the application of verbal concepts.[22]

Even those who are sympathetic to this picture of thought must make an exception for consciousness (in the sense, as always in this paper, of phenomenality). We can be happy with the view that there is a science of human thought and another science of machine thought, but no science of thought per se. But we should not be happy with the idea that there is a science of human phenomenality, another of machine phenomenality, and so on. For since the overlap of these phenomenalities, *phenomenality*, is something real and not merely nominal as in the case of thought, it must have a scientific basis. If a phenomenal property is nomically coextensive with a heterogeneous neural disjunction, it would not be at all obvious that we should conclude that the phenomenal property is nonnomic and non-"real" because the disjunction is. The phenomenal-realist naturalist point of view would be more friendly to the opposite, that the disjunction is nomic and "real" because the phenomenal property is.

The real problem with Disjunctivism is that whether it is true or not, we could have no good reason to believe it. To see this, we will have to have a brief incursion into the epistemology of reductive theoretical identity.

The Epistemology of Theoretical Identity

Why do we think that water = H_2O, temperature = mean molecular kinetic energy and freezing = lattice formation?[23] The answer begins with the fact that water, temperature, freezing, and other magnitudes form a family of causally interrelated "macro" properties. This family corresponds to a family of "micro" properties: H_2O, mean molecular kinetic energy, formation of a lattice of H_2O molecules. And the causal relations among the macroproperties can be explained if we suppose the following relations between the families: that water = H_2O, temperature = mean molecular kinetic energy, and freezing = lattice formation. For example, as water is cooled, it contracts until about 4 degrees F above freezing, at which point it expands. Why? Why does ice float on water? Here is a sketch of the explanations: the oxygen atom in the H_2O molecule has two pairs of unmated electrons, which attract the hydrogen atoms on other H_2O molecules. Temperature = mean molecular kinetic energy. When the temperature (that is, kinetic energy) is high, the kinetic energy of the molecules is high enough to break these hydrogen bonds, but as the kinetic energy of the molecules decreases, each oxygen atom tends to attract two hydrogen atoms on the ends of two other H_2O molecules. When this process is complete, the result is a lattice in which each oxygen atom is attached to four hydrogen atoms. Ice is this lattice and freezing is the formation of such a lattice. Because of the geometry of the bonds, the lattice has an open, less dense structure than amorphously structured H_2O (that is, liquid water)—which is why ice (solid water) floats on liquid water. The lattice forms slowly, beginning about 4 degrees above freezing. (The exact temperature can be calculated on the basis of the numerical values of the kinetic energies needed to break or prevent the bonds.) The formation of large open lattice elements is what accounts for the expansion of water on the way to freezing. (Water contracts in the earlier cooling because decreasing kinetic energy allows more bonding, and until the bonding reaches a stage in which there are full lattice elements, the effect of the increased bonding is make the water more densely packed.)

Suppose we reject the assumption that temperature is identical to mean molecular kinetic energy in favor of the assumption that temperature is merely correlated with mean molecular kinetic energy? And suppose we reject the claim that freezing is lattice formation in favor of a correlation thesis. And likewise for water/H_2O. Then we would have an explanation for how something that is *correlated* with decreasing temperature causes something that is *correlated* with frozen water to float on something *correlated* with liquid water, which is not all that we want. Further, if we assume identities, we can explain why certain macroproperties are spatiotemporally coincident with certain microproperties. The reason to think that the identities are true is that assuming them gives us explanations that we would not otherwise have and does not deprive us of explanations that we already have or raise explanatory puzzles that would not otherwise arise. The idea is not that our reason for thinking these identities are true is that it would be nice if they were true. Rather, it is that assuming that they are true yields the *most explanatory overall picture*. In other words, the epistemology of theoretical identity is just a special case of inference to the best explanation.

Some suppose that substance identities such as "water = H_2O" are on a different footing from "property" identities, and that substance identities can be established on purely spatiotemporal grounds. (Jaegwon Kim gave a paper at Columbia University in December 1999 making this suggestion, and Tim Maudlin argued that all theoretical identities are established on spatiotemporal grounds when I gave this paper at Rutgers.) But deciding that water and H_2O *are spatiotemporally coincident* is part of the same package as deciding that they are one and the same. For example, the air above a glass of water buzzes with bits of water in constant exchange with water in the atmosphere, a fact that we can acknowledge only if we are willing to suppose that those H_2O molecules *are* bits of water. The claims that water is H_2O and that water and H_2O are spatiotemporally coincident stand or fall together as parts of one explanatory package. And once we conclude that the substance liquid water = amorphous H_2O and that the substance frozen water = lattice-structured H_2O, we would be hard pressed to deny that freezing = lattice formation, since the difference between liquid and frozen water is that the former has an amorphous structure and the latter a lattice structure. Substance identities and property identities often form a single explanatory package.

Back to Disjunctivism

With the epistemology of identity in place, we can now ask whether there could be an argument from inference to the best explanation to the conclusion that consciousness is a heterogeneous physical disjunction, the disjunction of our realization of the consciousness role and Commander Data's corresponding realization. Of course without a prior decision as to whether Commander Data's states are actually conscious, there could be no such argument. Putting this point aside, let us suppose, temporarily, that Commander Data is conscious. Even so, the prospects for an argument from inference to the best explanation to the identity of a phenomenal property with a disjunctive physical property are dubious. We can see this in two ways. First, let us attend to our explanatory practice. We have an important though vague notion of "fundamentally different" that governs our willingness to regard some differences in realization as variants of the same basic type and others as fundamentally different. When we regard two realizations as fundamentally different, we prefer two nondisjunctive identities to one disjunctive identity. Here is an example: molten glass hardens into an amorphous solidlike substance. (If there are absolutely no impurities, fast continuous cooling of water can make it harden without lattice formation in a similar manner.) We could give a disjunctive explanation of solidlike formation that included both freezing and this kind of continuous hardening. And if we preferred that disjunctive explanation to two distinct explanations, we would regard the hardening of glass as a kind of freezing and glass as a solid. But we do not take the disjunctive explanation seriously and so we regard glass as (strictly speaking) a supercooled liquid rather than a solid. And we do not regard amorphous hardening as freezing. We prefer two nondisjunctive identities, freezing = lattice-formation and hardening = formation of an amorphous supercooled liquid to one disjunctive identity. Of course, the two processes (freezing and hardening) are functionally different in all sorts of fine-grained ways. But the functional roles of Commander Data's functional analogs of our conscious states are also functionally different from ours in all sorts of fine-grained ways. Commander Data is functionally equivalent to us in those functional roles known to common sense and anything else nomologically or logically required by that equivalence, but everything else can be presumed to be different. Since we can stipulate that our physical realizations of our conscious states are fundamentally different from Data's, whatever exactly fundamental difference turns out to be, the methodology that applies to the hardening/freezing case can reasonably be applied to the case at hand.

Of course, there are cases in which we accept disjunctive identities—for example, jade is nephrite or jadeite. But *jade* is a merely nominal category, which makes disjunctive identities acceptable even if not explanatory.

A second factor is that the disjunctive identity, if accepted, would rule out questions that the phenomenal realist naturalist does not want to rule out. The question of why it is that water is correlated with H_2O or why it is that heat is correlated with molecular kinetic energy are bad questions, and they are ruled out by the identity claims that water = H_2O and heat = molecular kinetic energy. Nor can the identities themselves be questioned. (See note 7.) If we were to accept that consciousness is a disjunction of the physical basis of our conscious states and Commander Data's realization of the functionally equivalent states, we would be committing ourselves to the idea that there is no answer to the question of why we overlap phenomenally with Data in one respect rather than in another respect or no respect at all. For the phenomenal realist, it is hard to imagine a ground for rational belief that these questions have no answers. One can imagine finding no other account remotely plausible, but why should the phenomenal realist accept a physicalist view that dictates that these questions are illegitimate rather than opt for a nonphysicalist view that holds out some hope for an answer? (Remember that physicalism is only a default view.) Even if we should come to believe that dualism is unacceptable as well, our reason for accepting Disjunctive physicalism would not seem to get up to the level of a ground for rational belief.

Objection You say identities cannot be explained, but then you also say that we can have no reason to accept a disjunctive physicalistic identity because it is not explanatory.

Reply Identities cannot be explained, but they can contribute to explanations of other things. My point about the epistemology of identity is that it is only because of the explanatory power of identities that we accept them and the disjunctive identity countenanced by disjunctivism does not pass muster.

Disjunctivism is one way of making naturalism compatible with Commander Data being conscious, but there are others. One is the view that consciousness is as a matter of empirical fact identical to the superficial functional organization that we share with Commander Data. We might call this view superficialism (with apologies to Georges Rey, who has used this term for a somewhat different doctrine). Recall that the phenomenal-realist/deflationist distinction is an epistemic one, so any ontological view could in principle be held as having either epistemic status. Superficialism is the *phenomenal-realist* claim that consciousness is identical to the superficial functional organization that we share with Commander Data—as distinct from the deflationist version of this claim mentioned earlier.

Note that superficialism says consciousness is a role property, not a property that *fills* or realizes that role. A role property is a kind of dispositional property. Now there is no problem about dispositions being caused: spraying my bicycle lock with liquid nitrogen causes it to become fragile. So if pain is a superficial functional state, we can perhaps make use of that identification to explain the occurrence of pain in neural terms. Whether dispositions are causes—as would be required by this identity—is a more difficult issue that I will bypass. (Does a disposition to say ouch cause one to say ouch?)

The difficulty I want to raise is that even if identifying pain with a superficial functional role does license explanations of the *superficial* causes and effects of being in pain, the identification cannot in the same way license explanations of the *nonsuperficial* causes and effects of being in pain. Suppose, for example, that psychologists discover that pain raises the perceived pitch of sounds. Even if we take the thesis that pain is a disposition to say ouch to help us to explain why pain causes saying ouch, it will not explain the change in pitch. The epistemic difficulty I am pointing to is that there is no good reason why the causal relations *known to common sense* ought to be explained differently from the ones not known to common sense. So the identification raises an explanatory puzzle that would not otherwise arise, and that puts an epistemic roadblock in the way of the identification. This is perhaps not a conclusive difficulty with the proposal, but it does put the burden of proof on the advocate of the identification to come up with explanatory advantages so weighty as to rule out the explanatory disadvantage just mentioned.[24]

Of course, this objection will not apply to the phenomenal realist identification of consciousness with its *total* functional role as opposed to its superficial functional role. Since the physiology of Commander Data's states differs from ours, their total functional roles will differ as well. So this would be a chauvinist proposal that would beg the question against Commander Data's consciousness.

Martine Nida-Rümelin objected that there are a vast number of properties, maybe infinitely many, that are entailed nomologically or logically by the superficial functional equivalence, and each of these is both shared with Data and is a candidate for the nature of consciousness. Certainly a full treatment would attempt to categorize these properties and assess their candidacy. Some—for example, possessing complex inputs and outputs—can be eliminated because they are also shared with mindless computers. Of course, there may be others that are not so easily dismissed.

The Upshot

I said earlier that it seemed at first glance that a form of physicalism that required that consciousness be constituted by a unitary physical property dictated that Commander Data is not conscious. We can now see that at second glance, this is not the case. Even if we preclude a disjunctive physical basis to the phenomenal overlap between us and Commander Data (assuming that there is such an overlap), still the physicalist could allow that Commander Data is conscious *on superficialist grounds*. And even if we reject superficialism, there are other potential meta-inaccessible physical bases of a phenomenal overlap between us and Commander Data.

The upshot is that physicalism in neither the stronger (unitary physical basis) nor weaker (physical basis that may or may not be unitary) versions mentioned above rules out Commander Data's being conscious. However, *the only epistemically viable naturalist or physicalist hypothesis*—the only naturalist or physicalist hypothesis we have a conception of a reason for accepting—is a deep unitary physical or otherwise scientific property in common to all and only conscious beings, a naturalistic basis that Commander Data does not share. So for the physicalist, Commander Data's consciousness is not epistemically viable.

Thus our knowledge of physicalism is *doubly* problematic: we have no conception of a ground of rational belief that Commander Data is or is not conscious, and we have no way of moving from a conclusion that Commander Data is conscious to any consequence for the truth of physicalism. And this holds despite the fact that physicalism is our default view. *Physicalism is the default and also inaccessible and meta-inaccessible.* The practical significance—if we ever make a robot that is functionally equivalent to us—is that the question of its consciousness and also of physicalism are inaccessible and meta-inaccessible. But even if we decide that the robot is conscious, we will have a choice between dualism and an epistemically nonviable version of physicalism (disjunctivism or superficialism). This is all part of the Harder Problem. A second part follows.

But first I will discuss the question of whether the epistemic tension itself is a good reason to conclude that Commander Data is not conscious. The short version of my answer is that while the epistemic tension is a bad consequence of our phenomenal realist view that it is an open question whether Commander Data is conscious, it is not the kind of bad consequence that justifies us in concluding that he is not conscious. I will justify this claim.

Objection   You say disjunctivism is epistemically defective, but isn't it also metaphysically defective? How could a unitary phenomenal property be identical to a physical property that is nonunitary?

Reply   There is no logical flaw in disjunctivism. If a unitary phenomenal property is identical to a nonunitary physical property, then one property is both unitary from the mental point of view and nonunitary from the physical point of view. We are willing to allow that unitary properties of economics, sociology and meteorology are nonunitary from the physical point of view. Why shouldn't we include mentality too?[25]

Of course, there are views that are worthy of being called "naturalism" that dictate that disjunctivism is metaphysically defective. But they are not the "naturalism" that I am talking about. The naturalist I am talking about, you will recall, is also a phenomenal realist. And being a phenomenal realist, this naturalist keeps the question open of whether creatures that are heterogeneous from a physical point of view nonetheless overlap phenomemenally. If you like, this is a naturalistic concession to phenomenal realism.

Objection   Silicon machinery of the sort we are familiar with is manifestly not conscious. The only reason we could have to suppose that Commander Data's brain supported consciousness would be to find some kind of physical similarity to the states that we know underlie human consciousness, and that possibility has been ruled out by stipulation. Moreover, we can explain away our tendency to think of Commander Data as conscious as natural but unjustified anthropomorphizing.

Reply Naturalism and phenomenal realism do not dictate that Commander Data is not conscious or that the issue of his consciousness is not open. Recall that disjunctivism and superficialism are metaphysically (though not epistemically) viable. Further, naturalism gives us no evidence against or reason to doubt the truth of either disjunctivism or superficialism. Hence naturalism (and physicalism) give us no reason to doubt the consciousness of Commander Data. Imagine arguing at Commander Data's trial that he is a zombie (or that there is no matter of fact as to whether he is conscious) while conceding that his zombiehood is not even *probabilified* by naturalism unless we set aside disjunctivism and superficialism, options on which he may be conscious. And imagine conceding that we are setting these options aside not because we have any evidence against them or reason to think they are false but because we cannot conceive of any way in which they may be known. He could reasonably say (or to be neutral, produce the noise), "Your lack of a conception of how to find out whether I am conscious is no argument that I am a zombie; I similarly lack a conception of how to find out whether you are conscious." In any case, phenomenal realism is a form of metaphysical realism, so the phenomenal realist cannot suppose that our ignorance, even necessary ignorance, is not a reason to suppose that Commander Data is not conscious or that there is no matter of fact as to whether he is.

Why should the phenomenal realist take the consciousness of anything other than humans seriously? One answer can be seen by considering what happens if one asks Commander Data whether red is closer to purple than blue is to yellow. Answering such questions requires, in us, a complex multidimensional phenomenal space—in part captured by the color solid—with phenomenal properties at many levels of abstractness (see Loar, op. cit.). Commander Data's functional equivalence to us guarantees that he has an internal space that is functionally equivalent to our phenomenal space. But anyone who grasps our phenomenal space from the first-person point of view has to take seriously the possibility that an isomorphic space in another being is grasped by him from a similar first-person perspective. Talking of our "functional equivalence" to Commander Data tends to mask the fact that we are like him in a complex structure or set of structures. If one thinks of the functional similarity as limited to saying "Ouch" when you stick a pin in him, it is easy to miss the positive phenomenal-realist rationale for regarding Commander Data's consciousness as an open question. Thus the phenomenal realist and the deflationist converge on not closing off the possibility that Commander Data is conscious.

To make the plausibility of Commander Data's consciousness vivid, I include in figure 20.1 stills from Commander Data's trial.

Figure 20.1
Stills from "The Measure of a Man," episode 35 of *Star Trek: The Next Generation*. Commander Data is on the left in the first, in which his hand is removed by his prosecutor after he has turned Data off, emphasizing his robotic nature, and in the middle on the right, in the dock.

Objection (Made by Many Critics)   Why should the mere epistemic possibility of a bad consequence of physicalism threaten physicalism? No one thinks that the mere epistemic possibility of an object that has mass traveling faster than light threatens relativity theory. If relativity is true, nothing can travel faster than light. Similarly, if physicalism is true, there is no conscious Commander Data.

Reply   Relativity theory gives us reason to believe that it is impossible for anything to travel faster than light. But physicalism does not give us reason to believe that there can be no Commander Data or that it is impossible that Commander Data is conscious. Disjunctivism is not metaphysically suspect but only epistemically suspect: we have no conception of how we can know whether it is true or not. Our lack of knowledge is no argument against the consciousness of Commander Data.

Brian McLaughlin has argued (in a response at a meeting of Sociedad Filosofica Ibero Americana, 2001) that I am mischaracterizing the epistemic role of functional similarity in our reasoning about other minds. The role of functional similarity is in providing evidence that others are like us in intrinsic physical respects, and that is the ground for our belief in other minds. In the case of Commander Data, that evidential force is canceled when we find out what Commander Data's real constitution is. He notes that we are happy to ascribe consciousness to babies even though they are functionally very different from us because we have independent evidence that they share the relevant intrinsic physical properties with us. The same applies, though less forcefully, to other mammals—for example, rabbits. He asks us to compare a human baby with a functionally equivalent robot baby. The robot baby's functional equivalence to the real baby gives us little reason to believe that the robot baby is conscious. Similarly, for the comparison between a real rabbit and a robot rabbit. Moving closer to home, consider a paralytic with Alzheimer's: little functional similarity to us, but we are nonetheless confident, on the basis of an inference from similarity in intrinsic physical properties, that the senile paralytic has sensory consciousness. The upshot, he says, is that material constitution and structure trumps function in our attribution of consciousness to others. And so, if we become convinced that Commander Data is unlike us in the relevant intrinsic physical respects, we should conclude that he is not conscious.

My Reply Is, first, Commander Data shares with us *disjunctivist* and *superficialist material constitution and structure*, and so no conclusion can be drawn about the consciousness of Commander Data, even if McLaughlin is right about material constitution and structure trumping function. Nothing in McLaughlin's argument supplies a reason to believe that disjunctivism or superficialism is false. (Recall that I have argued that these views are epistemically defective, not that they are false.) He says that the relevant physical properties are "intrinsic" but if that is supposed to preclude disjunctivism or superficialism, we are owed an argument.

Second, I do agree with McLaughlin that a substantial element of our belief in other consciousnesses depends on an inference to a common material basis. However, it would be a mistake to conclude that this inference provides the entire basis for our attribution of other consciousnesses. Our justification is an inference from like effects to like causes. Even if we find out that the causes of behavioral similarity are not alike in material constitution and structure, it remains open that the common cause is a similarity in *consciousness itself* and that consciousness itself has a disjunctive or superficial material basis or no material basis. (Recall that naturalism is committed to physicalism as a default, but a default can be overridden.)

Third, function is not so easy to disentangle from material constitution and structure, at least epistemically speaking. The opponent-process theory of color vision originated in the nineteenth century from common sense observations of color vision such as the fact that afterimages are of the complementary color to the stimulus and that there are colors that seem, for example, both red and blue (purple) or red and yellow (orange), but no color that seems both red and green or both blue and yellow. The basic two-stage picture of how color vision works (stage 1: three receptor types; stage 2: two opponent channels) was discovered before the relevant physiology on the basis of behavioral data. To the extent that Commander Data behaves as we do, there is a rationale for supposing that the machinery of Commander Data's color vision shares an abstract structure with ours that goes beyond the color solid.

The first of the epistemic difficulties on the right hand side of our conditional is that *physicalism is the default, but also inaccessible and meta-inaccessible.* We are now ready to state the second epistemic difficulty. Let us introduce a notion of the "subjective default" view that we have rational ground for believing on the basis of background information—but only ignoring escape hatches—such as disjunctivism and superficialism—that we have no evidence against but that are themselves inaccessible and meta-inaccessible. Then the second epistemic difficulty is that of holding *both that it is an open question whether Commander Data is conscious and that it is the subjective default view that he is not.* These two epistemic difficulties constitute the Harder Problem.

Before I go on to consider further objections, let me briefly contrast the point of this paper with Nagel's famous "bat" paper (op. cit.). Nagel's emphasis was on the functional differences between us and bats, creatures which share the mammalian physical basis of sensation. My example, however, is one of a functionally identical creature, the focus being on the upshot of physical differences between us and that creature.

The issue of the application of our phenomenal concepts to exotic creatures is often mentioned in the literature, but assimilated to the Hard Problem (the "explanatory gap"). (I am guilty too. That was the background assumption of the discussion of "universal psychology" in my "Troubles with Functionalism," op. cit.) For example, Levine (*Purple Haze*, op. cit.) notes that we lack a principled basis for attributing consciousness to creatures that are physically very different from us. He says, "I submit that we lack a principled basis precisely because we do not have an explanation for the presence of conscious experience even in ourselves" (p. 79). Later he says, "Consider again the problem of attributing qualia to other creatures, those that do not share our physical organization. I take it that there is a very real puzzle whether such creatures have qualia like ours or even any at all. How much of our physicofunctional architecture must be shared before we have similarity or identity of experience? This problem, I argued above, is a direct manifestation of the explanatory gap" (p. 89).

It might be objected that naturalism says the concept of consciousness is a natural-kind concept and phenomenal realism denies it, so the tension is not epistemic, but is simply a matter of contradictory claims. But this is oversimple. Naturalism entails that the concept of consciousness is a natural-kind concept in one sense of the term, since one sense of the term is just that it is the default that there is a scientific nature. Phenomenal realism does not deny this. Phenomenal realism denies something importantly different, which could be put in terms of Putnam's famous "twin-earth" example. We find that twin-water has a fundamentally different material basis from water, and that shows twin-water is not water. But if we find that Martian phenomenality has a fundamentally different material basis from human phenomenality, that does not show Martian phenomenality is not phenomenality. According to phenomenal realism, if it feels like phenomenality, it is phenomenality, whatever its material basis or lack of it.

Those who apply the scientific worldview to consciousness often appeal to analogies between consciousness and kinds that have been successfully reduced. As noted earlier in connection with the Hard Problem, there is some mileage in analogies to the identity of water with H_2O, heat with molecular kinetic energy, and so on. But the fact that our concept of consciousness is not straightforwardly a natural-kind concept puts a crimp in these analogies.

VIII   More Objections

One can divide objections into those that require clarification of the thesis and those that challenge the thesis as clarified. The objections considered so far are more in the former category, while those below are more in the latter.

Objections from Indeterminacy

Objection   The issue of whether Commander Data is conscious is just a matter of vagueness or indeterminacy in the word "conscious." If we reject property dualism, then the issue of whether Commander Data is conscious depends on extrapolating a concept of consciousness grounded in our physical constitution to other physical constitutions. If those other physical constitutions are sufficiently different from ours as is stipulated for Commander Data, then the matter is indeterminate and so a decision has to be made. Similarly, in extending the concept "wood" to an alien form of life, we might find that it resembles what we have already called "wood" in certain ways but not others and a decision will have to be made. (Hartry Field and David Papineau have pressed such views in commenting on an earlier version of this paper.)

Reply   No phenomenal realist—physicalist or not—should accept the assumption that the decision whether to attribute consciousness to Commander Data is a decision about whether to extrapolate from our *nondisjunctive and nonsuperficial* physical constitution to his. For as I have emphasized, the physical basis of our conscious states may be of the sort supposed by disjunctivism or superficialism, in which case there will be a matter of fact about Commander Data's consciousness—from a physicalist point of view.

I do not want to give the impression that phenomenal realism is incompatible with indeterminacy about consciousness. For example, perhaps a fish is a borderline case of consciousness. Similarly, Commander Data might be a borderline case of consciousness and therefore indeterminate. On the phenomenal realist view of consciousness, it is an open question whether Commander Data is conscious, not conscious, or a borderline case. But there is no reason to think that Commander Data *must* be a borderline case. From the phenomenal-realist point of view, epistemic considerations alone do not show metaphysical indeterminacy.

There is another kind of indeterminacy, exemplified by a familiar example of the Eskimo word for the whale oil that they use in daily life. Does their category include a petroleum product that looks and functions similarly, but is fundamentally different at a chemical level? There may be no determinate answer. If the Eskimo term is a natural-kind term, the chemical specification is important; if the Eskimo term is not a natural-kind term, perhaps the chemical specification loses out to function. But, as Gareth

Evans once commented (in conversation), it may be indeterminate whether the Eskimo term is a natural-kind term or not. So there may be no determinate answer to the question of whether the Eskimos should say that the petroleum product is "oil." David Lewis takes a similar stance toward consciousness. He supposes that in ascribing consciousness to an alien, we rely on a set of criteria that determine the population of the alien. If the alien has no determinate population, it is indeterminate in consciousness.[26]

The indeterminacy in the application of the Eskimo word can be resolved in the petroleum company's favor by introducing a coined expression (as Evans noted). For example, if there is an issue as to whether "oil" is determinately a natural-kind term, we can get rid of any indeterminacy of this sort by introducing "oily stuff," stipulating that anything that has the appearance and utility of oil is oily stuff (Chalmers, op. cit.; Block and Stalnaker, op. cit.). But in the case of consciousness, no such stipulation will help. Suppose I coin "consciousish," stipulating that comparisons do not depend on any hidden scientific essence. "Consciousish" is not a natural-kind term in the relevant sense. We may now ask: "How could we get scientific evidence of whether or not Commander Data's current sensation is the same as my current sensation in respect of consciousishness?" The stipulation does not help. Alternatively, we could decide that "consciousish" is a natural-kind term, so Data is not consciousish. But the original question would recur as: "Does Commander Data's state of consciousishness feel the same as ours?" I do not see how any coined term that was adequate to the phenomenon—from a phenomenal-realist point of view—would fare any differently.

Another type of indeterminacy is exemplified in the question whether H_2O made out of heavy hydrogen (that is, D_2O) is a kind of *water* or not? There is no determinate answer, for our practice does not determine every decision about how the boundaries of a natural kind should be drawn. To decide the question of whether D_2O is a kind of water, we could either decide that water is a wide natural kind, in which case the answer is yes, or we could decide that water is a narrow natural kind, in which case the answer is no. The issue would be settled. Suppose we try this technique to settle the issue of whether Commander Data is conscious. We could decide to construe "consciousness" widely in case he is, or we could decide to construe "consciousness" narrowly, in which case. . . . What? Even if we decide to construe "consciousness" narrowly, we can still wonder if the phenomenon picked out by it *feels the same* as what Commander Data has when he is in a functionally identical state! One can stipulate that "Tuedaysconsciousness" designates consciousness that occurs on Tuesday, but it still is in order to ask whether Tuesdayconsciousness feels the same as, say, Thursdayconsciousness. Stipulations need not stick when it comes to the phenomenal realist conception of consciousness; any *adequate* concept of consciousness or phenomenality generates the same issue.

Closure of Epistemic Properties

In a response to this paper at a meeting of Sociedad Filosofica Ibero Americana in 2001, Martine Nida-Rümelin gave a formalization of the argument that involved a principle of closure of epistemic properties such as being open or being meta-inaccessible. (Brendan Neufeld made a similar point.) For instance, Nida-Rümelin supposes that part of the argument goes something like this: supposing physicalism requires a deep unitary property in common to conscious creatures, if Data is conscious, then physicalism is false; Data's consciousness is meta-inaccessible; so the falsity of physicalism is meta-inaccessible.

One can easily see that the form of argument is fallacious. If Plum did it, then it is false that the butler did it. But if it is inaccessible whether Plum did it, it does not follow that it is inaccessible whether or not the butler did it. We might find evidence against the butler that has nothing to do with Plum. The application of the point to the argument that Nida-Rümelin attributes to me is that even if Data's consciousness is inaccessible, we might have some independent reason to believe physicalism is false. I explicitly noted (and did in the earlier version) that I think the standard arguments against physicalism do not work.

Here is a standard problem with closure. (See my discussion of the tacking paradox in "Anti-Reductionism Slaps Back," op. cit.) Consider a meta-inaccessible claim, I, and an accessible claim, A. The conjunction I & A is meta-inaccessible, but a consequence of it, Λ, is not. So meta-inaccessibility is not transmitted over entailment. Briefly and metaphorically: fallacies of the sort mentioned seem to arise with respect to an epistemic property that applies to a whole even if only one of its parts has that property. The whole can then entail a different part that does not have that epistemic property. I doubt that my argument has that form, but if someone can show that it does, that will undermine it.

Objections Concerning Empirical Evidence

Objection Suppose my brain is hooked up to Commander Data's and I have the experience of seeing through his eyes. Isn't that evidence that he has phenomenal consciousness? Reply: maybe it is evidence, but it does not get up to the level of a rational ground for believing. Perhaps if I share a brain in that way with a zombie, I can see through the zombie's eyes because whatever is missing in the zombie brain is made up for by mine.

Objection Suppose we discover what we take to be laws of consciousness in humans and discover that they apply to Commander Data. That is, we find that the laws that govern human consciousness also govern the functional analog of consciousness in

Commander Data. Doesn't that get up to the level of rational ground for believing that Commander Data is conscious? (I am grateful to Barry Smith for getting me to take this objection more seriously.)

Reply   Since Commander Data's brain works via different principles from ours, it is *guaranteed that his states will not be governed by all of the same laws* as the functionally equivalent states in us. Two computers that are computationally equivalent but physically different are inevitably different in all sorts of physical features of their operation, for example, how long they take to compute various functions, and their failure characteristics—such as how they react to humidity or magnetic fields. The most that can be claimed is that the state that is the functional analog of human consciousness in Commander Data obeys *some* of the laws that our conscious states obey. The problem is: are the laws that Commander Data does *not* share with us laws of consciousness or laws of his *different physical realizer*? Without an understanding of the scientific nature of consciousness, how are we supposed to know? A zombie might share some laws of consciousness, but not enough or not the right ones for consciousness. So long as Commander Data does not share all the laws of our conscious states, there will be room for rational doubt as to whether the laws that he does share with us are decisive. Indeed, if we knew whether Commander Data was conscious or not, we could use that fact to help us in deciding which laws were laws of consciousness and which were laws of the realization. But as this point suggests, the issue of whether Commander Data is conscious is of a piece with the epistemic problem of whether a given law is a law of consciousness or a law of one of the realizers of its functional role.

An example will be useful to clarify this point. All human sensory systems obey a power function, an exponential function relating stimulus intensity to subjective intensity as judged by subjects' reports. That is, subjective intensity = stimulus intensity raised to a certain exponent, a different exponent for different modalities. For example, perceived brightness is proportional to energy output in the visible spectrum raised to a certain exponent. This applies even to outré parameters of subjective judgments such as how full the mouth feels as a function of volume of wads of paper stuck in the mouth or labor pains as a function of size of contractions. Should we see the question of whether Commander Data's sensations follow the power law as a litmus test for whether Commander Data has conscious experiences? No doubt the power law taps some neural feature. Is that neural feature essential or accidental to the nature of consciousness? Roger Shepard has argued in his unpublished William James Lectures that the power law form would be expected in any naturally evolved creature. But that leaves open the possibility of artificial creatures or evolutionary singularities (subject to unusual selection pressures) whose sensations (or "sensations") do not obey the power law. The question whether this is a law of consciousness or a law of the human realization of consciousness that need not be shared by a conscious Commander Data is of a piece with the question of whether creatures like Commander Data (who, let us suppose, do not obey the law) are conscious. We cannot settle one without the other, and the epistemic problem I am raising applies equally to both.

Skepticism and the Problem of Other Minds

Recall that I am arguing for a conditional. On the left are naturalism, phenomenal realism, and the denial of skepticism. There is a superficial resemblance between the Harder Problem and the problem of other minds. But the problem of other minds is a form of skepticism. The nonskeptic has no doubt that *humans* are (sometimes) conscious, but when we find out that Commander Data is *not human*, denying skepticism does not help.

What is it about being human that justifies rejecting skepticism? It is not part of my project here to attempt an answer, but I have to say something to avoid the suspicion that our rationale for regarding other humans as conscious or rocks as not conscious might apply equally to Commander Data.

Elliot Sober's "Evolution and the Problem of Other Minds"[27] argues plausibly that our rationale for attributing mental states to other humans is a type of "common-cause" reasoning. But such common-cause reasoning is vulnerable to evidence against a common cause—for instance, evidence for lack of genealogical relatedness or evidence for different scientific bases for the similarity of behavior that is exhibited. Thus the rationale for attributing mentality to humans does not fully apply to Commander Data.

Stephen White raises the skeptical worry of how we know that creatures whose brains are like ours in terms of principles of operation but not in DNA are conscious.[28] But this worry may have a *scientific* answer that would be satisfying to the nonskeptic. We might arrive at a partial understanding of the mechanisms of human consciousness that is sufficient to assure us that a creature that shared those mechanisms with us is just as conscious as we are even if its DNA is different. For example, we might discover a way to genetically engineer a virus that replaced the DNA in the cells of living creatures. And we might find that when we do this for adult humans such as ourselves, there are no noticeable effects on our consciousness. Or we might come to have something of a grip on why corticothalamic oscillation of a certain sort is the neural basis of human consciousness and also satisfy ourselves that many changes in DNA in adults do not change corticothalamic oscillation. By contrast, the Harder Problem may remain even if we accept the dictates of nonskeptical science.

IX   Supervenience and Mind-Body Identity

Much of the recent discussion of physicalism in the philosophy of mind has centered on supervenience of consciousness on the brain rather than on good old-fashioned mind-body identity. Chalmers (op. cit., xvii) recommends this orientation, saying "I find that discussions framed in terms of identity generally throw more confusion than light onto the key issues, and often allow the central difficulties to be evaded. By contrast, supervenience seems to provide an ideal framework within which key issues can be addressed."

But the Harder Problem depends on the puzzling nature of multiple physical constitution of consciousness, a problem that does not naturally arise from the perspective that Chalmers recommends. Supervenience prohibits any mental difference without a physical difference, but multiple constitution is a physical difference without a mental difference. Of course nothing prevents us from stating the issue in supervenience terms. In those terms, it is the problem of how a unitary phenomenal property can have a nonunitary (heterogeneously disjunctive) supervenience base. But there is no reason why this should be puzzling from the supervenience point of view. Heterogeneous supervenience bases of unitary properties—for example, adding—are common. What makes it puzzling is the thought that a phenomenal overlap between physically different creatures ought to have a unitary physical basis. That puzzle can be appreciated from the point of view of old-fashioned mind-body identity—which says that a phenomenal overlap is a physical overlap. (No one would identify adding with a physical (e.g., microphysical) property—it is obviously functional.) But it is not puzzling from the supervenience point of view.

X   The Hard and the Harder

Are the Hard and Harder Problems really different problems? The Hard Problem is: why is the scientific basis of a phenomenal property the scientific basis of that property rather than another or rather than a nonphenomenal property? The question behind the Harder Problem could be put so as to emphasize the similarity: why should physically different creatures overlap phenomenally in one way rather than another or not at all? This way of putting it makes it plausible that the Harder Problem includes or presupposes the Hard Problem. In any case, the Harder Problem includes an issue that is more narrowly epistemic than the Hard Problem The Hard Problem could arise for someone who has no conception of another person, whereas the Harder Problem is closely tied to the problem of other minds. Finally, the Harder Problem involves an epistemic discomfort not involved in the Hard Problem. My claim is that the "Harder Problem" differs from the "Hard Problem" in these ways independently of whether we choose to see them as distinct problems or as part of a single problem.

Is the Harder Problem harder than the Hard Problem? If the Harder Problem is the Hard Problem plus something else problematic, then it is trivially harder. As indicated above, the Harder Problem has an epistemic dimension not found in the Hard Problem, so they are to that extent incomparable, but the epistemic difficulty involved in the Harder Problem makes it harder in one way.

Both the Hard and Harder Problems depend on what we cannot now conceive. Even the epistemic difficulty may be temporary, unlike the epistemic difficulty of the concept of *the gold mountain that no one will ever have evidence of.* Perhaps we will come to understand the nature of human consciousness, and in so doing, develop an objective theory of consciousness that applies to all creatures, independently of physical constitution. That is, perhaps the concepts developed in a solution to the Hard Problem will one day solve the Harder Problem, though I think our relation to this question is the same as to the Harder Problem itself, namely, we have no conception of how to find an answer.

XI What to Do?

Naturalism dictates that physicalism is the default, but also inaccessible and meta-inaccessible; and in the "subjective" sense mentioned earlier, it is the default that Commander Data is not conscious, but at the same time phenomenal realists regard his consciousness as an open issue. This is the Harder Problem. Alternatively, we could see the problem this way: if Commander Data is conscious, then we have a choice of superficialism, disjunctivism, and dualism. The naturalist will want to reject dualism, but it is cold comfort to be told that the only alternatives are doctrines that are epistemically inaccessible. So this may lead us to want to say that Commander Data is not conscious. But we have no *evidence* that he is or is not conscious.

What to do? To begin, one could simply live with these difficulties. These are not paradoxical conclusions. Physicalism is the default and at the same time meta-inaccessible. It is the subjective default that androids like Commander Data are not conscious, but it is an open question whether they are. Consciousness is a singularity—perhaps one of its singular properties is these epistemic discomforts.

Another option would be to reject or restrict the assumption of naturalism or of phenomenal realism. One way to slightly debase naturalism would be to take the problem itself as a reason to believe the disjunctivist or superficialist form of naturalism. Those who prefer to weaken phenomenal realism can do so without adopting one of the deflationist views mentioned at the outset (functionalism, representationism, and cognitivism). One way to restrict phenomenal realism is to adopt what Shoemaker (op. cit.) calls the "Frege-Schlick" view, that comparisons of phenomenal character are only meaningful within the stages of a single person and not between individuals. Another proposal is slightly weaker than the Frege-Schlick view in allowing only interpersonal comparisons across naturalistically similar persons. That is, though comparisons of phenomenal character among subjects who share a physical (or other naturalistic) basis of that phenomenal character make sense, comparisons outside that class are nonfactual. Or else a significant group of them are false. That is, Commander Data either has no consciousness or there is no matter of fact about his consciousness.

Naturalistic phenomenal realism is not an unproblematic position. We cannot completely comfortably suppose both that consciousness is real and that it has a scientific nature. This paper does not argue for one or another way out, but is only concerned with laying out the problem.

Notes

Reprinted in *The Philosophers' Annual*, 2002, 5–49. Expanded version in *Disputatio* 15, November 2003.

This is a longer version of a paper by the same name that appeared in the *Journal of Philosophy* 99(8): 391–425, August 2002. I would like to thank David Barnett, Paul Boghossian, Tyler Burge, Alex Byrne, David Chalmers, Hartry Field, Jerry Fodor, Paul Horwich, Brian Loar, Tom Nagel, Georges Rey, Stephen Schiffer, Stephen White, and the editors of *The Journal of Philosophy* for comments on earlier drafts. I am also grateful to Alex Byrne and Jaegwon Kim for reactions when an ancestor of this paper was delivered at a Central APA meeting in 1998. My thanks to the Colloquium on Language and Mind at NYU at which an earlier version of this paper was discussed in 2000, and especially to Tom Nagel as the chief inquisitor. I am also grateful to the audience at the 2001 meeting of Sociedad Filosofica Ibero Americana (SOFIA) and especially to my respondents, Brian McLaughlin and Martine Nida-Rümelin. And I would also like to thank my graduate students at NYU, particularly Declan Smithies, for their comments. In addition, I am grateful for discussion at a number of venues where earlier versions of this paper were delivered, beginning with the Society for Philosophy and Psychology meeting, June 1997.

1. T. H. Huxley, *Lessons in Elementary Physiology* (London: Macmillan, 1986), 193; also see Güven Güzeldere, "The Many Faces of Consciousness: A Field Guide," in Ned Block, Owen Flanagan, and Güven Güzeldere, eds., *The Nature of Consciousness: Philosophical Debates*, 1–67, (Cambridge, MA: MIT Press, 1997), note 6.

2. See Thomas Nagel, "What is it like to be a bat?", *Philosophical Review* 83 (1974): 435–450. Joe Levine introduced the "explanatory-gap" terminology to be used later; see his "Materialism and qualia: The explanatory gap," *Pacific Philosophical Quarterly* 64 (1983): 354–361. David Chalmers and Galen Strawson distinguished between the hard problem and various "easy problems" of how consciousness functions. See David Chalmers, *The Conscious Mind* (New York: Oxford University Press, 1996), xxii–xxiii; Galen Strawson, *Mental Reality* (Cambridge, MA: MIT Press, 1994), 93–96.

3. David Lewis, "An Argument for the Identity Theory," *The Journal of Philosophy* 63 (1966): 17–25.

4. Deflationism with respect to truth is the view that the utility of the concept of truth can be explained disquotationally and that there can be no scientific reduction of truth. (See Paul Horwich, *Truth* (Oxford: Blackwell, 1990); 2nd ed. (Oxford: Oxford University Press, 1998). Also see Hartry Field, "Deflationist Views of Meaning and Content," *Mind* 103 (1994): 249–285.) Deflationism with respect to consciousness in its most influential form is, confusingly, a kind of reductionism—albeit armchair reductionism rather than substantive scientific reductionism—and thus

the terminology I am following can be misleading. I may have introduced this confusing terminology (in my 1992 reply to Dennett and Kinsbourne, reprinted in Block, Flanagan, and Güzeldere, op. cit., p. 177; and also in my review of Dennett in *The Journal of Philosophy*, pp. 181–193, 1993).

5. Georges Rey, "A Reason for Doubting the Existence of Consciousness," R. Davidson, G. Schwartz, and D. Shapiro, eds., in *Consciousness and Self-Regulation*, vol 3. (New York: Plenum, 1983), 1–39. In previous publications ("On a Confusion about a Function of Consciousness," *Behavioral and Brain Sciences* 18/2 (1995): 227–247), I have argued that Rey's alleged incoherence derives from his failure to distinguish between phenomenal consciousness and other forms of consciousness (what I call access consciousness and reflexive consciousness). The difficulty that is the subject of this paper, by contrast, is a difficulty in phenomenal consciousness itself.

6. Francis Crick and Christof Koch, "Towards a neurobiological theory of consciousness," *Seminars in the Neurosciences* 2 (1990): 263–275.

7. We can reasonably wonder how it is that Mark Twain and Samuel Clemens married women with the same name, lived in the same city, and so on. But we cannot reasonably wonder how it is that Mark Twain *is* Samuel Clemens. Imagine two groups of historians in the distant future finding a correlation between events in the life of Clemens and Twain. The identity explains such correlations, but it cannot itself be questioned. This point is made in Ned Block, "Reductionism," *Encyclopedia of Bioethics*, 1419–1424 (New York: Macmillan, 1978). See also Ned Block and Robert Stalnaker, "Conceptual Analysis and the Explanatory Gap," *Philosophical Review* 108 (1999): 1–46; David Papineau, "Consciousness, Physicalism and the Antipathetic Fallacy," *Australasian Journal of Philosophy* 71 (1993): 169–183. For a statement of a contrary view, see Chalmers, op. cit.

8. *Purple Haze* (Oxford: Oxford University Press, 2001).

9. The articles by Paul Churchland, Brian Loar, William Lycan, and Robert van Gulick in Block, Flanagan, and Güzeldere, op. cit., all take something like this line. So also do Scott Sturgeon, "The Epistemic View of Subjectivity," *The Journal of Philosophy* 91/5 (1994): 221–235, as well as Perry, op. cit.

10. Note that my account of subjective concepts allows for subjective concepts of many more colors or pitches than we can recognize, and thus my account differs from accounts of phenomenal concepts as *recognitional* concepts such as that of Loar, op. cit. In my view, one can have a phenomenal concept without being able to reidentify the same experience again. (See Sean Kelly, "Demonstrative Concepts and Experience," *Philosophical Review* 110/3 (2001): 397–420, for arguments that experience outruns recognition.)

11. Ned Block, "Troubles with Functionalism," in C. W. Savage, ed., *Minnesota Studies in the Philosophy of Science*, vol. 9, 261–325 (Minneapolis: University of Minnesota Press, 1978).

12. Hilary Putnam, "Psychological Predicates," later titled "The Nature of Mental States," in W. Capitan and D. Merrill, eds., *Art, Mind, and Religion* (Pittsburgh: Pittsburgh University Press, 1967); J. A. Fodor, "Materialism," *Psychological Explanation*, 90–120 (New York: Random House, 1968); Ned Block and Jerry Fodor, "What Psychological States Are Not," *Philosophical Review* 81 (1972): 159–181.

13. The most important criticism is given in a paper by Jaegwon Kim (Jaegwon Kim, "Multiple Realization and the Metaphysics of Reduction," *Philosophy and Phenomenological Research* 52/1 (1992): 1–26; see also J. Kim, *Mind in a Physical World: An Essay on the Mind-Body Problem and Mental Causation* (Cambridge, MA: MIT Press, 1998). I believe that Kim's argument does not apply to phenomenality, as he himself hints. I will briefly summarize Kim's argument in this note and the reason it does not apply to phenomenality later in section VII. In "Multiple Realization and the Metaphysics of Reduction," Kim says, correctly I think, that Putnam (op. cit.), Block and Fodor (op. cit.), and Fodor (op. cit.) reject without adequate justification the option of identifying a multiply realizable special science property with the heterogeneous disjunctive property whose disjuncts are its physical realizers. (P is the disjunctive property whose disjuncts are F and G. $P = \lambda x(Fx \text{ or } Gx)$. "$\lambda xFx$" is read as the property of being an x such that Fx, i.e., F-ness.) Kim says that the nomic covariance of the special science property with the disjunction of physical realizers shows that the special science property is just as nonnomic as the heterogeneous physical disjunction. The upshot, he says, is that there are no special sciences. My "Anti-reductionism Slaps Back," *Mind, Causation, World, Philosophical Perspectives* 11 (1997): 107–133, replies by arguing that whether a property is nomic is relative to a *level* of science. Both the multiply realizable special science property and the disjunction of physical realizers are nomic relative to the special science level and both are nonnomic relative to the physical level. (A sketch of a different challenge is given in section VII.)

Philip Kitcher and Elliott Sober have persuasively argued that certain biological kinds (e.g., fitness) are both multiply realizable and causal explanatory. See Kitcher, "1953 and All That: A Tale of Two Sciences," *Philosophical Review* 93 (1984): 335–373; Sober, *The Nature of Selection: Evolutionary Theory in Philosophical Focus* (Cambridge, MA: MIT Press, 1984). See also Alex Rosenberg, "On Multiple Realization in the Special Sciences," *The Journal of Philosophy* 98/7 (2001): 365–373. See also the wonderful example in Brian Keeley's "Shocking Lessons from Electric Fish: The Theory and Practice of Multiple Realization," *Philosophy of Science* 67 (2000): 444–465.

14. Kim accepts the standard argument that functionalism shows physicalism is false, though I do not think he would like that way of putting it. His stance is that of a deflationist functionalist about the mental. What makes human mental state M and Martian M both M is something functional, not something physical. However, he endorses structure-restricted physical identities: Martian M is one physical state, human M is another, and in that sense he is a physicalist. Since he is a physicalist—in that sense—and also a functionalist, he would not find the verbal formula that functionalism shows physicalism is false congenial.

Incidentally, the issue of multiple realization/reduction discussed here is quite different from the explanatory issue also discussed by Putnam and Fodor concerning whether macrophenomena always have microexplanations that subsume the macroexplanations. See Elliot Sober, "The Multiple Realizability Argument against Reductionism," *Philosophy of Science* 66 (1999): 542–564, on this issue.

William Bechtel and Jennifer Mundale, "Multiple Realizability Revisited: Linking Cognitive and Neural States," *Philosophy of Science* 66 (1999): 175–207, argue that mental states of actual animals and people are not multiply realized. (In my terminology, they mean multiply constituted.) They note that when we are offered real examples of multiple realization, a closer analysis reveals small functional differences. The putative multiple realizers are at best *approximately* realizers of the same functional state. For instance, though language is normally based in the left hemisphere, people without a left hemisphere can learn language pretty well; but there are differences in their abilities to master difficult syntactic constructions.

But recall the issue of the conflict between functionalism and physicalism. Pain cannot be brain state B if creatures that lack B (or even lack brains) have pain. *Even if pain in humans has a somewhat different role from pain in the imagined creature that has pain without B, still if the creature both lacks B and has pain, it is false that pain = B.* So the difference in role is irrelevant, once the logic of the argument is seen clearly. The point is clearest if one sees the issue of functionalism versus physicalism in terms of a mind-body identity thesis (but that is not necessary). If humans and the imagined creature share a mental property, M, then the issue of functionalism versus physicalism can be seen as the issue of whether M can be explained in terms of something physical that is shared between the two creatures. Even if M differs between the two creatures both mentally and in function, still there is an issue of whether M can be explained by a shared physical property. The issue is not whether there are inevitably functional differences between different realizers, but whether the *functional resemblances are explained by unitary properties at the realizer level.*

15. The restriction to first-order properties is unnecessary. See my "Can the Mind Change the World," in G. Boolos, ed., *Meaning and Method: Essays in Honor of Hilary Putnam* (Cambridge: Cambridge University Press, 1990).

16. An alternative notion of realization appeals to the notions of supervenience and explanation. The realized property supervenes on the realizer and the realizer explains the presence of the realized property. Possessing the realizer is one way in which a thing can possess the realized property. See Ernest Lepore and Barry Loewer, "Mind Matters," *The Journal of Philosophy* 93 (1987): 630–642; Lenny Clapp, "Disjunctive Properties: Multiple Realizations," *The Journal of Philosophy* 98/3 (2001): 111–136.

Dormitivity in the sense mentioned is a second-order property, the property of having some property that causes sleep. But one could also define dormitivity as a first-order property, the property of causing sleep. That is, by this different definition, F is dormitive just in case F causes sleep. But if we want to ascribe dormitivity to *pills*, we will have to use the second-order sense. What it is for a pill to be dormitive is for it, the pill, to have some property or other that causes sleep. Similarly, if we want a notion of functional property that applies to properties, the first-order variant will do. But if want to ascribe those properties to people, we need second-order properties. What it is for a person to have pain, according to the functionalist, is for the person to have some property or other that has certain causal relations to other properties and to inputs and outputs.

17. Here is a brief synopsis by Timothy Lynch (tlynch@alumni.caltech.edu, quoted with permission), http://www.ugcs.caltech.edu/st-tng/episodes/135.html: "While at Starbase 173 for crew rotation, Picard runs into an old acquaintance, Captain Phillipa Louvois, who once prosecuted him in the Stargazer court-martial, but is now working for the JAG (Judge Advocate General) office in this sector. Also on hand is Commander Bruce Maddox, who once on board the Enterprise, announces his intention to dismantle Data. Maddox is an expert in cybernetics, and has worked for years to recreate the work of Dr. Soongh, and he believes examining Data will give him the boost he needs to create many more androids like Data. However, when Picard, wary of Maddox's vagueness [actually, Maddox appears to have no idea whether he can put Data back together],

declines the offer, Maddox produces orders transferring Data to his command. After talking to Data, Picard goes to Phillipa to find a way to block the transfer. Unfortunately, the only option is for Data to resign from Starfleet. This he does, immediately, but is interrupted while packing by Dr. Maddox, who claims Data cannot resign. Data says that he must, to protect Soongh's dream. Maddox takes his complaint to Phillipa, and claims that since Data is property, he cannot resign. As she starts looking into this possibility, Data is thrown a going-away party and wished well in whatever he chooses to do. However, Phillipa then tells Picard and Riker that, according to the Acts of Cumberland, Data is the property of Starfleet, and thus cannot resign, or even refuse to cooperate with Maddox. Further, if a hearing is held to challenge this ruling, since Phillipa has no staff, serving officers must serve as counsel, with Picard defending and Riker prosecuting. Riker does some research and presents a devastating case for the prosecution, turning Data off while talking about cutting Pinocchio's strings. Picard, taken aback, asks for a recess, and talks to Guinan. Guinan subtly gets Picard to realize that if Data, and his eventual successors, are held to be "disposable people," that's no better than slavery all over again. Picard, renewed, presents his defense. He asks Data why he values such things as his medals, a gift from Picard, and especially a holographic image of Tasha (surprising Phillipa with Data's statement that they were "intimate"). He calls Maddox as a hostile witness, and demands from him the requirements for sentience. Finally, Picard points out…the possibility of thousands of Datas…becoming a race, and claims that 'Starfleet was founded to seek out new life—well there it sits!!' Phillipa rules in favor of Data, who refuses to undergo Maddox's procedure. Maddox cancels the transfer order, and Data comforts Riker, saying he will not easily forget how Riker injured himself (by prosecuting) to save Data."

18. Following Putnam, op. cit. This stipulation needs further refinement, which it would be digressive to try to provide here.

19. See Sydney Shoemaker, "The Inverted Spectrum," *The Journal of Philosophy* 79/7 (1982): 357–381. Shoemaker makes assumptions that would dictate that Commander Data overlaps with us in the most general phenomenal property, *having phenomenality*—by virtue of his functional likeness to us. But by virtue of his lack of physical overlap with us, there are no shared phenomenal states other than phenomenality itself. So on Shoemaker's view, phenomenality is a functional state, but more specific phenomenal states have a partly physical nature.

20. "Author's Response," *Behavioral and Brain Sciences* 3 (1980): 450–457.

21. Colin McGinn, *The Problem of Consciousness* (Blackwell: Oxford, 1991).

22. See my replies to Kim, "Anti-reductionism Slaps Back," *Mind, Causation, World, Philosophical Perspectives* 11 (1997): 107–133; also see my paper, "Do Causal Powers Drain Away," *Philosophy and Phenomenological Research* 67/1 (2003): 110–127, with a response by Kim.

23. The temperature identity is oversimplified, applying in this form only to gases. Paul Churchland raises doubts about whether there is a more abstract identity in *Matter and Consciousness* (Cambridge, MA: MIT Press, 1984). I think those doubts are deflected in Simon Blackburn's "Losing Your Mind: Physics, Identity and Folk Burglar Prevention," chap. 13 of *Essays in Quasi-Realism* (Oxford: Blackwell, 1993).

24. I am grateful to David Chalmers for pressing me for a better treatment of this issue.

25. See my "Anti-reductionism Slaps Back," op. cit., for more on this topic.

26. David Lewis, "Mad Pain and Martian Pain," in N. Block, ed., *Readings in Philosophy of Psychology*, vol. 1 (Cambridge, MA: Harvard University Press, 1980). Actually, Lewis's view is even weirder than I mention in the text. In Lewis's view, a creature that is both physically (and therefore functionally) just like us and that is now undergoing a state physically and functionally like one of our pains does not have pain if it is determinately a member of an appropriately different population. See Sydney Shoemaker's convincing refutation of Lewis, "Some Varieties of Functionalism," *Philosophical Topics* 12/1 (1981): 357–381.

27. *The Journal of Philosophy* 97/7 (2000): 365–386.

28. Stephen White, "Curse of the Qualia," *Synthese* 68 (1983): 333–368. Reprinted in Block, Flanagan, and Güzeldere, op. cit. The DNA issue is also mentioned in the version of Shoemaker's "The Inverted Spectrum," in Block, Flanagan, and Güzeldere, op. cit., 653–654.

21 Max Black's Objection to Mind-Body Identity

In his famous article advocating mind-body identity, J. J. C. Smart (1959) considered an objection (Objection 3) that he says he thought was first put to him by Max Black. He says "it is the most subtle of any of those I have considered, and the one which I am least confident of having satisfactorily met." This argument, the "Property Dualism Argument," as it is often called, turns on much the same issue as Frank Jackson's (1982, 1986) "Knowledge Argument," or so I will argue. This chapter is aimed at elaborating and rebutting the Property Dualism Argument (or rather a family of Property Dualism Arguments) and drawing some connections to the Knowledge Argument.[1] I will also be examining John Perry's (2001) book which discusses both Max Black's argument and the Knowledge Argument, and some arguments drawn from Stephen White's (1983) paper on the topic and some arguments inspired by unpublished papers by White.

I discovered rather late in writing this chapter (from Rozemond 1998[2]) that some of my arguments, especially those in the last third of the chapter, amount to a physicalistic adaptation of Arnauld's criticisms of Descartes. As I understand it, Arnauld criticized Descartes's idea that we have a complete intuition of the mental substance by arguing that nothing in our intuitive grasp of the mental rules out an objective "backside" to the mental whose objective description is out of reach of our intituitive grasp.

I will say a bit about what the basic idea of the Property Dualism Argument is and compare it with the Knowledge Argument. Then I will discuss Perry's view of both issues. Next, I will introduce an ambiguity in the notion of mode of presentation and use that to give a more precise statement and rebuttal of one version of the Property Dualism Argument. That is the first half of the chapter. In the second half, I will use this long set-up to exposit and rebut another version of the Property Dualism Argument and mention some related arguments. This chapter is long and detailed. Those who are very familiar with the issues will find it too long and detailed, but given the prevalence of confusion on these matters, I felt it was better to err on the side of explicitness.

I   What Is the Property Dualism Argument?

Smart said "suppose we identify the Morning Star with the Evening Star. Then there must be some properties which logically imply that of being the Morning Star, and quite distinct properties which entail that of being the Evening Star." And he goes on to apply this moral to mind-body identity, concluding that "there must be some properties (for example, that of being a yellow flash) which are logically distinct from those in the physicalist story." (1959: 148) He later characterizes the objection to physicalism as "the objection that a sensation can be identified with a brain process only if it has some phenomenal property ... whereby one-half of the identification may be, so to speak, pinned down" (149), the suggestion apparently being that the problem of physicalism will arise for that phenomenal property even if the original mind-body identity is true. This concern motivated the "dual-aspect" theory, in which mental events are held to be identical to physical events even though those mental events are alleged to have irreducible mental properties. (See also Schaffer 1963.) Smart did not adequately distinguish between token events (e.g. this pain) and types of events (e.g. pain itself), or between token events and properties such as the property of being a pain, the property of being pain, or the property of being in pain—the first being a property of pains, the second being a property of a property, and the last being a property of persons. (For purposes of this chapter, I will take types of events to be properties—any of those just mentioned will do.) But later commentators have seen that the issue arises even if one starts with a mind-body property identity, even if the mind-body identity theory that is being challenged says that the property of being in pain (for example) is identical to a physical property. For the issue arises as to how that property is "pinned down," to use Smart's phrase. If the mind-body identity says that phenomenal property Q = brain property B_{52}, then the question raised by the argument is: is the property by which Q is pinned down non-physical or is something non-physical required by the way it is pinned down?[3]

John Perry (2001: 101) states the argument as follows: "even if we identify experiences with brain states, there is still the question of what makes the brain state an experience, and the experience it is; it seems like that must be an additional property the brain state has.... There must be a property that serves as our mode of presentation of the experience as an experience." Later in discussing Jackson's Knowledge Argument, Perry considers the future neuroscientist, Mary, who is raised in a black and white room (which Perry calls the Jackson Room) and learns all that anyone can learn about the scientific nature of the experience of red without ever seeing anything red. While in the room, Mary uses the term "Q_R" for the sensation of red, a sensation whose neurological character she knows but has never herself had. Perry (ibid.) says:

If told the knowledge argument, Black might say, "But then isn't there something about Q_R that Mary didn't learn in the Jackson room, that explains the difference between 'Q_R is Q_R' which she already knew in the Jackson room, and (5) [Perry's (5) is: 'Q_R is this subjective character'], which she didn't?" There must be a new mode of presentation of that state to which "Q_R" refers, which is to say some additional and *apparently non-physical* aspect of that state, that she learned about only when she exited the room, that explains why (5) is *new* knowledge.[4]

On one way of understanding Perry, he uses "mode of presentation" here, not in the usual Fregean sense of something cognitive or semantic about a representation, but rather for a property of the represented referent. It seems that he sees Black's problem as arising from the question of the physicality of the mode of presentation in that non-Fregean sense of the term. Smart speaks in the same spirit of a property that pins down one half of the identification.

The idea of the Property Dualism Argument, and, I will argue, the Knowledge Argument, is that the mind-body identity approach to phenomenality fails in regard to the phenomenality that is involved in a certain kind of subjective mode of presentation (in both the Fregean and non-Fregean senses mentioned) of a phenomenal state. Even if a mind-body identity claim is true, when we look at the mode of presentation of the mental side of the identity, we are forced to accept a "double aspect" account in which unreduced phenomenal properties remain. However, don't expect a full statement of the main version of the Property Dualism Argument until nearly the halfway point. The next items on the agenda are connections to the Knowledge Argument, then (section II) Perry's solutions to both problems. Then (section III) I will take up the question of the difference between and respective roles of the Fregean and non-Fregean notions of mode of presentation.

Consider a specific phenomenal property, Q, e.g., the property of feeling like the pain I am having right now. (If pain just is a type of feel, then Q is just pain.) The physicalist says, let us suppose, that Q = cortico-thalamic oscillation of such and such a kind. (I will drop the last six words.) This is an a posteriori claim. Thus the identity depends on the expressions on either side of the "=" expressing distinct concepts, that is, having distinct modes of presentation, for if the concepts and modes of presentation were the same, it is said, the identity would be a priori. (An ambiguity involved in this reasoning—involving (surprise!) the distinction between Fregean and non-Fregean modes of presentation—will be scrutinized in section IV.)

"Q" in my terminology is very different from "Q_R" in Perry's terminology since "Q_R" is a term that Mary understands in the black and white room. "Q" by contrast is meant (by me even if not by Perry and Smart) as the verbal expression of a *phenomenal* concept. A phenomenal concept of the experience of red is what Mary lacked in the black and white room and what she gained when she went outside it. (She also lacked a phenomenal concept of the color red, but I will not depend on that.) Why do I insist that "Q" express a phenomenal concept? Because the mind-body identity claim under consideration must be one in which the phenomenal property is referred to *under a phenomenal concept of it* for the Property Dualism Argument—in any of its forms—*even to get off the ground.* (The Knowledge Argument also depends on the use of a phenomenal concept in my sense.) Suppose that in the original identity claim we allowed *any old concept* of Q—e.g., "the property whose onset of instantiation here was at 5 p.m." or "the property whose instantiation causes the noise 'ouch'." There is no special problem having to do with phenomenality for the physicalist about the cognitive significance of such properties or how such properties could pick out their referents. The modes of presentation of these properties raise no issues of the metaphysical status of phenomenality. If the original paradigm of mind-body identity were "the property whose onset of instantiation here was at 5 p.m. = cortico-thalamic oscillation," the property in virtue of which the left-hand term presents the referent would not be a special candidate for non-physicality. It would be the property of being instantiated here starting at 5 p.m. The Property Dualism Argument depends on an identity in which a *phenomenal concept* is involved on the mental side. To allow a non-phenomenal concept is to discuss an argument that has only a superficial resemblance to the Property Dualism Argument.

With all this emphasis on phenomenal concepts, you might wonder what they are supposed to be. A phenomenal concept is individuated with respect to fundamental uses that involve the *actual occurrence* of phenomenal properties. In these fundamental uses, a simultaneously occurring experience is used to think about that very experience. No one could have a phenomenal concept if they could not in some way relate the concept to such fundamental uses in which the subject actually has a simultaneous instance of the phenomenal quality.

That is what I mean by a phenomenal concept, but in the rest of this chapter, I will often adopt a simplification: the fundamental uses will be taken to be all the uses of the concepts. That is, I will assume that in the exercise of a phenomenal concept, the subject actually has to have an experience. Phenomenal concepts in this heavy-duty sense do not really correspond to the kind of general ability that we take concepts to be individuated by. But since it is really these fundamental uses that figure in this chapter, it will make matters simpler if we usually talk about the concepts as if their only uses were the fundamental uses. The idea of these heavy duty phenomenal concepts is that an instantiation of a phenomenal property is used in the concept to pick out a phenomenal property (a type). Of course, the experience involved in the fundamental use need not be an *additional* experience, that is, additional to the referent. A single experience can be both the object of thought and part of the way of thinking about that object. Further, one does not *have* to have an experience of red in order to think about an experience of red. One can think about the experience of red using, for example a purely descriptive concept of it, e.g., "the color of ripe tomatoes."[5]

Perry (2001, 2004*a,b*) uses what may be a more relaxed notion of phenomenal concept, in which a phenomenal concept is a kind of mental folder that contains what he calls a "Humean idea" of the experience. He says (2004*b*: 221):

Thinking of having the experience of some kind in this way is not having the experience, but it is in some uncanny way like it. Usually the same kinds of emotions attach to the thinking as to the having, although in a milder form. It is usually pleasant to anticipate or imagine having pleasant experiences, and unpleasant to anticipate or imagine having unpleasant ones, for example.

Perry's notion of a phenomenal concept is vague on the crucial point. Sure, thinking of having the experience is not just having the experience. Dogs can have experiences but presumably they can't think about them. The question is: does a phenomenal concept in Perry's sense require that the subject relate the concept to the fundamental uses I mentioned that involve an actual experience? Or, putting the point more clearly in terms of my simplified notion of a phenomenal concept, does the exercise of a phenomenal concept in Perry's sense involve an actual experience? As I shall argue in the section on Perry below, the problem for Perry's treatment hinges on whether phenomenal concepts in his sense are phenomenal enough to give the Knowledge Argument and the Property Dualism Argument a fighting chance.

It is time to turn to my claim that the Knowledge Argument hinges on the same requirement of a phenomenal concept in my sense as the Property Dualism Argument. Mary is reared in a colorless environment but learns all there is to know about the physical and functional nature of color and color vision. Yet she acquires new knowledge when she leaves the room for the first time and sees colored objects. Jackson concludes that there are facts about what it is like to see red that go beyond the physical and functional facts, and so dualism is true. From the outset, the following line of response has persuaded many critics.[6] Mary knew about the subjective experience of red via an objective concept from neuroscience. On leaving the room, she acquires a subjective concept of the same subjective experience. In learning what it is like to see red, she does not learn about a new property. She knew about that property in the room under an objective concept of it and what she learns is a new concept of that very property. One can acquire new knowledge about old properties by acquiring new concepts of them. I may know that there is water in the lake and learn that there is H_2O in the lake. In so doing, I do not learn of any new property instantiated, and in that sense I do not learn of any new fact. I acquire new knowledge that is based on a new concept of the property that I already knew to be instantiated in the lake. When Mary acquires the new subjective concept that enables her to have new knowledge, the new knowledge acquired does not show that there are any properties beyond the physical properties. Of course it does require that there are concepts that are not physicalistic concepts; however, that is not a form of dualism but only garden-variety conceptual pluralism: concepts of physics are also distinct from concepts of, say, economics and concepts of biology. The idea of the argument is to substitute a dualism of concepts for a dualism of properties and facts: there is a new concept but no new properties or facts in the relevant sense.

A natural rejoinder from the dualist is this. After seeing red for the first time, how does Mary "pin down" (to use Smart's obscure phrase) that old property? Or, to use an equally obscure phrase, what is Mary's "mode of presentation" of that old property?[7] When she acquires a subjective concept of the property that she used to have only an objective concept of, *a new unreducible subjective property* is required to pin down the old objective property. *This is the key stage in the dialectic about Mary, and this stage of the dialectic brings in the same considerations that are at play in the Property Dualism Argument.* Just to have a name for it, let us call this idea that the phenomenal concept that Mary acquires itself contains or else requires unreducible phenomenality the "metaphenomenal" move in the dialectic.[8]

The issue is sometimes put in terms of a distinction between two kinds of propositions. (See van Gulick 1993, 2006.) Coarse-grained propositions can be taken to be sets of possible worlds (or, alternatively, Russellian propositions that are n-tuples of objects and properties but contain no (Fregean) modes of presentation). The proposition (in this sense) that Harry Houdini escaped is the same coarse-grained proposition as the proposition that Erich Weiss escaped, in that the possible worlds in which Harry Houdini escaped are the same as the worlds in which Erich Weiss escaped, because Harry Houdini is Erich Weiss. (Alternatively, these are the same Russellian propositions because the proposition ⟨Houdini, escaped⟩ is the same proposition as ⟨Weiss, escaped⟩.) Fine-grained propositions include (Fregean) modes of presentation, and so the different names determine different fine-grained propositions. When we say that Harry Houdini escaped, we express a different fine-grained proposition from the one we express when we say that Erich Weiss escaped. In these terms, the issue is: does Mary's new knowledge involve merely a new fine-grained proposition (in which case physicalism is unscathed because Mary's new knowledge does not eliminate any possibilities), or does it require a new coarse-grained proposition (as well)? *It is the phenomenal (Fregean) mode of presentation of Mary's new subjective concept of the property that she already had an objective concept of that motivates the idea that she gains new coarse-grained knowledge.* The metaphenomenal move is at play: the thought is that that phenomenal mode of presentation brings in something fundamentally ontological and not something on the order of (merely) a different description. The idea is that when something phenomenal is part of a (Fregean) mode of presentation, it will not do for the physicalist to say that that phenomenal item is unproblematically physical. Whether one agrees with this or not, if one does not recognize it, one misses a crucial step in the dialectic about Mary.

I said that the standard reply to Jackson's argument attempts to substitute a dualism of concepts for a dualism of properties and facts. But the dualist rejoinder that I have been describing—exploited in pretty much the same way by the Knowledge Argument and the Property Dualism Argument—is that the dualism of concepts *requires* a dualism of properties and facts.

I said that Mary acquires a subjective concept of the experience of red, whereas what she already had was an objective concept of it. However, it is a particular kind of subjective concept she acquires, namely a phenomenal concept of the experience of red. If it was an objective concept that she acquired, say the concept of the type of experience that occurred at 5 p.m., the argument would have no plausibility. But even some subjective concepts would not do, e.g., the concept of the type of experience that happened five minutes ago. This concept is subjective in that it involves the temporal location of the subject from the subject's point of view ("now"), but it is no more suitable for the Knowledge Argument than the objective concept just mentioned. What is required for the metaphenomenal move in the dialectic about the Knowledge Argument is that Mary acquires a mode of presentation that is either itself problematic for physicalism or that requires that the referent have a property that is problematic for physicalism. And in this regard, it is just like the Property Dualism Argument.

What Mary learns is sometimes put like this: "Oh, so *this* is what it is like to see red," where "what it is like to see red" is a phrase she understood in the black and white room, and the italicized 'this' is supposed to express a phenomenal concept. Since there is some doubt as to whether a demonstrative concept can really be a phenomenal concept (I'll explain the doubt below), we could put the point better by saying that what Mary learns is that P = the property of being an experience of red, where it is stipulated that "P" expresses a phenomenal concept (of a phenomenal property) and "is an experience of red" is a term Mary understood in the black and white room. But there is nothing special about this item of knowledge in the articulation of the point of the Knowledge Argument as compared with other items of knowledge that use 'P'. In particular, one could imagine that one of the things that Mary learns is that P = the property of being cortico-thalamic oscillation. She already knew in the room that the experience of red = cortico-thalamic oscillation (where it is understood that 'the experience of red' is something she understood in the black and white room), but she learns that P = the property of being cortico-thalamic oscillation. The proposition that P = the property of being cortico-thalamic oscillation is supposed to be a new coarse-grained proposition, one that she did not know in the black and white room. This version of the Knowledge Argument makes the overlap with the Property Dualism Argument in the metaphenomenal move explicit: there is supposed to be something problematic about physicalism *if it is stated using a phenomenal concept*. That is, what is problematic is something about the "mode of presentation" of the phenomenal side of the identity. Both arguments can be put in the form: even if we take physicalism to be true, that supposition is undermined by the phenomenal mode of presentation in the knowledge or statement of it.[9]

I have used, more or less interchangeably, terms such as "pin down," "mode of presentation," "concept," and "way of thinking." But there is an ambiguity (the ambiguity between Fregean and non-Fregean readings) that must be resolved in order to focus on a precise statement of these arguments. Before I turn to that topic, however, I will give a critique of Perry's approach to Max Black, the Knowledge Argument and modal arguments for dualism.

II Perry's Treatment of the Two Arguments

Perry's (2001, 2004*a*,*b*) approach to the Knowledge Argument is roughly along the lines mentioned above: that Mary does something like acquiring a new subjective concept of a property that she had an objective concept of already in the black and white room. But Perry gives that response two new twists with two ideas: that the new concept is part of what he calls a "reflexive content" and that Mary need not actually acquire the new concept so long as she is appropriately sensitive to it.

Here is a quotation from Perry (2001) that gives his response both to Max Black's problem and to the Knowledge Argument.

We can now, by way of review, see how Black's dilemma is to be avoided. Let's return to our imagined physicalist discovery, as thought by Mary, attending to her sensation of a red tomato:

"This$_i$ sensation = B$_{52}$" [where 'this$_i$' is an internal demonstrative and B$_{52}$ is a brain property that she already identified in the black and white room—NB]

This is an informative identity; it involves two modes of presentation. One is the scientifically expressed property of being B$_{52}$, with whatever structural, locational, compositional and other scientific properties are encoded in the scientific term. This is not a neutral concept. The other is being a sensation that is attended to by Mary. This is a neutral concept; if the identity is true, it is the neutral concept of a physical property. Thus, according to the antecedent physicalist [who takes physicalism as the default view—NB], Mary knows the brain state in two ways, as the scientifically described state and as the state that is playing a certain role in her life, the one she is having, and to which she is attending. The state has the properties that make it mental: there is something it is like to be in it and one can attend to it in the special way we have of attending to our own inner states. (2001: 205)

If Mary's concept were "being the sensation attended to by Mary" it could not be regarded as a topic-neutral concept unless the terms "sensation" and "attend" are themselves understood in a topic-neutral manner. (Ryle introduced the term "topic-neutral" for expressions that indicate nothing about the subject matter. Smart offered topic-neutral analyses of mental terms that were supposed neither to entail that the property is physical nor that it is non-physical. But it is clear that mentalistic terminology was supposed to be precluded, for otherwise no topic-neutral analyses would be needed—the terms would already have been topic-neutral.)

If Mary's concept is topic-neutral, it is not a phenomenal concept in the sense required by the Property Dualism Argument. Although Perry rejects the "deflationist" view that phenomenal concepts are analyzable a priori in non-phenomenal terms (as Smart advocated), his approach to arguments for dualism is to appeal to topic-neutral demonstrative/recognitional concepts as surrogates for phenomenal concepts. To explain what he has in mind, we need to introduce what he calls "reflexive content." Propositional attitudes have "subject matter" contents which are a matter of the properties and objects the attitudes are concerned with. The subject matter content of your belief that the morning star rises could be taken to be the Russellian proposition ⟨Venus, rises⟩. But there are other contents that are concerned with the same subject matter and have the same truth condition: for example, that the heavenly object which you are now thinking of is in the extension of the property that is the object of your concept of rising. Before I mentioned it and brought it to your explicit attention, this might have been a reflexive content but not a subject matter content of your thought. ("Reflexive" is meant to indicate that what is being brought in has to do with the way thought and language fit onto the world or might fit onto the world.) The subject matter content of the claim that $this_i$ (where "$this_i$" is an internal demonstrative) = B_{52}, if physicalism is right, is the same as that $this_i = this_i$ or that $B_{52} = B_{52}$. Perry's intriguing idea is that my belief can have reflexive contents, the concepts of which are not concepts that I actually have, or even if I have them, those concepts are not ones that I am exercising in using demonstrative or recognitional concepts that have those reflexive contents. However, he argues persuasively that these concepts may be psychologically relevant nonetheless if the subject is "attuned" to the concepts in reasoning and deciding. Attunement is a doxastic attitude that can have contents that are not contents of anything the subject believes or has concepts of. For example, I can be attuned to a difference in the world that makes a perceptual difference without conceptualizing the difference in the world. Perry's view is that our intuitions about contents are often a matter of reflexive contents that we are attuned to rather than to subject matter contents that we explicitly entertain.

Perry's solution to Max Black's problem and his reply to Jackson is to focus on a topic-neutral version of what Mary learns. I am not totally sure whether it is just the demonstrative/recognitional concept ("$this_i$") that is topic-neutral, or whether the reflexive content of it is also supposed to be topic-neutral. But both proposals evade the Max Black problem without solving it. In the passage quoted earlier, he says what Mary learns can be put in terms of "$This_i$ sensation is brain state B_{52}," where "$this_i$" is a topic-neutral internal demonstrative/recognitional concept. If the suggestion is that Mary acquires the belief that $this_i$ is brain state B_{52}, the problem is that the topic-neutral concept involved in this belief is not a phenomenal concept, so the real force of the Knowledge Argument (and Max Black's argument) is just ignored. However, it seems that Perry's suggestion is that Mary comes to be *attuned* to the relevant reflexive content instead of coming to believe it. He thinks that what Mary learns can be expressed in terms of something she is attuned to and Max Black's problem can be solved by appealing to attunement to the same content. That is, in using demonstrative and recognitional concepts in the thought "$This_i$ sensation = B_{52}," Mary becomes

attuned to a reflexive content like "the sensation Mary is attending to is the scientifically described state" without explicitly exercising those concepts.

But does substituting attunement for belief avoid the problem of ignoring the real
force of the argument? Does attunement help in formulating a response to the Mary
and Max Black arguments that takes account of the metaphenomenal move in the
Mary dialectic? I think not.

Distinguish between two versions of Jackson's "Mary." Sophisticated Mary acquires a
genuine phenomenal concept when she sees red for the first time. Naive Mary is much
less intellectual than Sophisticated Mary. Naive Mary does not acquire a phenomenal
concept when she sees red for the first time (just as a pigeon presumably would not acquire a new concept on seeing red for the first time), nor does she acquire an explicit
topic-neutral concept, but she is nonetheless *attuned* to certain topic-neutral nonphenomenal content like that of "The sensation I am now attending to is the brain
state I wrote my thesis on earlier." In addition, we might suppose (although Perry
does not mention such a thing) that Naive Mary is also attuned to a genuine phenomenal concept of a color even though she does not actually acquire such a concept.

As I mentioned earlier, there is a well-known solution to the Mary problem that takes
Mary as Sophisticated Mary. What Sophisticated Mary learns is a phenomenal concept
of a physical property that she already had a physical concept of in the black and white
room. Any solution to the Mary problem in terms of Naive Mary is easily countered by
a Jacksonian opponent who shifts the thought-experiment from Naive to Sophisticated
Mary. Consider this dialectic. Perry offers his solution. The Jacksonian opponent says
"OK, maybe that avoids the problem of Naive Mary, but the argument for dualism is
revived if we consider a version of the thought experiment involving Sophisticated
Mary, that is a version of the thought-experiment in which Mary actually acquires
the phenomenal concept instead of merely being attuned to it (or attuned to a topic-
neutral surrogate of it). What Sophisticated Mary learns is a content that contains a
genuine phenomenal concept. And that content was not available to her in the room.
What she acquires is phenomenal knowledge (involving a phenomenal concept),
knowledge that is not deducible from the physicalistic knowledge she had in the black
and white room. So dualism is true." Indeed, it is this explicit phenomenal concept
that makes it at least somewhat plausible that what Mary acquires is a new coarse-
grained belief as well as a new fine-grained belief. Perry cannot reply to *this* version of
the thought experiment (involving Sophisticated Mary) by appealing to the *other* one
(that involves Naive Mary). And the thought experiment involving Sophisticated Mary
is not avoided by appeal to attunement to a topic-neutral concept or even to a phenomenal concept.

As I indicated earlier, the crucial point in the dialectic about Mary is this: the dualist
says "The concept that Mary acquires (or acquires an attunement to) has a mode of
presentation that involves or requires unreducible phenomenality." If Perry appeals to

the idea that the concept is topic-neutral or has a topic-neutral reflexive content, the dualist can reasonably say "But that isn't the concept I was talking about; I was talking about a genuinely phenomenal concept."[10]

Let us now turn to Perry's solution to the Max Black problem. Although the Max Black problem is mentioned a number of times in the book, Perry's solution is expressed briefly in what I quoted above. He clearly intends it to be a by-product of his solutions to the other problems. I take it that that solution is the same as the solution to the Mary problem, namely that the problem posed by the alleged non-physical nature of the mode of presentation of the phenomenal side of a mind-body identity or what is required by that mode of presentation can be avoided by thinking of what Mary learns in terms of a demonstrative/recognitional topic-neutral concept that—perhaps—has a topic-neutral reflexive content. The proponent of the Max Black argument (the Property Dualist) is concerned that in the mind-body identity claim "P = B_{52}" where "P" expresses a phenomenal concept, the phenomenal mode of presentation of "P" undermines the reductionist claim that P = B_{52}. Someone who advocates this claim—and who, like Perry, rejects deflationist analyses of phenomenal concepts—is certainly not going to be satisfied by being told that the content that Mary is attuned to is topic-neutral. The Property Dualist will say "So what? My concern was that the mode of presentation of 'P' introduces an unreducible phenomenality; whether Perry's topic-neutral content is something we believe or are merely attuned to is not relevant." And even if what Mary is attuned to is a reflexive content that contains a genuine phenomenal concept, that also evades the issue without solving it, since the dualist can reasonably say that it is the actual phenomenal concept on which the argument for dualism is based.

Perry also applies his apparatus to the modal arguments for dualism such as Kripke's and Chalmers's. Why do we have the illusion that "This$_i$ sensation = B_{52}" is contingent, given that (according to physicalism) it is a metaphysically necessary truth? Perry's answer is that the necessary identity has some *contingent* reflexive contents such as: that the subjective character of red objects appears like so and so on an autocerebroscope, is called "B_{52}," and is what I was referring to in my journal articles. The illusion of contingency comes from these reflexive contents. Here the metaphenomenal move I mentioned earlier has no role to play. I think Perry's point here has considerable force.

However, the dualist can respond to Perry by saying, "Look, I can identify the brain state by its *essential properties* and still wonder whether I could have that brain state (so identified) without *this$_i$* phenomenal property." *A version of this argument, will be explored in section IV below.*

Though I agree with Perry on many things about phenomenality, and find his book with its notion of attunement to reflexive concepts insightful and useful, there is one key item from which all our disagreements stem. He does not recognize the need for, or rather he is vague about the need for, a kind of phenomenal concept that itself requires fundamental uses that are actually experiential. When saying what it is that Mary learns, he says, "This new knowledge is a case of recognitional or identificational knowledge.... We cannot identify what is new about it with subject-matter contents; we can with reflexive contents" (2004a: 147). The physicalist will agree that what Mary learns is not a *new* subject matter content (in the sense explained earlier). But the problem is that it is unclear whether the recognitional or identificational concepts that Perry has in mind have the phenomenality required to avoid begging the question against the advocate of Max Black's argument. When he proposes to explain away the intuitions that motivate the Max Black argument and the Knowledge Argument by appeal to a topic-neutral concept, he loses touch with what I called the metaphenomenal move and with it the intuitive basis of these arguments in phenomenal concepts, or so it seems to me.

The reader may have noticed that there has still not been an explicit statement of the Property Dualism Argument. I have postponed the really difficult and controversial part of the discussion, the explanation of an ambiguity in "mode of presentation," a matter to which I now turn.

III Modes of Presentation

The "mode of presentation" of a term is often supposed to be whatever it is on the basis of which the term picks out its referent. The phrase is also used to mean the cognitive significance of a term, which is often glossed as whatever it is about the terms involved that explain how true identities can be informative. (Why is it informative that Tony Curtis = Bernie Schwartz but not that Tony Curtis = Tony Curtis?) However, it is not plausible that these two functions converge on the same entity, as noted in Tyler Burge (1977) and Alex Byrne and Jim Pryor (2006).[11]

I believe that these two functions or roles are not satisfied by the same entity, and so one could speak of an ambiguity in "mode of presentation." However, perhaps confusingly, the Property Dualism Argument depends on a quite different ambiguity in "mode of presentation."[12] I will distinguish between the cognitive mode of presentation (CMoP) and the metaphysical mode of presentation (MMoP). The CMoP is the Fregean mode of presentation mentioned earlier, a constellation of mental (cognitive or experiential) or semantic features of a term or mental representation that plays a role in determining its reference, or, alternatively but not equivalently, constitutes the basis of explanation of how true identities can be informative (and how rational disagreement is possible—I will take the task of explaining informativeness and rational disagreement to be the same, using "cognitive significance" for both. I will also tend to simplify, using "cognitive" to describe the relevant constellation of features. Since semantic and experiential differences make a cognitive difference, they don't need to be mentioned separately.). The importantly different, non-Fregean, and less familiar mode of presentation, the MMoP, is a property of the referent. There are different notions of MMoP corresponding to different notions of CMoP. Thus if the defining feature of the CMoP is taken to be its role in determining reference, then the MMoP is the property of the referent in virtue of which the CMoP plays this role in determining reference. If the defining feature of the CMoP is taken to be explaining cognitive significance, then the MMoP is the property of the referent in virtue of which cognitive significance is to be explained.

For example, suppose, temporarily, that we accept a descriptional theory of the meaning of names. On this sort of view, the CMoP of "Hesperus" might be taken to be cognitive features of "the morning star." "The morning star" picks out its referent in virtue of the referent's property of rising in the morning rather than its property of being covered with clouds or having a surface temperature of 847 degrees Fahrenheit. The property of the referent of rising in the morning is the MMoP. (And this would be reasonable for both purposes: explaining cognitive significance and determining the referent.) The CMoP is much more in the ballpark of what philosophers have tended to take modes of presentation to be, and the various versions of what a CMoP might be are also as good candidates as any for what a concept might be. The MMoP is less often thought of as a mode of presentation—perhaps the most salient example is certain treatments of the causal theory of reference in which a causal relation to the referent is thought of as a mode of presentation. (Devitt 1981).

In the passage quoted earlier from Perry's statement of Max Black's argument, Perry seemed often to be talking about the MMoP. For example, he says: "even if we identify experiences with brain states, there is still the question of what makes the brain state an experience, and the experience it is; it seems like that must be an additional *property* the brain state has ... There must be a *property* that serves as our mode of presentation of the experience as an experience" (2001: 101, italics added). Here he seems to be talking about the MMoP of the brain state (i.e. the experience if physicalism is right). When he says what Max Black would say about what Mary learns, he says: "'But then isn't there something about Q_R that Mary didn't learn in the Jackson room, that explains the difference between 'Q_R is Q_R' which she already knew in the Jackson room, and (5) [(5) is: Q_R is this subjective character], which she didn't?" There must be a new mode of presentation of that state to which 'Q_R' refers, which is to say some additional and *apparently non-physical aspect* of that state, that she learned about only when she exited the room, that explains why (5) is *new* knowledge." (ibid., italics added) Again, "aspect" means property, a property of the state. So it looks like in Perry's rendition, a mode of presentation is an MMoP. However, his solution to Max Black's problem involves the idea that the concept that Mary acquires or acquires sensitivity to is topic-neutral, and that makes it look as if the issue in the Property Dualism Argument is centered on the CMoP. He says, speaking of a mind-body identity: "This is an informative identity; it involves two modes of presentation. One is the scientifically expressed *property* of being B_{52}, with whatever structural, locational, compositional and other scientific properties are encoded in the scientific term. This is not a neutral *concept*. The other is being a sensation that is attended to by Mary. This is a neutral *concept*; if the identity is true, it is the neutral *concept* of a physical property" (italics added). The properties of being B_{52} and being a sensation that is attended to by Mary are said by Perry to be properties, but also concepts. The properties are modes of presentation in the metaphysical sense, but concepts are naturally taken to be or to involve modes of presentation in the cognitive sense. The view he actually argues for is: "We need instead the topic-neutrality of demonstrative/recognitional concepts" (205).

When I described the metaphenomenal move in the dialectic concerning the Knowledge Argument, I said the phenomenal concept that Mary acquires itself contains or else requires unreducible phenomenality. Why "contains or else requires"? In terms of the CMoP/MMoP distinction: if the CMoP that Mary acquires is partly constituted by an unreduced phenomenal element, then we could say that the concept contains unreduced phenomenality. If the MMoP that is paired with the CMoP involves unreduced phenomenality, one could say that the concept that Mary acquires *requires* an unreduced phenomenal property, as a property of the referent.

In the next section (IV) I will state a version of the Property Dualism Argument in terms of MMoPs. But as we shall see, that argument fails because of what amounts to equivocation: one premise is plausible only if modes of presentation are MMoPs, the other premise is plausible only if modes of presentation are CMoPs. A second version of the Property Dualism Argument (V) will also be couched initially in terms of MMoPs, but that treatment is tactical, and the argument will involve some degree of separate discussion of CMoPs and MMoPs.

I will pause briefly to say where I stand on the main issue. The Property Dualism Argument is concerned with a mind-body identity that says that phenomenal property $Q = $ brain property B_{52}. The worry is that the mode of presentation of Q brings in a non-physical property. But mode of presentation in which sense? Start with the CMoP. Well, a phenomenal CMoP has a constituent that is phenomenal and is used to pick out something phenomenal. Let me explain.

If I think about the phenomenal feel of my pain *while I am having it*, I can do that in a number of different ways. I could think about it using the description "the phenomenal feel of this pain." Or I could think about it using the phenomenal feel of the occurring pain itself as part of the concept. But if a token phenomenal feel does double duty in this way (as a token of an aspect of both the pain and our way of thinking of the pain), no extra specter of dualism arises. If the phenomenal feel is a physical property, then it is a physical property even when it (or a token of it) does double duty. The double duty is not required by a phenomenal concept. One could in principle use one phenomenal feel in a CMoP to pick out a different phenomenal feel; e.g., the phenomenal feel of seeing green could be used to pick out the phenomenal feel of seeing red if the concept involves the description "complementary" in the appropriate way. But there is no reason to think that such a use brings in any new specter of dualism.

Move now to the MMoP. We can think about a color in different ways, using different properties of that color. I might think of a color via its property of being my favorite color or the only color I know of whose name starts with "r." Or, I may think about it via its phenomenal feel. And what holds of thinking about a color holds for thinking about the phenomenal feel itself. I can think of it as my favorite phenomenal feel or I can think about it phenomenally, for example, while looking at the color or imagining it. If the referent is a phenomenal property P, the MMoP might be taken to be the property of being (identical to) P. If P is physical, so is being P. So the MMoP sense generates no new issue of dualism. That is where I stand. The Property Dualist, by contrast, thinks that there are essential features of modes of presentation that preclude the line of thought that I expressed. That is what the argument is really about.[13]

I have not given a detailed proposal for the nature of a phenomenal CMoP, since my case does not depend on these details. But for concreteness, it might help to have an example. We could take the form of a phenomenal CMoP to be "the experience: —," where the blank is filled by a phenomenal property, making it explicit how a CMoP might mix descriptional and non-descriptional elements.[14] If the property that fills the blank is phenomenal property P, the MMoP that is paired with this CMoP might be the property of *being P* and the referent might be P itself.

I will turn now to a bit more discussion of the CMoP/MMoP distinction and then move to stating and refuting the Property Dualism Argument.

Different versions of the Property Dualism Argument presuppose notions of CMoP and MMoP geared to different purposes. I have mentioned two purposes, fixing reference and accounting for cognitive significance. A third purpose—or rather a constraint on a purpose—is the idea that the MMoP is a priori accessible on the basis of the CMoP. And since one cannot assume that these three functions (cognitive significance, fixing reference, a priori accessibility) go together, one wonders how many different notions of CMoP and MMoP there are. Burge (1977) and Byrne and Pryor (forthcoming) give arguments that—although put in different terms—can be used to make it plausible that these three *raisons d'être* of modes of presentation do not generally go together. However, I will rebut the Property Dualism Argument without relying—except at one point—on any general claim that this or that function does not coincide with a different function. All of the versions of the CMoP that I will be considering share a notion of a CMoP as a cognitive entity, for example a mental representation. The MMoP, by contrast, is always a property of the referent. One way in which the different *raison/s d'être* matter is that for fixing reference, the MMoP must not only apply to the referent but uniquely pick it out—and further, have been in effect given a special authority in picking out the referent by the subject. But when it comes to cognitive significance, the MMoP need not even apply to the referent (as Byrne and Pryor note in somewhat different terms), so long as it seems to the subject to apply. However, I will not be making use of this difference.

Physicalists say that everything is physical and thus they are committed to the claim that everything cognitive, linguistic, and semantic is physical. However, not all issues for physicalism can be discussed at once, and since the topic of this chapter is the difficulty for physicalism posed by phenomenality, I propose to assume that the cognitive, linguistic, and semantic features of CMoPs do not pose a problem for physicalism so long as they do not involve anything phenomenal.

I will argue that the key step in the Property Dualism Argument can be justified in a number of ways, assuming rather different ideas of what MMoPs and CMoPs are (so there is really a family of Property Dualism Arguments). There are many interesting and controversial issues about how to choose from various rather different ways of fleshing out notions of CMoP and MMoP. My strategy will be to try to avoid these interesting and controversial issues, sticking with the bare minimum needed to state and critique the Property Dualism Argument. In particular, I will confine the discussion to CMoPs and MMoPs of singular terms, since the mind-body identities I will be concerned with are all of the form of an "=" flanked by singular terms (usually denoting properties). I will not discuss belief contexts or other oblique contexts. The reader may wonder if all these different and underspecified notions of mode of presentation are really essential to any important argument. My view, which I hope this chapter vindicates, is that there is an interesting family of arguments for dualism involving a family of notions of mode of presentation and that this family of arguments is worth spelling out and rebutting.

Am I assuming the falsity of a Millian view, according to which modes of presentation do not figure in a proper understanding of concepts? Without modes of presentation, the Property Dualism Argument does not get off the ground, so if Millianism assumes that there are no modes of presentation involved in concepts, then I am assuming Millianism is false. However, the view of phenomenal concepts that I will be using has some affinities with a Millian view. In addition, I will be considering a version of the Property Dualism Argument (in the next section) in which metaphysical modes of presentation on both sides of the identity are assumed to be identical to the referent.

Modal arguments for dualism such as Kripke's and Chalmers's attempt to move from epistemic premises to metaphysical conclusions. (For example, the epistemic possibility of zombies is appealed to in order to justify a claimed metaphysical possibility of zombies.) A similar dynamic occurs with respect to the Property Dualism Argument. One way it becomes concrete in this context is via the issue of whether in an identity statement with different CMoPs there must be different MMoPs. That is, is the following principle true?

D(CMoP) → D(MMoP): A difference in CMoPs in an identity statement entails a difference in MMoPs

Prima facie, the D(CMoP) → D(MMoP) principle is false. Consider the identity "the wet thing in the corner = the thing in the corner covered or soaked with H_2O." Suppose the CMoP associated with the left-hand side of the identity statement to be the description "the wet thing in the corner." Take the corresponding MMoP to be the property of being the wet thing in the corner. Analogously for the right-hand side. But the property of being the wet thing in the corner = the property of being the thing in the corner covered or soaked with H_2O. $MMoP_1 = MMoP_2$, i.e., there is only one MMoP, even though here are two CMoPs.

Of course, a theorist who wishes to preserve the D(CMoP) → D(MMoP) principle, seeing MMoPs as shadows of CMoPs, can postulate different, more fine-grained quasi-linguistic-cognitive MMoPs that are individuated according to the CMoPs. There is no matter of fact here but only different notions of CMoP and MMoP geared to different purposes. In the discussion to follow, I will focus on the cognitive significance purpose of the CMoP/MMoP pair, since I think that rationale is the most favorable to the view I am arguing against, that we must—that we are forced to—individuate MMoPs according to CMoPs.[15]

Consider the familiar "Paderewski" example. Our subject starts out under the false impression that there were two Paderewskis of the turn of the twentieth century, a Polish politician and a Polish composer. Later, he has forgotten where he learned the two words and remembers nothing about one Paderewski that distinguishes him from the other. That is, he remembers only that both were famous Polish figures of the turn of the twentieth century. Prima facie, the cognitive properties of the two uses of "Paderewski" are the same. For the referent is the same and every property associated by the subject with these terms is the same. However, there is a cognitive difference. We could give a name to the relevant cognitive difference by saying that the subject has two "mental files" corresponding to the two uses of "Paderewski." We could regard the difference in mental files as a semantic difference, or we could suppose that semantically the two uses of "Paderewski" are the same, but that there is a need for something more than semantics—something cognitive but non-semantic—in individuating CMoPs. In either case, there are two CMoPs but only one MMoP, the MMoP being, say, the property of being a famous turn-of-the-twentieth-century Pole named "Paderewski." Thus "Paderewski = Paderewski" could be informative to this subject, despite identical MMoPs for the two terms.

As Loar (1988) notes, Paderewski-type situations can arise for general terms, even in situations where the subject associates the same description with the two uses of the general term. An English speaker learns the term "chat" from a monolingual French speaker who exhibits cats, and then is taught the term "chat" again by the same forgetful teacher exhibiting the same cats. The student tacitly supposes that there are two senses of 'chat' which refer to creatures that are different in some respect that the student has not noticed or perhaps some respect that the student could not have noticed, something biological beneath the surface that is not revealed in the way they look and act. We can imagine that the student retains two separate mental files for "chat." Each file has some way of specifying some observable properties of chats, for example that they are furry, purr, are aloof, are called 'chat', and most importantly, each of the files says that there are two kinds of creatures called "chat": chats in the current sense are not the same as chats in the other sense. So if the student learns "this chat = this chat" where the first "chat" is linked to one file and the second is linked to the other, that will be informative. It is certainly plausible that there are different CMoPs, given that there are two mental files. But the MMoP associated with both CMoPs would seem to be the same—being furry, purring, being aloof, and being called "chat."[16]

It may be objected that there cannot be only one MMoP since explaining cognitive significance requires postulating a difference somewhere—if not in the MMoP of the referent, perhaps there are two different MMoPs of that MMoP, or two different MMoPs of the MMoP of the MMoP of the referent.[17] But these higher-order MMoPs need not exist! The MMoP of chats in both senses of "chat" is something like: being one of two kinds of furry, purring, aloof pet with a certain look, called "chat." There will not be any further MMoP of that MMoP unless the subject happens to have a thought about the first MMoP. What, then, explains the difference in cognitive significance between the two "chat"'s? Answer: the difference in the CMoPs, the difference I have given a name to with the locution of different mental files. Objection: "But that difference in CMoP must correspond to a difference in MMoP!" To argue this way is simply to beg the question against the idea that there can be two CMoPs but only one MMoP.

Objection: "But the cognitive difference between the two CMoPs has to correspond to a difference in the world in order to be explanatory; e.g. the subject will think "The chat on my left is of a different kind from the chat on my right"." Answer: No, the example has been framed to rule out this kind of difference. The subject does not remember *any* differences between the two kinds of chat, not even differences in the situations in which he learned the terms.

It may seem that, wherever there is a difference in CMoP, there *has* to be *some* difference in MMoP of some kind, for otherwise how would the difference in CMoP ever arise? Thus, corresponding to the different CMoPs "covered with water" and "covered with H_2O" one might imagine that "water" is learned or applied on the basis of properties such as, e.g. being a colorless, odorless, tasteless liquid coming out of the tap, and "H_2O" is learned and applied on the basis of something learned in a chemistry class having to do with hydrogen and oxygen. Similarly, one might say that in the "chat" case, there must be some difference between the property instantiated in the first and second introductions of the word "chat" to the student. For example, perhaps the first one was introduced on a cloudy day and the second on a sunny day. Or at any rate, they were introduced at different times and so there is a difference in *temporal* MMoPs. For if there were no difference at all in the world, what would explain—that is explain as rational—why the subject thinks there are different referents?

But this reasoning is mistaken. Maybe there has to be some difference in properties in the world that explain the *arising* of the different CMoPs, but that difference can *fade away leaving no psychological trace*. After the student learns the word "chat" twice, and tacitly assumes that it applies to different animals, the student may forget *all the specific facts* concerning the occasions of the learning of the two words, while still tacitly supposing that things that fit 'chat' in one sense do not fit it in the other. The *ongoing* use of two cognitive representations corresponding to the two uses of "chat" do not require any *ongoing* difference in MMoPs in order to be completely legitimate and rational. Likewise for the "Paderewski" example. To suppose otherwise is to *confuse ontogeny with metaphysics*.

The following reply would fit the view of many dualists such as Chalmers and White: "But doesn't there have to be a possible world, different from the actual world, that the subject rationally supposes he is in, in which the two CMoPs are CMoPs of different referents? For the subject who believes there are two different Paderewskis, a musician and a politician, the rationalizing world is a world that contains two persons named 'Paderewski', both born around the turn of the century, one famous as a politician, the other famous as a musician. Now in your version of the *chat* and Paderewski stories as you tell them, you have eliminated all differences in specific properties available to the subject. You have postulated that the subject does not believe that one is a politician and the other is a musician—but the same strategy can be followed all the same. The world that rationalizes the subject's view that there are two Paderewskis is a world in which there are two persons named Paderewski, both Europeans born around the turn of the century. The subject knows that there are bound to be many properties that distinguish them (if only their spatial locations) and he can single out two of them in his imagination, X and Y, such that one has property X but lacks Y, the other has property Y but lacks X. If the subject were rationalizing his belief, he could appeal to X and Y, so they can constitute his different MMoPs. One of his MMoPs, call it, $MMoP_A$, is X; the other, $MMoP_B$, is Y. The fact that the subject does not know what X and Y are does not change the fundamental strategy of rationalizing the subject's error in which the cognitive difference, $CMoP_A$ vs. $CMoP_B$, requires a metaphysical difference, that between $MMoP_A$ and $MMoP_B$."

This territory will be familiar to those who have thought about modal arguments for dualism. The dualist supposes that the conceivability of zombies justifies the claim that there is a possible world in which there is a zombie, and that leads by a familiar route to dualism.[18] The physicalist resists the argument from epistemology to metaphysics in that case, and the physicalist should resist it here as well. We can explain the erroneous view that Paderewski is distinct from Paderewski by reference to *epistemic possibilities only*: The epistemically possible situation (not a genuine metaphysically possible world) in which, as one might say, Paderewski is not Paderewski. This is an epistemic situation in which Paderewski—who has property X but not Y (and, as we the theorists might say, is identical to the actual Paderewski) is distinct from Paderewski, who has property Y but not X (and who, as we the theorists might say is also identical to the actual Paderewski). Of course there is no such world, but this coherently describable epistemic situation accurately reflects the subject's epistemic state. We need only this coherently describable epistemic situation, not a genuine difference in properties in a genuinely possible world. (I follow the common convention of calling a genuinely possible situation a world and reserving "situation" for something that may or may not be possible.) Likewise for the chat example. *The rationality of error can be explained epistemically with no need for metaphysics.* This is a basic premise of this chapter and it links the physicalist position on the Property Dualism Arguments to the physicalist position with regard to the Kripke-Chalmers modal arguments. Given this principle, I believe that the Property Dualism Argument, the Knowledge Argument, and the familiar modal arguments can be defanged, so the residual issue—not discussed here—is whether this principle is right. Chalmers and White argue that genuine worlds are needed to rationalize the subject's behavior, but I have not seen anything in which they argue against situations as rationalizers.

In my view, the issue I have been discussing is the key issue concerning all forms of the Property Dualism Argument (and some modal arguments for dualism as well). If the D(CMoP) → D(MMoP) principle does not come up in some form or other, the main issue has been skipped.

There is one reason for the view that a difference in CMoPs entails a difference in MMoPs that I have not yet mentioned and will not go into in detail until the end of the chapter in the "thin/thick" part of section VI: the view that MMoPs must be thin in the sense of having no hidden essence in order to account for their role in determining reference and explaining cognitive significance.

Of course, as before, those who prefer to see MMoPs as shadows of CMoPs can think of the property of being a chat—relative to the link to one mental file—as distinct from the property of being a chat—relative to the link to the other mental file. That is, the MMoP would be individuated according to the corresponding CMoP to preserve one-one correspondence. According to me, one can individuate MMoPs as shadows of CMoPs—or not—but as we will see, the Property Dualist has to insist on individuating MMoPs as shadows of CMoPs.

What about the converse of the cases we have been talking about—one CMoP, two MMoPs? People often use one mental representation very differently in different circumstances without having any awareness of the difference. Aristotle famously used the Greek word we translate with 'velocity' ambiguously, to denote in some circumstances instantaneous velocity, and in other circumstances, average velocity. He did not appear to see the difference. And the Florentine "Experimenters" of the seventeenth century used a term translated as "degree of heat" ambiguously to denote both heat and the very different magnitude of temperature. Some of their measuring procedures for detecting "degree of heat" measured heat and some measured temperature (Block and Dworkin 1974). For example, one test of the magnitude of "degree of heat" was whether a given object would melt paraffin. This test measured whether the temperature was above the melting point of paraffin. Another test was the amount of ice an object would melt. This measured amount of heat, a very different magnitude (Wiser and Carey 1983). One could treat these cases as one CMoP which refers via different MMoPs, depending on context. Alternatively, one could treat the difference in context determining the difference in CMoP, preserving the one-one correspondence. This strategy would postulate a CMoP difference that was *not available from the first-person point of view*, imposed on the basis of a difference in the world. That is, it would take a conceptual revolution for theorists of heat phenomena to see a significant difference between their two uses of "degree of heat," so the cognitive difference was not one that they could be aware of, given their conceptual scheme. A CMoP difference that is not available to the subject is not acceptable for purposes that emphasize the relevance of the CMoP to the first person.

In what follows, I will assume independently individuated CMoPs and MMoPs. However, at one crucial point in the dialectic, I will examine whether individuating MMoPs according to CMoPs makes any difference to the argument, concluding that it does not. Why does it matter whether or not there is a one-one correspondence between CMoPs and MMoPs? I will now turn to a member of the family of Property Dualism Arguments that turns on this issue. The argument of the next section, or something much like it, has been termed the "property dualism argument" by McGinn (2001), though I think a somewhat different argument is more closely related to what Smart, Perry, and White have in mind, what I will call the "orthodox" property dualism argument in sections V and VI. The two arguments depend on nearly the same issues.

IV   E → 2M Version of the Property Dualism Argument

Saul Kripke (1980) argued for dualism as follows. Identities, if true, are necessarily true. But cases of mind without brain and brain without mind are possible, so mind-brain identity is not necessary, and therefore not true.[19] A standard physicalist response is that the mind-body relation is necessary, but appears, misleadingly, to be contingent: there is an "illusion of contingency." Most of the discussion of an illusion of contingency has focused on the mental side of the identity statement, but Richard Boyd (1980) noted that one way for a physicalist to explain the illusion of contingency of "Q = cortico-thalamic oscillation" would be to exploit the gap between cortico-thalamic oscillation and its mode of presentation. When we appear to be conceiving of Q without the appropriate cortico-thalamic oscillation (e.g., a disembodied mind or a version of spectrum inversion), all we are managing to conceive is Q in a situation in which we are misled by our mode of epistemic access to cortico-thalamic oscillation. What we are implicitly conceiving, perhaps, is a situation in which our functional magnetic resonance scanner is broken. So the physicalist is free to insist that cortico-thalamic oscillation is part of what one conceives in conceiving of Q, albeit not explicitly, and, conversely, Q is part of what one conceives in conceiving of cortico-thalamic oscillation.

But the sole reason for believing in *implicit* commitment to epistemic failure such as failing brain measurement devices in these thought experiments is that it avoids the non-physicalist conclusion, and that is not a very good reason. The conceivability of zombies, inverted spectra, disembodied minds, etc. does not seem *on the surface* to depend on implicit conceiving of malfunctioning apparatus. For example, it would seem that one could conceive of the brain and its cortico-thalamic oscillation "neat" (as in whiskey without ice or water), i.e., without conceiving of any particular apparatus for measuring cortico-thalamic oscillation.

However, the idea that one can conceive of cortico-thalamic oscillation "neat," is useful not just in combating Boyd's objection to Kripke's argument for dualism, but also in a distinct positive argument for dualism.[20]

Consider an empirical mind-body property identity claim in which *both* terms of the identity—not just the mental term—have MMoPs that are identical to the referent. (MMoPs are, of course, properties, and we are thinking of the referents of mind-body identity claims as properties as well.) McGinn (2001) claims—albeit in other terms—that this would be true for a standard physicalist mind-body identity claim. He says "it is quite clear that the way of thinking of C-fiber firing that is associated with "C-fiber firing" is simply that of having the property of C-fiber firing ... it connotes what it denotes" (294). Is cortico-thalamic oscillation or potassium ion flow across a membrane its own metaphysical mode of presentation? That depends on what a metaphysical mode of presentation is supposed to be, and that depends on the purpose we have for them. I have mentioned a number of different conceptions of MMoPs, explaining cognitive significance, determining the referent, a priori graspability (on the basis of understanding the term it is the MMoP of).

Suppose we took explaining cognitive significance as primary. How can we explain why "cortico-thalamic oscillation = cortico-thalamic oscillation" is less informative than "Q = cortico-thalamic oscillation"? Do we need to appeal to an MMoP of *being cortico-thalamic oscillation* for "cortico-thalamic oscillation"? First, if the identity is true, it is not clear that an MMoP of *being cortico-thalamic oscillation* is of any use. For if the MMoP of Q is *being* Q, then the MMoP of the left-hand side would be the same as for the right-hand side for both the trivial and the cognitively significant identity so that MMoP is useless. Second, other MMoPs can explain the difference in cognitive significance. For example, a scientist might conceive of Q from the first-person point of view but think of cortico-thalamic oscillation in terms of the machinery required to detect it. A scientist might even think of it perceptually, in terms of the experience in the observer engendered by the apparatus, as radiologists often say they do in the case of CAT scans.

Suppose instead that we take the special reference-fixing authority as the *raison d'être* of the MMoP. This conception has the advantage that if we have given the special reference-fixing authority to an MMoP, then it is a priori graspable that the referent, if it exists, has that property (Byrne and Pryor, 2006). Again, it is not very plausible that the MMoP of "cortico-thalamic oscillation" or "potassium ion flow" is *being cortico-thalamic oscillation* or *being potassium ion flow*. What would be the point of giving the special reference-fixing authority for 'cortico-thalamic oscillation' to the property of *being cortico-thalamic oscillation*? (Recall that uniquely determining the referent is not enough for reference fixing—the subject must also have decided (even if implicitly) that that uniqueness property governs the term, as noted by Byrne and Pryor.)

But there is a kind of mind-body identity in which the right-hand term does more plausibly have an MMoP on both the cognitive significance and the reference-fixing sense that is identical to the referent (or at any rate has the relation of *being X* to X), namely a mental-functional identity claim. I will skip the cognitive significance rationale, focusing on determination of reference. What is our way of fixing reference to the property of being caused by A and B and causing C and D if not that property itself (or the property of having that property itself): that is, *being caused by A and B and causing C and D*? For many complex functional properties, it is hard to imagine any other reference-fixing property that could be taken very seriously, since it is hard to see how such functional properties could be singled out without singling out each of the causal relations. Further, the functional property would be plausibly a priori graspable on the basis of a typical concept of it. These considerations suggest that a mental-functional identity claim is a better candidate for the kind of identity claim being discussed here than the standard mental-physical identity claim.

Since the candidate identity claim has to be plausibly empirical, let us think of the physical side as a *psycho*functional property (see Block 1978, where this term was introduced), that is, a functional property that embeds detailed empirical information that can only be discovered empirically. For example, we can take the functional definition to include the Weber-Fechner Law (which dictates a logarithmic relation between stimulus intensity and perceptual intensity). To remind us that we are taking the right-hand side of the identity to be a psychofunctional property, let us represent it as "PF."

Let our sample mind-body identity be "Q = PF," where as before, "Q" denotes a phenomenal property. As before, let us use "M" for the metaphysical mode of presentation of Q, and let us assume that M = *being Q*. Ex hypothesi, the metaphysical mode of presentation of PF is *being PF*. But since M = *being Q*, and the MMoP of PF = *being PF*, if

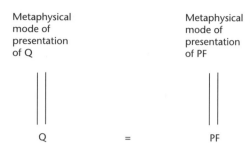

Metaphysical
mode of
presentation
of Q

Metaphysical
mode of
presentation
of PF

Q   =   PF

Figure 21.1

Empirical → 2MMoP Argument for Dualism

MMoP (i.e., metaphysical mode of presentation) of Q = *being* Q, MMoP of PF = *being PF*, so if it is true that Q = PF, then the MMoP of PF = the MMoP of Q. But if the two MMoPs are the same, the identity is supposed to be a priori. However, since the identity is not a priori, the argument concludes, it is not true. The vertical "=" signs represent the relation between X and *being X*.

the identity is true (Q = PF) it follows that the MMoPs of both sides are the same. (See fig. 21.1.) But if the MMoPs of both sides are the same, then—supposedly—the identity cannot be a posteriori. Here I assume the principle that an empirical identity must have distinct MMoPs for the two sides of the identity. Call that Empirical → 2MMoP, or E → 2M for short. That would show that the original a posteriori identity claim—which embeds, you will recall, the Weber-Fechner Law and so cannot be supposed to be a priori—cannot be true: psychofunctionalism is refuted (or so it may seem).

The upshot would be that if we want a functionalist mind-body identity thesis, it can only be a priori (in which case deflationism—in the sense of conceptual reductionism about consciousness—holds). Or if we reject deflationism, the upshot is that functionalist mind-body identity is false (i.e. the relevant form of dualism is true). So the conclusion is the same as that of the Property Dualism Argument, but restricted to functionalist mind-body identity claims: only dualism and deflationism are viable.

Why accept the E → 2M Principle? Suppose that different CMoPs entail different MMoPs (i.e., the D(CMoP) → D(MMoP) principle). An empirical identity requires different CMoPs, since, it may be said (but see below) if two of one's terms have the same cognitive significance, that fact is a priori available to the subject. An empirical identity requires different CMoPs, different CMoPs require different MMoPs, so an empirical identity requires different MMoPs. So it would follow that an empirical identity requires different MMoPs. This is one way of seeing why the considerations of the last section about the one-one correspondence between CMoPs and MMoPs matter for dualism.[21]

You will not be surprised to learn that my objection to the argument is to the E → 2M Principle and the claim that different CMoPs require different MMoPs which engenders the E → 2M Principle. As I mentioned, a priority is better taken to be a matter of sameness of CMoPs, not a matter of sameness of MMoPs. In the example given above, before the subject learns that there is only one kind of creature called 'chat', he has two CMoPs but only one MMoP.[22]

The argument could be resuscitated if the CMoP of each side were identical to the referent. But at least on the right-hand side, this seems like a category mistake: our concept of a psychofunctional state (or something cognitive about it) is a poor candidate for identity with the psychofunctional state itself.

In comments on this chapter, David Chalmers suggested a variant of the E → 2M Argument. Instead of "Q = PF," consider "Q = P," where P is a physical property. Assume the E → 2M Principle—that an empirical identity must have distinct MMoPs for the two sides of the identity. If "Q = P" is empirical, then it follows that the MMoP of Q is distinct from any MMoP of a physical property. For if the MMoP of P is just P and the MMoP of Q is just Q, and since the E → 2M principle requires that the two MMoPs be distinct, it follows by transitivity of identity that Q must be distinct from P, and so dualism is true.

My objections to this variant are, as before:

1. The argument assumes the E → 2M principle in the first step, in which it is argued that the MMoP of Q is distinct from any MMoP of any physical property, and as mentioned above, I reject the E → 2M principle.
2. The argument presupposes the view that it is reasonable to take the MMoP of a physical property, P, to be just P itself. (It would be better to take it to be being P, but I will ignore this glitch.) As I emphasized above, I find this doubtful for physical properties although more plausible for functional properties. So at most, the argument is an argument against empirical functionalism (psychofunctionalism) rather than against physicalism.

V   Back to Stating the Orthodox Property Dualism Argument

The E → 2M Argument raises many of the same issues as the Smart, Perry, and White argument, to which I now turn, but is not quite the same.

To frame the orthodox Property Dualism Argument, we need to use a contrast between deflationism and phenomenal realism about consciousness.[23] In its strong form, deflationism is *conceptual reductionism* concerning concepts of consciousness. More generally, deflationism says that a priori or at least armchair analyses of consciousness (or at least armchair sufficient conditions) can be given in non-phenomenal terms, most prominently in terms of representation, thought or function.[24] (If the analyses are physicalistic, then deflationism is a form of what Chalmers (1996) calls Type A physicalism.) The deflationist says phenomenal properties and states do exist, but that commitment is "deflated" by an armchair analysis that reduces the commitment. The conclusion of the orthodox Property Dualism Argument is that physicalism and phenomenal realism are incompatible: the phenomenal realist must be a dualist and the physicalist must be a deflationist.

In what follows, I will drop the term "orthodox," referring to the argument I am spelling out simply as the "Property Dualism Argument."

The Property Dualism Argument in the form in which I will elaborate it depends on listing all the leading candidates for the nature of the MMoP of the mental side. My emphasis on the MMoP at the expense of the CMoP is artificial but has some dialectical advantages. The metaphenomenal move is what is really being explored, the view that with the statement of mind-body identity, either or both of the MMoP or the CMoP brings in unreducible phenomenality. Most of the issues that come up with respect to the MMoP could also have been discussed with respect to the CMoP. In rebutting the Property Dualism Argument, I will go back to the CMoP occasionally.

Recall that the phenomenal side (which I will always put on the left side of the sentence on the page) of the identity is "Q." Let the metaphysical, mode of presentation of Q be M (for *m*ental, *m*etaphysical and *m*ode of presentation). The basic idea of the Property Dualism Argument is that even if Q is physical, there is a problem about the physicality of M. I will discuss five proposals for the nature of M. M might be (one or more of)

1. mental,
2. physical,
3. non-physical,
4. topic-neutral or
5. non-existent, i.e. the reference is "direct" in one sense of the term.

Here is a brief summary of the form of the argument. (1) is correct but useless in the sense that both the physicalist and the dualist will agree on it. The problem for the physicalist is to show how M can be both physical and mental. (2) is (supposed to be) ruled out by the arguments given below, which will be the main topic of the rest of this chapter. (5) changes the subject by stipulating a version of the original property identity "Q = cortico-thalamic oscillation" in which Q is not picked out by a genuine phenomenal concept. So the remaining options are the dualist option (3), and the topic-neutral option (4). White (1986) argues that (4) is deflationist as follows: The topic-neutral properties that are relevant to the mind-body problem are functional properties. If M, the metaphysical mode of presentation of Q, is a topic-neutral and therefore—according to White—a functional property, then that could only be because the phenomenal concept has an a priori functional analysis; e.g., the concept of pain might be the concept of a state that is caused by tissue damage and that causes certain reactions including interactions with other mental states. But an a priori functional analysis is deflationist, by definition. The upshot is supposed to be that only (3) and (4) remain; (3) is dualist and (4) is deflationist. The conclusion of the Property Dualism Argument is that we must choose between dualism and deflationism: phenome-nal realist physicalism is not tenable.

Of course the argument as I have presented it makes the title "Property Dualism Ar-gument" look misguided. Anyone who does take the argument to argue for dualism would presumably want to add an argument against deflationism. However, Smart and Armstrong (and in a more convoluted version, David Lewis (1980)) use the argu-ment the other way around: the threat of dualism was brought in to argue for defla-tionism. Their view is that 'pain' contingently picks out a physical state, for 'pain' is a non-rigid designator whose sense is *the item with such and such functional role*. But the view that stands behind this picture is that the nature of the mental is given a priori as functional. 'Pain' is a non-rigid designator, but what it is to have pain, that which cases of pain all share in virtue of which they are pains, is a certain functional property, and that functional property can be rigidly designated by, for example, the phrase "having pain."[25] So the view is a version of deflationism.

White (1986) adds an anti-dualist premise to the argument whose conclusion is *dual-ism or deflationism*, but in some papers in preparation (White (unpublished *a, b*)), he drops that premise, arguing instead for dualism. The point of view of the present chapter is phenomenal realist and physicalist, the very combination that the argument purports to rule out. (Though see Block 2002 for a different kind of doubt about this combination.) As we will see when I get to the critique of the Property Dualism Argu-ment, the argument fares better as an argument for dualism than for deflationism, so the name of the argument is appropriate.

There are some well-known problems concerning the notion of a physical property.[26] But not all philosophy concerned with physicalism can be about the problem of how to formulate physicalism. For some purposes, physicalism is clear enough.[27] In particular, the debate about the Property Dualism Argument seems relatively insensitive to issues about what exactly physicalism comes to. (If not, that is an objection to what follows.)

I will take the notions of physicalistic vocabulary and mentalistic vocabulary to be unproblematic. A physical property is a property canonically expressible in physicalis-tic vocabulary. (I won't try to explain "canonically.") For example, the property of being water is a physical property because that property = the property of being H_2O. The predicate "— is H_2O" is a predicate of physics (or anyway physical science), the property of being H_2O is expressed by that predicate, and so is the property of being water, since they are the same property. (Note that the relation of "expression" is dis-tinct from referring.) A mentalistic property is a property canonically expressible in mentalistic vocabulary. "— is a pain" is a mentalistic predicate and thus expresses (or connotes) a mental property (that of being a pain). A non-physical property is a prop-erty that is not canonically expressible in physicalistic vocabulary. (So physicalism dictates that mental properties are canonically expressible in both physicalistic and mentalistic vocabularies.) I don't know if these notions can ultimately be spelled out in a satisfactory manner, but this is another of the cluster of issues involved in defining physicalism that not every paper concerning physicalism can be about.

Smart said that a topic-neutral analysis of a property term entails neither that the property is physical nor that it is non-physical. It would not do to say that a topic-neutral property is expressible in neither physicalistic nor non-physicalistic terms, since if physicalistic terms and non-physicalistic terms are all the terms there are, there are no such properties. The key kind of topic-neutral property for present purposes is a functional property, a second-order property that consists in the having of certain other properties that are related to one another (causally and otherwise) and to inputs and outputs, all specified non-mentalistically. One could say that a topic-neutral property is one that is expressible in terms of logic, causation and non-mentalistically specified input-output language. The question may arise as to whether these terms are to be counted as part of physicalistic vocabulary or not. For purposes of this chapter, I will leave that issue undecided.

I will briefly sketch each of the proposals mentioned above for the nature of M (the metaphysical mode of presentation of Q, which you recall was introduced in the sample identity, "Q = cortico-thalamic oscillation") from the point of view of the Property Dualism Argument, adding some critical comments at a few places. Then, after a section on phenomenal concepts, I will rebut the Property Dualism Argument.

Proposal 1: M is Mental

If M is mental, then the same issue of physicalism arises for M, the metaphysical mode of presentation of Q, which arises for Q itself. It isn't that this proposal is false, but rather that it presents a challenge to the physicalist of showing how it could be true.

Proposal 2: M is Physical

The heart of the Property Dualism Argument is the claim that M cannot be physical.[28] I will discuss three arguments for that claim. The first proceeds as follows. If M is physical, it will not serve to account for cognitive significance: specifically, the informativeness of identities and the possibility of rational error. For example, suppose the subject rationally believes that Q is instantiated here and now but that cortico-thalamic oscillation is absent. He experiences Q, but also has evidence (misleading evidence, according to the physicalist) that cortico-thalamic oscillation is absent. We can explain rational error by appeal to two different MMoPs of the referent, only one of which is manifest. Let us take the metaphysical mode of presentation of the right-hand side of the mind-body identity "Q = cortico-thalamic oscillation" to be a matter of the instrumentation that detects cortico-thalamic oscillation. We can think of this instrumentation as keyed to the oxygen uptake by neural activity. (Functional magnetic resonance is a form of brain imaging that detects brain activity via sensitivity to metabolism of the oxygen that feeds brain activity.)

The focus of this argument is on the left-hand side, the metaphysical mode of presentation of Q, namely M. According to the argument, if M is physical, it cannot serve the purpose of explaining rational error. For, to explain rational error, we require a metaphysical mode of presentation that makes rational sense of the subject's point of view. But the physical nature of M is not available to the subject. (The subject can be presumed to know nothing of the physical nature of M.) The problem could be solved if there was a mental mode of presentation of M itself, call it "M*." But this is the first step in a regress in which a physical metaphysical mode of presentation is itself presented by a mental metaphysical mode of presentation. For the same issue will arise all over again for M* that arose for M. Explaining rational error requires two modes of presentation, the manifestations of which are available to the first person at some level or other, so postulating a physical metaphysical mode of presentation just takes out an explanatory loan that has to be paid back at the level of modes of presentation of modes of presentation, etc. The upshot is that physical metaphysical modes of presentation do not pass the test imposed by one of the stipulated purposes of metaphysical modes of presentation.

There is also a related non-regress argument: if M is physical, a subject could believe he is experiencing Q, yet not believe he is in a state that has M. But there can be no epistemic gap of this sort between the metaphysical mode of presentation of a phenomenal property and the property itself.

Another argument that M cannot be physical is given by White (1986). He notes, plausibly enough, that "Since there is no physicalistic description that one could plausibly suppose is coreferential a priori with an expression like "Smith's pain at t," no physical property of a pain (i.e., a brain state of type X) could provide the route by which it was picked out by such an expression." (See ibid. 353, reprinted in Block, Flanagan, and Güzeldere 1997: 706). Or in the terms of this chapter, there is no physicalistic description that one could plausibly suppose is coreferential a priori with a mentalistic expression such as "Q," so no physical property could provide the route by which it was picked out by such an expression. The property that provides the route by which Q is picked out by "Q" is just the metaphysical mode of presentation (on one way of understanding that term) of Q, that is, M. So the upshot is supposed to be that M cannot be physical because there is no physicalistic description that is coreferential a priori with a phenomenal term.

A third argument that M cannot be physical is that MMoPs must be "thin." We can take a thin property to be one that has no hidden essence. "Thick" properties include Putnamian natural kinds such as water. According to the Property Dualist, the explanatory purpose of MMoPs precludes thick properties serving as modes of presentation. For, it might be said, it is not *all* of a thick property that explains rational error but only an *aspect* of it. The same conclusion can be reached if one stipulates that the MMoP is a priori available on the basis of the CMoP. Since hidden essences are never a priori available, hidden essences cannot be part of MMoPs. I will indicate later how the claim that MMoPs must be thin can be used to argue against the phenomenal realist physicalist position. This consideration can also be used to bolster the regress argument and the argument of the last paragraph.

I said earlier that the standard reply to Jackson's argument attempts to substitute a dualism of concepts for a dualism of properties and facts. And then I noted that the objection that is exploited by both the Knowledge Argument and the Property Dualism Argument is that the dualism of concepts is held to *require* a dualism of properties and facts. Thin MMoPs are in effect individuated according to the corresponding CMoPs. So the attempt to substitute a dualism of concepts for a dualism of properties and facts is opposed by the claim that properties and facts should be individuated according to concepts, and so if Mary acquires a new concept, she acquires a concept that involves new properties and facts.

Earlier I discussed the D(CMoP) → D(MMoP) principle, suggesting that there could be cases of two CMoPs with the same MMoP. One example was the identity 'the thing in the corner covered with water = the thing in the corner covered with H_2O'. The CMoP associated with the left-hand side is the description "the thing in the corner covered with water," and the corresponding MMoP is the property of being the thing in the corner covered with water. Analogously for the right-hand side. But the property of being the thing in the corner covered with water = the property of being the thing in the corner covered with H_2O, so there is only one MMoP. But if MMoPs cannot be "thick," being covered with water cannot be an MMoP. The relevant MMoP would have to be some sort of stripped-down version of being covered with water that does not have a hidden essence.[29]

These three arguments are the heart of the orthodox Property Dualism Argument. I regard the three arguments as appealing to MMoPs in different senses of the term, and when I come to critiquing these three arguments later in the chapter, I will make that point more explicitly. In my critique, I will argue that two of the arguments do not stand on their own, but rather presuppose the third ("thick/thin") argument. Then I will examine that argument.

Proposal 3: M is Non-physical

If M is non-physical, dualism is true. So this proposal will not preserve the compatibility of phenomenal realism with physicalism and will not be considered further here.

Proposal 4: M is Topic-neutral

In effect, I covered this topic earlier, in my discussion of Perry. A genuinely phenomenal concept is required for getting the Property Dualism Argument (and the Mary argument) off the ground so a topic-neutral concept will not do.

Proposal 5: There is no M: the Relation between "Q" and its Referent is "Direct" in One Sense of the Term

A phenomenal concept is a phenomenal way of thinking of a phenomenal property. Phenomenal properties can be thought about using non-phenomenal concepts of them, for example, the concept of the property occurring at 5 p.m. As I keep mentioning, the Property Dualism Argument requires a phenomenal concept in my sense of the term, and so if the mind-body identity at issue does not make use of a phenomenal concept, the Property Dualist will simply substitute a mind-body identity that does make use of a phenomenal concept. Of course, if it could be shown that there could not be any phenomenal concepts, then the Property Dualism Argument will fail. But I believe in phenomenal concepts and so will not discuss this view further.

Phenomenal concepts are often said to refer "directly," but what this is often taken to mean in philosophy of mind discussions is not that there is no metaphysical mode of presentation, but rather that the metaphysical mode of presentation is a necessary property of the referent.

Loar (1990) says:

Given a normal background of cognitive capacities, certain recognitional or discriminative dispositions suffice for having specific recognitional concepts ... A recognitional concept may involve the ability to class together, to discriminate, things that have a given objective property. Say that if a recognitional concept is related thus to a property, the property triggers applications of the concept. Then the property that triggers the concept is the semantic value or reference of the concept; the concept directly refers to the property, unmediated by a higher order reference-fixer.[30]

Consider the view that a phenomenal concept is simply a recognitional concept understood as Loar suggests whose object is a phenomenal property that is a physical property. I don't know if this would count as a concept that has no metaphysical mode of presentation at all, but certainly it has no phenomenal metaphysical mode of presentation, and so is not a phenomenal concept in the sense required for the Property Dualism Argument. For one can imagine a case of totally unconscious triggering of a concept by a stimulus or by a brain state. As Loar notes, there could be an analog of "blindsight" in which a self-directed recognitional concept is triggered blankly, without any phenomenal accompaniment. (Of course this *need* not be the case—the brain property doing the triggering could itself be phenomenal, or else the concept triggered could be phenomenal. In either case, phenomenality would have to be involved in the triggering of the concept.) And for this reason, Loar (1990: 98; 1997: 603) argues, a phenomenal concept is not merely a self-directed recognitional concept.

To sum up, the central idea of the Property Dualism Argument (and the Knowledge Argument) is the metaphenomenal move, the idea that in thinking about a phenomenal property, a further phenomenal property must be brought in as part of the CMoP or with the MMoP and that further phenomenal property poses a special problem for

physicalism, because of its connection to a mode of presentation. There are three functions of modes of presentation on one or another conception of them that putatively
lead to this resistance to physicalism, a function in explaining cognitive significance,
of determining reference, and of a priori availability on the basis of understanding the
term.

The Property Dualism Argument says that in the identity "Q = cortico-thalamic oscillation," the metaphysical mode of presentation of Q (namely, M) must be either
mental, physical, non-physical, topic-neutral, or "direct" (in which case there is no
metaphysical mode of presentation). The mental proposal is supposed to be useless.
The physical proposal is supposed to be ruled out because there is no a priori available
physicalistic description of Q, because of supposed regress, and because the metaphysical mode must be "thin." The "direct reference" proposal appears to be ruled out by
the fact that the concept of Q needed to get the argument off the ground is a phenomenal concept with a phenomenal metaphysical mode of presentation. So the only proposals for M that are left standing are the non-physical and topic-neutral proposals.
The topic-neutral proposal involves a form of deflationism. So the ultimate metaphysical choice according to the Property Dualism Argument is between deflationism and
dualism. The upshot is that the phenomenal realist cannot be a physicalist. The argument is a way of making the metaphenomenal move described earlier concrete: the
statement of a mind-body identity claim is supposed to be self-defeating because the
MMoP (or the CMoP—but I have focused on the MMoP) of the phenomenal term
of the identity is supposed to bring in unreduced phenomenality. The only way to
avoid that unreduced phenomenality is to give a deflationist analysis; the alternative
is dualism.

Objections Concerning Phenomenal Concepts

I have been using a notion of phenomenal concept based on the observation that there
is a fundamental exercise of it in which a token of a phenomenal property can serve in
thought to represent a phenomenal property. In such a case, there is a phenomenal
property that is part of the CMoP. There is a special case that I mentioned earlier in
which a token of a phenomenal property can serve in thought to represent that very
phenomenal property. In such a case, the phenomenal property does double duty: as
part of the concept and also as the referent of that concept. Before I go on to rebutting
the Property Dualism Argument, I will briefly consider two objections to this conception of a phenomenal concept.

Objection (put to me by Kirk Ludwig)   I can truly think "I am not having an experience as of red now" using a phenomenal concept of that experience, but that would
not be possible on your view of what phenomenal concepts are.

Reply Ludwig is right that one can truly think "I am not having a red experience now" using a phenomenal concept of that experience. As I mentioned, a phenomenal concept has non-fundamental uses in which there is nothing phenomenal going on in exercising the concept. But even in one of the fundamental uses in which a token of an experience as of red is being used to represent that experience, it is possible to think a false thought to the effect that one is not having that experience. For example, one might set oneself to think something that is manifestly false, saying to oneself, "I am not having an experience as of red now," using a phenomenal concept—in my heavy-duty sense of phenomenal concept—of the experience.

Objection On your view, a phenomenal property does double duty: as the referent but also as part of the mode of presentation of that referent. But if physicalism is true, cortico-thalamic oscillation would be part of its own mode of presentation. Does that really make sense?

Reply The claim is not that the right-hand side of the identity "Q = cortico-thalamic oscillation" has an associated mode of presentation (CMoP or MMoP) that involves cortico-thalamic oscillation. I have been supposing that the modes of presentation of the right-hand side have to do with the physical properties of oxygen metabolism that are exploited by scanning technology. Modes of presentation—both cognitive and metaphysical—are modes of presentation associated with *terms* or the concepts associated with the terms, and the identity involves *two* terms. There is no conflict with the indiscernibility of identicals if one keeps use and mention distinct. That is, cortico-thalamic oscillation is part of its own mode of presentation only as *picked out by the phenomenal concept of it*.[31]

VI Critique of the Property Dualism Argument

The Property Dualism Argument says that the metaphysical mode of presentation of Q, namely M, cannot be physical (using the identity "Q = cortico-thalamic oscillation" as an example). I mentioned three (subsidiary) arguments to that effect, a regress argument, an argument concerning a priori availability, and an argument based on the thin/thick distinction. I also mentioned three different *raisons d'être* of modes of presentation, each of which could be used with respect to any of the three arguments, yielding in principle, nine distinct arguments—even eighteen if one counts the CMoP/MMoP dimension—making refutation potentially unmanageable. I will try to finesse this multiplicity by taking the strongest form of each argument, and bringing in the other *raisons d'être* as they are relevant. (I have already mentioned my focus on the MMoP in most of the argument at the expense of the CMoP.) The exposition of the argument has been long, but the critique will be much shorter. As we will see, the first two arguments do not really stand alone, but require the thin/thick argument. My critique of the thin/thick argument is aimed at depriving the conclusion of support rather than outright refutation.

Regress

The first argument mentioned earlier against the physical proposal is a regress argument. The idea is that if M is physical, it will not serve to account for cognitive significance (informativeness). For example, suppose the subject rationally believes that he has Q but not cortico-thalamic oscillation. As noted earlier, there can be rational error in supposing A is present without B when in fact A = B. That error can be explained if, at a minimum, there is a metaphysical mode of presentation of A, $MMoP_A$ and a metaphysical mode of presentation of B, $MMoP_B$, such that $MMoP_A$ is manifest and $MMoP_B$ is not.

Applied to the case at hand, the physicalist thesis that Q = cortico-thalamic oscillation, let us assume that the MMoP of "cortico-thalamic oscillation" is the one mentioned earlier having to do with oxygen uptake by neural processes that affects a brain scanner. It is the other metaphysical mode of presentation that is problematic, namely M, the metaphysical mode of presentation of the left-hand side of the identity. The Property Dualist says that if M is physical, then M cannot serve to account for cognitive significance, since the subject need have no access to that physical description just in virtue of being the subject of that metaphysical mode of presentation. The problem could be solved if there was a *mental* mode of presentation *of M itself*, call it "M*". But this is the first step in a regress in which a metaphysical mode of presentation that is physical is itself presented by a metaphysical mode of presentation that is mental. For the same issue will arise all over again for M* that arose for M. Accounting for the different cognitive significances of the two sides of an identity statement requires two modes of presentation that are available to the first person at *some level or other*, so postulating a physical metaphysical mode of presentation just takes out an explanatory loan that has to be paid back at the level of modes of presentation of modes of presentation, etc.

This argument is question-begging. The argument supposes that if M is physical, it could not serve to account for cognitive significance, since accounting for cognitive significance requires a mental MMoP. But the physicalist thesis is that M is *both* mental and physical, so the physicalist will not be concerned by the argument.[32] Thus, the regress argument in the form I described is like the old objection to physicalism that says that brain states involve the instantiation of, e.g., electrochemical properties, but since pain does not involve the instantiation of such properties, pain can't be a brain state.

Of course if MMoPs must be thin, then M, which is an MMoP, cannot have a hidden physical nature, and so it cannot be both mental and physical. But if that is the claim, the regress argument depends on the "thick/thin" argument to be discussed below, and does not stand on its own.

I assumed that the MMoP of "cortico-thalamic oscillation" is unproblematic, having to do, for example with oxygen metabolism as a result of brain activity. But the Property Dualist may say that this MMoP does not uniquely determine the referent and need not be a property to which the subject has given a special reference-fixing authority. (I will use the phrase "fixes the referent" to mean uniquely determines the referent and has been given the special authority.) Why is this a reply to my point concerning the question-begging nature of the regress argument? The question arises: if the regress argument's appeal to cognitive significance requires an MMoP for "cortico-thalamic oscillation" that *does* fix the referent, what would that MMoP be? Someone could argue that that MMoP could only be the property *being cortico-thalamic oscillation itself*. And then it could be claimed that both sides of the identity statement are such that the MMoP of that side is identical with the referent. And this may be said to lead to dualism via the route canvassed earlier in the section on the E → 2M Argument. (If the MMoP of the right-hand side of an identity of the form X = Y is being Y; and the MMoP of the left-hand side is being X, then, if it is true that X = Y, it follows that being X = being Y, so the MMoPs of the two sides are the same. The E → 2M argument goes on to conclude that the identity must therefore be a priori if true, so therefore false.) I will not go into the matter again, except to note that it cannot be assumed that a property of the referent that accounts for cognitive significance also fixes the referent, and what counts in this argument is cognitive significance. As Burge (1977) and Byrne and Pryor (forthcoming) note, it is easy to see that properties of the referent that account for cognitive significance need not fix the referent. As Burge notes, the determination of reference depends on all sorts of non-conceptual contextual factors that "go beyond what the thinker 'grasps' in thought" (1977: 358). Byrne and Pryor give the example that *being a raspy-voiced singer* may give the cognitive significance for "Bob Dylan," even though there are other raspy-voiced singers. And *being a raspy-voiced singer* need only be a property that the subject saliently associates with the referent, not a property to which the subject has given the special authority.[33] (This, incidentally, is the one point at which I appeal to general considerations about whether the three *raisons d'être* for modes of presentation mentioned earlier go together.)

In sum, the regress argument depends on the "thin/thick" argument and does not stand alone.

To avoid confusion, let me just briefly mention something the Property Dualism Argument is *not*. Someone might ask the question: in the identity 'A = B', how does one think of the metaphysical mode of presentation of A, MMoP$_A$? Doesn't one need a metaphysical mode of presentation of MMoP$_A$, which we could call MMoP$_{A'}$? And another of that, MMoP$_{A''}$? And the series won't end without some kind of "direct acquaintance" which does not require an MMoP (cf. Schiffer 1990: 255). Answer: One does not *need* to think about MMoP$_A$ in order to use MMoP$_A$ to think about A. However, if one does *happen* to want to think about MMoP$_A$, then one does need a concept of MMoP$_A$ with its own MMoP. "And don't we have to have a way of thinking of MMoPs that don't involve further MMoPs to avoid a regress?" Answer: No. To frame a thought about anything, we need a concept of it, including both a CMoP and an MMoP. To think about that CMoP, we need a further concept of it and to think about the MMoP we need a further concept of that. Every layer of thinking about a concept of a concept of … makes it harder and harder to do the mental gymnastics required to form the thought, and for most people, the ability to think these ever more complex thoughts will run out pretty quickly. So there is no regress—the mental gymnastics are voluntary. By contrast, the allegation of the Regress Argument that is part of the Property Dualism Argument, is that we *must* go up a level in order to explain cognitive significance at the preceding level. This is logically required and not just voluntary mental gymnastics.

A Priori Availability

The second argument presented above was that (to quote White 1983: 353), "Since there is no physicalistic description that one could plausibly suppose is coreferential a priori with an expression like 'Smith's pain at t,' no physical property of a pain (i.e., a brain state of type X) could provide the route by which it was picked out by such an expression." So the MMoP of the mental side of a mind-body identity claim could not be physical.

The first thing to notice about this argument is that if "Smith's pain at t" is taken to be the relevant mental concept in the Property Dualism Argument, it has the flaw of being purely linguistic and not a phenomenal concept of the sort I have argued is required for the argument. Still, it might seem that the argument goes through, for a genuinely phenomenal concept does not make a physical description of anything that could be called the route of reference any more available a priori than the description "Smith's pain at t."

Note that the *raison d'être* of modes of presentation assumed here is not the cognitive significance appealed to in the regress argument but rather: the property of the referent (i.e., MMoP) that provides "the route by which it is picked out." What is "the route by which it is picked out"? I think the right thing to mean by this phrase is what I have called fixing the referent, but I doubt that anything hangs on which of a number of candidates is chosen. Consider a case in which the subject conceives of the referent as being the local wet thing. Let us suppose that:

• The property of being the local wet thing is a priori available to the subject on the basis of understanding the term and therefore grasping its CMoP.
• The property of being the local wet thing uniquely determines the referent.

▪ The subject has given this property the special reference-fixing authority mentioned earlier.

My strategy is to concede all that could reasonably be said to be involved in reference fixing and to argue that nonetheless the argument does not work. For being wet = being at least partially covered or soaked with H_2O. But the subject whose metaphysical mode of presentation it is need not have a priori access to "being at least partially covered or soaked with H_2O" or know a priori that this physical description is coreferential with the original description. The subject can give the property of being the local wet thing the special reference fixing authority and thus have that property a priori available from the first-person point of view, without ever having heard the description "H_2O." I hereby stipulate that the name "Albert" is the name of the local wet thing. In virtue of my grasp of the term "Albert," the property of Albert's being the local wet thing is a priori available to me. Also, I have stipulated that the property of being the local wet thing has the special reference-fixing authority. But I can do all that without knowing *all* descriptions of that property. That property *can be and is physical* even though I do not know, and therefore do not have a priori available, its physicalistic description.

Earlier, I considered the idea that MMoPs should be individuated according to CMoPs and thus that the property of being the local wet thing—considered as an MMoP-individuated-according-to-CMoP—is not identical to the property of being covered or soaked with H_2O because the *terms* "water" and "H_2O" are not identical. And of course this way of individuating the MMoP would provide an objection to the argument of the last paragraph.

However, the question then arises of what it is for such properties to be physical and what the physicalist's commitments are with respect to such properties. I believe that this question is best pursued not by inquiring about how to think of such strange entities as MMoPs-individuated-according-to-CMoPs but by focusing on the CMoPs themselves. And a further reason for turning the focus to CMoPs is that although the subject need have no a priori access to the physical descriptions of the physical properties that provide the metaphysical route of access, it may be thought that this is not so for CMoPs. After all, CMoPs are certainly good candidates for something to which we have a priori access!

Let us distinguish two things that might be meant by saying that a CMoP (or MMoP) is physical. First, one might have an *ontological* thesis in mind—that the CMoP (or MMoP) is identical to a physical entity or property or some conglomeration involving a physical properties or entities. In this sense, a CMoP (or MMoP) can be physical whether or not the subject has a priori access to any physicalistic description of it. (The issue with which the Property Dualism Argument is concerned is whether phenomenal properties are, ontologically speaking, physical properties. I said at the outset that the issue of whether the cognitive apparatus involved in a CMoP is ontologically physical should be put to one side (except to the extent that that apparatus is phenomenal). My rationale, you will recall, is that although there is an important issue as to whether physicalism can handle cognitive (and semantic) entities or properties, in a discussion of whether *phenomenal* properties are physical, a good strategy is to suppose that non-phenomenal cognitive and semantic entities are not physically problematic.)

A second interpretation of the claim that a CMoP is physical is that it is *explicitly* physical or explicitly analyzable a priori in physical terms. In this chapter, I have been using "physical*istic*" to mean explicitly physical. It is not obvious what it would mean to say that an MMoP is or is not physicalistic (since it is not a cognitive, linguistic, or semantic entity), but it does make sense to say that something that involves conceptual or linguistic or semantic apparatus is or is not physicalistic. For example, the CMoP 'being covered with water' is not physicalistic (at least if we restrict physics to microphysics), whereas "being covered with H_2O" is physicalistic.

Is the CMoP of a phenomenal concept physical? Physicalistic? Recall, that according to me, a phenomenal concept uses a (token of a) phenomenal property to pick out a phenomenal property. Thus the CMoP of a phenomenal concept contains a non-descriptional element: a phenomenal property. And a phenomenal property is certainly not *explicitly* physical, i.e., physicalistic, that is, it does not contain conceptual apparatus or vocabulary of physics. A phenomenal property is not a bit of conceptual apparatus and it contains no conceptual apparatus. So, focusing on the 'physicalistic' sense of 'physical', the CMoP of a phenomenal concept is not physical. Must the physicalist therefore admit defeat? *Hardly, for physicalism is not the doctrine that everything is explicitly physical.* Physicalism does not say that all descriptions or conceptual apparatus are couched in physical vocabulary or analyzable a priori in physical vocabulary. Physicalists allow that there are domains of thought other than physics. Physicalists do not say that economics, history, and anthropology use physicalistic vocabulary or conceptual apparatus. This is an absurd form of conceptual or terminological reductionism that cannot be equated with physicalism.

Physicalism does not require that the CMoP of a phenomenal concept be physicalistic, but it does require that it is (ontologically) physical. Is it physical? That depends partly on whether all semantic and cognitive apparatus is physical, an issue that I am putting aside in this chapter. So the remaining issue is whether the phenomenal property that is part of the CMoP is physical. And that of course is the very issue of physicalism vs. dualism that this chapter is about. The Property Dualism Argument cannot *assume* that it is not physical—that is what the argument is supposed to show.

Where are we? Here is the dialectic: the Property Dualist says that in order for physicalism to be true, the physical description of the property that provides the route of reference (of the phenomenal term in a phenomenal-physical identity) has to be a priori available to the subject; it is not a priori available; so physicalism is false. I pointed out that even on very liberal assumptions about the role of the MMoP, a priori availability of a physical description of a physical property is an unreasonable requirement. But then I imagined a Property Dualist reply which said that I had failed to individuate the MMoP according to the CMoP. I then suggested that we eliminate the middleman, looking at the CMoP itself instead of considering the MMoP-individuated-according-to-the-CMoP. I pointed out that there is a sense of 'non-physical' (namely non-physicalistic) in which the CMoP of a phenomenal concept is indeed non-physical. I noted however that physicalists are not committed to all language or conceptual apparatus being physicalistic. Physicalists are committed to ontological physicalism, not conceptual reductionism. How does this apply to the MMoP-individuated-according-to-the-CMoP? It is true that if you individuate MMoPs according to CMoPs, then if there is no a priori available physical description, the MMoP is not "physical", and in this sense White's argument is correct. But all "physical" comes to here is *physicalistic*, and it is no part of physicalism to make any claim to the effect that phenomenal MMoPs or CMoPs are physicalistic. Thus the assumption of the second argument (namely, the topic of this section, the a priori availability argument) that the physicalist requires an a priori available description of the MMoP of the mental side of the mind-body identity is false.

If MMoPs have to be thin, then perhaps the distinction between an MMoP being ontologically physical and explicitly physical does not come to as much as would otherwise seem. Since a thin physical property has no hidden essence, it might be said to wear its physicality on its sleeve. However, if this is the only way to save the argument from a priori availability, that argument does not stand on its own but depends on the thin/thick argument, to which we now turn.

But first a brief reminder of what has been presupposed so far about the nature of MMoPs and CMoPs. In rebutting the regress argument, I assumed, along with the argument itself, that the *raison d'être* of MMoPs is to account for cognitive significance. The issue arose as to whether an MMoP defined according to its explanatory purpose must also fix reference or determine the referent. I noted that this cannot be assumed. The issue of the nature of CMoPs did not arise. In rebutting the second argument, I did not make any assumption about MMoPs or CMoPs that should be controversial, allowing a priori availability of the MMoP on the basis of the CMoP, reference-fixing authority and determination of the referent.

Thin/Thick

The third argument that the MMoP of a phenomenal concept cannot be physical involves the distinction mentioned between "thin" and "thick" properties. As we have seen above, the first two parts of the Property Dualism Argument fall flat on their own, but can be resuscitated using the thin/thick distinction. However, if it could be shown that MMoPs must be thin, these other arguments would be superfluous, since the claim that MMoPs must be thin leads to dualism by a shorter route, as I will explain shortly.

First, I must consider what exactly the thick/thin distinction is. I have been taking it that whether a property is thick or thin is a matter of whether it has a hidden essence. On this view, the primary bearer of thickness is a property, and a thick concept would be a concept that purports to be a concept of a thick property. However, this definition will be wrong if fundamental physical properties are thin. For since being water = being H_2O, if being H_2O is thin and being water is thick, whether a property is thick or thin is relative to what concept one has of that property. (Of course, being H_2O is not a candidate for a fundamental physical property—I used that description as a surrogate since I don't know how to describe water in terms of electrons, quarks, etc.) On the picture of the thick/thin distinction in which whether a property is thin is concept-relative, one could define a thin concept as follows: the extension of the concept in a possible world does not depend on its extension in the actual world. (In terms of Chalmers's apparatus, the primary intension is the same as the secondary intension.) And thin properties would be defined in terms of their relation to thin concepts.[34]

Are fundamental physical properties thin? Or, to put the matter from the other perspective, are fundamental physical concepts concepts of thin properties? We could approach the issue via the question of whether there could be a "twin earth" case for fundamental physical concepts. In my view, the answer is yes. I gave an example long ago (Block 1978) in terms of matter and antimatter. The idea is that there is a counterfactual situation in which people who are relevantly like us—functionally like us—use the term "electron" to refer to anti-electrons. That is, the counterfactual situation is one in which our doppelgängers inhabit a universe or a place in our universe in which anti-matter plays the role played here by matter. And as a result, their Ramsey sentence for fundamental physics is the same as ours.[35] Which suggests that the functional role of a concept inside the head is not enough to determine its full nature, since the concept of an electron is not the same as the concept of an anti-electron.

But what if science can delve further into the matter/antimatter distinction, coming up with structure that explains the distinction and that will make a difference between the functional role of our concept and the doppelgängers' concept? The problem is that what we regard as fundamental physics is full of symmetries that can ground further examples, the idea being that there is more to physical reality than can be cashed out in a Ramsey sentence.

Of course, I don't think this mere suggestion settles the matter. Rather, I take the upshot to be that the issue of whether fundamental physical properties are thin cannot be settled here. Another argument in favor of that view is the point (Block 2003) that it is compatible with much of modern physics that for each level there is a still more fundamental level, the upshot being that there is something defective about the notion of a "fundamental" level in physics.

Ideally, I would consider the issues concerning the thick/thin distinction using both approaches, thin properties defined in terms of thin concepts and the other way around. However, this chapter is already much too long, so I will simply make a choice based on ease of discussion: taking properties as basic. I don't think any issues will depend on this choice.

Whether a property is thick or thin, then, will be considered here to be a matter of whether it has a hidden essence. For example, water or the property of being water is thick, since whether something is water goes beyond superficial manifestations of it. Examples of thin properties are mathematical properties, at least some functional properties, and phenomenal properties if dualism is true. (The last point about dualism could be challenged—see Nagel (2001)—but I will put the issue aside.) Artifact properties such as being a telephone might also be taken by some to be thin. As I mentioned, fundamental properties of physics might be alleged to be thin.

Note that it is not necessary for the Property Dualist to claim that *all* MMoPs are thin properties; it would be enough if this were true only for the MMoPs of phenomenal concepts. I do not have a blanket argument against all attempts to show that MMoPs for phenomenal concepts must be thin, but I do have arguments for a number of specific attempts.

Why believe that MMoPs must be thin? I will start with two arguments.

1. The A Priority Argument, which appeals to the idea mentioned earlier that the MMoP is a priori available on the basis of the CMoP.
2. The Aspect Argument, according to which, the cognitive significance role of MMoPs precludes thick properties serving as modes of presentation. For, as mentioned earlier, the Property Dualist may say that it is not *all* of a thick property that explains rational error but only an *aspect* of it, the thin aspect.

These two arguments for MMoPs (at least for phenomenal concepts) being thin appeal to different features of MMoPs and their relations to CMoPs. Although I have registered doubt as to whether the same entities can serve both functions, I will put that doubt aside.

The A Priority Argument for Thin MMoPs

Let us assume that the MMoP of a concept is a priori available on the basis of the CMoP. For example, if one grasps the term "Hesperus," and if its CMoP is the meaning or other mental features of "the morning star," then the MMoP of rising in the morning is supposed to be a priori available in virtue of one's grasp of the term and its CMoP. This constraint might be taken to rule out thick MMoPs, for it might be said that I do not know a priori whether I am on Earth or Twin Earth (McKinsey 1991). A thick MMoP might vary as between Earth and Twin Earth, which would be incompatible with a priori availability on the basis of the CMoP which is shared between me and my twin on Twin Earth.

I will give a fuller treatment of such arguments in the next section, but for now I will reply for the special case of phenomenal concepts, using the points made earlier about a phenomenal property doing "double duty."

I mentioned that a phenomenal property might be part of a CMoP, but also be brought in by the MMoP. For example, the CMoP might be taken to be the meaning or other mental features of: "the experience: ____," where the blank is filled by phenomenal property P. And the MMoP might be the property of *being P*. Such a relation between the CMoP and the MMoP allows for the MMoP to be a priori available on the basis of the CMoP, even if the property P is a thick property with a hidden essence. That is, the property of *being P* is a priori available on the basis of grasp of a CMoP that has property P as a constituent whether or not P is thick.

Although the a priori relation in itself does not appear to pose an obstacle to thickness of the MMoP, it might be thought to pose a problem combined with another argument, to which we now turn.

The Aspect Argument

As mentioned, the idea of the Aspect Argument is that it is not *all* of a thick property that explains cognitive significance in general and rational error in particular, but only an aspect of it, the aspect that is available a priori on the basis of the CMoP. But on the face of it, *that aspect can itself be thick*. Recall the example of Albert, which I pick out on the basis of its being the local wet thing. Albert's property of being the local wet thing fixes reference, uniquely determines the referent, is a *priori available and also thick*.

The Property Dualist may say that the property that would serve in explanations of error is not that it is wet but that it *looks* wet. However, consider a non-perceptual case: I infer using inductive principles that something in the corner is wet, and pick it out via its property of being wet. In this case, the substitution of *looks wet* for *wet* is unmotivated. The MMoP just does not seem perceptual. Nor artifactual, nor, more generally, functional. On the face of it, the MMoP is a thick property, the property of being wet, i.e., (roughly) at least partially covered or soaked with water (which is thick because being covered or soaked with water is being covered or soaked with H_2O).

But perhaps this rebuttal misses the significance of aspects to the first-person point of view. Perhaps the Property Dualist will say something like this: "If phenomenal property Q is a physical property, then it can be picked out by a physical—say neurological—concept that identifies it in neurological terms. But those neurological identifications are irrelevant to first-person phenomenal identifications, showing that the first-person phenomenal identification depends on *one aspect* of the phenomenal property—its "feel"—rather than *another aspect*—its neurologically identifying parameters. You have suggested that "cortico-thalamic oscillation" picks out its referent via the effect of cortico-thalamic oscillation on instruments that monitor oxygen uptake from blood vessels in the brain. But this effect is not part of the first-person route by which we pick out Q, so it follows that not every aspect of the physical property is relevant to the first-person route. Therefore the identity "Q = cortico-thalamic oscillation" is supposed to be one in which the terms pick out a single referent via different properties of it, different MMoPs. And so the Property Dualism Argument has not been avoided."

I agree that the two terms of the identity "Q = cortico-thalamic oscillation" pick out the referents via different aspects of that referent, different MMoPs. And I also agree that the aspect used by the mental term of the identity is available to the first-person whereas the aspect used by the physical term is not. But it does not follow that the aspect used by the mental term is thin. It is true that no neurological property is explicitly part of the first-person route, but that does not show that it is not part of the first-person route, albeit ontologically rather than explicitly. The MMoP of "Q" is stipulated to be phenomenal, and may be taken to be the property of *being* Q. But being identical to Q, on the physicalist view, is *both* a thick property, and available to the first person. Being identical to Q is a physical property (being identical to cortico-thalamic oscillation) but is nonetheless distinct from the MMoP I have been supposing for "cortico-thalamic oscillation," which has to do with the oxygen uptake that fMRI scanners use to identify it. On the physicalist view, the feel and the neurological state are not different aspects of one thing: they are literally identical. If they are aspects, they are identical aspects. But the MMoP of the right-hand term of the identity is still different from the MMoP of the left-hand term.

As mentioned earlier, some will say that oxygen uptake cannot provide the MMoP for the term "cortico-thalamic oscillation," which should be taken to be cortico-thalamic oscillation itself, or perhaps being identical to cortico-thalamic oscillation. In this supposition, there is a germ of a different argument for dualism, the E → 2M Argument discussed earlier.

I say that the aspect of a property that accounts for cognitive significance can itself be thick, appealing to examples. But the Property Dualist may suppose that if we attend to the mental contents that are doing the explaining, we can see that they are *narrow* contents, contents that are shared by Putnamian twins, people who are the same in physical properties inside the skin that are not individuated by relations to things outside the skin. If the relevant explanatory contents are narrow contents, then the corresponding explanatory properties—MMoPs—will be thin.

Here is the argument, the Narrow → Thin Argument, in more detail, offered in the voice of the Property Dualist:

N → T Argument: Suppose my CMoP is "the wet thing in the corner" (in a non-perceptual case) and my twin on Putnam's twin earth would put his CMoP in the same words. Still, the difference between what he means by "wet" and what I mean by "wet" *cannot matter to the rationalizing explanatory force* of the CMoPs. And since CMoPs are to be individuated entirely by rationalizing explanatory force, my twin and I have the same CMoPs: so, the CMoPs are narrow. But since the MMoP is a priori available to anyone who grasps the CMoP, the twins must have the same MMoP as well as the same CMoP, so the MMoP must be thin. Narrow CMoP, therefore thin MMoP.

The N → T Argument presupposes the familiar but controversial idea that only narrow content can serve in intentional explanations. However, on the face of it, my "water"-concept can be used in an explanation of my drinking water ("I wanted water, I saw water, so I drank water") but would not explain my drinking twin-water.[36] The idea that only narrow contents can serve in a rationalizing explanation is certainly controversial. I will not enter into this familiar dispute here, since there is another less familiar problem with the reasoning.

The inference from narrow content/narrow CMoP to thin MMoP has some initial plausibility, but it is actually question-begging. I agree with the premise of the N → T Argument that phenomenal CMoPs are narrow. (I won't go into the possibility that there is a descriptive part of the CMoP that is wide.) However, it does not follow that the MMoP is thin. The physicalist says that since phenomenality supervenes on the physical, Putnamian doppelgängers will share CMoPs: CMoPs are narrow. For example, a phenomenal CMoP containing phenomenal property P for one twin will also contain phenomenal property P for the other twin. The MMoP, *being P*, will also be the same for both twins, but that MMoP can nonetheless be thick. In short, the phenomenal part of a CMoP and the corresponding phenomenal MMoP will in general be narrow in virtue of being necessarily shared by doppelgängers, but will nonetheless be thick on the physicalist view. That is, what the doppelgängers necessarily share will be a property with a scientific essence.

The point can be approached by looking at the anomalous nature of phenomenal kinds. Phenomenal concepts of the sort that I have described here are natural kind concepts in that they purport to pick out objective kinds, and if the physicalist is right, those kinds have scientific natures whose scientific descriptions cannot be grasped a priori simply on the basis of having the concept. But they differ from most natural kind concepts in that the Twin Earth mode of thought experiment does not apply. The Twin Earth mode of thought experiment involves a pair of people who are the same in physical properties inside the skin (that are not individuated by relations to things outside the skin) but with a crucial physical difference. In Putnam's classic version (1975), twins who are relevantly the same in physical properties inside the skin pick out substances using the term "water" that have physically different natures, so (it is claimed), the meanings of their "water" terms and "water"-thought contents differ. They are (relevantly) physically the same, but different in "water"-meaning and "water"-content.

But how is the Twin Earth thought experiment supposed to be applied to phenomenality? If physicalism is true, the twins cannot be the same in physical properties inside the skin (that are not individuated by relations to things outside the skin) and also differ in the physical natures of their phenomenal states! (That's why I say the N → T Argument begs the question against physicalism.) So there is no straightforward way to apply the Putnamian Twin Earth thought experiment to phenomenal concepts. (The issue concerning Burgean thought experiments is more complex, since it hinges on the ways in which our terms express phenomenal concepts. I can't go into the matter here.)

But perhaps only a superficial analysis of Twin Earth thought experiments require that the twins be the same in physical properties inside the skin (that are not individuated by relations to things outside the skin). One way to think of Twin Earth cases is that what is important is that they be *mentally* alike in ways that don't involve relations to things outside the skin. (Thus, for some purposes, functional alikeness might seem more relevant than microphysical alikeness. This line of thought was what I used in my earlier discussion of whether fundamental physical properties are thin.) But phenomenality is certainly part of mentality, so if twins are to be the same in phenomenal CMoPs, there had better not be any physical difference between them that makes a phenomenal difference. However, from the physicalist point of view, the shared phenomenality of the twins' CMoPs has to be explained by a shared physical basis of it. So the shared narrow CMoP is compatible with a shared thick MMoP.

The upshot is that phenomenal concepts are an *anomaly*—at least from the physicalist point of view. They are natural kind concepts in that they allow for objective scientific natures that are "hidden" (the scientific descriptions are not a priori available on the basis of merely having the concept). But they are different from other natural kind concepts in that no reasonable facsimile of a Putnamian Twin Earth scenario is possible.

So even if the inference from narrow CMoP to thin MMoP applies in a variety of other cases, it should not be surprising that it fails to apply in this anomalous case. The CMoPs for phenomenal concepts can be narrow even though the corresponding MMoPs are thick. Indeed, the CMoPs themselves can be both narrow *and* thick. Narrow because non-relational, thick because they involve a phenomenal element that has a hidden scientific nature.

I have rebutted the Aspect and A Priority Arguments and a subsidiary argument, the N → T Argument, which all push for the conclusion that MMoPs of phenomenal concepts must be thin. But one can also look at the thesis itself independently of the arguments for it. Here are two considerations about the thesis itself.

Issues about the Claim of Thin MMoPs for Phenomenal Concepts

First, the assumption of thin MMoPs is perhaps sufficient for the conclusion of the Property Dualism Argument *all by itself*. For what are the candidates for a thin MMoP for a phenomenal concept? Artifact properties such as being a telephone (even assuming that they are thin) and purely mathematical properties are non-starters. Some kind terms that are not natural kind terms, e.g., "dirt," may yield thin properties. But phenomenal MMoPs are not artifactual or mathematical and they are or purport to be natural kinds as just pointed out. It is not clear whether there are any natural kind terms that express thin properties. Even if there are fundamental physical properties that are thin, the Property Dualist can hardly suggest fundamental physical properties as candidates for MMoPs for phenomenal concepts, since that has no independent plausibility and in any case would be incompatible with the conclusion of the Property Dualist's argument. So it would seem that the only remotely plausible candidates for thin MMoPs by which phenomenal concepts refer are (1) purely functional properties, in which case deflationism would be true, and (2) phenomenal properties that are non-physical, in which case dualism is true. The conclusion would be the same as the conclusion of the Property Dualism Argument itself: that phenomenal realist physicalism is untenable.

The upshot is that much of the argumentation surrounding the Property Dualism Argument can be dispensed with if the arguments of this chapter are correct. The most obvious arguments that MMoPs of phenomenal concepts cannot be physical (the Regress Argument and the A Priori Availability Argument, presented earlier) do not stand alone but rather depend on the Thin/Thick Argument. I have not shown that there is no good argument for the claim that MMoPs of phenomenal concepts are thin, but I have rebutted some obvious candidates, and it is hard to see how the Regress and A Priori Availability Arguments could be used to justify the thinness claim since they presuppose it. So if my arguments are right, the burden of proof is on the Property Dualist to come up with a new argument for the claim that MMoPs of phenomenal concepts are thin.

Here is the second point. So far, I have argued that the assumption of thin MMoPs leads directly to dualism or deflationism, putting a heavy burden of proof on the Property Dualist to justify that assumption. But actually I doubt that deflationism really is an option. Let me explain. The functionalist characterizes functional properties in terms of the Ramsey sentence for a theory. Supposing that "yellow teeth" is an "observation term," the Ramsey sentence for the theory that smoking causes both cancer and yellow teeth is $\exists F_1 \exists F_2 [F_1$ causes both F_2 and yellow teeth], i.e., the Ramsey sentence says that there are two properties one of which causes the other and also yellow teeth. Focusing on psychological theories, where the "observation terms" (or "old" terms in Lewis's parlance) are terms for inputs and outputs, the Ramsey sentence could be put as follow: $\exists F_1 \ldots \exists F_n [T(F_1 \ldots F_n, i_1 \ldots i_m, o_1 \ldots o_p)]$. The "i" terms are input terms and the "o" terms are output terms. Functional properties of the sort that can be defined in terms of the Ramsey sentence are properties that consist in having certain other properties that have certain causal relations to inputs, outputs, and other properties.[37] The inputs and outputs can be characterized in many ways. For example, an output might be characterized neurally, or in terms of movements of a hand or leg, or distally, in terms of, e.g., water in the distance, or distally and mentalistically in terms of drinking water. *But all these characterizations are plausibly thick, not thin.* Perhaps you will think that some of them are *themselves* to be cashed functionally, but then the issue I am raising would arise for the input and output specification of *those* functional properties. Since the problem I am raising depends on the thickness of the input and output properties, I put those terms for those properties, ("i_1" … "i_m," "o_1" … "o_p"), in bold in the Ramsey sentence earlier. The only functional properties I know of that are plausibly thin are *purely formal* functional properties that abstract from the specific nature of inputs and outputs, the kind of functional property that could be shared by a person and an economy. (See Block 1978.) For example, in the case of the theory that smoking causes cancer and yellow teeth, a purely formal Ramsey property would be: being an x such that $\exists F_1 \exists F_2 \exists F_3 ([F_1$ causes F_2 and $F_3]$ and x has $F_1)$. This is the property of having a property which causes two other properties. Such a property could be shared by a person and an economy. Since not even a deflationist should agree that the metaphysical modes of presentation of our phenomenal states are *purely* formal, the only remaining option is dualism. So the assumption of thin properties plausibly leads right to dualism.

To sum up the points about the thin/thick argument: The "aspect" rationale for MMoPs being thin seems doubtful because the aspect can itself be thick. And the rationale for thin MMoPs in terms of the supposed a priori relation between CMoP and MMoP is problematic because the key phenomenal feature of the MMoP can also be present in the CMoP, when the relevant concept is phenomenal. At least this is so on one plausible notion of phenomenal concepts, which the Property Dualist would have to challenge. Narrow CMoPs can be used to argue for thin MMoPs, but this reasoning begs the question against the physicalist. I explained at the outset that the emphasis on MMoPs at the expense of CMoPs was tactical: the metaphenomenal move—that says that modes of presentation bring in unreduced phenomenality—can be discussed equally with respect to either mode of presentation. This was the place in the argument where the artificiality is most apparent—CMoPs must be discussed explicitly.

Moving to the thesis itself independently of arguments for it, the assumption of thin MMoPs amounts to much the same thing as the Property Dualism Argument itself. Further, the only remotely plausible candidates for thin MMoPs are purely formal properties that we do not have ordinary concepts of and phenomenal properties, dualistically conceived. The purely formal properties, though more plausible than some other candidates, are not very plausible, even from a deflationist point of view.

Deflationist functionalism is based on analyses of mentality in terms of sensory input and behavioral output. Purely formal properties do not adequately capture such analyses, and cannot without thick input and output terms. The upshot is that the assumption of thin MMoPs for phenomenal concepts adds up to dualism itself. To assume thin MMoPs begs the question against the physicalist.

Of course, I have not shown that there cannot be an argument for thin phenomenal MMoPs, but I hope I have shown that a number of candidates do not succeed.

VII   The Relation between the Property Dualism Argument and Some Other Arguments for Dualism

Loar (1997) locates the flaw in Jackson's "Mary" argument and Kripke's modal argument in a certain principle: the "semantic premise."[38] The semantic premise (on one understanding of it) says that if a statement of property identity is a posteriori, then at least one of the MMoPs must be contingently associated with the referent. The idea behind the principle is that if the two concepts pick out a property non-contingently, it must be possible for a thinker who grasps the concepts to see, a priori, that they pick out the same property. Again the issue arises as to what notion of MMoP is at stake. Consider, for example, the reference-fixing notion of MMoP. In this sense, the "semantic premise" is plainly false. Note that the person formed by a certain sperm = the person formed by a certain egg. This identity is a posteriori, yet both terms pick out their referents via essential and therefore necessary properties of it, assuming that Kripke is right about the necessity of origins. Call the sperm and egg that formed George W. Bush "Gamete-Herbert" and "Gamete-Barbara" respectively. The person formed from Gamete-Herbert = the person formed from Gamete-Barbara. "The person formed from Gamete-Herbert" does not pick out George W. contingently, nor does "The person formed from Gamete-Barbara." My example is put in terms of individuals but it is easy to see how to frame a version of it in terms of properties. Even if Kripke is wrong about the necessity of origins, the logic of the example remains. One thing can have two necessary but insufficient properties, both of which can be used to pick it out, neither of which a priori entails the other. Thus the terms in a true a posteriori identity can pick out that thing, each term referring by a different necessary property as the MMoP.

Of course there is some contingency in the vicinity. Gamete-Herbert might have joined with an egg other than Gamete-Barbara or Gamete-Barbara might have joined with a sperm other than Gamete-Herbert. And this might suggest a modification of the principle (one that White (2006b) suggests in response to an earlier version of this chapter), namely, if a statement of property identity is a posteriori, then it is not the case that both terms refer via MMoPs that are necessary and sufficient conditions for the property that is the referent. Or, more minimally, if a property identity is a posteriori, then it is not the case that one term refers via a sufficient property of it and the other refers via a necessary property of it. But a modification of my example (contributed by John Hawthorne) suggests that neither of these will quite do. Let the identity be: the *actual* person formed from Gamete-Herbert = the *actual* person formed from Gamete-Barbara. Arguably, each designator refers via a property that is both necessary and sufficient for the referent. So the revised version of the semantic premise is also false.

The reference of the terms "Gamete-Herbert" and "Gamete-Barbara" need not be fixed via properties that involve George Bush. The gametes can be identified independently, for example before George Bush was conceived. But perhaps the names will pick them out via some contingent reference-fixing property, e.g., a perceptual demonstrative ("that egg") or by description. And that motivates White (ibid.) to suggest a beefed up form of the semantic premise that says that there must be contingency either in the relation between MMoPs and referent or in the relation between MMoPs and the MMoPs of those MMoPs, or ... I reject the beefed-up semantic premise for the reason given earlier: I don't think these further MMoPs need exist. That is, in the identity "a = b," there will be MMoPs associated with both sides. But there will be no MMoPs of those MMoPs unless the subject happens to refer to the first level MMoPs in another voluntary cognitive act.

VIII Conclusion

Both the Knowledge Argument and Max Black's Property Dualism Argument for dualism hinge on the idea that there is something special about phenomenality in our phenomenal concepts that eludes physicalism. Both arguments are ways of making concrete what I called the metaphenomenal move: the idea that in a phenomenal mind-body identity claim, the CMoP is partly constituted by something with unreduced phenomenality or the MMoP is an unreduced phenomenal property.

My response has been to argue that phenomenality in modes of presentation is no different from phenomenality elsewhere. I tried to dissolve apparent impediments to the phenomenal element in the CMoP and the MMoP being physical. My way out involves a notion of a phenomenal concept that has some affinities with the "directness" story in which there is no metaphysical mode of presentation at all, since my phenomenal MMoPs are not very different from the referent itself. I considered a family of arguments based on the idea that MMoPs must be thin, arguing that appeal to narrow content does nothing to establish thinness. According to me, phenomenal concepts are both narrow and thick, which is why the phenomenality in the CMoP can be physical. I also considered a different version of the Property Dualism Argument that assumes that an empirical identity must have different MMoPs, so that if the MMoPs of the two terms of an identity are the same, then the identity is a priori. I argued that whereas sameness of CMoP makes for a priority of the identity, sameness of the MMoP does not.

Much of the argumentation involved the principle that a difference in CMoP requires a difference in MMoP (D(CMoP) → D(MMoP)). I argued that nothing forces us to adopt notions of CMoP and MMoP on which this principle is true. However, at a key point in the dialectic I considered a notion of MMoP individuated with respect to CMoP, which I argued did not rescue the Property Dualism Argument.

Although I expressed skepticism about whether any one thing can explain rational error, fix reference, and be relevantly a priori available, I have not claimed that these *raisons d'être* fail to coincide except at one point at which I noted that an explanatory MMoP need not fix the referent. The other rebuttals were keyed to one or another specific version of MMoPs and CMoPs and their relation. My strategy was to avoid multiplying arguments based on different notions of CMoP/MMoP by choosing what seemed to me the strongest argument of each type. In the end, everything hinges on the claim that MMoPs of phenomenal concepts are thin, and I attempted to remove the most straightforward motivations for that view.

I have pursued a divide-and-conquer strategy, distinguishing among different senses of "mode of presentation" and further dividing those by the *raisons d'être* of modes of presentation in those senses. My claim is that once we do that, the Property Dualism Argument dribbles away. I have not claimed to refute these arguments conclusively but I believe that the ball is in the Property Dualist's court.

Appendix on a Variant of the E → 2M Argument Using Primary Intensions Instead of MMoPs

I mentioned that there is a version of the E → 2M Argument using the notion of a primary intension instead of the notion of an MMoP. The primary intension of "water" is the function from worlds considered as actual (as actual world candidates in Davies and Humberstone's (1980) sense) to what water turns out to be in that world. (Or so I will understand the term. Chalmers uses various different ways of specifying what a primary intension is but since this is a very brief discussion, I will just pick that one.) Thus the primary intension of "water" picks out water in the actual world and XYZ ("twin-water") on Putnam's Twin Earth. Since Putnam's Twin Earth could have both XYZ and H_2O in it, the primary intension is a function from "centered" worlds— worlds with a privileged point—to referents. What makes the primary intension of "water" pick out the XYZ in Putnam's Twin Earth is that the center of that world has the relevant relation to XYZ rather than H_2O. (For example, the center might be surrounded by XYZ whereas there might be only a few molecules of H_2O that are light years away. If there are people on twin earth, we can suppose causal commerce of the relevant sort between XYZ (but not H_2O) and uses of the term "water" that have some appropriate relation to the center.)

I read Chalmers (1996) as stipulating that the primary intension captures the a priori component of content, and on this reading the primary intension would be more like a CMoP than an MMoP. Given this stipulation, my complaint that MMoPs are not what is relevant to a priority would fall away, the pressure instead being on the issue of whether primary intensions in the sense in which they are stipulated to capture the a priori aspect of content are indeed the same as secondary intensions. That is, the analog of the E → 2M principle, the "E → 2 PI principle," would be a stipulation, but the other premise of the argument—that the phenomenal and functional primary intensions are identical to the secondary intensions—would then take the heat. The secondary intension of "water" is the function from worlds to what 'water' denotes in those, worlds, namely, water, if there is any. The worlds are considered "as counterfactual" (as familiar from Kripke): we take reference of "water" in the actual world as fixed, and given that fixed reference, the function picks out what is identical to the actual referent in each counterfactual world, namely H_2O if there is any (assuming the usual philosophical myth that "water" refers to H_2O in the actual world). So the doubtful premise—according to me—would be whether primary intensions stipulated to capture the a priori component of content are the same as secondary intensions for both the phenomenal and the psychofunctional term.

Of course, there is no plausibility of the primary intension being identical to the secondary intension for "water." Twin Earth is a counterexample since the primary intension picks out XYZ whereas the secondary intension picks out H_2O. To the extent that the right-hand side of mind-body identity claims are natural kind terms like 'water', the version of the Property Dualism Argument presented in this Appendix has no plausibility whatsoever. You can see why by noting that primary intensions in this incarnation correspond to my CMoPs—which can also be stipulated to capture the a priori aspect of content. As noted in the text, there is no plausibility at all that the CMoP of, say a functional term, is identical to the referent. Consider a very simple functional term, "solubility." The CMoP of "solubility" is something like a meaning, but the referent is a property of sugar and salt. Why should we suppose that the solubility of sugar and salt is a kind of *meaning*? This seems like a category error.

In many of his writings, Chalmers has one notion—primary intension—corresponding to the two notions of my apparatus—CMoP and MMoP. But in Chalmers (2006), he considers dividing the primary intension into two notions. As I understand it, the *epistemic* intension of 'water'—which is stipulated to capture the a priori aspect of content—is a function from situations (situations, not worlds) to what turns out to be water in those situations. The primary intension—which, on this version is not stipulated to capture the a priori aspect of content—is a function from worlds to what turns out to be water in those worlds. So on this scheme, epistemic intensions roughly correspond to my CMoPs, whereas primary intensions roughly correspond to MMoPs. On this new notion of a primary intension, it becomes a substantive question whether primary intensions capture an a priori component of content. If it turns out that they do for phenomenal terms and psychofunctional terms, then the Property Dualism Argument of this section would avoid the first of the two objections I mentioned above to the E → 2M analog for primary intensions. So it is worth taking a closer look at the prospects for the substantive—as opposed to stipulated—claim that primary intensions capture an a priori component of content.

I will start with a criticism of the notion of a primary intension as stipulated to capture an a priori component of content (see Block 1991, Block and Stalnaker 1999, and Chalmers (2006: s. 5.8) for a response). Take the value of the primary intension of 'water' to be what turns out to be water in a world considered as actual. How do we know what turns out to be water in a world considered as actual? By consulting our intuitions about what one should say about various worlds considered as actual. We ask ourselves what we should say if, for example, we became convinced we were living on Putnam's Twin Earth. These intuitions are the epistemic basis of the primary intension, that is how we know what it is. And they are or at least index its metaphysical basis. That is, these intuitions constitute the metaphysical basis or they index an underlying property that is responsible both for the intuitions and the primary intension.

Now ask yourself about another of Putnam's (1970) thought experiments, which we could put like this. Suppose we discover that cats are actually robots controlled from Mars that were put on earth 100 million years ago to spy on the intelligent beings they predicted would evolve. There never were any naturally evolving catlike creatures, since the robot cats killed off anything that had a chance of becoming one. When intelligent primates finally evolved, the robot cats made themselves appealing to people and came to develop the close relation to people portrayed in *Garfield*. We are wrong about many of the properties we take cats to have. The robot cats pretend to be aloof but are actually very interested in us and love us. They would like nothing better than to act more like dogs, but their orders are to act aloof. They do not actually purr but use mind-control to make us think so.

I think the story is intelligible and I hope you think so too. But notice that other stories would have been equally intelligible in which cats fail to have other properties that we ordinarily think they have. The world I mentioned is a world considered as actual in which cats are not cute aloof purring animals. But there are other worlds considered as actual in which they lack other properties that we ordinarily think they have. Perhaps all the properties we ascribe to cats—or at least the ones that distinguish them from, say dogs—are in this sense dispensable. Some may want to retreat to *seeming* to have such properties, but in this direction lies the phenomenalism of C. I. Lewis. If the primary intension of "cat" is determined or indexed by such intuitions and captures the a priori component of content, it looks as if there is very little to the a priori component of content. Maybe one can't imagine a world considered as actual in which cats are not moving middle-sized physical entities—but that will not distinguish a putative a priori component of "cat" from that of "dog." The Chalmers-Jackson response is to note that our intuitions about worlds considered as actual do in fact distinguish between "cat" and "dog," so the primary intensions are not so thin as to be the same for these two words. This response, however, sets up the real worry, which is that given that these intuitions are (or at least index) the foundation of the semantics of these terms, how we are supposed to know whether, in having these intuitions, that is, in considering a world as actual, we end up *covertly changing the meaning of "cat."* That is, how do we know whether in coming up with the best way of thinking about a world as actual, one of the variables we can implicitly adjust is the meanings of the words we use to describe the world?

The problem would be avoided if one had some other notion of the a priori component of content that could be used in defining primary intensions, for example an account along the lines of the suggestion from Kripke that some words can be defined metalinguistically or Katz's more orthodox definitions. The primary intension of "cat" would be the function from worlds considered as actual to what is picked out in that world by the proposed definition. But then we would not need the primary intension as an account of the a priori component of content because we would already have such an account: the definition.

Note that the problem is not one of indeterminacy in our intuitions or of cases not decided by our intuitions—of course there are cases our intuitions do not decide. The problem is with cases that our intuitions *do* decide, like the robot cat case. Our intuitions are a function of the simplest overall account, and as Quineans have long said, *there is no guarantee that anything putatively a priori will be preserved in the simplest account.* If one believes in determinate a priori intensions, the thing to say is that our intuitions present us with situations in which we find it natural to change those a priori intensions. That is, in considering the Putnam robot cat world, we tacitly change our meaning of "cat" (Katz 1972, 1975).

So there is a dilemma for the advocate of primary intensions as stipulated to capture an a priori component of content. If our advocate goes with Katzian or metalinguistic definitions, then there is no need for the notion of a primary intension. However, if our advocate rejects those definitions, then it is not clear why we should believe that our linguistic intuitions index any interesting a priori aspect of content or the primary intensions that are stipulated to capture it. Of course, primary intensions are just functions, and so the primary intension of 'cat' can be said to exist trivially. Yes, but that function may include inputs in which the word "cat" is used in a different sense from the normal one and so could not be said to capture anything semantic. (See the coumarone example in Block and Stalnaker 1999.) The question is: Why should we believe

in a primary intension that *does* capture an a priori aspect of content? *Given the unreli-*
ability of the intuitions about cases as a pipeline to an a priori notion of content, primary
intensions which are stipulated to capture an a priori notion of content become highly doubtful
theoretical entities. The upshot for the E → 2M form of the Property Dualism Argument
is this. If an intension—primary or epistemic—is simply stipulated to capture an a priori aspect of content, then it is in doubt for the reasons just given. If we put this doubt
aside, accepting the analog of the E → 2M principle, the identity of those intensions
with secondary intensions is in doubt—that is, the other premise of the argument is
in doubt. What if the intension is not stipulated to have this a priori significance, but
it is claimed to have it nonetheless? The Putnamian considerations I raised cast doubt
on that claim, but putting that doubt aside, my view is that to the extent we can show
an intension to capture an a priori aspect of content, it will be doubtful that that intension can be identified with a secondary intension, so the two premises of the E → 2M
argument will never be satisfied together.

Notes

Reprinted from Dean W. Zimmerman, ed., *Oxford Studies in Metaphysics*, vol. 2, 3–78 (Oxford:
Oxford University Press, 2006).

I gratefully thank the following persons for commenting on a remote ancestor of this paper:
Paul Horwich, Brian Loar, David Pitt, Stephen Schiffer, Susanna Siegel, Stephen White, and Dean
Zimmerman; and my thanks to Tyler Burge, David Chalmers, and Stephen White for comments
on a more recent version. I also thank students in my graduate seminar, participants in the NEH
Santa Cruz Summer Institute of 2002, participants at an ANU Workshop ("Themes from Ned
Block") in the summer of 2003, and the audience at the University of Houston for reactions to
parts of the remote ancestor.

1. Stephen White (1986, 2006*a, b*) has done more than anyone to elucidate the Property Dualism
Argument. John Perry's (2001) book develops machinery that he uses against modal arguments
for dualism, Jackson's Knowledge Argument and the Property Dualism Argument. Christopher
Hill (1991, 1997), Joseph Levine (2001), and Colin McGinn (2001) have also put forward versions
of the argument. Some of David Chalmers's (1996, 2004) arguments for dualism involve similar
ideas. Brian Loar's (1990 and 1997) papers are also immersed in the territory of the argument, although not explicitly about it. Jerome Schaffer (1963) discusses the argument but in somewhat
different terms than those used more recently. I will focus on a version of the Property Dualism
Argument similar to the arguments given by Smart (though see n. 4), White, and Perry, and I
will contrast my refutation with Perry's.

2. I am indebted to Tyler Burge for drawing the Rozemond book to my attention.

3. White (1986, 2006*b*) runs the Property Dualism Argument against both token and type mind-
body identities, but I am ignoring the issue of token identity.

4. Part of what Smart says is hard to interpret. I left out a crucial phrase in the Smart quotation
that seems confused. What I left out is the italicized phrase in the following: "the objection that

a sensation can be identified with a brain process only if it has some phenomenal property, *not possessed by brain processes*, whereby one-half of the identification may be, so to speak, pinned down." The italicized phrase is puzzling since Smart gives every indication of thinking that the threat from Max Black's objection is from a "double aspect" theory that says that token pains are token brain states, but that the token pains have irreducible *phenomenal properties*. The dualism is supposed to derive from the non-physicality of the phenomenal property, not a failure of the phenomenal property to apply to the brain processes. Perry explicitly avoids Smart's error when he says: "even if we identify experiences with brain states, there is still the question of what makes the brain state an experience, and the experience it is; it seems like that must be an additional property the brain state has."

5. The heavy duty notion of phenomenal concepts has its origins in Brian Loar (1990, 1997); a version that is closer to what I have in mind is described briefly in Block (2002) and accounts that share the structure I am talking about appear in David Chalmers (2003), David Papineau (2002), and in an unpublished paper by Kati Balog.

6. The articles by Paul Churchland, Brian Loar, William Lycan, and Robert van Gulick in Block, Flanagan, and Güzeldere (1997) all take something like this line, as do Horgan (1984) and Sturgeon (1994).

7. Here, and in the rest of the discussion of Mary, unless otherwise stated, I intend both the Fregean and non-Fregean senses of "mode of presentation."

8. I have the sense from a remark in Jackson (2004) that he might agree with this. On another issue: Jackson says that the matter should not be put in terms of whether there is a new fact involved in Mary's acquiring the subjective concept of the experience. When Mary closes her books and steps across the threshold, *everything* she does constitutes a new fact that was not described in her books. However, this would be motivation for a somewhat different way of setting up the Knowledge Argument in which Mary predicts everything that will happen to her in the first day of leaving the room *in physical terms*. So she does know about the fact of what she sees after leaving the room, albeit in physical terms. Using this device, one could then state the issue in terms of whether Mary learns any new facts.

9. Although it would take me too far afield to go into the differences between the Knowledge Argument and the Property Dualism Argument, I should mention one: that the Knowledge Argument as usually stated concerns a supervenience form of physicalism (no mental difference without a physical difference) whereas the Property Dualism Argument is directed against mind-body identity. Indeed, Jackson is thinking of a really extreme form of physicalism which makes a commitment to all the facts following a priori from a set of base physical facts. Chalmers (1996) also regards this view as entailed by physicalism. On that view of physicalism, the Knowledge Argument is much more persuasive, since all that has to be shown is that what Mary learns does not follow a priori from what she already knows. On that form of physicalism, the move made here and in Perry's book of thinking of Mary as learning (or in Perry's case acquiring a sensitivity to) a new subjective concept of a property she already had an objective concept of has little purchase. However, the Knowledge Argument can be discussed as it is here and in Perry's book from the perspective of a mind-body identity account of physicalism. The standard reply I have discussed

is from that perspective, so even though some of the adherents of the Knowledge Argument are thinking of physicalism in a different way, that is irrelevant to the points made here.

10. Chalmers (2003) argues that phenomenal concepts cannot be demonstrative concepts. The main argument could be put as follows: for any demonstrative concept, say "this$_i$," this$_i$ has phenomenal property P would be news. But if the demonstrative concept was genuinely a phenomenal concept, there would be some claims of that form that are not news. I agree with the "not news" rule of thumb, though I would not go so far as to agree that it shows no demonstrative concept can be phenomenal. However, whether or not it shows that there can't be a concept that is both demonstrative and phenomenal, the demonstrative concepts that Perry is talking about are not phenomenal concepts in the sense required to motivate the Knowledge Argument and the Property Dualism Argument, the sense required to ground the metaphenomenal move.

11. Burge describes the two functions of Fregean sense as sense$_1$ and sense$_2$. (He also mentions a third function, sense$_3$, providing entities to be denoted in oblique contexts, which will not be discussed here. Byrne and Pryor talk of two different roles, the informativeness or cognitive significance role and the reference-determination role.

12. A similar but not identical distinction is introduced in arguing for Property Dualism in two papers by Stephen White (White, 2006a,b). These are my terms, not White's, and I do not agree with White about key features of the distinction. I will attribute very little specific content to White's unpublished papers, since those papers are in draft form as of the writing of this chapter.

13. Although I am defending physicalism in this chapter, I do think there is a genuinely troubling argument for dualism, one that is completely different from Kripke's and Chalmers' modal arguments, the Knowledge Argument, and the Property Dualism Argument. What I have in mind is the multiple realization argument discussed in Block (2002): if there could be a creature whose phenomenology has a sufficiently different physical basis from ours, but whose phenomenology is similar to ours, then there would be a phenomenal similarity which is not explained by a physical similarity.

I spoke earlier of double duty. A phenomenal feel in a concept is used to pick out a phenomenal feel. But what I have just suggested amounts to "triple duty." A phenomenal feel in the CMoP serves to pick out a phenomenal feel as referent via a closely related phenomenal feel as MMoP. I don't want to make much of this "triple duty." The notions of CMoP and MMoP are artificial notions that make more intuitive sense in some cases than in others.

14. I take this formulation from Papineau (2002), although he does not use the CMoP/MMoP distinction. See also Block (2002) for a somewhat different formulation.

15. This (putative) example of the failure of the D(CMoP) → D(MMoP) principle is suboptimal in a number of ways. Something can be wet by being soaked with a liquid other than water and paint can be wet without being soaked at all. The words "water" and "H$_2$O" are different, and that might be said to provide a genuine metalinguistic difference in properties. Further, "Water" is simple and "H$_2$O" is compositional giving rise to another difference in properties. (Despite these flaws, I will use the example later in the chapter.) These flaws are corrected in a type of counterexample to come now. (See n. 29 as well.)

16. Schiffer (1990) has a similar example. Another case of two CMoPs but only one MMoP might be constructed from a variant of Austin's (1990) two tubes case. The subject looks through two fiber optic "tubes," one for each eye, and sees what he would describe as a red circular patch via each eye—with no differences between the patches. Further, the subject cannot tell which experience comes from the tube on the right and which from the tube on the left. A further wrinkle: unknown to the subject, the two fiber optic channels merge into one, so the object of the two experiences is exactly the same. From the subject's point of view, there are two experiences that may for all he knows be experiences of different things, so there are two CMoPs, but since they are in fact of the redness of one thing, there is only one MMoP.

17. See the discussion of the "semantic premise" in Section VII, The Relation between the Property Dualism Argument and Some Other Arguments for Dualism.

18. The familiar point is put in a rather neat way in Perry's (2004a) rendition: If the putative zombie world contains cortico-thalamic oscillation, then according to the physicalist, it contains phenomenality and so is not a zombie world; but if the putative zombie world does not contain cortico-thalamic oscillation, then it does not fit the physical requirement of a zombie world. So physicalism cannot allow a zombie world.

19. See n. 18.

20. I presented a version of the argument in a reply to David Chalmers at the Philadelphia APA in 1997, partly as a result of conversations with Brian Loar. There is an argument in Loar (2000) that has some similarity to it. McGinn (2001) takes something of this sort to be the Property Dualism Argument, i.e. the one that Smart (1959) and White (1983) had in mind. I have heard unpublished versions of similar arguments by Martine Nida-Rümelin and John Hawthorne.

21. A similar argument can be framed using Chalmers's and Jackson's primary intension/secondary intension apparatus (Chalmers 1996; Jackson 1998). The idea would be that for phenomenal and functional concepts, the primary intension is identical to the secondary intension. (Both views are endorsed by Chalmers (1996).) So if the secondary intension of a phenomenal/functional identity claim is true, so is the primary intension, and hence a phenomenal/psychofunctional identity claim is if true, a priori true. And since for reasons just given it is not a priori true, it is false. I will discuss the E → 2M Argument in this section, and then—in the Appendix—the variant using Chalmers's and Jackson's apparatus. So I will postpone saying what I take a primary intension to be until then.

22. The point can be made with another more controversial type of example. Consider 'This property = this property' where the first demonstrative picks out the property of being water and the second picks out the property of being H_2O. (See Austin 1990). It could be said that each demonstrative picks out the property directly in the sense that the MMoP just is the property picked out. But if so, the form of the E → 2M Argument would give us a general argument against any empirical property identity!

23. Deflationism with respect to truth is the view that the utility of the concept of truth can be explained disquotationally and that there can be no scientific reduction of truth (Horwich 1990, 1998; Field 1994). Deflationism with respect to consciousness in its most influential form

is, confusingly, a kind of reductionism—albeit armchair reductionism rather than substantive scientific reductionism—and thus the terminology I am following can be misleading. I may have introduced this confusing terminology (in Block 1992, 1993), and though it is both confusing and misleading, it has already taken firm hold, and so I will use it here.

24. Why "a priori or armchair"? Many philosophers adopt forms of functionalism, representationism, or cognitivism that, it would seem, could only be justified by conceptual analysis, while nonetheless rejecting a priority.

25. The rationale for the functionalist understanding of this point of view is spelled out in Block (1980) and in more streamlined form in Block (1994). Lewis (1980) adopts a more complex mixture of functionalism and physicalism.

26. As Hempel (1969) noted, physicalism has a serious problem of obscurity. Physicalism about properties could be put as: all properties are physical. But what is a physical property? Hempel noted a dilemma (that has been further elaborated by Chomsky (2000); but see the critique by Stoljar (2001)): Horn 1 is: we tie physicalism to current physics, in which case physicalism is unfairly judged false, since there are no doubt physical entities and properties that are not countenanced by *current* physics. These entities and properties would be counted as non-physical by this criterion, even if the physics of next week will unproblematically acknowledge them. Horn 2 is: we define physicalism in terms of future physics. But what counts as physics? We cannot take physics as given in an inquiry about whether physicalism can be unproblematically defined. And we surely don't want to count as physics whatever is done in academic departments called "Physics Departments." For if theologians hijacked the name "Physics," that would not make God physical.

27. The big problem in defining physicalism is getting an acceptable notion of the physicalistically non-problematic without simply using the notion of the physical. One approach is to use a paradigm of the physicalistically unproblematic. I have suggested (1978) defining physicalism as the view that everything is decomposable into particles of the sort that make up inorganic matter. This definition uses "inorganic" as a way of specifying what is physicalistically unproblematic (following Feigl 1958, 1967), and so would get the wrong result if the inorganic turns out to be physicalistically problematic, e.g., if pan-psychism obtains (electrons are conscious). Thus it fails as a sufficient condition of physicalism. It does not capture the meaning of "physicalism" (and it does not even try to define "physical property"), but it does better as a necessary condition of physicalism. (See also Montero 1999.) Papineau (2002) takes the tack of specifying the physicalistically unproblematic by (in effect) a *list*. He suggests defining physicalism as the thesis that everything is identifiable non-mentally, that is, non-mental concepts can be used to pick out everything, including the mental. One problem with this way of proceeding is that "mental" has the same problem as "physical." We may one day acknowledge "mental" properties that we do not acknowledge today (much as Freudian unconscious mental properties are said to not always have been part of our conception of the mind). We can define the mental in terms of a list of currently acknowledged mental properties, which would be as problematic as defining the physical by a list. Or we could appeal to what will be recognized later as "mental," hitching our concept wrongly to the use of a term by future generations.

28. All three arguments are inspired by conversation with or published or unpublished (at the time of writing) papers by Stephen White. I doubt, however, that he would agree with my renditions or the conceptual apparatus they use.

29. The second example I gave involving Loar's "chat" case is, prima facie, not vulnerable to this objection. Or rather what it suggests is that the version of "thin property" needed by the property dualist is something more like "concept-individuated" rather than lacking a hidden essence. So the "chat" MMoPs will be something like *being a furry purring aloof creature*—relative to mental file 1, and *being a furry purring aloof creature*—relative to mental file 2.

30. The quotation is from the 1990 version of Loar's "Phenomenal States," 87. This picture is abandoned in the 1997 version of Loar's paper in which he retains talk of triggering and the direct reference terminology, but with a new meaning, namely: refers, but not via a contingent property of the referent. The view common to both the 1990 and 1997 paper is that a theoretical concept of e.g., neuroscience might pick out a neurological property "that triggers a given recognitional concept, and so the two concepts can converge in their reference despite their cognitive independence" (1990: 88).

31. There is an outstanding issue involving phenomenal concepts that I will raise briefly without attempting to resolve. What makes it the case that a token phenomenal property in a phenomenal concept serves as a token of one phenomenal type or property rather than another? For example, suppose that a token of a mental image of red serves in a phenomenal concept to pick out an experience as of red. Why red rather than scarlet or colored? One answer is an appeal to dispositions. Suppose you are looking at chips in an ideal paint store that has a chip for every distinct color. (Robert Boynton estimates that there would be about a million such chips.) You are looking at Green$_{126,731}$, thinking that color-experience is nice, using a phenomenal concept of that experience. But what experience is it that your phenomenal concept is of? The experience as of Green$_{126,731}$? The experience as of green? The answer on the dispositionalist view is that it depends on the subject's disposition to, for example, treat another experience as falling under the same concept. You are thinking that the experience is nice—but what will you count as another one of those? If only another experience as of Green$_{126,731}$ will count as an experience of the same type, the phenomenal concept is maximally specific; if any bluish-green experience will count as an experience of the same type, the concept is more abstract. If any experience of green will count as an experience of the same type, the concept is still more abstract. (Views of this general sort have been defended in conversation by Brian Loar and Kati Balog.)

This sort of view is similar to one interpretation of Berkeley's answer to the question of how an image of an isosceles triangle can be a concept of triangle, a concept that covers non-isosceles triangles as well as isosceles triangles. His answer (on this interpretation) was: because the image functions so as to apply to all types of triangles rather than just to isosceles triangles. There is a problem with Berkeley's answer that also applies to the view of phenomenal concepts I am talking about: namely, that it would seem that it is because one is *taking* the image of an isosceles triangle as a *triangle-image* rather than as an *isosceles-triangle-image* that it functions as it does, rather than the other way around. (This is not to impugn the functionalist idea that the role is what makes the concept the concept it is; rather, the point is that in some cases, there is something about the entity that has the role that makes it the case that it has that role.) Similarly, it is because one is taking the experience of a specific shade of green as a green-experience rather than as a Green$_{126,731}$ experience that makes it function as a concept of the experience of green rather than the concept of that highly specific shade of green. The dispositionalist view seems to get things backwards. However, no view of phenomenal concepts can sign on to the idea that an experience functions in a concept only under *another* phenomenal concept, since that would lead to a regress. My tentative thought is that there is a form of "taking" that does not amount to a further concept but is enough to explain the dispositions. However, I cannot go into the matter further here.

32. I did say the mental option was "useless" in the sense that the dualist and the physicalist could agree on it. The mental option is useful, however, for the physicalist in avoiding the regress argument.

33. Perhaps it will be said that not any old "associated property" is enough to rationalize error. Let us use the notation RF['Dylan'] to mean the property to which the subject has given the special reference-fixing authority for using "Dylan." The view I expect to hear is that to rationalize error, we must ascribe to the subject a justified belief that RF["Bob Dylan"] is instantiated here, whereas, say RF['Robert Zimmerman'] is not. But this is a false picture of what it takes to rationalize error. If I have reason to believe that some abiding property, X, of Bob Dylan is instantiated here but that some abiding property, Y, of Robert Zimmerman is not, then other things equal, I have reason to think Dylan and Zimmerman are different people, no matter how unconnected X and Y are from reference-fixers.

34. Another reason for taking thinness to be a matter of the relation between concepts and properties—say, properties individuated according to concepts—is given in n. 29.

35. Ramsey sentences are defined in the text connected with n. 37.

36. This dialectic appears in Fodor (1982) and Burge's (1982) reply. See also Burge (1986, 1989, 1995).

37. More specifically the functional definitions work as follows. If "F_{17}" is the variable that replaced "pain," "pain" could be defined as follows: pain = the property of being an x such that $\exists F_1 \ldots \exists F_n [T(F_1 \ldots F_n, i_1 \ldots i_m, o_1 \ldots o_p)$ and x has $F_{17}]$.

38. Loar (1999*a*) extends this analysis to Chalmers's and Jackson's modal arguments. White (2006*b*), argues for a weakened version of the semantic premise and for its relevance to the Property Dualism Argument.

References

Austin, D. F. (1990) *What's the Meaning of "This"?* (Ithaca, NY: Cornell University Press).

Block, Ned (1978) "Troubles with Functionalism", *Minnesota Studies in the Philosophy of Science* 9, ed. C. W. Savage (Minneapolis: University of Minnesota Press); 261–325. Reprinted in N. Block (ed.), *Readings in Philosophy of Psychology*, Vol. 1, (Cambridge, Mass.: Harvard University Press, 1980). Reprinted (shortened version) in W. Lycan (ed.), *Mind and Cognition*, (Oxford: B. H. Blackwell, 1990), 444–69. Reprinted (shortened version) in D. M. Rosenthal (ed.), *The Nature of Mind*

(Oxford: Oxford University Press, 1991), 211–29. Reprinted (somewhat longer shortened version) in David Chalmers (ed.), *Philosophy of Mind: Classical and Contemporary Readings* (Oxford: Oxford University Press, 2002).

——— (1980) "What is Functionalism?" in *Readings in Philosophy of Psychology* (Cambridge, Mass.: Harvard University Press), 171–84.

——— (1991) "What Narrow Content is Not", in B. Loewer and G. Rey (eds.), *Meaning and Mind: Fodor and his Critics* (Oxford: Blackwell).

——— (1992) "Begging the Question Against Phenomenal Consciousness", *The Behavioral and Brain Sciences* 15/2, repr. in Block, Flanagan, and Güzeldere (1997: 177).

——— (1993) Review of Daniel Dennett, *Consciousness Explained, in The Journal of Philosophy* 90/4: 181–93.

——— (1994) "Functionalism", in S. Guttenplan (ed.), *Blackwell's Companion to Philosophy of Mind* (Oxford: Blackwell).

——— (2002) "The Harder Problem of Consciousness", *Journal of Philosophy* 49/8 (August), 1–35. A longer version is in *Disputatio* 15 (November 2003).

——— (2003) "Do Causal Powers Drain Away?" *Philosophy and Phenomenological Research* 67/1 (July 2003), 110–27.

——— and Dworkin, G. (1974) "IQ, Heritability and Inequality. Part I", *Philosophy and Public Affairs* 3/4: 331–409.

——— and Stalnaker, Robert (1999) "Conceptual Analysis, Dualism and the Explanatory Gap", *Philosophical Review* 108 (January), 1–46.

——— and Flanagan, O., G. Güzeldere, G. (1997) *The Nature of Consciousness: Philosophical Debates* (Cambridge, Mass.: MIT).

Boyd, Richard (1980) "Materialism without Reductionism: What Physicalism Does Not Entail", in Block (1980: 67–106).

Burge, Tyler (1977) "Belief *De Re*", *Journal of Philosophy* 74/6: 338–62.

——— (1982) "Two Thought Experiments Reviewed," *Notre Dame Journal of Formal Logic* 23: 284–93.

——— (1986) "Individualism and Psychology", *Philosophical Review* 95: 3–45.

——— (1989) "Individuation and Causation in Psychology", *Pacific Philosophical Quarterly* 707: 303–22.

——— (1995) "Intentional Properties and Causation", in C. Macdonald and G. Macdonald (eds.), *Philosophy of Psychology: Debates about Psychological Explanation* (Oxford: Blackwell).

Byrne, Alex, and Pryor, James (2006) "Bad Intensions", in Manuel Garcia-Carpintero and Josep Macia (eds.), *The Two-Dimensionalist Framework: Foundations and Applications.*

Chalmers, David (1996) *The Conscious Mind* (New York: Oxford University Press).

——— (2003) "The Content and Epistemology of Phenomenal Belief", in A Jokic and Q. Smith (eds.), *Consciousness—New Philosophical Perspectives* (Oxford: Oxford University Press).

——— (2004) "Phenomenal Concepts and the Knowledge Argument", in Peter Ludlow, Yujin Nagasawa, and Daniel Stoljar (eds.), *There's Something About Mary* (Cambridge, Mass.: MIT).

Chalmers, David (2006) "The Foundations of 2D Semantics", in M. Garcia-Carpintero and J. Macia (eds.), *Two-Dimensional Semantics: Foundations and Applications* (Oxford: Oxford University Press). An abridged version, "Epistemic Two-Dimensional Semantics", is in *Philosophical Studies* 118/1–2 (2004), 153–226.

Chomsky, N. (2000) *New Horizons in the Study of Language and Mind* (Cambridge: Cambridge University Press).

Davies, Martin, and Humberstone, Lloyd (1980) "Two Notions of Necessity", *Philosophical Studies* 38: 1–30.

Devitt, Michael (1981) *Designation* (New York: Columbia University Press).

Feigl, Herbert (1958, 1967) *The "Mental" and the "Physical": The Essay and a Postscript* (Minneapolis: University of Minnesota Press). Originally published in 1958 in *Minnesota Studies in the Philosophy of Science*.

Field, Hartry (1994) "Deflationist Views of Meaning and Content", *Mind* 103: 249–285.

Fodor, Jerry (1982) "Cognitive Science and the Twin-Earth Problem", *Notre Dame Journal of Formal Logic* 23: 98–119.

Hempel, Carl G. (1969) "Reduction: Ontological and Linguistic Facets", in S. Morgenbesser, P. Suppes, and M. White (eds.), *Philosophy, Science, and Method: Essays in Honor of Ernest Nagel* (New York: St Martin's Press), 179–99.

Hill, Christopher (1991) *Sensations: A Defense of Type Materialism* (New York: Cambridge University Press), 98–101.

——— (1997) "Imaginability, Conceivability, Possibility and the Mind-Body Problem", *Philosophical Studies* 87.

Horgan, Terrence (1984) "Jackson on Physical Information", *Philosophical Quarterly* 34: 147–83.

——— and Tienson, John (2001) "Deconstructing New Wave Materialism," in Carl Gillett and Barry Loewer (eds.), *Physicalism and Its Discontents* (New York: Cambridge University Press).

Horwich, Paul (1990, 1998) *Truth* (Oxford: Blackwell. Second edn. 1998 (Oxford: Oxford University Press).

Jackson, Frank (1982) "Epiphenomenal Qualia", *American Philosophical Quarterly* 32: 127–36.

——— (1986) "What Mary Didn't Know", *Journal of Philosophy* 83: 291–5.

—— (1998) *From Metaphysics to Ethics: A Defense of Conceptual Analysis* (Oxford: Oxford University Press).

—— (2004) Review of Perry (2001) in *Mind* 113/449 (January), 207–10.

Katz, Jerrold (1972) *Semantic Theory* (New York: Harper & Row).

—— (1975) "Logic and Language: An Examination of Recent Criticisms of Intentionalism", in *Minnesota Studies in the Philosophy of Science* 7, ed. K. Gunderson (Minneapolis: University of Minnesota Press).

Kripke, Saul (1980) *Naming and Necessity* (Cambridge, Mass.: Harvard University Press).

Levine, Joseph (1993) "On Leaving Out What It's Like", in M. Davies and G. Humphreys (eds.), *Consciousness* (Oxford: Blackwell), 137–49. Reprinted in Block, Flanagan, and Güzeldere (1997: 543–55).

—— (2001) *Purple Haze: The Puzzle of Consciousness* (Oxford: Oxford University Press).

Lewis, David (1980) "Mad Pain and Martian Pain", in N. Block (ed.), *Readings in the Philosophy of Psychology* (Cambridge, Mass.: Harvard University Press), 216–22.

—— (1988) "What Experience Teaches", *Proceedings of the Russellian Society*, Sydney, Australia. Reprinted in Lycan 1990*a*.

—— (1990) "What Experience Teaches", in Lycan (1990*a*).

Loar, B. (1988) "Social Content and Psychological Content", in R. Grimm and P. Merrill (eds.), *Contents of Thoughts* (Tucson: University of Arizona Press).

—— (1990) "Phenomenal states", in J. Tomberlin (ed.), *Philosophical Perspectives*, iv. *Action Theory* (Northridge, Calif.: Ridgeview).

—— (1997) *Phenomenal states* (2nd version), in Block, Flanagan, and Güzeldere (eds.).

—— (1999*a*) "David Chalmers' *The Conscious Mind*". *Philosophy and Phenomenological Research* 59: 464–71.

—— (2000) "Should the Explanatory Gap Perplex Us?", in T. Rockmore (ed.), *Proceedings of the Twentieth World Congress of Philosophy* (Charlottesville, Va.: Philosophy Documentation Center), ii. 99–104.

McGinn, Colin (2001) "How Not to Solve the Mind-Body Problem", in Carl Gillett and Barry Loewer (eds.), *Physicalism and Its Discontents* (New York: Cambridge University Press).

McKinsey, Michael (1991) "Anti-individualism and Privileged Access", *Analysis* 51: 9–16.

Montero, Barbara (1999) "The Body Problem", *Nous* 33/3: 183–200.

Nagel, Thomas (2002) "The Psychophysical Nexus", *Concealment and Exposure and Other Essays* (New York, Oxford University Press, 2002), ch. 18. An earlier version appeared in Paul Boghossian and Christopher Peacocke (eds.), *New Essays on the A Priori* (Oxford, Clarendon 2000).

Nemirow, L. (1980) Review of Thomas Nagel, Mortal Questions. *Philosophical Review* 89/3: 473–7.

Papineau, David (2002) *Thinking about Consciousness* (Oxford: Oxford University Press).

Perry, John (1979) "The Problem of the Essential Indexical", *Nous* 13/1.

——— (2001) *Knowledge, Possibility and Consciousness* (Cambridge Mass.: MIT).

Perry, John (2004*a*) "Précis of *Knowledge, Possibility and Consciousness*", *Philosophy and Phenomenological Research* 68/1 (January), 172–82.

——— (2004*b*) Replies, *Philosophy and Phenomenological Research* 68/1 (January), 207–29.

Putnam, Hilary (1970) "Is Semantics Possible?", in H. Kiefer and M. Munitz (eds.), *Language, Belief, and Metaphysics* (Albany, NY: State University of New York Press), 50–63. Reprinted in Putnam, *Mind, Language and Reality* (Cambridge: Cambridge University Press), 139–52.

——— (1975) "The Meaning of 'Meaning'", in K. Gunderson (ed.), *Language, Mind, and Knowledge* (Minneapolis: University of Minnesota Press).

Rozemond, Marleen (1998) *Descartes's Dualism* (Cambridge Mass.: Harvard University Press).

Schaffer, Jerome (1963) "Mental Events and the Brain", *The Journal of Philosophy* 60/6: 160–6.

Schiffer, Stephen (1990) "The Mode-of-Presentation Problem", in C. A. Anderson and J. Owens (eds.), *Propositional Attitudes* (Stanford: CSLI), 249–68.

Smart, J. J. C. (1959) "Sensations and Brain Processes", *Philosophical Review* 68: 141–56.

Stoljar, Daniel (2001) "Physicalism", *The Stanford Encyclopedia of Philosophy* (Spring) ed. Edward N. Zalta, ⟨http://plato.stanford.edu/archives/spr2001/entries/physicalism/⟩, accessed 4 July 2005.

Sturgeon, Scott (1994) "The Epistemic View of Subjectivity", *Journal of Philosophy* 91/5.

van Gulick, Robert (1993) "Understanding the Phenomenal Mind: Are We All Just Armadillos?" in M. Davies and G. Humphrey (eds.), *Consciousness* (Oxford: Blackwell).

——— (2006) "Jackson's Change of Mind: Representationalism, *A Priorism* and the Knowledge Argument", in Ian Ravenscroft.

White, Stephen (1986) "The Curse of the Qualia", in Block, Flanagan, and Güzeldere, 695–718.

——— (2006*a*) "A Posteriori Identities and the Requirements of Rationality", in Dean Zimmerman (ed.), *Oxford Studies in Metaphysics, Volume 2* (Oxford: Oxford University Press).

——— (2006*b*) "Property Dualism, Phenomenal Concepts, and the Semantic Premise", in T. Alter and S. Walter (eds.), *Phenomenal Concepts and Phenomenal Knowledge: New Essays on Consciousness and Physicalism.*

Wiser, M., and Carey, S. (1983) "When Heat and Temperature Were One", in D. Gentner and A. Stevens (eds.), *Mental Models* (Hillsdale, NJ: Lawrence Erlbaum).

V Consciousness and Representation

Qualia include the ways things look, sound and smell, the way it feels to have a pain; more generally, what it's like to have mental states. Qualia are experiential properties of sensations, feelings, perceptions and, in my view, thoughts and desires as well. But, so defined, who could deny that qualia exist? Yet, the existence of qualia is controversial. Here is what is controversial: whether qualia, so defined, can be characterized in intentional, functional or purely cognitive terms. Opponents of qualia think that the content of experience is intentional content (like the content of thought), or that experiences are functionally definable, or that to have a qualitative state is to have a state that is monitored in a certain way or accompanied by a thought to the effect that I have that state. If we include the idea that experiential properties are not intentional or functional or purely cognitive in the definition of "qualia," then it is controversial whether there are qualia.

This definition of "qualia" is controversial in a respect familiar in philosophy. A technical term is often a locus of disagreement, and the warring parties will often disagree about what the important parameters of disagreement are. Dennett, for example, has supposed in some of his writings that it is of the essence of qualia to be nonrelational, incorrigible (to believe one has one is to have one) and to have no scientific nature (see Flanagan, 1992, 61). This is what you get when you let an opponent of qualia define the term. A proponent of qualia ought to allow that categorizations of them (beliefs about them) can be mistaken, and that science can investigate qualia. I think that we ought to allow that qualia might be physiological states, and that their scientific nature might even turn out to be relational. Friends of qualia differ on whether or not they are physical. In my view, the most powerful arguments in favor of qualia actually presuppose a physicalistic doctrine, the supervenience of qualia on the brain. (See Horgan 1994.)

Perhaps the most puzzling thing about qualia is how they relate to the physical world. Sometimes this is put in terms of the explanatory gap, the idea that nothing we know or can conceive of knowing about the brain can explain why qualia feel the way they do. The explanatory gap is closely related to the thought experiments that dominate the literature on qualia.

The Knowledge Argument

One of these thought experiments is the case of Jackson's (1986) Mary, who is raised in a black and white environment in which she learns all the functional and physical facts about color vision. Nonetheless, when she ventures outside for the first time, she learns a new fact: what it is like to see red. So, the argument goes, what it is like to see red cannot be a functional or physical fact. Dennett (1991) objects that perhaps she could have figured out which things are red, but that is beside the point for two reasons. The question is does she know what it is like to see red, not which things are red. And does she know it simply in virtue of knowing all the functional and physical facts about color vision, whether or not she is clever enough to figure it out on the basis of what she knows.

Lewis (1994) denies that Mary acquires any new knowledge-that, insisting that she only acquires knowledge-how, abilities to imagine and recognize. But as Loar points out, the knowledge she acquires can appear in embedded contexts. For example, she may reason that if this is what it is like to see red, then this is similar to what it is like to see orange. Lewis's ability analysis of Mary's knowledge has the same problem here that noncognitive analyses of ethical language have in explaining the logical behavior of ethical predicates.

Here is a different (and in my view more successful) objection to Jackson (Horgan 1984b; Peacocke 1989; Loar 1990; Papineau 1993; van Gulick 1993): What Mary acquires when she sees red is a new phenomenal concept, a recognitional disposition that allows her to pick out a certain type of phenomenal feel. This new phenomenal concept is a constituent of genuinely new knowledge—knowledge of what it is like to see red. But the new phenomenal concept picks out old properties, properties picked out by physical or functional concepts that she already had. So the new knowledge is just a new way of knowing old facts. Before leaving the room, she knew what it is like to see red in a third-person way; after leaving the room, she acquires a new way of knowing the same fact. If so, what she acquires does not rule out any possible worlds that were not already ruled out by the facts that she already knew, and the thought experiment poses no danger to physicalistic doctrines. Incidentally, the recognitional disposition account indicates how qualia could turn out to be relational; perhaps the recognitional disposition picks out a relational physical state of the brain or even a functional state. But see the criticism of Loar in Block 1994.)

Absent Qualia

Another familiar conundrum is the absent qualia hypothesis. If human beings can be described computationally, as is assumed by the research program of cognitive science, a robot could in principle be built that was computationally identical to a human. But would there be anything it was like to be that robot? Would it have qualia? (See Shoemaker 1975, 1981; White 1986.) Some thought experiments have appealed to oddball realizations of our functional organization—for example, by the economy of a country. If an economy can share our functional organization, then our functional organization cannot be sufficient for qualia. Many critics simply bite the bullet at this point, saying that the oddball realizations do have qualia. Lycan (1987) responds by making two additions to functionalism as spelled out in Block 1994. The additions are designed to rule out oddball realizations of our functional organization of the ilk of the aforementioned economy. He suggests thinking of the functional roles in teleological terms and thinking of these roles as involving the details of human physiology. Economies don't have the states with the right sort of evolutionary "purpose", and their states are not physiological. On the first move, see Block 1994. On the second, note that including physiology in our functional definitions of mental states will make them so specific to humans that they won't apply to other creatures that have mental states. Further, this idea violates the spirit of the functionalist proposal, which, being based on the computer analogy, abstracts from hardware realization. Functionalism without multiple hardware realizations is functionalism in name only.

The Inverted Spectrum

One familiar conundrum that uses a physicalistic idea of qualia against functionalist and intentionalist ideas is the famous inverted spectrum hypothesis, the hypothesis that things we both call "red" look to you the way things we both call "green" look to me, even though we are functionally (and therefore behaviorally) identical. A first step in motivating the inverted spectrum hypothesis is the possibility that the brain state that I have when I see red things is the same as the brain state that you have when you see green things, and conversely. (Nida-Rümelin 1996, presents evidence that this is a naturally occurring phenomenon.) Therefore, it might be said, our experiences are inverted. What is assumed here is a supervenience doctrine, that the qualitative content of a state supervenes on physiological properties of the brain.

There is a natural functionalist reply. Notice that it is not possible that the brain state that I get when I see things we both call "red" is exactly the same as the brain state that you get when you see things we both call "green." At least, the total brain states can't be the same, since mine causes me to say "It's red," and to classify what I'm seeing as the same color as blood and fire hydrants, whereas yours causes you to say "It's green," and to classify what you are seeing with grass and Granny Smith apples. Suppose that the brain state that I get when I see red and that you get when you see green is X-oscillations in area V4, whereas what I get when I see green and you get when you see red are Y oscillations in area V4. The functionalist says that phenomenal properties should not be identified with brain states quite so "localized" as X-oscillations or

Y-oscillations, but rather with more holistic brain states that include tendencies to classify objects together as the same color. Thus the functionalist will want to say that my holistic brain state that includes X-oscillations and your holistic brain state that includes Y-oscillations are just alternative realizations of the same experiential state (Harman 1990). So the fact that red things give me X-oscillations but they give you Y-oscillations does not show that our experiences are inverted. The defender of the claim that inverted spectra are possible can point out that when something looks red to me, I get X-oscillations, whereas when something looks green to me, I get Y-oscillations, and so the difference in the phenomenal aspect of experience corresponds to a local brain state difference. But the functionalist can parry by pointing out that this difference has only been demonstrated intrapersonally, keeping the larger brain state that specifies the roles of X-oscillations in classifying things constant. He can insist on typing brain states for interpersonal comparisons holistically. And most friends of the inverted spectrum are in a poor position to insist on typing experiential states locally rather than holistically, given that they normally emphasize the "explanatory gap," the fact that there is nothing known about the brain that can adequately explain the facts of experience. (See Horgan 1994.) So the friend of the inverted spectrum is in no position to insist on local physiological individuation of qualia. At this stage, the defender of the inverted spectrum is stymied.

One move the defender of the possibility of the inverted spectrum can make is to move to an intra-personal inverted spectrum example. Think of this as a four stage process. (1) You have normal color vision. (2) You have color inverting devices inserted in your retinas or in the lateral geniculate nucleus, the first way-station behind the retina, and red things look the way green things used to look, blue things look the way yellow things used to look, etc. (3) You have adapted, so that you naturally and spontaneously call red things "red," etc., but when reminded, you recall the days long ago when ripe tomatoes looked to you, colorwise, the way Granny Smith apples do now. (4) You get amnesia about the days before the lenses were inserted. Stage 1 is functionally equivalent to Stage 4 in the relevant respects, but they are arguably qualia-inverted. So we have an inverted spectrum over time. The advantages of this thought experiment are two. First, the argument profits from the force of the subject's testimony at stages 2 and 3 for qualia inversion. Second, the four-stage setup forces the opponents say what stage is the one where my description goes wrong. (See Shoemaker 1981; Block 1990.) Rey (1993) attacks (3), Dennett (1991) attacks (2) and (3), and White (1993) attacks (4). In my view, the most vulnerable stage is (3) because the functionalist can raise doubts about whether what its like to see red things *could* remain the same during the changes in responses that have to go on in the process of adaptation.

Why, an opponent might ask, is the inverted qualia argument against functionalism any more powerful than the inverted qualia argument against physicalism? After all, it might be said, one can imagine particle for particle duplicates who have spectra that are inverted with respect to one another. But though physical duplicates with inverted spectra may be imaginable, they are ruled out by a highly plausible principle that any materialist should accept: that qualia supervene on physical constitution. The thought experiments that I have been going through argue that even materialists should accept the possiblity of an inverted spectrum, and further, that for all we know, such cases are feasible via robotics or genetic engineering or even actual. And in so doing, they make the case for conceptual possibility stronger, for one is surer that something is genuinely conceptually possible if one can see how one might go about making it actual.

Inverted Earth

An interesting variant of the inverted spectrum thought experiment is Inverted Earth (Block 1990). Inverted Earth is a planet that differs from Earth in two relevant ways. First, everything is the complementary color of the corresponding earth object. The sky is yellow, the grass-like stuff is red, etc. (To avoid impossibility, we could imagine, instead, two people raised in rooms in which everything in one room is the complementary color of the corresponding item in the other room.) Second, people on Inverted Earth speak an inverted language. They use "red" to mean green, "blue" to mean yellow, etc. If you order paint from Inverted Earth, and you want yellow paint, you fax an order for "blue paint." The effect of both inversions is that if you are drugged and kidnapped in the middle of the night, and inverters are inserted behind your eyes (and your body pigments are changed), you will notice no difference if you are placed in the bed of your counterpart on Inverted Earth. (Let's assume that the victim does not know anything about the science of color.)

Now consider the comparison between you and your counterpart on Inverted Earth. The counterpart could be your identical twin who was fitted with inverting lenses at birth and put up for adoption on Inverted Earth, or the counterpart could be you after you have been switched with your twin and have been living there for a long while. Looking at blue things give you Z-oscillations in the brain, yellow things give you W-oscillations; your twin gets the opposite. Now notice the interesting difference between this twin case and the one mentioned earlier: there can be perfect inversion in the *holistic* brain states as well as the local ones. At this moment, you both are looking at your respective skies. You get Z-oscillations because your sky is blue, he gets Z-oscillations because his sky is yellow. Your Z-oscillations make you say "How blue!", and his Z-oscillations make him say "How blue!" too. Indeed, we can take your brains to be molecular duplicates of one another. Then the principle of the supervenience of qualia on holistic brain state dictates that experientially, at the moment of looking at the skies, you and your twin have the same qualia.

But though you and your twin have the same qualia, you are functionally and intentionally inverted. If you are asked to match the color of the sky with a Munsell color chip, you will pick a blue one, but if your twin is shown the same (earth-made) Munsell chips, he will pick a yellow one. Further, when he says "How blue!" he *means* "How yellow!" Recall that the Inverted Earth dialect, of which he is a loyal member, has color words whose meanings are inverted with respect to ours. You and your twin are at that moment functionally and intentionally inverted, but qualitatively identical. So we have the converse of the inverted spectrum. And there is no problem about local vs. holistic brain states as in the intersubjective inverted spectrum; and no problem about whether qualia could persist unchanged through adaptation as in the intrasubjective inverted spectrum.

The argument that you and your twin are qualitatively the same can work either of two ways. We can assume the principle of supervenience of qualia on the brain, building the brain identity of the twins into the story. Or we can run the story in terms of you being kidnapped, drugged, and placed in your twin's niche on Inverted Earth. What justifies the idea that your qualia are the same is that you notice no difference when you wake up in your Twin's bed after the switch; not appeal to supervenience is required.

Notice that the functional differences between these qualia-identical twins are long-arm functional differences (see Block 1994) and the intentional differences are external intentional differences. Perhaps, you might say, the twins are not inverted in short-arm functional roles and narrow intentional content. The cure for this idea is to ask the question of what the purely internal functional or intentional differences could be that would define the difference between an experience as of red and an experience as of green. The natural answer would be to appeal to the internal aspects of beliefs and desires. We believe, for example, that blood is red but not that it is green. However, someone could have color experience despite having no standing beliefs or desires that differentiated colors. Imagine a person raised in a room where the color of everything is controlled by a computer, and nothing retains its color for more than 10 seconds. Or imagine a person whose color perception is normal but who has forgotten all color facts.

There is no shortage of objections to these lines of reasoning. I will very briefly mention two closely related objections. It has been objected (Hardin 1988) that red is intrinsically warm, whereas green is intrinsically cool, and thus inversion will either violate functional identity or yield an incoherent cool-red state. (Note, incidentally, that this is not an objection to the inverted earth thought experiment, since that is a case of qualitative identity and functional *difference*—no functional identity is involved.) But the natural reply (Block 1990) is that warm and cool can be inverted too. So long as there is no intrinsic connection between color qualia and behavior, the inverted spectrum is safe. But is there such an intrinsic connection? Dennett (1991) says there is. Blue calms, red excites. But perhaps this is due to culture and experience; perhaps people with very different cultures and experiences would have color experiences without this asymmetry. The research on this topic is equivocal; Dennett's sole reference, Humphrey (1992), describes it as "relatively second-rate," and that is also my impression. The fact that we do not know is itself interesting, however, for what it shows is that this asymmetry is no part of our color concepts. As Shoemaker (1981) points out, even if human color experience is genetically asymmetrical, there could nonetheless be people much like us whose color experience is not asymmetrical. So an inversion of the sort mentioned in the thought experiments is conceptually possible, even if it is not possible for the human species. But then color inversion may be possible for a closely related species whose color qualia are not in doubt, one which could perhaps be produced by genetic engineering. Functionalism would not be a very palatable doctrine if it were said to apply to some people's color experiences but not to others.

The Explanatory Gap Again

At the outset, I mentioned the "explanatory gap," the idea that nothing now known about the brain, nor anything anyone has been able to imagine finding out would explain qualia. We can distinguish inflationary and deflationary attitudes towards this gap among those who agree that the gap is unclosable. McGinn (1991) argues that the gap is unclosable because the fundamental nature of consciousness is inaccessible to us, though it might be accessible to creatures with very different sorts of minds. But a number of authors have favored a deflationary approach, arguing that the unclosability of the explanatory gap has to do with our concepts, not with nature itself. Horgan (1984), Levine (1993), Jackson (1993), as well as Chalmers (1993) (and interestingly, McGinn (1991) too) have contributed to working out the idea that reductive explanation in science depends on a priori analyses of the phenomena to be explained, usually in functional terms. (A version of this point was made in Nagel 1974.) Consider Chalmers's example of the reductive explanation of life. Life can be roughly analyzed in terms of such general notions as metabolism and adaptation, or perhaps more specific notions such as digestion, reproduction and locomotion, and these concepts can themselves be given a functional analysis. Once we have explained these functions, suppose someone says "Oh yes, I see the explanation of those functions, but what about explaining *life*?" We can answer that, a priori, to explain these functions *is* to explain life itself.

In some cases, the a priori analysis of the item to be explained is more complicated. Consider water. We cannot give an a priori analysis of water as the colorless, odorless liquid in rivers and lakes called "water," because water might not have been colorless, it might have been called "glue," there might not have been lakes, etc. But we can formulate an a priori reference fixing definition of the sort that Kripke has emphasized: water = R(the colorless, odorless liquid in rivers and lakes called "water"), where the

"R" is a rigidification operator that turns a definite description into a rigid designator. (A rigid designator picks out the same thing in all possible worlds in which the thing exists; for example, "Aristotle" is rigid. To rigidify a definite description is to treat it as a name for whatever the definite description *actually* picks out.) Thus, suppose we want to explain the fact that water dissolves salt It suffices to explain that H_2O dissolves salt and that H_2O is the colorless, odorless liquid in rivers and lakes called "water." If someone objects that we have only explained how something colorless, odorless, etc. dissolves salt, not that water does, we can point out that it is a priori that water is the actual colorless, odorless, etc. substance. And if someone objects that we have only explained how H_2O dissolves salt, not how water does, we can answer that from the fact that H_2O is the colorless, odorless, etc. stuff and that, a priori, water is the (actual) colorless, odorless, etc., stuff, we can derive that water *is* H_2O.

The upshot is that closing the explanatory gap requires an a priori functional analysis of qualia. If Kripke (1980) is right that we pick out qualia by their qualitative character and not by their functional role, then no a priori reference fixing definition can be given for qualitative concepts of the sort that can be given for "water" and "life." (Of course, if there is a true functional analysis that picks out a quale, it can be rigidified, but it still will not be an a priori characterization. Pain = R(Aunt Irma's favorite sensation) can be true and necessary without being a priori. And if the arguments about qualia inversion just sketched are right, there is no a priori conceptual analysis of qualitative concepts either, and so the explanatory gap is unclosable. As Chalmers points out, with a physical or a functional account, we can explain the functions associated with qualia, the capacity to classify things as red, for example. But once we have explained these functions, there will be a further question: why are these functions accompanied by qualia? Such a further question does not arise in the case of life and water precisely because of the availability of an a priori functional analysis.

It would be natural to suppose that the explanatory gap derives from the fact that neuroscientists have not yet come up with the required concepts to explain qualia. Nagel (1974) gives an analogy that suggests this idea. We are in the situation, he suggests, of a caveman who is told that matter is energy. But he does not have the concepts to appreciate how this could be so. These concepts, however, are ones that some of us do have now, and it is a natural thought that a few hundred years from now, the concepts might be available to explain qualia physically. But the deflationary account of reductive explanation denies this, blaming the explanatory gap on our ordinary concepts, not on science.

Note

Reprinted from S. Guttenplan, ed., *Blackwell's Companion to Philosophy of Mind* (Oxford: Blackwell, 1994).

References

Block, N. 1990. Inverted earth. In J. Tomberlin, ed., *Philosophical Perspectives 4*. Atascadero: Ridgeview.

Block, N. 1994. *Functionalism*. In Guttenplan 1994, 323–332.

Chalmers, D. J. 1993. *Toward a Theory of Consciousness*. University of Indiana doctoral dissertation.

Davies, M., and Humphreys, G., eds. 1993. *Consciousness*. Oxford: Blackwell.

Dennett, D. 1988. Quining qualia. In A. Marcel and E. Bisiach, eds., *Consciousness in Contemporary Society*. Oxford: Oxford University Press.

Dennett, D. 1991. *Consciousness Explained*. New York: Little, Brown.

Flanagan, O. 1992. *Consciousness Reconsidered*. Cambridge, MA: MIT Press.

Guttenplan, S. 1994. *Blackwell's Companion to Philosophy of Mind*. Oxford: Blackwell.

Hardin, C. 1988. *Color for Philosophers*. Indianapolis: Hackett.

Harman, G. 1990. The intrinsic quality of experience. In J. Tomberlin, ed., *Philosophical Perspectives 4*. Atascadero: Ridgeview.

Horgan, T. 1984a. Supervenience and cosmic hermeneutics. *Southern Journal of Philosophy Supplement* 22: 19–38.

Horgan, T. 1984b. Jackson on physical information and qualia. *Philosophical Quarterly* 34: 147–152.

Horgan, T. 1994. *Physicalism*. In Guttenplan 1994, 471–479.

Jackson, F. 1986. What Mary didn't know. *Journal of Philosophy* 83: 291–295.

Jackson, F. 1993. Armchair metaphysics. In J. O'Leary-Hawthorne and M. Michael, eds., *Philosophy in Mind*. Dordrecht: Kluwer.

Kripke, S. 1980. *Naming and Necessity*. Cambridge, MA: Harvard University Press.

Levine, J. 1993. On leaving out what it is like. In M. Davies and G. Humphreys, eds., *Consciousness*. Oxford: Blackwell.

Lewis, D. 1994. Reduction of mind. In Guttenplan 1994, 412–431.

Loar, B. 1990. Phenomenal properties. In J. Tomberlin, ed., *Philosophical Perspectives: Action Theory and Philosophy of Mind*. Atascadero: Ridgeview.

Lycan, W. 1987. *Consciousness*. Cambridge, MA: MIT Press.

McGinn, C. 1991. *The Problem of Consciousness*. Oxford: Blackwell.

Nida-Rümelin, M. 1996. Pseudonormal vision: An actual case of qualia inversion? *Philosophical Studies* 82: 145–157.

Papineau, D. 1993. Physicalism, consciousness and the antipathetic fallacy. *Australasian Journal of Philosophy* 71(2): 169–184.

Peacocke, C. 1989. No resting place: A critical notice of The View from Nowhere. *Philosophical Review* 98: 65–82.

Rey, G. 1993. Sensational sentences switched. *Philosophical Studies* 70(1): 73–103.

Shoemaker, S. 1975. Functionalism and qualia. *Philosophical Studies* 27: 291–315.

Shoemaker, S. 1981. Absent qualia are impossible—a reply to Block. *Philosophical Review* 90(4): 581–599.

Van Gulick, R. 1993. Understanding the phenomenal mind: Are we all just armadillos? In M. Davies and G. Humphreys, eds., *Consciousness*. Oxford: Blackwell.

White, Stephen L. 1986. Curse of the qualia. *Synthese* 68: 333–368.

White, Stephen L. 1993. Color and the narrow contents of experience. Paper delivered at the Eastern Division meeting of the American Philosophical Association.

23 Inverted Earth

The Fallacy of Intentionalizing Qualia

To a first approximation, the inverted spectrum hypothesis is that things we agree are red look to you the way things we agree are green look to me (and we are functionally identical). There is a simple argument from the possibility of an inverted spectrum to the falsity of functionalism: if two different mental states can play exactly the same functional role, then there is an aspect of mentality (the "qualitative" aspect) that eludes characterization in terms of functional role. In terms of the machine version of functionalism: even if we are computers, if nonetheless you and I could be computationally exactly alike though mentally different (in what it is like to see something red), then the mental outruns the computational.

The "containment response"[1] to the inverted spectrum would be to give up on functionalism as a theory of experience (or at least of its qualitative aspect), retaining functionalism as a theory of the cognitive aspect of the mind. I favor this approach, but I will not pursue it here. This chapter is directed against the thoroughgoing functionalist who insists on functionalism as a theory of the whole of the mind.[2] The drawback of the containment response is that it arguably commits its proponents to the possibility of a "zombie," a being that is like us in cognitive states but totally lacking in qualia.[3]

I gave a first approximation to the inverted spectrum hypothesis above. But a proper statement of it must make use of a distinction between two kinds of content of experience, one of which is a matter of the way the experience represents the world, the other of which is a matter of "what it is like" (in Tom Nagel's phrase) to have it. The former has been called intentional or representational content; the latter, qualitative or sensational content.[4] In terms of this distinction, the inverted spectrum hypothesis is this: when you and I have experiences that have the intentional content *looking red*, your qualitative content is the same as the qualitative content that I have when my experience has the intentional content *looking green* (and we are functionally identical). This chapter will be concerned with this rather dramatic version of the claim that there is a gap between intentional and qualitative contents of experience. But the emphasis here and in the literature on this dramatic case should not make us forget that if the functionalist theory of qualia were correct, it would also preclude less systematic qualitative differences among functionally identical people, differences the hypothesizing of which though hard to work out in detail is also less vulnerable to the abuse that has been heaped on the inverted spectrum hypothesis.

If blood looks red to both of us, then in the *intentional* sense of "looks the same," blood looks the same to us. (In respect of color, that is. I will leave out this qualification from now on, and I will also ignore the fact of different shades of red for simplicity.) The *qualitative* sense of 'looks the same' can be defined via appeal to such notions as "what it's like," or alternatively, by direct appeal to the inverted spectrum hypothesis itself. If your spectrum is inverted with respect to mine, then red things look the same to you—in the qualitative sense—as green things look to me.

As Shoemaker points out, it is easy to go from these senses of 'looks' to kinds of content. If blood looks the same to us in the intentional sense, then the intentional contents of our experiences of it are the same. If blood looks the same to you in the qualitative sense as grass looks to me, then the qualitative contents of our experiences are the same.[5]

Now that the intentional/qualitative distinction has been introduced I can correct a vital error made by both sides of the inverted spectrum debate. My point is that if an inverted spectrum is possible, then experiential contents *that can be expressed in public language* (for example, *looking red*) are not qualitative contents, but rather intentional contents. *For suppose that spectrum inversion is rife*: there is no spectrum of the vast majority, despite widespread functional similarity in relevant respects. How could I justify the claim that red things look red to me but not to you? How could I claim that the qualitative content of my experience as of red things is *looking red*, whereas yours is, say, *looking blue*? Any argument I could use against you could equally well be used by you against me. And it will not do to say we are both right, each with our own sense of 'red'. 'Red' is a public language word, not a word that means one thing in your mouth and another thing in mine.

Since I will be appealing to this point later it will be useful to have a name for it. I will tendentiously describe the supposition that experiential contents that can be expressed in public language such as *looking red* are qualitative contents as the fallacy of intentionalizing qualia.[6]

Note that the intentional contents of color experience must be referentially based— these contents are "Californian," not neo-Fregean. The reason is that "modes of presentation" of color experiences are qualitative contents, and qualitative contents are precisely that in which our experiences as of red things—our contents of *looking red*— can differ. What gives an experience the content of *looking red* is its relation to red things, not its qualitative content. One way to put the point would be that each of us may have our own "concept" of the look of red, where a concept is a qualitative content, but such differences in "concept" of red need make no difference to whether something looks red to us. Whether something looks red to us depends on whether we are having an experience as of something red, not on our different "concepts" of red. (Recall that I am ignoring the fact of different shades of a single color.)[7]

I want to note two points about the argument against intentionalizing qualia. First, the argument is not really directed against qualia skeptics like Harman and Dennett, since they don't accept the inverted spectrum premise. Also, they already believe the conclusion on one formulation of it, namely that *looking red* is an intentional content.[8] The second point is that although I hope qualia realists are convinced. I do not intend to go into the matter in much detail here. I mentioned above that the point could be avoided by supposing that 'red' and hence 'looking red' is ambiguous, being privately defined by each of us in terms of his own qualitative content. I scoffed, saying that "red" is a univocal public language word. But of course the matter need not end here. And there are other more sophisticated ploys the determined defender of a qualitative definition of 'red' might make. I will not pursue the matter because since this paper is directed against the qualia skeptics, a rear-guard action against other members of my team would not be good strategy. Qualia realists who are tempted to intentionalize qualia should note the power of the view that *looking red* is an intentional content in defending qualia realism in the face of the functionalist challenge.

One route to the fallacy of intentionalizing qualia among qualia realists is to define secondary quality terms in terms of the qualitative contents of the experiences they normally produce, a view shared (despite many differences of opinion) by McGinn (op. cit.) and Peacocke (op. cit.). Peacock defines 'red''' as the name he gives to "the" quale produced by red things. Since the semantic content of "looks red" is given by that of 'looks' and 'red', and 'red' is linked definitionally to 'red''', the meaning of 'looks red' can be given in terms of 'red'''. Such a view would not be very attractive if there is no "the" quale produced by red things.

McGinn considers the possibility that things to which we and Martians both apply 'red' look to us the way things we and the Martians agree are 'green' look to them. Though he remains agnostic on whether such Martians could be totally functionally identical to us (and thus agnostic on the possibility of an inverted spectrum), he concludes that in such a case, things that are red relative to us (e.g., ripe tomatoes) are green relative to them, even though both groups apply 'red' to things that are the color of ripe tomatoes. Thus, according to McGinn, the Martians might have always spoken a language in which 'red' is applied to things just as we apply it, but nonetheless they mean green by it. But if we are willing to consider such a possibility, why not consider the possibility that those of us with short ear lobes bear a relation to those of us with long ear lobes that McGinn's Earthians bear to McGinn's Martians? This is not as absurd as might appear, given that there are enormous differences among normal people in the physiological machinery of color vision (see Hardin, op. cit.). Why should we try to define 'red' in terms of a quale that red things are supposed to produce in all of us when we don't have any good reason to believe that there is any such thing?

My argument is not based on the idea that spectrum inversion is merely possible (though not actual). I claim that we simply do not know if spectrum inversion obtains or not. Further, even if we were to find good evidence against spectrum inversion actually obtaining, there could be a race of people otherwise very like us who have color vision, color sensations, and color terms for whom spectrum inversion does obtain. Presumably, any good theory of the semantics of color terms will apply to them as well as us.[9]

A defender of a McGinn-Peacocke analysis of color in terms of qualia might wish to allow the possibility of spectrum inversion, but insist that nonetheless our color concepts preclude spectrum inversion. The reasoning might go like this: prior to general relativity, the concept of a straight line presupposed the axioms of Euclidean Geometry, along with the idea that a straight line is the shortest distance between two points, the path of a stretched string or a light ray, the path along which travel uses up the least fuel, and the like. But general relativity plus observations revealed that Euclidean straight lines were not the paths that had the other properties just listed—those properties accompanied Riemmanian straight lines—hence the generally accepted view that space is Riemmanian. The point of the story is that before the development of general relativity and alternative geometries, the unsticking of the notion of a Euclidean straight line from the cluster of other properties was precluded by our concepts—literally inconceivable, though not actually impossible. To conceive of it required a conceptual revolution.

The application of this model to spectrum inversion is this: the application of 'red' to red things, and the production by red things of the same quale in all of us, are joined by our concepts, conceptual revision being required for their unsticking. The analogy is not persuasive. In wondering whether the sunset looks to you as it does to me, I may be imagining you with an experience qualitatively like mine. In daily life, we do not usually take the possibility of spectrum inversion into account. But it would be a mistake to jump from this fact about practice to the idea that spectrum inversion is precluded by our concepts. Spectrum inversion can be understood easily by children (assuming it can be understood at all). Try it out on the next seven-year-old you encounter. Indeed, they sometimes come up with the idea themselves. (My eleven-year-old daughter offered spectrum inversion as an explanation of why people seem to have different favorite colors. Everyone has the same favorite color quale.)

My brand of qualia realism is quasi-functional. According to me, the *intentional* content of experience is functional. An experience has the intentional content of looking red if it functions in the right way—if it is caused by red things in the right circumstances, and used in thought about red things and action with respect to red things rightly.[10] The functional roles I am talking about are what I call "long-arm" roles, roles that include real things in the world as the inputs and outputs. They are to be distinguished from the "short-arm" roles that functionalists sometimes prefer, roles that stop at the skin. It is essential to the functional role that characterizes the intentional content of *looking red* that it be caused (appropriately) by red things and cause appropriate thought about and action on red things.

So this is why my brand of qualia realism is quasi-*functional*; here is why it is *quasi*-functional: the *qualitative* content of experience is *not* functionally characterizable. Two experiences can differ functionally, hence have different intentional contents, but have the same qualitative content, that is, be alike in "what it is like" to have them. Further, two experiences can be alike in function (and hence have the same intentional content), but have different qualitative contents.

So quasi-functional qualia realism is functionalist about the intentional content of experience. And it is also functionalist about the belief that blood is red, the concept of red, and the meaning of "red."[11]

But didn't I identify color "concepts" with qualitative contents earlier? Yes, and this is certainly one reasonable way to use the concept of a concept, but one can equally well individuate concepts in line with public language meanings, as Harman does. Harman says that what makes a concept the concept of red is its production in a natural and immediate way by red things, its role in thinking about and manipulating red things, in causing the subject to judge that two things are the same color, and the like. This is something about which the quasi-functional qualia realist may as well agree with Harman. So let it be common ground that possession of the concept of red is a matter of how our experiences function, not their intrinsic qualitative properties.[12]

Harman's refutation of the inverted spectrum depends on rejecting the distinction I've been talking about between qualitative and intentional content. He claims that experience has only one kind of content: intentional content. According to Harman, two experiences with the same intentional content must be the same in all mental respects. His rejection of the distinction leads him to state and refute a version of the inverted spectrum hypothesis that involves only intentional content. His version of the inverted spectrum hypothesis is: "Things that look red to one person look green to the other, things that look orange to the first person look blue to the second, and so forth," where the people referred to are functionally the same.[13] But this inverted spectrum hypothesis is made of straw. According to this straw inverted spectrum hypothesis, the experience you get on looking at red things, your experience as of red, the one that produces sincere utterances like "This is red," in the normal way—this experience might be one whose intentional content is *looking green*. But no proponent of the inverted spectrum should accept *this* inverted spectrum hypothesis. The proponent of the inverted spectrum hypothesizes inverted qualitative contents, not inverted *intentional* contents.

Perhaps misunderstanding on this matter is partly responsible for the fact that both sides of the inverted spectrum argument tend to see nothing at all in the other side. To quote Harman on the inverted spectrum from an earlier paper, "I speak of an "argument" here, although (as D. Lewis has observed in a similar context), the "argument" really comes down simply to denying the functionalist account of the content of concepts and thoughts without actually offering any reason for that denial."[14] The straw inverted spectrum hypothesis does indeed have this question-begging flavor, supposing as it does that there could be inverted intentional contents. The supposition that there could be inverted intentional contents amounts to the supposition that someone's concept of red might function as a concept of green without thereby being a concept of green. And that does just deny the functionalist account of concepts.

The Inverted Spectrum and Inverted Earth

Let us consider positive arguments for the possibility of an inverted spectrum. If the proponent of the inverted spectrum could establish that the burden of proof is on those who deny the possibility, then positive arguments would be unnecessary. But since no one has succeeded in establishing the burden of proof, the emphasis in the literature has been *epistemic*: science fiction cases which (allegedly) would be *evidence* for an inverted spectrum are produced and discussed.[15] The idea is that if there could be evidence for an inverted spectrum, then it is possible. For example, imagine genetically identical twins one of whom has had color-inverting lenses placed in its eyes at birth.[16]

Both twins are raised normally, and as adults, they both apply 'red' to red things in the normal way. But though the twins are functionally identical in the relevant respects, we may suppose that the internal physiological state that mediates between red things and "red" utterances in one is the same as the internal physiological state that mediates between green things and 'green' utterances in the other. And one can argue from this to the claim that things that they both call red look to one the way things they both call green look to the other. There is much to be said on both sides of this debate. I do not wish to enter into the argument here.

Interpersonal inverted spectrum cases such as the one just mentioned have not been taken very seriously by the opposition. They suppose (as does Harman) that there is no reason to think that the different physiological realizations of the experience of red things involves any *experiential* difference. Like any mental state, the experience of red has alternative physiological realizations, and this is held to be just a case of alternative realizations of the very same experience.

The qualia realist reply to Harman is that when we put on the inverting lenses, grass looks red, ripe strawberries green, the sky yellow, and the like. So shouldn't we suppose that the same is true of the twin who wears the inverting lenses? Here, as elsewhere in the disputes about qualia we would do well to follow Searle's (op. cit.) advice of looking to the first-person point of view. This appeal to what happens when we ourselves put on the inverting lenses suggests a version of the inverted spectrum example that involves just such a case—the *intra*personal inverted spectrum.[17]

I think it is best to treat the intrapersonal inverted spectrum as having four stages. First, we have a functionally normal person. Second, inverting lenses are placed in his eyes and he says grass looks red and blood looks green.[18] Third, after a period of confused use of color terms, he finally adapts to the point where he uses color language normally. That is, he naturally and immediately describes blood as 'red' and grass as 'green'. At the third stage, he is functionally normal except in one important respect: he recalls the period before the insertion of the lenses as a period in which "grass looked to me the way blood now looks." Fourth, he has amnesia about the period before the lenses were inserted and is functionally totally normal—just as in the first period. The crucial stage is the third. Here we have the evidence of the victim's testimony that grass used to look to him the way blood now looks. Note that as I have described it there is no use of "quale" or other technical terms in what he says—he's just talking about the way red things look and used to look as compared with green things. At this point, he is functionally abnormal precisely because he is saying such odd things. But if we are prepared to believe him, then when he gets amnesia and is functionally normal, why should we think that his qualia have reinverted?

The main advantage of the intrapersonal case over the interpersonal case is the availability of the subject's introspective report at stage 3. Suppose the subject is *you*. By hypothesis, you recall what grass used to look like, and you realize that it used to look to you the way ripe tomatoes now look. Is there anything incoherent about this? Dennett and Rey say yes. Dennett insists that your inclinations to say such things can reflect a memory malfunction, which, if it exists, could not be detected—and so the question of whether or not there is such a memory malfunction makes no sense. And Rey says that you are so confused that we cannot interpret what you say.[19] I concede that there is some justice in these complaints (though I disagree with them). After all, the adapted subject is not a normal person. Perhaps it can be shown that the hypothesis of confusion will always be more plausible than the hypothesis of spectrum inversion. Certainly if you think the distinction between intentional and qualitative content is a confusion, it will be natural to look for some way of avoiding taking the subject's memory reports at stage 3 at face value.

I believe that these criticisms can be defeated on their own terms, but instead of trying to do that here, I propose to take a different tack. I will describe a case that is the "converse" of the usual inverted spectrum case, a case of inverted *intentional* content and functional inversion combined with identical qualitative content. In the usual inverted spectrum case, we have two persons (or stages of the same person) whose experiences are functionally and intentionally the same but qualitatively inverted. I will describe a case of two persons/stages whose experiences are qualitatively the same but intentionally and functionally inverted. If I am right about this case, the distinction between the intentional and qualitative content of experience is vindicated, and the functionalist theory of qualitative content is refuted.

As with the usual inverted spectrum argument, mine hinges on a science fiction example. (The fancifulness of my example could be much reduced. For example, imagine rooms to which our subjects are confined for their whole lives instead of whole planets.) I will make use of an example of Harman's: Inverted Earth.[20] Inverted Earth differs from Earth in two respects. Firstly, everything has the complementary color of the color on Earth. The sky is yellow, grass is red, fire hydrants are green, and so forth. I mean everything *really* has these oddball colors. If you visited Inverted Earth along with a team of scientists from your university, you would all agree that on this planet, the sky is yellow, grass is red, and so forth. Secondly, the vocabulary of the residents of Inverted Earth is also inverted: If you ask what color the (yellow) sky is, they (truthfully) say "Blue!" If you ask what color the (red) grass is, they say "Green." If you brought a speaker of the Inverted Earth dialect to a neutral place (with unknown sky color, unfamiliar vegetation, and the like) and employed a team of linguists using any reasonable methods to plumb his language, you would have to come to the conclusion that he uses 'red' to mean what we mean by 'green', 'blue' to mean what we mean by 'yellow', and so on. You would have to come to the conclusion that the Inverted Earth dialect differs from ours in "inverted meanings" of color words. If commerce develops between the two planets and painters on Inverted Earth order paint from one of our paint stores, we shall have to translate their order for "green paint" into an order to our stockboy to get red paint. Inverted Earth differs from earth in switched words and switched stimuli.

Further, the intentional contents of attitudes and experiences of Inverted Earthlings are also inverted. If a foreigner misreads a phrase book and comes to the conclusion that "trash can" means a type of sandwich, despite what he says, he does not actually want a trash can for lunch—he wants a sandwich. Similarly, when a resident of Inverted Earth wonders, as he would put it, "why the sky is blue," he is wondering not why the sky is blue, but why it is yellow. And when he looks at the sky (in normal circumstances for Inverted Earth), the experience he has that he would describe as the sky looking "blue" is actually the experience of the sky looking yellow. There is no mystery or asymmetry here. I am using our language to describe his intentional contents; if he used his language to describe ours, he would correctly describe us as inverted in just the same way.

These two differences that I have mentioned "cancel out" in the sense that the talk on Inverted Earth will *sound* just like talk on Earth. Radio programs from Inverted Earth sound to us like radio programs from faraway places where English is spoken, like New

Zealand. Children on both planets ask their parents, "Why is the sky blue?" "Why is grass green?"

Now let's have the analog of the intrasubjective inverted spectrum example. A team of mad scientists knock you out. While you are out cold, they insert color-inverting lenses in your eyes, and change your body pigments so you don't have a nasty shock when you wake up and look at your feet. They transport you to Inverted Earth, where you are substituted for a counterpart who has occupied a niche on Inverted Earth that corresponds exactly (except for colors of things) with your niche at home. You wake up, and since the inverting lenses cancel out the inverted colors, you notice no difference at all. "What it's like" for you to interact with the world and with other people does not change at all. For example, the yellow sky looks blue to you, and all the people around you describe yellow objects such as the sky as "blue." As far as the qualitative aspect of your mental life is concerned, nothing is any different from the way it would have been had you stayed home. Further, we may suppose that your brain is exactly the same in its physiological properties as it would have been had you stayed at home. (Of course, the statements in the science of color would have to be different on both planets. Pure light of 577 nm is described by us as 'yellow' and by them as 'blue'. So let us suppose that you and the twins in the examples to follow know nothing of the science of color, and hence these scientific differences make no difference to you.)[21]

There you are on Inverted Earth. The qualitative content of your experience of the (local) sky is just the same as the day before, when you looked at the sky at home. What about the intentional content of this experience? Here there may be some disagreement. The causal rooting of your color words is virtually entirely at home; your use of 'blue' is grounded in references to blue things and to the uses of 'blue' by other people to refer to blue things. For this reason, I would say that on your first day on Inverted Earth, your intentional contents remain the same as they were—that is, different from the natives. At first, when you look at the sky, thinking the thought that you would express as "It is as blue as ever," you are expressing the same thought that you would have been expressing yesterday at home, only today you are *wrong*. Also, your thought is not the same as the one a native of Inverted Earth would express with the same words. Nonetheless, according to me, after enough time has passed on Inverted Earth, your embedding in the physical and linguistic environment of Inverted Earth would dominate, and so your intentional contents would shift so as to be the same as those of the natives. Consider an analogy (supplied by Martin Davies): if you had a Margaret Thatcher recognitional capacity before your journey to Inverted Earth, and on arriving misidentify twin MT as MT, you are mistaken. But eventually your 'That's MT' judgments get to be about twin MT, and so become right having started out wrong. If you were kidnapped at age 15, by the time 50 years have passed, you use 'red' to mean green, just as the natives do. Once your intentional contents have inverted, so do your functional states. The state that is now *normally* caused by blue things is the same state that earlier was normally caused by yellow things. So once 50 years have passed, you and your earlier stage at home would exemplify what I want, namely a case of functional and intentional inversion together with the same qualitative contents—the converse of the inverted spectrum case. This is enough to refute the functionalist theory of qualitative content and at the same time to establish the intentional/qualitative distinction.

But what if the facts of human physiology get in the way of the case as I described it? My response is the same as the one mentioned earlier (based on Shoemaker's rebuttal of Harrison), namely that it is possible for there to be a race of people very much like us, with color vision, and color sensations, but whose physiology does not rule out the case described (or spectrum inversion). The functionalist can hardly be satisfied with the claim that our experiences are functional states but the other race's experiences are not.

The functionalist theory that I have in mind is a functional state identity theory, a theory that says that each and every mental state *is* some functional state. If mental state M = functional state F, then any instance of M must also be an instance of F. But in the Inverted Earth case just described, two instances of the same qualitative state—yours and Twin's—have different functional roles. And the qualitative state that you share with Twin cannot be identical to *both* your functional state and Twin's functional state, since that would be a case of $Q = F_1$, $Q = F_2$ and $\sim(F_1 = F_2)$, which contravenes transitivity of identity. There is still one loose end to the argument: the existence of one sort of functional description on which the two qualitatively identical states are functionally different does not rule out the possibility of another sort of functional description on which they are the same. I will return to this matter when I consider objections to the Inverted Earth argument later.

Note that this intrapersonal Inverted Earth case does not have the weakness that we saw in the intrapersonal inverted spectrum case. In the latter case, the subject's internal disturbance renders his first-person reports vulnerable to doubt. But you, the subject of the Inverted Earth case, have had no internal disturbance. Your move to Inverted Earth was accomplished without your noticing it—there was no period of confusion or adaptation. All the inversion went on outside your brain—in your inverting lenses, and in your physical and linguistic environment. The intrapersonal case has the considerable advantage of testimony for Inverted Earth as for the inverted spectrum case. But some readers may feel some doubt about the claim that after 50 years your intentional contents and language are the same as that of the Inverted Earth natives. For this reason, it may be helpful to move briefly to the interpersonal Inverted Earth case. I will be talking in terms of the interpersonal case later, but I hope the reader will refer back from time to time to the first-person point of view that is better captured in the intrapersonal case.

Imagine a pair of genetically identical twins, one of whom is adopted on Inverted Earth after having had inverting lenses inserted into his eyes and body pigment changes, the other of whom grows up normally on Earth (without special lenses). To try to bring in the first-person point of view, let the home twin be you. When you two look at your respective skies, you both hear 'blue', and the same retinal stimulation occurs. We may suppose that you and Twin are in relevant respects neurologically the same. (We could even suppose that your brains are molecular duplicates.) But then you two are the same in the qualitative contents of your experiences; just as in the intra-subjective example, your qualitative contents were the same before and after your trip to Inverted Earth. For qualitative contents supervene on physical constitution, and your physical constitutions are relevantly the same.

Though you and Twin have the same qualitative contents at every moment, you are inverted functionally and with respect to intentional contents of experience. For in his intentional contents, Twin is the same as his friends on Inverted Earth. When Twin or any other resident of Inverted Earth thinks the thought that he would express as "The blue of the sky is very saturated," his thought is about *yellow*. Thus your intentional contents of experience are inverted with respect to Twin's. What about functional inversion?

One's mental representation of blue—one's concept of blue, in the psychologists' sense of the term "concept"—plays a familiar role in being produced in a natural and immediate way by blue things, and in controlling one's behavior toward blue things. (Harman assumes that one's experience of blue *is* one's concept of blue; I am happy to go along; the issue is not relevant to the controversy discussed here.) I speak of the familiar role of one's concept of blue. Perhaps it would help here to think of you and Twin of both being engaged in a game. You are shown something of a certain color, and your task is to find something of the same color. I show you a ripe strawberry, and you look around, finding a matching English double-decker bus. Twin, in his corresponding situation, matches his green strawberries with a green bus.

There you and Twin are, looking at your respective skies, having experiences with just the same qualitative contents. At this very moment, you are in a state produced in a natural and immediate way by blue things, one that plays the aforementioned familiar functional role in controlling your responses to blue things. At the same time, Twin is in a state produced by yellow things, one that plays the same familiar functional role in controlling his responses to yellow things, so you are functionally inverted with respect to Twin. Think of the color-matching game. The qualitative state that functions so as to guide you in matching blue target with blue sample also functions so as to guide Twin in matching yellow target with yellow sample. Of course there is considerable functional similarity between you and Twin; indeed you are functionally exactly alike if we take the border between the inside and the outside so as to exclude the inverter, including your production of the same noise, "Blue again!," when you see the sky. Later I will take up the matter of whether this internal functional description can be used to avoid the criticism of functionalism that I am making.

Further, your perceptual state is about blue things whereas Twin's is about yellow things, so you are intentionally inverted. (The "inversion" has to do with the fact that yellow and blue are simply examples of complementary colors.)

Notice that the argument against functionalism depends on an intentional way of individuating responses. If you and Twin were brought together into my study and asked the color of a red thing, you and Twin would make different noises. You would say "red," Twin would say "green." But Twin would *mean* red by "green," as would any member of the Inverted Earth Inverted English speech community. In this respect, the Inverted Earth case gets a bit less of a grip on the imagination than the inverted spectrum case, for which no such distinction between ways of individuating responses need be made. And it also points up the fact that the argument is more powerful as a refutation of intentionalism about qualia than of functionalism about qualia. (The issue will be discussed below of whether there is a functionalist theory of qualia that is left untouched by the argument.)

The upshot is that if you and Twin are looking at your respective skies, saying "Still blue," you have experiences that have the same qualitative content, but inverted intentional content, and they are functionally inverted. Conclusion: the distinction between intentional and qualitative content is vindicated, and the functional and intentional theory of qualia is refuted.

The Inverted Earth argument just given can be attacked in a variety of ways. I will examine a few of them shortly, but first I want to make some comparisons with the more traditional inverted spectrum argument.

The Inverted Earth case is meant to exemplify qualitative identity plus functional and intentional inversion, whereas the inverted spectrum case is meant to exemplify the converse, qualitative inversion plus functional and intentional identity. As I mentioned earlier, the qualitative difference in the best version of the inverted spectrum case (the intrasubjective inversion) is meant to be established by the testimony of the inverted subject. As I also mentioned, the weakness of the case is that unusual things have happened inside this subject (the "adaptation" period), and so there is some doubt (taken more seriously by some philosophers than by others) that the subject's words can simply be taken at face value. The contrast with the Inverted Earth case is strong. When you are kidnapped and wake up on Inverted Earth, there is no difference at all in what it is like for you. In this case unlike the intrasubjective inverted spectrum, there is no internal disturbance to throw doubt on the subject's testimony. (Of course, any subject may miss a series of small changes, but there is no reason to suspect these in the Inverted Earth case.) Further, in the intersubjective Inverted Earth case, we have supervenience on our side. Your brain is a molecular doppelganger of Twin's, and since intrinsic properties such as qualitative content are presumably supervenient on physical properties, we can conclude that you are qualitatively identical to Twin. Note that supervenience is asymmetrical with respect to sameness and difference. That is, the molecule-for-molecule identity of your brain with Twin's establishes that intrinsic properties like qualia are the same. But the physical difference between the brains of the inverted spectrum twins does not establish any qualitative difference between them, because the critic can always allege (as Harman does) that the physical difference is just a matter of alternative realizations of the same mental state.

The advantage of the Inverted Earth case is that there is no *internal* switch as in the inverted spectrum case. The switching goes on outside the brain. So far, the Inverted Earth argument is a better argument against functionalism than the inverted spectrum argument. But does it fare as well with respect to objections?

The first objection I want to consider is that Twin does not have the same intentional contents as his friends on Inverted Earth because when he looks at the sky he has a qualitatively different experience from the one his friends have (because he has inverting lenses and they don't). And his color judgments are answerable to the qualitative contents of his experiences. So when he says and his friends echo "The sky looks blue," what they say is true whereas what he says is false because the sky does not look yellow to *him*.[22]

The first thing to note about this objection is that it assumes an inverted spectrum; it claims that Twin's spectrum is inverted with respect to that of his friends, and it uses that claim to argue that Twin's intentional contents are not the same as those of his friends. For this reason, no functionalist can accept this objection, least of all Harman. Harman insists (as I have) that the intentional content of the experience as of yellow consists in its natural and immediate production by yellow things, its role in manipulating yellow things, and the like. And since Twin is the same as his friends in this respect, Harman cannot suppose he differs from them in intentional content.

Further, those of us who accept the possibility of an inverted spectrum cannot accept the objection either, since it commits the fallacy of intentionalizing qualia. If inverted spectra are possible, then the natives of Inverted Earth may differ from one another in the qualitative content produced by the sky. No one of them can be singled out as the one whose qualitative content on looking at the sky is *really* that of *looking yellow*. Intentional content cannot be reduced to qualitative content.

Note that I have not used the possibility of an inverted spectrum to defend Inverted Earth. The objection assumes an inverted spectrum, and I simply pointed out the consequences of that assumption.

Now onto a more serious objection. I have said that you are qualitatively identical to but functionally inverted with respect to Twin. At the moment when each of you are looking at your respective skies, you are in a state produced by blue things that controls manipulation of blue things, whereas Twin is in a state produced by yellow things that controls manipulation of yellow things. (Recall the example of the color-matching game.) My reasoning involves thinking of inputs and outputs as involving objects in the world. But this is just one way of thinking of inputs and outputs according to one type of functional description. The existence of one functional description according to which you are an invert of Twin does not preclude other functional descriptions according to which you and Twin are functionally the same. If there are other functional descriptions according to which you and Twin are functionally the same, how can I claim to have refuted functionalism?

Indeed, there are a variety of functional descriptions according to which you are functionally the same as Twin. For example, your brain is physically identical to Twin's, so any functional description that draws the line between the inside and the outside at the surface of the brain will be a functional description according to which you and Twin are functionally the same. For internal functional organization is just as supervenient on internal physical state as is qualitative state.

But brain-internal functional states cannot capture the intentional content of experience. For that content depends on the colors in the outside world. Here is a way of dramatizing the point. The inverting lenses (and the post-retinal inverter as well) invert the color solid 180 degrees.[23] But one can just as well imagine inverters that invert the color solid by smaller amounts, for example, 90 degrees. Imagine a series of clones of yours (and Twin's) whose lenses contain a series of different inverters. Imagine each of these clones confronted with a color patch so chosen as to produce exactly the same neural signal in each of the identical brains. If your brain is confronted with a red patch, another will be confronted with a yellow patch, another with a blue patch, and so forth. But you will all be having exactly the same qualitative content. If * is the neural signal that we are counting as input to your brain, * would be produced by red in your brain, by yellow in one of your clones, and by blue in another clone. So neither * nor any brain-internal functional state triggered by it can correspond to any single color in the world. The intentional content of your experience is *looking red*, whereas that of your clones are *looking yellow*, *looking blue*, and so forth.[24] Your intentional contents are all different, but since your brains are exactly the same (by hypothesis), and since internal functional organization is supervenient on the brain, *all* internal functional descriptions will be shared by all of you. So no purely brain-internal functional description can capture the intentional content of experience.[25]

What I have just argued is that no brain-internal functional state could be suitable for identification with an intentional content of experience. If intentional contents of experience are functional states, they are "long-arm" functional states that reach out into the world of things and their colors. But though Harman commits himself to recognizing *only* long-arm functional states, there is no good reason why the functionalist cannot recognize *both* these long-arm functional roles *and* short-arm functional roles that are purely internal. Why can't the functionalist identify intentional contents with long-arm functional states and qualitative content with short-arm functional states? The result would be a kind of "dualist" or "two-factor" version of functionalism.[26]

My response: perhaps such a two-factor theory is workable, but the burden of proof is on the functionalist to tell us what the short-arm functional states might be. Without some indication of what these functional states would be like we have no reason to believe in such a functional theory of qualia.[27] In terms of machine versions of functionalism, the responsibility of the functionalist is to find a characterization of qualia in terms of the "program" of the mind. Good luck to him![28]

I have conceded that *if* there is some functional characterization of qualia, that will sink the Inverted Earth Argument. But this concession does not yield any superiority of the inverted spectrum over Inverted Earth. For the same possibility would sink the inverted spectrum argument as well. The inverted spectrum twins are supposed to be qualitatively different but functionally identical. And that is supposed to show that qualitative states are not functional states. But if there is a functional theory of qualia, it will be one on which the inverted spectrum twins are functionally different after all.

Perhaps a physiological theory of qualia is possible. If there is a physiological theory of qualia, it can be functionalized.[29] Such a move is changing the subject in the context of the inverted spectrum argument, however. Functionalism in that context is linked to the computer model of the mind. The idea is rather as if two machines with different hardware might have different qualia despite computational identity: having the same computational structure and running all the same programs. Since the issue is whether qualia are computational states, you can't legitimately defend a computationalist theory by appealing to the hardware difference itself.

Let us now turn to what is the most plausible candidate for an alternative functional description designed to make you functionally identical to Twin, namely one that exploits the fact of the inverting lenses. Let's focus on the version in which the inverting lens is installed inside the lens of the eye. Then it may be objected that when you and Twin are looking at your respective skies, you have the *same* inputs. There is blue light in *both* of your eyes, despite the fact that Twin is looking at a yellow sky. So there is no functional inversion.

I've been using a functional description (as does Harman) in which the inputs relevant to experiences as of red are red objects in the world. The objection I am considering is that the boundary between the inside and the outside should be moved inward, and inputs should be thought of in terms of the color of the light hitting the retina, not in terms of colored objects. Here is a first approximation to my reply: you give me an independently motivated conception of the boundary between the inside and the outside of the system, and I will tailor an inverted earth example to suit. In this case the tailoring is done. You will recall that I mentioned an alternative to the inverting lenses, one that seems to me more physically plausible than the lenses, namely a neural inverter behind the retina. The retina reacts in a well-understood way to triples of light wavelengths, transforming them into impulses in the optic nerve. I don't know any reason why it shouldn't be in principle possible for a miniaturized silicon chip to register those impulses and substitute transformed impulses for them.

Sensation is generally the product of the action of the world on a transducer that registers some feature of the world and outputs some corresponding signal that conveys information to the brain. The visual apparatus registers light, the auditory apparatus sound, and so forth. The natural way of thinking of inputs and outputs is in terms of impingements on such transducers. With any real transducer, there is often indeterminacy as to exactly where transduction starts or finishes. The lens of the eye could be thought of as the visual transducer, or alternatively the visual transducer could be thought of as ending at the rods and cones or one of the other layers of the retina, or in the optic nerve, or in the lateral geniculate nucleus. I could locate my inverter at any of those places. However, I suppose it could be discovered that there is a "visual sensorium" in the brain with a sharp natural boundary such that any change within it changes qualia and any change outside it does not (except by affecting its inputs). In that case, the choice of the boundary of the sensorium as the border between inside and outside would require placement of the inverter in a place that would change qualia. My response to this possibility is to note as I did in the section on the fallacy of intentionalizing qualia that there could be a type of person otherwise very like us who has color vision and color sensations but no sharp sensorium boundary. Thus I can run my thought experiments on a sort of being (perhaps hypothetical, perhaps us) that has color experience but no sharply bounded sensorium.

Awareness of Intrinsic Properties

Thus far, I have been arguing against Harman's objections to the inverted spectrum, and giving my own argument in terms of Inverted Earth for accepting the qualitative/intentional distinction, and the falsity of a functionalist theory of qualia. But there is one consideration raised by Harman that I have not yet mentioned. He says that the qualitative/intentional distinction depends on the view that we are aware of intrinsic properties of our experience. This latter view is one that he spends more than half the paper arguing against. So in order fully to examine his objection to the inverted spectrum hypothesis, we shall have to turn to his objection to the view that we are aware of intrinsic features of our experience.

Harman's primary argument is, as far as I can see, an appeal to—of all things—introspection. He says that the idea that we are aware of the "mental paint" is "counter to ordinary visual experience." Here is the main passage where the argument is given.

When Eloise sees a tree before her, the colors she experiences are all experienced as features of the tree and its surroundings. None of them are experienced as intrinsic features of her experience. Nor does she experience any features of anything as intrinsic features of her experience. And that is true of you too ... Look at a tree and try to turn your attention to intrinsic features of your visual experience, I predict you will find that the only features there to turn your attention to will be features of the presented tree ...

In my view, Harman's appeal to introspection here is an error in philosophical method. When I look at my blue wall, I *think* that in addition to being aware of the color I can also make myself aware of what it is like for me to be aware of the color. I'm sure others will disagree. The one thing we should all agree on is that this is no way to do philosophy. Our intuitions can tell us something about our concepts and our experiences so long as we use them rightly. One principle is: *Elicit simple intuitions about complex cases rather than complex intuitions about simple cases.* Looking at a blue wall is easy to do, but it is not easy (perhaps not possible) to answer on the basis of introspection alone the highly theoretical question of whether in so doing I am aware of intrinsic properties of my experience. The point of the complicated science fiction stories described above is to produce complex cases about which one can consult simple intuitions. Harman hopes to argue against the inverted spectrum by appealing to the introspective judgment that we are not aware of intrinsic features of our experience. I think he proceeds the wrong way around. If arguments such as the one I gave convince us that it is possible for qualitative content to remain the same while intentional content is inverted (or conversely), then that will settle the issue of whether we are aware of intrinsic features of our experience. Or at any rate, it will settle the matter that is really at stake: whether *there are* intrinsic mental features of our experience.

Finally, let me turn to Harman's critique of Jackson. Let us put the issue in terms of Jackson's Mary, the scientist who knows all the physical and functional facts about color perception that can be learned in a black-and-white environment. The issue Jackson poses is this: does Mary acquire new knowledge on seeing red? The qualia realist says she acquires genuine knowledge *that*, genuine new information, namely, knowledge that this is what it is like to see red. Lewis, Nemirow, Shoemaker, and other critics have said that what Mary acquires is something more like knowledge *how*: new skills, not new information. Harman's line is that Mary *does* genuinely acquire new information, genuine knowledge *that*, but he goes on to say that functionalism is not refuted because Mary did not know all the functional facts before seeing red. Harman says that knowledge of all the functional facts requires possession of the full concept of red, and that is a matter of being in a certain functional state. More specifically, the full concept of red must be produced in a natural and immediate way by red things and must play a certain role in thought and action with respect to red things. While she is still locked in the black-and-white room, Mary has no state that is produced in a natural and immediate way by red things, and plays the appropriate role in thought and action. So Mary had no such functional state before seeing red; hence she did not know all the functional facts. When she sees a red thing for the first time she acquires the concept of red, and with it the functional facts that she lacked for lack of that concept. Further, she now can be said to know that blood is red, apples are red, and the like, whereas earlier she could mouth those words, but lacking the concept of red, she did not really possess the knowledge.

In sum: Jackson says that Mary knows all the functional facts before she sees anything red, yet she learns a new fact, so the functional facts do not include all the facts. Some of Jackson's critics deny that Mary learns a new fact. Harman, by contrast, allows that Mary learns new facts on seeing red, but he denies that Mary knew all the functional facts before she saw anything red. He says she acquires a new functional fact as well, in acquiring the concept of red itself.

If Harman is right about all this—and for the sake of argument, let's suppose that he is—he has provided no argument against qualia realism; rather, he has shown that the Jackson argument does not serve very well as a locus of controversy between the qualia realist and the qualia skeptic. The knowledge that Harman shows Mary lacks in the black-and-white room has little to do with the real issues about qualia. Until Mary sees green for the first time, she cannot have the full concept of green, and so she cannot have the knowledge that some olives are green. Indeed, she can't even have the false belief that all olives are green. This fact has little to do with the disagreement between the qualia skeptic and the qualia realist.

If one accepts Harman's claim that Mary can't have any beliefs about the colors of things until she leaves the black-and-white room, then the real issue between the qualia realist and the qualia skeptic about Mary is that the qualia realist says Mary acquires *two* types of knowledge *that* when she sees colors for the first time, whereas the qualia skeptic says she acquires only one. All can agree that she acquires knowledge involving *intentional* contents. For example, she acquires the concept of green and having already read the *Encyclopaedia Brittanica*, she acquires the knowledge that olives are green. However, the qualia realist says she acquires knowledge involving qualitative contents in addition to the intentional contents. This is the crux of the matter, and on this, Harman's reply to Jackson is silent.

Notes

Reprinted from J. Tomberlin, ed., *Philosophical Perspectives, Volume 4: Action Theory and Philosophy of Mind*, 53–79 (Atascadero: Ridgeview, 1990).

This chapter started life as a response to Gilbert Harman's "The Intrinsic Quality of Experience," in the same volume, and it retains that format even though the aim of the chapter is to argue that there is an "inversion" argument for qualia realism and against functionalism that is better than the traditional inverted spectrum argument. (Qualia realism in the sense that I will be using the term is the view that there are intrinsic mental features of our experience.) Those who have not read Harman's chapter may want to skip the last section of this chapter.

The reply was delivered at the Chapel Hill Colloquium, October 17, 1987. A later version of this paper was delivered at the Universities of Oxford, Cambridge, and Edinburgh; at Birkbeck College and Kings College London; and at a meeting of the Anglo-French Philosophy Group. I am grateful for support from the American Council of Learned Societies and from the National Science Foundation (DIR88 12559). I am also grateful to Martin Davies and Christopher Peacocke for comments on an earlier version, and I am grateful for useful discussions on these matters with Davies and with Sam Guttenplan.

1. John Haugeland, "The Nature and Plausibility of Cognitivism," *The Behavioral and Brain Sciences* 1/215–226, 1978.

2. In "Functionalism and Qualia," *Philosophical Studies* 27/291–315, 1975 (reprinted in my *Readings in Philosophy of Psychology*, Vol 1, Harvard University Press, 1980). Sydney Shoemaker shows how functionalism can provide identity conditions for qualia even if it abandons an attempt to characterize particular qualiatative states. Shoemaker's technique does, however, assume that "absent" qualia are impossible, an assumption that I dispute.

3. For arguments against the possibility of such a zombie, see Shoemaker, op. cit.; see also Colin McGinn, *The Subjective View*, Oxford University Press: Oxford, 1983; and John Searle, *The Rediscovery of the Mind*, MIT Press: Cambridge, 1992. I reply to Shoemaker in "Are Absent Qualia Impossible?," *The Philosophical Review* 89/257–274, 1980. Shoemaker responds in "Absent Qualia are Impossible—a Reply to Block," *The Philosophical Review* 90, 4/581–599, 1981.

4. The intentional/qualitative terminology is from Shoemaker's, "The Inverted Spectrum," *The Journal of Philosophy* 74, 7, 1981, 357–81. This essay is reprinted with a new postscript together with other papers of Shoemaker's on the same topic (including "Functionalism and Qualia") in *Identity, Cause and Mind: Philosophical Essays*, Cambridge University Press: Cambridge, 1984. The representational/sensational terminology is from Christopher Peacocke, *Sense and Content*, Oxford University Press: Oxford, 1983, chapters 1 and 2. Peacocke uses "what it is like" in a way that includes both representational and sensational content. Frank Jackson's distinction between comparative and phenomenal senses of "looks" comes to much the same thing. See chapter 2 *of Perception*, Cambridge University Press: Cambridge, 1977.

5. Peacocke, op. cit., uses a number of intriguing examples to argue for the representational/sensational distinction without any commitment to an inverted spectrum. For example, he argues that in looking at a room through one eye, one has an experience with a representational content that is the same as that of the experience one gets on looking with two eyes (the same objects are represented to be the same distances away), but the sensational contents differ. If he is right, then there is a much greater distance between the representation/sensational distinction and the inverted spectrum than I suppose. I will sidestep the issue by individuating intentional contents *functionally*. So the monocular and binocular intentional contents will be different because they function differently. For example, since we are fully aware of the difference, and can make use of it in our verbal reports of our experiences, the binocular experience can produce different reports from those produced by the monocular experience. See Michael Tye's review of Peacocke's book in *Canadian Philosophical Reviews* V/173–175, 1985, for a discussion of another of Peacocke's examples from the same point of view.

6. One qualification: It is useful to have some terms to refer to that content of experience that is mental without being intentional. I have used "what it is like" and "qualitative content" in this way, and so I do not wish to regard these terms as referring to intentional contents.

7. The point I have been making does assume that it is often the case that objects have colors, for example, the book I am now looking at is blue. It does not assume that questions of what color something is always have a determinate answer, nor does it deny that what color an object is is relative to all sorts of things, for example, the position of the perceiver. An expanse of color in a comic strip may be orange from a distance yet also be red and yellow from close up. If this is objectivism, I am happy to be an objectivist. See C. L. Hardin, *Color for Philosophers: Unweaving the Rainbow*, Indianapolis: Hackett Publishing Co, 1988, for a forceful argument against objectivism (and subjectivism).

8. Some qualia skeptics hold that there is no such thing as qualitative content whereas others believe that there is such a thing but that it is identical to intentional content. Dan Dennett seems to me to have vacillated on this issue. In "Quining Qualia," 1988 in A. Marcel and E. Bisiach, eds., *Consciousness in Contemporary Society*. Oxford: Oxford University Press, 1988. He takes a functionalist view of qualia, as he does in "Toward a Cognitive Theory of Consciousness," in *Brainstorms: Philosophical Essays on Mind and Psychology*, MIT Press: Cambridge, 1978, 149–173. But in other papers he has been more of an eliminativist about qualia. See especially "On the Absence of Phenomenology," in *Body, Mind and Method: Essays in Honor of Virgil Aldrich*, D. Gustafson and B. Tapscott, eds., D. Reidel: Dordrecht, 93–113, 1979; and "Why You Can't Make a Computer that Feels Pain," *Synthese* 38.3, 1978, reprinted in *Brainstorms*, 190–229. The answer to the title question (why you can't make a computer that feels pain) is that there isn't any such thing as pain.

9. This point is stimulated by Shoemaker's (op. cit.) argument against Harrison.

10. Note that I've said that the function of *an experience* is what gives it the intentional content of *looking red*; I did not say that anything at all (even something that isn't an experience) that has that function has that content. This issue—the issue of "absent qualia"—is not taken up in this chapter.

11. But it is not functionalist, for reasons mentioned earlier, about the meaning of "what it is like" and "qualitative content." The view I'm defending of the semantics of color terms is similar to Paul Churchland's in *Scientific Realism and the Plasticity of Mind*, Cambridge: Cambridge University Press, 1979, chapter 2.

12. So long as the experience has *some* qualitative content or other—which it must have, being an experience. As I said in the last note, whether a non-experience could have the functional role of an experience is a matter I do not intend to discuss here.

13. W. Lycan, *Consciousness*, MIT Press: Cambridge, 1987 also puts the inverted spectrum hypothesis in this way.

14. "Conceptual Role Semantics," *The Notre Dame Journal of Formal Logic* 23, 2, 1982, p. 250. Lycan, op. cit., p. 60, says that proponents of the inverted spectrum hypothesis "simply ... deny the truth of Functionalism ... without argument."

15. See, for example, Sydney Shoemaker, "The Inverted Spectrum," op. cit., and William Lycan, "Inverted Spectrum," *Ratio* 15, 1973.

16. A perhaps more realistic possibility would be that of a miniature computer placed in a sinus cavity hooked into the optic nerve behind the retina that registers the output of the retina and changes the signals that represent red to signals that represent green, and so forth, feeding the transformed signals to the lateral geniculate nucleus. Many of the objections to the empirical possibility of an inverted spectrum by Harrison and Hardin are also objections to the possibility of a color inverter. See Bernard Harrison, *Form and Content*, Oxford University Press: Oxford, and C. L. Hardin, op. cit. See also Shoemaker's comment on Harrison in the paper referred to earlier (p. 336 of *Identity, Cause and Mind*). Harrison and Hardin both argue in different ways that the color solid has asymmetries that prevent indetectable color inversion. As will become clear later, the main claim of this paper is one that would not be damaged if they are right, for I am claiming only that the "Inverted Earth" argument to be presented is a better argument against functionalism than the inverted spectrum argument. (Further, both arguments can avoid inverting spectacles.) However, I cannot resist mentioning that neither Harrison's nor Hardin's objections work. Hardin points out the main problems with Harrison. For example, Harrison argues that there may be more shades between some unique (primary) colors than others, rendering an inversion detectable. Hardin points out that the number of shades seen between any two colors is a highly variable matter among people with perfectly normal color vision. Hardin's own objection is that some colors (red and yellow) are warm whereas others (blue and green) are cool. But he gives no argument against the possibility of warm/cool inversion. That is, he gives no argument against the possibility that things we agree have a warm color produce the same qualitative character in you that things we agree have a cool color produce in me.
    Hardin also argues that if the color-inverted person sees blood as green plus cool, epiphenomenalism would have to be true, whereas supposing he sees blood as green plus warm verges on incoherence. These claims—at least the first—draw their plausibility from the fallacy of intentionalizing qualia. The reason that the possibility of seeing blood as green plus cool is supposed to involve epiphenomenalism is that it is supposed that seeing blood as cool-colored would lead to talking and acting as if it were cool-colored, which is incompatible with the functional (and therefore behavioral) identity presupposed in the inverted spectrum hypothesis. But this claim depends on thinking of the inverted spectrum as intentional inversion. Suppose that the qualitative property that leads you to say something is red and leads me to say something is green is Q_a, whereas Q_b has the opposite effect. And suppose that the qualitative property that leads you to say something is warm-colored and leads me to say something is cool-colored is Q_x, whereas Q_y has the opposite effect. There is no threat of epiphenomenalism in my experiencing red things via the qualitative content $Q_b + Q_y$. The appearance of an epiphenomenalism problem comes only from the fallacy of intentionalizing qualia via thinking of $Q_b + Q_y$ as having an intentional content involving coolness.

17. I said that when we put on the inverting lenses, grass looks red, so am I not committed to the claim that for the inverted twin as well grass looks red? No. Grass looks to the *temporary* wearer of the lenses the way red things normally look. But the inverted twin is not a temporary wearer: grass looks to him the way green things normally look.

18. This stage is broken into parts in a way that adds to its power to convince in Shoemaker, op. cit.

19. See Dennett's "Quining Qualia," op. cit., and Rey's *Contemporary Philosophy of Mind: A Contentiously Classical Approach*, Cambridge: Blackwell, 1997.

20. "Conceptual Role Semantics," op. cit., p. 251. I have an earlier but clumsier example to the same effect, in "Troubles with Functionalism," pp. 302–303 (note 21), in my *Readings in Philosophy of Psychology*, Vol 1, Harvard University Press, 1980 and pp. 98–99, this volume. See also Ron McClamrock's use of Harman's example for a different purpose in his 1984 Ph.D. thesis, MIT.

21. In my clumsier example (mentioned in the last footnote) I had the inverting lenses and the switched color words, but instead of the yellow sky and the like on Inverted Earth, I had my events take place in a remote Arctic village where (I supposed) the people had no standing beliefs about the colors of things.

22. This objection is suggested by the McGinn-Peacocke view mentioned earlier according to which the intentional content ("representational content" in Peacocke's terminology) of an experience as of red is defined in terms of its qualitative content (sensational content).

23. I am thinking of an inversion of the constant brightness hue-saturation wheel.

24. Since your qualitative contents are the same but your intentional contents are all different, *looking red* is not a qualitative content. Thus we see that the Inverted Earth case can be used to unmask the fallacy of intentionalizing qualia, just as the inverted spectrum case can.

25. What makes the difference between the intentional content of the experience of *looking red* and *looking blue* is the connection between these experiences and the colored objects in the world. Therefore any conception of content that leaves out the connection between experience and the world will have no way of distinguishing between these different intentional contents. "Narrow content," the aspect of content that is "inside the head" is just such a conception of content, and so it is not hard to see that the "narrow content" of *looking red* and *looking green* must be the same. In my "Functional Role and Truth Conditions," *Proceedings of the Aristotelian Society*, suppl. vol. 61/157–181, I argue that a theory that uses Harman's "long-arm" functional roles (the ones that I have adopted here) is equivalent to a "two-factor" theory utilizing "short-arm" functional roles plus a referential component.

26. See the paper referred to in the last note for a discussion of such a two-factor theory in the context of propositional attitudes.

27. I also think an "absent qualia" argument would doom any such proposal, but I cannot go into that here.

28. I take the view that thought is functional, but that the best bet for a theory of qualia lies in neurophysiology. See my "Troubles with Functionalism," op. cit.

29. As advocated by Lycan, op. cit., 1987. I described this idea as "physiofunctionalism" in my "Troubles with Functionalism," op. cit.

The greatest chasm in the philosophy of mind—maybe even all of philosophy—divides two perspectives on consciousness. The two perspectives differ on whether there is anything in the phenomenal character of conscious experience that goes beyond the intentional, the cognitive, and the functional. A convenient terminological handle on the dispute is whether there are "qualia," or qualitative properties of conscious experience. Those who think that the phenomenal character of conscious experience goes beyond the intentional, the cognitive, and the functional believe in qualia.[1]

The debates about qualia have recently focused on the notion of representation, with issues about functionalism always in the background. All can agree that there are representational contents of thoughts, for example the representational content *that virtue is its own reward*. And friends of qualia can agree that experiences at least sometimes have representational content too, for example, *that something red and round occludes something blue and square*. The recent focus of disagreement is on whether the phenomenal character of experience is *exhausted* by such representational contents. I say no. Don't get me wrong. I think that sensations—almost always perhaps even always—*have* representational content in addition to their phenomenal character. What's more, I think that it is often the phenomenal character itself that has the representational content. What I deny is that representational content is all there is to phenomenal character. I insist that phenomenal character *outruns* representational content. I call this view "phenomenism." Phenomenists believe that phenomenal character outruns not only representational content but also the functional and the cognitive; hence they believe in qualia.

This paper is a defense of phenomenism against representationism. Hence issues of reduction of the phenomenal to the functional or the cognitive won't play much of a role. First I will briefly discuss an internalist form of representationism, and then I will go on to the main topic of the paper, externalist forms of the view.

Internalism

One form of representationism holds that the phenomenal character of experience is its "narrow intentional content," intentional content that is "in the head" in Putnam's phrase. That is, heads that are the same in ways that don't involve relations to the environment share all narrow intentional contents. A full dress discussion of this view would discuss various ideas of what narrow intentional content is supposed to be. But this isn't a full dress discussion. I will simply say that all versions of this view that I can think of that have even the slightest plausibility (and that aren't committed to qualia) are functionalist. They are functionalist in that they involve the idea that narrow intentional content supervenes on internal functional organization as well as physico-chemical configuration. That is, there can be no differences in narrow intentional contents without corresponding differences at the level of causal interactions of mental states within the head. The view comes in different flavors: Functional organization can be understood in terms of the interactions of common-sense mental states or in terms of the causal network of computational states. In both cases, there is a level of "grain" below which brain differences make no difference. One functional organization is multiply realizable physico-chemically in ways that make no difference in narrow intentional content. In other words, there is a level of organization above the level of physiology ("mental" or "computational") that determines narrow intentional content. (Tye 1994 takes this view and I understand Rey 1992a,b and White 1995 as endorsing it.)

Of course phenomenists can (and should) be internalists about phenomenal character too. But phenomenists can allow that phenomenal character depends on the details of the physiology or physico-chemical realization of the computational structure of the brain. Of course, there are also dualist forms of phenomenism, but both the physicalist and dualist forms of phenomenism agree that there is no need to suppose that qualia supervene on functional organization.

There is a very simple thought experiment that raises a serious (maybe fatal) difficulty for any such (functionalist) internalist form of representationism. Suppose that we raise a child (call her Erisa) in a room in which all colored surfaces change color every few minutes. Further, Erisa is allowed no information about grass being green or the sky being blue, and so on. The result is that Erisa ends up with no standing beliefs that distinguish one color from another. Suppose further that she is not taught color words, nor does she make them up for herself. (There are many languages that have only two words for colors, for example the language of the Dani famously studied by Rosch 1972.) Now we may suppose that the result is that there is little in the way of abiding functional differences among her color experiences. Most important, Erisa has no associations or behavioral inclinations or dispositions toward red that are any different from her associations or inclinations or dispositions toward blue. Of course, she responds to color similarities and differences—she groups blue things together as having the same color, and she groups red things together as having the same color. But her ability to group under the *same color* relation does not distinguish her reaction to red from her reaction to blue. The experience as of red is vividly different from the experience as of blue. But what difference in function in this case could plausibly constitute that difference?

The challenge to the internalist representationist, then, is to say what the difference is in internal intentional content between the experience of red and the experience of blue. The only resources available to the internalist representationist are functional. There is a difference in phenomenal character, so the internalist representationist is committed to finding a difference in function. But the example is designed to remove all abiding differences in function.

The functionalist can appeal to *temporary* differences. Erisa will say "The wall is now the same color that adorned the table a second ago," and "For one second, the floor matched the sofa." But these beliefs are fleeting, so how can they constitute the *abiding* differences between the phenomenal character of her experience of red and green? The differences between these phenomenal characters stay the same (for us) from moment to moment, day to day, and there is no reason to suppose that the same cannot be true for Erisa. The point of the thought experiment is to make it plausible that color experiences can remain just as vivid and the differences between them just as permanent as they are for us even if the functional differences between them attenuate to nothing that could plausibly constitute those differences.

Of course, there is one abiding difference in functional role between the experience of red and the experience of green—the properties of the stimuli. Since we are talking about *internalist* representationism, the stimuli will have to be, for example, light hitting the retina rather than colored surfaces. But these differences in the stimuli are what *cause* the differences in the phenomenal character of experience, not what *constitute* those phenomenal differences. I don't expect diehard functionalists to recant in response to this point, but I really don't see how anyone with an open mind could take being caused by certain stimuli as constituting phenomenal characters of color experiences.

Of course, there may be innate behavioral differences between the experience of red and the experience of blue. Perhaps we are genetically programmed so that red makes us nervous and blue makes us calm. In my view it is a bit silly to suppose that the phenomenal character of the experience as of blue is constituted by such factors as causing calmness. But since so many philosophers feel otherwise, I will also note that despite claims of this sort (Dennett 1991), such assertions are empirical speculations. (See Dennett's only cited source, Humphrey, 1992, which emphasizes the poor quality of the empirical evidence.). And of course anyone who holds that representationism is a conceptual truth will be frustrated by the fact that we don't know without empirical investigation whether it is a truth at all.

Perhaps the internalist will say that there would be no differences among Erisa's experiences. Red would of necessity look just the same to her as yellow. But this is surely an extraordinary thing for the internalist to insist on. It *could* be right of course, but again it is surely an unsupported empirical speculation.

I claim that an Erisa of the sort I described is conceptually possible. The replies I have just considered do not dispute this, but instead appeal to unsupported empirical claims.

But physicalism is an empirical thesis, so why should the representationist be embarrassed about making an empirical claim? Answer: Physicalism is a very general empirical thesis having to do with the long history of successes of what can be regarded as the physicalist research program. Internalist representationism, by contrast, depends on highly specific experimental claims. For example, perhaps it will be discovered that newborn babies hate some colors and love others before having had any differential experience with these colors. I doubt that very many opponents of qualia would wish their point of view to rest on speculations as to the results of such experiments.

The defender of qualia does not depend on a prediction about the results of such experiments. Our view is that even if such experiments do show some asymmetries, there are *possible* creatures—maybe genetically engineered versions of humans—in whom the asymmetries are ironed out. (See Shoemaker 1982.) And those genetically engineered humans could nonetheless have color experience much like ours. Any view that rests an argument against qualia on the existence of such asymmetries would seem to be committed to the peculiar claim that qualia are possible in creatures that differ from us in ways so subtle that we are not now sure whether we are these possible creatures. Further, given the necessity of identity, if phenomenal characters are identical to internal functional states, then there are no creatures, even possible creatures, who have different phenomenal characters that do not differ functionally.

Externalism

That is all I will have to say about internalist representationism. Now I will move to the main topic of this paper, externalist representationism. In this section, I will try to motivate externalist representationism. The consideration I will advance in motivating it will be of use to me later. Then I will advance various considerations that cause one or another sort of difficulty for the view.

Often, when I see water I see it *as* water; that is, my visual experience represents it as water. Most of you have seen water as water all your lives, but I'm different, I'm a foreigner. I was born on Twin Earth and emigrated to Earth at age 18. When I was 15 and looked at the sea on Twin Earth, my visual experience represented the twin-water as twin-water (though of course we didn't call it that). Perhaps you are skeptical about whether visual experience represents such properties, but please bear with me. When I first got here, I saw water as twin-water, just as you, if you went to Twin Earth, would see the twin-water in the oceans as water. Now, many years later, my practices of applying concepts are relevantly the same as yours: My practices show that I am committed to the concepts of my adopted home, Earth. Now when I look at the sea of my adopted home, my visual experience represents the water as water just as yours does. (This is controversial but again, let's suppose.) So the representational content of my experience of looking at the sea has changed. But my visual experience is nonetheless indistinguishable from what it was. If you took me up in a space ship and put me down by some seaside, I wouldn't know whether I was on Earth or Twin Earth. (See Stalnaker's 1996 commentary on Lycan 1996c on Block 1990.) The representational content of my experience has changed, but the phenomenal character has stayed the same. And that shows, someone (but not me) might argue, that there is some sort of gap between representational content and phenomenal character. (I think that there is such a gap, but this case doesn't reveal it.)

One way for the representationist to answer would be to note that though all phenomenal character is (according to representationism) representational content, the converse is not true. Not all representational contents are phenomenal characters. For example, the thought content that mumesons have odd spin is not a phenomenal character. But how is this point supposed to apply to the issue at hand? The putative gap between representational content and phenomenal character has to do with the representational content of visual experience, not thought. Here is one way of extending the representationist response. The representationist should hold that visual experience has two kinds of representational content: One kind of representational content can be identified with phenomenal character, and another kind of representational content is distinct from phenomenal character. The (relevant) phenomenal character of experience that has remained the same throughout my life is a matter of the observable or appearance properties of the liquids in oceans, rivers, and streams, their color, sheen, motion, taste, smell, and so on. It is these properties that my experience has represented liquids as having that have been shared by my experiences of both twin-water and water. *Those* are the representational contents that make my visual experience of the Twin Earth ocean at age 15 indistinguishable from my visual experience of the ocean now. (Many representationists go further, saying that these observational representational contents are nonconceptual, but nothing I will be saying here will depend on whether or not this is so.)

Of course, as Burge (1979 and elsewhere) has noted, color concepts and other "appearance concepts" are vulnerable to the same sort of Twin Earth arguments for externalism as is the concept of water. (Perhaps only truly phenomenal concepts are invulnerable to such arguments—as is suggested by Burge's 1979 remark that in his thought experiment, phenomenal character does not change.) Further, as I will argue later in the essay, a sort of Twin Earth argument can be run on perceptual contents whether or not they are conceptual. So in my view, the reply just discussed will ultimately fail to sustain the representationist point of view. But for the moment, we can take the representationist reply just given as a success for representationism. We started with an experiential continuity despite representational change that challenged the representationist. But then it turned out that the representationist can give a representational explanation of the difference. The main burden of this essay is to explore some reasons for thinking that the representationist cannot always repeat this success.

Two preliminary issues: First, one might object to my claim that visual experience can ever represent anything *as water*. Perhaps, you might say, visual experience can represent something as round or at least red, but not as water. I use the notion of visual experience representing water as a way of setting up the issue, but it does not play any essential role in my argument. Further, it should be noted that disallowing visually representing water as water has the effect of limiting the resources available to the representationist.

Next, a terminological reminder. I take a qualitative character or quale as a phenomenal property of an experience that eludes the intentional, the functional, and the purely cognitive. "Phenomenal character" is a more neutral term that carries no commitment to qualia. Both the representationist and the phenomenist can agree that there are phenomenal characters, even though the former but not the latter thinks phenomenal characters are wholly representational.

Supervenience

If phenomenal character supervenes on the brain, there is a straightforward argument against representationism. For arguably, there are brains that are the same as yours in internal respects (molecular constitution) but whose states represent *nothing* at all. Consider the Swampman, the molecular duplicate of you who comes together by chance from particles in the swamp. He is an example of total lack of representational content. How can he refer to Newt Gingrich when he has never had any causal connection with him; he hasn't ever seen Newt or anyone else on TV, never seen a newspaper, and so on. But although he has no past, he does have a future. If at the instant of creation, his brain is in the same configuration that yours is in when you see a ripe tomato, it might be said that the Swampman's state has the same representational content as yours in virtue of that state's role in allowing him to "track" things in the future that are the same in various respects (e.g., color) as the tomato. It might be said that he will track appearances of Bill Clinton in the future just as well as you will. But this invocation of the Swampman's future is not very convincing. Sure, he will track

Bill Clinton if he materializes in the "right" environment (an environment in which Bill Clinton exists and has the superficial appearance of the actual Bill Clinton), but in the wrong environment he will track someone else or no one at all. And the same point applies to his ability to track water and even color. If put on Twin Earth, he will track twin-water, not water. Of course, you will have the same tracking problems if suddenly put in "wrong" environments, but your references are grounded by the very past that you have and the Swampman lacks.

If we can assume supervenience of phenomenal character on the brain, we can refute the representationist. The phenomenal character of the Swampman's experience is the same as yours but its experiences have no representational content at all. So phenomenal character cannot be representational content. And the case of two different Swampmen who have different phenomenal characters but the same (null) representational content shows phenomenal character does not even supervene on representational content. If this point is right, there will be a great temptation for the representationist to deny supervenience of phenomenal character on the brain. And in fact, that's what representationists often do (Dretske 1995; Lycan 1996a,b; McDowell 1994). This seems to me to be a desperate maneuver with no independent plausibility. The independent arguments against representationism to follow constitute a partial justification of supervenience, since if representationism were true, supervenience would be false.

What Is the Issue?

One of the ways that I have been framing the issue is this: Is there more to experience than its representational content? But if experiences are brain states, there will be more to experiences than their representational contents just as there is more to sentences in English than their representational contents. For example, the size of the font of this sentence is something more than (or anyway, other than) its representational content. So the question is better taken as: Is there anything *mental* in experience over and above its representational content? I say yes, the representationist says no.

Harman (1990, 1996) expresses his version of representationism about experience by claiming that in experience we are aware only of properties of what is *represented*, not the vehicle of representation. When we look at a red tomato, no matter how hard we try to introspect the aspect of the experience that *represents* redness, all we succeed in doing is focusing our attention on the redness of the tomato itself. Harman relies on the diaphanousness of perception (Moore 1922), which may be defined as the claim that the effect of concentrating on experience is simply to attend to and be aware of what the experience is of. As a point about attention in one familiar circumstance— for example, looking at a red tomato—this is certainly right. The more one concentrates on the experience, the more one attends to the redness of the tomato itself. But attention and awareness are distinct, and as a point about awareness, the diaphanousness claim is both straightforwardly wrong and misleading. One can be aware of what one is not attending to. For example, one might be involved in intense conversation while a jackhammer outside causes one to raise one's voice without ever noticing or attending to the noise until someone comments on it—at which time one realizes that one was aware of it all along. Or consider the familiar experience of noticing that the refrigerator compressor has gone off and that one was aware of it for some time, even though one didn't attend to it until it stopped. (These and other examples of attention without awareness are discussed in Block 1995a, and in Tyler Burge's reply to this volume. I am grateful to Burge for discussion of this issue.)

So Harman is wrong about awareness, even if he is right about attention. Further, though Harman is right about attention in one common circumstance, I believe he is wrong about attention in other circumstances. For example, close your eyes in daylight and you may find that it is easy to attend to aspects of your experience. If all experiences that have visual phenomenology were of the sort one gets with one's eyes closed while awake in daylight, I doubt that the thesis that one cannot attend to or be aware of one's experience would be so popular. Another way to appreciate the point: Stick your finger in front of your face, then focus on something distant. It does not seem so hard (at least to me) to attend to and be aware of aspects of the experience of the finger as well as of the finger.

The points just made are preliminary. They are just appeals to introspection—mine, and I hope yours—that go against representationism. If you agree, you are ready to reject representationism. But the main purpose of this section is to get clearer on what exactly you would be rejecting.

Harman can allow that there are many properties of experience that we are aware of. For example, we know when an experience happens and how long it lasted. But that will no doubt be glossed by him as a matter of when we looked at the tomato and how long we looked. Harman concludes that introspection gives us no access to anything "nonrepresentational" about the experience, nothing whose identity is not given representationally, no access to mental paint. He argues that the contrary view confuses properties of what is represented, the intentional object of perception, with properties of the vehicle of representation, what is doing the representing. I don't agree with the imputation of fallacy. But my point right now is more preliminary: that if Harman means to define representationism in this way, his definition is too narrow.

Harman writes as if the issue is whether we can introspect the representational features of the experience, the mental paint that represents the redness of the tomato. But there are two deeper issues.

1. The first is whether there *is* mental paint, even if Harman were right that we cannot become aware of it when we are seeing a tomato. One way—not the only way—of seeing why there is a real issue here is to consider the idea that the possibility of an

inverted spectrum shows that there is more to experience than its representational content. According to this argument (Shoemaker 1982; Block 1990; see also Block and Fodor 1972), your experience and my experience could have exactly the same representational content, say, as of red, but your experience could have the same phenomenal character as my experience as of green. Shoemaker (1994a,b) agrees with Harman's views about introspection. He agrees that we cannot be aware of mental paint, that when we try to introspect the experience of the redness of the tomato, all we succeed in doing is attending to and being aware of the represented color of the tomato itself. But according to Shoemaker, we have a kind of indirect introspective access to the phenomenal character of the experience via our intuitions about the inverted spectrum. By imagining that things we both call red look to you the same way that things we both call green look to me, we succeed in gaining indirect introspective access to mental paint. Thus there is mental paint. So Shoemaker's view gives us an example of how on certain assumptions it would be reasonable to think that there is mental paint even if we can't be directly aware of it, and that is one way of illustrating the distinction.

Shoemaker's view is highly paradoxical—there is mental paint but it is a theoretical entity. It is of the essence of mental paint to be something of which we are aware. This view would be less paradoxical if Shoemaker's "phenomenal properties" of objects were really just phenomenal characters of experiences projected onto objects. The phenomenal character of an experience determines what phenomenal property it represents, and the phenomenal property is individuated in accord with and gets its identity from the phenomenal character that determines it. Thus far, Shoemaker's phenomenal properties look like mere projections of phenomenal characters onto the world. But there is one crucial feature of Shoemaker's view that resists this attempt to blunt the paradox, namely that Shoemaker takes phenomenal properties to be causally efficacious, indeed to cause the instantiation of the phenomenal characters that help to individuate them. Shoemaker's view is discussed in more detail in note 2.

2. A second issue is whether there are phenomenal features of experience that are not *even* vehicles of representation. For example, according to me, the phenomenal character of the experience of orgasm is partly nonrepresentational. Such a nonrepresentational mental feature would be (in this respect) like the oil in oil-based paint. So we could put the two issues as whether there is mental paint and whether there is mental oil.

To sum up then, we can distinguish three things:

1. The intentional content of an experience. I am currently looking at a tomato and my experience represents the tomato as red.
2. Mental properties of the experience that represent the redness of the tomato. This is mental paint. According to me, the phenomenal character of the experience is such a

mental property: It represents the tomato as red. According to me, one can attend to this phenomenal character and be aware of it even when one is not attending to it. Representationists would deny both.

3. Mental properties of the experience that don't represent anything. This is mental oil. I don't know whether there are any such properties in the case of a normal experience of a red tomato, but I do claim that such properties are involved in orgasm-experience, pain, and other bodily sensations.

These distinctions allow us to see an ambiguity in 'nonrepresentational'. In the most straightforward sense, if as I claim there are phenomenal properties of orgasm-experience that don't represent anything (the ones that make orgasm experience something one wants to have), then those properties are nonrepresentational. But there is also a weaker sense: The phenomenal character of color experience, for example, could be said to be nonrepresentational in that the identity of that phenomenal character is not given by its representational content. In this weak sense, we can agree that color experience *has* representational content while at the same time regarding it as nonrepresentational because that representational content is not the whole essence of the experience.

As I mentioned, Harman says that we are aware only of what is represented by our experience, the intentional object of the experience, not what is doing the representing, not the vehicle of representation. But what will Harman say about illusions, cases where the intentional object does not exist? Surely, there can be something in common to a veridical experience of a red tomato and a hallucination of a red tomato, and what is in common can be introspectible. This introspectible commonality cannot be constituted by or explained by the resemblance between something and nothing. It would be better for the representationist to say that what is in common is an intentional content, not an intentional object. Disjunctivists like McDowell deny that there is anything introspectible in common. But how can they understand the perceptual situations in which one can be reliably fooled, in which one has no idea whether the perception is veridical or not? "It only *seems* that there is something perceptual in common." But why doesn't whatever mental aspect that grounds the seeming constitute the phenomenal similarity?

On the face of it, the disjunctivist has a liability beyond those of the representationist. The representationist can appeal to the intentional content that is shared by the two experiences, the content that there is a red tomato in front of me. Suppose Harman were to hold that we are aware of the shared intentional content; what would that come to? What is it to be aware of the intentional content that I am seeing a red tomato or that two experiences have that intentional content? I don't see what awareness *of* an intentional content could come to if not awareness *that* some state has that intentional content. And, one might speculate, awareness that two experiences have the same intentional content requires awareness that each has that intentional content. So if Harman were to give this representationist account of the introspectible similarity, he would have to concede that we have introspective awareness of some mental properties of experience, not just of the intentional objects of experience.

The representationist view I've just mentioned is taken by Lycan (1995)—that one can be aware of a family of mental properties of an experience, namely *that* the experience represents something, that it represents a tomato, that it represents the tomato as red, and so on. So Lycan can deal with illusions by saying that when one hallucinates a red tomato, there is something introspective in common with a normal veridical perception of a tomato, namely in both cases one is aware that the experience represents a red tomato.[2] Though Lycan's position does accommodate common sense better than the disjunctivist, it is nonetheless implausible. A child who has no concept of representation or of intentional content can be aware of what is in common to two experiences that represent that a tomato is red.

Some representationists combine externalism and internalism. For example, Rey (1992a,b) individuates color experience partly in terms of what colors it represents and partly in terms of what he sees as syntactic properties of the vehicle of representation. (There is a similar view in Lycan 1996b.) I won't try to consider such mixed views here.

Those who deny both mental paint and oil are representationists; those who countenance one or the other are phenomenists. The representationists include Byrne and Hilbert (1997a), Dretske (1995, 1996), Harman (1990, 1996), Lycan (1995, 1996), McDowell (1994), Rey (1992a,b) and Tye (1995, 1996). (See also White 1995 for a representationist view of color experience.) The phenomenists include Burge (1997), Block (1990, 1994a), Loar (1990), McGinn (1991), Peacocke (1983), and Shoemaker (1982, 1994a,b). (Shoemaker's view combines aspects of both representationism and phenomenism, though I count him as a phenomenist here.)[3] Shoemaker and I hold that the Inverted Spectrum argument and the Inverted Earth argument make strong cases for phenomenism. (Loar, McGinn, and Peacocke have declared doubts about the Inverted Spectrum arguments; I don't know what they think of the Inverted Earth argument.) I won't go into the Inverted Spectrum argument here, and I will only be able to mention Inverted Earth briefly. I will mention some other considerations that are less effective, but which I hope put some pressure on the representationist.

Bodily Sensations

Is the experience of orgasm completely captured by a representational content *that there is an orgasm?* Orgasm is phenomenally *impressive* and there is nothing very impressive about the representational content *that there is an orgasm.* I just expressed it and you just understood it, and nothing phenomenally impressive happened (at least not on my end). I can have an experience whose content is that my partner is having an orgasm without *my* experience being phenomenally impressive. In response to my raising this issue (Block 1995a,b), Tye (1995a) says that the representational content of orgasm "in part, is that something very pleasing is happening down *there*. One also experiences the pleasingness alternately increasing and diminishing in its intensity." But once again, I can have an experience whose representational content is that my *partner* is having a very pleasing experience down *there* that changes in intensity, and although that may be pleasurable for me, it is not pleasurable in the phenomenally impressive way that that graces my own orgasms. I vastly prefer my own orgasms to those of others, and this preference is based on a major league phenomenal difference. The location of "down there" differs slightly between my perception of your orgasms and my own orgasms, but how can the representationist explain why a small difference in represented location should matter so much? Of course, which subject the orgasm is ascribed to is itself a representational matter. But is that the difference between my having the experience and my perceiving yours? Is the difference just that my experience *ascribes* the pleasure to you rather than to me (or to part of me)? Representational content can go awry in the heat of the moment. What if in a heated state in which cognitive function is greatly reduced, I *mistakenly* ascribe your orgasm to me or mine to you? Would this difference in ascription really *constitute* the difference between the presence or absence of the phenomenally impressive quality? Perhaps your answer is that there is a *way* in which my orgasm-experience ascribes the orgasm to me that is immune to the intrusion of thought, so there is no possibility of a confused attribution to you in *that way*. But now I begin to wonder whether this talk of "way" is closet phenomenism.

No doubt there are functional differences between my having an orgasm-experience and merely ascribing it to you. Whether this fact will help to defend representationism depends on whether and how representationism goes beyond functionalism, a matter to be discussed in the section after next.

Lycan (1996c) appeals to the following representational properties (of male orgasm): It is "ascribed to a region of one's own body," and the represented properties include "at least warmth, squeezing, throbbing, pumping and voiding. (On some psycho-semantics, I suppose, impregnating is represented as well)" (p. 136). Lycan says that it is "impracticable to try to capture detailed perceptual content in ordinary English words, at least in anything like real time," but he thinks he has said enough to "remove reasonable suspicion that there are nonintentional qualitative features left over in addition to the functional properties that are already considered characteristic of the sensation." But Lycan's list of properties represented seems to me to *increase* the suspicion rather than removing it. *Everything* that matters (phenomenally speaking) is left over.

According to me, there are features of the experience of orgasm that don't represent anything; so mental oil exists. I don't expect this example to force representationists to concede that mental oil exists. Appeals to intuitions about relatively unstructured cases are rarely successful. That is why the complex thought experiments such as those involving the inverted spectrum and inverted earth are useful. I believe that complex cases can be framed that reflect our concepts so directly that everyone can be brought to agree with them. The argument can leave the intuitions behind and move to the philosophical question of what they show.

Of course, we should not demand that a representationist be able to capture his contents in words. But if we are to try to believe that the experience of orgasm is nothing over and above its representational content, we need to be told something fairly concrete about what that representational content is. Suppose the representational content is specified in terms of recognitional dispositions or capacities. One problem with this suggestion is that the *experience* of orgasm seems on the face of it to have little to do with *recognizing* orgasms. Perhaps when I say to myself "There's that orgasm experience again" I have a somewhat different experience from the cases where no recognition goes on. But there is no plausibility in the insistence that the experience *must* involve some sort of categorization. And if you are inclined to be very intellectual about human experience, think of animals. Perhaps animals have the experience without any recognition.

The representationists should put up or shut up. The burden of proof is on them to say what the representational content of experiences such as orgasm is.

Phosphene-Experiences

Harman (1990) says "Look at a tree and try to turn your attention to intrinsic features of your visual experience. I predict you will find that the only features there to turn your attention to will be features of the represented tree." But the diaphanousness of perception is much less pronounced in a number of visual phenomena, notably phosphene-experiences. (I use the cumbersome "phosphene-experience" instead of the simpler "phosphene" by way of emphasizing that the phenomenist need not have any commitment to phenomenal individuals.) If all of our visual experiences were like these, representationism would have been less attractive. Phosphene-experiences are visual sensations "of" color and light stimulated by pressure on the eye or by electrical or magnetic fields. (I once saw an ad for goggles that you could put on your eyes that generated phosphenes via a magnetic field.) Phosphene-experiences have been extensively studied, originally in the nineteenth Century by Purkinje and Helmholz. Close your eyes and place the heels of your hands over your eyes. Push your eyeballs lightly for about a minute. You will have color sensations.

Can you attend to those sensations? I believe I can. Even if you can't attend to them, are you aware of them? According to the representationist, all awareness of those sensations could consist in is awareness of the colored moving expanses that are represented by them. My view is that one can be aware of something more. Again, I don't think this sort of consideration can change anyone's mind, but I hope it will have an impact on the noncommitted.

Lycan (1987) says: "given any visual experience, it seems to me, there is *some* technological means of producing a veridical qualitative equivalent—e.g. a psychedelic movie shown to the subject in a small theater" (p. 90). But there is no guarantee that phosphene-experiences produced by pressure or electromagnetic stimulation could be produced by light. (Note I don't say there is a guarantee that phosphene-experiences could *not* be produced by light, but only that there is no guarantee that they could; I have no idea whether they could or not.) I do wonder if Lycan's unwarranted assumption plays a role in leading philosophers to suppose that the phenomenal characters of phosphene-experiences, afterimage-experiences, and the like are exhausted by their representational content.

Bach-y-Rita

According to me, in normal perception one can be aware of the mental paint—the sensory quality that does the representing. This idea can be illustrated (this is more of an illustration than it is an argument) by Bach-y-Rita's famous experiment in which he gave blind people a kind of vision by hooking up a TV camera that produced tactual sensations on their backs. Bach-y-Rita says that the subjects would normally attend to what they were "seeing." He says "unless specifically asked, experienced subjects are not attending to the sensation of stimulation on the skin of their back, although this can be recalled and experienced in retrospect" (quoted in Humphrey 1992, p. 80). The retrospective attention of which Bach-y-Rita speaks is a matter of attending in retrospect to a feature of one's experience that one was aware of but not attending to when the perception originally happened, as with the jackhammer and refrigerator examples mentioned earlier. Of course, the analogy is not perfect. In attending to visual sensations, we are not normally attending to sensations of the eye (Harman 1996).

I think that the Bach-y-Rita experiment is useful in thinking about the two versions of representationism mentioned above. Let me remind you about the difference. Harman seems to say that all we can introspect in experience are the intentional objects of experience. Lycan, however, allows that we can actually introspect certain properties of the experiences themselves. At first glance, reflection on the Bach-y-Rita experiment provides support for Lycan over Harman. For the ability of Bach-y-Rita's subjects to introspect their tactual sensations helps to remind us that we really can notice features of our own visual sensations. But Lycan's concession, you will recall, was to allow introspection of *the property of having certain intentional properties*. But is that what Bach-y-Rita's subjects were doing? Were they introspecting *that the sensations on their backs represented, say, a couch?* Perhaps occasionally, but I doubt that that's what Bach-y-Rita was talking about. I think he meant that they were attending to the experiential quality of the feelings on their backs. And I think that this case helps to remind us that at least sometimes when we introspect visual experience, we are attending to the phenomenal properties of experience, not the fact that they have certain intentional properties. So although Lycan's version of representationism is superior to Harman's in allowing *the existence of* introspection of something other than intentional properties of experience, it is not true to what that introspection is often like.[4]

Moving now to the orgasm and pain cases, as I mentioned earlier, there is a challenge here for the representationist. Just what is the representational content of these states? In vision, it often is plausible to appeal to recognitional dispositions in cases where we lack the relevant words. What's the difference between the representational contents of the experience of color A and color B, neither of which has a name? As I mentioned earlier, one representationist answer is this: The recognitional dispositions themselves provide or are the basis of these contents. My experience represents A as *that* color, and I can *mis*represent some other color as *that* color. But note that this model can't straightforwardly be applied to pain. Suppose I have two pains that are the same in intensity, location, and anything else that language can get a handle on—but they still feel different. Say they are both twinges that I have had before, but they aren't burning or sharp or throbbing. "There's *that* one again; and there's that other one" is the best I can do. If we rely on my ability to pick out *that* pain, (arguably) we are demonstrating a phenomenal character, not specifying a representational content. (Note the difference between Loar's 1990 proposal of a recognitional view of phenomenal *concepts* and the current suggestion that a recognitional disposition can specify phenomenal character itself. Phenomenal character is what a phenomenal concept specifies or refers to.) The appeal to recognitional dispositions to fill in representational contents that can't be specified in words has some plausibility, so long as the recognitional dispositions are directed outward. But once we direct them inward, one begins to wonder whether the resulting view is an articulation of representationism or a capitulation to phenomenism. I will return to this point.[5]

Is Representationism Just a Form of Functionalism?

Consider what I call *quasi-representationism*. Quasi-representationists agree with phenomenists that there are differences between sensory modalities that cannot be cashed out representationally. One modality is flashing lights, another is tooting horns. But quasi-representationists agree with representationists that *within* a single modality, all phenomenal differences are representational differences. (I think that this is the view that Peacocke 1983, ch. 1 argues against.)

Some philosophers are attracted to representationism but can't bring themselves to treat the experiential differences between, say, vision and touch as entirely representational. So they appeal to the fact that visual and touch representations of, say, an edge, function differently. They plug a gap in representationism with functionalism. (Block 1996 and Robinson 1998 interpret Lycan 1996c in this way.) But they should tell us why they don't reject representationism altogether in favor of functionalism. Some philosophers start with functionalism, but don't see how to handle afterimages (and perhaps other putatively intentional phenomena) functionally (Lycan 1996a,b). So they add representationism (Lycan 1996c). Perhaps both doctrines are wrong by themselves, but there is a third that draws on the resources of both that works.

Many philosophers in the representationist ballpark are rather vague about whether they are pure representationists or quasi-representationists, but Tye (1995b) makes it clear that he is a pure representationist. (Harman tells me he is a quasi-representationist and Lycan 1996c declares quasi-representationism.)

How can we decide whether the antiphenomenist needs both representationism and functionalism? Suppose I both touch and see a dog. Both experiences represent the dog as a dog, but they are different phenomenally. Representationists are quick to note that the two experiences also differ in all sorts of other representational ways. (See Tye 1995a, for example.) The visual experience represents the dog as having a certain color, whereas the tactual experience represents it as having a certain texture and temperature. In Block (1995a,b) I tried to avoid this type of rejoinder by picking experiences with very limited representational content. If you wave your hand in the vicinity of your ear, your peripheral vision gives you an awareness of movement without size, shape, or color. You have a visual experience that plausibly represents something moving over there *and nothing else*. And I imagined that there were auditory experiences with the same content. But my expert consultants tell me that I was wrong. There is no auditory analogue of peripheral vision. For example, any auditory experience will represent a sound as having a certain loudness. But that does not ruin the point. It just makes it slightly harder to see. Imagine the experience of hearing something and seeing it in your peripheral vision. It is true that you experience the sound as having a certain loudness, but can't we abstract away from that, concentrating on the perceived location? And isn't there an obvious difference between the auditory experience *as of that location* and the visual experience *as of that location*? If so, then there is either mental paint or mental oil. (The ways in which representationally identical experiences might be phenomenally different could involve differences in either paint or oil.)[6]

Seeing Red for the First Time

Marvin is raised in a black and white room, never seeing anything of any other color. Further, as with Erisa, he never learns that fire engines and ripe tomatoes are red or that grass is green, and so on. Then he is taken outside and shown something red without being told that it is red. (I've changed "Mary" to "Marvin" so as to emphasize the small differences between this and Jackson's 1982 argument.) He learns what it is like to see red, even though, unlike Mary, he is not told what that color is *called*. He might say: "So *that's* what it is like to see *that* color."

Lewis (1990) (following Nemirow) says that Marvin aquires an ability, some sort of recognitional know-how. But as Loar (1990) notes, this idea can't account for embedded judgements. Here's an example that fits the Marvin case: "If *that's* what it is like to see red, then I will be surprised." (Loar is applying a standard argument against nondescriptivism in ethics. Perhaps followers of Lewis and Nemirow will try to utilize nondescriptivist attempts to deal with the problem by Blackburn 1993 and Gibbard 1990.)

What does the representationist say about what Marvin has learned? If Marvin is told that what he sees is red, the representationist might say that he has acquired a visual representational concept, the concept of red. But can the representationist say this if Marvin doesn't know *that* it is red? Perhaps the representationist will say this:

He acquires the concept of red without the name 'red'. What Marvin acquires is a recognitional concept. After all, he can say "There's *that* color again." He has a recognitional concept that he applies on the basis of vision, even though it doesn't link up to his linguistic color concepts.

But there is a trap for the representationist in this reply. For what, according to the representationist, is the difference between Marvin's concept of red and Marvin's concept of blue? He recognizes both. When he sees a red patch he says "There's *that* color again" and when then sees a blue patch he says "There's *that other* color again," each time collating his outer ostension with an inner ostension. But what, according to the representationist, is the difference between Marvin's concept of red and Marvin's concept of blue? The phenomenist will link the difference to an internal difference, the difference in the phenomenal qualities of the experience of blue and the experience of red. But the representationist can't appeal to that without changing sides. What else is there of a suitably internal sort for the representationist to appeal to? (Remember, we are supposing, as with Erisa raised in the room of changing colors, that Marvin knows nothing that distinguishes the unnamed colors, no abiding beliefs to the effect that this color has certain properties that that color doesn't have.) The appeal to a recognitional disposition suggests that the representationist is appealing to the *colors* themselves. What makes his concept of red different from his concept of blue is that he applies the former in recognizing red and the latter in recognizing blue.

In a response to an earlier version of this objection to representationism (Block 1996), Lycan (1996c, p. 137) gives an answer to my question about what the difference is between Marvin's concept of red and Marvin's concept of blue. "Answer: that the former represents the (or a) physical property of objective redness while the latter represents objective blueness." I believe that this is an important concession on the part of the externalist representationists because it eases the way for a variety of thought experiment arguments, some of which will be considered later in this essay. (Here's one that won't be considered later: Imagine that Marvin has somewhat different color vision in one eye from the other. Can't he have phenomenally *different* experiences of the *same* color? Here's another: Suppose a Cartesian demon fools Marvin. His two concepts that he takes to pick out different colors actually pick out the same color. But surely the concepts are different independently of what they pick out!) But even independently of such thought experiments, if the representationist is willing to recognize a color concept that has been cut loose from everything but recognition, why shouldn't he also recognize such concepts turned inward? Why can't he have a recognitional concept of his own phenomenal state—"There's *that* experience again." And that would just be a phenomenal concept. (I don't mean to imply that I think it would be natural for Marvin to invoke such a highly sophisticated concept in recognizing that he is seeing the same color again. Phenomenal concepts, that is concepts of phenomenal characters, are highly sophisticated.)

Rey (1992a,b) postulates that color experiences involve the tokenings of special restricted predicates in the language of thought. So he would say that Marvin tokens 'R' when he sees red and 'B' when he sees blue. Is that a suitable representationist answer? Recall that we are now discussing *externalist* representationism, and Rey's view would deal with this problem by bringing in an internalist element. Recall my objection to internalism in terms of Erisa, the girl raised in the room in which everything changes colors. Erisa perhaps has more or less normal color experience but may have no abiding asymmetrical associations in her color experience. So what's the *representational* difference between her 'R' and 'B'? Suppose Rey says: "who needs a representational difference; the syntactic difference is enough." Then it becomes difficult to see why he is not just an old-fashioned eliminativist. Let me explain. I am a reductionist, a *physicalist* phenomenist. I believe that the difference between Marvin's experience of red and of blue is a physical difference. I suspect it is a difference in brain events that is not naturally capturable in terms of "syntax," since talk of syntax in connection with brain processes will most likely apply, if anywhere, to language areas of the brain rather than to visual areas, but I am flexible on this issue. Certainly no position on the syntax issue is an important feature of the physicalist-phenomenist position. I allow that it is an empirical question (of course) what the physical natures of phenomenal qualities are. Perhaps these natures are syntactical or even functional (psychofunctional, that is, in the terminology of Block 1978). In sum, no doubt the internalist antiphenomenist can find some physicalistic surrogate for qualia, but a suitable surrogate will be the very item that the physicalist phenomenist will think of qualia as reduced to. And then the difference will be like the difference between the reductionist who says that there is water and it is H_2O and the eliminativist who says there is H_2O but no water. And eliminativism about phenomenal character is even less plausible than eliminativism about water.

Jackson uses his "Mary" case to argue against physicalism. Mary knows all the physico-functional facts, but nonetheless learns a new fact, so there are facts that aren't among the physico-functional facts. I accept the familiar refutation of this argument along the lines of: Mary learns a new concept of something she already knew. She acquires a phenomenal concept of a physical fact that she was already acquainted with via a physical concept (Loar 1990). The point of this section is that an adaptation of Jackson's case is more effective in setting up an argument against representationism than it is against physicalism.

Externalist Memory

At the beginning of the discussion of externalism, I discussed the thought experiment in which I, a native of Putnam's Twin Earth, emigrated to Earth. When I first looked at water, I thought it was twin-water and, we are agreeing to suppose, my visual experience represented it as twin-water. Much later, after learning everything that I've just told you, my allegiances shifted; in effect, I decided to become a member of the Earth language community, to speak English, not Twenglish. Now, when I look at the sea, I take what I am seeing to be water and my visual experience represents it as water (let's suppose), not twin-water.

(How could a *conceptual* change affect a *visual* representation? Though nothing here depends on the matter, I will briefly mention the rationale. There is a difference between seeing a group of buildings as a hospital and seeing them as a nuclear reactor. These are conceptual differences but they make a visual difference. *Seeing as* is both conceptual and visual.)

Though my conceptual and visual representation of water has changed during my stay on earth, in some very obvious sense, water looks the same to me as it did the first time I saw it even though my representational content has changed. If you blindfolded me and put me down at the seaside, I would not know from looking at the liquid in the ocean whether it was water or twin-water. My phenomenal character has stayed the same even though the representational content of my visual experience changed. But this doesn't yet show that there is anything nonrepresentational about phenomenal character. For the shared *representational* contents can be appealed to explain why there's no difference in what it's like to see water. Here is the representationist picture: Experiences have representational properties of two types, and the phenomenal character of an experience can be identified with one of those two types. The nonphenomenal type includes the representation of water as water, the phenomenal type includes representations of such "appearance properties" as color. (See Block 1995a,b and Tye 1995a.) The visual representation of these appearance properties includes non-conceptual representations according to many representationists, and these are the ones whose representational content is identified with phenomenal character. (This is the view of Dretske, Lycan, and Tye.) What I will argue is that there is a Twin Earth case that turns on a property that does not allow a reply corresponding to the one just made with respect to water. The property is color, which is an "appearance property" if anything is. The upshot, I will argue, is that there is mental paint (but there is no argument here for mental oil). I will illustrate this point with an argument from Block (1990, 1994a) about color. I won't go into this argument in full detail.[7]

Inverted Earth is a place that differs from Earth in two important ways. First, everything is the complementary color of the corresponding Earth object. The sky is yellow, the grasslike stuff is red, and so on. Second, people on inverted earth speak an inverted language. They use "red" to mean green, "blue" to mean yellow, and so forth. If you order a sofa from Inverted Earth and you want a yellow sofa, you fax an order for a "blue" sofa (speaking their language). The two inversions have the effect that if wires are crossed in your visual system (and your body pigments are changed), you will *notice no difference* when you go to Inverted Earth. After you step off the spaceship, you see some twin-grass. You point at it, saying it is a nice shade of "green," but you are wrong. You are wrong for the same reason that you are wrong if you call the liquid in a Twin Earth lake "water" just after you arrive there. The grass is red (of course I am speaking English not Twenglish here). But after you have decided to adopt the concepts and language of the Inverted Earth language community and you have been there for fifty years, your word "red" and the representational content of your experience as of red things (things that are *really* red) will shift so that you represent them *correctly*. Then, your words will mean the same as those of the members of your adopted language community and your visual experience will represent colors veridically.

Your color words and color concepts shift in meaning and content, and your color experiences shift in representational content, but the explanations are not exactly the same. Concepts shift for reasons familiar from the work of Burge and Putnam. But the representational contents of color experience may be nonconceptual and therefor not linked to the use of concepts in the language community. Still, nonconceptual contents arguably get their content causally. My dog recognizes me and has experiences that represent me even if my dog has no concept of me. If my dog goes to Twin Earth, she will react to Twin Block in just the way she reacts to me. She will mistakenly represent Twin Block as Block. But a Block-recognitional capacity is not a Twin-Block recognitional capacity, and that has to be because the Block-recognitional capacity involves causal contact with Block rather than Twin-Block. Further, any recognitional capacity can be "swamped" by a new causal source. Suppose that my dog meets Erisa for ten minutes and develops an Erisa recognitional capacity. Then the dog goes to Twin Earth and meets Twin Erisa, whom she misrecognizes as Erisa. Twin Erisa then adopts the dog. After ten years, the dog's Erisa-recognitional capacity has been replaced by a Twin-Erisa recognitional capacity. Evans introduced the dominant causal source account of reference, but the account covers some aspects of visual representation as well as linguistic representation.

It may be said that whereas the visual or olfactory representation of Erisa has a current causal source, the visual representational of colors has its source in evolutionary history. That issue will be taken up later.

In the old version of the thought experiment, you are kidnapped and inserted in a niche in Inverted Earth without your noticing it (your twin having been removed to make the niche). In the new version, you are aware of the move and consciously decide to adopt the concepts and language of the Inverted Earth language community. The change has the advantage of making it clearer that you become a member of the new community. On the old version, one might wonder what you would say if you found out about the change. Perhaps you would insist on your membership in the old language community and defer to it rather than to the new one. Your color concepts might be regarded as indeterminate in reference. Dennett (1991) made objections to the inverted spectrum case, which, applied to Inverted Earth, would say that there is no coherent interpretation of the conceptual representational contents of the traveler in the thought experiment. The point concerns conceptual contents, but applies nonetheless to nonconceptual contents. For suppose the traveler's memory images of the sky on his fifth birthday, taken to represent the same color as now, are intimately involved in every identification of the color of any yellow thing on Inverted Earth. We may feel that radical error suffuses all his color representations, nonconceptual as well as conceptual. But thinking of the traveler as knowing all along all we know shows how incoherence can be avoided. (In Block 1990, this problem—though with respect to the inverted spectrum rather than inverted earth—is dealt with by changing the thought experiment to involve amnesia for the earlier life. The same idea would work here as well, as Burge hints in his response.)

The upshot is:

1. The phenomenal character of your color experience stays the same. That's what you say, and why shouldn't we believe you?
2. But the representational content of your experience, being externalist, shifts with external conditions in the environment. (Recall that I am now discussing representationists who are externalists; I discussed internalist representationism at the beginning of the essay.)

Your phenomenal character stays the same, but what it represents changes. This provides the basis of an argument for mental paint, not mental oil. Mental paint is what stays the same; its representational content is what changes.

What exactly is the argument for mental paint? Imagine that on the birthday just before you leave for Inverted Earth, you are looking at the clear blue sky. Your visual experience represents it as blue. Years later, you have a birthday party on Inverted Earth and you look at the Inverted Earth sky. Your visual experience represents it as yellow (since that's what color it is and your visual experience by that time is veridical, let us suppose—I'll deal with an objection to this supposition later). But the phenomenal character stays the same, as indicated by the fact that you can't tell the difference. So there is a gap between the representational content of experience and its phenomenal character. Further, the gap shows that phenomenal character outruns representational content. Why? How could the representationist explain what it is about the visual experience that stays the same? What representational content can the representationist appeal to in order to explain what stays the same? This is the challenge to the representationist, and I think it is a challenge that the representationist cannot meet.

The comparison with the water case is instructive. There, you will recall, we also had phenomenal continuity combined with representational change. But the representationist claimed that the phenomenal continuity itself could be given a representational interpretation. The phenomenal character of my visual experiences of twin-water and water were the same, but their representational contents differed. No problem, because the common phenomenal character could be said by the representationist to be a matter of the representation of color, sheen, flow pattern, and the like. But what will the representationist appeal to in the Inverted Earth case that corresponds to color, sheen, flow pattern, and the like?

Objections

There are many obvious objections to this argument, some of which I have considered elsewhere. I will confine myself here to two basic lines of objection.

Bill Lycan has recently objected (1996a,b) that the testimony of the subject can show only that the phenomenal character of color experience is indistinguishable moment to moment, and that allows the representationist to claim that the phenomenal character shifts *gradually*, in sync with the shift in the representational content of color experience. (I raised this objection in my 1990, p. 68.) The gradual shift of phenomenal character in sync with the gradual shift of representational content avoids any gap between them. But this objection ignores the *longer-term* memories. The idea is that you remember the color of the sky on your birthday last year, the year before that, ten years before that, and so on, and your long-term memory gives you good reason to think that the phenomenal character of the experience has not changed gradually. You don't notice any difference between your experience now and your experience five years ago or ten years ago or sixty years ago. Has the color of the American flag changed gradually over the years? The stars used to be yellow and now they are white? No, I remember the stars from my childhood! They were always white. Of course, memory *can* go wrong, but why should we suppose that it *must* go wrong here? Surely, the scenario just described (without memory failure) is both conceptually and empirically possible. (As to the empirical possibility, note that the thought experiment can be changed so as to involve a person raised in a room who is then moved to a different room where all the colors are changed. No need for a yellow sky, a yellow ceiling will do.)

Now a different objection may be mounted on Lycan's behalf—that the externalist representationist should be externalist about *memory*. According to the first version of my story, the representational contents of the subject's color experience have shifted without his knowing about it. So if my story is right, Lycan (if he is to be an externalist about memory) should say that the subject's color experience has shifted gradually without the subject's knowing it. And that *shows* that the subject's memory is defective.[8]

Why should we believe that memory is defective in this way? One justification is simply that the nature of phenomenal character is representational (and externalist), so the phenomenal character of experience shifts with its representational content. Since memory is powerless to reveal this shift, memory is by its nature defective.

But this justification is weak, smacking of begging the question. The Inverted Earth argument challenges externalist representationism about phenomenal character, so trotting in an "error theory," an externalist representationism about memory of phenomenal character to defend it is not very persuasive. The idea of the Inverted Earth argument is to exploit the first-person judgment that in the example as framed the subject *notices no difference*. The subject's experience and memories of that experience reveal no sign of the change in environment. Yet his representational contents shift. Since the contents in question are color contents, the move that was available earlier about a set of representational contents that capture what stays the same is not available here. And that suggests for reasons that I just gave that there is more to experience than its representational content. The defender of the view that memory is defective must blunt or evade the intuitive appeal of the first-person point of view to be successful. It is no good to simply invoke the doctrine that experience is representational. But the reply to the Inverted Earth argument as I presented it above does something close to it. It says that the memories of the representational contents are wrong, so the memories of the phenomenal characters are wrong too. But that is just to *assume* that as far as memory goes, phenomenal character is representational content. For the argument to have any force, there would need to be some independent reason for taking externalism about phenomenal memory seriously.

The representationist may reply that there is no question begging going on, but only thoroughgoing externalism about the phenomenal character of experience in all domains—in both perception and memory. But externalism about phenomenal memory has nothing to recommend it aside from its use in defending externalist representationism about phenomenal character. It is an error theory—it postulates that ordinary memory, for example about what it was like to see the sky a few minutes ago, is inherently defective. It has the consequence that there can be changes in the phenomenal character of my experience (due to changes in the world) that I am in principle incapable of detecting, no matter how large they are or how fast they happen. The founders of externalism (such as Tyler Burge) should not be pleased by such an invocation of the externalist point of view.

It will be useful to consider briefly a related objection to the Inverted Earth argument. Suppose it is said that the subject's (that is, your) representational contents don't ever switch. No matter *how* long you spend on Inverted Earth, the sky *still* looks blue to you. After all, as I have insisted, you notice no difference. So doesn't the sky continue to look *the same*, namely blue? This line of objection has more than a little force,[9] but it can easily be seen not to lead away from my overall conclusion. For it is hard to see how anyone could accept this objection without *also* thinking that the subject (viz., you) on Inverted Earth has an "inverted spectrum" relative to the other denizens of Inverted Earth. The sky looks yellow to them (recall that the sky there *is* yellow) but blue to you. And you are as functionally similar to them as you like. (We could even imagine that your monozygotic twin brother is one of them.). The sky on earth is blue and looks blue to normal people. The sky on Inverted Earth is yellow and looks yellow to normal residents. But the sky on Earth looked the same to you as the sky on Inverted Earth now looks. So you must be inverted either with respect to Earthians or Inverted Earthians.[10]

Shifted Spectra

A shifted spectrum would obtain if, for example, things that we both call "orange" look to you the way things we both call "reddish orange" look to me. There is an argument for shifted spectra that appeals to the fact that color vision varies from one *normal* person to another. There are three kinds of cone in the retina that respond to long, medium, and short wave light. The designations "long," "medium," and "short" refer to the peak sensitivities. For example, the long cones respond most strongly to long wavelengths but they also respond to medium wavelengths. Two normal people chosen at random will differ half the time in peak cone sensitivity by 1–2 nm (nanometers) or more. (More precisely, the standard deviation is 1–2 nm. See Lutze et al. 1990.) This is a considerable difference, given that the long wave and middle wave cones only differ in peak sensitivities by only about 25 nm. Further, there are a number of specific genetic divisions in peak sensitivities in the population that are analogous to differences in blood types (in that they are genetic polymorphisms, discontinuous genetic differences coding for different types of normal individuals). The most dramatic of these is a 51.5 percent/48.5 percent split in the population of two types of long wave cones that differ by 5–7 nm, roughly 24 percent of the difference between the peak sensitivities of long and middle wave cones (Neitz and Neitz 1998).[11] This characteristic is sex-linked. The distribution just mentioned is for men. Women have smaller numbers in the two extreme categories and a much larger number in between. As a result, the match on the Rayleigh test (described below) *most frequently made by female subjects occurs where no male matches* (Neitz and Jacobs 1986).[12]

These differences in peak sensitivities don't show up in normal activities, but they do reveal themselves in subtle experimental situations. One such experimental paradigm uses the anomalo-scope (devised in the nineteenth century by Lord Rayleigh), in which subjects are asked to make two halves of a screen match in color, where one half is lit by a mixture of red and green light and the other half is lit by yellow or orange light. The subjects can control the intensities of the red and green lights. Neitz et al. 1993 note that "People who differ in middle wavelength sensitivity (M) or long wavelength sensitivity (L) cone pigments disagree in the proportion of the mixture primaries required" (p. 117). That is, whereas one subject may see the two sides as the same in color, another subject may see them as different   for example, one redder than the other. When red and green lights are adjusted to match orange, women tend to see the men's matches as too green or too red (Neitz and Neitz 1998). Further, variation in peak sensitivities of cones is just one kind of color vision variation. In addition, the shape of the sensitivity curves varies. These differences are due to differences in macular pigmentation, which vary with "both age and degree of skin pigmentation" (Neitz and Jacobs 1986). Hence races that differ in skin pigmentation will differ in macular pigmentation. There is also considerable variation in amount of light absorption by preretinal structures. And this factor also varies with age.

I emphasize gender, race, and age to stifle the reaction that one group should be regarded as normal and the others as defective. There are standard tests for defective color vision such as the Ishihara and Farnsworth tests, and it is an empirical fact that most men and almost all women have nondefective color vision as measured by these tests. My point is only that the facts about variation that I have presented give us no reason at all to regard any gender, race, or age as abnormal in color vision.

Hardin (1993) mentions a classic study (by Hurvich, Jameson, and Cohen 1968) of the spectral location of unique green in a group of 50 normal subjects. Here is a table of locations:

5 subjects located unique green at	490 nm
11	500 nm
15	503 nm
11	507 nm
5	513 nm
2	517 nm

As Hardin notes, this is an enormous range, as can be seen in a number of ways. Take a look at a spectrum (such as the one in Hardin's book) and block off the other areas. Or look at the Munsell chips, noting that this range goes from 5 blue-green to 2.5 green. Or simply note that the 27 nm span of this group's location of unique green is 9 percent of the visible spectrum.

The upshot is that if we take a chip that any one subject in this experiment takes as being unique green, most of the others will see it as slightly off. Thus we are justified in supposing that the way any chip looks (colorwise) is unlikely to be exactly the same as the way that chip looks to most other people, especially if they differ in sex, race, or age. So now we have the beginnings of an argument against representationism. Jack and Jill have experience that represents red things as red even though they very likely experience red slightly differently.

But the argument doesn't quite work, for as representationists could reply, the representational contents of Jack's and Jill's color categories may differ too, so there is still no proven gap between representational content and phenomenal character. "Color categories?" you say. "I thought the representationist was talking about *nonconceptual* contents?" True, but the representationist has to allow that our visual experiences represent a scarlet thing as red as well as scarlet. For we experience scarlet things as both red and as scarlet. We experience two red things of different shades as having the same color, though not the same shade, so a representationist has to concede a component of the representational contents of experience that captures that fact about experience. The representationist has to allow representational content of both color and shade. Further, pigeons can be conditioned to peck when presented with things of a certain color, as well as of a certain narrow shade. Even if the pigeon lacks color concepts, it has something short of them that involves some kind of categorization of colors as well as shades, red as well as scarlet. Let's use the term "category" for this aspect of the nonconceptual contents that are conceptlike but can be had by animals that perhaps can't reason with the contents. Now we can see why the argument I gave doesn't quite work against the representationist. Jack's and Jill's experiences of a single red fire hydrant may differ in phenomenal character *but also* in representational content, because, say, Jack's visual category of red may include a shade that is included instead in Jill's visual category of orange. Furthermore, because of the difference in Jack's and Jill's color vision, the fire hydrant may look more red than orange to one, more orange than red to the other. So we don't yet have the wedge between phenomenal character and representational content.

Indeed, it is quite plausible that the varying nature of our perceptual apparatuses determines different extensions for common color words. (By "extension," I don't mean just what they apply or would apply their color words to, but what they would apply their words to in ideal conditions.) Some things that Jack categorizes as blue will be categorized by Jill as green, and it is implausible to regard either as mistaken. A sensible conclusion is that they use the words blue and green in somewhat different senses, both correctly. The objective nature of color, it might be said, derives from the overlap between persons with normal color perception. There are objects which should be agreed to be blue by everyone with normal color vision, and that's what makes them objectively blue. The objects that are not objectively blue, but are said to be blue by one normal person but not another are indeterminate in color. I endorse this point of view, though I think that it is of less value to the representationist than might appear at first glance.

The way to get the wedge between phenomenal character and representational content is to apply the argument just given to shades rather than colors. Let us co-opt the word "aquamarine" to denote a shade of blue that is as narrow as a shade can be, one that has no discriminable subshades. If Jack's and Jill's visual systems differ slightly in the ways that I described earlier, then we can reasonably suppose that aquamarine doesn't look to Jack the way it looks to Jill. Maybe aquamarine looks to Jack the way turquoise (a different minimal shade, let's say) looks to Jill. But why should we think that there is any difference between the representational contents of Jack's experience as of aquamarine and Jill's? They both acquired their categories of aquamarine by being shown (let's suppose) a standard aquamarine chip. It is that objective color that their (different) experiences of aquamarine both represent. The upshot is that there is an empirically based argument for a conclusion—what one might call "shifted spectra" that, while not as dramatic as an inverted spectrum, has much the same consequences for representationism and for the issue of whether there are uniform phenomenal characters corresponding to colors. There probably are small phenomenal differences among normal people that don't track the colors that are represented. Genders, races, and ages probably differ by shifted spectra. Thus, if representationism is right, if aquamarine things look aquamarine to men, they probably don't look aquamarine to women. And if aquamarine things look aquamarine to one race or age group, they probably don't look aquamarine to others. In sum: If representationism is right, color experience probably cannot be veridical for both men and women, both blacks and whites, both young and old. Hence representationism is not right.

I mentioned above that there is an objection to my first try at refuting representationism: Maybe Jack's visual category that represents red includes a shade that is included in Jill's visual category that represents orange. The present point is that the same argument does not apply to minimal shades themselves.[13]

This possibility should not disturb the functionalist, however, for even if there are phenomenal differences among representationally identical experiences as just supposed, the phenomenal differences might be revealed in subtle empirical tests of the sort I mentioned. That is, perhaps shifted spectra always result in different matches on a Rayleigh anomaloscope or other devices. But shifted spectra would still count against representationism.

There is a complication that I can't treat fully here. If you regard a certain mixture of blue and green as matching the aquamarine chip, but I don't, then our categories of aquamarine are applied by us to different things, and in that sense have different extensions. I don't regard this as showing our categories have different representational contents, since representational contents have to do with what objective colors are represented and the example given exploits an indeterminacy in objective color. There is no determinate answer as to whether the color of the mixture of blue and green (that matches aquamarine according to me but not you) actually *is* aquamarine. It is an objective fact that the standard aquamarine chip is aquamarine, but there is no fact of the matter as to whether the two mixtures of blue and green are aquamarine.

Representationist Objections

I will put an objection in the mouth of the representationist:

Whatever the differences in their visual systems, if Jack and Jill are normal observers, then in normal (or anyway ideal) conditions, the standard aquamarine chip has to look aquamarine to Jack and it also has to look aquamarine to Jill. After all, "looks aquamarine" just *means* that their perceptual contents represents the chip *as aquamarine*, and you have already agreed [above] that both Jack's and Jill's visual experience represent the chip as aquamarine. You have argued that the representational content of their visual experience is the same (viz., aquamarine), but the phenomenal character is different. However, we representationists don't recognize any kind of phenomenal character other than that which is given by the representational content—which is the same for Jack and Jill. The chips look aquamarine to both Jack and Jill, so they look the same to both Jack and Jill, so Jack and Jill have the same phenomenal characters on viewing the chips in any sense of "phenomenal character" that makes sense. If Jack and Jill have different brain states on viewing the aquamarine chip, that just shows that the different brain states differently realize the same phenomenal character.

Reply: We phenomenists distinguish between two senses of "looks the same." In what Shoemaker (1981) calls the intentional sense of "looks the same," the chips look the same (in respect of color) to Jack and Jill just in case both of their perceptual experiences represent it as having the same color. So I agree with the objection that there is a sense of "looks the same" in which the aquamarine chip does look the same to Jack and Jill. But where I disagree with the objection is that I recognize another sense of "looks the same," (the qualitative or phenomenal sense) a sense geared to phenomenal character, in which we have reason to think that the aquamarine chip does not look the same to Jack as to Jill. (The same distinction is made in somewhat different terms in Shoemaker 1981, Peacocke 1983, and Jackson 1977.) But the case at hand supports the phenomenist rather than the representationist. For we have reasons to believe that there is a sense in which the aquamarine chip does not look the same to Jack as to Jill.

One reason was given earlier: The chip that Jack regards as unique green (green with no hint of blue or yellow) is not regarded as unique green by most other people. So it looks different to Jack from the way it looks to most others, including, we may suppose, Jill. And the same is likely to be true for other chips, including the aquamarine chip. But there is another reason that even functionalists should agree to: Jack and Jill match differently on the anomaloscope. Recall that the match "most frequently made by female subjects occurs where no male matches." If Jack produces a mixture of blue and green which he says matches the aquamarine chip, Jill will be likely to see that mixture as either "bluer" than the chip or "greener" than the chip.

The big division in the ballpark we are talking about is between those who accept and those who reject qualia, that is, features of experience that go beyond the experience's representational, functional, and cognitive features. In effect, the argument just given uses functionalism against representationism. The functional differences between different perceivers suggest phenomenal differences, but we have yet to see how those phenomenal differences can be cashed out representationally, even if they can be cashed out functionally. So the argument does not show that there are qualia, though it does go part way, by challenging one of the resources of the anti-qualia forces.

Another representationist objection:

These empirical facts show that colors are not objective. A given narrow shade looks different to different groups, so the different groups represent it as having slightly different colors. Thus it *does* in fact have slightly different colors relative to these different groups. Famously, phenylthiocarbamide tastes bitter to many people but not to many others. Phenylthiocarbamide is not objectively bitter, but it is objectively bitter relative to one group and objectively nonbitter relative to another. Color is the same, though not so dramatically. There are no absolute colors—color is relative, though only slightly so.

Reply: The problem with this objection derives from a difference between our concept of taste and our concepts of at least some colors, or rather shades. We are happy to agree that phenylthiocarbamide has no objective taste—it tastes bitter to some but not others. But we do not agree that Munsell color chip 5 Red has no objective hue. Its objective hue is 5 Red no matter whether it looks different to people of different genders, races, and ages. The whole point of the Munsell color scheme, the Optical Society of America Uniform Color Space, and other color schemes is to catalog objective colors (see Hardin 1988). Every American grade school child knows the colors named by the Crayola company, despite differences in the way Burnt Sienna or Brick Red probably looks to different children. If you paint your living room wall Benjamin Moore Linen White, it is an objective fact that you have not painted it Cameo White, Dove White, Opal White, or Antique White. If you have ordered White 113 but the paint store gives you White 114, you can get your money back. (The premixed colors have names in the Benjamin Moore scheme; the custom colors, of which there are very many, as anyone who has ever picked out one of their paint colors knows, have numbers.) If the paint dealer says, "Hey, color is relative to gender and we are different genders. Your white 113 is my 114, so I didn't make a mistake," he is wrong.

So the problem for the representationist is this: The standard aquamarine chip is objectively aquamarine. If it looks different to men and to women, then at least one gender's visual experience is representing it as some other shade, and that is an unacceptable consequence. Representationism is empirically false.[14]

There is a type of difficulty with the argument presented that I have not been able to discuss here. Perhaps Jack sees aquamarine as greener than Jill does, so there is a representational difference after all. For example, Jill may see aquamarine as greenish blue whereas Jack sees it as greenish greenish blue. I argue in Block (1999) that given that there are tens of thousands of shades of greenish blue that persons with normal vision can discriminate, it is unlikely that we (or our visual systems) have available to us (as part of our normal visual competence) representational resources that would distinguish close shades of greenish blue. Alternatively, suppose that Jack and Jill both see aquamarine as greenish blue, but their visual categories corresponding to the terms "green" and "blue" have slightly different extensions. Can their different phenomenal impressions of aquamarine be explained in terms of different representations of green and blue? I argue not. See the discussion of "subjective color" in Block (1999).

Now we are in a position to counter another of Lycan's (1996a,b) arguments. He notes that I concede that our inverted earth subject has experiences whose representational contents (on looking at the inverted earth sky) shift from *looking blue* to *looking yellow*. And he concludes that this undermines the subject's claim that there is no difference between the way the sky looked to him on earth and the way the sky looks to him now fifty years later on inverted earth. I have admitted that the sky looked blue to him at the beginning of our story on earth, and that the sky looks yellow to him at the end of our story on inverted earth. So how can I (or he) claim that the sky looks the same to him as it always did? Since he can't remember any change, we must conclude that the reason is that the change was gradual. But this argument ignores the distinction made earlier between the two senses of "looks the same." "Looks blue" does not express a phenomenal character but rather a representational content! We can all agree that his color representational contents have changed. But it is phenomenal character, not representational content, that is relevant to noticing a difference, and phenomenal character has remained the same. Representational content has changed purely externally without any corresponding change in phenomenal character.

Tyler Burge suggests (see his reply to me in Hahn and Ramberg 2003) that commonly, the phenomenal character of color perception is a factor in individuating the sense component of color concepts. He leaves it open whether phenomenal character is literally a part of the sense of color concepts or part of the intentional content of thoughts involving color concepts. For simplicity, let's take phenomenal character to constitute the sense of color concepts. Then inverted spectrum cases fail to show that phenomenal character doesn't supervene on representational content. For if representational content *includes* phenomenal character, any difference in phenomenal character will, *ipso facto*, constitute a difference in representational content. But representationists of the sort I have been talking about here should not be pleased by this Pickwickian victory. They have tried to cash phenomenal character of color experience in terms of the *color represented*. That is, representationists have construed phenomenal character purely referentially. The phenomenal experience as of red is a matter of visual experience representing something as red. My arguments are supposed to show that view is wrong even if we follow Burge in taking phenomenal character to be an individuating factor in the representational content of color experience.

I began the discussion of externalism by discussing a thought experiment involving Putnam's Twin Earth. The idea was that I had emigrated from Twin Earth to Earth and that after many years on Earth the representational contents of my visual experiences of the liquid in the oceans shifted even though the phenomenal character of the experiences stayed the same. I noted that there is no immediate problem for the representationist here, since the constant phenomenal character can be understood in representational terms. However, there is no corresponding move available to the representationist in the case of an emigration to or from Inverted Earth. This is one of a number of reasons given in this essay to resist the identification of the phenomenal character of the experience as of red with representing red.

Notes

Reprinted from Martin Hahn and Bjorn Ramberg, eds., *Reflections and Replies: Essays on the Philosophy of Tyler Burge*, 165–200 (Cambridge, MA: MIT Press, 2003).

I am grateful for discussions with Tyler Burge, Brian Loar, Paul Horwich, Pierre Jacob, and Georges Rey, and to Bill Lycan and his NEH Summer Seminar, 1995. I am grateful to Burge, Lycan, Rey, and Sydney Shoemaker for helpful comments on an earlier draft. This essay is a descendant of "Mental Paint and Mental Latex," in E. Villaneuva, ed., *Philosophical Issues 7* (Atascadero: Ridgeview, 1996).

1. Controversially, I think that the scientific nature of qualia could be discovered to be functional or representational or cognitive. Thus I actually prefer a definition of qualia as features of experience that cannot be *conceptually* reduced to the nonphenomenal, in particular the cognitive, the representational, or the functional. But this view will play no role in this essay.

2. These mental properties aren't mental paints because they don't represent. However, my definition of mental oil does, unfortunately, count them as mental oils because they are mental properties of experience that do not represent. So let's understand the definition of mental oil as containing a qualification: The property of having certain intentional contents does not count as a mental oil.

3. Shoemaker (1994a,b) holds that when one looks at a red tomato one's experience has a phenomenal character that represents the tomato as having a certain phenomenal property *and also* as being red, the latter via the former. On his view, the objects have certain phenomenal characters. Each phenomenal property of an object can be defined in terms of its production in certain circumstances of a certain nonrepresentational phenomenal character of experience. The view is motivated in part by a consideration of the Inverted Spectrum. For concreteness, suppose that George's spectrum is inverted with respect to Mary's. George's experience of the apple represents it both as red *and* as having phenomenal property Q (the former via the latter). Mary's experience represents the apple as red and as having phenomenal property P. (George's experience represents grass as green and Q.) What determines that George's experience represents phenomenal property Q is that it has the nonrepresentational phenomenal character Q^*; and Q gets its identity (with respect to George) from the (normal) production of Q^*. Red can be identified with the production of Q^* in George, P^* in Mary, etc. The phenomenal character Q^* is in a certain sense more basic than the phenomenal property Q, for Q^* is what makes the experience represent Q. Still, it could reasonably be said that there is nothing in Q^* over and above its representation of Q, and so Shoemaker's view qualifies as representationist about phenomenal character Q^* on my definition. However, there is more to Q^* than the representational content *red*. Shoemaker's view could therefore be said to be representationist with respect to phenomenal character Q^*; so phenomenal character supervenes on the representation of phenomenal properties. But phenomenal character does not supervene on the representation *of colors*. George and Mary both have experiences that represent red, but one has phenomenal character Q^*, the other P^*. So if inverted spectra are possible, representationism with respect to colors is wrong. It is that kind of representationism that is at issue in this essay (except in the internalism section). That is, the argument against representationism in this essay is directed against the view that the representational content of color experience is *color content*. In my view as well as in Shoemaker's the phenomenal character of an experience as of red is not exhausted by the representation of what is seen as red.

I say that representationists hold that the phenomenal character of an experience is or at least is determined by its representational content. I use the phrase 'is determined by' rather than 'supervenes on' because I think the supervenience relation as it is normally interpreted is too weak to capture the representationist ideology. Suppose, for example, that a dualist agrees that phenomenal character supervenes on representational content, but only because the dualist believes in irreducible phenomenal—representational laws of nature, laws of nature that describe the effect of representational content on the soul. This would fit most definitions of supervenience but would certainly be incompatible with the doctrine that representationists intend.

4. Harman tells me that his view is actually the same as what I ascribe to Lycan.

5. As I mentioned earlier, there is also a problem for the recognitional view in the plausibility of the idea that we (or animals) can have an experience without any sort of categorization or recognition.

6. See the papers in Crane (1992) for more on this issue.

7. I will make use of Harman's (1990) Inverted Earth example. In my 1978 essay, I used a cruder example along the same lines. (Pages 302–303 of Block 1978—reprinted on pp. 98–99 of this

volume, p. 466 of Lycan 1990 and p. 227 of Rosenthal 1991). Instead of a place where things have the opposite of their normal colors, I envisioned a remote arctic village in which almost everything was black and white, and the subject of the thought experiment was said to have no standing color beliefs of the sort of 'grass is green'. Two things happen to him: He confuses color words, and a color inverter is placed in his visual system. Everything looks to have the complementary of its real color, but he doesn't notice it because he lacks standing color beliefs.

Harman used the Inverted Earth example to make a point orthogonal to the point made here. His conclusion is that representational content does not supervene on the brain. He does not consider someone emigrating to Inverted Earth or a pair of twins one of whom is on earth the other on Inverted Earth. Instead, he describes the Inverted Spectrum thought experiment in a form in which a person puts on color-inverting lenses. Then he describes Inverted Earth and notes that the inverting lenses could be donned by someone on Inverted Earth with the upshot that the brain state that normally represents blue would then represent orange. There is no discussion of sameness or difference of phenomenal character. Here is Harman's complete discussion of the matter:

Consider Inverted Earth a world just like ours, with duplicates of us, with the sole difference that there the actual colors of objects are the opposite of what they are here. The sky is orange, ripe apples are green, etc. The inhabitants of Inverted Earth speak something that sounds like English, except that they say the sky is 'blue', they call ripe apples 'red,' and so on. Question: what color does their sky look to them? Answer: it looks orange. The concept they express with the word 'blue' plays a relevantly special role in the normal perception of things that are actually orange.

Suppose there is a distinctive physical basis for each different color experience. Suppose also that the physical basis for the experience of red is the same for all normal people not adapted to color inverting lenses, and similarly for the other colors. According to (nonsolipsistic) conceptual role semantics this fact is irrelevant. The person who has perfectly adapted to color inverting lenses\will be different from everyone else as regards the physical basis of his or her experience of red, but that will not affect the quality of his or her experience.

Consider someone on Inverted Earth who perfectly adapts to color inverting lenses. Looking at the sky of Inverted Earth, this person has an experience of color whose physical basis is the same as that of a normal person looking at Earth's sky. But the sky looks orange to the person on Inverted Earth and blue to normal people on Earth. What makes an experience the experience of something's looking the color it looks is not its intrinsic character and/or physical basis but rather its functional characteristics within an assumed normal context.

8. I took this point to be raised by some of the discussion of Lycan's paper at the meeting of Sociedad Filosofica Ibero-Americano in Cancun in June, 1995. If I had to credit it to anyone, it would be Alan Gibbard.

9. In my (1998) I give a different response in terms of the Swampman visiting Inverted Earth. The Swampman response is also used there to deal with Dretske's and Tye's plausible view (shared by Burge) that color representation is a product of evolution, hence if the sky on Inverted Earth continues to produce the same phenomenal experience in our traveler, it also is represented as blue.

10. It may be thought that the Inverted Spectrum argument is superior because it is a case of same representational content, different phenomenal character, and that this yields a more direct argument that phenomenal character goes beyond representational content. Inverted earth might be said to provide only the converse: same phenomenal character, different representational content. The upshot, it might be said, is that I have had to resort to a burden of proof argument. I have had to challenge the representationist with the question: What kind of representational content

of experience stays the same? This thought, which I have been guilty of, makes a simple error. Both the Inverted Spectrum and Inverted Earth cases involve counterexamples in both directions. Consider the Inverted Earth twin looking at a lemon and compare that with the Earth twin looking at the sky. This is a case of same representational content (both states represent blue, the color of Inverted Earth lemons), different phenomenal character. So we can squeeze both same representational content/different phenomenal character and same phenomenal character/different representational content out of the thought experiment. Similarly, we can imagine an Inverted Spectrum subject looking at a lemon while his inverted twin looks at the sky. This is a case of same phenomenal character/different representational content, the converse of the usual Inverted Spectrum conclusion.

11. Neitz, Neitz, and Jacobs (1993) report a figure of 62 percent/38 percent.

12. Neitz and Neitz (1998) explain the result as follows. Genes for long and medium wave pigment are on the X chromosome. Men have a single X chromosome, which is roughly equally likely to be each of the two forms, and hence they show a matching distribution with two spikes corresponding to the peak sensitivities of the two kinds of cones. Women have two X chromosomes, and in roughly half the cases, they have different alleles of the long wave gene in the two chromosomes. When this happens, one gene deactivates the other. But that happens independently in each cell, the result being that the average in these women is intermediate between the extreme values, and so they have long wave absorption peaks roughly in between the two groups of men.

13. Some may wish to try to avoid this conclusion by insisting that colors are not real properties of things, that our experience ascribes phenomenal properties to physical objects that the objects do not and could not have (Boghossian and Velleman 1989, p. 91). Recall that representationism as I am understanding it says that the phenomenal character of a visual experience as of red consists in its representing something as red. Are the phenomenal properties (1) colors or (2) phenomenal properties in something like Shoemaker's (1994a,b) sense? If the latter, the view countenances unreduced phenomenal characters and is therefore incompatible with representationism as I understand it. (See the discussion of Shoemaker's views in the penultimate section of this essay.) The former interpretation is that our experiences represent objects as having colors such as red or orange, but objects do not and could not have those colors. Colors are in the mind, not in the world outside the mind. The point I will be making contains the materials for refuting this view. Briefly, the picture of colors as in the mind rather than in the world has to explain our agreement on which Munsell chip is 4 Red. But how can the Boghossian-Velleman picture, on this interpretation of it, explain this agreement, given that we have somewhat different experiences, colorwise, when we see that chip? If your experience represents the 4 Red chip the way mine represents the 5 Red chip, how can we explain our agreement on which chips are 4 Red and 5 Red? Perhaps Boghossian and Velleman will say that you and I have different phenomenal characters that represent the same color. But this line of thought only makes sense if phenomenal characters are in the mind and colors are in the world, contrary to the current interpretation of Boghossian and Velleman.

14. I present the Shifted Spectrum argument in more detail in Block (1999).

References

Berlin, Brent and Paul Kay. 1969. *Basic Color Terms*. Berkeley: University of California Press.

Blackburn, Simon. 1993. *Essays in Quasi-Realism*. New York: Oxford University Press.

Block, Ned. 1978. Troubles with Functionalism. *Minnesota Studies in the Philosophy of Science* (C. W. Savage, ed.), vol. IX: 261–325. Reprinted (in shortened versions) in Block (ed.), 1980, *Readings in Philosophy of Psychology* 1; in W. Lycan (ed.), 1990, *Mind and Cognition*, Oxford: Blackwell: 444–469 (435–440 in the second edition); in D. M. Rosenthal (ed.), 1991, *The Nature of Mind*, Oxford: Oxford University Press: 211–229; in B. Beakley and P. Ludlow (eds.), 1992, *Philosophy of Mind*, Cambridge, MA: MIT Press; and in Goldman, Alvin (ed.), 1993, *Readings in Philosophy and Cognitive Science*, Cambridge, MA: MIT Press.

———. 1980. *Readings in Philosophy of Psychology*. Cambridge, MA: Harvard University Press.

———. 1981. Psychologism and Behaviorism. *Philosophical Review* 90(1): 5–43.

——— 1990. Inverted Earth. *Philosophical Perspectives* 4: 51–79. Reprinted in W. Lycan (ed.), 1999, *Mind and Cognition* (second edition), Oxford: Blackwell. Also reprinted in Block, Flanagan, and Güzeldere (1997).

———. 1994a. Qualia. In *A Companion to Philosophy of Mind*, S. Guttenplan (ed.), 514–520. Oxford: Blackwell.

———. 1994b. Consciousness. In *A Companion to Philosophy of Mind*, S. Guttenplan (ed.), 209–218, Oxford: Blackwell.

———. 1995a. On a Confusion about a Function of Consciousness. *Behavioral and Brain Sciences* 18: 227–247. Reprinted in Block, Flanagan, and Güzeldere (1997).

———. 1995b. How Many Concepts of Consciousness? *Behavioral and Brain Sciences* 18.

———. 1996. Mental Paint and Mental Latex. In *Philosophical Issues 7: Perception*, E. Villanueva (ed.). Ridgeview: Atascadero.

———. 1998. Is Experiencing Just Representing? *Philosophy and Phenomenological Research* 58(3): 663–670.

———. 1999. Sexism, Racism, Ageism, and the Nature of Consciousness. In *The Philosophy of Sydney Shoemaker, Philosophical Topics*, Richard Moran, Jennifer Whiting, and Alan Sidelle (eds.), 26 (1&2).

Block, Ned and Jerry Fodor. 1972. What Psychological States Are Not. *The Philosophical Review* 81(2): 159–181. Reprinted in Block (ed.), *Readings in Philosophy of Psychology*, volume 1, 1980.

Block, Ned, Owen Flanagan, and Güven Güzeldere. (eds.). 1997. *The Nature of Consciousness: Philosophical Debates*. Cambridge, MA: MIT Press.

Boghossian, Paul and David Velleman. 1989. Color as a Secondary Quality. *Mind* 98: 81–103.

Burge, Tyler. 1979. Individualism and the Mental. *Midwest Studies in Philosophy* 4: 73–121.

———. 1997. Two Kinds of Consciousness. In Block, Flanagan, Güzeldere (1997).

Byrne, Alex and David Hilbert. 1997a. Colors and Reflectances. In Byrne and Hilbert (1997b).

———. 1997b. *Readings on Color: The Philosophy of Color*, volume 1. Cambridge, MA: MIT Press.

Crane, Tim (ed.). 1992. *The Contents of Experience: Essays on Perception*. New York: Cambridge University Press.

Dennett, Daniel C. 1991. *Consciousness Explained*. Boston: Little Brown.

Dretske, Fred. 1995. *Naturalizing the Mind*. Cambridge: MIT Press/A Bradford Book.

———. 1996. Phenomenal Externalism, or If Meanings Ain't in the Head, Where Are Qualia? In *Philosophical Issues 7: Perception*, E. Villanueva (ed.). Atascadero: Ridgeview.

Gibbard, Alan. 1990. *Wise Choices, Apt Feelings: A Theory of Normative Judgment*. Cambridge, MA: Harvard University Press.

Hahn, Martin and Ramberg, Bjorn, eds. 2003. *Reflections and Replies: Essays on the Philosophy of Tyler Burge*. Cambridge, MA: MIT Press.

Hardin, C. L. 1988. *Color for Philosopher*. Indianapolis: Hackett.

Harman, Gilbert. 1982. Conceptual Role Semantics. *Notre Dame Journal of Formal Logic* 23: 242–256.

———. 1990. The Intrinsic Quality of Experience. In *Philosophical Perspectives 4, Action Theory and Philosophy of Mind*, James Tomberlin (ed.), pp. 31–52. Atascadero: Ridgeview.

———. 1996. Explaining Objective Color in Terms of Subjective Reactions. In *Philosophical Issues 7: Perception*, E. Villanueva (ed.), pp. 1–17. Atascadero: Ridgeview.

Humphrey, N. 1992. *A History of the Mind*. New York: Simon and Schuster.

Hurvich, L. M., D. Jameson, and J. D. Cohen. 1968. The Experimental Determination of Unique Green in the Spectrum. *Perceptual Psychophysics* 4: 65–68.

Jackson, Frank. 1982. Epiphenomenal Qualia. *Philosophical Studies* 32: 127–36.

———. 1997. *Perception*. Cambridge: Cambridge University Press.

Lewis, David. 1990. What Experience Teaches. In *Mind and Cognition: A Reader*, W. Lycan (ed.). Oxford: Blackwell.

Loar, Brian. 1990. Phenomenal States. In *Philosophical Perspectives 4, Action Theory and Philosophy of Mind*, James Tomberlin (ed.), pp. 81–108. Atascadero: Ridgeview. A much revised version of this paper is found in Block, Flanagan, and Güzeldere (1997), pp. 597–616.

Lutze, M., N. J. Cox, V. C. Smith, and J. Pokorny. 1990. Genetic Studies of Variation in Rayleigh and Photometric Matches in Normal Trichromats. *Vision Research* (30)1: 149–162.

Lycan, William G. 1987. *Consciousness*. Cambridge, MA: MIT Press.

———. 1990. *Mind and Cognition, A Reader*. Oxford: Blackwell.

———. 1995. We've Only Just Begun. *Behavioral and Brain Sciences* 18: 262–263.

———. 1996a. Layered Perceptual Representation. In *Philosophical Issues 7: Perception*, E. Villa-nueva (ed.), pp. 81–100. Atascadero: Ridgeview.

———. 1996b. *Consciousness and Experience*. Cambridge, MA: MIT Press.

———. 1996c. Replies to Tomberlin, Tye, Stalnaker, and Block. In *Philosophical Issues 7: Perception*, E. Villanueva (ed.). Atascadero: Ridgeview.

McDowell, John. 1994. The Content of Perceptual Experience. *Philosophical Quarterly* 44(175): 190–205.

McGinn, Colin. 1991. *The Problem of Consciousness*. Oxford: Blackwell.

Moore, G. E. 1922. *Philosophical Studies*. London: Routledge.

Neitz, J. and G. Jacobs. 1986. Polymorphism of Long-wavelength Cone in Normal Human Color Vision. *Nature* 323: 623–625.

Neitz, J., M. Neitz, and G. Jacobs. 1993. More than Three Different Cone Pigments among People with Normal Color Vision. *Vision Research* (33)1: 117–122.

Neitz, M. and J. Neitz. 1998. Molecular Genetics and the Biological Basis of Color Vision. In W. G. Backhaus, R. Kliegl, and J. S. Werner, (eds.), *Color Vision: Perspectives from Different Disciplines*. Berlin: de Gruyter.

NIH. 1993. Mixed-up Genes Cause Off-Color Vision. *Journal of NIH Research* 5(February): 34–35.

Peacocke, Christopher. 1983. *Sense and Content*. Oxford: Oxford University Press.

Rey, Georges. 1992a. Sensational Sentences. In *Consciousness: Psychological and Philosophical Essays*, M. Davies and G. Humphreys (eds.). Oxford: Blackwell.

———. 1992b. Sensational Sentences Switched. *Philosophical Studies* 68: 289–331.

Robinson, William. 1998. Intrinsic Qualities of Experience: Surviving Harman's Critique. *Erkenntnis* 47: 285–309.

Rosch, Eleanor. 1972. [E. R. Heider]. Probabilities, Sampling and Ethnographic Method: The Case of Dani Colour Names. *Man* 7: 448–466.

Rosenthal, David. 1991. *The Nature of Mind*. Oxford: Oxford University Press.

Shoemaker, Sydney. 1981. Absent Qualia are Impossible: Reply to Block. *Philosophical Review* 90: 581–600.

———. 1982. The Inverted Spectrum. *Journal of Philosophy* 7(79): 357–381.

———. 1994a. Self-Knowledge and Inner Sense; Lecture III: The Phenomenal Character of Experience. *Philosophy and Phenomenological Research* 2(54): 291–314.

———. 1994b. Phenomenal Character. *Noûs* 28: 21–38.

Stalnaker, Robert. 1996. On a Defense of the Hegemony of Representation. In *Philosophical Issues 7: Perception*, E. Villanueva (ed.). Atascadero: Ridgeview.

Strawson, Galen. 1994. *Mental Reality*. Cambridge, MA: MIT Press.

Tye, Michael. 1994. Qualia, Content, and the Inverted Spectrum. *Noûs* 28: 159–183.

———. 1995a. Blindsight, Orgasm, and Representational Overlap. *Behavioral and Brain Sciences* 18: 268–269.

———. 1995b. *Ten Problems of Consciousness*. Cambridge, MA: MIT Press.

White, Stephen. 1994. Color and Notional Content. In *Philosophical Topics* 22: 471–504.

25 Sexism, Racism, Ageism, and the Nature of Consciousness

Everyone would agree that the American flag is red, white, and blue. Everyone should also agree that it looks red, white, and blue to people with normal color vision in appropriate circumstances. If a philosophical theory led to the conclusion that the red stripes cannot look red to both men and women, both blacks and whites, both young and old, we would be reluctant (to say the least) to accept that philosophical theory. But there is a widespread philosophical view about the nature of conscious experience that, together with some empirical facts, suggests that color experience cannot be veridical for both men and women, both blacks and whites, both young and old.

Qualia are features of experience that go beyond the experience's representational, functional, and cognitive features.[1] Current debates about whether there are qualia have focused on whether there is anything experiential that goes beyond the *representational* content of experience. All can agree that there are representational contents of thoughts, for example, the representational content *that virtue is its own reward*. And friends of qualia, or phenomenists as I will call them, can agree that experiences at least sometimes have representational content too, e.g. *that something red and round occludes something blue and square*. The recent focus of disagreement is on whether the phenomenal character of experience is *exhausted* by such representational contents. Representationism holds that the phenomenal character of an experience is its representational content. For example, the phenomenal character of an experience as of red consists in its representing something as red. (This view is advanced by Byrne and Hilbert, Dretske, Harman, Lycan, Tye, and less clearly by McDowell. Stalnaker's view is certainly in the spirit of representationism. And representationism is disputed by Shoemaker, Peacocke, and Block.)[2] I will give an argument that representationism is empirically false. I think the representationist can evade the refutation, but at a cost, so the real upshot will be that representationists are forced to adopt certain problematic views. Some observations about the semantics of color terms will be a by-product of the argument. A sub-theme of the paper is that the facts of individual differences in color perception require some conceptual adjustment.

I can lead into the empirical argument against representationism by a brief discussion of the much-maligned inverted spectrum hypothesis. Even philosophers who smile on qualia often regard the inverted spectrum hypothesis as empirically or conceptually flawed or both. Don't worry, this paper isn't about the inverted spectrum. I'm just using it to lead into my argument.[3] According to the inverted spectrum hypothesis, things which you and I agree are red—and which our visual experience represents as red—look to you the way things we agree are green look to me. If there are inverted spectra, the dominant philosophical views of the nature of experience are wrong, including representationism. Not surprisingly, it is widely held that the inverted spectrum is a confusion, or if not a confusion, impossible, or if not impossible, not actual. Suppose, for the moment, that spectrum inversion is not only coherent, possible, and actual, but rife. The way red things look to me = the way blue things look to your cousin = the way green things look to your neighbor = the way yellow things look to your mother-in-law. Assuming that I, your cousin, your neighbor, and your mother-in-law all have normal color vision; no one should suppose that red things look red to me but blue to your cousin and green to your neighbor. Any argument that *my* color vision reveals the way things *really* look, whereas your cousin and neighbor have color vision that misleads them, could equally well be used by any one of us against the other two. All of us have normal color vision, so none of us systematically misperceives colors in normal or at least in ideal circumstances. But since our experiences that all veridically represent a red thing as red have phenomenal characters that are different from one another, phenomenal character cannot be representational content. Thus, anyone who supposes phenomenal character is identical to representational content has to deny the possibility or coherence or actuality or at least rifeness of such spectrum inversion.[4] As I noted, there are both conceptual and empirical reasons that make many (though not me) suspicious of spectrum inversion, but this paper will consider a phenomenon that evades these suspicions: *shifted* spectra. Probably, shifted spectra are indeed rife.

As I mentioned, representationists say that the phenomenal character of an experience as of red consists in the experience representing something *as red*. These representational contents are usually supposed to be "non-conceptual," as distinct from the contents of thoughts. If a cat and I both see a torus (doughnut shape), I may see it as falling under the torus concept, but the cat may not even have the concept of a torus, so the cat's experience cannot represent the torus via that concept. The representational content that is common to my experience and the cat's experience of the torus is the non-conceptual content which consists in representing space as being filled in a certain way.[5] We concept users can think with such contents, but only by conceptualizing and therefore transforming them. I won't try to spell out the concept of non-conceptual content further.[6]

Another preliminary matter: The inverted spectrum refutes representationism be-cause it is a case of two people whose experiences are representationally alike—they represent something as red—but phenomenally different. But if phenomenal character is included in representational content as a sense component, then the inverted spec-trum would not be a case of same representational content but different phenomenal character. For the inverted pair would have experiences with different representational contents. Burge has suggested that phenomenal character is involved in the indivi-duation of such a sense component but is perhaps not a part of it.[7] But the represen-tationists I'm after would never accept unreduced phenomenal characters as senses or as involved in individuating senses. The representationism this paper is directed against is referential: the experience as of red consists in its representing something as red.

Although the kind of inverted spectrum needed to refute functionalism requires be-havioral (and functional) isomorphism, representationism can perhaps be refuted em-pirically without these isomorphisms, as I shall now argue. My argument appeals to the fact that color vision varies from one *normal* perceiver to another. There are three kinds of cone in the retina that respond to long, medium, and short wave light. (Light is electromagnetic radiation in the wavelength zone of 400–700 nm (nanometers).) The designations "long," "medium," and "short" refer to the peak sensitivities. For example, the long cones respond most strongly to long wavelengths but they also re-spond to medium wavelengths. Two normal people chosen at random will differ half the time in peak cone sensitivity by 1–2 nm or more. (More precisely, the standard de-viation is 1 2 nm.)[8] This is a considerable difference, given that the long wave and middle wave cones only differ in peak sensitivities by about 25 nm. Further, there are a number of specific genetic divisions in peak sensitivities in the population that are analogous to differences in blood types (in that they are genetic polymorphisms, dis-continuous genetic differences coding for different types of normal individuals). The most dramatic of these is a 51.5 percent/48.5 percent split in the population of two types of long wave cones that differ by 5–7 nm, roughly 24 percent of the difference between the peak sensitivities of long and middle wave cones.[9] This characteristic is sex-linked. The distribution just mentioned is for men. Women have smaller numbers in the two extreme categories and a much larger number in between. As a result, the match on the Rayleigh test (described below), as Neitz and Jacobs put it, "most fre-quently made by female subjects occurs where no male matches."[10]

Neitz and Neitz, "Molecular Genetics," explain the result as follows. Genes for long and medium wave pigments are on the X chromosome. Men have a single X chromo-some which is roughly equally likely to be either of the two forms, and hence they show a matching distribution with two spikes corresponding to the peak sensitivities of the two kinds of cones. Women have two X chromosomes. In roughly half the cases,

they have the same allele in both chromosomes—in the other half the alleles are different. That is, a quarter of the cases are $X_A X_A$, a quarter $X_B X_B$, and a half are $X_A X_B$. In the
$X_A X_B$ case, one gene de-activates the other. But that happens independently in each
cone cell in the retina, the result being that the average cell in these women is intermediate between the extreme values, and so these women have long wave absorption
peaks roughly in between the two groups of men.

These differences in peak sensitivities don't show up in common activities, but they
do reveal themselves in subtle experimental situations. One such experimental paradigm uses the anomaloscope (devised in the nineteenth century by Lord Rayleigh), in
which subjects are asked to make two halves of a screen match in color, where one half
is lit by a mixture of red and green light and the other half is lit by yellow or orange
light. The subjects can control the intensities of the red and green lights. Neitz, et al.
note that "People who differ in middle wavelength sensitivity (M) or long wavelength
sensitivity (L) cone pigments disagree in the proportion of the mixture primaries
required."[11] That is, whereas one subject may see the two sides as the same in color,
another subject may see them as different—e.g., one redder than the other. When red
and green lights are adjusted to match orange, women tend to see the men's matches
as too green or too red.[12] Further, variation in peak sensitivities of cones is just one
kind of color vision variation. In addition, the shape of the sensitivity curves vary.
These differences are due to differences in macular pigmentation, which, as Neitz and
Jacobs point out, vary with "both age and degree of skin pigmentation."[13] Hence, races
that differ in skin pigmentation will differ in macular pigmentation. There is also
considerable variation in amount of light absorption by pre-retinal structures. And
this factor also varies with age.

I emphasize gender, race, and age to stifle the reaction that one group should
be regarded as normal and the others as defective. (That would be sexism, racism, or
ageism—hence the title of the essay.) There are standard tests for defective color vision,
such as the Ishihara and Farnsworth tests, and it is an empirical fact that most men
and almost all women have non-defective color vision as measured by these tests. My
point is only that the facts about variation that I have presented give us no reason at all
to regard any gender, race, or age as abnormal in color vision.

The fact that people match differently gives us reason to suppose that the phenomenal character of an experience of a narrow shade—say, a specific Munsell chip—may
not be the same for any two persons if they differ in sex, race, or age. (The Munsell
chips are a set of 1600 one-inch square shade samples organized by hue, saturation,
and brightness that are widely used for commercial and scientific purposes.) The differences noted in matching colored lights will presumably also apply to chips that have
the same dominant wavelengths as the colored lights, if such chips can be made. There
is another sort of evidence for a similar conclusion. Hardin mentions a classic 1968

study of the spectral location of unique green in a group of fifty normal subjects.[14] (Unique green is green that does not appear to be at all reddish, yellowish, or bluish.) Here is a table of locations:

5 subjects located unique green at	490 nm
11 at	500 nm
15 at	503 nm
12 at	507 nm
5 at	513 nm
2 at	517 nm

Note that the 27 nm span of this group's location of unique green is 9 percent of the visible spectrum. Hardin also mentions a more recent study that indicated a much larger range—from 486 nm to 535 nm, 13 percent of the visible spectrum. In this study, there was an overlap of 7 nm for unique green and unique blue. That is, there were lights that some people classified as unique green and others classified as unique blue.

The upshot is that if we take a chip that any one subject in this experiment takes as being unique green, *most* of the others will see it as at least slightly bluish or yellowish. Thus it is reasonable to say that any given chip will look a bit different to a randomly chosen subject than to most others. And we have no reason to think that this phenomenon is limited to that particular shade of chip. (Although it is a fact that there is less agreement about unique green than about other colors.) Hardin mentions an estimate by Ralph Evans that "a perfect match by a perfect 'average' observer would probably be unsatisfactory for something like 90 percent of all observers because variation between observers is very much greater than the smallest color differences which they can distinguish."[15] Thus we are justified in supposing that the way any chip looks (colorwise) is unlikely to be exactly the same as the way that chip looks to most other people, especially if they differ in sex, race, or age.

In sum, there are three arguments for the conclusion that any chip is likely to look different to different people, especially those who differ in sex, race or age. First, there is the fact of variation in relevant aspects of the visual systems of different people. The reasoning here does presuppose a limited form of supervenience. But the supervenience claim involved is a scientific claim about the dependence of experience on absorption curves, not a general metaphysical doctrine that can easily be set aside. Second, the differences in matching give a reason that even a functionalist would have to take seriously. Third, we have the argument just mentioned that appeals to the variation in the location of unique colors.

So now we have the beginnings of an argument against representationism. Jack and Jill both have experiences that represents red things as red even though they very likely experience red slightly differently.

But the representationist could reply that the representational contents of Jack's and Jill's visual color categories, say that of red, may differ too, so there is still no proven gap between representational content and phenomenal character. Before we can see what justice there is in this complaint, we should briefly examine its perhaps surprising invocation of color categories. "Color categories?" you say. "I thought the representationist was talking about *non-conceptual* contents?" True, but the representationist has to allow that our visual experiences can represent a scarlet thing as red as well as scarlet. For we can experience scarlet things as both red and as scarlet. We can experience two red things of different shades as having the same color, though not the same shade, so a representationist has to concede a component of the representational contents of experience that captures that fact about experience. The representationist has to allow representational content of both color and shade. Further, pigeons can be conditioned to peck when presented with things of a certain color, as well as of a certain narrow shade. Even if the pigeon lacks color concepts, it has something short of them that involve some kind of categorization of colors as well as shades, red as well as scarlet. Let's use the term "category" for this aspect of the non-conceptual contents that are concept-like but can be had by animals which perhaps can't reason with the contents. Now we can see why the argument I gave against the representationist can be challenged. Jack's and Jill's experiences of a single red fire hydrant may differ in phenomenal character *but also* in representational content, because, say, Jack's visual category of red may include or comprise a shade that is included instead in Jill's visual category of orange. Furthermore, because of the difference in Jack's and Jill's color vision, the fire hydrant may look more red than orange to one, more orange than red to the other.

The reader may wonder: if Jack's and Jill's visual categories of red differ from one another, how can there be objective (i.e., intersubjectively available) colors? Perhaps there are some things that Jill would categorize as "green" and Jack would categorize as "blue," even in ideal circumstances. And perhaps this difference in color word usage is grounded in a corresponding difference in visual color categories. If so, it is implausible to regard either as mistaken. A sensible conclusion is that they use the words "blue" and "green" in somewhat different senses, both correctly. The objective nature of color, then, derives from the overlap between persons with normal color perception. There are objects which would be categorized as "blue" under ideal circumstances by everyone with normal color vision, and that's what makes them objectively blue. The objects that are not objectively blue, but are categorized as "blue" under ideal circumstances by one normal person but not another are indeterminate in objective color. One aspect of the characterization I just gave is misleading: it makes objective color look more linguistic than it is. In principle, there could be objective color even without language. Our non-linguistic color behavior includes, for example grouping things together in same-color piles. Visual color categories could be externalized in that way even without language. I endorse this point of view, though I shall argue that it is of less value to the representationist than might appear at first glance.[16]

Jack's and Jill's color categories *may* differ, but *must* they? That is, does a phenomenal difference require a representational difference? I think the answer is no. Verbal color categories are certainly partly social and the same may be true of visual color categories. Before the introduction of the orange into England, the color of the orange was included in red. Public categorization may make visual color categories more uniform than they would be if each person developed his or her own color categories from scratch. The representationist may suppose that the very evidence that I have appealed to for phenomenal difference also supports representational difference. I noted that location of unique hues differ from person to person. Perhaps Jack will see the colored object they are both looking at as closer to unique red than Jill will. But it remains to be shown that we have visual representational resources capable of expressing such fine grained differences. No doubt there are differences in dispositions which could be made explicit. If a set of ultimately fine grained chips were set up, perhaps Jack would reckon the sample he and Jill are looking at as 50,003 chips from unique red, whereas Jill would categorize it as 49,901 chips from unique red. But these representational resources have been constructed, and the representationist has not shown that such resources are available at the moment of perception, i.e. on the fly.

The argument just given puts the ball in the representationist's court. But it will be of interest to move to a slightly different form of the argument.

Even if Jack's and Jill's visual color categories differ, a wedge between phenomenal character and representational content can be inserted by applying the argument just given to narrow shades rather than broad colors. Let us co-opt the word "aquamarine" to denote a shade of blue that is as narrow as a shade can be, a shade that is the shade of one chip from the densest set of chips that people with normal color perception can distinguish from one another, one that has no discriminable subshades. If Jack's and Jill's visual systems differ slightly in the ways that I described earlier, then we can reasonably suppose that aquamarine doesn't look to Jack the way it looks to Jill. Maybe aquamarine looks to Jack the way turquoise (a different minimal shade, let's say) looks to Jill. But why should we think that there is any difference between the representational contents of Jack's experience as of aquamarine and Jill's? (I will consider some suggestions on behalf of representationists later.) Neither is abnormal and they both acquired their categories of aquamarine by being shown (let's suppose) a standard aquamarine chip. Their visual experiences both represent aquamarine things as aquamarine. Their aquamarine representations can't comprise different shades since they already are minimal shade representations. Alternatively, we can think of Jack's and Jill's representational contents as *that shade*. Jack's and Jill's representational contents both represent that shade as that shade. Of course, both of their representations are no doubt temporary. (A trained observer can discriminate ten million surface colors. No one has that many permanent shade representations.) But even temporary representations can have content.

The upshot is that there is an empirically based argument for a conclusion—what one might call "shifted spectra"—that, while not as dramatic as an inverted spectrum, has much the same consequences for representationism and for the issue of whether there are uniform phenomenal characters corresponding to colors. There probably are small phenomenal differences among normal perceivers that don't track the colors or shades that are represented. Genders, races, and ages probably differ by shifted spectra. Thus, if representationism is right, if aquamarine things look aquamarine to men, they probably don't look aquamarine to women. And if aquamarine things look aquamarine to one race or age group, they probably don't look aquamarine to others. In sum: If representationism is right, color experience probably cannot be veridical for both men and women, both blacks and whites, both young and old. Hence, representationism is not right. Alternatively, assuming that most men and women, blacks and whites, old and young have veridical color vision, two experiences can have the same representational content but different phenomenal character so representationism is wrong. (A possible escape route will be mentioned later.)

I mentioned above that there is an objection to my first try at refuting representationism: maybe Jack's visual category that represents red includes or comprises a shade that is included in Jill's visual category that represents orange. (More later on the exact meaning of the terms "includes" and "comprises.") Does the same objection apply to minimal shades themselves? As just mentioned, a minimal shade can't include or comprise any shades other than itself, so it would seem that the problem can't arise.[17]

The shifted spectrum should not disturb the functionalist, however, for even if there are phenomenal differences among representationally identical experiences as just supposed, the phenomenal differences might be revealed in subtle empirical tests of the sort I mentioned. That is, perhaps shifted spectra always result in different matches on a Rayleigh Anomaloscope or other devices. But shifted spectra would still count against representationism.

Should the phenomenon I'm talking about really be called a "shifted spectrum"? One way in which the name is appropriate is that the Munsell 4 Red chip may look to Jack the way the 5 Red chip looks to Jill. But there is one misleading implication involved in calling the phenomena I describe as a "shifted spectrum," namely, that there is no reason to believe that there is any sort of uniform displacement of the color wheel, a mini version of the traditional inverted spectrum. Differences in absorption peaks for long wave cones, for example, would be expected to cause differences that are more "ragged" than that.

Representationist Objections

I will put an objection in the mouth of the representationist:

Whatever the differences in their visual systems, if Jack and Jill are normal observers, then in normal (or anyway ideal) conditions, the standard aquamarine chip has to look aquamarine to Jack and it also has to look aquamarine to Jill. After all, "looks aquamarine" just *means* that their perceptual contents represent the chip *as aquamarine*, and you have already agreed (above) that both Jack's and Jill's visual experience represent the chip as aquamarine. You have argued that the representational content of their visual experience is the same (viz., aquamarine), but the phenomenal character is different. However, we representationists don't recognize any kind of phenomenal character other than that which is given by the representational content—which is the same for Jack and Jill. The chips look aquamarine to both Jack and Jill, so they look the same to both Jack and Jill, so Jack and Jill have the same phenomenal characters on viewing the chips in any sense of "phenomenal character" that makes sense. If Jack and Jill have different brain states on viewing the aquamarine chip, that just shows that the different brain states just differently realize the same phenomenal character.

Reply: We phenomenists distinguish between two senses of "looks the same." In what Shoemaker calls the intentional sense of "looks the same," the chips look the same (in respect of color) to Jack and Jill just in case both of their perceptual experiences represent it as having the same color.[18] So I agree with the objection that there is a sense of "looks the same" in which the aquamarine chip does look the same to Jack and Jill. But where I disagree with the objection is that I recognize another sense of "looks the same" (the qualitative or phenomenal sense), a sense geared to phenomenal character, in which we have reason to think that the aquamarine chip does not look the same to Jack as to Jill. (The same distinction is made in somewhat different terms by Shoemaker, Peacocke, and Jackson.)[19] But the case at hand supports the phenomenist rather than the representationist. For we have reasons to believe that there is a sense in which the aquamarine chip does not look the same to Jack as to Jill. One reason was given earlier: the chip that Jack regards as unique green (green with no hint of blue or yellow) is not regarded as unique green by most other people. So it looks different to Jack from the way it looks to most others, including, we may suppose, Jill. And the same is likely to be true for other chips, including the aquamarine chip. Another reason given earlier, one that even functionalists should agree to: Jack and Jill match differently on the anomaloscope. Recall that the match "most frequently made by female subjects occurs where no male matches." If Jack produces a mixture of blue and green which he says matches the aquamarine chip, Jill will be likely to see that mixture as either "bluer" than the chip or "greener" than the chip.

The big difference of opinion on the topic of the nature of experience is between those who accept and those who reject qualia; that is, features of experience that go beyond the experience's representational, functional, and cognitive features. The argument I just gave depends in part on using functionalism against representationism. The functional differences between different perceivers suggest phenomenal differences, but we have yet to see how those phenomenal differences can be cashed out representationally, even if they can be cashed out functionally. So the argument does not show that there are qualia, though it does go part way, by challenging one of the resources of the anti-qualia forces.

Another Representationist Objection:

These empirical facts show that colors are not objective (in the sense of intersubjectively available). A given narrow shade looks different to different groups, so the different groups represent it as having slightly different colors. Thus it *does* in fact have slightly different colors relative to these different groups. Famously, phenylthiocarbamide tastes bitter to many people but not to many others. Phenylthiocarbamide is not objectively bitter, but it is objectively bitter relative to one group and objectively non-bitter relative to another. Color is the same, though not so dramatically. There are no absolute colors—color is relative, though only slightly so. You have argued that Jack and Jill represent a given chip as the same objective shade even though they experience that shade differently. But if there are no objective shades, your argument collapses.

Reply: The problem with this objection derives from a difference between our concept of taste and our concepts of at least some colors, or rather shades. We are happy to agree that phenylthiocarbamide has no objective taste—it tastes bitter to some but not others. But we do not agree that Munsell color chip 5 Red has no objective hue. Its objective hue is 5 Red no matter whether it looks different to people of different genders, races, and ages. The whole point of the Munsell color scheme, the Optical Society of America Uniform Color Space, and other color schemes, as Hardin points out, is to catalog objective shades.[20] Every American grade-school child knows the shades named by the Crayola company, despite differences in the way Burnt Sienna or Brick Red probably look to different children. If you paint your living room wall Benjamin Moore Linen White, it is an objective fact that you have not painted it Cameo White, Dove White, Opal White, or Antique White. If you have ordered White 113, but the paint store gives you White 114, you can get your money back. (The premixed colors have names in the Benjamin Moore scheme; the custom colors, of which there are very many, as anyone who has ever picked out one of their paint colors knows, have numbers.) If the paint dealer says "Hey, color is relative to gender and we are different genders. Your white 113 is my 114, so I didn't make a mistake," he is wrong. In short, there are at least some objective colors, the shades systematized by the various organizations mentioned above.

Another representationist objection:

Your point depends on special regimented objective color systems such as the Munsell or OSA system or commercial paint company systems. You say that if Jack and Jill are looking at Benjamin Moore chip Green 121 and their visual experiences are representing it as that very shade, still it will probably look different to them. Same representational content, different phenomenal character—according to you. But the existence of these regimented systems does not make our normal, everyday color categories disappear. Perhaps the chip looks bluish green to Jack but greenish blue to Jill, in which case we have a representational difference. So you don't have a case of same representational content, different phenomenal character after all.

Reply: The objection assumes a case in which the phenomenal difference between Jack and Jill results in a verbal disagreement, one saying "greenish blue," the other saying "bluish green." First, note that there is no reason to suppose that the phenomenal character of a perception of a thing of a specific shade must also represent it as having a less specific color. Ignoring this point, suppose instead that Jack and Jill *agree!* Suppose that they are looking at a chip—say Benjamin Moore Green 126—that they both categorize as "greenish blue." The representationist doesn't get to make up my thought experiment. Even one case of same representational content/different phenomenal character is enough to make my point against the representationist, even though there are other similar thought experiments that don't make the point. Will there be any chips on which Jack and Jill have verbal agreement? Boynton estimates that a maximally fine grained set of color chips would have about a million chips.[21] "Blue-green" is one of ten categories in the Munsell system, so a rough estimate of how many chips of blue-green hue there would be if the system were maximally fine grained is about 100,000. Of those, we might suppose that half would fall into greenish blue and half into bluish green. So there are somewhere in the vicinity of 50,000 different chips that would be widely agreed to be greenish blue. Though this is a back-of-the-envelope calculation, I think the upshot is clear: we can safely assume that there will be very many chips for which Jack and Jill will have no verbal disagreement. In these cases in which Jack's and Jill's verbal categorizations of a chip are the same, what will the representationist appeal to in order to justify a representational difference?

Any given chip is likely to look different to Jack from the way it looks to Jill. And we are considering one of the many cases where Jack and Jill have no verbal disagreement about the color of the chip. How can the representationist justify a representational difference? Here is one approach the representationist might try. Let us assume that human color experience represents colors via a combinatorial apparatus that we can think of as in an internal language, mentalese. In appropriately ideal circumstances, when someone says they are seeing something as "greenish blue," their visual system represents it as GREENISH BLUE (mentalese is capitalized English). Both Jack's and Jill's visual systems represent Green 126 as GREENISH BLUE. The apparatus can be used by the representationist to explain or at least accommodate the fact that Green 126 looks different to them. Perhaps, despite verbal agreement, one has the representation "GREENISH SIDE OF GREENISH BLUE" whereas the other has "BLUISH SIDE OF GREENISH BLUE." Maybe they could be brought to say something like that in English. But how far can such an apparatus be pushed? What if Jack and Jill agree on "bluish side of greenish blue"? Will the representationist postulate different mentalese representations of ever-increasing complexity? Remember there are on the order of 50,000 "greenish blue" chips. Whatever plausibility attached to the introduction of the mentalese color term apparatus in the first place derived from the idea that there was something in our visual experience that corresponded to combining "green" and "blue," but that plausibility quickly dissipates as the representations get further from anything that one can get an explicit handle on.

The upshot is that there probably are many chips on which Jack and Jill can agree on the verbal description, but which still look different to them. The challenge to the representationist is to tell us why we should not see such cases as cases of same representational content, different phenomenal character.[22]

Subjective Color

Except very briefly early in the paper, when I considered the possibility that Jack's and Jill's visual categories of red might differ, I have been supposing objective color representations (shared by normal perceivers in virtue of being normal) as I think representationists also suppose. However, there is a problem with objective color representation in the light of the facts about individual variation: an objective sense of "looks red" has to give up one or the other of two plausible principles. The two principles are:

(1) If something looks red under conditions that are as ideal as can be, it is red.
(2) One can tell whether something looks red "from the inside" without need of a survey of the judgments of others, so long as the conditions of perception are as ideal as can be.

Suppose something looks red to me in conditions that are as ideal as can be. I consult others and determine that normal perceivers in ideal conditions disagree about whether it is red. It follows that the item is not objectively red. Thus looking red to me is not sufficient for being red. There are two possibilities: Looking red to me (even under ideal conditions) isn't sufficient for looking red, or looking red (even under ideal conditions) isn't sufficient for being red. Both options reveal a counterintuitive aspect of objective color in the light of the facts about individual variation. I would suppose that any view that takes colors as objective will have to embrace the former, holding that data about all normal perceivers is required to find out whether something looks red even under ideal conditions (giving up on (2)). In effect, the objective view of color will have to regard "looking red" as looking red to all normal perceivers, and that is something I cannot ascertain simply by looking at something, even if I am a normal perceiver and know I am and the conditions are ideal and known to be so. (Note that switching from "all" to "most" won't help.) I can tell by looking whether something looks red to me but not whether it looks red, *simpliciter*. Thus, in the light of the facts about individual variation, *looking red*, where red is an objective color is not what one might have supposed—it is not an observational concept but rather a social concept. One assumes naturally that the properties one detects in color perception are both observational and objective—the same color properties that are detected by others— but if this argument is right they can't be both.

We should not suppose that this is a conclusive reason for preferring subjective color to objective color, since the former has its own peculiarities, but it does motivate taking a closer look at subjective color.

There is a second reason for taking a closer look at subjective color. Here is a version of my argument against representationism:

1. Jack's and Jill's perception is equally veridical; they see colors as they are (in ideal circumstances).
2. Their experiences of chip Green 126, a single objective shade, are different, even in ideal circumstances.
3. If phenomenal character = representational content, chip Green 126 is colored all over at the same time with 2 different colors or 2 different shades of one color.
4. Perhaps this is impossible. In any case, Green 126 has one shade, viz., Green 126, so representationism is wrong.

Putting the argument in this way points to an obvious representationist response: that Jack and Jill represent the chip has having one *objective* color, Green 126, but that they represent it also as having different subjective person-relative colors.

Let us suppose that each person has visual color categories and corresponding color terms that differ slightly from the color categories of some others. For example, Jack's visual category of red and hence Jack's sense of "red" may differ from Jill's, comprising somewhat different minimal shades. But person relative color categories can be used against the reply I just gave to the representationist. If Jack and Jill have visual experiences that represent the chip as (as they would each say) "on the greenish side of greenish blue," and if Jack and Jill have different categories of "green" and "blue," then there is a representational difference between them despite their verbal agreement. "On the greenish side of greenish blue" has compositional semantics. If the meanings of Jack's "green" and "blue" differ from Jill's, so do their meanings of "on the greenish side of greenish blue." As I mentioned early on in the paper, Jack's and Jill's visual color categories may differ, but that doesn't show they must differ, even if their phenomenal characters differ. The grid of public use of color terms and public categorization may impose a certain degree of uniformity on people's color categories. All I need is a mismatch between representational content and phenomenal character, and I have made a prima facie case. The representationist response that visual color categories may differ does not seem to me to be an adequate reply.

But even supposing it is adequate, the move to subjective color does not get the representationist out of the soup. The same problem arises in a slightly different form. Recall that Jack and Jill are looking at Green 126, which they describe in exactly the same way verbally (e.g., "on the greenish side of greenish blue"). But they differ, we are supposing, in the shades comprised, and therefore the contents of their words "green" and "blue" and the corresponding visual categories. But note that we can also expect them to describe Green 127 in exactly the same way. Recall that by my back-of-the-envelope calculation, there are roughly 50,000 distinct ultimately fine-grained chips that are in some sense a "bluish green" category. But now we can ask the question: what is the representational content of *Jill's* experience of Green 126 and *Jill's* experience of Green 127 such that there is a representational difference between them? We can't appeal to any difference in her contents of "green" and "blue" since they remain the same. As earlier, we could impose a representational system of ultimately fine-grained chips which Jill could use to represent the difference, but that doesn't show that she has that representational system on the fly. Alternatively, we could postulate a mentalese difference as before. Her representation of Green 126 is "ON THE GREENISH SIDE OF THE GREENISH SIDE OF GREENISH BLUE" whereas her representation of Green 127 is "ON THE BLUISH SIDE OF THE GREENISH SIDE OF GREENISH BLUE." But this is no more plausible in the intrasubjective comparison than it was in the case of the intersubjective comparison made before.

I put the question for the representationist in a stilted way to avoid misunderstanding of it: What is the representational content of Jill's experience of Green 126 and Jill's experience of Green 127 such that there is a representational difference between them? The question consists of 3 parts:

1. What is the content of Jill's visual representation of Green 126?
2. What is the content of Jill's visual representation of Green 127?
3. In terms of 1 and 2, what is the difference?

It is no good just saying something like "Green 127 looks slightly greener to Jill than Green 126," without saying what the content of her representation of each chip is such that that is the difference. The challenge to the representationist is to say what these contents are in a way that accommodates the difference.

The link between the intra-subjective case and the intersubjective case can be made explicit by noting that the difference between Jack's and Jill's experience of Green 126 could be the same as the difference between Jill's experience of Green 126 and Green 127. If the complicated apparatus of mentalese predicates could be harnessed to accommodate one, then presumably it could be harnessed to accommodate the other. But both are unsupported empirical speculations.

No doubt there is a tacit color space as revealed in similarity judgments and as systematized in the color solid. And as adults who know about it, we can achieve imaginal access to it. But that is a far cry from evidence that phenomenal awareness of such a space is part and parcel of color perception, something which I doubt. For example, is the color experience of monkeys and babies informed by such a space? My argument is an empirical one and this is an area of empirical vulnerability.

In sum, I have not been able to imagine a representationist objection that gives me any good reason to depart from my earlier conclusion that representationism is probably empirically false. Of course the representationist side of the dialectic has been up to me, and real supporters of the view may see their portion of the dialectic rather differently than I have on their behalf. So we should regard the arguments I have given as a challenge to them. I now turn to the one consideration in the literature that I know of concerning issues of this sort.

Byrne and Hilbert, in a defense of representationism,[23] discuss the objection that one subject might locate unique green[24] at 490 nm, whereas another might locate it at 520 nm.[25] Their defense makes two points. First, they appeal to the analogy of the square and the diamond. It would seem at first glance that nothing could be both a square and a diamond, but once one sees that a tilted square is a diamond, on second thought, the two properties are compatible. Similarly, they suggest, perhaps "some ways of being unique green are also ways of being bluish green."[26] Byrne and Hilbert see themselves as floating a possibility, and so they give no hint as to how the square/diamond analogy could possibly apply to color. (They appear to have objective color in mind, otherwise it would be trivial that something could be unique green—relative to one person, yet bluish green—relative to another.) But then it is hard to see why we should take that possibility seriously. Further, even if it applies to colors, there would be a further burden on them to show how it could apply to minimal shades. Byrne and Hilbert conclude their discussion (and this is the second point) of this matter as follows: "But even if bluish green and unique green are in fact contraries, this is not a disaster. That many of us *misperceive* unique green objects is certainly an unwelcome result; but at least (for all the objection says) we veridically perceive them as green, and perhaps that is enough."[27] But what is the rationale for taking some locations of unique green to be veridical and others as misperceptions?

Byrne notes in correspondence that I concede that the individual differences in color vision that I have been talking about result in some indeterminacies about the objective shade of some mixtures of light. (See the following two sections.) He wonders why this fact doesn't count in his favor. I conceded that there are some objects whose fine-grained shade is indeterminate, but there are many whose fine-grained (objective) shade is not indeterminate. Any of us can see huge numbers of them in a paint store. If Jack and Jill are both looking at Benjamin Moore Red 123, they can agree on the objective fact that that is what shade it is, even though very likely their phenomenal experience of it will be slightly different. Even a single example of experiences that have the same representational content but different phenomenal character is enough to disprove representationism.

Representationism's Last and Best Chance

Suppose that Jack and Jill are looking at the aquamarine chip in ideal circumstances. Their experiences represent it as aquamarine or as "that shade," but the phenomenal characters of their experiences differ, hence representationism is false. So I have argued. But it should be noted that one of the items of evidence that I presented for the different phenomenal characters of their experiences was different matching experiences and behavior. Thus we may suppose that there is a mixture of colored lights that Jack takes as matching the aquamarine chip but Jill takes as not matching it. So, it seems, the idealized extensions of their terms "aquamarine" or their visual categories indicated by "that shade" as applied to the aquamarine chip are different. Jack's includes the mixture of lights and Jill's does not. So their contents are different. Hence my argument appears to be refuted.

The argument just mentioned was my second one, but the response against the second argument can be used against the first one. The difference, you will recall, was that the first was based on broad colors, the second on narrow shades. The first argument supposed that Jack's and Jill's experiences both represented something as red, but were nonetheless phenomenally different. But it is open to the representationist to argue that one only sees something as red via seeing it as a particular shade of red, so if there is bound to be a difference in the shade content, that could be the source of the difference in phenomenal character of the broad color experience.

Representationists say the phenomenal character of the experience as of red consists in a visual state representing something as red. They depend on the fact that in color experience a property is represented. But what property would be involved if the objector's point of view is right? Here is one option: Two representations represent the same property for a person just in case they would be applied by that person to exactly the same things in ideal circumstances. Or perhaps the representationist would prefer a vaguer alternative. The subjective extensional criterion could be taken as merely a sufficient condition of difference: If two representations would be applied to different objects in ideal circumstances, then the properties represented are different. The distinction is more promissory than actual, although the representationist is invited to make the view less vague. In the absence of a representationist proposal, I will use the biconditional form. Thus the view is a version of extensionalism in that content is a matter of idealized extension. And it is a form of subjectivism in that a person's color and shade contents are a matter of *that person's* idealized applications of color and shade properties. I will call the view "subjective extensionalism." (Of course, subjective extensionalism is a form of representationism, but I will tend to leave out the "representationism" for brevity.)

One line of reply to the subjective extensionalist (representationist) would be to deny that the mixture of lights is part of Jack's or anyone else's extension of the visual category of aquamarine. Jill makes a finer discrimination and sees a shade (or at least a shade difference) that Jack does not see, a different shade from aquamarine. The mixture of lights is not aquamarine at all, but a distinct shade that Jack cannot distinguish from aquamarine. On this view, ultimately fine-grained shade distinctions should distinguish shades that can be distinguished by some normal perceivers in optimal circumstances, even if other normal perceivers can't distinguish them. This line of thought would individuate shades more according to exact profiles of reflected or emitted wavelengths than is ordinarily done, for if the mixture of wavelengths is different, there will be room for a pair of persons who agree on colors and shades of the usual sort but differ in experimental setups like the Rayleigh anomaloscope in which colored lights are mixed. The technical term for objects which match in exact spectral profile is "isomers." On one version of this view, then, shades would be isomer equivalence classes.

However, the subjective extensionalist has a ready reply: Subjective extensionalists are talking about subjective shades, not objective shades. Perhaps the mixture of lights is not the same objective shade as the aquamarine chip, but if Jack can't distinguish them in ideal circumstances, the two items are of the same *Jack*-shade. If Jack can't distinguish between red and green, we wouldn't take the representational content of his experience of red as *red* but rather as something more like a disjunction of red and green. Similarly, assuming that the representational content of Jill's experience of the aquamarine chip is aquamarine, we shouldn't take Jack's representational content of the aquamarine chip as aquamarine—precisely because she can and he can't distinguish the aquamarine chip from the mixture of lights. If the mixture is a different shade than the aquamarine chip, then the content of Jack's representation of the color of the aquamarine chip would be better regarded as the disjunction of the two shades rather than just aquamarine itself. So Jack's and Jill's visual categories are different after all. Thus the subjective extensionalist can withstand an objective difference in shade between the aquamarine chip and the mixture of lights that Jack matches to it.

Another line of reply to the subjective extensionalist would be to deny that there is any matter of fact as to whether the mixture of lights is the same shade as the aquamarine chip. After all, two normal perceivers in ideal conditions disagree about whether the mixture of lights is the same shade as the aquamarine chip, so how could there be a matter of fact? And since there is no matter of fact, the mixture of lights is not in either Jack's or Jill's extension of the aquamarine category. I regard this reply as correct, but it does presuppose objective color. Again, the subjective extensionalist can insist on subjective (person-relative) color, saying that Jack's and Jill's contents differ according to their extensions, independently of the facts about sameness and difference in objective shade.

My favored reply to the subjectivist extensional conception is that its coherence is dubious. For the extensionalist part of the doctrine depends on conceptions of ideal circumstances and normal perceiver—if one normal perceiver applies and the other witholds a given representation in ideal circumstances, that ensures that the representations differ in content. The notion of normal perceiver is relevant to subjective color in the form of normal *state* of a perceiver. Even if Fred is highly abnormal by the standards of humanity, still Fred's representations can have idealized extensions. But the idealized extensions will depend on Fred's being in a normal state—for Fred. Fred's applications of color or shade representations while dead drunk won't count. The problem is this: it is unclear that there is any content to optimality of conditions and normality of perceiver independently of what it is to get colors *right*. That is, it is unclear that subjectivism is compatible with extensionalism. The dependence on objective color is trivial if normality and optimality are given what Crispin Wright calls the "whatever-it-takes" reading: optimal conditions for detecting aquamarine are just the infallibly aquamarine-detecting conditions.[28] But the same holds in a less direct manner if optimality and normality are given substantive readings.

It is natural to take optimal or ideal (I use these as stylistic variants) circumstances to include a certain intensity of lighting and field and angle of view. And it is natural to take normal state of a perceiver to include no finger pressing on the eyeball (which induces phosphenes, illusions of colored swirls), no electrical stimulation to the cortex and no ingestion of hallucinogenic drugs. But the rationale for including or excluding any such factor involves a conception of objective color and what it is to see things as having the objective colors that they in fact have. There is a famous illusion known as the McCullough Effect.[29] To prepare yourself to experience the McCullough Effect, look at a pattern of red and black stripes along with green and black stripes at right angles to the first stripes for five or ten minutes. To experience the McCullough Effect, look at a similar configuration of black and white stripes. You will see images of the complementary colors in the white areas even as much as a month later. If the first grid had horizontal red stripes, you will see the horizontal white stripes of the black and white grid as greenish. The colors you see in the black and white grid are illusory, hence a perceiver so prepared is not normal. The grid that looks reddish and black is actually white and black, so if you want to see the grid colors as they really are, don't set yourself up for the McCullough Effect. Those who set themselves up for the McCullough Effect are not perceivers in a normal perceptual state, but what makes them not normal is that they will not see a black and white grid of the appropriate size and orientation *as* black and white. So normality of perceiver only makes sense relative to objective color.

The same point applies to ideal conditions. As Hardin has persuasively argued, there are many different ways of standardizing viewing conditions, and the relevant type of condition depends on what is to be viewed and the purpose of viewing it. For example, some color samples will look to be one color on a light background, another color on a dark background. One remedy is to use a narrow viewing tube. But a narrow viewing tube will be very suboptimal for viewing brown, a color that depends on contrast effects. What *makes* the tube suboptimal for viewing a brown chip is that the chip is objectively brown, but the normal perceiver won't see it that way in those circumstances. If we cut our conception of color loose from objectivity, it is not clear that there is any substance in the invocation of normality of a perceiver or ideality of circumstances. There are conceptual connections among the issue of the nature of objective color, normality of a perceiver and optimality of conditions of perception. We have no choice but to determine these things together. (I am indebted here to conversation with Tyler Burge.)

There is an obvious subjective-extensionalist response, which can be introduced by considering the debate between those who regard colors as primary qualities against dispositionalists. The primary quality theorist says to the dispositionalist: you say that what it is for an object to be red consists in normal perceivers having a certain response to it in ideal conditions. But ideal conditions are arbitrary given that all there is to something being red is causing a certain reaction in those very conditions. Any conditions would do. The dispositionalist counters that the ideal conditions are only ideal in that it is part of our concept that an object's having a color *consists in* causing a certain response in *those very* conditions. And this is the natural response by the subjective extensionalist: We don't need objective colors to anchor our understanding of optimality and normality because the concepts of optimality and normality are supplied by our concepts of color and shade themselves.

But the key questions are beyond the reach of common-sense concepts. Some color judgments are made better in a 2-degree viewing field with a dark surround, others in a 4-degree viewing field with a dark surround. It isn't our concepts that tell us that one is more ideal than another for a specific judgment, but rather empirical testing against a background view of what the colors really are. Of course, our concepts are deployed in empirical testing, but that is not the use of concepts that is at issue.

Difficult color viewing tasks such as fine grained judgments of matching depend on highly specific viewing conditions, often known as "standard conditions," whose details involve empirically determined parameters. Further, it is an interesting fact about the conceptions of standard or ideal conditions that are found in the literature that they differ slightly but significantly from one another. For example, Boynton suggests that ideal conditions involve looking through a hole in a luminous hemisphere that provides the illumination of a cloudy sky at a 45-degree angle at an object placed at the center of a horizontal plane that is rotating at 12 rpm, the plane being covered by a 40 percent neutral reflecting surface that suffusely reflects all wavelengths equally.[30]

By contrast, the instructions for viewing Munsell chips stated in the *Munsell Book of Color* are "that the samples should be placed against a dark achromatic background and 'colors should be arranged under North Daylight or scientific daylight having a color temperature of from 6500 degrees to 7500 degrees Kelvin. Colors should be illuminated at 90 degrees and viewed at 45 degrees, or the exact opposite of these conditions.' "[31] Does anyone think that such precise viewing angles are to be derived from our color concepts alone without empirical testing? Further, are differences between them to be resolved by appeal to concepts alone? These differences are insignificant for most purposes, but they loom large when we are thinking of perceptual judgments that are at the limit of human capacity. Suppose Jill sees a difference between two chips in one set of conditions but no difference in the other. Do our *concepts* tell us that one circumstance is more ideal than the other? You may suppose that the way our concepts come in is by dictating that the ideal conditions are the ones in which we make the most distinctions. But what if the two conditions yield the same number of distinctions, just slightly different ones? (See the discussion three paragraphs below.)

Further, even if our concepts supply standard conditions for viewing colored chips, it is doubtful that these considerations would extend to viewing the mixtures of colored lights I have mentioned, much less stars, TV screens, color photos printed in newspapers and rainbows.[32] Averill tries to answer via a divide and conquer strategy.[33] In some cases, he seems to claim that our concepts do supply standard conditions, in others, the colors are not what they seem. (Rainbows have no colors, TV screens are the colors of the 3 phosphors, newspaper photos are the colors of the individual dots.) Discussing these issues would take us beyond the scope of this paper, though I hope I can rely on a sense that such proposals are prima facie implausible.[34]

You may suppose that the indeterminacies in ideal conditions can be handled by postulating indeterminacies in representational contents. But that raises a different issue, for there is no reason to think that phenomenal character is similarly indeterminate. The burden would then be on the representationist to show that any indeterminacy in representational content is matched by an indeterminacy in phenomenal character.

In thinking about this problem with subjective extensionalism, it may be of use to have an alternative more objective conception at hand. I will attempt to sketch one here that is extensionally based but not subjective.

I spoke of Jack's and Jill's visual categories of red as including or comprising somewhat different shades. What does that come to? I have been speaking of ultra-fine-grained shades as systematized in the densest set of chips that all people with normal color vision can distinguish from one another. The key property of the set of chips is that there are no colored objects that can be discriminated (colorwise) by any normal perceiver from every one of the chips in ideal conditions. That is, every colored object is seen as matching one of the chips by normal perceivers in ideal circumstances. (If a normal perceiver finds something that does not match one of the chips, that just shows the set of chips was incomplete, and the new item or a new chip based on it should be added.) And it would make sense to define ideal conditions and the normality of a perceiver in terms of this requirement. Minimal shades as represented by the set of chips are objective in the sense that they can be agreed upon to be the minimal shades by all normal perceivers. Different normal perceivers may clump the chips differently into broad color categories, but they will all be able to discriminate no fewer and no more shades. Colors such as red and green are sets of shades, though perhaps somewhat different sets for different persons. Let's call the set of ultra-fine-grained chips the Ultimate Color System. As I mentioned earlier, there will be roughly a million chips in such a system. Perhaps there will be ties for the ultimate set. If so, we will choose one of the tied systems.[35]

In terms of this apparatus, then, Jack and Jill would each classify a set of Ultimate Color System chips as "red" in ideal circumstances, and those sets perhaps would not coincide exactly. That's what I mean by saying that their categories of red comprise or include somewhat different shades. The content of color perception can be defined in terms of this notion of comprising shades. Two color representations are different in content just in case they comprise different shades. One could say that what makes two representations different in content is that they carve out different chunks of objective color space. So my conception has a place for subjective color—but it is based on objective color.

Now let us return to Jack and Jill and the aquamarine chip, which, let us suppose, is one of the Ultimate Color System chips. There is a mixture of lights that Jack sees as matching the chip but Jill does not. Then Jack matches the mixture of lights to one of the Ultimate Color System chips whereas Jill matches the mixture of lights to another chip. That is, Jack sees both the chip and the mixture of lights as matching one chip (since the chip matches itself), whereas Jill sees them as matching two chips. For every colored thing is seen by normal perceivers as matching *some* chip in the Ultimate Color System. The fact that Jill makes a discrimination that Jack does not make does not show that Jill discriminates more *shades* than Jack. The Ultimate Color System chips include all shades discriminable by normals from one another and Jack and Jill are normal. Thus Jack and Jill have visual representations of aquamarine (or "that chip") with exactly the same representational contents. The mixture of lights is indeterminate in shade, being seen as having one shade by one normal perceiver and as having another shade by another normal perceiver. It is not in the extension of "aquamarine" or of the visual category indicated by "that shade" as applied to aquamarine. So on this conception of shade, the argument against representationism works.

The upshot is that the subjective extensionalist conception has a chance of evading the refutation of representationism. But the subjective extensionalism used in the evasion raises some difficult issues for representationism.

Observations on the Semantics of Color Terms

I now move to some questions about we should think of the semantics of color terms in the light of the facts of individual variation that I have been discussing. The issues here are closely related to my critique of representationism. We can start with the question: What is the status of unique green? It can't be an objective minimal shade like the Munsell or OSA shades (or the Ultimate Color System), since Jack and Jill will disagree about which chip is unique green, yet both can be correct. And it can't be a phenomenal character. If Jack and Jill are each looking at the shades that they classify as "unique green" (say Green 21 for Jack, Green 22 for Jill), we have no guarantee that their phenomenal characters would be the same.

In order to cope with this problem, I am first going to summarize some views of Sydney Shoemaker's, since they are needed in order to introduce the notion of a phenomenal property. Shoemaker's views will also allow me to sharpen up the representationist position, since his position combines elements of phenomenism with elements of representationism.

Shoemaker is a representationist on one definition of the term.[36] He holds that when one looks at a red tomato, one's experience has a phenomenal character that represents the tomato as having a certain phenomenal property *and also* as being red, the latter via the former. On his view, the objects have certain phenomenal properties in virtue of standing in causal relations to experiences which have certain phenomenal characters.[37] Each phenomenal property of an object can be defined in terms of production by it in certain circumstances of a certain non-representational phenomenal character of experience. (Note that phenomenal properties are therefore causally efficacious.) The view is motivated in part by a consideration of the inverted spectrum. For concreteness, suppose that George's spectrum is inverted with respect to Mary's. George's experience of the apple represents it both as red *and* as having phenomenal property Q (the former via the latter). Mary's experience represents the apple as red and as having phenomenal property P. (George's experience represents grass as green and P, whereas Mary's experience represents grass as green and Q.) What determines that George's experience represents phenomenal property Q is that it has the non-representational phenomenal character Q*; and Q gets its identity (with respect to George) from the (normal) production of Q*. Red can be identified with the production of Q* in George, P* in Mary, etc. The phenomenal character Q* is in a certain sense more basic than the phenomenal property Q, for Q* is what makes it the case that the experience represent Q. Still, it could reasonably be said that there is nothing in Q* over and above its representation of Q, and so Shoemaker's view qualifies as representationist about phenomenal character Q* on my definition. However, there is more to Q* than the representational content *red*. Shoemaker's view could therefore be said to be representationist with respect to phenomenal properties but not colors. If two experiences have the same representational content Q, then they must both have the same phenomenal character, in this case Q*; so phenomenal character supervenes on the representation of phenomenal properties. But phenomenal character does not supervene on the representation *of colors*. George and Mary both have experiences that represent red, but one has phenomenal character Q*, the other P*. So if inverted spectra are possible, representationism with respect to colors is wrong. It is that kind of representationism that is at issue in this paper. That is, the argument against representationism in this paper is directed against the view that the representational content of color experience is color content. In my view as well as in Shoemaker's, the phenomenal character of an experience as of red is not exhausted by the representation of what is seen as red.

Now back to the question of unique green. Here are some options:

1. Objective shade   The Benjamin Moore Paint Company has wisely refrained from using "unique" in any of its color names, perhaps to avoid any appearance of lack of objectivity as to what color the customer is buying. "Unique green" cannot name an objective minimal shade, since as noted above, Jack and Jill may disagree about which shade it is, yet they can both be correct. Different people would single out different chips as "unique green" from Benjamin Moore samples or from the Munsell or Optical Society of America Uniform Color Space samples even under the most ideal conditions, and no one should choose one of them as more correct than the others. So this is not a live option.

2. Phenomenal character   If Jack and Jill are each looking at the (different) chips that they classify as "unique green," we have no guarantee that their phenomenal characters would be the same. So unique green cannot be a phenomenal character.

3. Person-relative phenomenal character   "Unique green" names for each of us the phenomenal character we get from a shade that does not appear to have any element of red or yellow or blue. It isn't that unique green is a single phenomenal character as in option 2, but rather that the semantics of at least this color term dictates reference to different phenomenal characters in many pairs of different perceivers. Your unique green is something in your mind; mine is something in my mind. My main objection to this view is one I could have raised to 2: on the face of it, "unique green" is a property of things in the world, not of our minds. We should resist pushing the reference of color terms into the head.

4. Person-relative phenomenal property in Shoemaker's sense   Unique green is a property of objects, a property determined in each of us by the phenomenal character we have (maybe a different one in different people) when something does not appear to have any element of red or yellow or blue. This option has the benefit of 3 over 2 without the problem that 2 and 3 share. I consider this one of the main options worth taking seriously, though I will argue against it.

5. *Person-relative shade*   Different people use "unique green" to describe somewhat different objective shades, each naming a shade that is unique green for them. There is no incompatibility between Jack's assertion and Jill's denial of "This is unique green." There are a number of ways of filling in this idea, notably that "unique green" is interpersonally ambiguous and that it is unambiguous but has a suppressed indexical reference.

I won't consider 1, 2, or 3 further, but both 4 and 5 have some initial plausibility. In order to explain my opposition to 4, I will have to say a bit more about Shoemaker's reason for postulating phenomenal properties in the first place. As I mentioned, Shoemaker accepts the possibility of inverted spectra. That is an assumption I share. But Shoemaker also accepts what he refers to as "Harman's phenomenological point," namely, that introspection is in the first instance of properties of objects and has no direct access to the phenomenal character of color experience. When we try to introspect our color experience, all we succeed in doing is focusing on certain properties of objects. But what are those properties? According to Shoemaker, they can't be colors themselves. Since these properties are introspectible, the inverted spectrum precludes their being objective colors. So they must be properties of objects whose individuation is bound up with the phenomenal character of color experience, viz., phenomenal properties.

I reject phenomenal properties because I reject Harman's phenomenological point. I believe that we can introspect phenomenal character, and hence there is no need to postulate phenomenal properties. An ontology of colors of things plus internal phenomenal characters of our perception of those colors is all that is needed. I think the only grain of truth in Harman's phenomenological point is that when we try to attend to our experience in certain circumstances, we only succeed in attending to what we are seeing, e.g., the color of the apple. But attention and awareness must be firmly distinguished. For example, we can experience the noise of the refrigerator (and be aware of it in that sense) but only notice it or attend to it when it ceases.[38] Further, as Burge emphasizes, what properties we are aware of depends on what concepts we apply. If we apply experiential concepts to our experiences, we can be aware of the phenomenal properties of those experiences. In my view, the issue of unique green that we are now discussing is the best reason for postulating phenomenal properties, but that motivation can be undermined by a better construal, a matter to which we now turn.

"Unique green" doesn't name a single objective shade since we don't agree on which shade that would be and none of us is privileged with respect to unique green. It doesn't name a phenomenal character since it names something in the world, not in the mind. And it doesn't name a phenomenal property since there is no independent motivation for believing in phenomenal properties in the first place. That leaves the last option above, option 5. One version of option 5 would say that "unique green" is ambiguous, being used by different people in somewhat different senses. Another view is that the phrase is univocal but there is an implicit "with respect to me" to be understood.

Let us consider the following way of thinking of unique green: "Unique green" means *shade that doesn't seem to have any blue, red, or yellow in it,* for short: green that seems pure. Seems to whom? Seems to a contextually indicated person. On this view, the relativity is a product of the invocation of *seeming.* Note that this is an intentional property, not a phenomenal character or phenomenal property. This proposal has the virtue of explaining how it can be that the Munsell or OSA shade that is unique green for me isn't for you. The shade that seems to you to have no blue, red, or yellow isn't the shade that seems to me to have no blue, red, or yellow. (It also explains the relativity of "unique green" without appealing to any relativity of "green.")

Hardin notes that "bluish green" is in the same boat as "unique green," since "bluish green" locates a color relative to unique green.[39] If Jill says something is bluish green and Jack says it isn't because it is unique green, then it would seem that they can't both be right. There is an obvious construal of "bluish green" along the same lines just given: "Bluish green" means green that seems to have some blue in it. If this is right, bluish green isn't an objective shade either.

In conversation, Shoemaker suggests that color terms have divided reference or unmarked ambiguity, picking out not only colors but associated phenomenal properties. Where Jack and Jill seem to disagree (in ideal conditions), he blames it not on the objective colors or shades they pick out, which are the same, but on their picking out slightly different phenomenal properties. Thus he preserves a common meaning in public language and in idiolects for color words. Shoemaker's suggestion is that if Jack and Jill disagree about whether "green" applies, we should construe the disagreement as concerning a phenomenal property rather than a color, but other uses of "green" pick out the color denoted univocally by both of their "greens." Sometimes color terms are used to indicate colors, other times to indicate phenomenal properties. I disagree with this line of thought for the reason mentioned earlier: I am doubtful about phenomenal properties.

The resolution I favor is to do without the "seems" in the analysis of "unique green." If a certain chip is green that doesn't *seem* to be at all blue, red, or yellow, then if that color experience is veridical, the chip *is* green without being at all blue, red or yellow, and that is what it is to be unique green. Unique green is green that is pure, not green that seems pure. How then can we account for the fact that your unique green is different from mine—yet neither of us should be said to be wrong? "Unique green," like "green" has two senses. In fact, the two senses of "unique green" derive from the two senses of "green," "blue," "yellow," and "red." All natural language color terms have a person-relative sense based in the person's visual phenomenology. That is, visual color representations differ from person to person, and there is an at least partially corresponding variation in color terminology. Color terms also have an objective sense based on overlap between people. There are objective colors because there is overlap of personal "greens," "blues," "yellows," and "reds." When we talk about the color something seems to be, we are using person-relative colors. But we sometimes use objective color terms. Suppose you complain to the judge that the color of the stoplight may have been red relative to the policeman, but it was green relative to you. The judge says "Dammit, I don't care about your visual apparatus. The light was red!" This is an (imperfect) objective use. The narrower the color category, the less likely there is to be any overlap. I suppose there is an overlap for "reddish yellow," but maybe not for "on the yellowish side of reddish yellow." There is no objective unique green. But there are objective shade names codified by Munsell, OSA, Benjamin Moore, and others, as mentioned earlier. Color terminology is ambiguous but color experience picks out the person-relative properties. When Jack's visual experience represents something as what Jack calls "green," it represents it as having a property that may encompass slightly different chips than the corresponding property represented by another person's color experience.

Jack's visual category of red is subjective in that it differs from Jill's category of red. But it is objective in that it comprises a set of objective color chips (in ideal circumstances). Jill's visual category of red comprises a different set of objective color chips. Jacks' unique green is also subjective in that it is different from Jill's, but both are objective in that the chip each picks out as "unique green" has an objective shade. Color terms like "red" or "bluish green" are ambiguous. Jill can use them subjectively to pick out the same intension as her visual category of red or bluish green; and she can also use them objectively to pick out the overlap of all normal perceivers. "Green 126," however, has only an objective sense.

Conclusion

This paper has offered a refutation of one form of representationism. The representationist can evade the refutation by embracing the subjective extensionalist point of view, but that point of view raises its own problems.

Notes

Reprinted from *Philosophical Topics* 26 (1–2): 39–70, 1999.

I am grateful to Eliza Block, Paul Boghossian, Tyler Burge, Alex Byrne, Susan Carey, Larry Hardin, Paul Horwich, Brian Loar, Adam Pautz, Chris Peacocke, Sydney Shoemaker, and Michael Tye for comments on an earlier draft, and I am grateful to the participants in my seminar at the University of Barcelona in June 1999 for their helpful discussion.

1. Functionalist accounts: see Ned Block, "What is Functionalism?" in *Readings in Philosophy of Psychology*, vol. 1, ed. Block (Cambridge, Mass.: Harvard University Press, 1980). Cognitivist accounts: I mean theorists like D. M. Armstrong, *A Materialist Theory of the Mind* (London: Routledge, 1968), and George Pitcher, *A Theory of Perception* (Princeton, N.J.: Princeton University Press, 1971), who, roughly speaking, tried to analyze appearing in terms of inclination to believe. See Frank Jackson, *Perception* (Cambridge: Cambridge University Press, 1977), 37–40, for a convincing refutation. Representationists: see below. The definition I give in the text of "qualia" is what is implicit in the literature, but I believe it involves a misconception. In my view, the real issue between friends and enemies of qualia is conceptual. The definition of "qualia" that I favor is: phenomenal features of experience that are not conceptually reducible to the experience's representational, functional, or cognitive features. In my view, qualia could turn out to be, e.g., functional states. I think qualia are entities whose scientific essence is at present entirely unknown, and we therefore cannot rule out a computational-functional theory of them. I have chosen to put my thesis in this paper in more traditional terms to avoid unnecessary conflicts with the way the issues are usually conceived. I will be giving an empirical counterexample to representationism on one conception of representationism. Since what is actual is also conceptually possible, the counterexample will work just as well even if "qualia" is defined as I prefer. In addition, I think that the semantics of color terms does depend on actual facts, e.g., whether inverted or shifted spectra are rife. There are many issues about this matter that I cannot go into here, e.g., whether the issues of the semantics of color terms that concern me would be settled by a priori conditionals which are independent of the actual facts. See Ned Block and Robert Stalnaker, "Conceptual Analysis and the Explanatory Gap," *Philosophical Review* (January 1999).

2. Alex Byrne and David Hilbert, "Colors and Reflectances," in their *Readings on Color: The Philosophy of Color*, vol. 1 (Cambridge, Mass. MIT Press, 1997); Fred Dretske, *Naturalizing the Mind* (Cambridge, Mass.: MIT Press, 1995); Gilbert Harman, "Explaining Objective Color in Terms of Subjective Reactions," in *Philosophical Issues 7: Perception*, ed. E. Villanueva (Atascadero, Calif.: Ridgeview, 1996); William G. Lycan, *Consciousness and Experience* (Cambridge, Mass.: MIT Press, 1996); Michael Tye, *Ten Problems of Consciousness* (Cambridge, Mass.: MIT Press, 1995); John McDowell, "The Content of Perceptual Experience," *Philosophical Quarterly* (April 1994). Sydney Shoemaker, "The Inverted Spectrum," *Journal of Philosophy* 74 (1981): 357–81; Christopher Peacocke, *Sense and Content* (Oxford: Oxford University Press, 1983); Ned Block, "Inverted Earth," *Philosophical Perspectives* 4 (1990): 51–79; reprinted in *Mind and Cognition*, 2d ed., ed. W. Lycan (Oxford: Blackwell, 1999); also reprinted in Ned Block, Owen Flanagan, and Güven Güzeldere, *The Nature of Consciousness: Philosophical Debates* (Cambridge, Mass.: MIT Press, 1997). Robert Stalnaker, "Comparing Qualia Across Persons" in the volume edited by Hahn and Ramberg mentioned in note 7. Some representationists are satisfied with a supervenience thesis: that phenomenal character supervenes on representational content. But this is compatible with a variety of views on which phenomenal character goes beyond representational content. These views can perhaps be ruled out by appropriate construals of the modalities implicit in supervenience, but I will bypass these issues by taking representationism as an identity thesis rather than as a supervenience thesis.

The representationists I am talking about are externalists. Rey is an internalist representationist about phenomenal character. See his *Contemporary Philosophy of Mind* (Cambridge: Blackwell,

1997). Shoemaker has a version of externalist representationism, but one which is representationist only about what he calls phenomenal properties rather than about colors. Shoemaker denies, as do I, that the phenomenal character of an experience as of red is a matter of its representing what is seen as red. Shoemaker's position will be explained further in the last sections of this paper. See Shoemaker, "Self-Knowledge and Inner Sense; Lecture III: The Phenomenal Character of Experience," *Philosophy and Phenomenological Research* 54 (2) (June 1994): 291–314; and Shoemaker, "Phenomenal Character," *Nous* 28 (1994): 21–38.

3. See Stephen Palmer, "Color, Consciousness and the Isomorphism Constraint," *Behavioral and Brain Sciences* 22 (1999): 923–943 for a detailed authoritative discussion of the empirical issues and Shoemaker, "The Inverted Spectrum," Block, "Inverted Earth," and Byrne and Hilbert, "Colors and Reflectances," for discussion of the philosophical issues.

4. I am assuming objective color and color representations—that is, colors that are intersubjectively available to normal perceivers and color representations that are shared by normal perceivers. Later, I will consider the possibility of subjective or person-relative color categories, those that may vary from person to person.

5. See Christopher Peacocke, *A Study of Concepts* (Cambridge, Mass.: MIT Press, 1992); T. Crane, "The Non-conceptual Content of Experience," in *The Contents of Experience: Essays on Perception*, ed. Crane (Cambridge: Cambridge University Press, 1992).

6. Why can't "unconscious" states have non-conceptual content? If a patch of say orange is presented for a very short exposure and followed by a longer stimulus of random gray characters (a "mask"), then orange can be identified faster than other colors, even though the subject says he saw the mask rather than any color at all. In the psychological lingo, masked presentation of a color primes recognition of that color. In some sense, the subject can be said to have perceived the color "unconsciously." Can the representationist allow that the content of an unconscious perception of red is the same as the content of a conscious perception of red? Friends of qualia can allow that states with non-conceptual content, e.g., an image as of something red, can be unconscious in the sense of inaccessible to machinery of reasoning and control of action (access-unconscious in the terminology of Block, "On a Confusion about a Function of Consciousness," *Behavioral and Brain Sciences* 18 (2) (1995) and chapter 9 of this volume. Reprinted in N. Block, O. Flanagan, G. Guzeldere, eds., *Consciousness* (Cambridge, Mass.: MIT Press, 1996), and in *The Philosophers' Annual*, 1996. German translation, "Über ein Missverständis bezüglich einer Funktion des Bewußtseins," in *Bewußtsein: Beiträge aus der Gegenwartsphilosophie*, ed. Thomas Metzinger (Schoningh: Paderborn, 1995). But a representationist who thinks that it is the content of a perceptual state that makes it conscious cannot say this. One way of avoiding the problem is to concede that a pure representationist theory cannot work and that a workable representationism must be combined with functionalism. A conscious state must have a certain functional role as well as a certain kind of representational content. Tye, *Ten Problems*, holds such a combined representationist/functionalist view.

7. Tyler Burge, Comments on my "Mental Paint," Hahn, Martin and Ramberg, Bjorn (eds.) 2003. *Reflections and Replies: Essays on the Philosophy of Tyler Burge* (Cambridge: MIT Press).

8. M. Lutze, N. J. Cox, V. C. Smith, and J. Pokorny, "Genetic Studies of Variation in Rayleigh and Photometric Matches in Normal Trichromats," *Vision Research* 30 (1) (1990): 149–62.

9. M. Neitz and J. Neitz, "Molecular Genetics and the Biological Basis of Color Vision," in *Color Vision: Perspectives from Different Disciplines*, ed. W. G. Backhaus, R. Kliegl and J. S. Werner (Berlin: De Greuter, 1998); A figure of 62 percent/38 percent is reported in J. Neitz, M. Neitz, and G. Jacobs, "More than Three Different Cone Pigments Among People with Normal Color Vision," *Vision Research* 33 (1) (1993): 17–122.

10. J. Neitz and G. Jacobs, "Polymorphism of Long-wavelength Cone in Normal Human Color Vision," *Nature* 323 (1986): 623–25. The quotation comes from 625.

11. Neitz, et al., "More than Three Different Cone Pigments," 117.

12. Neitz and Neitz, "Molecular Genetics."

13. Neitz and Jacobs, "Polymorphism," 624.

14. C. L. Hardin, *Color for Philosophers*, 2d ed. (Indianapolis: Hackett, 1993); L. Hurvich, D. Jameson, and J. Cohen, "The Experimental Determination of Unique Green in the Spectrum," *Perceptual Psychophysics* 4 (1968): 65–68.

15. Hardin, *Color for Philosophers*, 193, citing Ralph Evans, *An Introduction to Color* (New York: Wiley, 1948).

16. Perhaps being categorized as blue by most normal perceivers is enough for being objectively blue. I don't think the difference between most and all will matter for my purposes. I'll stick with all. Note that objectivity in my use of the term is a matter of intersubjectivity. Even subjective, that is person-relative, colors are factual. That is, it is a fact that this object is blue relative to me.

If there are many perceivers who have no identifiable defect in color vision but are rather just extreme outliers who have so little overlap with others so as to reduce the space of objective color to virtually nothing, there will be considerable pressure to regard outliers as abnormal. For if we have to choose between regarding extreme outliers as abnormal and giving up objective color, I think we should and would choose the former.

17. Some may wish to try to avoid this conclusion by insisting that colors are not real properties of things, that our experience ascribes phenomenal properties to physical objects that the objects do not and could not have. See Paul Boghossian and David Velleman, "Physicalist Theories of Color," *Philosophical Review* 100 (1991): 67–106; reprinted in *Readings on Color*, ed. Byrne and Hilbert. Recall that representationism as I am understanding it says that the phenomenal character of a visual experience as of red consists in its representing something as red. Are the phenomenal properties (1) colors or (2) phenomenal properties in something like Shoemaker's sense described in "Self-Knowledge and Inner Sense" and "Phenomenal Character"? If the latter, the view countenances unreduced phenomenal characters and is therefore incompatible with representationism as I understand it. (See the discussion of Shoemaker's views in the penultimate section of this paper.) The former interpretation is that our experiences represent objects as having colors such as red or orange, but objects do not and could not have those colors. Colors are in the mind, not in the world outside the mind. The point I will be making contains the materials for refuting this

view. Briefly, the picture of colors as in the mind rather than in the world has to explain our agreement on which Munsell chip is 4 Red. But how can the Boghossian-Velleman picture on this interpretation of it explain this agreement, given that we have somewhat different experiences, colorwise, when we see that chip? If your experience represents the 4 Red chip the way mine represents the 5 Red chip, how can we explain our agreement on which chips are 4 Red and 5 Red? Perhaps Boghossian and Velleman will say that you and I have different phenomenal characters that represent the same color. But this line of thought only makes sense if phenomenal characters are in the mind and colors are in the world, contrary to the current interpretation of Boghossian and Velleman.

18. Shoemaker, "The Inverted Spectrum."

19. Ibid.; Peacocke, *Sense and Content*; Jackson, *Perception*.

20. Hardin, *Color for Philosophers*.

21. R. M. Boynton, "Insights Gained from Naming the OSA Colors," in *Color Categories in Thought and Language*, ed. C. Hardin and L. Maffi (Cambridge: Cambridge University Press, 1997). Hardin mentions the estimate that a trained normal observer can discriminate ten million surface colors under optimal conditions and he also notes an estimate that there are about half a million commercially different colors (*Color for Philosophers*, 182).

22. Hardin criticizes the standard philosopher's way of thinking in terms of responses instead of probabilities of responses. I admit to using the philosopher's standard model here, but I think it is useful if what one is interested in are responses in conditions that are as ideal as can be. For example, let the subject take all day to respond.

23. Byrne and Hilbert, "Colors and Reflectances."

24. See Hardin, *Color for Philosophers*, especially the new "Further Thoughts" for more on variation in the location of unique green and unique blue. Hardin says that locations of unique green and unique blue actually overlap. That is, there are wavelengths that are classified by some normal people as unique green and by others as unique blue. The criterion for normality here is that of passing standard tests for color deficiency, such as the Ishihara or Farnsworth tests. Thus by this criterion of normality, an outlier whose color classifications were very different from 99.9 percent of other normal humans could be normal. As mentioned earlier, I doubt that this notion of normality can be sustained. Note that my argument does not depend on this notion of normality (although some of the studies quoted do use it). Recall, for example, my appeal to fact that the Rayleigh match "most frequently made by female subjects occurs where no male matches." Even if the population includes males and females who differ so much from the average that they should not be counted as normal, it would be true even if they were eliminated.

25. My objection to representationism on the basis of individual variation was arrived at independently of Byrne and Hilbert. I have been giving this argument in classes since I happened to read NIH, "Mixed-Up Genes Cause Off-Color Vision," *Journal of NIH Research* 5 (February 1993): 34–35.

26. Byrne and Hilbert, "Colors and Reflectances," 273.

27. Ibid., 274 (my italics).

28. Mark Johnston, "Objectivity Refigured: Pragmatism without Verificationism," in *Reality, Representation and Projection*, ed. Haldane and Wright (Oxford: Oxford University Press, 1993), 85–130; Crispin Wright, "Realism: The Contemporary Debate—W(h)ither Now?" in *Reality, Representation and Projection*, ed. Haldane and Wright, 63–84.

29. See the cover of Block, *Imagery* (Cambridge, Mass.: MIT Press, 1981), or Hardin, *Color for Philosophers*, pl. 5.

30. Described in Evan Thompson, Colour Vision: A Study in Cognitive Science and the Philosophy of Perception (London: Routledge, 1995), 119.

31. Hardin, *Color for Philosophers*, 68.

32. Hardin, *Color for Philosophers*.

33. Edward Averill, "The Relational Nature of Color," *Philosophical Review* 101 (3): 551–88.

34. Hardin, *Color for Philosophers*, xxiv.

35. One qualification: Chips that don't actually look different can be discriminated in a sense if they are adjacent and the border is visible because of contrast. Think of contrast effects as being eliminated in the discrimination of chips.

36. See Shoemaker, "Self-Knowledge and Inner Sense," and "Phenomenal Character."

37. Shoemaker distinguishes between qualitative character and phenomenal character, a distinction which I am ignoring here.

38. See Block, "On a Confusion," for more on this type of case, and Burge, Comments on my "Mental Paint."

39. Hardin, Color for Philosophers, xxiii.

26   Is Experiencing Just Representing?

Representationism says that the phenomenal character of experience is reducible to its representational content. Michael Tye's book responds to two problems for this view; I will argue that these two responses conflict.

1   Swampman

The first problem concerns the famous Swampman who comes into existence as a result of a cosmic accident in which particles from the swamp come together, forming a molecular duplicate of a typical human.[1] Reasonable people can disagree on whether Swampman has intentional contents. Suppose that Swampman marries Swampwoman and they have children. Reasonable people will be *inclined* to agree that there is something it is like for Swampchild when "words" go through his mind or come out of his mouth. Fred Dretske (1995) claims that if the materialist is to have any theory of intentional content at all, he has no option other than denying it. He is committed to the view that since phenomenal character is a kind of representational content that derives from evolution, the swampchildren have no phenomenal character. Zombiehood is hereditary. (So long as there is no evolution.) If your grandparents are all swamp-people, you are a zombie.

Many philosophers hate fanciful examples like this one. Some say weird thought experiments like this one are so distant from anything we can really take in that our intuitions about them show nothing about our concepts. Others add that even if they show something about our concepts, they are ridiculous from a scientific point of view. Both are wrong, at least in the context of evolutionary views of content. The swampman example is one in which a *real* empirical possibility is stretched so as to allow us to focus on it more easily. There is a famous dispute between the adaptationists (Dawkins, Dennett, Pinker) and the anti-adaptationists (Gould, Lewontin, Eldridge). The anti-adaptationists emphasize that there may be features of the human mind and body that were not selected for but are in one or another sense accidental by-products of evolution. Both sides allow the possibility of such cases. What is controversial is whether (as the adaptationists claim) the default assumption should be that a complex useful character is adaptive. The adaptationists are on defensible ground when it comes to intentional content, but there is far more controversial empirical issue about the adaptational value of phenomenal character. Putting the point somewhat dramatically: *in the relevant respect, we all are swamp-people, for all we know.* Hence Dretske is committed to the claim that if an open scientific question is resolved in a certain way, our experience has no phenomenal character. Philosophers should not rest basic metaphysical views on empirical claims that are as wide open as this one.

Despite his general sympathy for evolutionary representationism, Tye rejects Dretske's view of the swampman. Tye gives pride of place to optimal conditions. Optimal conditions for a mechanism obtain when it is discharging its biological function. In the case of an evolved creature, this coincides with Dretske's evolutionary account. But Tye sees optimal conditions as relative to the sort of system or creature in question. In the case of Swampman, Tye thinks not in terms of actual history, but in terms of well-functioning. Conditions of well-functioning are met when there is an appropriate match between behavior and the states tracked in the environment. If the swampman has his needs met and flourishes, then his actual environment meets that condition and can supply the representational content. Hence the swampman can have phenomenal character, and so can his grandchildren. (How bitter a pill for the poor swampman who is not flourishing to find out that precisely *because* he is not flourishing, his agony is unreal!)

I will be focusing on the incompatibility between Tye's strategy in the swampman case and in the Inverted Earth case.

2   Earth Inverted Earth

Inverted Earth is a variant of Putnam's famous "Twin Earth". Everything is the complementary color of the corresponding Earth object. The sky is yellow, the grass (or at least the "grass") is red, etc. In addition, people on Inverted Earth speak an inverted language. They use "red" to mean green, "blue" to mean yellow, and so forth. If you order a sofa from Inverted Earth and you want a yellow sofa, you FAX an order for a "blue" sofa (speaking their language). The two inversions have the effect that if "wires are crossed" in your visual system (and your body pigments are changed), you will notice no difference when you go to Inverted Earth. After you step off the space-ship, you see some Twin-grass. You point at it, saying it is a nice shade of "green," but you are wrong. You are wrong for much the same reason that you are wrong if you call the liquid in a Twin-Earth lake "water" just after you arrive there. The grass is red (of course we are speaking English not Twenglish here). Suppose you left Earth at age 8, remaining on Inverted Earth for the rest of your life, not as a visitor but as an immigrant; you identify with the local culture and in effect adopt the concepts and language of the

Inverted Earth language community. Then (according to me) the representational content of your experience as of red things (things that are really red) will eventually shift so that you represent them correctly. See Block 1990, 1994, 1996.[2]

The key features of the example are these:

1. The phenomenal character of your color experience stays the same as suggested by (though not entailed by) the fact that you don't notice any difference.

2. But the representational content of your experience, being externally determined, shifts with external conditions in the environment and the language community.

Your phenomenal character stays the same but what it represents changes. Why is this a problem for representationists? Imagine that on the birthday just before you leave for Inverted Earth, you are looking at the clear blue sky. Your visual experience represents it as blue. Years later, you have a birthday party on Inverted Earth and you look at the Inverted Earth sky. Your visual experience represents it as yellow (since that's what color it is and your visual experience by that time is veridical let us suppose—I'll deal with an objection to this supposition later). But the phenomenal character stays the same, as indicated by the fact that you can't tell the difference. (An alternative will be mentioned later.) So there is a gap between the representational content of experience and its phenomenal character. Further, the gap shows that phenomenal character is not reducible to representational content, and it is easy to extend the example to show that phenomenal character does not supervene on representational content. (Compare the traveler as an old man looking at something blue (e.g., a banana) on Inverted Earth with the same person as a child looking at something blue (the sky) on Earth. Same representational color content, different phenomenal character.)

A comparison with Putnam's Twin Earth is instructive. If I emigrate to Twin Earth, the representational content of my experience of water changes (let us suppose). After a great deal of time has passed and I have committed to my new language community and new experts, I see twater as twater instead of as water (let us suppose). But I cannot tell from looking at the liquid in the oceans whether it is water or twater. My phenomenal character stays the same even though the representational contents of my experiences change. But representationists needn't be bothered by Twin Earth, since they can give the phenomenal continuity a *representational interpretation*. The common phenomenal character is a matter of representation of color, sheen, flow pattern and the like. But what will the representationist appeal to in the Inverted Earth case that corresponds to color, sheen, flow pattern, etc.? This is the problem for representationists posed by the Inverted Earth case.

Once again, many philosophers are skeptical about such fanciful examples. I will respond to only one point: feasibility. In its essential features, the Inverted Earth thought experiment could *actually* be performed with present day technology. We could substitute large isolated buildings for the two planets. And a version of the visual "wire-crossing" could be done today with "virtual reality" goggles.

3   Tye's Solution to the Inverted Earth Problem

Tye's view of phenomenal character is that it is "nonconceptual" representational content. He concedes that the conceptual contents of the traveler's experience eventually change. If there is reason to see the new language community as the one he relies on and defers to, we have reason to link his concepts to theirs. And the dominant causal source of his concepts shifts to Inverted Earth, as his commitments there outweigh his initial commitments. Tye allows that an externalist theory of meaning and concepts link the concept of red with the meaning of a person's word "red." But the *non*conceptual contents do not shift in this way according to Tye. They are biologically based in the emigrant's evolutionary history. According to Tye, when the emigrant looks at the sky, saying, "Very blue," his words are correct even though his visual experience *misrepresents* the color of the sky. In sum, Tye's view is that the phenomenal character of experience is to be identified with its non-conceptual content. That does not shift upon immigration to Inverted Earth. It is the conceptual contents of experience that shift, but they are distinct from phenomenal character.

4   The Swampman's Grandchild Goes to Inverted Earth

Without inquiring further about nonconceptual content, we can now see why there is a conflict between Tye's view of the swampman and his view of Inverted Earth travelers.

Suppose Swamp-grandchild emigrates to Inverted Earth. The environments of both Earth and Inverted Earth are well matched to the swamp-grandchild's behavior: there is equal "well-functioning" in both cases. So on what basis could Tye choose to ascribe to the swamp-grandchild the phenomenal character that goes with representing the Inverted Earth sky as blue (as a normal Earthian emigrant, according to Tye) rather than the phenomenal character that goes with representing the sky as yellow (like normal Inverted-Earthians)? A choice here would be arbitrary. Suppose Tye chooses the Earthian phenomenal character. But what makes *that* the privileged phenomenal character for the swamp-grandchild? The fact that his grandparents materialized on Earth as opposed to Inverted Earth? But that is a poor reason. Suppose the swamp-grandchild is born on Inverted Earth while his parents are on a visit and stays there. Are his phenomenal characters determined by his birth place or by his grandparents' birth place? There is no good reason for either choice and there is no plausibility in the idea that there is no matter of fact about what the phenomenal characters are.

In his original discussion of traveling to Inverted Earth, Tye was happy to say that the nonconceptual contents of experience remained fixed, agreeing with me that the phenomenal character of experience remains the same on Inverted Earth after emigration. But there is no way he can say this about the traveling swamp-grandchild, for he has no reason to choose the nonconceptual content of a native Earthian as opposed to the nonconceptual content of a native Inverted Earthian. Unable to choose either option, he is forced to go environmental, postulating that these nonconceptual contents of the traveling swamp-grandchild change. And hence the phenomenal characters change.

So he is forced to recognize changes in phenomenal character that are due solely to changes in the external determiners of content (and when I raised this problem in correspondence, Tye took exactly that line). We all can agree that there are some possible changes in intentional content due solely to changes in its external determiners. But it is another matter to allow that there can be changes in phenomenal character that are due solely to changes in external determiners of content. To claim this is to cut phenomenal character loose from its conceptual moorings. (See Shoemaker's contribution to this symposium.)

Lycan (1996a, 1996b) responds to the original (nonswampman) Inverted Earth Problem in the same way. He puts it in terms of memory. According to him, memories of the color of the sky, for example, are necessarily defective in cases of purely external change like the Inverted Earth Immigration case.

5 Perception of Change

I believe that the postulation of externalist memory to defend externalist perception begs the question, but I won't argue that here. (See Block 1996.) Instead, I'll stick to some points about perception. In certain circumstances, externalist representational content can change without the subject, the person whose representational content is changing, having any possibility of noticing it, no matter how big the change is or how fast it happens. But *it is a necessary feature of phenomenal character that if a change is big enough and happens fast enough, we can notice it.* It follows that phenomenal character cannot be externalist representational content.

We can be concrete about this point. Differences in the hue wheel can be thought of in terms of degrees of separation. For example, a 180 degree difference separates blue from yellow and red from green. For a given person in given circumstances, there will be color changes that are just fast enough to notice. Let's say, just guessing, that 10 degrees per second is fast enough to notice for most people in normal circumstances. If color changes of 10 degrees per second are noticeable, so are changes in the phenomenal character of color experience corresponding to 10 degrees per second. But purely external representational changes (changes that do not affect physical properties of the body that do not involve relations to things outside the body) of more than 10 degrees per second, if they could happen, would not be noticeable.

What is the likelihood that independent externalist considerations about the nature of representation would converge on 10 degrees per second as the maximum rate of change for purely external change? But this is precisely what would be required for the externalist to explain why purely externalist change in phenomenal character is not noticeable to the subject. The burden is on the representationist to show how externalism yields this result without begging the question by assuming that phenomenal character is reducible to representational content.

Let us see how these points apply to Inverted Earth. Suppose that I am looking intently at a blue sky on Earth; then I am beamed (as in Star-Trek) to Inverted Earth (the matter transmitter also is programmed to switch wires in my visual system) where I am looking at a yellow sky (but my wires have been switched so I don't notice the difference). The transition is so seamless that I don't notice any change at all. Eventually, my representational contents shift half way across the color wheel. How long does this take? We can put this question to one side for the moment. The important point is that there is nothing in the nature of externalist representational content that precludes a fast change. But there is something in the nature of phenomenal character that precludes a fast change half way across the color wheel, because that's a big change, one that could not happen in a short time without my noticing it. In short, the problem for Lycan and Tye is that they are committed not only to an ad hoc externalist theory of memory, but also to an ad hoc restriction on noticing phenomenal change.

As I mentioned above, a natural response on behalf of Tye would be that nonconceptual representational contents can't shift so fast as to be problematic. A blue to yellow shift would take years, and no one could notice a chameleon changing from blue to yellow if it took years. Such a reply raises the question of what it is that determines the rate of change of non-conceptual contents. As mentioned above, one plausible view of change in conceptual content appeals to the notion of a dominant causal source. The Spanish explorers originally named the island of Puerto Rico "San Juan," and the potentially rich port of San Juan was called "Puerto Rico." But the cartographer mixed up the labels on the way back to Spain. What makes our "Puerto Rico" refer to the island, not the port? The dominant causal source of our word is the island. Let's apply this idea to nonconceptual content.

Our swampman materializes on Earth where he is looking intently at a blue sky. After a total of one minute of life there, he is beamed (without noticing it) to Inverted Earth where he is looking at the yellow sky. (Again, the wires in his visual system are crossed by the transponder, which is why he notices no difference.) After 10 minutes of looking intently at the Inverted Earth sky, the dominant causal source of the phenomenal experience linked to his word "blue" is yellow, since 10 of his 11 minutes of existence has been on Inverted Earth. So on the dominant causal source view, the representational content of his experience changed during that 10 minutes. But he didn't notice it. Indeed, he couldn't have noticed it. No matter how fast it happened, he couldn't have noticed it.

But perhaps the dominant causal source view isn't right. Or perhaps it applies to conceptual content but not to nonconceptual content. Never mind: its role in my argument is to serve as an example of an independently motivated account of change in representational content, one that arguably allows big fast changes. The main point is that the burden is on anyone who claims that there is something in the nature of representational content that excludes big fast unnoticeable changes. Since there is something in the nature of phenomenal character that precludes big fast unnoticeable changes, we should conclude that phenomenal character can't be representational content.

Notes

Reprinted from *Philosophy and Phenomenological Research* 58 (3): 663–670, 1998. Reprinted in John Heil, ed., *Philosophy of Mind: A Guide and Anthology* (Oxford: Oxford University Press, 2004).

1. The Swampman example is usually attributed to Davidson (1987) but it was commonly discussed in the early 1980s. My (1981) uses an example of a swamp-machine.

2. I make use of Harman's (1982) Inverted Earth example. Block (1980) uses a cruder example along the same lines (pp. 302–303 of Block 1980—reprinted pp. 98–99 of this volume, on p. 466 of Lycan 1990 and p. 227 of Rosenthal 1991). Instead of a place where things have the opposite from the normal colors, I envisioned a remote Arctic village in which almost everything was black and white, and the subject of the thought experiment was said to have no standing color beliefs of the sort of "Grass is green". Two things happen to him: he confuses color words, and a color inverter is placed in his visual system. Everything looks to have the complementary of its real color, but he doesn't notice it because he lacks standing color beliefs. Harman used the Inverted Earth example to motivate a very different point from that made here: that the representational content of experience does not supervene on the brain.

References

Block, Ned, 1980. "Troubles with Functionalism." In Block (ed.), *Readings in Philosophy of Psychology*, Vol. 1. Cambridge: Harvard University Press.

Block, Ned, 1981. "Psychologism and Behaviorism." *The Philosophical Review* 90, no. 1, January 1981, 5–43.

Block, Ned, 1990. "Inverted Earth." In James Tomberlin (ed.), *Philosophical Perspectives 4, Action Theory and Philosophy of Mind*, 53–79. Atascadero: Ridgeview.

Block, Ned, 1994. "Qualia." In S. Guttenplan (ed.), *A Companion to Philosophy of Mind*. Oxford: Blackwell, 514–520.

Block, Ned, 1996. "Mental Paint and Mental Latex." In E. Villanueva (ed.), *Perception, Philosophical Issues 7*. Atascadero: Ridgeview.

Davidson, Donald, 1987. "Knowing One's Own Mind." *Proceedings and Addresses of the American Philosophical Association* 60, 441–458.

Dretske, Fred, 1995. *Naturalizing the Mind*. Cambridge: MIT Press.

Harman, Gilbert, 1982. "Conceptual Role Semantics." *Notre Dame Journal of Formal Logic* 23.

Lycan, William G., 1990. *Mind and Cognition: A Reader*. Oxford: Blackwell.

Lycan, William G., 1996a. "Layered Perceptual Representation." In E. Villanueva (ed.), *Perception, Philosophical Issues 7*. Atascadero: Ridgeview.

Lycan, William G., 1996b. *Consciousness and Experience*. Cambridge: MIT Press.

Rosenthal, David, 1991. *The Nature of Mind*. Oxford: Oxford University Press.

Tye, Michael, 1995a. "Blindsight, Orgasm and Representational Overlap." *Behavioral and Brain Sciences* 18, 268–269.

Tye, Michael, 1995b. *Ten Problems of Consciousness*. Cambridge: MIT Press.

27 Bodily Sensations as an Obstacle for Representationism

Representationism,[1] as I use the term, says that the phenomenal character of an experience just is its representational content, where that representational content can itself be understood and characterized without appeal to phenomenal character. Representationists seem to have a harder time handling pain than visual experience. (I say 'seem' because in my view, representationists cannot actually handle either type of experience successfully, but I will put that claim to one side here.) I will argue that Michael Tye's heroic attempt (in Aydede 2005b) at a representationist theory of pain, although ingenious and enlightening, does not adequately come to terms with the root of this difference.

Representationism is in part an attempt to make an account of phenomenal character comport with G. E. Moore's diaphanousness intuition, the idea of which is that when I try to introspect my experience of the redness of the tomato, I only succeed in attending to the color of the tomato itself, and not to any mental feature of the experience. The representationist thinks we can exploit this intuition to explain phenomenal character in nonphenomenal terms. To understand representationism, we need to know what to make of the phrase 'representational content' as applied to an experience. There is no clear *pretheoretical* notion of representational content as applied to an experience, certainly none that will be of use to the representationist. True, I can speak of seeing *that* and seeing *as*, and more generally of experiencing that and experiencing as. Looking at the gas gauge, I can say that I see that the tank is empty (Dretske 1995). And I can say that I experience my wound as a medical emergency. These (and other) pretheoretical ways of thinking of something that could be called the representational content of experience have little to do with phenomenology or with the kind of properties that the representationist takes the phenomenology to constitutively represent. Thus the representationist thesis involves a partially stipulated notion of representational content. This is not, in itself, a criticism, but as I shall argue, there is a problem about how the stipulation should go in the case of pain.

Thus in my view, the dispute between Tye and Colin McGinn over whether pain even *has* representational content is not a dispute about a matter of fact, but a dispute about how to talk. The same applies to Tye's claim that a referred pain (e.g., a pain in the inside of the left arm caused by malfunction in the heart or a pain in the groin caused by malfunction in the kidney) is nonveridical. Pretheoretically, we might (might!) regard such a pain as misleading but not false or inaccurate or nonveridical. We are willing to allow hallucinations in which it seems to us that there is a colored surface in front of us when there is no colored surface that we are seeing, in front or elsewhere. However, we do not acknowledge pain hallucinations, cases where it seems that I have a pain when in fact there is no pain. Tye does not argue for pain hallucinations in which there seems to be a pain when there is no pain at all, but since he does say that referred pain is nonveridical, he must think that a referred pain in the arm is not actually in the arm. Where, then, is it? In the heart? It is not our practice to assign locations to referred pain in this way, so such a claim is at best stipulative.

In the case of representationism about some aspects of visual phenomenology, there is a fairly natural line of stipulation. My color experience represents colors, or colorlike properties. (In speaking of colorlike properties, I am alluding to Sydney Shoemaker's "phenomenal properties" [1994, a,b], "appearance properties" [2001], and Michael Thau's [2002] nameless properties.) According to me, there is no obvious candidate for an objectively assessable property that bears to pain experience the same relation that color bears to color experience. But first, let us ask a *prior* question: what in the domain of pain corresponds to the *tomato*, namely, the thing that is red? Is it the chair leg on which I stub my toe (yet again), which could be said to have a pain-ish or painy quality to it in virtue of its tendency to cause pain-experience in certain circumstances, just as the tomato causes the sensation of red in certain circumstances? Is it the stubbed toe itself, which we experience as aching, just as we experience the tomato as red? Or, given the fact of phantom-limb pain, is it the toeish part of the body image rather than the toe itself? None of these seems obviously better than the others.

Once we have stipulated what we mean by the representational content of pain, it is a substantive and nonstipulative question whether the phenomenal character of pain is that stipulated representational content. The stipulative aspect of the issue is reflected in Tye's presentation by the fact that two-thirds of the way through the paper, he has not yet quite stated what he intends to stipulate. He says "What, then, is the phenomenal character of pain?" and considers the possibility that one might say the representational content of pain is a matter of its representing *subjective qualities* of the bodily region in which the pain occurs. He rejects this proposal on the ground that the phenomenal character of a pain in the leg can be present even when there is no such bodily region (as in phantom-limb pain), suggesting instead that "the phenomenal character of pain is representational content of a certain sort, content into which the *experienced qualities* enter" (emphasis added). The "certain sort" alludes to his view that the relevant contents are nonconceptual, abstract, and poised.

The problem that is worrying me is what these "subjective qualities" or "experienced qualities" are in terms of which Tye characterizes the representational contents of the phenomenal character of pain. (I will use the former phrase and indicate the problem of the obscurity typographically by talking of Subjective Qualities.) Examples of Subjective Qualities in Tye's sense are what we speak of when we describe a pain as sharp, aching, throbbing, or burning. Here is the problem: why don't these Subjective Qualities bring in the very unreduced phenomenality that the representationist is seeking to avoid?

Let me explain via the comparison with Shoemaker's (1994a,b; 2001) version of representationism mentioned above. Shoemaker honors the diaphanousness intuition without the reductionist aspect of representationism. He holds that when one looks at a red tomato, one's experience has a phenomenal character that represents the tomato as having a certain appearance property *and also* as being red, the latter via the former. Each appearance property of an object can be defined in terms of production by it in certain circumstances of a certain phenomenal character of experience. The view is motivated *in part* by the possibility of an inverted spectrum. If Jack and Jill are spectrum inverted, Jack's experience of the tomato represents it both as red *and* as having appearance property A (the former via the latter). Jill's experience represents the tomato as red and as having appearance property A^*. (Jack's experience represents grass as green and A^*, whereas Jill's experience represents grass as green and A.) What determines that Jack's experience represents appearance property A is that it has phenomenal character PC, and A gets its identity (with respect to Jack) from the production of PC in normal viewing conditions. Red can be identified with the production of PC in Jack, PC^* in Jill, and so on. PC is metaphysically more basic than A since PC is what makes it the case that the experience represents A. But A is epistemically more basic than PC in that in perception of colors one is aware of A rather than PC. And in introspection, one is aware that one's experience represents A. Awareness of PC, by contrast, is at least in part theoretical (which I see as a big problem with Shoemaker's view). Shoemaker's view of the relation between phenomenal character and appearance properties has been in flux, but what I think has been constant is something I can agree with, that PC and A are a pair such that each could be defined in terms of the other taken as basic. Or, if the two are defined in terms of one another as a "package deal," with neither as basic, the definition would not capture the difference between the $\langle PC, A \rangle$ pair and the very different $\langle PC^*, A^* \rangle$ pair. Shoemaker's appearance properties are in that sense of a piece with phenomenal characters.

Shoemaker's (2001) view of pain is that pain experiences are perceptions that represent a part of the body as instantiating an appearance property. Such a view is not problematic for Shoemaker since if he is to be called a representationist, his representationism is nonreductionist: he is not attempting to explain phenomenal character in nonphenomenal terms. But if Tye's Subjective Qualities are appearance properties, then Tye cannot be a representationist in the sense that he at least used to endorse, in which phenomenal character is supposed to be explained in nonphenomenal terms.

Does Tye give us any reason to think that his Subjective Qualities are *not* appearance properties in a sense that undermines his (former?) project? Well, if he said that as a matter of empirical fact, these Subjective Qualities turn out to be (aspects of) tissue damage, then I think they could not be taken by him to be appearance properties. But Tye's view is not that Subjective Qualities are features of tissue damage. Rather, what he says is something importantly different, namely that "pain" applies to tissue damage when it is within the content of a pain experience. And it is good that he does not identify Subjective Qualities with aspects of tissue damage, since that identification would be most implausible given that exactly the same tissue damage in the foot can give rise to a more intense pain—or one that is different in other ways—in me than in you because of differences between my fibers leading from the foot to the brain and yours.

The representationist says that when I try to introspect my experience of the stubbed toe, I only succeed in attending to the Subjective Quality of the toe. My question to Tye has been: why think of the Subjective Quality of the toe as like the redness of the tomato rather than like an appearance property of the tomato? Of course, Tye is a representationist about visual experience as well as about pain, so presumably he will reject the question or regard it as a choice between a correct option (red) and a confused option (an appearance property).

To see the difficulty in such a position, we have to recognize that colors are objective in a way that Subjective Qualities are not. There is an appearance-reality distinction for red but not for a Subjective Quality such as achiness. (Aydede [2005] quotes a characterization of pain from the International Association for the Study of Pain that pretty much makes the point that there is no appearance-reality distinction for pain.) The tomato is red whether or not anyone is looking at it, but the achy toe cannot have its Subjective Quality if no one is having pain. That is, there can be unseen red but not unfelt achiness. Indeed, tomatoes would still be red even if there never had been any people or other creatures who could see them. But in a world without pain-feeling creatures, there would be no Subjective Qualities at all, no burning limbs or achy toes. In the case of color, a physicalist theory has some plausibility. For example, colors may be held to be sets of reflectances. This account fits with the idea that there could be colors in a world with no perceivers, since tomatoes could reflect light even if no one was there to see it. But a physicalist account of Subjective Qualities in terms of tissue damage is not remotely plausible, for the reason given above—the Subjective Qualities of a toe depend not only on the tissue damage but on the connection between tissue damage and the brain. Whether something is red can be an objective matter, but whether my toe aches is something others know about only because of my special privileged relation to it. Finally, as Shoemaker (2001) notes, there is a many-one relation between color-appearance properties and color. Looking around the room, I see all four walls as white, but the color-relevant appearance properties are nonetheless different because of differences in lighting. However, there is no corresponding distinction in the domain of pain. Every slight difference in appearance is a difference in Subjective Quality, indicating that Subjective Qualities are mentalistic in a way that colors are not.

That is why bodily sensations have been a challenge for representationism. If the representationist proposes to explain phenomenal character in nonmentalistic and especially nonphenomenal terms, there must be something for the phenomenal character to (constitutively) represent that is *not itself individuated with respect to phenomenal character*. Color is a better bet to pass this test (even if it does not pass in the end) than are Subjective Qualities.

Of course the view of color that I have been presupposing is itself controversial. It may be said that a physicalistic theory of color ignores the fact that what color something has is relative to the perceiver. Colored objects produce slightly different phenomenal characters in different normal observers in normal circumstances, because the various parts of the eye differ among *normal* perceivers—perceivers who can be assumed to perceive correctly—male versus female, young versus old, black versus white (Block 1999). Perhaps color is not objective after all. So perhaps we should say that in a world without perceivers, nothing has colors. Or perhaps we should say that they have *all* colors— each relative to a different possible but nonactual perceiver. And once we have gone that far, we might say instead that there are no colors even in the actual world, rather merely the projection of phenomenal characters onto objects (Boghossian and Velleman 1989, 1991). But these are all views of color that would deprive representationism of its reductionist point The challenge to Tye is to manage to assimilate Subjective Qualities to color as an objectivist would see color.[2]

Notes

Reprinted from Murat Aydede, ed., *Pain*, 137–142 (Cambridge, MA: MIT Press, 2005).

1. Some say "representationalism," but I prefer "representationism." "Representationism" is shorter and "representationalism" is ambiguous, being used also to mean the doctrine in epistemology that seeing is mediated by awareness of a representation, namely, indirect or representative realism. As Aydede (2005) notes, representationism is more akin to direct rather than indirect realism, so the ambiguity is confusing. Since we still have a chance for the more rational use of terms, I hope readers will adopt "representationism."

2. I am grateful to Sydney Shoemaker for some comments on an earlier draft.

References

Aydede, Murat. 2005a. "Pain." In the *Stanford Encyclopedia of Philosophy*, ed. Ed Zalta. Available at http://plato.stanford.edu/.

Aydede, Murat. 2005b. *Pain* (Cambridge, MA: MIT Press).

Block, Ned. 1999. "Sexism, Racism, Ageism, and the Nature of Consciousness." In the special issue of *Philosophical Topics* 26 (1 and 2) on Sydney Shoemaker's work, edited by Richard Moran, Jennifer Whiting, and Alan Sidelle, 1999.

Boghossian, Paul, and David Velleman. 1989. "Color as a Secondary Quality." *Mind* 98: 81–103. Reprinted in Byrne and Hilbert 1997.

———. 1991. "Physicalist Theories of Color." *Philosophical Review* 100: 67–106. Reprinted in Byrne and Hilbert 1997.

Byrne, Alex, and David Hilbert, eds. 1997. *Readings on Color: The Philosophy of Color*, volume 1. Cambridge, Mass.: MIT Press.

Dretske, F. 1995. *Naturalizing the Mind*. Cambridge, Mass.: MIT Press.

Shoemaker, Sydney. 1994a. "Self-Knowledge and Inner Sense, Lecture III: The Phenomenal Character of Experience." *Philosophy and Phenomenological Research* 54(2): 291–314.

———. 1994b. "Phenomenal Character." *Noûs* 28: 21–38.

———. 2001. "Introspection and Phenomenal Character." *Philosophical Topics* 28(2): 247–273. This paper is reprinted with some omissions in David Chalmers, ed., *Philosophy of Mind: Classical and Contemporary Readings*, New York: Oxford University Press, 2002.

Thau, Michael. 2002. *Consciousness and Cognition*. New York: Oxford University Press.

Name Index

Subject Index

I am grateful to Daniela Dover and Dustin Peskuric for preparing these indexes.